Computer Design and Architecture

Computer Design and Architecture

L. HOWARD POLLARD

University of New Mexico

Prentice-Hall International, Inc.
Englewood Cliffs, N.J.

ISBN 0-13-162629-9

© 1990 by **PRENTICE-HALL, INC.**
A Division of Simon & Schuster
Englewood Cliffs, N.J. 07632

Printed in the United States of America

10 9 8 7 6 5 4 3 2 1

Prentice-Hall International (UK) Limited, *London*
Prentice-Hall of Australia Pty. Limited, *Sydney*
Prentice-Hall Canada Inc., *Toronto*
Prentice-Hall Hispanoamericana, S.A., *Mexico*
Prentice-Hall of India Private Limited, *New Delhi*
Prentice-Hall of Japan, Inc., *Tokyo*
Simon & Schuster Asia Pte. Ltd., *Singapore*
Editora Prentice-Hall do Brasil, Ltda., *Rio de Janeiro*
Prentice-Hall, Inc., *Englewood Cliffs, New Jersey*

This book is dedicated to my wife,
Sybil,
and my daughters,
Ashley and **Lauren**,
with thankful appreciation for their
love, encouragement, and patience
throughout the entire project.

Contents

CHAPTER 4

Instruction Set Processing, 128

CHAPTER 5

Control System Design, 193

CHAPTER 6

Input and Output Operations, 271

Preface

This text was created to gather into one place many of the practical things that have been beneficial as I have designed various types of digital machines. Many texts about computer design deal with the block diagram level of design, which is interesting and instructive only if a person has sufficient background to put real devices into the blocks. However, it has been my experience that not a sufficient amount of real constraints and real design information accompanies the information that many people learn about computer design and computer architecture. That is, the design of the components of the system—the adders, the multipliers, the interface elements, and other hardware items—is understood to some degree at the conceptual level, but often people are unable to match devices to the functions. Thus, this text is about real examples and real systems.

In an attempt to identify the concepts and put real devices and methods with them, some examples are selected from a variety of real machines, while other examples stand alone. Thus, in the discussion of the instruction sets, rather than select a single instruction set and use it as a model to follow, instruction types are described. Also, examples of instructions are selected from different processors to illustrate different methods of performing some operation. Thus, the inferences are, I hope, that there are many ways to accomplish an objective, and that a designer needs to weigh the use of the available resources (time, silicon, power, etc.) against the design objectives. The design methodology must permit different solutions to different problems, not modifications of a single solution to meet different system needs.

The emphasis is on designs that work. The design examples are done with various "flavors" of TTL, and this is done on purpose. The ideas presented can be tested in the lab with off-the-shelf components, and different designs can be tested quickly to ascertain correctness and feasibility. Many of the ideas presented using TTL building blocks can be extended to on-chip designs of computer systems. However, even when a CPU chip has been created, it must be interfaced with memory, buses, and other functional modules. For much of the currently available equipment, interfaces, and memory, this is accomplished with different forms of TTL. Hence the use of TTL devices.

It has been my experience that the concepts offered in this book can be most effectively adsorbed by examination of a number of different designs, done in different ways. For that reason, many designs are available in a separate volume, *The Design Book: Techniques and Solutions for Digital Computer Systems.* This book contains designs to demonstrate features of number systems, combinational and sequential systems, interfaces, and memory systems.

Although the emphasis of the text is TTL, the methods presented here will be applicable in different technologies as well. Rather than assume the existence of an adder or a multiplier, the mechanisms and tradeoffs are discussed. A multiplier can be designed in many ways, and different solutions lead to various ways to utilize resources. A microprogrammed shift and add algorithm is slower than a pipelined high speed algorithm, but uses fewer parts and power. The designer that is aware of both solutions can effectively select the one that will fit the requirements of the system. So different mechanisms are described in the various chapters, and real examples given of each, so that both the method and its application can be examined.

This text assumes that the reader has had a basic course in logic design, both combinational and sequential, and some experience with microprocessor architecture and interfacing. However, in Chapter 3 is a review of the fundamentals in the setting of the combinational design of arithmetic units. Also, Chapter 5 includes examples and methods for four different approaches to synchronous sequential design. Each of the methods has characteristics that will lead to application in different systems, and a designer who is cognizant of more than one way to do a design can benefit by finding the most appropriate solution for a particular problem. Again, rather than allude to the process of microprogramming or state machine design, specific examples and solutions are given.

One of the intents of this text is to provide real examples that draw together the skills and ideas that seem diverse and unrelated to some observers. One example of this is the discussion of number systems in Chapter 2. Although much of this material has been presented by the time students get to the computer design level, many do not fully understand the limitations of number systems, and the range of effect that information representation decisions can have. Number systems take on real meaning when they are directly applied to a specific problem. Floating point numbers lose some of their mystique when examples of differing mechanisms are presented.

The information in Chapter 2 also highlights one of the problems of this type of a text. Although efforts have been made to be thorough, each of the topics presented could be expanded to include an entire text by itself. For example, whole books deal solely with computer arithmetic. For that reason, the information in this text should be used in conjunction with information in the areas of design for testability, operating systems, computer system performance evaluation, and networking, to name just a few of the applicable fields.

Another topic that is missing from this text concerns the use of computer tools to aid in the design/evaluation process. A number of schematic capture and simulation tools are very helpful in performing some of the design tasks presented in the text. Indeed, these tools can reduce some of the drudgery associated with producing the final product, as well as helping in the design process itself. However, the designer or system architect must not become too dependent on the tools. If this dependence is pronounced, then perceived limitations may be provided by the tools, not by the technique or digital system itself.

As with any project of this size, a number of people and organizations have contributed to the knowledge and experience that culminated with this text. My earliest experiences with digital systems were at Utah State University under the guidance of Bill Fletcher and Al Despain. I then gained experience with stand-alone systems at Reticon, Corp., and also benefited from experience with attached processors at Lockheed Missiles and Space Co. The most recent contributions have been made by my colleagues at the Parallel Processing Research Group at UNM, with special thanks for the opportunities to practice the craft with the Data Systems group (MEE-10) of the Mechanical and Electronics Engineering Division of Los Alamos National Laboratory. To all of these people and organizations I extend my sincere thanks.

L. HOWARD POLLARD

1

Introduction

Computers have become a common fixture in today's society, prevalent not only as a computational tool for scientific use, but also providing the control mechanism for a wide variety of systems. Computers and computer-like devices are found in appliances, automobiles, supermarket checkout stands, telephones, radios, and televisions, where they are used to control the function of the device. They are also found in information systems, such as office computer systems, inventory control systems, and library reference systems. Computers form the basis for engineering workstations, personal computers, and intelligent communication systems. These applications have become reasonable since the cost and size of computer devices have decreased. Not only have computers proliferated into many different areas, but the power of large "mainframe" computers has continued to increase. These large machines provide the tools necessary for research and applied technology in science, engineering, medicine, and many other areas. New machines with more capabilities will permit development of new techniques for analysis and research in many areas.

The field of computer design encompasses a wide variety of disciplines, each of which forms a necessary part of the whole system. The electrical nature of the systems is understood through applications of principles of electrical engineering. Included in this area is the semiconductor technology used to create the logic, memory, processors, and other devices of a computer system. Different technologies provide devices with different speeds, different power, and different capabilities, and the task left to the system architect and computer designer is to use these devices in reasonable ways to meet the design objectives of the system.

Other areas of electrical engineering are required in computer systems. The power needed to drive the system must be transported, converted, isolated from noise, and delivered to the active devices in the system. Also, steps must be taken to ensure that the devices do not generate noise which can propagate back into the power supply system of the machine. The signals used to communicate between

1

devices also present a number of problems. As time allotted for information transfer decreases, the connection can no longer be treated strictly as a wire; the transmission line characteristics of the interconnect must be considered, and steps taken to reduce any noise which may arise from reflections and impedance mismatches. In short, all electrical aspects of the system are important in producing a computer system which will be both functional and reliable.

Another type of information needed to understand computer systems has traditionally been the domain of computer science. This includes a knowledge of the operating system, which provides a mechanism for control, not only of the processor, but also of the input and output (I/O) system, the memory system, and the user interface. It includes an understanding of semaphore operations, why they are needed for resource management within both operating systems and programs, and the responsibilities of the processor architecture and implementation in creating and managing semaphores. It includes a working knowledge of data structures and their applications, both in the operating systems and in application programs. It includes a knowledge of the operation and function of compilers, the languages they work with and desirable characteristics of programs and subroutines. It includes a wide variety of ideas and concepts utilized to apply the computational and control capabilities of a computer system to the solution of problems encountered in different facets of science and industry.

Application of the computational capabilities of a computer system to real problems also mandates an understanding of numerical analysis. A mathematical model of a process can be created to provide a vehicle for studying the various aspects of the problem. Conversion of the mathematical model into a computer program results in representation of information in a limited fashion. That is, the computer system can represent a limited number of values, and the user must ascertain that the limits of the representation mechanisms and the arithmetic interactions of the variables will not introduce unacceptable errors into the results.

Many of the aspects of the computer system relating to its logical structure, its speed of operation, and its interconnection mechanisms are the domain of computer engineering. This includes:

- The design of the arithmetic elements used in a system, analyzing algorithms and methods to produce the desired answers within an acceptable time.

- The creation of the set of instructions used to control the system, which define the apparent structure of the system.

- The interconnection methods for arithmetic units, memorys, registers, and other units, which define the actual structure of the system.

- The method used to define and control the data flow between the major portions of the systems.

- The techniques used to provide communication between the computer and other devices, such as disks, tape units, and terminals.

An understanding of these aspects of the computer system provide a basis on which reasonable decisions can be made — both in the design process, where a computer system is being created, and in the application process, where the use of different techniques results in improved performance for various problem areas.

This text has been written to address these computer design issues. Design techniques and architectural issues for each of the above areas will be discussed and tradeoffs will be illustrated. However, before we consider some of the details of computer systems, let us look at the origin of the modern computer.

1.1. Early Computational Devices

The early history of computers is fascinating, and we will not attempt here to give a complete list of the machines and activities. This information is available in a variety of texts [Haye88, Stal87], as well as the series *Annals of the History of Computing*. Since necessity is the mother of invention, computers came into being to provide a mechanism for removing the drudgery from repeated calculations. As the techniques were explored, modified, and refined, new ideas and concepts continued to emerge. There has always been tradeoff between the available technology and the capabilities of the computing machinery (based on that technologies). As the limits of one technique were reached, other ideas were generated and explored to utilize different techniques to provide faster machines with more features. As different technologies were used, alternate solutions and new features were added to machines, and new machines (based on the new technologies) were developed. This process continues to provide new devices and new capabilities as the number of available computer systems expands.

One of the earliest calculating devices was created by the French philosopher/scientist Blaise Pascal around 1642. This device, basically a mechanical counter, was created to automate the addition and subtraction process. Numbers were expressed in decimal form on two sets of six wheels, one wheel for each digit. Thus, the unit had the capability of manipulating six-digit numbers. The digits of each number were represented by the position of the wheels, each of which had the ten numerals engraved on it. One set of wheels acted as an accumulator register, and another number was entered onto the second set of wheels. The two sets were connected by gears, and when one set of wheels was turned, the other set was incremented accordingly. The principle innovation of the system was the creation of a mechanical carry device, which automatically incremented the appropriate wheel position by one when the wheel of one lower significance rolled over another decade. To handle negative numbers or subtraction, a complements representation was used.

Another mechanical calculating system was created around 1671 by the German philosopher/mathematician Gottfried Leibniz. This unit incorporated the addition/subtraction capability of the Pascal device, and extended it to perform multiplication and division automatically. The multiplication operation was implemented by using chains and pulleys, deriving the appropriate information from sets of wheels which were used to identify the multiplier and multiplicand. Like the Pascal device, this one utilized mechanical mechanisms to provide the basic functions needed for computation. In fact, one could say that the Leibniz device was the first four-function calculator.

A prolific scientist in the field of computing was Charles Babbage, an Englishman who worked on two different computing systems, as well as creating a wealth of supporting material that was ahead of its time. The first machine, called the Difference Engine, was created around 1823 to automatically generate mathematical tables. The machine was to not only calculate a number, but also directly transfer this information to the plates used for printing the tables. The only operation supported was addition, but the addition mechanism could be used repeatedly to create the desired result, using the method of finite differences to represent or approximate the functions needed. The Difference Engine consisted of a number of mechanical registers, each of which stored a decimal number. The registers were connected in pairs by an mechanical addition mechanism that functioned much like Pascal's calculator. To form a result, initial values were entered into the registers, and the system could then be driven by a motor of some kind to produce the final result. Although some difference engines were built, the unit proposed by Babbage was never completed, partly because of mechanical difficulties and partly because Babbage became more interested in a new device, the Analytical Engine.

Whereas the Difference Engine was designed to create answers using the technique of finite differences, the Analytical Engine was designed to perform any mathematical function in an automatic fashion. The basic organization of the Analytical Engine is shown in Figure 1.1; this system bears a striking resemblance to the computers of today. The principle parts were the store, the mill, the control section, and the output section. The store was a memory unit composed of sets of counter wheels; the design called for storage of 1,000 numbers, each consisting of 50 digits. The mill, corresponding to the arithmetic/logic unit (ALU) in more modern machines, was capable of performing the four basic arithmetic operations. The output unit was intended to be either printed on paper or punched on cards. The system was controlled by two sets of punched cards: the operation cards identified the basic operation that was to be performed by the mill, and the variable cards identified the source of the operands used in the calculation, as well as the destination of the result. One of the most significant contributions of the Analytical Engine was a mechanism for altering the sequence of operations depending on the state of the machine, basically a conditional branch capability. The testable condition was the sign of a number; if the number was positive, one course of action was followed; if the number was negative, a different set of instructions was identified.

Although the system was proposed and the design was worked on for many years, only a small portion of the system was actually constructed. Had he been successful in construction of the system, Babbage estimated that the time required for an addition operation was on the order of a second, and the time required for a multiplication was on the order of a minute. It is doubtful that a mechanical computer of the size and complexity of the Analytical Engine could ever be built.

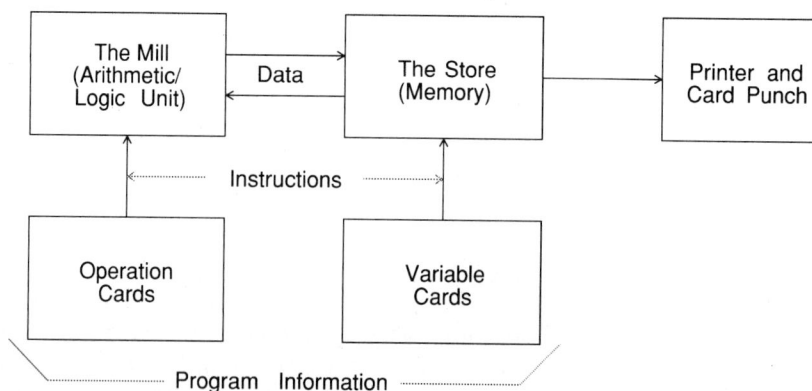

Figure 1.1. Block Diagram of Babbage's Analytical Engine.

A number of mechanical calculators were implemented in the early 1900s, and these contributed to the general idea of automating the computing process. Other mechanical devices would play a role in the advancement of computing devices. One of these was the Jacquard Loom, a device that automated the weaving of rugs by using patterns punched on cards. This device was actually operational by about 1801, and the idea of using cards for controlling machines was used by Babbage and others. Another card-oriented machine was the punched-card tabulating machine, invented by an American, Herman Hollerith. One of the first use of Hollerith's card system was processing data taken in the 1890 census of the United States. The characteristics of the population were punched on cards, entered into the system, and counted mechanically. Hollerith formed the Tabulating Machine Company in 1911, which later merged with several other companies into a venture that would become International Business Machines. Card systems were used for data entry and output in computer systems for many years.

During the late 1930s a German engineering student named Konrad Zuse created several models of electromechanical computational systems. He chose as the active unit of the system a mechanical relay, and used a binary number system, rather than a decimal system, to represent the numbers. The first model, the Z1, was a primitive machine, with minimal processing capability and a memory based on mechanical relays. The third model, the Z3, was completed in 1941. This machine was also based on electromechanical relays, and is perhaps the first operational program-controlled general purpose computer. The input was through a punched tape mechanism, which utilized discarded photographic film in which instructions were represented by hole patterns punched by the programmer. Most of Zuse's machines were destroyed by the bombing of Berlin, and although Zuse later received support from IBM and Remington Rand, his efforts did not greatly influence the other computational systems that followed.

Another electromechanical system was created by Howard Aiken, a physicist and mathematics professor at Harvard University. Whereas it appears that Zuse was not aware of the work of Babbage, Aiken did know of the previous work, and followed some of the ideas presented there. The effort was initiated in 1939, and the Mark I became operational in 1944. Information was stored in wheels like the Babbage machines, but the computational system was composed of relays. It could store 72 23-digit decimal numbers, and instructions were input into the system with a punched paper tape; each instruction contained an operation and two addresses. Once operational it, could do an addition in 6 seconds and a division in 12 seconds.

Perhaps the first electronic computer system was created by John V. Atanasoff, a physicist at Iowa State College, which later became Iowa State University. Between 1937 and 1942 he and a graduate student, Clifford E. Berry, worked on a system that would perform gaussian elimination solutions for sets of equations. Their system was totally electronic in nature, and used capacitors to store information, in much the same way that dynamic RAMs (random access memories) store information on capacitors created with semiconductor technology. He also used a binary number system for information representation, and organized the functional units by separating the logic and arithmetic portion of the system from the memory portion, as well as the I/O portion. The resulting computational system performed adequately, but the punched card I/O system introduced an error about once every 10,000 operations. This portion of the system was used extensively in the operation of the unit, and so the errors were unacceptable. However, before the source of the problem could be located and corrected, World War II interrupted work on the system, and further efforts were suspended.

1.2. The Computer Generations: Technology and Innovation

The early efforts in devising computing systems inspired the creation of other systems to perform automatic computation functions. As more experience was obtained with computing machines, and as the technology changed, different computational systems emerged. One of the ways of classifying the machines that have followed is to group them into generations, using not only the chronological position of the system, but also the characteristics and capabilities of the systems.

1.2.1 The first generation (??–1953)

The first generation includes the early machines, as well as machines created until the mid-1950s. These machines used either electromechanical elements or tubes for logic, and a variety of mechanisms for memory. Some of the systems were organized in a bit serial manner to more effective utilize the expensive hardware devices. Some of the systems operated on entire words simultaneously, to provide high speed operation. The first generation systems were primarily for scientific purposes, with business applications a low priority. For the most part, these machines were programmed at the machine level, and users of the systems were expected to provide all data and all of the required program control.

One of the first well-known computers to use electronic components was the ENIAC system (electronic numerical integrator and calculator). This system was built at the University of Pennsylvania by John W. Mauchly and J. Presper Eckert. Like many machines of this era, one of the principal motivations for the system was the need to generate tables automatically. Work on the ENIAC project began in 1943, and it was completed in 1946. The system was physically very large, with over 18,000 vacuum tubes. The electronic nature of the unit resulted in a system that was considerably faster than any previous computer system, with an addition time of approximately 3 ms. The data memory of the system consisted of 20 accumulator registers, each of which could store a 10-digit decimal number with its sign. Each digit of storage required ten flip-flops, which were organized as a ring counter: the active flip-flop indicated the value of the digit stored in that digit position. Each of the accumulators in the system combined arithmetic (addition and subtraction) logic with the storage logic. Hardware units were also provided for multiplication, division, and square root calculation. As can be seen from the ENIAC block diagram included in Figure 1.2, data input to the system was provided by a card reader system, and output was either printed or punched. The connections within the system were physically made with wires configured on panels; to connect one accumulator to another, the appropriate points were manually connected to one another. The programming was also accomplished manually, setting switches and establishing connections with cables between control points. In addition, constants used during the computation could be stored in the function tables and used as needed.

The ENIAC system was very cumbersome to program, since the program was actually determined by the physical arrangement of the cables in the system. The next step was to create a system in which the program would be stored in memory along with the data, so that the program could be altered by modifying

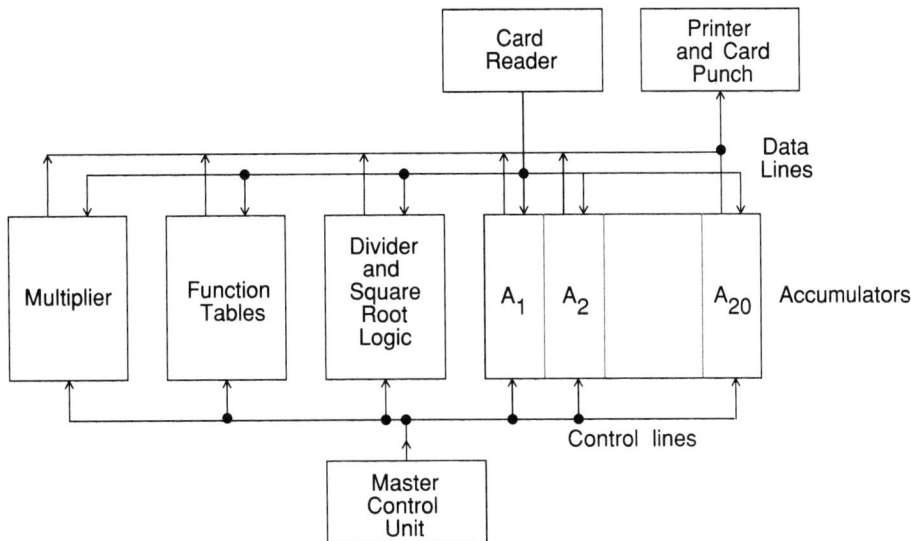

Figure 1.2. Block Diagram of ENIAC.

the contents of the memory during program execution. It is interesting to note that, in the Harvard Mark I and other machines (see the block diagram of ENIAC in Figure 1.2), the data was kept separate from the program. This mechanism, often called the Harvard architecture, can be found in many systems today, especially systems like real time digital signal processing units. The benefit is that there are independent paths to data memory and control memory, and both can be used simultaneously; this leads to a higher effective system speed. The cost of this mechanism is that two separate memory units must be provided, with their data paths, addressing decoders, and other costs. This not only results in a higher costs associated with the memory, but also imposes different limits on the system. That is, one program may utilize all of the available program space and need more, while not making use of all of the data memory; another program may require very little program memory, but need more data memory than is available. The next architectural change combined the two memories, which permitted the program to be modified as mentioned above, but which also allowed the available memory to be used by program or data as required by the system.

In 1945 John von Nuemann, a Hungarian-born mathematician who was a consultant working with Mauchly and Eckert on the ENIAC, proposed the creation of a new system, the EDVAC (electronic discrete variable computer). This system was to operate on what is called the stored program concept, where the program and data share the same memory, and thus the program could be modified to extend the possible execution modes. Although there is evidence that this concept did not uniquely originate with von Neumann and his colleagues, his name is most often attached to it. The EDVAC system was developed at the University of Pennsylvania, and differed in many respects from the previous systems. Like Atanasoff's machine, it utilized a binary number system to represent the information. The storage area was much larger than earlier systems, capable of storing 1,024, or 1K, words of information. In addition, the system had a secondary storage unit capable of storing 20K words. Both of these memories were made from serial delay lines, the main memory from mercury delay lines, and the larger storage unit from magnetic delay lines. Because of the serial nature of the delay line storage, and to minimize hardware costs, the arithmetic was performed in a serial fashion, working on a single bit at a time. The words were 44 bits long, and there were three basic types on instructions. Arithmetic instructions were of the form:

$$A_1 \quad A_2 \quad A_3 \quad A_4 \quad OP$$

The OP identified the operation to be performed ($+$, $-$, $\times$, or $\div$), and the A_i specified the addresses involved. The function was performed on the information stored at the locations specified by A_1 and A_2, and the result was placed at the location specified by A_3. The next instruction to execute was found at location A_4. The format for the conditional branch instructions was similar:

$$A_1 \quad A_2 \quad A_3 \quad A_4 \quad C$$

If the number stored at A_1 is not less than the number stored at A_2, the next instruction to execute is located at A_3; otherwise, the next instruction to execute is located at A_4. The other type of instruction was an input/output instruction of the following format:

$$A_1 \quad \{1,2\},N \quad A_3 \quad A_4 \quad W$$

If the $\{1,2\}$ choice was a 1, then the words from A_1 to A_3 were stored on the delay line wire N. If the $\{1,2\}$ choice was a 2, then information from delay line wire N was transferred to locations starting at A_1 and ending at A_3. Again, the next instruction to execute was located at A_4. Actual input and output operations moved information directly to and from the delay lines.

A number of observations can be made about this system, two of which we will identify here. First, this was a memory-to-memory architecture, and no registers were involved in the instructions. Second, there was no default "next" instruction; each instruction identified the location of the instruction which was to follow. These architectural decisions resulted in some unique system characteristics, and incurred one set of costs. In comparing architectures, much can be learned by comparing their use of specific system resources. For example, instructions that required four separate addresses necessitated instruction words long enough to include all four identifiers; for 1K locations, this was 10 bits per address, or 40 bits total for the four addresses. Thus, only four bits were left to identify the instruction itself.

In 1946, von Neumann, along with Arthur W. Burks and Herman H. Goldstine, made a proposal to the Army for a new computer system that combined many of the characteristics of the previous machines and added some new concepts. This machine was called the IAS after the Institute for Advanced Studies at Princeton, where the work was done. The machine was worked on for many years, and finally became operational in 1952. This system formed a basis for many of the computers that followed, so we will describe some of its characteristics.

The unit was constructed from a few basic modules: the memory, the arithmetic units, the control unit, and the input/output capabilities. Since IAS was principally a computer, the four primary arithmetic functions were supplied in specialized hardware. One of the operands required for the arithmetic functions was located in a predefined register, the other operand was obtained from memory, as with EDVAC. The result of the operation was placed in the accumulator. Thus, only one address was required with the instruction, and the instruction length could be correspondingly smaller. Also, instead of having each instruction identify the location of the subsequent instruction, the next instruction to execute was assumed to be located in the next location in memory; this further reduced the address requirement in an instruction. This type of organization became known as a single address machine, since only one address was required in any instruction.

The memory of the IAS system was provided by an array of X-Y cathode ray tubes, each storing a 64×64 array of bits. Thus, the memory had 4,096 locations for storage of either data or instructions; an address to specify a unique location in the memory required 12 bits. Transfer of information between the memory and the other portions of the system occurred over a parallel path, which provided a higher speed system than the serial information transfers used in EDVAC.

The word size was selected based on the expected numerical accuracy required by the workload, in conjunction with the number of bits required to represent the instruction and the address. The formats are shown in Figure 1.3. Eight bits were selected to represent the operation code of the instruction, although fewer bits could have been used. The single address required by an instruction required an additional 12 bits. These two elements could be contained in a word size of 20 bits, but the arithmetic precision offered by 20-bit words was not sufficient to solve the problems for which it was intended. Therefore, the word length was extended to 40 bits, and two instructions were included in each program word in memory. The data was represented in a fixed point scheme, with a sign bit, an assumed radix point, and 39 bits of fractional data. This format also permitted the bits to represent integers, if appropriate assumptions were made about the data manipulation techniques.

The instructions of IAS are included in Table 1.1; the original nomenclature has been changed to a more descriptive method similar to the instruction sets of more recent machines. The instructions identify the manipulations that can be controlled by a programmer in moving data in the system. A block diagram of the organization of IAS, its modules and their interconnection paths is given in Figure 1.4. Table 1.1 identifies several types of instructions that move information within the system. The data transfer instructions move information between the memory and the two data registers: the ACCUMULATOR and the MQ (multiplier-quotient) register. The arithmetic instructions operate on the data

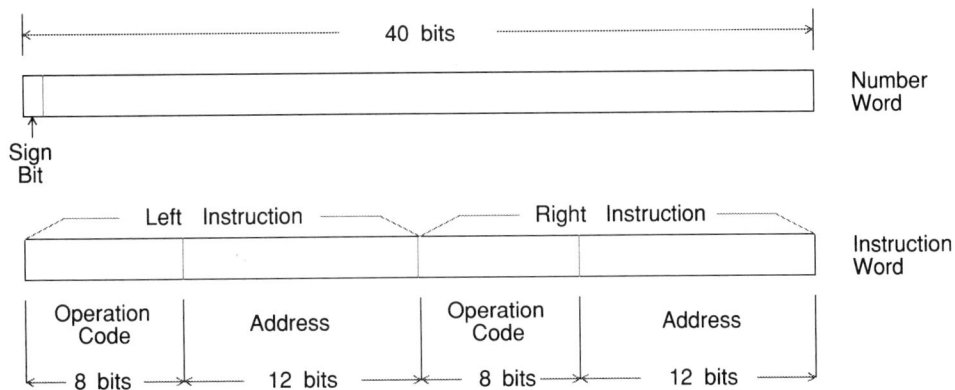

Figure 1.3. Data and Instruction Formats for IAS.

Table 1.1 Instructions for IAS.

Data transfer instructions	
Instruction	*Description*
LDA X	Load ACCUMULATOR with value stored at location X.
LDAM X	Load ACCUMULATOR with negative of value stored at location X.
ABS X	Load ACCUMULATOR with absolute value of number stored at location X.
ABSM X	Load ACCUMULATOR with negative of absolute value of number stored at location X.
LDM X	Load MQ register with value stored at location X.
MQA	Load ACCUMULATOR with value stored in MQ register.
STOR X	The value of the ACCUMULATOR is transferred to location X.

Arithmetic instructions	
Instruction	*Description*
ADD X	Add number stored at location X to ACCUMULATOR.
SUB X	Subtract number stored at location X from ACCUMULATOR.
ADDABS X	Add absolute value of number stored at location X to ACCUMULATOR.
SUBABS X	Subtract absolute value of number stored at location X from ACCUMULATOR.
MULT X	Multiply the number stored in MQ register by value stored in location X, leave 39 most significant bits in ACCUMULATOR, and leave 39 least significant bits in MQ register.
DIV X	Divide value in ACCUMULATOR by value stored at location X; leave remainder in ACCUMULATOR and quotient in MQ register.
LFTSHFT	Multiply the number in the ACCUMULATOR by 2, leaving it there.
RGTSHFT	Divide the number in the ACCUMULATOR by 2, leaving it there.

Jump instructions	
Instruction	*Description*
JMPL X	Next instruction to execute is in most significant half of location X.
JMPR X	Next instruction to execute is in least significant half of location X.

Conditional branch instructions	
Instruction	*Description*
BRANCHL X	If number in ACCUMULATOR is nonnegative, next instruction to execute is in most significant half of location X.
BRANCHR X	If number in ACCUMULATOR is nonnegative, next instruction to execute is in least significant half of location X.

Address modification instructions	
Instruction	*Description*
CADRL X	The address bits (12 least significant bits) of the most significant half of location X are replaced with the 12 least significant bits of the ACCUMULATOR.
CADRR X	The address bits (12 least significant bits) of the least significant half of location X are replaced with the 12 least significant bits of the ACCUMULATOR.

located in the data registers; operands are retrieved from memory as needed, and the results are left in the registers. The jump instructions and the branch instructions allow program control to be moved to another location in the memory by

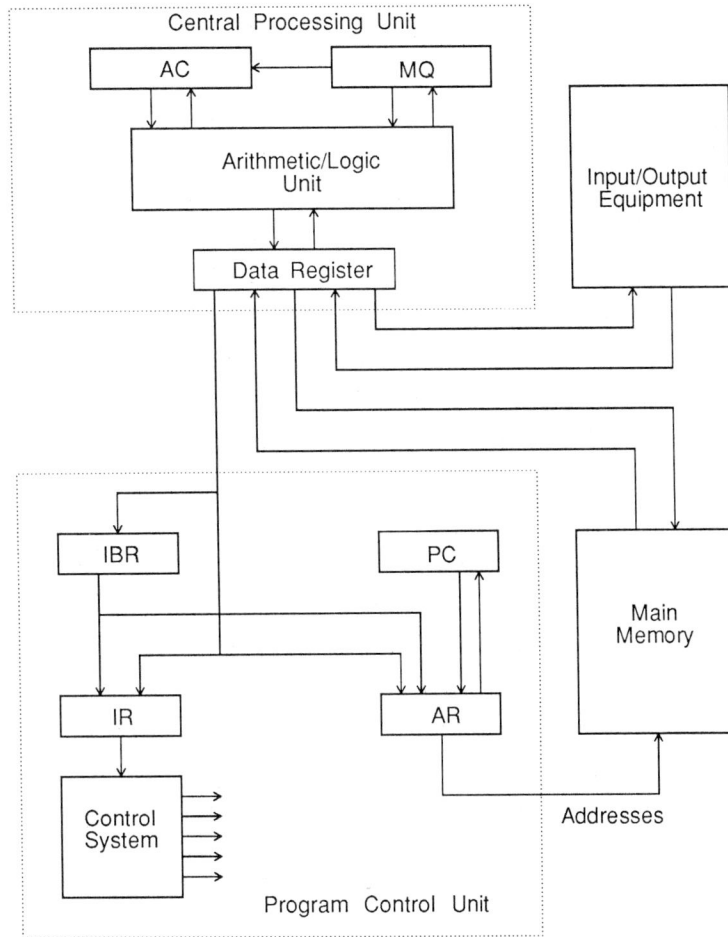

Figure 1.4. Block Diagram Representation of IAS.

modifying the contents of the control registers. The address modification instructions allow a program to dynamically modify the instruction stream. The registers in the program control portion of the system include the program counter (PC), the address register (AR), the instruction register (IR), and the instruction buffer register (IBR). The PC is responsible for identifying the location in memory where the next instruction will be found. The contents of the PC and the instruction stream are used by the AR, which specifies the address to be used in main memory. Memory interaction is accomplished by transferring information to and from the data register. When an instruction pair is extracted from memory, the active instruction is directed to the IR, and the other instruction is sent to the IBR to await the time of execution. Note that instructions listed do not support input/output operations; transferring information to and from IAS was accomplished by moving blocks of data to and from main memory via the registers in the data processing unit.

Note that the instruction set had three different ways to deal with the locations in memory. If the location was used in a data transaction, the entire word was used. If the location was used as the target of a jump or a conditional branch, then the appropriate half of the word was utilized. Finally, modification of the address bits of one the two instructions is possible.

Although this machine was more capable in many respects than the earlier machines, a number of shortcomings became evident as the machine was used. The address modification mechanism was awkward to utilize in an efficient way, and later machines extended the accessing methods to facilitate identification of operands. One of the obvious omissions is a method of structuring programs, that is, a subroutine call-return mechanism. This would facilitate using a single section of code to implement often occurring functions. The scientific nature of the expected workload is evident from the instruction set; programming logical or nonnumerical types of operations was somewhat difficult to accomplish. Systems that handled these problems in a different way, as well as those using different technologies, became more prevalent as new systems moved into another generation of machines.

1.2.2 The second generation (1952–1963)

Many of the first machines were single systems, created for a specific problem or set of problems. As the possible applications of the systems became evident, commercial systems were created. IBM and Sperry enjoyed the most commercial success, being joined later by other firms. The second generation of machines brought to light the methods and lessons learned earlier, together with new technology for both functional units and storage. The transistor, invented in the late 1940s, became one of the principle active devices in computer systems, although tubes continued to play a role. The use of transistors greatly reduced the power required to run a computer system, as well as increasing the speed of operation. Core memories provided a faster, more reliable storage medium for the main memories needed in the new systems. New methods were used to identify the location of operands used in the transactions in the machine. Floating point arithmetic was introduced to remove from the computer user the burden of scaling all of the data and arithmetic to fit the available operations. This period also saw the start of computer languages, such as Fortran and Cobol, which allowed the users of the machines to create programs without knowing all of the details of the internal operations of the machines. Independent input/output processors removed the time-consuming transfer of information to and from the system from the CPU (central processing unit) itself; this allowed the CPU to spend its time doing useful work. These systems also provided the user with some system software: batch processing facilities, libraries, and compilers.

The influence of the first generation on the machines of the second generation is evident by comparing block diagrams of machines from each era. Figure 1.5 gives a block diagram representation of the IBM 7094. The IBM 709X series of machines were 36-bit systems, with the data formats shown in Figure 1.6. The system is a single address machine, but with this system the address register can specify information based not only on the contents of the program counter, but also on the content of index registers and combinations of registers. This additional capability adds to the flexibility of the system, but it also requires additional complexity in the control unit and in the specification method. The instruction format has expanded to fill the entire 36-bit word; the operation code must not only identify the desired function, but also the manner in which the address must be treated to identify the location of the operand. This requires several bits of the operation code to identify one of the eight index registers, and the manner in which the address is to be constructed. In addition to the instruction format, Figure 1.6 identifies two different data formats, one for integer data, and one for

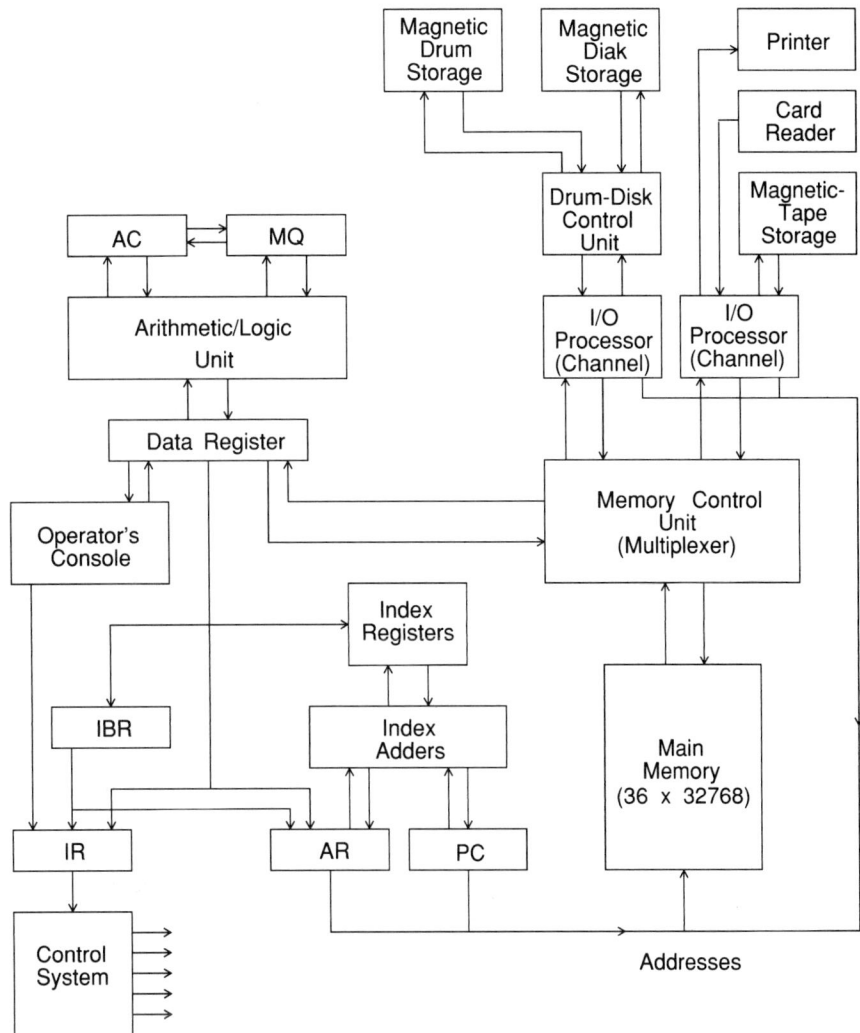

Figure 1.5. Block Diagram Representation of the IBM 7094.

floating point data. The integer capability allows for "normal" incremental functions, and the floating point capability provides for a combination of large and small values to be used with minimal user worry. Also, a double precision floating point format provides for a double length mantissa.

The IBR in this system is an instruction backup register, but it serves the same purpose as the IBR in the IAS. However, in this case, the provision arises not because two instructions can fit into the characteristic word length of the system, but rather because the data path from main memory to the central processing unit is 72 bits wide, and so two transfers can be effected simultaneously. The AR and the PC specify the address and the location in memory where the program is executing. The AC and MQ registers provide a similar function to the corresponding registers in the IAS system.

Another difference in the system capabilities is evident by examining the peripheral devices and their communication paths to the system. The I/O processors, called channels, have the responsibility of coordinating the transfer of

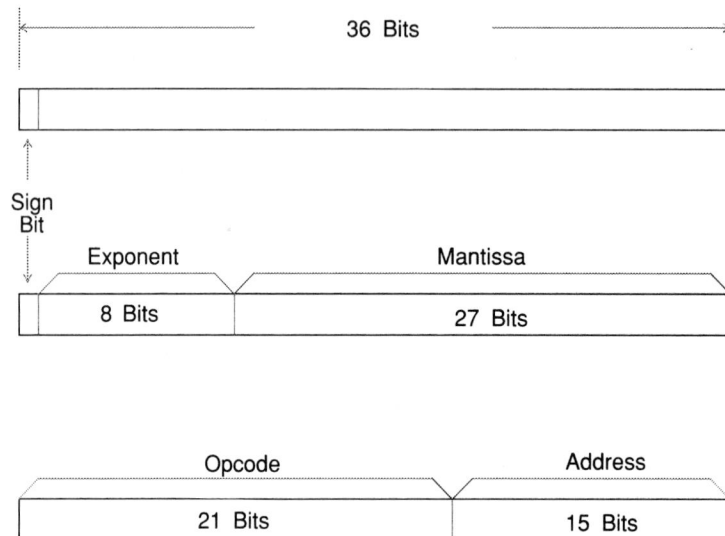

Figure 1.6. Data and Instruction Formats for IBM 709X.

information to and from the mass storage devices and the input/output devices. These transfers are initiated by action of the CPU, but are carried out by the channels. When the transfer has been completed, the channel has the capability to interrupt the action of the CPU, which will indicate the completion of the specified action.

The more elaborate I/O system also added to the flexibility and efficiency of the system. In earlier systems, the operation of the device was strictly single user — whoever had physical access to the machine controlled the operation of the system. The system then was dedicated to the task of one user, until that user finished and relinquished the machine. This resulted in a large amount of dead time when the system was idle. With the second generation systems, programs were collected together into a "batch," and then fed one at a time into the memory and executed. This increased the apparent speed of the machine, because it minimized the time the central processing system was idle.

The creation of the transistor and related technology provided higher performance in a much smaller package. The availability of these devices prompted efforts to create machines capable of much higher execution rates than the "normal" computer systems. These machines are called supercomputers, and involve a variety of techniques to improve the processing speed. One of the first efforts was the LARC system (Livermore Atomic Research Computer), made by UNIVAC. Another early system was the IBM 7030, also called the Stretch. These systems pushed the technology to create faster systems, and also explored the use of parallelism to increase system speed.

The parallelism at this stage took two basic forms: overlapped instruction execution and the use of parallel processing elements. Overlapping the fetch and execute portions of the computational process resulted in an apparent speed increase by doing more than one thing at at time. While one instruction was being executed, the next instruction was being fetched from memory. Higher degrees of overlap could be achieved by dividing the processing into even smaller pieces. The use of multiple processors allowed one program to execute on one processor while another executed on a second processor. The benefit came when the systems resources (memory, I/O processors, disks, etc.) were more fully utilized because of the increased processing. These early attempts at supercomputing led the way to further advances in the next set of computers.

1.2.3 The third generation (1962–1975)

Early in the 1960s the promise of semiconductor technology began to make itself felt. Integrated circuits, which combined many transistors in a single chip, reduced the size and cost of computer systems. Not only did the integrated circuits have a great impact on the logic, but semiconductor memories became a significant factor in the creation of computer systems. These memories would eventually replace core memories as the primary memory element in a computer. The high speed memories provided the needed technology to implement a technique known as microprogramming. This technique had been proposed by Maurice Wilkes in England as early as 1951, but the technology was not available to effectively utilize it. However, with memory speeds an order of magnitude faster than the main memory speed, microprogramming was widely used. The regularity involved in microprogramming allowed the complexity of the instruction sets increase, without an undue increase in the complexity of the control system needed to assert the control signals of the system.

The utilization of a CPU was raised above that of the second generation systems by means of multiprogramming, in which the system resources are shared among several programs on "time-shared" basis. This resulted in part from the advances made in the set of programs that controlled the operation of the system, which have become known as the operating system (OS). Operating systems continue to provide additional capabilities, such as improved compilers, shared libraries, utilities, and accounting information.

The concurrent use of hardware segments in parallel or pipelined processing was utilized in a variety of ways. Again, the objective of the mechanism was to increase the apparent speed of the system. Along with the increased processing speeds, a new technique for numerical programming was introduced, which is called vector processing. A vector processor seeks to enhance system speed by organizing the information into uniform sets called vectors, and applying the same operation to all of the elements of the vector. This saves time because a single instruction is used to specify many operations, and because the hardware can be organized to take advantage of the one-after-another nature of the operands being used in the vector operations.

One of the most prolific systems of this period was the IBM 360. This system is interesting from a number of aspects, one of which is the manner in which it came into existence. In 1964 an article in the *IBM Journal* [AmBl64] described the various members of the 360 family. To this point in time, and in many cases after, members of a "family" of computers came into existence as newer technology made speed improvements possible, and as a customer base made investment in the new machines reasonable. However, with the announcement of the 360 series of computers, the various members of the family were identified, and their specific characteristics enumerated. Thus, if a customer wanted one level of performance, one machine was purchased; a different level of performance, either higher or lower, dictated a different choice. However, from the view of an assembly language programmer, the systems were identical. This initiated into the computer jargon the phrase, "instruction set architecture," which refers to the appearance of the machine, not as defined by the functional units and interconnections of the hardware, but rather the apparent functional units and interconnections that are activated or controlled by the instruction set. This leaves the hardware designer free to create a system that uses whatever techniques are economically or technically justifiable to create a system with a certain set of characteristics.

From the creation of the notion of an instruction set architecture, there have been two uses of the term "architecture": one is to describe the actual functional elements of a system and their interconnections; the other is to describe the apparent structure of the machine as defined by the instruction set. In this text we will be examine the instructions used to define a system, but also the interconnection methods and some of their implications.

A system level block diagram of a typical IBM 360 installation is shown in Figure 1.7. The system is controlled by the CPU, which not only manipulates the data in the main memory, but also controls the action of the I/O channels. The channels transfer information directly to and from the memory, and the CPU is informed of the completion of the specified operation by use of an interrupt. Two different types of channels are indicated, one for high speed operation (selector channel), and one for low to medium speed operation (multiplexer channel). The channels handle device specific I/O requirements, and communicate with each device over a common set of interface lines.

The instruction set architecture of an IBM 360 system is shown in Figure 1.8. The fundamental size of the system is 32 bits, which was chosen for a number of pragmatic reasons. This width is a multiple of 4 bits, which is the size of the representation of BCD (binary coded decimal) digits; instructions are

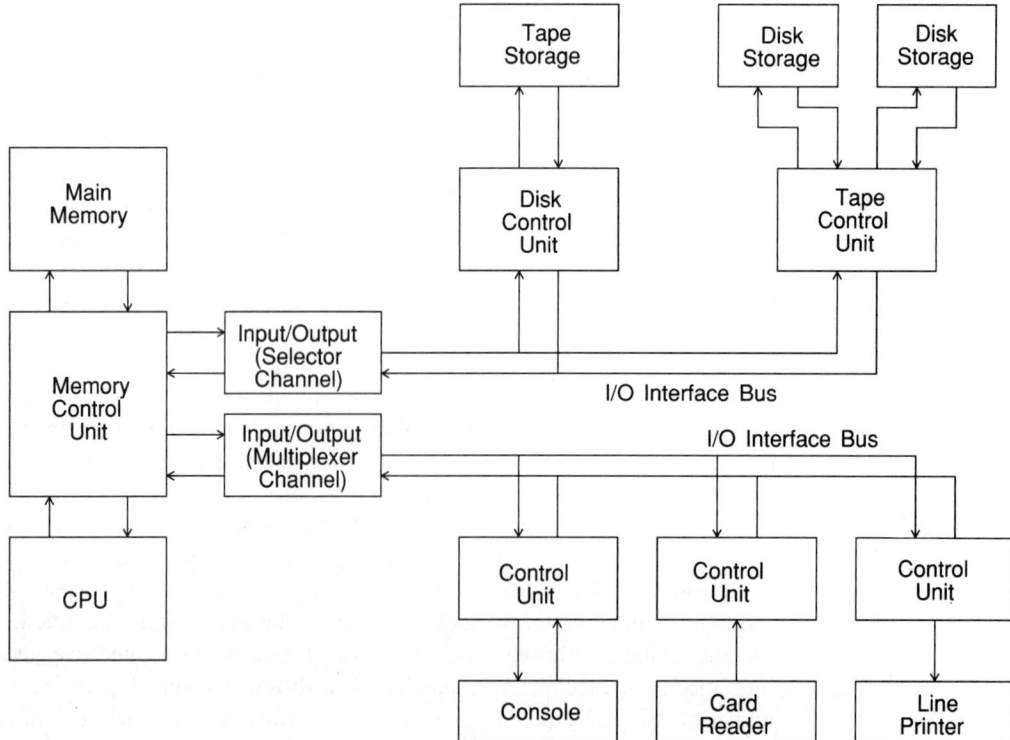

Figure 1.7. Block Diagram Representation of an IBM 360 Installation.

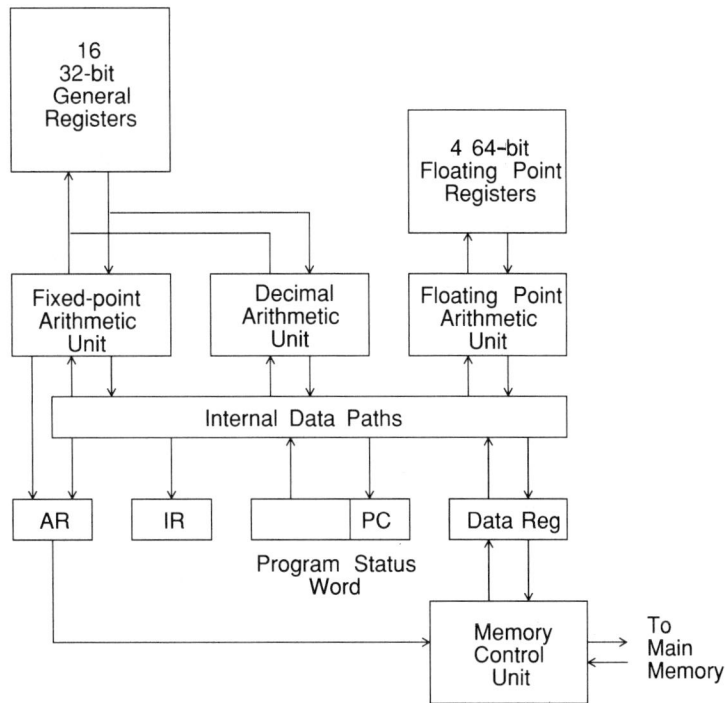

Figure 1.8. Instruction Set Architecture of an IBM 360 CPU.

available to operate on BCD digits. It is also a multiple of eight bits, which is used for character storage. Integers can be represented with either one or two words, for single or double precision information. Floating point numbers can be represented with one, two, or four words, for a variety of numerical capabilities. Finally, instructions are composed of two, four, or six bytes, and will fit easily into a 32-bit format.

The instruction set processor of an IBM 360 identifies 16 registers used for storage of general purpose values. These can hold data to be used in normal calculations, or they can be used to hold addresses that identify the location of operands in main memory. In addition to the general registers, there are four 64-bit floating point registers. These are used to hold operands in the execution of floating point operations. The AR is used to identify the location of information in main memory, which is accessed via the memory control unit. The IR holds the instruction being executed, and the PC is used to identify locations in the execution of the program. The PC is considered part of a set of information known as the program status word (PSW). The PSW contains not only the PC, but also information about the current status of the system, such as whether the last operation resulted in a positive or negative number, and so on. Also shown in the figure are the apparent communication paths connecting the various units. These connections may or may not be extant, which also applies to the functional units. In smaller systems the functional units appear to be there, because the instructions function as expected. However, the actions may be orchestrated by a microprogrammed control system which utilizes a single arithmetic/logic unit to accomplish all of the various capabilities of the system. However, on the higher end models the functional units are there as expected, providing additional speed to the system.

Along with the advances in hardware, operating system advances continued to modify the manner in which users interacted with the computer systems. During this time, concepts were developed that led to the implementation of virtual memory systems. These systems present a uniform view to user programs of the available system memory, and then map address requests in the user space (virtual addresses) into the actual location of the information (real addresses). The operating system also presented to users an easily manageable access to the file system for program and data storage, to the system utilities (editors, file manipulation, etc.), and to the workhorse programs (compilers, etc.) As the systems became more readily controlled and managed, the application areas in which computers were utilized expanded.

As a result of the use of semiconductor technology to reduce the space and power requirements required by computer logic, small computers could be created with very useful capabilities. The result was the minicomputer, which provided computational and control capabilities for a variety of applications. These systems utilized the same concepts as the larger machines, but worked on smaller quantities of information, such as 12- or 16-bit words. This proliferation of machines made the capabilities of computing systems available to a larger community of users. The computer lost some of its mystery, and became an inexpensive, useful tool in the solution of a large variety of problems in science, industry, business, and education.

1.2.4 Additional generations of computers (1974-?)

Each advance in technology brings with it computer systems with more capabilities. As the amount of logic and memory contained in a single integrated circuit continued to increase, a new generation of computers emerged. This is sometimes called the fourth generation of computers. These computers utilize semiconductor devices almost exclusively for main memory as well as the active logic required in the CPU and I/O controllers. The use of virtual memory systems has become a standard feature of systems, in both large and small computers. The proliferation of active devices and semiconductor memories has allowed the virtual memory techniques to be applied to high speed memories, called cache memories. These units provide a relatively small high speed memory between the CPU and main memory. The net result is an increase in the apparent system speed, since the amount of time that a processor is idle decreases.

As the relative cost of the hardware portion of a system continues to decrease, techniques that were at one time reserved for high performance machines are routinely applied to smaller systems. The complexity available in integrated circuits has allowed creating entire systems on a single chip. These processors have progressed from the 4- or 8-bit processing elements, which were available in the mid-1970s, to systems with complete 32-bit computer systems on a single chip, such as the Motorola 68000 series of processors, which form a popular 32-bit processor system. Contained within the chip are not only the registers and arithmetic units of a complex processing element, but also the virtual memory facility and the interface to the physical system memory. Along with the immense amount of processing capability, memory technology also provides storage capacities unavailable in previous systems. In the late 1980s, a single chip can now provide up to 4 megabits of storage capability, and 16-megabit memories are in the experimental stage.

The availability of low cost, high performance processors and memory devices resulted in personal computers for the home or office, in workstation computers for engineering and scientific use, and in multiprocessing systems useful in many areas of computing. With the proliferation of computers have come different ways to provide communication between processors, such as token ring networks, collision detection, common wire networks, broadcast networks, and direct connection networks. Fiber optics have opened new dimensions in speeds and capabilities, and other communication mechanisms continue to evolve. Each of these advances opens new doors to computer architects, and application of the new technologies will result in even more exciting systems.

Another generation of computers, sometimes called the fifth generation, is the target of different research and development efforts. This generation of machines is not identified by the technology used to implement it, but rather by the capabilities of the machine. The target is to create a system that is oriented to human interaction, so that minimal specific knowledge on the part of the user is necessary to make use of the system. This "user friendly" type of a system will result in improved abilities to use computers to meet needs in all endeavors which can make use of computers. In addition, this new generation will be capable of handling immense amounts of data. This will facilitate not only the traditional mathematically intense programming, but also areas such as artificial intelligence and natural language translation.

As advances in technology continue to give us new capabilities and improved tools to work with, our challenge is to create systems that will not only solve an immediate need, but which will also be capable of growth to solve future needs.

1.3. Computer Design and Architecture: The Organization of This Book

The preceeding brief history highlights the fact that the various architectures and design techniques used in system implementation change and grow as more experience is gained and as the available technology changes. A number of different design issues are involved in any design, and what is a good design or a good architecture will not be the same from one implementation to another. How "good" a design or an architecture is depends on how well it matches the goals of the system, and the intended application area of the system will have a great impact on the characteristics of the unit. To compare one technique against another requires that a metric or a set of metrics be chosen, and that the relative performance of the systems be compared using the chosen metrics as a measure of how "good" the system is. The number and type of metrics chosen will directly impact the comparison method and results of the evaluation. We will not try to establish a specific set of metrics; rather, we will present different metrics throughout the text to provide a basis for evaluation. The task of a system architect is to select the set of metrics that most closely reflects the goals for the system.

An example of the evaluation mechanism and the metrics involved is available with the numerical calculation of the Fourier transform. The Fourier transform can be used as a tool in a number of areas of research, and it has provided a wealth of knowledge in a variety of fields. The transform is simply defined, and utilizes a set of input values to create a set of output values. The complexity arises because each of the input values must interact with all other input values, which results in a computation requiring on the order of N^2 multiplications, which we represent as $O(N^2)$. In the mid-1960s a number of researchers independently developed an algorithm, or a set of algorithms, known as the fast fourier transform (FFT). The FFT follows a carefully planned pattern to allow the interaction between inputs required by the Fourier transform, but the operations are done in such a way that some values are used a number of times. The net result is a reduction in the number of multiplications required, from an algorithm that requires $O(N^2)$ multiplies, to an algorithm which requires only $O(N \times \log_2 N)$ multiplies. This greatly increased the size of transforms that could be economically produced, since it reduced the amount of computer time required for the calculation of a transform. The choice of the number of multiplies as the metric was reasonable in 1965, since the multiply was the most time-consuming portion of the algorithm. However, in today's technology, the multiply can be done very rapidly with inexpensive hardware, so other metrics could be more useful and result in algorithms that exhibit better performance than the straightforward FFT algorithm. For example, instead of using a base 2 radix algorithm, a base 4 radix algorithm could be used. This would actually result in more multiplies, but fewer data transfers would be required to complete the calculation. By using both the multiply time and the data transfer time, and the number of each required, better choices can be made for the architecture of an algorithm or a computer system created to do FFTs. A clearer picture of the overall response of the system will be obtained as more metrics are included in the evaluation.

The design process involves application of basic principles to solve engineering problems. In the process of learning the basic principles of computer design and the application of those principles to solve the problems posed by computer systems, it is not enough to simply explain the principle and to assume that the application of the principle will automatically follow. For that reason, this text makes extensive use of examples to illustrate the principles being discussed. It is hoped that the examples chosen and the design methods used will illustrate not only the principle, but the application of that principle as well. Thus, not only do the examples include block diagram representations of a solution, but the example will also, where appropriate, carry the application of the principle to a hardware level, so that a real implementation is presented. In some cases, the hardware included in the example is extensive, and the actual schematics and further explanations are included in Appendix B.

The design examples follow the ideas detailed by Fletcher [Flet80] in his design text. Uniform application of these ideas will result in designs that are not only functionally correct, but are also easily understood and debugged. Some of the specific ideas we will mention here include the consistent use of:

- The shape of gates to identify function.
- The use of polarized mnemonics.
- The use of logical state indicators.
- The use of incompatibility triangles.

All of these ideas are related to one another, and all deal with the issue of communication of ideas.

In the creation of a design to perform a specific function, a designer can implement a system that performs the desired work and matches all system criteria. But if the designer is unable to communicate these ideas and this design to anyone else, then no benefit is derived. One of the greatest challenges encountered by technically oriented people is to communicate their ideas not only to their colleagues, but also, perhaps more importantly, to the people who would benefit from application of those ideas. By following a consistent method for providing drawings and presenting designs, the ideas and concepts can be more readily understood.

Random logic is used extensively in computer design, not only to create the functional units of a system, such as adders and registers, but also to test conditions and create control signals. The logic provides an active function, and is not simply created to check for "true" or "false" conditions. This active nature of logic is reflected in the creation of the designs used in this book. We do not refer to signals as "true" or "false," but rather, a signal is either ASSERTED or UNASSERTED. A signal will be ASSERTED when the conditions required for the appropriate action are satisfied. If these conditions are not satisfied, then the signal will be UNASSERTED. In order to identify the action of the signal, polarized mnemonics will be used; that is, the names used to identify a signal will also identify its function. For example, a signal used to enable a data value onto a bus might be called DATA_ENABLE. If a name is too long, it can be shortened in a manner that will maintain the information. For example, the previous name could be shortened to D_ENBL. The other information that needs to be added to the name is an indication of the binary level at which the signal will be ASSERTED. This is done by appending to the end of the name a polarization indicator. If the signal is ASSERTED when the voltage of the line is high, then a hyphen and the letter H is added to the name. If the signal is ASSERTED when the voltage of the line is low, then a hyphen and the letter L is added to the name. If the data enable line is asserted low, then the name could be D_ENBL-L. The consistent use of polarized mnemonics will provide a basis for better understanding of the design and for better communication. It also will help the designer when, six months later, the design is revisited.

When representing the gates used to perform the logic work in a digital system, the shape of the gate should indicate the function being performed. The three basic shapes are the AND shape, the OR shape, and the BUFFER shape:

AND shape   OR shape   BUFFER shape

Like the names of signal lines, the inputs and outputs of a logic gate should identify the assertion levels involved. This is done by the use of logical state indicators, which are the "bubbles" appearing on some of the leads of a gate or a logical block. If a logical state indicator is present, then that line is asserted low. If a logical state indicator is not present, then that line is asserted high. For example, consider the equation used to implement the carry of a full adder:

$$C_{OUT} = A \cdot B + B \cdot C_{IN} + A \cdot C_{IN}$$

We know from basic digital design implementations that this can be implemented with two levels of NAND gates, one for the ANDing function and one for the

ORing function. However, when the shape of the gate, the use of polarized mnemonics, and the use of logical state indicators all come into play, then the gating will appear like:

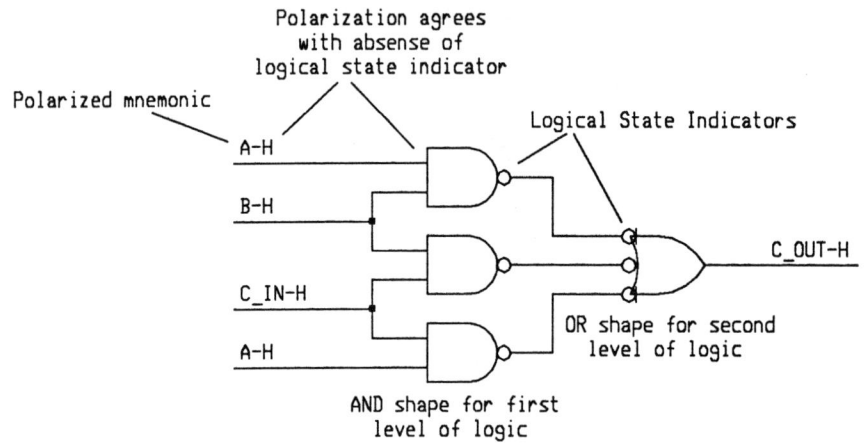

The various configurations for the basic gates is shown in Figure 1.9. Each can be used in either an ANDing or an ORing function, and the buffer can provide level conversion or not, as needed by the logic.

As can be seen from the gating for the carry shown above, the normal situation is for an output with a logical state indicator to supply a signal to an input

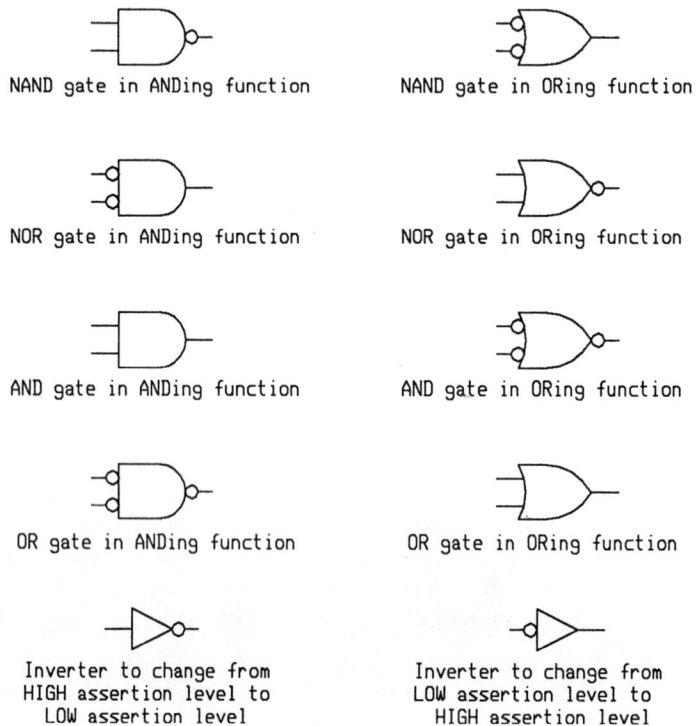

Figure 1.9. Basic Gates in and Their DeMorgan Representations.

with a logical state indicator. Also, an output with no logical state indicator will normally drive inputs that do not have a logical state indicator. However, sometimes this does not happen, and this condition is called an incompatibility. There are two times when this incompatibility will occur: at the input of an ANDing function and at the input of an ORing function. Consider the two functions below:

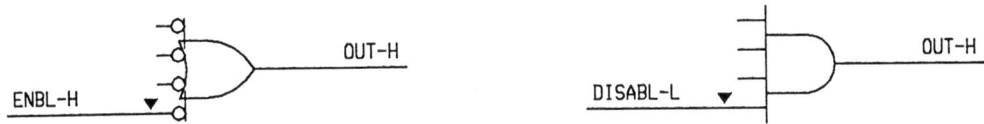

The first function shows an incompatible signal at the input of an OR function. When the signal (ENBL-H) is asserted, then the output (OUT-H) will be the logical OR of the remaining inputs. When the signal is not asserted, then OUT-H will be asserted, regardless of the level of the other inputs. Thus, an incompatibility at the input of an ORing function provides an enabling action: when the signal is asserted, the OR function is enabled; when the signal is not asserted, the OR function is disabled. The second function shows an incompatible signal at the input of an AND function. This time the incompatibility provides a disabling function. When the signal is asserted, the AND function is disabled, and the output will not be asserted, regardless of the level of the other inputs. When either of these cases arise, the fact that the designer created the incompatibility on purpose is indicated by the use of the small incompatibility triangle at the input. This is a signal from the creator of the design to anyone looking at the circuit that a high asserted signal feeding a low asserted input, or a low asserted signal that provides input to a high asserted signal, is not an oversight or a mistake, but rather a result of the design process.

These simple procedures will lead to systems that are easily understood and implemented. As an example, consider the task of creating a gating circuit to detect the address 776000_8 on an address bus that consists of 18 lines. One logic circuit to do this is shown in Figure 1.10. The drawings used in this book make extensive use of buses, which are merely a collection of wires. The name of the bus should follow the same polarized mnemonic convention mentioned above. The width of the bus and the range of the elements contained in it are identified by the use of the pair of numbers in parentheses: the ADDRESS(17:0)-H nomenclature identifies that the address lines range from ADDRESS(17)-H to ADDRESS(0)-H. The H on the end identifies the fact that the assertion level is high for this bus. Note also that the elements that are split off from the bus will identify which wire of the bus is involved. The gates used to detect the address include two NAND gates used in an ANDing function, and two OR gates, also used in an ANDing function. The incompatibility triangles identify the fact that the high asserted bus is knowingly directed to the low asserted input. The AND shape of the lower gate indicates that the output will be asserted (high) if ADDRESS(0)-H is not asserted, AND ADDRESS(1)-H is not asserted, AND ADDRESS(2)-H is not asserted, AND ADDRESS(3)-H is not asserted, AND ADDRESS(4)-H is not asserted. The shape of all of the gates in this book can be similarly interpreted to identify the function performed.

As mentioned above, information transfer within a computer system is often performed on a collection of wires called a bus. To provide an additional piece of information about the transfer of information on the bus, the direction of information flow will sometimes be indicated with a small arrow, as shown with the

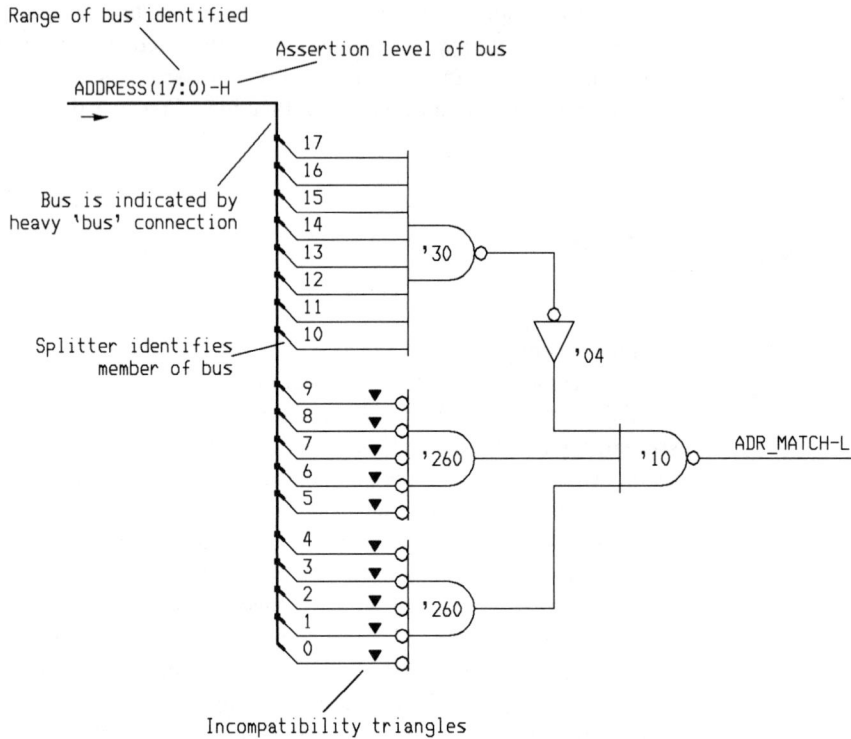

Figure 1.10. Implementation of an Address Decode Logic Circuit.

address bus above. If information can be transferred in both directions along a bus, this is indicated with a double ended arrow.

Since buses will be very important in the structure of systems, and in the logic used to implement examples in the text, a brief word about their function is in order. Buses can be created with a number of techniques, but we will mention only two, both diagramatically shown in Figure 1.11.

The first technique shown in the figure is the open collector method, in which the collector of the final transistor of a gate (or a functional block, such as a register) is not connected internally to any element. The effect of this mechanism is that, when the transistor is turned "on," the output will sink current, and the output voltage will go to a small value, usually near 0.4V. When the output transistor is not turned "on," no current is requested from the output, and the output voltage level is not influenced by that transistor/gate. Thus, an external pullup of some kind must be provided, so that the output voltage will go high when there is no transistor pulling it down. This mechanism will allow multiple outputs to be connected together; the level of this common node will be allowed to go high only if all output transistors are turned "off." This ability can be used effectively in a number of circumstances, as we shall see. A gate is often identified as an open collector gate by the presence of a mark at the output of the gate, as shown in Figure 1.11.

The other prevalent mechanism used for busing is also shown in Figure 1.11. This is called a tri-state capability, so named because the output can assume one of three states. Two of the states are the "normal" states of a TTL gate: low

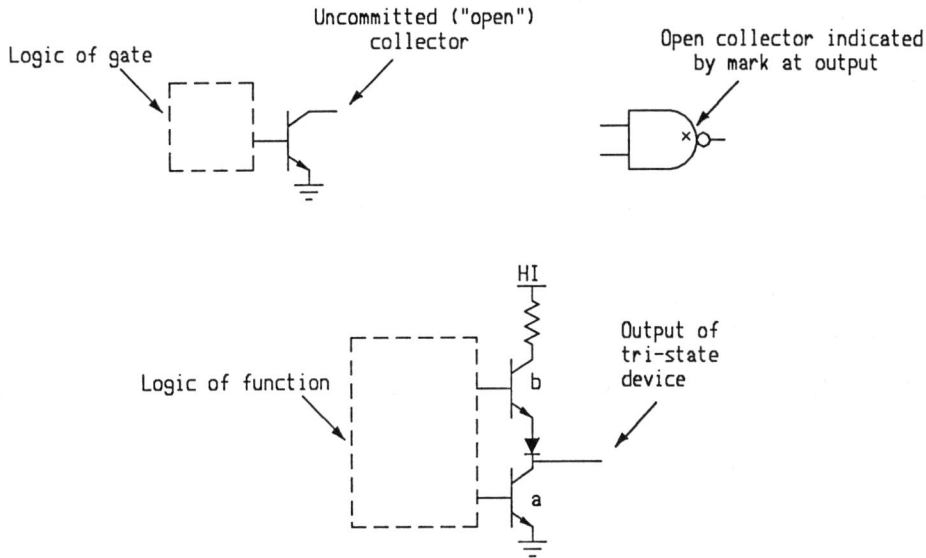

Figure 1.11. Busing Configurations: Open Collector and Tri-state.

and high. The output will be low when the logic of the function creates a situation in which transistor "a" is turned "on," and transistor "b" is turned "off"; the output will be high when transistor "a" is turned "off" and transistor "b" is turned "on." The third state occurs when the logic of the function creates a situation where both transistors "a" and "b" are turned off. In this case, the output is electrically disconnected from the system, since the paths through transistor "a" and through transistor "b" present an extremely high impedance. This third, high impedance state is usually created by an enable (or disable) input to the function.

The enable line used to control the tri-state capabilities of a gate of function can be included with a simple gate or with more complex functions. Figure 1.12 includes several examples of tri-state functions. Figure 1.12(a) shows a buffer shape (from the basic shapes shown above), which also has an enable line. From the presence of the logical state indicator on the enable line, it is evident that the buffer function will occur when the enable line is asserted low; if the enable line is high, then the buffer is electrically disconnected from the wire connected to the output. The buffer shown in Figure 1.12(b) operates in exactly the same fashion, except that the assertion level for the enable line is high. To require an enable line for each output would be excessive, so often a single enable line is used for an entire IC. Such is the situation depicted in Figure 1.12(c), which is often called a tri-state driver: eight buffers are packaged in a single IC, and the enable lines (in this case, asserted low enable lines) are connected together and made available on a single pin. Finally, since it is possible to transfer information in both directions through a tri-state port, Figure 1.12(d) shows a device configured to provide this capability. The device is a transceiver, and both an enable input and a direction input are used. Internal to the transceiver, two tri-state buffers are used for each line, one in either direction (A to B, or B to A). When the enable line is not asserted, the transceiver is electrically disconnected from both the A lines and the B lines. However, when the enable line is asserted, the direction line will determine which set of buffers is enabled.

Before continuing, we will mention one final set of devices to be used again and again in the text. These are the register and the latch:

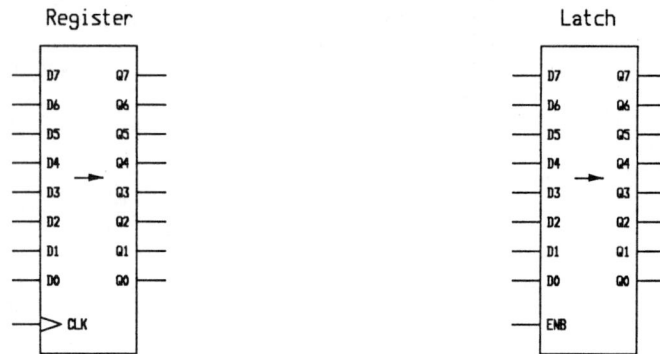

Register   Latch

Like the buffer of Figure 1.12(c), the register contains several elements ganged together for a common function. In this case, the joined elements are flip-flops, and in this configuration they are capable of storing a byte, or 8 bits. The clock lead on the register is marked with a special symbol that indicates that the function (in this case, a storage function) occurs on the rising edge of the clock. That is, when a low-to-high transition occurs on the clock line, information available at the input is transferred to the output. The next time at which a

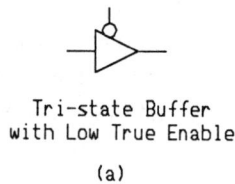

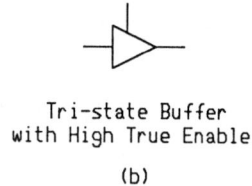

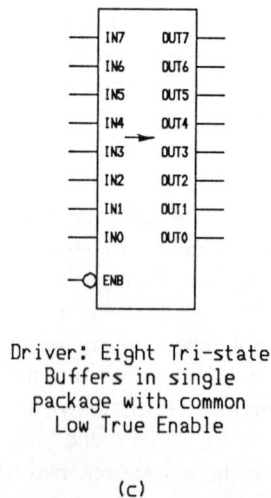

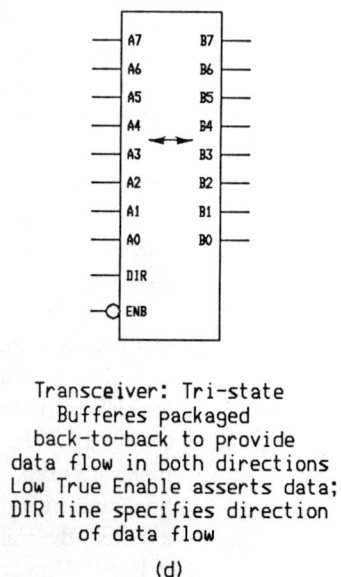

Tri-state Buffer
with Low True Enable

(a)

Tri-state Buffer
with High True Enable

(b)

Driver: Eight Tri-state
Buffers in single
package with common
Low True Enable

(c)

Transceiver: Tri-state
Bufferes packaged
back-to-back to provide
data flow in both directions
Low True Enable asserts data;
DIR line specifies direction
of data flow

(d)

Figure 1.12. Tri-state Buffer Configurations.

data input can have an effect on its corresponding output is when the clock again makes a low-to-high transition.

The latch function, as shown above, can also store a byte. Note, however, that there is no dynamic indication on the enable line of the latch. The latch function is described as follows: as long as the enable line is NOT ASSERTED (a low voltage level for this example), the outputs will be maintained at the value previously entered. So long as the enable line is ASSERTED (a high voltage level for this example), the output will follow the input, until the enable line is DEASSERTED, at which point the information will be stored in the latch. Thus, a register, as used in this text, is an edge-triggered function, while the latch is a level-sensitive function. (Note that latches can be created in other configurations than 8 bits, such as a single bit latch.)

Registers and tri-state devices can be packaged together, which can save board space and power. Registers, tri-state drivers, buffers, and transceivers will be used extensively in the examples in this text. The elements will be identified by their TTL device numbers, but the same functions are often available in other technologies as well. The open collector and tri-state capabilities can be provided with CMOS and other technologies, and the functions shown in the examples are often available in device libraries for designing functions on a single IC chip.

From the days of Pascal to the present, computers have been used to work with information, to do arithmetic, and to manipulate a variety of quantities. Some of the machines have implemented schemes to do the work with decimal quantities, but most of them use binary systems to represent the information. In Chapter 2 we look at the representation of information, as well as mechanisms that can be utilized to present different kinds of information. Not all number schemes are created equal, and different methods will lead to different characteristics in the ability of a system to represent values and in the amount of logic required to work in a number system. Once a designer or a system architect knows the limits to the various representations and schemes, then reasonable engineering choices can be made about the use of number systems.

The techniques used to manipulate data is the subject of Chapter 3. Here we examine techniques for doing not only addition and subtraction, but multiplication and division as well. All of the basic operations can be implemented in more than one way, and we will examine some of the assorted implementations. Each method will present a different set of characteristics, and so the choice of a metric will determine which type of algorithm or structure will be best suited for an application.

Armed with the number systems and the arithmetic methods, we are ready to consider the mechanisms used to specify work to be done by a computer. Thus, Chapter 4 looks at instruction specification: what is both useful and necessary at the instruction set level of a computer. Here we also introduce a register transfer language (RTL), which can be used to specify the elementary operations used to accomplish the work of the instruction. Again, the use of metrics, such as the time and number of steps required, provides a basis on which to compare different ideas or implementation techniques. One of the instruction set ideas to be examined is the ongoing debate on the complexity of the instruction set.

The control section of the computer coordinates the action of the various modules making up the machine, the buses, arithmetic units, registers, and so on. The action of the instruction set and the basic register transfers required to implement it are discussed in Chapter 4, and the creation of a control system to implement the instruction set is discussed in Chapter 5. Here we look at different techniques that can be utilized to assert the control signals required to move data throughout the system. Again, these techniques are represented as both principles and specific examples.

The subject of Chapter 6 is the input/output process — the techniques and methods used to move information to and from the computer. From the earliest days of computing machinery, this has been a requirement: how does the information get transferred to the machine to start a computation, and what is required to get the information out of the system? A number of methods are available, from the simple programmed I/O to the more complex direct memory access. The methods and their relative merits are presented, along with a discussion of different bus techniques utilized in the I/O process.

The storage and retrieval of the information required by a computer system is discussed in Chapter 7. As the technology of memories has changed over the years, the implementations have also changed. Memories have become larger, and this trend will continue for the foreseeable future. In order to maintain all of the information needed in a system, a hierarchical memory system is utilized. At one end of this system are the registers and cache memory systems needed to keep pace with a high speed processor. At the other end of the system are the slow speed devices, such as tape systems, where immense amounts of information are maintained. In Chapter 7 we will discuss not only the implementation of memories, but also some of the methods used in this hierarchy of storage devices, such as virtual memory techniques and cache memory systems.

The desire for higher performance always pushes designers and system architects to select approaches that most effectively utilize the overall system resources. One mechanism for obtaining higher performance is to utilize concurrent events. That is, if two things can happen simultaneously, then the overall system speed should increase. One method of doing this would be to have parallel computer systems, which greatly increases the complexity of the hardware and software problems needed to utilize a computer system. Another method to achieve some of the benefits of parallel processing is to create a pipeline of events. That is, the processing required by a system is divided into sections, and independent operations are carried out in hardware created to perform each of the sections. This technique is called pipelining, and in Chapter 8 we will examine some of the issues involved. Pipelining will result in performance benefits, but only if we are successful in keeping the pipe busy.

The following chapters provide some insights into the design process, along with some techniques for comparing the benefits of one technique with another. These techniques and ideas will be valid only when fully understood and applied in reasonable ways.

1.4. References and Readings

[AmBl64] Amdahl, G. M., G. A. Blaauw, and F. P. Brooks, Jr., "Architecture of the IBM System/360," *IBM Journal of Research and Development.* Vol. 8, No. 2, April 1964, pp. 87–101.

[Baer84] Baer, J. L., "Computer Architecture," *Computer.* Vol. 17, No. 10, October 1984, pp. 77–87.

[Baer80] Baer, J. L., *Computer Systems Architecture.* Rockville, MD: Computer Science Press, 1980.

[BaJo86] Bashe, C. J., L. R. Johnson, J. H. Palmer, and E. W. Pugh, *IBM's Early Computers*. Cambridge, MA: MIT Press, 1986.

[BeNe71] Bell, C. G. and A. Newell, *Computer Structures: Readings and Examples*. New York: McGraw-Hill Book Co., 1971.

[BlBr64] Blaauw, G. A., and F. P. Brooks, Jr., "The Structure of System/360 Part I: Outline of Logical Structure," *IBM Systems Journal*. Vol. 3, No. 2, 1964, pp. 119–135.

[BoTj78] Borgerson, B. R., G. S. Tjaden, and M. L. Hanson, "Mainframe Implementation with Off-the-Shelf LSI Modules," *Computer*. Vol. 11, No. 7, July 1978, pp. 42–48.

[BoHa78] Borgerson, B. R., M. L. Hanson, and P. A. Hartley, "The Evolution of the Sperry Univac 1100 Series: A History, Analysis, and Projection," *Communications of the ACM*. Vol. 21, No. 1, January 1978, pp. 25–43.

[BuCa84] Burger, R. M., R. K. Calvin, W. C. Holton, et al., "The Impact of ICs on Computer Technology," *Computer*. Vol. 17, No. 10, October 1984, pp. 88–96.

[CaPa78] Case, R. P., and A. Padegs, "Architecture of the IBM System/370," *Communications of the ACM*. Vol. 21, No. 1, January 1978, pp. 73–95.

[CoGi68] Conti, C. J., D. H. Gibson, and S. H. Pitkowski, "Structural Aspects of the System 360/85: General Organization," *IBM System Journal*. Vol. 7, No. 1, 1968, pp. 2–14.

[Dasg89] Dasgupta, S., *Computer Architecture: A Modern Synthesis*. New York: John Wiley & Sons, 1989.

[Dasg84] Dasgupta, S., *The Design and Description of Computer Architectures*. New York: John Wiley & Sons, 1984.

[FlWa86] Fleming, P. J., and J. J. Wallace, "How Not to Lie with Statistics: The Correct way to Summarize Benchmark Results," *Communications of the ACM*. Vol. 29, No. 3, March 1986, pp. 218–221.

[Flet80] Fletcher, W. I., *An Engineering Approach to Digital Design*. Englewood Cliffs, NJ: Prentice Hall, 1980.

[Flynn80] Flynn, M. J., "Directions and Issues in Architecture and Language," *Computer*. Vol. 13, No. 10, October 1980, pp. 5–22.

[FoME85] Fossum, T., J. B. McElroy, and W. English, "An Overview of the VAX 8600 System," *Digital Technical Journal*. Hudson, MA: Digital Equipment Corporation, 1985, pp. 8–23.

[FoIb85] Foster, C. C., and T. Iberall, *Computer Architecture*. 3rd Edition. New York: Van Nostrand Reinhold Co., 1985.

[Gold72] Goldstine, H. H., *The Computer from Pascal to von Neumann*. Princeton, NJ: Princeton University Press, 1972.

[HaVr78] Hamacher, V. C., Z. G. Vranesic, and S. G. Zaky, *Computer Organization*. New York: McGraw-Hill Book Company, 1984.

[Haye88] Hayes, J. P., *Computer Architecture and Organization*, 2nd Edition. New York: McGraw-Hill Book Company, 1988.

[HeJo82] Hennessy, J. L., N. Jouppi, S. Przybylski, et al., "MIPS: A Microprocessor Architecture," *Proceedings of the 15th Annual Workshop on Microprogramming*. New York: IEEE Computer Society Press, Los Angeles, CA, 1982, pp. 17–22.

[HwBr84] Hwang, K., and F. A. Briggs, *Computer Architecture and Parallel Processing*. New York: McGraw-Hill Book Company, 1984.

[IbCa78] Ibbett, R. N., and P. C. Capon, "The Development of the MU5 Computer System," *Communications of the ACM.* Vol. 21, No. 1, January 1978, pp. 13–24.

[Kain89] Kain, R. Y., *Computer Architecture, Software and Hardware.* Englewood Cliffs, NJ: Prentice Hall, 1989.

[Kane87] Kane, Gerry, *MIPS R2000 RISC Architecture.* Englewood Cliffs, NJ: Prentice Hall, 1987.

[Kate85] Katevenis, M. G. H., *Reduced Instruction Set Computer Architectures for VLSI.* Cambridge, MA: MIT Press, 1985.

[KuLa77] Kuck, D. J., D. H. Lawrie, and A. H. Sameh (Eds.), *High Speed Computer and Algorithm Organization.* New York: Academic Press, Inc., 1977.

[Lang82] Langdon, G. G., Jr., *Computer Design.* San Jose, CA: Computeach Press, Inc, 1982.

[Lavi78] Lavington, S. H., "The Manchester Mark I and Atlas: A Historical Perspective," *Communications of the ACM.* Vol. 21, No. 1, Jan 1978, pp. 4–12.

[Lavi80] Lavington, S., *Early British Computers.* Digital Press, 1980.

[Lund87] Lundstrom, D. E., *A Few Good Men from Univac.* Cambridge, MA: MIT Press, 1987.

[Mano82] Mano, M. M., *Computer System Architecture.* Englewood Cliffs, NJ: Prentice Hall, 1982.

[MeHo80] Metropolis, N., J. Howlett, and G. C. Rota (Eds.), *A History of Computing in the Twentieth Century.* New York: Academic Press, 1980.

[MoIb79] Morris, D., and R. Ibbett, *The MU5 Computer Systems.* London: Macmillan, 1979.

[Myer82] Myers, G. J., *Advances in Computer Architecture.* New York: John Wiley & Sons, 1982.

[Patt85] Patterson, D. A., "Reduced Instruction Set Computers," *Communications of the ACM.* Vol. 28, No. 1, January 1985, pp. 8–21.

[Prep85] Preparata, F. P., *Introduction to Computer Engineering.* New York: Harper & Row, 1985.

[Rand75] Randell, B. (ed.), *Origins of Digital Computers.* New York: Springer-Verlag, 1975.

[SaCh81] Saur, C. H., and K. M. Chandy, *Computer Systems Performance Modeling.* Englewood Cliffs, NJ: Prentice Hall, 1981.

[Schn85] Schneider, G. M., *The Principles of Computer Organization.* New York: John Wiley & Sons, 1985.

[Seit85] Seitz, C. L., "The Cosmic Cube," *Communications of the ACM.* Vol. 28, No. 1, January 1985, pp. 22–33.

[Shiv85] Shiva, S. G., *Computer Design and Architecture.* Boston, MA: Little, Brown, 1985.

[SiBe82] Siewiorek, D. P., C. G. Bell, and A. Newell, *Computer Structures: Principles and Examples.* New York: McGraw-Hill Book Co., 1982.

[Stal87] Stallings, W., *Computer Organization and Architecture.* New York: Macmillan Publishing Co., 1987.

[Ston80] Stone, H. S. (Ed.), *Introduction to Computer Architecture.* Chicago, IL: Science Research Associates, 1980.

[Ston87] Stone, H. S., *High-Performance Computer Architecture*. Reading, MA: Addison-Wesley Pub. Co., 1987.

[Swar76] Swartzlander, E. E., Jr. (Ed.), *Computer Design Development: Principal Papers*. Rochelle Park, NJ: Hayden Book Company, 1976.

[Tane84] Tanenbaum, A. S., "Implications of Structured Programming for Machine Architecture," *Communications of the ACM*. Vol. 21, No. 3, March 1978, pp. 237–246.

[Tane84] Tanenbaum, A. S., *Structured Computer Organization*. Englewood Cliffs, NJ: Prentice Hall, 1984.

[ThPa77] Thurber, K. J., and P. C. Patton, *Data Structures and Computer Architecture: Design Issues at the Hardware Level*. Lexington MA: Lexington Books, 1977.

[Thur76] Thurber, K. J., *Large Scale Computer Architecture, Parallel and Associative Processers*. Rochelle Park, NJ: Hayden Book Company, 1976.

[Tibe84] Tiberghien, J. (Ed.), *New Computer Architectures*. New York: Academic Press, 1984.

[Wall85] Wallich, P., "Toward Simpler, Faster Computers," *IEEE Spectrum*. Vol. 22, No. 8, August 1985, pp. 38–45.

[Wulf81] Wulf, W. A., "Compilers and Computer Architecture," *IEEE Computer*. Vol. 14, No. 7, July 1981, pp. 41–47.

2

Information Representation

One definition of a computer is a black box that manipulates information. First, information is entered into the computer. Then some form of processing is applied to the input information. Finally, the result is output to the user. In order to make any sort of evaluation of the computer or the proposed manipulation, some knowledge is required of the methods used for information storage and transfer. The purpose of this chapter is to examine the methods used for representing information. This includes not only numeric information, but also textual information, address representation, error coding information, boolean values, and status information. Each of these types of information is useful, and each type will be used by the computer at the appropriate time for a specific function. First, let us examine number representation, both integer and floating point, to determine the capabilities and limitations of available types of number systems. In addition, we will examine some of the difficulties introduced by numeric manipulation. Then we will move on to representation of status information, boolean information, and addresses. Finally we will consider the problems associated with integrating all of these types of information into the same system.

2.1. Integer Number Systems: Bounded Usefulness

Representation of information within a computer, and in most communication methods associated with computers, relies on the concept of a "bit." We will consider a bit to be a variable capable of assuming one of two distinct values. For numbers, these values are considered ones and zeros. Other interpretations are possible: true and false, asserted and unasserted, and so on. Collections of bits form numbers; each bit position doubles the possible representations of the system. Thus, the number of bits available for representation determines the number of representable values. For N bits, there are 2^N possible representations. Table 2.1 summarizes the number of representable values for popular computer sizes.

Table 2.1. Number of Representable Values.

Number of Bits	Number of Representable Values	Machines, Uses
4	16	4004, control
8	256	8080, 6800, control, communication
16	65,536	PDP11, 8086, 32020
32	4.29×10^9	IBM 370, 68020, VAX11/780
48	1.41×10^{14}	Unisys
64	1.84×10^{19}	Cray, IEEE (dp)

The number of bits used in a particular format identifies the total number of representable values, but does not directly specify the range of those values. The assumptions made about the representations actually identify the range and usefulness of the system. The simplest assumption is to let the binary numbers represent unsigned integers. If this is the case, then the range of representable numbers is from 0 to $2^N - 1$. These numbers are equally spaced, with a value of 1 between each representation. The system is a positional system, in every respect like the base 10 system with which we are familiar. Each bit position k has associated with it a value of 2^k, and the value represented by the collection of bits is represented by:

$$V_{\text{UNSIGNED INTEGER}} = \sum_{i=0}^{N-1} b_i \times 2^i$$

where b_i is the one or zero in position i. Thus, in unsigned binary the pattern 101101 means $1 \times 2^5 + 0 \times 2^4 + 1 \times 2^3 + 1 \times 2^2 + 0 \times 2^1 + 1 \times 2^0 = 45_{10}$.

While the unsigned integer representation is simple and easily manipulated, negative numbers cannot be represented. Hence, other integer systems are more often used for information representation. Perhaps the most widely utilized system is the two's complement system. Here, the 2^N representable values range from $-(2^{N-1})$ to $2^{N-1} - 1$. To negate a value, the value is subtracted from 2^N. Table 2.2 gives a few of the 256 values of an 8-bit two's complement system. This representation has also a positional nature, and the value of a particular representation is given by:

$$V_{\text{TWO'S COMPLEMENT}} = -b_{N-1} \times 2^{N-1} + \sum_{i=0}^{N-2} b_i \times 2^i$$

Thus, in two's complement representation, the pattern 101101 means $-1 \times 2^5 + 0 \times 2^4 + 1 \times 2^3 + 1 \times 2^2 + 0 \times 2^1 + 1 \times 2^0 = -19$. One thing to note here is that, even though the most significant bit is not defined as a sign bit, it can be considered such. The reason for this is that, if the most significant bit is set, then the value will be negative, since the most significant bit carries more weight than all of the other bits combined.

Example 2.1: Finding values in two's complement number system: What is the bit representation of 87_{10} in an 8-bit two's complement number system?

There are a variety of algorithms for converting between bases; it is not our intention to promote one or another. And since this number is a positive number within the representable values of the system, the various

Table 2.2. 8-Bit Two's Complement Representations.

Bit Pattern	Value	Note
01111111	127	Largest representable value.
01111110	126	
01111101	125	
...	...	
...	...	
00000010	2	Note that leading zero indicates
00000001	1	positive number.
00000000	0	Unique representation of zero.
11111111	−1	Minus one is always all ones.
11111110	−2	Note that leading one indicates
11111101	−3	negative number.
...	...	
...	...	
10000010	−126	
10000001	−127	
10000000	−128	Smallest (most negative) representable value.

bit positions can each be checked to ascertain that the desired bit pattern is 01010111.

What is the bit representation of -76_{10} in an 8-bit two's complement number system?

Again, the solution begins by finding the bit pattern for 76_{10}, which is 01001100. To negate this, the number is then subtracted from 2^8:

$$
\begin{array}{r}
1\ 00000000 \\
-\ 01001100 \\
\hline
10110100
\end{array}
$$

It is not necessary to do these calculations in binary:

$$
\begin{array}{r}
256 \\
-\ 76 \\
\hline
180
\end{array}
$$

The representation 10110100 is equivalent (in unsigned binary) to 180. Also note that negative numbers are negated to positive numbers in exactly the same way:

What is the representation of the negative of 11010110_2?
Base two:

$$
\begin{array}{r}
1\ 00000000 \\
-\ 11010110 \\
\hline
00101010
\end{array}
$$

Base 10:

$$
\begin{array}{r}
256 \\
-\ 214 \\
\hline
42
\end{array}
$$

The answer 42 converts to 00101010, as above.

The last portion of the example demonstrates the method utilized by many people to arrive at the correct bit representation for negating a two's complement number: complement all of the bits and add 1, which is the same as complement and increment. This also demonstrates the method for subtracting one number from another: the number to be subtracted is complemented and fed into one input of an adder, the other number forms the other adder input, and the carry in of the adder is asserted. The result is that a complement and increment have been performed on the number to be negated, and the result out of the adder will be the desired value.

One of the extremely attractive features of the two's complement system is its circular nature. This is graphically demonstrated in Figure 2.1 for a 4-bit two's complement system. The numbers are arranged around a circle from 1000 to 0111. As can be seen from the figure, progressing from one point to the next, or from one number to the next is accomplished by simply increasing or decreasing the values by one. When this happens at the 0111 to 1000 border, the number changes from a positive to a negative value. The net result is a discontinuity in the desired numeric sequence. The name given to this discontinuity is an overflow — we have exceeded our ability to represent information in the number system. The same thing will happen if you specify successively more negative numbers: decrementing 1001 to 1000 works fine, but decrementing 1000 results in 0111, which is a positive number. We have again crossed the discontinuity boundary, and exceeded our ability to represent information in the number system. When an arithmetic operation causes this to occur, many computers will respond by setting an "overflow bit." This bit can be included as one of the several bits making up the status word of a processor; these bits will be further described in the next chapter. In addition, the benefit of the circular nature of the two's complement system will be further discussed after consideration of a fractional representation of information.

The numbers to this point have been described as integers, which is the correct interpretation only if we make the proper assumptions concerning the placement of the radix point of the system. Unless otherwise stated, we naturally assume that the radix point is located directly to the right of the least significant bit. With this assumption the patterns do indeed represent integers, and all of the

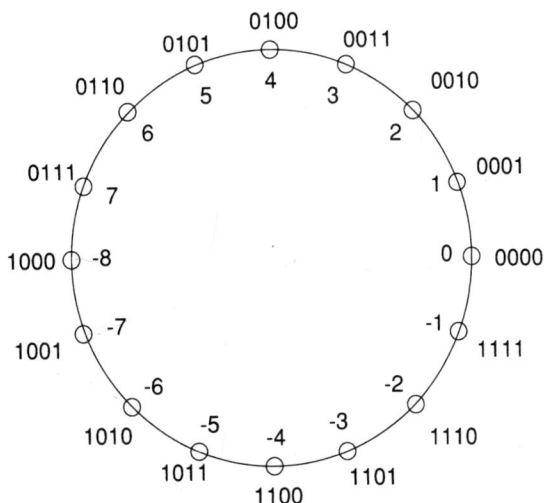

Figure 2.1. Graphical Representation of the Circular Nature of Two's Complement Numbers.

statements made concerning integer manipulation apply. However, if we assume that the radix point is located at some point other than to the right of the least significant bit position, then the range and granularity of the representable values changes.

The placement of the radix point (we are used to base 10, where it is the decimal point) is a matter of definition; no piece of hardware is installed on circuit boards to identify the location of the radix point. The radix point is established to satisfy the needs for which the processing element is utilized. If the information to be represented contains fractional values, then assumption of a radix point establishes a fixed point system that is so adjusted that it can cover the necessary range. Addition and subtraction operations for this type of a system are exactly the same as integer operations. However, for multiplication and division, care must be taken to assure that the radix point is in the correct place after an operation, and that the correct bits are saved. For example, multiplication of two 16-bit numbers, regardless of the placement of a radix point, results in a 32-bit number. However, if the result of the multiplication of two 16-bit numbers is to be stored in a 16-bit number, then there are limits to the size of the number. In the case of a fixed point system, the correct bits must be selected so that the assumptions made about the radix point of the multiplier and multiplicand are also true for the result.

A fixed point, noninteger system is also a positional system, just like the positional systems already described. The only difference is that the position of the radix point introduces a new factor into the equation. Let p represent the location of the radix point; this is the number of bit positions to the left of the least significant digit (bit) where the assumed radix point is found. Thus, the value of p for an integer system would be zero. Then the equation for the value of a two's complement fixed point number would be given by:

$$V_{\text{FIXED POINT}} = -b_{N-1} \times 2^{N-p-1} + \sum_{i=0}^{N-2} b_i \times 2^{i-p}$$

This gives the user the flexibility to choose a system that will fulfill the needs of a specific project. That is, a designer can determine the smallest value required to meet the needs of the system, and select a number system accordingly. Therefore, one of the characteristic values of a number system that will help determine its usefulness is the difference (in absolute value) between adjacent numeric representations. We will call this difference Δr. Note that Δr for all integer systems is 1; Δr for fixed point systems will be 2^{-p}.

A simple example of this is a 5-digit decimal number system for representation of monetary values. If p is equal to 0, then the system can represent values from \$0 to \$99999, and Δr has a value of \$1. Thus, any value less than a dollar cannot be represented in the system. If the system designer needs to represent cents as well as dollars, then p can be assumed to have a value of 2. The five digits can then represent values from \$0.00 to \$999.99, and Δr has a value of \$0.01. Both systems have the same number of representable values, but the range and the Δr differ with the use of the system and the assumed value for p.

Example 2.2: Fixed point number system: Consider a fixed point 16-bit two's complement system with a value of p equal to 8. What is the smallest representable number? What is the largest representable number? What is the Δr? We know that addition and subtraction will not have any effect on the position of the radix point, but what is the correct procedure for selecting the bits to retain after a multiplication?

The smallest representable number can be defined to be either the smallest absolute value that can be represented or the most negative number. The smallest absolute value for this system is zero; the next smallest absolute value is represented by the bit pattern 00000000.00000001. This has the value of 2^{-8}, which is just 3.9×10^{-3}. The most negative representable number has the bit pattern 10000000.00000000; this has the value of -2^7, which is -128. The Δr for this system is the same as the smallest representable value, 2^{-8}. To ascertain the effect that multiplication has upon the radix point, notice what happens when we multiply two of these numbers: the least significant bit will represent 2^{-16}, while the most significant bit will be 2^{14}. Thus, to get a properly aligned value when the process is over, the 31-bit result must be right shifted 8 bits, and then the next 16 bits form the desired result. Note that this dictates that the multiplication of the two input numbers has a maximum value if the number of bits saved as a result is to be the same as the number of bits used for the inputs. If the number of bits required to represent the value of the result exceeds 16, then an overflow has occurred.

A fixed point system is often used in applications like digital signal processing (DSP), where the values are scaled as they enter the system, and the intermediate values are sufficiently represented by the number of bits in the system. The Fujitsu 8764 DSP chip uses a 16-bit value with p equal to 14, while some components, such as the AMD29517, are set up for a 16-bit system with p equal to 15. If p is equal to 15 then all representable values (except for -1.0) have an absolute value less than one, and the system scales easily. These systems utilize integer arithmetic units, which are faster and require fewer devices than their floating point counterparts.

Some applications, such as the digital signal processing applications mentioned above, are able to take full advantage of the circular nature of the two's complement number system. These applications have a characteristic, inherent in the application itself, that will permit the number system to cross the overflow boundary without causing a disruption in the overall flow of instructions and data. For example, one of the frequently used digital signal processing algorithms is a finite impulse response (FIR) filter function. It can be shown that certain FIR filters will always result in a value within the ability of the number system to represent information; hence, intermediate overflows in the addition process can be ignored.

The two's complement number system is the most widely used integer system in machines, but it is not the only one. Another method used in some machines is the one's complement system. Mathematically, the one's complement of an N-bit number with value V is defined as $2^N - 1 - V$. The $2^N - 1$ portion of the equation is merely N one's, and subtracting V from a pattern of all 1's results in zeros where the ones were, and ones where the zeros were. Hence, the negative of a number is formed by complementing all of the bits in the number. Therefore, to negate any number, all that is required is to invert every bit position, which is a very fast operation. The range covered by this method is from $2^{N-2} - 1$ to $-(2^{N-2} - 1)$, which is just one different from the range of the two's complement number system. However, some "features" of this system limit its usefulness in digital systems. Unlike the other systems discussed above, this system does not follow a positional notation methodology. The bits have different significance depending on the sign of the number. Also, this system has two legal representations for the number zero, both of which must be checked by any operation that tests for zero. Finally, treatment of the carry in this system is different from other systems, because of its "end-around" feature. The proof of this feature will be left as an exercise, but the effect can be seen from the following example:

Example 2.3: One's complement arithmetic: Consider a 6-bit one's complement system. Represent 15, –15, 13, and –13 in this system. Then perform the following additions: 15 + 13, 15 + (–13), 13 + (–13), and 13 + (–15).

The numbers are derived in a simple fashion:

Decimal Value	One's Complement	Comment
15	001111	Positive numbers same as two's complement.
– 15	110000	Complement bits to negate.
13	001101	Positive numbers same as two's complement.
– 13	110010	Complement bits to negate.

Now for the additions:

15	001111	This proceeds just like the two's
+ 13	+ 001101	complement version.
28	0 011100	No carry out: number is correct, and the result is as we expect.

15	001111	The addition is done in the normal
+ –13	+ 110010	fashion, but
2	1 000001	the result of one is incorrect; however, the presence of a carry says we
	+ 000001	should add that as a 1 in the LSB
	000010	which gives the expected result.

13	001101	This time we will add a positive number
+ –13	+ 110010	to its negative (which is just complement)
0	111111	and end up with all ones — a valid zero.

13	001101	Here the positive number is smaller
+ –15	+ 110000	than the negative number, so result
–2	0 111101	is negative; no carry — the value is correct.

Note that, in all of the above cases, the carry out can be added to the intermediate result (hence the name of end-around carry) to produce the correct final result.

The one's complement number system can be used in many of the same ways that other systems can be used, but care must be taken to operate within the constraints that it imposes.

Another system utilized to represent numbers is the excess system. Here an excess is purposely added to the value to be represented, and the resulting bit pattern is stored or used as required. One of the most prevalent uses of excess codes is to store exponents in floating point numbers. If we let S represent the value that will be stored or otherwise utilized, V the true value of the number, and E the excess, then the relationship between them is defined as:

$$S = V + E$$

In operations utilizing this type of representation care must be taken to be sure that the result is within the desired range. That is, if two numbers are added together, the following will happen:

$$S1 + S2 = (V_1 + E) + (V_2 + E)$$

$$= (V_1 + V)_2 + 2 \times E$$

To obtain the correct result $[(V_1 + V_2) + E]$, a value equal to E must be removed from the calculated result. In some systems, where E is a power of 2, this is a simple operation. However, in other systems the operation can become more complicated.

> *Example 2.4: Number representation in excess codes:* What is the representation of $+37_{10}$ in an 8-bit excess 128 code? What is the representation of -23_{10} in an 8-bit excess 128 code? What is the sum of the two numbers, in the 8-bit excess 128 code?
>
> An 8-bit unsigned number can represent values between 0 and 255. The excess representation can then represent values from -128 to $+127$.

+ 128	10000000	This is the excess.
+ 37	00100101	The value to be represented.
165	10100101	The representation of 37_{10} in excess 128 code.
+ 128	10000000	This is the excess.
− 23	00010111	The value to be represented.
105	01101001	The representation of -23_{10} in excess 128 code.
165	10100101	This is +37 in excess 128.
+ 105	+ 01101001	This is −23 in excess 128.
270	1 00001110	Note the carry out in this operation. 270 is too big to represent in 8 bits; to correct for the $2 \times E$ that is in this sum, subtract 128.
− 128	− 10000000	In binary, is this add or subtract?
142	10001110	This is the representation of 14, the correct result, in excess 128.

Another use for the excess code is in representing decimal numbers. A 4-bit integer representation can assume values between 0 and 15. If we limit ourselves to decimal numbers, the desired values are 0 to 9. These are represented in excess 3 by the numbers 3 to 12. One of the beneficial effects of this type of representation is that, when two numbers are added together by a 4-bit binary adder, if the addition of those decimal values would have resulted in a carry out, then there will be a carry out of the binary adder. Note that if D_1 and D_2 are decimal numbers represented by $V_1 = D_1 + 3$ and $V_2 = D_2 + 3$, then $V_1 + V_2 = D_1 + D_2 + 6$. Then if the sum of D_1 and D_2 would result in a value greater than 9, which would cause a carry in a decimal adder, $V_1 + V_2$ would cause a carry in a binary adder. Note also that the resulting value $(D_1 + D_2 + 6)$ must have 3 removed from it before it is the valid representation in excess 3 for the resulting number, assuming that no carry out resulted. If a carry out did result, then the 4-bit representation is actually the correct value, since the excess is 6, and there are 6 unused representations in the 4-bit scheme. This code can be very useful for systems that work with 4-bit quantities.

Example 2.5: BCD excess 3 system: Consider a system that works with 3-digit decimal numbers, and it stores the digits in excess 3 format. What is the representation of 573? What is the representation of 142? Add the two numbers, and give the correct result in excess 3 format.

The numbers are handled on a digit-by-digit basis, with the excess being included with each digit:

Decimal	*Binary*	
+ 3 3 3	0011 0011 0011	This is the excess.
5 7 3	0101 0111 0011	And the number to be represented.
8 10 6	1000 1010 0110	The excess 3 representation.
+ 3 3 3	0011 0011 0011	This is the excess.
1 4 2	0001 0100 0010	This is the number to be represented.
4 7 5	0100 0111 0101	The excess 3 representation.
573	1000 1010 0110	Do the addition in decimal and in
+ 142	0100 0111 0101	binary. Correct as needed to make output correct.
715	1100 1 0001 1011	

Carry out of second set of 4 bits indicates that the most significant digit should be incremented by one. Also indicates that this value is correct as it stands (since $2 \times E = 6$ and the carry out indicates that the number overflowed into the next digit) so we need to add 3. Therefore, the MSD needs to be incremented by one and decremented by 3; the middle digit needs to have 3 added; and the LSD needs to be decremented by 3.

$$-0010 + 0011 - 0011$$

1010 0100 1000		Which is the correct excess 3 representation for 715_{10}.

The excess representation for decimal numbers does have some useful characteristics, but usually this information is represented in the more natural binary coded decimal format (BCD). This code is listed in Table 2.3. Here, the numbers 0–9 are represented by the equivalent binary representations 0000 to 1001. Thus, 4 bits are used for each decimal number. To represent all of the decimal numbers from 0 to 99_{10}, 8 bits would be required. The smallest number (zero) would be represented as 00000000; the largest would be 10011001. But we already know that with 8 bits we should be able to represent 256 values; why are we limited to 100 values with BCD? The other representations (1010 to 1111) are not used with BCD, which does not fully utilize all of the representable values. Thus, a BCD system is capable of $10^{N/4}$ different representations.

Table 2.3. Binary Coded Decimal
(BCD) Representations.

Bit Pattern	Value
0000	0
0001	1
0010	2
0011	3
0100	4
0101	5
0110	6
0111	7
1000	8
1001	9
1010	Not valid
1011	Not valid
1100	Not valid
1101	Not valid
1110	Not valid
1111	Not valid

The above representations point out some very important characteristics of the representation of information with bit patterns:

- For a representation of N bits, 2^N different values can be represented. This is true whether the information represented is numerical in nature, an address, or any other information, such as an instruction.
- The meaning associated with a bit pattern depends on the assumptions made.
- The assumptions about bit meaning will impact on the design of the hardware that manipulates the bits. Note that a one's complement adder is a different piece of hardware than a two's complement adder.
- The Δr for each representation is the same for the entire range of representable values.
- The assumption of a radix point will allow representation of fractional values. Note that the assumption of a radix point does not impact on the addition process; however, multiplication and division must account for shifts in the radix point due to an increased number of bits in the result.
- The choice of a coding method is based on available hardware, the desired range of values, and other system goals.

Regardless of the mechanisms chosen for information representation, the resulting collection of bits must be represented and communicated. Internal to a machine, the data is just that: a collection of bits in a register, in a memory location, or on a bus. But how humans see and remember or communicate this information is not usually in bit pattern format. We generally group bits together and utilize a different base to represent them; the most common systems are octal and hexadecimal. These representations will be utilized as appropriate throughout this book.

Example 2.6: Alternate representations for bit patterns: Represent -157_{10} and $+25,477_{10}$ in binary, octal, and hexadecimal. Do this for the 16-bit two's complement representation and a 16-bit excess 32,768 representation.

+157	= 0000000010011101	The binary representation, to 16 bits.
−157	= 1111111101100011	To negate, complement and increment.
	= 1 111 111 101 100 011	Group in groups of 3 for octal.
	= 177543	
	= 1111 1111 0110 0011	Group in groups of 4 for hexadecimal.
	= FF63	
25,477	= 0110001110000101	the binary representation, to 16 bits.
	= 0 110 001 110 000 101	Group in groups of 3 for octal.
	= 061605	
	= 0110 0011 1000 0101	Group in groups of 4 for hexadecimal.
	= 6385	

32,611	= 0111111101100011	Excess code for −157.
	= 0 111 111 101 100 011	Group for octal.
	= 077543	Compare with two's complement.
	= 0111 1111 0110 0011	Group for hexadecimal.
	= 7F63	Compare with two's complement.
58,245	= 1110001110000101	Excess code for 25477.
	= 1 110 001 110 000 101	Group for octal.
	= 161605	Compare with two's complement.
	= 1110 0011 1000 0101	Group for hexadecimal.
	= E385	Compare with two's complement.

2.2. Floating Point Number Systems: Coding for Range

The previous section pointed out the fact that for an N-bit number, there are 2^N different representable values. If we assume an integer interpretation to the bit pattern, then we have a numerical range of 2^N. Throughout this range Δr is equal to one. The coding mechanism (two's complement, one's complement, excess code, etc.) identifies the low point and the high point of that range. If we assume a radix point within the word, then the range is smaller; however, now we have the ability to represent fractional values. Many problems require the ability to represent information of a much greater or smaller magnitude than possible with fixed point systems, and for these problems we need a different type of information representation system. We are familiar with the use of scientific notation to represent large numbers, such as Avogadro's number (6.022×10^{23}), or small numbers, such as the mass of a proton (1.673×10^{-24} g). This same scheme is used to represent large and small numbers in computers, and has the name of a floating point number system (FPNS). This type of number system does not expand the quantity of representable values; rather, it modifies the way in which the 2^N values is interpreted.

To specify a floating point number, seven different pieces of information are necessary: base of the system, sign, magnitude, and base of the mantissa, and the sign, magnitude, and base of the exponent. We will first look at scientific notation, which is used to identify these pieces, and then examine methods used in computers to do the same things. The numbers in scientific notation above have the following format:

$$\text{(Sign) Mantissa} \times \text{Base}^{\text{EXPONENT}}$$

The "base" in the above equation is the radix of the system. For "normal" scientific numbers this radix is 10, because that is the base of the number system with which we are most familiar. Most computers do arithmetic in a binary fashion, so this choice would not be advantageous for a computer. The radix of the system is a constant that is decided at the time the system is defined, and it has a direct bearing on the range of values that the system can represent, as we shall see. The value used for the radix is not stored in the computer, but forms part of the definition of the number system. We will denote the radix of the system as r_b.

The radix of the system also applies to the mantissa. The mantissa is used to identify the significant digits of a value. In practice, we may use mantissas with few digits or many digits. In a machine representation, the number of digits used for mantissa representation is the same for all numbers (of the same type, i.e., single precision or double precision). One of the characteristics of the floating point number is the number of digits used to represent the mantissa. This number will be identified simply as m. Thus, for a specific floating point number system, each mantissa will consist of m base r_b digits. Let us designate the value of a mantissa as V_M. In the consideration of the range of the system, we will need to know the maximum and minimum allowable values for the mantissa, which we will designate as $V_{M_{MAX}}$ and $V_{M_{MIN}}$.

The location of the value of a floating point number on the real number line will be determined by the exponent. If the exponent is a large positive number, then the value of the floating point number is very large. If the exponent is zero then the value of the floating point number is just the value of the mantissa. If the exponent is a large negative number, then the value of the floating point number is very small. Determining the value of the exponent requires information concerning the sign, the radix, and the number of digits in the representation. We will let the radix of the exponent be designated by r_e. Like the radix of the system, the choice of r_e is made at design time, and is part of the number definition. For the scientific number examples above, $r_b = r_e = 10$, but in most computers, $r_e = 2$.

The number of digits in the exponent specifies the maximum size of the exponent, which, in conjunction with the radix of the system, identifies the range of the number system. We will designate this number (the number of digits in the exponent) with the letter e. Note that the exponent will contain e base r_e digits, and that, like the mantissa, r_e and e are decisions made at the time the number system is defined.

The sign of the exponent also needs to be identified. For our scientific examples, this was directly identified by the presence or absence of the minus sign. It is possible to do the same for exponents stored in floating point numbers in computers: identify a bit that is a sign bit for the exponent, and let the exponent be stored in sign-magnitude format. However, most computers use not this method, but rather a coding technique to represent positive and negative values. The method most often used is the excess code technique, although other methods could be used as well. We will examine the reason for excess codes in the exponent a little later. Whatever the coding scheme chosen, each of the allowable representations for the exponent results in a unique value for the exponent. Let the value of the exponent be represented as V_E. As with the mantissa, we will need to know the maximum and minimum representable values of the exponent. We will designate these as $V_{E_{MAX}}$ and $V_{E_{MIN}}$.

The sign of the number itself must also be known. In the scientific representation above it is identified explicitly by a sign. This sign-magnitude mechanism is also the most prevalent mechanism for the storage of floating point numbers in computers. However, this information may be coded into the number by any of the coding schemes which allow for positive and negative representations.

The final piece of information we need is the placement of the radix point. In scientific notation, we explicitly designate the location of the radix point. However, in the machine we will need to make provisions for identifying the location of the radix point, or make appropriate assumptions about the system at design time. As with the fractional systems discussed above, let p designate the location of the radix point with respect to the least significant digit. This p will be used in determining the value of the mantissa, since, for an unsigned mantissa,

$$V_M = \sum_{i=0}^{N-1} d_i \times r_b^{i-p}$$

where the mantissa is composed of N r_b digits labeled d_{N-1} to d_0. So, the value of the floating point number, V_{FPN}, is given by

$$V_{FPN} = (-1)^{SIGN} V_M \times r_b^{V_E}$$

The location of the radix point of the mantissa is directly connected to the value of the exponent. Consider the following representations for the number $32,768_{10}$.

$$3.2768 \times 10^4 = 32.768 \times 10^3 = 3276.8 \times 10^1$$

Each of the representations is a correct number in scientific notation, and the location of the decimal point is reflected in the value of the exponent. If the location of the radix point within the word is allowed to vary from number to number, then provisions must be made to record p and use that information in all of the calculations. This could be confusing and cumbersome, so in most systems an assumption is made concerning the location of the radix point (that is, the value of p) to minimize the amount of stored information and to make the arithmetic easier. The process of representing all of the numbers such that the mantissas all have the same value for p is called normalization. This process also identifies the allowable mantissa values. The assumption that we will make for our examples is that $p = M$, and that the leftmost digit of the mantissa is nonzero. This means that the mantissa is a fraction that can have values between $1/r_b$ and almost 1. Specifically, the maximum value is $V_{M_{MAX}} = 0.d_m d_m d_m \ldots$ to the length of the mantissa, where $d_M = r_b - 1$; this number is very close to one $(1 - r_b^{-N}$, for N digits). And the minimum mantissa value is $V_{M_{MIN}} = 0.100 \ldots = 1/r_b$. The value of this number varies with each r_b. Thus, the only legal values for the mantissas vary from $V_{M_{MIN}}$ to $V_{M_{MAX}}$, and the numbers represented by the FPNS must be obtained by combining a member of this set of mantissas and one of the available exponents. This leads to the following observations concerning nonzero values in a normalized floating point number system:

$$\text{Maximum representable value} = V_{\text{FPN}_{\text{MAX}}} = V_{M_{\text{MAX}}} \times r_b^{V_{E_{\text{MAX}}}}$$

$$\text{Minimum representable value} = V_{\text{FPN}_{\text{MIN}}} = V_{M_{\text{MIN}}} \times r_b^{V_{E_{\text{MIN}}}}$$

$$\text{Number of legal mantissas} = \text{NLM}_{\text{FPN}}$$

$$= (r_b - 1) \times r_b^{m-1}$$

$$\text{Number of representable values} = \text{NRV}_{\text{FPN}}$$

$$= \text{Number of legal mantissas}$$

$$\times \text{Number of legal exponents}$$

These values help to identify the characteristics of a floating point number system, and are useful to determine if the system can be used in a specific application.

Example 2.7: Characteristics of a FPNS: Consider a normalized floating point number system which has $r_b = 10$, $r_e = 10$, $m = 3$, $e = 2$, both exponent and number itself stored in sign/magnitude format. What is the largest representable fraction? What is the smallest representable fraction? What is the largest representable exponent? What is the smallest representable exponent? What is the largest representable number? What is the smallest representable positive nonzero number? How many nonzero numbers can be represented in this system?

From the equations given above,

$$V_{M_{\text{MAX}}} = 0.999 = 1.000 - 10^{-3}$$

$$V_{M_{\text{MIN}}} = 0.100$$

$$V_{E_{\text{MAX}}} = 99$$

$$V_{E_{\text{MIN}}} = -99$$

Note that this is the most negative exponent. The smallest exponent in absolute value is 0, but that exponent does not lead to the smallest representable numbers.

$$V_{\text{FPN}_{\text{MAX}}} = 0.999 \times 10^{99}$$

$$V_{\text{FPN}_{\text{MIN}}} = 0.100 \times 10^{-99}$$

$$\text{NLM}_{\text{FPN}} = 9 \times 10 \times 10$$

$$= 900$$

$$\text{NRV}_{\text{FPN}} = 2 \times 900 \times 199$$

$$= 358,200$$

There are 199 representable exponents: 99 greater than zero, 99 less than zero, and zero. At this point we will make an observation concerning the number system, but leave the discussion of the problem until a later section. The number system can represent very large values, and very small values. The question is, can the value 1.00 be added to 10,000? The representation of 1.00 is 0.100×10^1. The representation of 10,000 is 0.100×10^5. But there is no legal representation for 10,001. This points out the fact that the Δr is different for each V_E. For the legal representation of 1.00, the Δr is $1/100$. For the representation of 10,000 the Δr is 100.

The above example provides a very interesting illustration. With five digits and two sign bits 358,200 different values can be represented with a normalized floating point system. If we assume that one of the sign bits can be interpreted as a number with a value of 0 or 1, then an integer number system with the same quantity of symbols (i.e., five base 10 digits, a base 2 digit, and a sign) would be capable of representing 399,998 values, more than the floating point system. But these numbers vary between –199,999 and 199,999. (Note that we are not counting the representation of zero in either case.)

The range of the system and the number of representable fractions are both affected by the choice of the base of the system. The example given above used base 10, but computers don't usually provide that capability. With the base 2 arithmetic capabilities of the machines, one would assume that the most natural base for floating point numbers would be two. However, grouping the bits into other base values, such as base 4 or base 8, can expand the range of the system. To demonstrate this let us compare two different normalized floating point number systems, simplified enough that we can enumerate all of the legal values in the systems.

Both of these systems are representable in six bits. The first system is enumerated in Table 2.4. This table identifies how each bit is used in the number system. Four bits are used in the mantissa, and two bits for the exponent. With the $r_b = 2$ for this system, $m = 4$. Also, $r_e = 2$, and $e = 2$. Missing from the number system are negative values, both for the exponent and for the number itself. Nevertheless, the system demonstrates some important points. First of all, the first bit in the mantissa gives no information. In our definition of a normalized FPNS, the first digit to the right of the radix point must be nonzero, and for a base 2 system, the only digit left is a one. Hence, this digit adds no information to the system. Second, the Δr changes for each value of the exponent: when the exponent is 0, the Δr is 1/16; when the exponent is 1, the Δr is 1/8. The Δr doubles for successive exponent values. The third observation is that the 32 values representable in this system is only half of the $2^6 = 64$ legal combinations of six bits. Thus, while an integer system would represent 64 equally spaced values (0 to 63), the system demonstrated in Table 2.4 represents 32 nonequally spaced values from $1/2$ to $7^1/2$.

In contrast to the system of Table 2.4 is another 6-bit normalized floating point system shown in Table 2.5. This system is constructed so that the bits are grouped into base 4 digits; thus, the permissible values for the first digit are 1, 2, and 3, all of which take two bits to represent. However, note that the digit 1_4 has a leading 0 ($1_4 = 01_2$). This increases the number of allowable mantissas from eight to twelve. Thus, the first bit of the mantissa in this representation is *not* redundant, as it was for the previous system. The Δr for this system varies by a factor of four for subsequent exponent values. Note that the Δr for $V_E = 0$ is the

Table 2.4. 6-Bit Normalized Floating Point System, Base 2.
$r_b = 2, \; r_e = 2, m = 4, \; e = 2$

V_M base 2				V_M	$V_E \rightarrow$ 00	01	10	11
					$2^{V_E} \rightarrow$ 1	2	4	8
					$V_M \times 2^{V_E}$			
1	0	0	0	$\frac{1}{2}$	$\frac{1}{2}$	1	2	4
1	0	0	1	$\frac{9}{16}$	$\frac{9}{16}$	$1\frac{1}{8}$	$2\frac{1}{4}$	$4\frac{1}{2}$
1	0	1	0	$\frac{5}{8}$	$\frac{5}{8}$	$1\frac{1}{4}$	$2\frac{1}{2}$	5
1	0	1	1	$\frac{11}{16}$	$\frac{11}{16}$	$1\frac{3}{8}$	$2\frac{3}{4}$	$5\frac{1}{2}$
1	1	0	0	$\frac{3}{4}$	$\frac{3}{4}$	$1\frac{1}{2}$	3	6
1	1	0	1	$\frac{13}{16}$	$\frac{13}{16}$	$1\frac{5}{8}$	$3\frac{1}{4}$	$6\frac{1}{2}$
1	1	1	0	$\frac{7}{8}$	$\frac{7}{8}$	$1\frac{3}{4}$	$3\frac{1}{2}$	7
1	1	1	1	$\frac{15}{16}$	$\frac{15}{16}$	$1\frac{7}{8}$	$3\frac{3}{4}$	$7\frac{1}{2}$

Smallest fraction $= 0.1000_2 \qquad = \frac{1}{2}$

Largest fraction $= 0.1111_2 \qquad = \frac{15}{16}$

Smallest number $= 0.1000_2 \times 2^0 = \frac{1}{2}$

Largest number $= 0.1111_2 \times 2^3 = 7\frac{1}{2}$

Number of fractions $= 1 \times 2 \times 2 \times 2 = 8$

Number of values $= 8 \times 4 \qquad\quad = 32$

Adapted from David J. Cooke, *The Structure of Computers and Computations,* Tables 3.2 and 3.3 (1978), p. 203.

same in both systems. Finally, the 64 element capability for a six-bit system is more closely approached by the 48 values representable in this system than the previous system. Note that these values range from 1/4 to 60 — a much greater range than the base 2 system. However, also note that this system does not have the capability to represent many of the numbers represented in the base 2 system, such as $1\frac{1}{8}$.

These examples (6-bit normalized floating point number systems) underline the fact that not all floating point number systems are created equal. One N-bit floating point representation with its set of values for r_b, m, r_e, e, and so on, will have different characteristics from another N-bit floating point system. The designer is left with the task of selecting a representation which will fit the required combination of needs.

The method of storing numbers in a machine underlines the differences and similarities in computer floating point number systems. The information stored (or sent, or manipulated, or ...) is the sign, the exponent, and the mantissa. This information is usually grouped in that way: the sign of the number is the most significant bit, followed by the exponent, and then the mantissa. This is

Table 2.5. 6-Bit Normalized Floating Point System, Base 4.

Table 2.5. 6-Bit Normalized Floating Point System, Base 4.
$r_b = 4,\ r_e = 2, m = 2,\ e = 2$

V_M base 4		V_M	$V_M \times 2^{V_E}$			
			$V_E \rightarrow$ 00	01	10	11
			$2^{V_E} \rightarrow$ 1	4	16	64
1	0	$\frac{1}{4}$	$\frac{1}{4}$	1	4	16
1	1	$\frac{5}{16}$	$\frac{5}{16}$	$1\frac{1}{4}$	5	20
1	2	$\frac{3}{8}$	$\frac{3}{8}$	$1\frac{1}{2}$	6	24
1	3	$\frac{7}{16}$	$\frac{7}{16}$	$1\frac{3}{4}$	7	28
2	0	$\frac{1}{2}$	$\frac{1}{2}$	2	8	32
2	1	$\frac{9}{16}$	$\frac{9}{16}$	$2\frac{1}{4}$	9	36
2	2	$\frac{5}{8}$	$\frac{5}{8}$	$2\frac{1}{2}$	10	40
2	3	$\frac{11}{16}$	$\frac{11}{16}$	$2\frac{3}{4}$	11	44
3	0	$\frac{3}{4}$	$\frac{3}{4}$	3	12	48
3	1	$\frac{13}{16}$	$\frac{13}{16}$	$3\frac{1}{4}$	13	52
3	2	$\frac{7}{8}$	$\frac{7}{8}$	$3\frac{1}{2}$	14	56
3	3	$\frac{15}{16}$	$\frac{15}{16}$	$3\frac{3}{4}$	15	60

$$\text{Smallest fraction} = 0.10_4 \qquad = \frac{1}{4}$$

$$\text{Largest fraction} = 0.33_4 \qquad = \frac{15}{16}$$

$$\text{Smallest number} = 0.10_4 \times 4^0 = \frac{1}{4}$$

$$\text{Largest number} = 0.33_4 \times 4^3 = 60$$

$$\text{Number of fractions} = 3 \times 4 \qquad = 12$$

$$\text{Number of values} = 12 \times 4 \qquad = 48$$

Adapted from David J. Cooke, *The Structure of Computers and Computations,* Tables 3.2 and 3.3 (1978), p. 203.

graphically depicted in Figure 2.2. The information that never changes is not stored. Examples of this nonstored information are the radix of the system and the radix of the exponent; not so obvious examples of this are the location of the radix point and the coding method for storing the exponent. All of these are decided at design time, and remain constant for the life of the data. Another piece of constant information is the leading "1" for normalized base 2 mantissas. There is no reason to store this bit, and so the usual way to store a normalized base 2 mantissa is shown in Figure 2.2. Only the bits that change are stored, so the most significant bit of the mantissa is said to be "hidden" behind the exponent. Some manufacturers refer to this as a "hidden bit" technique. The net result is to double the number of representable mantissas.

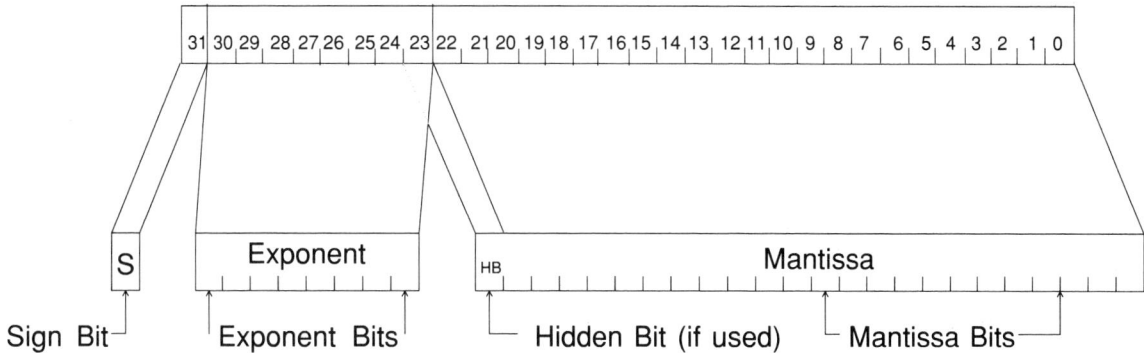

Storage Location (register or memory)

Figure 2.2. Normalized Floating Point Number Storage.

Some interesting observations can be made by considering the use of the "hidden bit" technique with the system depicted in Table 2.4. If this technique were adopted, then the number of legal mantissas would double, as would the representable values. Thus, all 64 combinations of bits would form correct floating point numbers. Note, however, the following: $V_{M_{\text{MIN}}}$ remains the same at $1/2$, and $V_{M_{\text{MAX}}}$ is $31/32$. The new representable values available by this technique are between each of the old values; the overall range is increased only from $7\frac{1}{2}$ to $7\frac{3}{4}$. So although the number of values has doubled, the range of representable numbers is basically the same. Finally, none of the values representable is zero; the smallest number is 000000, which turns out to be (with the hidden bit coming into play), $0.1000_2 \times 2^0 = 1/2$.

This raises the question: how is the number zero represented? We will examine this more closely in the examples to follow, but the general technique is to make an assumption concerning the exponent. A common method is to use an excess 2^{e-1} code for exponent representation. As the binary representations of this code vary from $2^e - 1$ to 1, the exponents vary from $2^{e-1} - 1$ to $-(2^{e-1} - 1)$. If the exponent bits are all zero, then the number is assumed to be zero, regardless of the values of the bits located in the mantissa field.

Example 2.8: Characteristics of a base 2 FPNS: Determine the characteristics, as defined by the above equations, of the DEC 32-bit normalized floating point number system.

This system has an r_b of 2, an r_e of 2, $m = 24$ with hidden bit, $p = 24$, $e = 8$, the exponent is stored in excess 128 code, and the number is stored in sign-magnitude form (mantissa is considered positive). So, from the above equations:

$$V_{M_{\text{MIN}}} = 0.1000..._2 = 1/2$$

$$V_{M_{\text{MAX}}} = 0.1111..._2 = 0.999999940395 = 1.0 - 2^{-24}$$

$$V_{\text{FPN}_{\text{MIN}}} = 0.1000..._2 \times 2^{-127} = 2.9387 \times 10^{-39}$$

$$V_{\text{FPN}_{\text{MAX}}} = 0.1111..._2 \times 2^{+127} = 1.7014 \times 10^{38}$$

$$\text{NLM}_{\text{FPN}} = 2^{23} = 8,388,608$$

$$\text{NRV}_{\text{FPN}} = 2^{23} \times (2^8 - 1) = 2.139 \times 10^9$$

Discussion: This system uses 99.6% of the available bit patterns for legal normalized floating point values. However, if the computations are very small or very large, then the system will not be able to provide the dynamic range needed for the calculations. One of the questions sometimes asked about a floating point system is how many significant digits are available. This is a subjective measure, since the amount of precision available is a function of the number only, not of the process producing the number. That is, for any V_E there are $2^{23} = 8.4 \times 10^6$ different values. A number in this system represented in base 10 scientific notation would require six digits; we say that there are six significant figures, even though a measurement represented by those figures may only be accurate to three places. DEC also provides a double precision format to increase the amount of precision with which calculations can be made. The double precision system is identical ($r_b = r_e = 2$, $e = 8$, exponent in excess 128 format, sign-magnitude representation for the number) except that the number of bits in the mantissa is extended from 24 to 56. Thus, the values cover the same sections of the real number line, but there are 2^{32} more values to represent the information to a greater precision. Thus for a given V_E there are 3.6×10^{16} values, or about 16 digits of significance.

The DEC format is prevalent simply because of the large number of DEC machines in use today. However, there are other systems available in both 32- and 64-bit formats. Another prevalent system is the IBM floating point system, which is analyzed in the next example.

Example 2.9: Characteristics of a base 16 FPNS: Determine the characteristics of the IBM 32-bit normalized floating point number system.
This system has an r_b of 16, an r_e of 2, $m = 6$ hexadecimal digits, $p = 6$, $e = 7$, the exponent is stored in excess 64 code, number is stored in sign-magnitude form (mantissa is considered positive).

$$V_{M_{\text{MIN}}} = 0.100000_{16} = 1/16$$

$$V_{M_{\text{MAX}}} = 0.\text{FFFFFF}_{16} = 0.999999940395 = 1.0 - 16^{-6}$$

$$V_{\text{FPN}_{\text{MIN}}} = 0.100000_{16} \times 16^{-63} = 8.636 \times 10^{-78}$$

$$V_{\text{FPN}_{\text{MAX}}} = 0.\text{FFFFFF}_{16} \times 16^{+63} = 7.237 \times 10^{75}$$

$$\text{NLM}_{\text{FPN}} = 15 \times 16^5 = 15,728,640$$

$$\text{NRV}_{\text{FPN}} = 15 \times 16^5 \times (2^7 - 1) = 1.9975 \times 10^9$$

This system has a far greater range than the DEC system, but actually has 7% fewer representable values. Nevertheless in certain applications, this is a reasonable system, and is chosen by some system designers. The IBM system has a double precision format which, like the DEC format, does not extend the range of the system, but includes 16^8 more values in the same basic area of the real number line.

One of the disappointing features of a normalized floating point system is that there is a large discontinuity when the values of the numbers approach zero. This is depicted graphically in Figure 2.3, which shows the smallest representable values of the DEC floating point system. The problem is, with the stipulation that the first digit to the right of the radix point be nonzero, the first representable value away from zero is disproportionately large. This is one of the problems addressed by the IEEE floating point system, which is the object of the next example.

Example 2.10: Characteristics of IEEE FPNS: Determine the characteristics, as defined by the above equations, of the IEEE 32-bit and 64-bit normalized floating point number systems.

First, the 32-bit system: This system has an r_b of 2, an r_e of 2, $m = 24$ with hidden bit, but here $p = 23$; $e = 8$, the exponent is stored in excess 127 code, and the number is stored in sign-magnitude form (mantissa is considered positive). The effect of p being 23 while m is 24 is that rather than range from 1/2 to almost 1, as in the DEC system, these mantissas range from 1 to almost 2. Another difference is that the exponent $V_E = 255$ is special. That is, when the exponent is 255, special values are possible, such as infinity. So, the system has the following characteristics for normalized numbers:

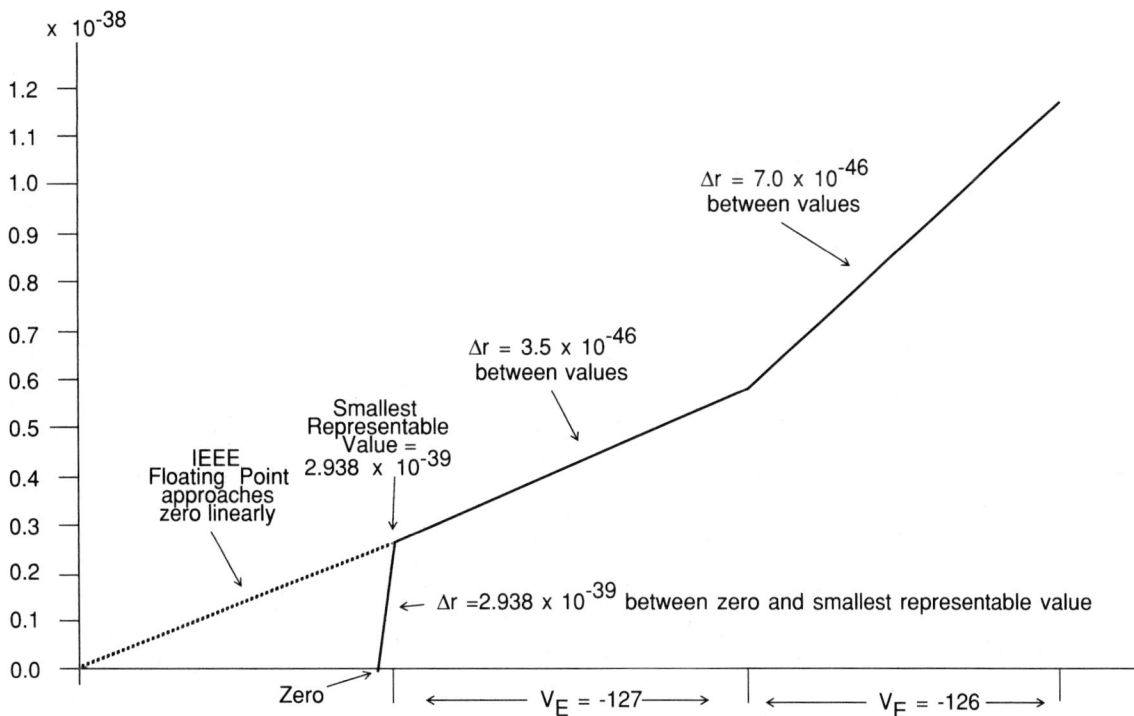

Figure 2.3. Values of the DEC Normalized Floating Point System Near Zero.

$$V_{M_{\text{MIN}}} = 1.000...{}_2 = 1$$

$$V_{M_{\text{MAX}}} = 1.111...{}_2 = 1.99999988 = 2.0 - 2^{-23}$$

$$V_{\text{FPN}_{\text{MIN}}} = 1.000...{}_2 \times 2^{-126} = 1.1755 \times 10^{-38}$$

$$V_{\text{FPN}_{\text{MAX}}} = 1.111...{}_2 \times 2^{+128} = 3.4028 \times 10^{38}$$

$$\text{NLM}_{\text{FPN}} = 2^{23} = 8,388,608$$

$$\text{NRV}_{\text{FPN}} = 2^{23} \times (2^8 - 2) = 2.131 \times 10^9$$

Discussion: Notice that the largest representable number in this system is twice as large as the $V_{\text{FPN}_{\text{MAX}}}$ of the DEC system. The reason for this is that the $V_{E_{\text{MAX}}}$ of both systems is the same (127), but the $V_{M_{\text{MAX}}}$ of the IEEE system is ~2, while the $V_{M_{\text{MAX}}}$ of the DEC system is ~1. At the other end of the normalized numbers, the smallest value ($V_{\text{FPN}_{\text{MIN}}}$) representable by the IEEE system is four times as large as the $V_{\text{FPN}_{\text{MIN}}}$ of the DEC system. One of the reasons the system is organized the way it is concerns the representation of zero, and the use of unnormalized numbers. The previous representations assumed that the number was zero if the exponent bits were all zero. The IEEE floating point system has a provision that lets the number become unnormalized as it approaches zero. That is, when the exponent bits are all zero, then the bits in the mantissa field continue to be significant, and the exponent remains at a −126. This allows the number to approach zero in a linear fashion, as opposed to the discontinuity depicted in Figure 2.3. There are two representations for zero: when all bits (excluding sign bit) are zero, the value of the number is zero. The use of unnormalized representations extends the range of the system down to 10^{-45}. The number of significant digits here is basically the same as the systems already discussed.

When V_E is 255, the system allows for representation of some specific information:

V_F	Sign	Meaning of Representation
$\neq 0$	1,0	Not a number (NaN)
0	0	$+\infty$
0	1	$-\infty$

The formal number system specification should be consulted for a complete explanation of the definition and use of the system. As shown above, the single precision system is very similar in many respects with the DEC system. However, the IEEE system changes the number of bits in the exponent for the double precision representation.

For the 64-bit representation, $r_b = r_e = 2$ as before, but $m = 53$, $p = 52$, $e = 11$, and the exponent is stored in excess 1,023 format. With these modifications, the characteristics of the number system change somewhat. The $V_{M_{\text{MIN}}}$ is still 1.0, and the $V_{M_{\text{MAX}}}$ gets closer to two ($2 - 2^{-52}$). But:

$$V_{\text{FPN}_{\text{MIN}}} = 1.000...{}_2 \times 2^{-1022} = 2.225 \times 10^{-308}$$

$$V_{\text{FPN}_{\text{MAX}}} = 1.111...{}_2 \times 2^{+1023} = 1.798 \times 10^{308}$$

$$\text{NLM}_{\text{FPN}} = 2^{52} \qquad\qquad = 4.5 \times 10^{15}$$

$$\text{NRV}_{\text{FPN}} = 2^{52} \times (2^{11} - 2) \quad = 9.214 \times 10^{18}$$

The double precision system provides 15 significant digits, and has a range much larger than either the DEC or IBM double precision formats.

The floating point number systems already mentioned are the ones that are most accessible for the majority of computer users. This is especially true in that the newer machines are utilizing chip sets that conform to the IEEE standard. This is true of the:

- 68020, which is the processor in many of the Sun computers.
- 80386, which is in the Sequent systems and many other computer systems.
- 32332, which is in the Encore systems and other computers.
- MIPS R2000, which is used in many engineering workstations.

In addition, many chip sets (see the AMD29C327, the ADP2100, etc.) are available for users to implement machines of their own design, utilizing the IEEE floating point format. And the DEC and IBM machines continue to be extremely prevalent throughout the computing community.

We will mention one more floating point system, that utilized by the Cray machines. This 64-bit format is utilized a great deal for scientific computing.

Example 2.11: Cray FPNS: Consider the Cray 64-bit floating point format. This system has an r_b of 2, an r_e of 2, $m = 48$, $p = 48$, $e = 15$, number is stored in sign-magnitude form (mantissa is considered positive). The exponent is stored in excess 16,384 format. With an exponent so large, Cray does not use the full range, but rather uses the uppermost (and also, the most negative) portions to identify underflow and overflow. This information is then stored in the number itself. The effect is to have a maximum positive exponent of 8,191, and a maximum negative exponent of –8,192. This gives rise to the following set of numbers:

$$V_{\text{FPN}_{\text{MIN}}} = 0.1000..._2 \times 2^{-8192} = 4.584 \times 10^{-2467}$$

$$V_{\text{FPN}_{\text{MAX}}} = 0.1111..._2 \times 2^{+8191} = 5.4537 \times 10^{2465}$$

$$\text{NLM}_{\text{FPN}} = 2^{48} \qquad\qquad = 2.815 \times 10^{14}$$

$$\text{NRV}_{\text{FPN}} = 2^{48} \times (2^{14} - 1) \quad = 4.6114 \times 10^{18}$$

This system has an extremely large range, and carries about 14 significant figures. The effect is to have a number system capable of extremely large and extremely small numbers, and sufficient significance for almost all necessary computations. Compare this system, for example, with the 64-bit IEEE format, which does not have the extreme range, but does carry over 15 digits of significance.

The information in this section points out the fact that not all floating point number systems are created equal. Each of the designers of the various systems has been influenced by a different set of real or perceived requirements in the choices made. Table 2.6 identifies a number of machines and the floating point choices made for them. We should add here that many manufacturers support floating point formats (as a special option) which go beyond those we have identified here. Some 128-bit and 256-bit formats allow calculations with extremely large and small numbers. However, the principles of data representation are the same, and an understanding of the principles discussed here will apply to the larger numbers.

As we have seen, a variety of floating point formats have been utilized in the design of different computer systems. One of the problems that arises is the exchange of data from one system to another: the bit patterns cannot be directly exchanged, even if the number of bits used in the representations is identical. However, if one is aware of the differences in the number systems, one can take the necessary steps to make sure that the numbers on one machine are correct on another. In any event, this should serve as a reminder that with N bits on a computer, 2^N different bit patterns are available. Floating point number systems allow the expression of large and small quantities, but do not expand the number of allowable representations.

2.3. Coding for Nonnumeric Information

The information utilized by computers in various tasks is not limited to numbers. Thus far, we have examined utilizing bit patterns to represent integer and floating point information. Other information must also be stored within the machine, or on electronic media such as tape or disks. This information may be instructions, text, addresses, status information, or other information needed by the machine. This information will be represented by bit patterns, just as the numbers were represented by bit patterns. And in a manner similar to the numeric data, the assumptions about the format of the information is made at design time. We will briefly examine several types of nonnumeric information in this section, including text, boolean, graphics symbols, and addresses.

Textual information has become one of the most often utilized forms of information for both storage and manipulation. This seems counterintuitive, since computers have historically been used to "compute," that is, doing calculations for a variety of applications. However, when one considers the fact that programs are input in text form, that compilers operate on strings of characters, and that answers are generally provided via some type of textual information, then the amount of character information begins to be appreciated. A more recent utilization for computers is in the office, where reports, letters, contracts, and other types of printed information are generated. In short, many applications must store, manipulate, and transfer textual information. How can this be accomplished?

One question in this regard is, what is the set of elements to be represented? Those interested in mathematical information would immediately respond with the characters needed to represent data: the digits (0–9), decimal point, plus, minus, and space. This gives a minimal character set with only 14 elements. However, there are severe limitations to the understandability of the results: no labels, no carriage returns or line feeds, and so on. So, at least add the alphabet (A–Z), punctuation, and formatting characters (comma, tab, carriage return, line feed, form feed, parenthesis). This gets the number of elements up to 46. We know that, in order to represent 46 different elements, we will need at least

Table 2.6. Floating Point Information Systems.

System	Word Size (# Bits)	r_b	Exponent # Bits	Exponent Code	Mantissa # Bits	Mantissa Repre.	Mantissa Code
Burroughs B6700/7700	48	8	7	SM	39	Int	SM
CDC 7600	60	2	11	Ex 1024	48	Int	1's C
DEC — single	32	2	8	Ex 128	24	Fra	SM
DEC — double	64	2	8	Ex 128	56	Fra	SM
Honeywell 8200	48	2 or 10	7	Ex 64	40 (base 2) 20 (base 10)	Fra Fra	SM
IBM — single	32	16	7	Ex 64	24	Fra	SM
IBM — double	64	16	7	Ex 64	56	Fra	SM
IEEE — single	32	2	8	Ex 127	24	Fra	SM
IEEE — double	64	2	11	Ex 1023	53	Fra	SM
Cray	64	2	15	Ex 16384	48	Fra	SM

Int = Integer representation

SM = Sign/magnitude

Fra = Fractional

1's C = One's complement

Ex = Excess code

$\lceil \log_2 46 \rceil = 6$ bits. With 6 bits we would be able to represent $2^6 = 64$ different bit patterns, or 64 different elements in the set. So we can represent most of the information that we need with 6-bit characters; however, note that this set is not large enough to include both upper- and lowercase letters. Character sets that are to represent both upper- and lowercase letters, control characters, punctuation marks, and other special characters must have at least 7 bits. The bit patterns can then be mapped to the characters or control information to be represented.

One of the early types of devices utilized to communicate with computers was the card reader. This mechanical marvel utilized a coding scheme to represent its various information. The information represented in the earliest machines included only uppercase letters, numbers, and special characters. To represent this information a code was developed for use with the card reader which was capable of this reduced set of characters. This 6-bit code, called the BCD code, should not be confused with the 4-bit representation mentioned earlier in this chapter used to represent the digits 0–9. Later, the 6-bit BCD code was extended to include the lowercase characters and additional information needed in computer communications. This code (given in Appendix A) is known as EBCDIC: Extended Binary Coded Decimal Interchange Code. It was used in the IBM 360/370 and other IBM equipment, but is not in general use in computers. However, this information can be useful if one needs to decode data generated by an EBCDIC machine. An examination of the code reveals that not all of the $2^8 = 256$ representations are used. However, all 8 of the bits are required to specify the various characters and control codes. It is also interesting to note that arithmetic using these codes may not always give the desired result. That is, if a routine were written to write out all of the standard letters (A–Z) in the alphabet, then one way to approach it would be to place the code for "A" in a register, and increment it to get the code for "B", and so on. However, note the discontinuity at "I": the code for the letter "J" is not the next in numeric sequence from "I." This illustrates one of the reasons that the code was not widely received.

Another code, which has received almost universal acceptance for the representation of textual information, is the ASCII code: American Standard Code for Information Interchange (also in Appendix A). In contrast to the EBCDIC format, the ASCII code is a 7-bit representation, which limits it to 128 different values. The difficulty mentioned in connection with the EBCDIC format does not apply to the ASCII code: incrementing the representation of a letter gives the successive letter, except for "Z." This code is used in most terminals, printers, and other devices that deal with character information.

The normal method for handling this information is to place the bit pattern in an 8-bit field called a byte. The EBCDIC format would utilize all of the bits in a byte, while the ASCII code would "waste" one of the bits. These bytes form 8-bit values, which are treated in exactly the same fashion as numbers. Thus, the hardware elements that operate on integers will also operate on characters. This allows one set of characters to be compared to a similar set of information, to be searched for specific patterns, or to be operated on by programs seeking statistical information. A spelling check program, for example, would identify a group of letters as a word, then compare that word against words that it knows are spelled correctly. If the program is unable to recognize the word, or construct it from a known word according to a set of rules, then the word is labeled as incorrect, and the operator is informed of this infraction. In all of these operations, the computer is operating on the bit patterns representing the characters, and the meaning of those characters becomes significant only to the humans at the end of the process.

The difficulty of expanding the set of representable elements can be overcome in a variety of ways. One obvious way would be to include the eighth bit of the ASCII code, doubling the available representations. Another method is exemplified by the character codes used in some 60-bit machines. Some machines have been built with 60-bit word lengths, a compromise between the needed accuracy and the expensive memory available at design time. It is not possible to equally divide the 60-bit word into either 7- or 8-bit quantities. So the system designers implemented a 6-bit system, which limited the number of available characters to 64. This system works well as long as the information output is in the specified characters, which consist of the numbers, the uppercase letters, common punctuation, and special characters. To represent the lowercase characters, a two-character sequence is used. The first character is an "escape" character, which informs the system that the desired character was not in the standard set, but rather in an alternate set. And the pattern identifying that character in the alternate set is found in the next 6-bit field. The effect of this method of information representation is to use 6 bits to represent some characters (preferably the most often used), and 12 bits to represent other characters. This method works well for data that is basically numbers and uppercase characters. But for text, such as correspondence or reports, this method is cumbersome and wasteful of bits.

The same type of arrangements can be utilized to enhance the number of representable elements for "standard" character sets. For example, nonstandard characters, such as Greek characters or special purpose characters ($\neq$, ∞, $\pm$, $\times$, ...) can be represented in this fashion. These characters become even more important as graphics-oriented devices become more prevalent.

Regardless of the coding scheme chosen, the computer deals with characters in the same fashion as it does with other data; the arithmetic is performed in the same way, and conditions are tested in much the same fashion. The result of a test is an example of another type of information: boolean. In general, the term "boolean" refers to information that can assume one of two possible values. For status information, this seems intuitively obvious: is the result of the arithmetic operation positive or negative? Is there an overflow or not? This type of information requires only a single bit to represent. In fact, a status register in a machine is nothing more than a collection of this type of single bits. Depending on the instruction set of the machine, these bits may or may not be individually setable/clearable/testable. We will examine this issue more closely when we discuss instruction sets.

Many languages also allow this type of variable to be declared. In general, the language will utilize an entire word to represent this information, which wastes a lot of bits. The smallest unit that could represent this under language control would be the smallest addressable unit of the computer. In most computers, the smallest addressable unit is the byte, but some large, mathematical type machines have a smallest addressable unit of a word (32 or 64 bits). In any case, compilers can be called upon to generate sequences of instructions that will allow storing of boolean information in individual bits of a word. This is a tradeoff between the use of time and the use of memory. Assigning a boolean variable to the smallest addressable unit of the machine will be faster than the alternative, which is to have boolean information limited to individual bits within a word. However, this method uses more memory. The alternative, using individual bits for storage of boolean information, requires a smaller amount of storage for the boolean information, but also requires more instructions to interact with this information.

In general, information is stored in locations within the memory of the machine, and those locations are identified by addresses. The addresses, which themselves form information that can be manipulated and utilized as needed, are simply numbers that can be considered integers. The number of bits in the address determines the number of uniquely identifiable items: N bits specifies one of 2^N unique items. The address is utilized by the machine to "point" to an item; hence, the use of the address in this manner gives rise to the term "pointer." Pointers are very useful to create within a machine an instantiation of an abstraction, such as a tree structure or queue.

Bit patterns, then, can be used to represent different types of information: numbers (integer, floating point, fixed point, ...), characters, symbols, addresses, and so on. The meaning attached to the bit pattern is a function of when it is used and where it is found.

2.4. Coding for Errors — Detection and Correction

Information can be represented in a variety of ways, and in the previous sections we examined some of the different coding techniques. We know that with N bits we can represent 2^N different values, or addresses, or instructions, or ... . To represent anything else requires more bits, and the number of additional bits needed is determined by the amount of information to be supplied. If we add one more bit to an N-bit representation, then the number of representable elements doubles, from 2^N to 2^{N+1}. So how are these additional elements identified and treated? That is, what rules exist to effectively utilize the additional information present? Let us examine rules (codes) for adding sufficient information to detect the presence of errors. And then we will examine some rules (codes) for adding enough information not only to detect that an error occurred, but also to correct that error.

Perhaps the simplest method of adding error detection to data is to include a parity bit. Here, the N bits of information is augmented by an additional bit, which doubles the representable patterns. However, this additional bit is so constructed that half of these patterns will not be legal representations. Hence, it is possible to detect the presence of a single bit that is incorrect. The fault can be a "stuck-at" fault, in which the incorrect bit is "stuck" at that incorrect value, or it can be transitory in nature. In either case, if only one bit is incorrect, the manner of constructing the correct code words enables us to detect that an error has occurred. The construction rule is to choose the value for the additional bit so that the number of "one" bits is odd (or even). Figure 2.4 gives a circuit that will create the proper signal for 8 bits. This circuit is available in integrated circuit form as a '280. Note that the expansion of the exclusive-OR tree by one bit would enable checking the parity across 9 bits, to identify if it is odd (or even). (The '280 is an exclusive-OR tree for nine bits.)

This type of error detection is useful wherever errors have a reasonable probability of occurrence. In general they are used in serial transmissions (terminal lines, etc.), in parallel data transmission systems (buses), or in memory systems. However, some conditions will invalidate the effectiveness of the use of a parity check. That is, if the assumptions of the fault model are exceeded or not applicable, then the effectiveness of the method is moot. For example, in one of the errors observed in bus systems the data is read (incorrectly) as all zero's. This would be a valid even parity condition, and so a system built to check for even parity would not detect the presence of an error. Likewise, for a 16-bit bus with

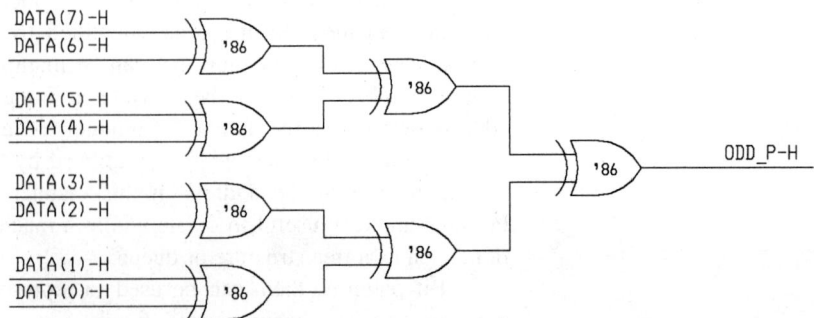

Figure 2.4. Generation of Parity Bits.

an additional bit for parity, the total number of lines is 17. And the similar error of reading all the lines as one's would be correct for a system using odd parity. One method suggested for this situation is to use two parity bits for the 16-bit bus, one for each byte. The parity sense of half of the bus would be set to odd, the other half to even. Then if all zero's were read, half of the bus would complain. And if the condition of all one's were read, then the other half of the bus would complain. In either case, the fact that an error had occurred would be correctly identified, even though the assumptions of the fault model had been violated.

> *Example 2.12: Parity detection and generation:* Construct a circuit providing a bidirectional data path that is 8 bits of data plus parity. That is, one side of the path is a byte-wide source/destination of information, and the other side is a tri-state data bus that includes a parity bit.
>
> The solution of this problem is to expand the circuit given in Figure 2.4 to include the generate/decode capability. An example of such a circuit is given in Figure 2.5. This figure shows that the data path is treated in the same way that a data path might be if no parity capability were required: the data is fed through a bidirectional tri-state transceiver ('245). So the only bit that needs to be dealt with is the parity bit (PARITY-H). When the direction line (IN-H) identifies incoming data, the parity line is enabled into the parity circuit to check consistency. If the parity sense is incorrect, then the error line (ERROR-L) is asserted. When the direction line identifies that this module provides information to the bus, then the outgoing parity generator is enabled, and the parity line is driven in the same way (by different physical circuits) that the bus lines are driven. Figure 2.5 shows the parity circuits as being separate, but they need not be, and cleverness in the design will match system requirements with an appropriate circuit. Some integrated circuits will do this function, such as the '286, a symbol of which is shown in Figure 2.6.

If we want be able to identify the location of an error, then more information must be added to the system than can be added by a single bit. A sufficiently

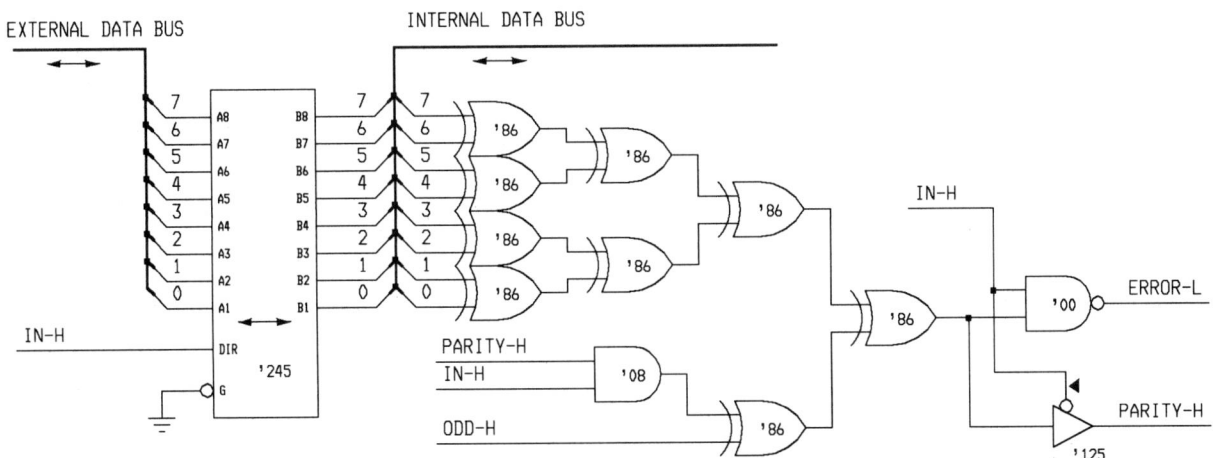

Figure 2.5. Byte-Wide Data Path with Bidirectional Parity Bit.

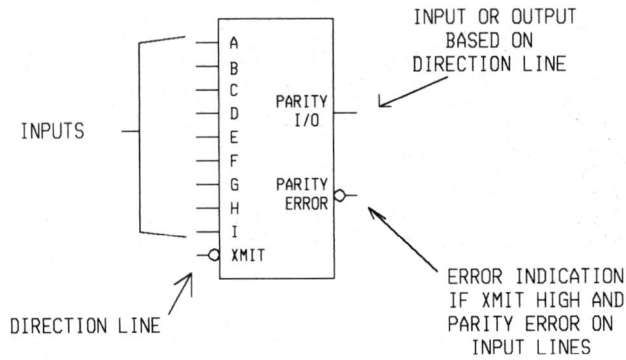

Figure 2.6. Functional Diagram for '286 Parity Checker/Generator.

large number of bits must be added to the data to not only identify the fact that one of the bits is in error, but also identify the faulty bit. Again, the fault model can be a stuck-at or a transient fault. But, for our discussion, we are limiting the errors to a single fault within the word. One class of codes that allows this type of information to be encoded into the extra bits is the set of Hamming codes. Many methods can be used to construct a code of this type. We will examine one method, but, once the principles are understood, the exact implementation and design choices can be driven by whatever constraints are imposed by the system. That is, the code could be chosen so that a minimal number of gates are required to identify errors, or the code could be chosen in an attempt to optimally position the 2^N valid code words in the total of 2^{N+p} choices, where p code bits are added to N data bits.

First, let us describe one method for construction of a code to identify the location of an error. To illustrate this method, we will utilize a system with 4 data bits and 3 code bits, or 7 bits in all. We will arrange these bits as shown in Figure 2.7, with the data bits labeled D_3, D_2, D_1, and D_0, and the code bits labeled C_2, C_1, and C_0. Note that the code bits physically occupy the positions corresponding to their binary weight. Thus, C_0 is in the $2^0 = 1$ position; C_1 is in the $2^1 = 2$ position; and C_2 is in the $2^2 = 4$ position. The remaining positions are occupied by the 4 data bits. Also shown in the figure is the fact that the code bits are constructed in such a way that parity is preserved across a subset of the bits of

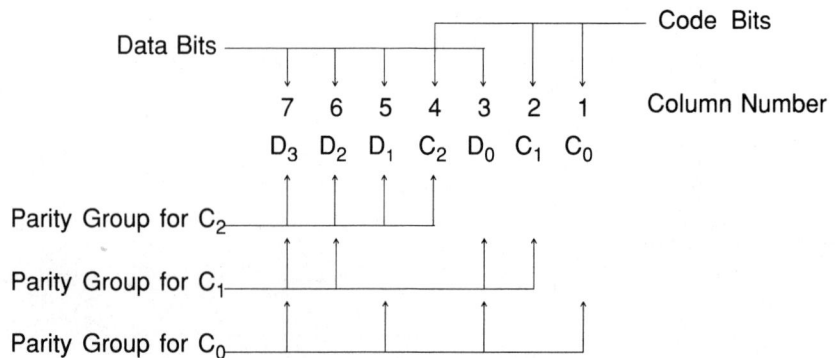

Figure 2.7. Construction of a Hamming Code for 7 Bits.

the entire word. The subsets are so constructed that when a single bit is in error, a unique pattern is identified by the code bits. Note that there is a single code bit in each subset; let the subset associated with code bit C_k be called set k. In this example, subset k contains all of the bits that have the 2^k bit set in the binary representation of bit position. The following table describes the situation for this system:

Set	Bit Positions	Bit Names
0	1, 3, 5, 7	C_0, D_0, D_1, D_3
1	2, 3, 6, 7	C_1, D_0, D_2, D_3
2	4, 5, 6, 7	C_2, D_1, D_2, D_3

Since three code bits are associated with this method, there must be three parity circuits to generate the three parity bits when the word is written — and three parity circuits to check the parity when the word is read. The ordering of these bits is such that they form a 3-bit word (set 2, set 1, set 0), which will identify a column. In Figure 2.8, the number 0101 is used as an example. The bits are placed in their proper position in the word, the code bits are generated assuming odd parity sense, and the result is presented as 0100110. If there are no errors, the output of the parity checkers for the subsets would be 000, which identifies a nonexistent bit position in our system. If the pattern 0100010 is detected, then the parity checks of the subsets identifies some errors. Set 2 is correct, set 1 is

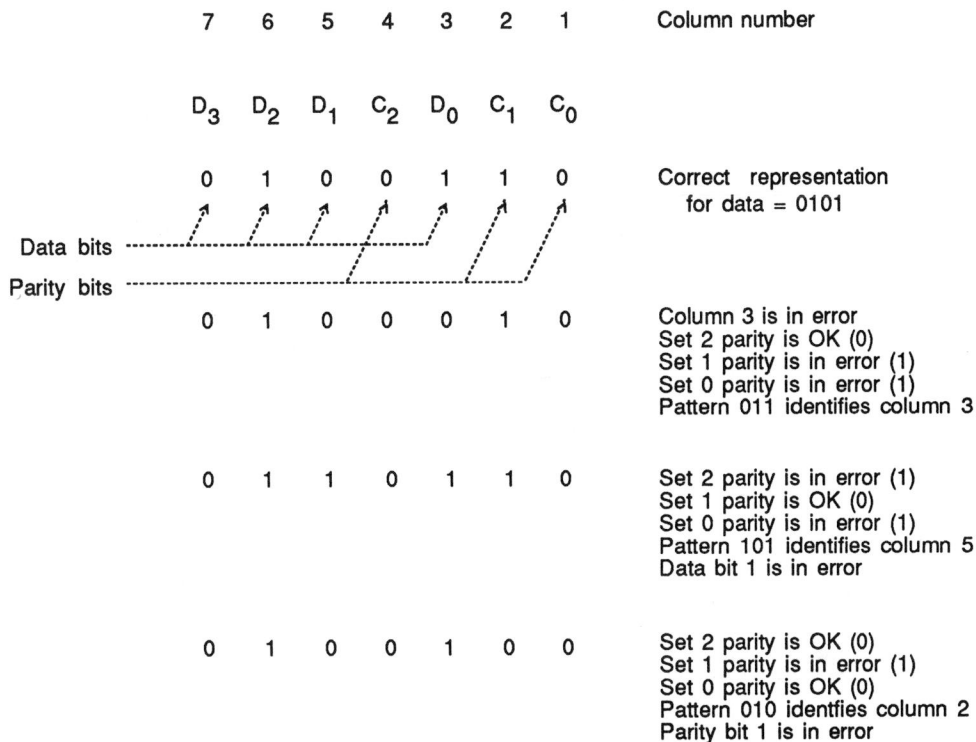

7	6	5	4	3	2	1	Column number
D_3	D_2	D_1	C_2	D_0	C_1	C_0	
0	1	0	0	1	1	0	Correct representation for data = 0101

Data bits

Parity bits

0	1	0	0	0	1	0	Column 3 is in error Set 2 parity is OK (0) Set 1 parity is in error (1) Set 0 parity is in error (1) Pattern 011 identifies column 3
0	1	1	0	1	1	0	Set 2 parity is in error (1) Set 1 parity is OK (0) Set 0 parity is in error (1) Pattern 101 identifies column 5 Data bit 1 is in error
0	1	0	0	1	0	0	Set 2 parity is OK (0) Set 1 parity is in error (1) Set 0 parity is OK (0) Pattern 010 identfies column 2 Parity bit 1 is in error

Figure 2.8. Hamming Code Examples for Data = 0101.

incorrect, and set 0 is incorrect, which results in an error syndrome of 011. This identifies the fact that the bit in position 3 is incorrect, and to make the word correct all that needs to happen is to invert the bit in position 3, D_0. Figure 2.9 indicates how some parity checkers, a decoder, and some exclusive-OR gates could be connected to perform this function.

The method described above was constructed to have the property previously mentioned: any single error will produce a unique bit pattern at the output of the parity check stages. Also, the placement of the code bits was done in such a fashion that decoding the location of the error from the pattern which the error created could be accomplished with a standard decoder IC. Other coding schemes are possible, as long as each single error causes a unique response, and a decoder system can be constructed to identify the location of the error from that response.

This method can effectively utilize $2^N - 1$ bits, N bits to create the data dependent code, and up to $2^N - 1 - N$ bits for data. For small N, $2^N - 1 - N$ data bits is also small; thus, for a small number of data bits the overhead is large. However, as the number of data bits becomes larger, then the overhead is reduced. For example, a system with 64 data bits would require 7 code bits, or about a 10% overhead. One of the problems incurred in using an error correcting code in a memory system is the fact that many machines are byte addressable. That is, even though the system memory may be organized in 32- or 64-bit elements for the error correction capability, the system must be able to modify only part of the data bits in a 32- or 64-bit word. This requires a read/modify/write capability, so that the other parts of the data word remain correct, and the code bits are

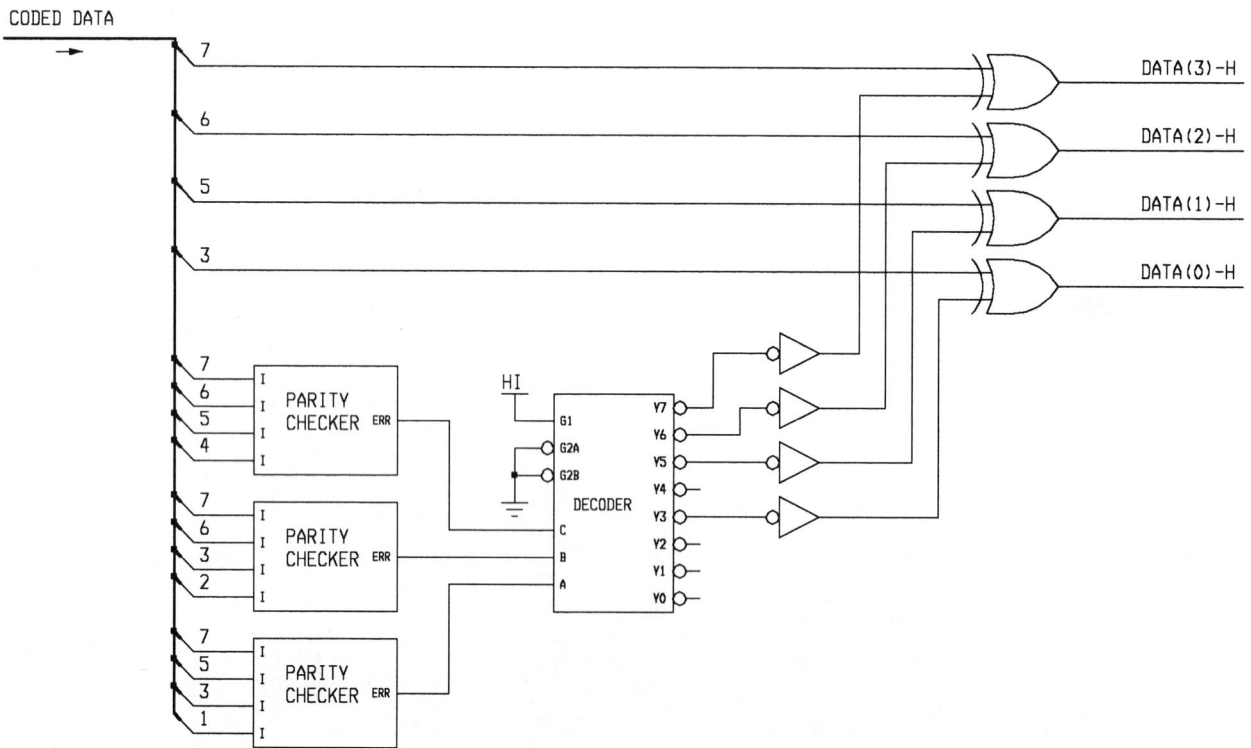

Figure 2.9. Correction Circuit for 7-Bit Hamming Code System..

appropriately set. In any case, this type of code will properly provide capability for single error correction (SEC).

This method is not sufficient to also provide double error detection (DED). Notice that, if two errors were to occur in the example just given, then an incorrect bit position would be identified, and the results would be wrong. Double error detection can be added to this method by including a single parity bit across the entire word, data bits and code bits alike. This bit would be created after the code bits had already been identified. So, the decoding system needs to take into account parity errors detected by the code bits, C_2, C_1, C_0, and occurrences of parity errors detected by the double error bit. These are then handled in the following fashion:

Parity Condition		Comment
Double Bit	Code Bits	
Correct	Correct	No error detected; normal condition.
Incorrect	Incorrect	Single error; location of error identified by binary weighting of code bits.
Incorrect	Correct	Single bit error; double bit is incorrect.
Correct	Incorrect	Double bit error; two bits in error — not correctable.

Example 2.13: Hamming Code for 8 bits: Consider a code for 8 data bits constructed after the pattern described above. In this code, what is the correct representation for 01011100? Also, describe the information available in the patterns.

This code will require 8 data bits (D_7 – D_0), 4 code bits (C_3 – C_0), and a double error bit (DEB). Following the pattern above, these will be arranged as follows:

(DEB — Double Error Bit; BW — Binary Weight)

13	12	11	10	9	8	7	6	5	4	3	2	1	Column number
DEB	D_7	D_6	D_5	D_4	C_3	D_3	D_2	D_1	C_2	D_0	C_1	C_0	Content of bit position
	1	1	1	1	0	0	0	0	0	0	0	0	BW of Column Number; 8-bit
	1	0	0	0	0	1	1	1	1	0	0	0	BW of Column Number; 4-bit
	0	1	1	0	0	1	1	0	0	1	1	0	BW of Column Number; 2-bit
	0	1	0	1	0	1	0	1	0	1	0	1	BW of Column Number; 1-bit

From the above information, set 3 consists of C_3, D_4, D_5, D_6, and D_7. Set 2 consists of C_2, D_1, D_2, D_3, and D_7. Set 1 consists of C_1, D_0, D_2, D_3, D_5, and D_6. Set 0 consists of C_0, D_0, D_1, D_3, D_4, and D_6. With this information, the desired pattern can be created:

	0 1 0 1	1 1 0	0										Placement of data bits
1 0 1 0 1 1 1 1 0 1 0 0 0														Code bits added to word

2.5. Information Representation — A Matter of Bits

We have discussed a number of different methods of representing information. A collection of bits will be interpreted by the computer in any of a number of ways, depending on the instruction being executed, the number systems adopted by the designers, and the coding schemes employed. It is not sufficient to know the pattern of ones and zeroes; we must know the rules concerning the interpretation of those bits. The rules for interpretation of the information are established at design time, and will be effective throughout the life of the system. These rules will enable the following pattern to be correctly interpreted:

$$01001110011100100000000000000000$$

If this is a DEC floating point number, it has the value of 2.537×10^8. If this is a IEEE floating point number, it has the value of 1.015×10^9. If it is an integer, it has the value 2.106×10^{10}. If this is a 68000 instruction, the computer should respond by performing a stop if the system is in the supervisor state; otherwise it will trap. If it is to be part of an ASCII character string, then it will provide the characters "Nr <nul> <nul>". In any case, the spectrum of possibilities of information content is limited in quantity, since N bits allows only for 2^N representable values. However, the interpretation of those values is influenced by the circumstance in which the value is found. The system designers make the choices that will allow representation of the information in a sensible and coherent fashion.

Information representation requires that both the supplier and the user of the patterns agree on the significance of the arrangements of digits (bits). The current technology represents information within a computing system in the form of bits, and those bits can be organized in many ways. However, the use of standard representations promotes systematic interpretation of the information. As we have seen,

- With N bits for the representation of information, 2^N different things can be represented.

- The coding of the N bits in an integer form allows representation of 2^N numerical values, all separated from their neighbors by one ($\Delta r = 1$).

- Integer representations can assume different coding schemes, such as ones complement, twos complement, excess codes, and the like, each of which has its own unique set of characteristics. The coding scheme for a number is a choice made at the definition/design stage of a computer system, and the choice is made in such a way that the system will behave in a predictable and appropriate fashion.

- Most computer systems use two's complement representations for integer values.

- Coding of information in a floating point format allows the range of the representable numbers to increase dramatically. This allows computer users to remove themselves from the scaling aspects of the data manipulation.

- The magnitude of the representable values in a floating point number system changes with each exponent. And the distance between representable values (Δr) doubles each time the exponent increases in value by one.

- Not all floating point number systems are created equal. They have different capabilities for storing information and different ranges, which effect their applicability for user problems. The choice of the radix, the placement of the radix point, and the coding schemes all influence the values that can be represented by the system.

- Bit patterns can be used to represent other types of information besides numbers. Characters, instructions, addresses, and status information are just a few of the kinds of information also represented as a collection of bits.
- By creating rules concerning the legal patterns of bits, sufficient information can be included in a pattern of bits to identify the fact that an error occurred, and find the location of the error. This reduces the total number of correct values represented by a number of bits, but can be very useful in identifying problems in data transfers.

2.6. Problems

2.1 If the technology were available for a wire or "bit" to represent three values rather than two, what would the result be? That is, consider a system with n tertiary bits, as opposed to n binary bits. Each "bit" in this system would be capable of representing the values 0, 1, or 2. How many different values could be represented with 8 tertiary bits? 16 tertiary bits? 32 tertiary bits? What is the general formula for the total number of values available in the tertiary system?

2.2 Examples were given in the chapter to demonstrate the mechanism involved in adding one's complement arithmetic, i.e., the end-around carry. Prove that the end-around carry works and is needed.

2.3 What does the bit pattern 10010101 represent in the following systems: unsigned binary, 8-bit two's complement, 8-bit one's complement, 8-bit BCD (2 digits), two 4-bit excess 3 coded base 10 digits.

2.4 Represent +95 and –95 as 8-bit one's complement and 8-bit two's complement numbers.

2.5 Express the following base 10 numbers in a 4-bit-per-digit excess 3 code: 45932 and 51373. Add the numbers together. Express the result in the same code.

2.6 Consider a 12-bit integer number system which is an excess 1,023 system. What is the smallest representable value? The largest representable value? What is the representation of zero?

2.7 Consider a 12-bit fixed point two's complement number system with $p=7$. What is the smallest representable (positive) value? What is the largest representable value? What is the most negative value? What is Δr for this system?

2.8 Consider an 8-bit fixed point two's complement number system. Give the equation for the value of a number. Multiply two such equations together to give the result of a multiplication. Give an algorithm for selecting the proper 8 bits from all of the bits available after a multiplication.

2.9 A base 10, 5-digit, sign-magnitude system has a value of p equal to 3. What is the largest representable number? What is the smallest representable (positive) number? What is the most negative representable number? What is Δr for this system?

2.10 Consider a 16-bit floating point number stored in the following format:

s eeeee ffffffffff

The "s" represents the sign of the number. The "eeeee" is the exponent, stored in excess 12. The "fff..." is the mantissa, which is a base 2 fraction, stored with the hidden bit technique. Give the characteristics ($V_{FPN_{MAX}}$, etc.) of this number system. What is Δr for this system when the value of the exponent is zero?

2.11 A floating point number system has the basic format given in 2.10, but the mantissa is a base 4 fraction, so that the hidden bit technique is not viable. Give the characteristics for this system. What is Δr for this system when the value of the exponent is zero?

2.12 Consider a floating point number system with the following characteristics: normalized, radix of the system is 4, radix of the exponent is 2, 12 bits total, with 4 bits in the exponent ($e = 4$), exponent stored in excess 8 format, 8 bits in the mantissa ($m = 4$, since base 4 number), mantissa stored in fractional form.

a. What is the smallest representable nonzero value?

b. What is the largest representable value?

c. What is the decimal equivalent of Δr when the exponent pattern is 0111?

d. What is the value, base 10, of the following pattern: 110001001011?

e. What is the pattern for the number $2\frac{3}{16}$?

f. What is the resulting pattern from adding the following positive numbers: 011001101011 and 100010110110? Use rounding for the result.

2.13 Given the following floating point format

s   exp   man

where the "s" is a 1-bit sign, "exp" is the 4-bit exponent field (exponent stored in excess 4 format), and "man" is the fractional mantissa, base 8, 6 bits wide. The format is for a normalized number system. Give the;

a. largest fraction.

b. smallest fraction.

c. largest number.

d. smallest number.

f. what number is represented by 00110101000?

g. represent the number 5/16 in this format.

2.14 A Hamming code has been created with the following pattern:

7	6	5	4	3	2	1	Column Number
D3	D2	D1	P2	D0	P1	P0	Data, parity designators

The code is constructed as discussed in the text. The parity sense is odd. Given that information, answer the following:

0	1	0	0	1	1	0	Part A
1	0	0	0	0	1	1	Part B
1	1	0	0	1	1	1	Part C
0	1	0	1	0	0	0	Part D

a. Is the representation correct? If not, is it correctable? To what?

b. Is the representation correct? If not, is it correctable? To what?

c. Is the representation correct? If not, is it correctable? To what?

d. What is the number represented?

e. Represent the number 6 in this code.

2.15 Consider the following floating point system:

$$a \quad b \quad c$$

a = sign of mantissa
b = 4-bit exponent in excess 8 code, radix = 4
c = 7-bit normalized mantissa

a. What number is represented by 010111001000?

b. What number is represented by 101111100000?

c. Represent –49 in this code.

d. Represent 1/4 in this code.

2.16 An error detecting/correcting code is constructed as described in the chapter, with the following format (parity sense is odd parity; PA is parity across the entire word):

$Col \rightarrow$	16	15	14	13	12	11	10	9	8	7	6	5	4	3	2	1
$Name \rightarrow$	PA	D_{10}	D_9	D_8	D_7	D_6	D_5	D_4	P_3	D_3	D_2	D_1	P_2	D_0	P_1	P_0
A	0	1	0	1	0	1	1	1	1	0	1	0	0	1	1	1
B	1	1	0	0	1	0	1	1	1	0	0	0	0	1	1	0
C	0	0	1	0	1	0	0	0	1	1	1	1	0	0	1	0
D	0	1	1	1	0	1	0	1	0	0	0	0	0	1	1	0
E																

For the first four numbers: if there is a single error, identify the bit in error; if there is a double error, indicate this result. For the final part, create the correct code for the decimal number 653.

2.17 Give the bit pattern for the following numbers in the 32-bit DEC, IEEE, and IBM floating point formats: 12, 127, 2.5, 768.

2.18 For the number systems listed in Table 2.6, find the minimum and maximum positive nonzero representable values.

2.19 Construct a 16-bit SECDED code using the technique demonstrated in Section 2.4. In this code, represent –512 and 183.

2.20 Design a combinational circuit that will correct single errors in a 7-bit Hamming coded word. The inputs thus are (all H asserted):

$$D_3 \quad D_2 \quad D_1 \quad P_2 \quad D_0 \quad P_1 \quad P_0$$

Odd parity is used. Outputs are H asserted also. Use any basic gates you choose, including EXORs, but make sure you maintain polarized mnemonics, incompatibility triangles, and so on. Explain any logic that is not intuitively obvious to the casual observer.

2.7. References and Readings

[Bart85] Bartee, T. C., *Digital Computer Fundamentals, 6th edition.* New York: McGraw Hill Book Company, 1985.

[Boot84] Booth, T. L., *Introduction to Computer Engineering: Hardware and Software Design.* New York: John Wiley & Sons, 1984.

[Bree89] Breeding, K. J., *Digital Design Fundamentals.* Englewood Cliffs, NJ: Prentice Hall, 1989.

[Cody84] Cody, W. J. et al., "A Proposed Radix-and Word-Length-Independent Standard for Floating-Point Arithmetic," *IEEE Micro.* Vol. 4, No. 4, August 1984, pp. 86–100.

[Flet80] Fletcher, W. I., *An Engineering Approach to Digital Design.* Englewood Cliffs, NJ: Prentice Hall, 1980.

[IEEE85] Institute of Electrical and Electronic Engineers, *Binary Floating Point Arithmetic,* IEEE Standard 754-1985. New York: IEEE, 1985.

[Knut73] Knuth, D. E., *The Art of Computer Programming: Volume 1, Fundamental Algorithms.* Reading, MA: Addison-Wesley, 1973.

[Knut69] Knuth, D. E., *The Art of Computer Programming: Volume 2, Seminumerical Alogrithms.* Reading, MA: Addison-Wesley, 1969.

[Kuck78] Kuck, D. J., *The Structure of Computers and Computations.* New York: John Wiley & Sons, 1978.

[Lang82] Langdon, G. G., Jr., *Computer Design.* San Jose, CA: Computeach Press Inc, 1982.

[LiCo83] Lin, S., and D. J. Costello, Jr., *Error Control Coding, Fundamentals and Applications.* Englewood Cliffs, NJ: Prentice Hall, 1983.

[Mano79] Mano, M. M., *Digital Logic and Computer Design.* Englewood Cliffs, NJ: Prentice Hall, 1979.

[Mano88] Mano, M. M., *Computer Engineering: Hardware Design.* Englewood Cliffs, NJ: Prentice Hall, 1988.

[PeWe72] Peterson, W. Wesley, and E. J. Weldon, Jr., *Error-Correcting Codes,* 2nd Edition. Cambridge, MA: MIT Press, 1972.

[RaFu89] Rao, T. R. N., and E. Fujiwara, *Error-Control Coding for Computer Systems.* Englewood Cliffs, NJ: Prentice Hall, 1989.

[Schn85] Schneider, G. M., *The Principles of Computer Organization.* New York: John Wiley & Sons, 1985.

[Wilk87] Wilkinson, B., *Digital System Design.* Englewood Cliffs, NJ: Prentice Hall International, 1987.

3

Arithmetic Units: Data Manipulation

If one considers that a computer is "one that computes," then perhaps the principle function of the machine is to operate on data. That is, we want to manipulate information in a predetermined fashion, according to some rules and methods that make sense. The earliest computers were built to do arithmetic at a higher rate than previously attainable, at an accuracy providing the detail needed. These machines were often used in some military capacity, such as building tables for ballistics operations. In the last chapter we examined some of the methods for information representation, and the limitations of those methods. In the next chapter we will discuss the instructions that the machines utilize, that is, instructions to manipulate the information and instructions to control the computer system itself. In this chapter, we are concerned with the design of the circuitry for doing the actual data manipulations, that is, how does one design circuitry for performing additions, multiplications, and divisions?

Many times in the discussion of a computer system we gather all of these functions together and consider them to be performed by a single block of logic called an arithmetic/logic unit (ALU). Such a block is shown in Figure 3.1. This diagram is directly applicable to LSI ALUs, such as the '181 or '381; however it is also applicable to dedicated units such as the THCT1010 Multiplier/Accumulator. Some ALUs may require additional lines to provide a carry input or to handle status bits on output. In the figure, the source of the operands is left unknown, as is the destination of the result. The interconnection of the components is a function of the type of computer and its intended application, as we will discuss later. But now our concern is with the ALU. Logical functions are achieved by gating the appropriate function to the output. For example, the function A AND B is achieved by having each A_I ANDed with the corresponding B_I to derive F_I. The logic operations can be achieved with minimal gate delays and is therefore a relatively fast operation. The more interesting operations are those required for the arithmetic manipulations.

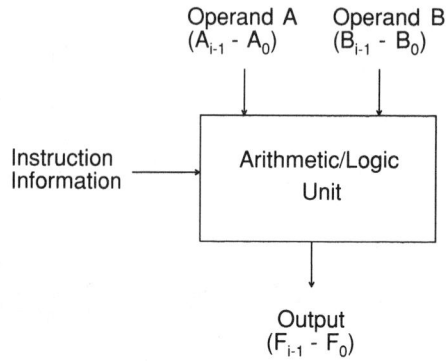

Figure 3.1. Connections for an
Arithmetic/Logic Unit.

3.1. Addition: the Universal Data Operation

One of the favorite questions asked by instructors teaching basic logic design is, what is a universal logic gate? The basic premise demonstrated by this question is that a NAND gate is considered a universal logic gate because all of the basic functions — AND, OR, EX-OR, and so on — can be derived by different combinations of NAND gates. In a similar fashion, NOR gates are also universal logic gates. The same type of statement can be made concerning arithmetic operations and the add function. All of the various arithmetic operations — add, subtract, multiply, and divide — can be implemented by appropriate combinations of the add function. First we will look at the full adder, and some variations of it, then we will consider the look-ahead carry process that can be used to speed up the add function. Other applications of add functions, such as the carry save adder or the Wallace tree adder, will be treated with other functions such as multiply.

A basic cell that can be used to perform additions is the full adder (FA), shown diagrammatically in Figure 3.2(a). As shown, the function of the FA is to add two bits (A_I and B_I) and the carry from a stage of lower significance (C_{IN}) to produce a single bit of output (F_I) and a carry out to the next stage of higher significance (C_{OUT}). The truth table for this function is shown in Figure 3.2(b). Several observations can be made after examination of the truth table. For example, the function of a FA is to take three bits of equal significance — A_I, B_I, and C_{IN}— and create two bits, F_I, which has the same significance as the three input bits, and C_{OUT}, which is one bit more significant. Another observation is that the output forms a 2-bit number (C_{OUT}, F_I) which indicates how many "one" bits there are in the three input bits. The four possibilities (0, 1, 2, 3) are the permissible number of asserted bits on the inputs.

Figure 3.2 also contains Karnaugh maps for C_{OUT} and F_I, and the resulting logic equations in sum-of-products form. The sum bit (F_I) is also shown in an exclusive-OR representation. The equations are then implemented with the appropriate logic. The implementation of the sum bit is shown in the sum-of-products NAND implementation as well as the exclusive-OR implementation. In either case, the output bits are formed from two levels of logic. That is, between any input and an appropriate output there are two gates, and hence two gate delays. (One set of gates is for the AND function; the other set of gates is for the OR function.) This is true for *any* combinational circuit: if one is willing to utilize enough gates, each of which has the requisite number of inputs, it is possible

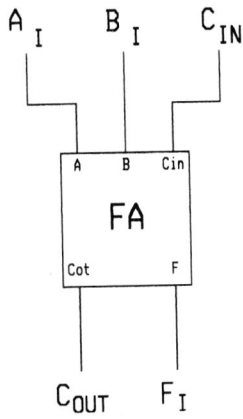

(a)

A_i	B_i	C_{in}	C_{out}	F_i
0	0	0	0	0
0	0	1	0	1
0	1	0	0	1
0	1	1	1	0
1	0	0	0	1
1	0	1	1	0
1	1	0	1	0
1	1	1	1	1

(b)

C_{in} \ A_iB_i	00	01	11	10
0	0	0	1	0
1	0	1	1	1

$$C_{out} = A_iB_i + B_iC_{in} + A_iC_{in}$$

C_{in} \ A_iB_i	00	01	11	10
0	0	1	0	1
1	1	0	1	0

$$F_i = \overline{A}_i\overline{B}_iC_{in} + \overline{A}_iB_i\overline{C}_{in} + A_iB_iC_{in} + A_i\overline{B}_i\overline{C}_{in}$$

$$F_i = A_i \oplus B_i \oplus C_{in}$$

(c)

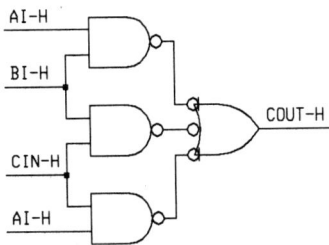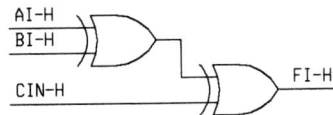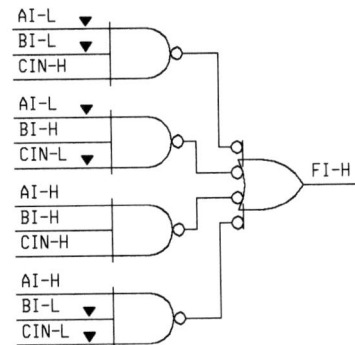

(d)

Figure 3.2. Design of a Full Adder (FA).

Chap. 3: Arithmetic Units: Data Manipulation

to accomplish any logical function in two gate delays. It may not be desirable or practicable, but it is possible. We will utilize this fact as we examine the times required to perform various functions. Thus, to perform the addition of the two bits A_I and B_I with carry, requires two gate delays from the time that the inputs are stable.

At this point it is useful to comment on the design methodology for combinational circuits, which is exemplified by the full adder. The first step in the design of any combinational system is to understand the problem at hand, which is a nontrivial requirement. Once the problem is understood, the problem and its solution can be stated succinctly in prose, identifying the input and output variables. From the problem statement, truth tables can be established, equations derived, and gating networks developed. When the solution is complete, simple tests can be performed to ascertain that the outputs do indeed perform the desired function, and that the requirements of the initial problem are satisfied.

For the full adder, the basic requirement is the addition of two numbers. As we discuss the various arithmetic operations in this chapter, we will first seek to understand the requirements of the underlying process, then proceed to determine a design which will perform the required work and meet the other needs of the system. The simplified block diagram shown in Figure 3.2(a) seems innocuous in appearance, but before progress can be made toward a reasonable design, the process which is being performed must be understood. One demonstration of the understanding required is a *correct* truth table, as shown in Figure 3.2(b). A designer's concept of what the device should do is identified by this table. If a design does not function properly, the usual debugging approach is to see if the wiring matches the logic as described by equations, and that the equations were correctly obtained from the truth table/Karnaugh maps. This approach will find errors that are implementation errors. However, it is often the case that the logic is an accurate implementation of the logic equations, and that the logic equations themselves are incorrect. This may be true not because the Boolean algebra was done incorrectly, but rather because the designer's understanding of the problem was flawed. And one place where that understanding will be displayed is in the truth table; thus, this step should also be examined in detail in both the design and checkout process.

In the design process, the logic equations are derived from the truth table representation of the problem. Each minterm can be written down individually from the truth table, and rules of logic utilized to find the minimal form. Or some other method can be used to find an acceptable logic equation. The Karnaugh map method is exemplified by Figure 3.2(c). From the equations, the proper arrangement of logic gates can be derived. The exact implementation techniques will be dictated by the design constraints established by the problem itself.

Portions of the process — from understanding to truth table to Karnaugh maps to logic equations to implementation — can be aided by CAE (computer aided engineering) systems or CAD systems (Computer Aided Design). However, it is imperative that a designer be able to understand the results of CAE/CAD systems, and be able to ascertain correctness of the final result. The computer aided systems will do a speedy and precise job, but the underlying algorithms used by the computer system may not coincide with the desires of the system designer. Therefore, care must be taken to assure that the final results provide a reasonable solution to the initial problem.

In general, we are not interested in computers operating on a single bit at a time. Rather, we are concerned with computers that operate on a collection of bits. Full adders can be cascaded to the width of the system, as shown in Figure 3.3. In the figure, two 8-bit numbers are added to produce an 8-bit result. An additional input is the carry in (C_{IN}), which may come from a status register or other source; and the carry out (C_{OUT}) from the addition is available for the system.

This is not the fastest method to perform an addition, as we will see, but it will provide the correct answer. The time required to perform addition by this method, as measured from the time that all inputs are stable, is directly proportional to the number of bits in the word. This kind of addition process can be called a ripple carry adder (RCA), since the carry at each stage is propagated to the next stage. We will label the time required by this type of addition as $T_{ADD_{RCA}}$, and this time is given as:

$$T_{ADD_{RCA}} = N \times T_{FA}$$

$$= N \times (2 \times G)$$

That is, the time for an N-bit addition is just N times the time for a single bit addition (T_{FA}), and the time for a single bit of addition is two gate delays. Thus, the time for a full adder implementation of an addition module is linear in the number of bits to be added.

The details mentioned above are often hidden inside integrated circuits. However, in designing or understanding the circuitry embedded in ICs, this information may be very beneficial. Full adders can be purchased in IC form, such as the '80. Or one can consider that four such stages are cascaded in a single unit, such as the '83, a 4-bit adder. However, if one examines the circuitry internal to the '83, the carry out of the chip is generated in a different fashion than the FA method just described. This method is the look-ahead method, which we will examine later. But first let's apply the add technique described above to a subtractor.

Example 3.1: Full subtractor: Using the methods described above, design a full subtractor (FS).

The first step in this process is to understand the requirements of the design. Figure 3.4(a) is a diagram that indicates the function of the full

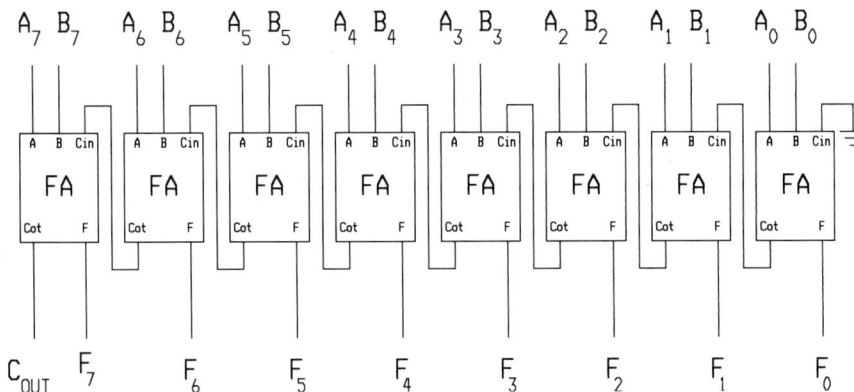

Figure 3.3. A Word Adder Composed of Full Adders.

X_I Y_I B_{IN}

X   Y   Bin

FS

Bot   F

B_{OUT} F_I

(a)

Borrow $\longrightarrow$ 0 1 1 1 1 0 0 0
X $\longrightarrow$ 1 1 1 0 0 0 1 0
Y $\longrightarrow$ 1 0 1 0 1 1 0 0
X-Y $\longrightarrow$ 0 0 1 1 0 1 1 0

(b)

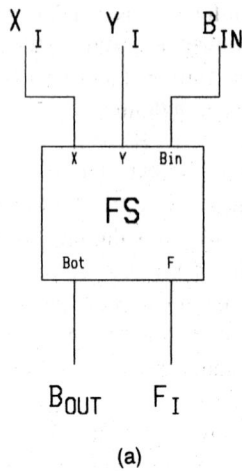

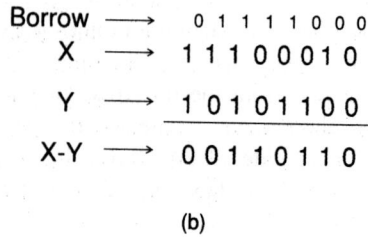

X_i	Y_i	B_{in}	B_{out}	F_i
0	0	0	0	0
0	0	1	1	1
0	1	0	1	1
0	1	1	1	0
1	0	0	0	1
1	0	1	0	0
1	1	0	0	0
1	1	1	1	1

(c)

X_iY_i

B_{in}	00	01	11	10
0	0	1	0	0
1	1	1	1	0

$B_{out} = \overline{X}_i Y_i + Y_i B_{in} + \overline{X}_i B_{in}$

X_iY_i

B_{in}	00	01	11	10
0	0	1	0	1
1	1	0	1	0

$F_i = X_i \oplus Y_i \oplus B_{in}$

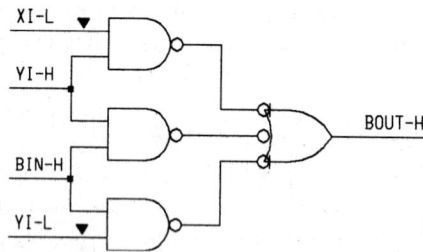

(d)

XI-L

YI-H

BIN-H

YI-L

BOUT-H

(e)

Figure 3.4. Design of a Full Subtractor (FS).

subtractor. Two bits from the data word (X_I, Y_I) are inputs to the FS, as is a line from the previous stage. This line is the borrow in, B_{IN}. The outputs are the subtract output for this stage, F_I, and the borrow output to the next stage, B_{OUT}. The algorithm for doing subtraction in base 2 is exactly the same as the algorithm used for the base 10 taught in grade school. One "borrows" bits (digits) from places of higher significance as needed to be able to perform the subtraction of a bit. Figure 3.4(b) is an example of a binary subtraction; this example is given because all of the information necessary to create the complete truth table is present. Figure 3.4(c) is the truth table for the full subtractor, which has been derived by examining the subtraction of Figure 3.4(b) and filling in the table as needed.

A good thing to do in unfamiliar circumstances (base 2 subtraction is not a daily occurrence for most people) is to convert to a familiar system and do the subtraction. The base 10 representation of this operation is 226 − 172 = 54; and since $00110110_2 = 54_{10}$, we feel much better about the accuracy of the results. Alternative derivations of an answer provide methods for checking the results of an algorithm, and should be employed as necessary to build confidence and prove correctness.

The Karnaugh maps for the subtractor are shown in Figure 3.4(d), as well as the resulting logic equations. Finally, the gating function for the borrow is given in Figure 3.4(e). The gating is not given for the subtract output since $F_I = X_I \oplus Y_I \oplus B_{IN}$ is exactly the same formula as the sum out for a full adder. The same circuitry can be used for both functions. Note also that the logic equation for the borrow has the same form as the logic equation for the carry out of the full adder, but the inputs are different. Thus, with a little ingenuity and some gating functions, the same circuitry could be used for the $A + B$, $A − B$, $B − A$, and $A \oplus B$. The latter function is achieved by disabling the carry function; forcing the carry to a logical zero allows $A \oplus B \oplus C$ to reduce to $A \oplus B$.

The timing for a multiple bit full subtractor is exactly the same as the timing for the carry propagate adder,

$$T_{SUB} = N \times T_{FS} = N \times 2 \times T_G .$$

Subtraction of two values can be accomplished by a system of subtractors created as described here. However, a subtraction system can also be created by using an adder system (composed, for example, of '283s) and the complement-and-increment method of negating a value. The value to be subtracted is complemented with a set of inverters, and the increment is supplied by asserting the carry-in of the adder system.

The similarity between the subtraction process and the addition process is not really surprising, but it points out a situation that often arises. In many circuits, both combinational circuits, such as those discussed here, and sequential circuits, such as direct multiplication methods discussed later, there are opportunities to utilize some of the same elements of the circuit for more than one function. Here, one set of gates can be utilized for both the addition and subtraction functions. The same concept applies in some sequential circuits, where counters (or other components) can be reused for different functions. The key to the effective use of system resources is to achieve a complete understanding of the functions to be performed by the system, and to combine that with a knowledge of the logic required to perform those functions and the capabilities of that logic. This combination will allow a designer to trade off system resources against system requirements to achieve an effective design.

Word adders composed of full adders are an example of a minimal gate solution to a problem, but the time required for the result may provide an unacceptable limit to system performance. Another approach is to add more complexity to the add process to do the function faster. In order to do this, we look again at the logic equations for the addition process:

$$F_I = A \oplus B \oplus C_{IN}$$

$$C_{OUT} = AB + AC_{IN} + BC_{IN}$$

$$= AB + C_{IN} \cdot (A + B)$$

Looking at these equations we make the following observations, some of which have been made before. The creation of the F_I signal requires but two gate delays from stabilization of input to output stable. The same can be said for the first form of the carry equation, but the second form requires three gate delays. However, the second form allows the addition process to proceed in a different fashion. Here the data inputs (as opposed to the carry input) are grouped into two terms: AB is called the carry generate (CG) function since if this term is asserted there *will* be a carry (hence, the carry is "generated") regardless of the value of the carry input. The $A + B$ term is called the carry propagate, since if this term is asserted any carry which is supplied to this stage is passed on to the next. (Note that the function $A \oplus B$ would also be a valid carry propagate function. Why?) Arrangement of the add operation to include the carry generate (CG) and carry propagate (CP) functions results in a module which produces:

$$F_I = A \oplus B \oplus C_{IN}$$

$$CG = AB$$

$$CP = A + B$$

Figure 3.5(a) shows a diagram of such an adder. Note that the time required to create the carry generate and carry propagate is a single time delay. But more importantly, note that the carry generate and carry propagate lines are *not* functions of the carry input. This means that if we arrange several look-ahead carry adder (LACA) modules as shown in Figure 3.5(b), then *all* of the CG and CP lines will be stable one gate delay after the inputs are stable. In Figure 3.5(b) these lines are inputs to another module, called a look-ahead carry generator (LACG). The LACG has the responsibility of creating the carry for each stage; it does this by looking at the carry generate and carry propagate signals from all of the stages. If C_{IN} is asserted then C_0 will be asserted. C_1 will be asserted if the carry generate of the previous stage (CG_0) is asserted, OR if CP_0 is asserted AND C_{IN} is asserted. As the carries become more significant, the amount of logic needed to generate the carry becomes larger. But it is important to note that, if the designer of the LACG is willing to supply a sufficient number of gates, then *all* of the carries will be generated in two gate delays. Thus, the addition shown in Figure 3.5(b) requires 5 gate delays: one to generate the CG and CP for each LACA, two to generate all of the appropriate carries, and two more to propagate the effect of the carries to the outputs. This is faster than the $4 \times 2 \times G = 8$ gate delays required for the FA implementation.

It is apparent that much of the complexity has been moved to the LACG, which becomes more complex as the number of modules that it services increases. A LACG that provided the carries for all 64 bits of an adder would be

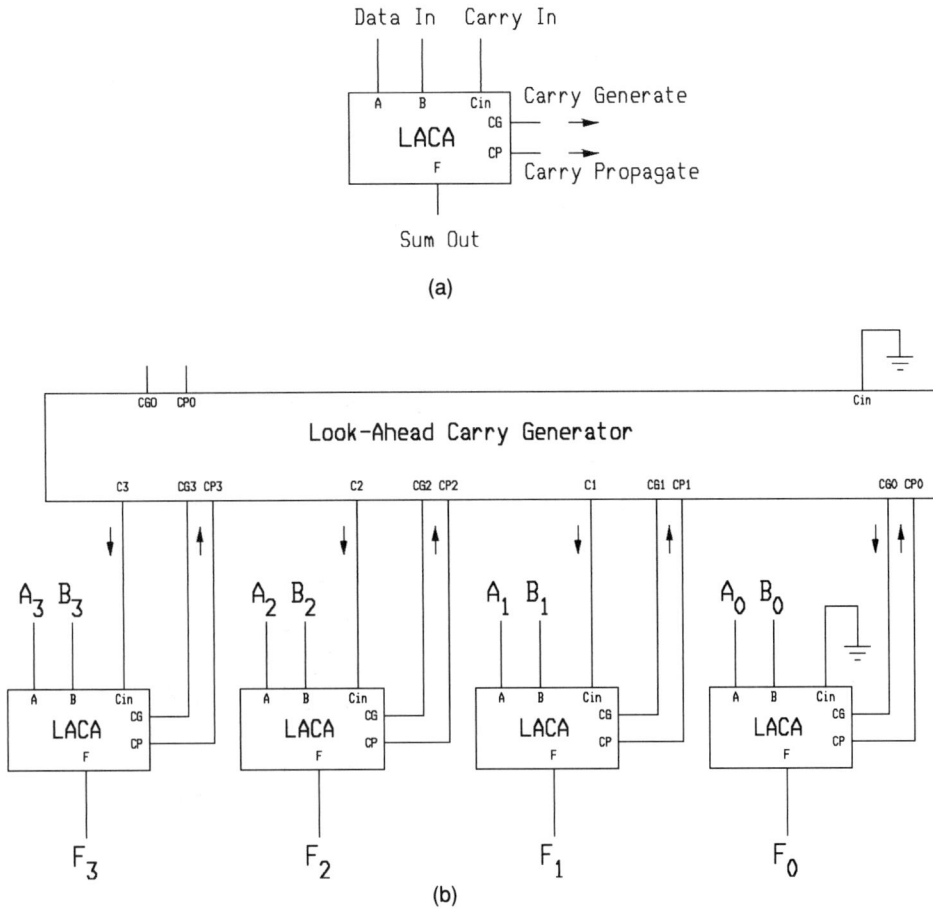

Data In   Carry In

A   B   Cin   Carry Generate
              CG
LACA
              CP
         F   Carry Propagate

Sum Out

(a)

Look-Ahead Carry Generator

Figure 3.5. Look-Ahead Carry Adder (LACA) and its Connection in an Adder Circuit.

prohibitively expensive in terms of numbers of gates, or IC real estate. So, the LACGs are designed to cascade in exactly the same fashion as the LACAs. That is, in addition to the carries, the LACG generates a CG and CP that can be utilized by a second stage of LACG; the process continues as far as necessary to perform the work required. Such a system is shown in Figure 3.6. This figure shows the connection of '181s, which are 4-bit ALUs that generate the CG and CP signals required, and '182s, which are the LACGs. These units are both 4-bit units; that is, the ALU performs the addition of 4 bits, as well as generating the CP and CG signals for those 4 bits, and the LACG handles the CG and CP signals from 4 modules. Because of this added complexity in the ALU module, the CG and CP signals will require a minimum of two gate delays to create, as opposed to the single gate delay for a single bit unit. The time required for a carry lookahead addition is then given by:

$$T_{\text{LACA}} = 2 + 4 \times (\lceil \log_b(N) \rceil - 1)$$

where there are N bits to be added, and the number of bits handled by the ALUs and LACGs is b. When no LACG is needed (up to b bits), then the time required

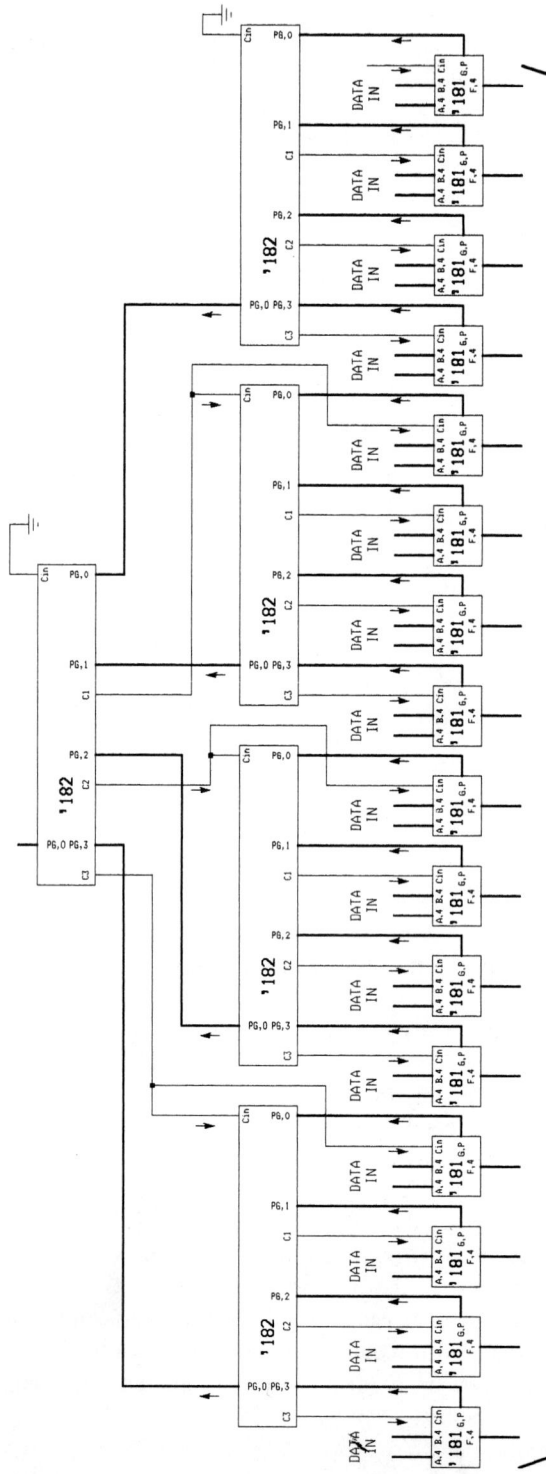

Figure 3.6. 64-Bit Addition with Carry Look-Ahead.

is simply two gate delays. Then, as the number of bits increases, the LACGs are added in a tree type of structure, where the fanout of each node of the tree is b. This gives rise to the second term in the above equation. As the number of bits (n) increases, each time the term $\log_b(N) -1$ crosses a b boundary, that is, when the number of bits to be added crosses an exponential integer (b^i), then the depth of the tree increases by one, and the number of gate delays required increases by four. By utilizing the look-ahead process, the time required for addition has been changed from function linear in the number of bits to a process that is logarithmic in the number of bits. And the base of the logarithm is the number of bits handled by the LACAs and LACG; a larger b results in a faster adder for a given number of bits. For the adder shown in Figure 3.6, the time would be:

$$T_{LACA} = 2 + 4 \times (\lceil \log_4(64) \rceil - 1)$$

$$= 2 + 4 \times (3-1)$$

$$= 10 \text{ gate delays}$$

The 10 gate delays for the look-ahead process of Figure 3.6 are a limit, which will not, in general, be fully attained by commercial parts. This is because parts such as the '181 and '182 will reduce the number of gates required for the final function by allowing three or four levels of gates, instead of the theoretically possible two. Nevertheless, the look-ahead method for addition is much faster than addition with chains of full adders. At this time we will introduce another term for the add process: carry propagate adder, abbreviated CPA. By this term we indicate that the carry will propagate all the way through the addition, but the method of carry implementation, whether ripple carry or carry look-ahead, is not specified.

The addition function provides an example of the tradeoffs available in creating a system. A carry propagate adder will perform a function with a minimal number of gates, but the time will be correspondingly long. A carry look-ahead adder will perform an addition in a minimal amount of time, but the number of gates required for the function has correspondingly increased. Each system designer must examine the resources available (time, gates, silicon real estate, etc.) and allocate those resources in an appropriate manner.

3.2. Status: Results of Arithmetic Operations

Often when arithmetic operations are performed, some information about the answer is as important as the answer itself. That is, many operations are performed simply to find out how things compare: is A larger than B? Is A equal to B? Is A negative? Many of these questions are answerable if certain information is available concerning arithmetic operations. For example, is A equal to B? Well, subtract A from B (or B from A); if the result is zero, then A is indeed equal to B. In general, four pieces of information are produced by these arithmetic operations, and these pieces can be used to form bits in a status register. The four bits are zero, sign, overflow, and carry. We should hasten to add that other types of information are often available in a status register, and we will deal with this type of information in Chapter 4. At this time, we are interested in the arithmetic operations and status that can result from them.

The sign bit is perhaps the easiest to generate: it is the sign of the result of whatever operation was performed by the ALU. For two's complement numbers, this is the MSB of the result; for most floating point number systems, this is also the most significant bit. In either case, the sign of the number is fed directly to the status register. Instructions that manipulate arithmetic values (ADD, SUBTRACT, COMPARE, etc.) will modify this bit; instructions that do not do arithmetic (JUMP, CALL, etc.) will not modify the bit. For a precise list of the instructions that do modify the various bits of the status register of an existing machine, the instruction set definition for that machine must be consulted. The opposite is true for a system architect in the process of creating a set of instructions. That is, based on the application area of the machine, the arithmetic operations required, and the number systems utilized, the system designer can, at the time of the definition of the system, identify which operations will have an effect on the status register.

In addition to the sign bit, the carry bit is also readily available from the ALU. If an arithmetic operation resulted in a carry, then this bit is asserted in the status register. Again, the instructions modifing the bit are obtained from the instruction set definition. The hardware of the system, then, must prevent instructions that cannot modify the bit (as defined by the instruction set) from actual modification capability. This is accomplished by disabling the load function of the status register bit (carry bit, in this case) within the status register.

The zero bit is also easy to visualize, conceptually. If the result of the operation is zero, then the bit should be set. Often this operation will be utilized by more instructions than strictly the arithmetic ones. For example, in some systems MOVE instructions will test the value being moved to see if it is zero. As before, the exact list of instructions that modify the zero bit will be obtained from the instruction set definition. The logic required is a test on each line to check its assertion level. For ALUs not providing this information on a separate status line, then all of the output lines must be checked. However, some ALUs provide a single line that will be asserted if any of the ALU lines are *not* zero. The advantage of this method is that these lines are constructed with open collector technology, and can be tied together without external gating. Thus, when all ALU outputs are zero, none of the lines is asserted, and the recognizable output is high, which is exactly what is needed by the status register.

The overflow bit is the condition that requires more than rudimentary logic. When should the overflow bit be set? The overflow bit indicates that the operation performed has exceeded the ability of the number system to represent information. Thus, one of the basic pieces of information needed (or assumed) is the number system being utilized. Our examples will concentrate on the two's complement number system. Other number systems may call for other conditions to identify an overflow. For example, consider an 8-bit, two's complement number system. From our previous considerations we know that this number system can represent values from -128 to $+127$. If we add 61_{10} to 45_{10}:

00111101	This is 61 in base 2.
00101101	This is 45 in base 2.
————	Now add them together.
01101010	The result is equivalent to 106, the correct answer.

This operation does not exceed the ability of the number system to represent information. However, if we add 75_{10} to 58_{10}:

01001011	This is 75 in base 2.
00111010	This is 58 in base 2.
10000101	In 2's complement, this is −123.

If the pattern is considered an unsigned integer, then the answer is correct (133_{10}). But as a two's complement number, the ability of the number system to represent information has been exceeded. Two positive numbers have been added together, and the result was a negative number. The same thing will happen if two large negative numbers are added together: a positive number will be the apparent result. Again, the ability of the system to represent information has been exceeded: an overflow has occurred. When this happens in an arithmetic operation, then the overflow bit of the status register will be set. If a number system other than the two's complement number system is to be used, then a similar set of operations must be checked, identified by the number system itself.

Example 3.2: Overflow circuit: Design a circuit that will detect the occurrence of an overflow condition for a two's complement system.

As stated above, the overflow will occur when two positive numbers are added together and a negative number results, or when two negative numbers are added together to form a positive result. So the observation points are the sign bits: if the two input sign bits are positive (zero), and the output sign bit is negative (one), then an overflow has occurred. Likewise, if the two input sign bits are negative (one), and the output sign bit is positive (zero), then an overflow has occurred. A circuit to detect this condition is shown in Figure 3.7.

If the internal carries of the addition process are available, this circuit can be replaced by a single exclusive-OR gate. The exclusive-OR gate would detect a difference between the carry-in and the carry-out of the most significant stage; these two lines will differ when the overflow condition exists.

The arithmetic bits included in the status register are set and cleared as directed by the control logic for the system. That is, not all of the instructions will be allowed to modify the status bits, and some status bits will be modified by more instructions than other bits. This will require a system which is capable of selectively controlling each of the bits. If we limit ourselves to fairly standard TTL parts, then such a circuit is shown in Figure 3.8. Note that each of the bits is individually setable and clearable, as well as being reset jointly by a system reset. If the instruction set does not require the ability to individually set and clear each of the bits, then the amount of logic required for this function will be reduced.

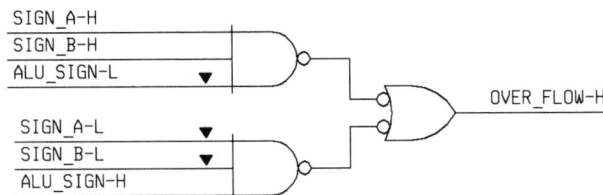

Figure 3.7. Circuit for Overflow Detection (Two's Complement System).

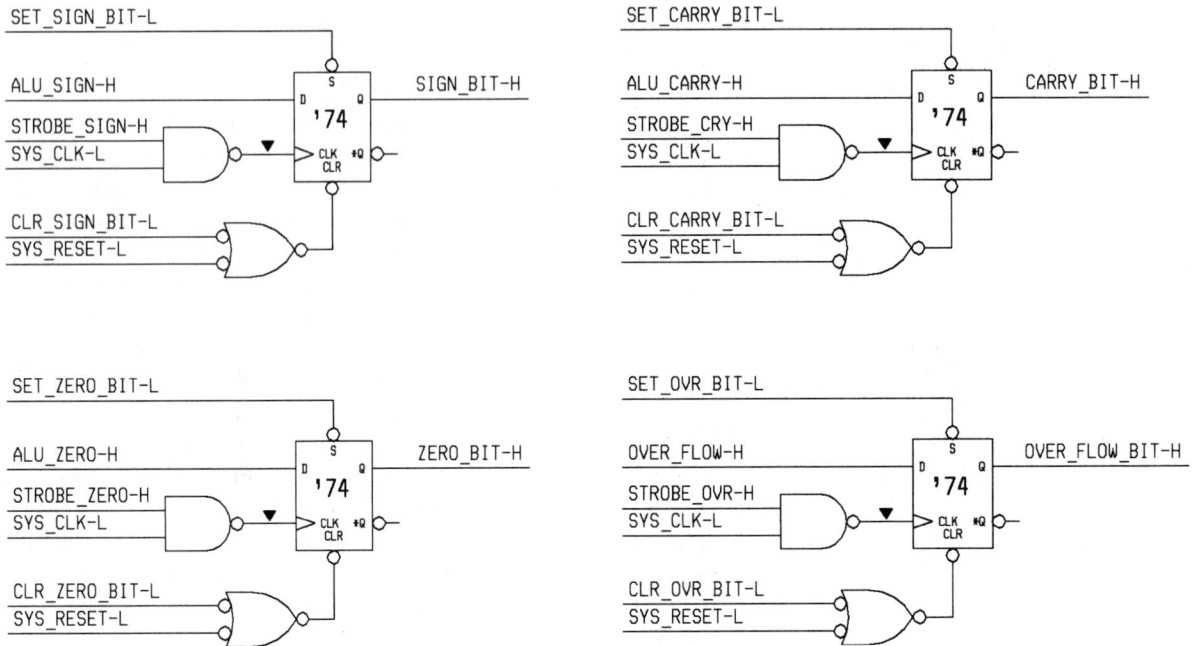

Figure 3.8. Arithmetic Bit Formation for a Status Register.

Some manufacturers provide many of these functions in a single IC, such as the AM2904. This reduces the number of chips required but not the control lines: The AM2904 has 17 control lines associated with this function.

These status bits form both a source and a destination of information in the performance of computer functions. Arithmetic operations often require a carry input, which is provided from the status register. Addition operations may change all four of the bits discussed above. Logical operations can also affect the zero bit. And program control operations can test status bits to control the flow of control in the system. Thus, these four bits can form a portion of a status register, which performs a central function in the overall system operation. We will include other kinds of status information in the discussion of instruction sets in Chapter 4.

3.3. Iterative Multiplication Methods

From the very early days of computers one of the things needed was a multiplication capability. Many of the early machines were funded by defense needs, such as calculation of ballistics tables and other strictly computational tasks. For these tasks a multiply was required, and many early machines had a hardware multiply instruction. Later, when memory speeds improved dramatically, subroutines could be used to do the multiply and still accomplish the function faster than the previous hardware systems. This allowed a sizeable reduction in hardware for the computer. Still, hardware multiplication capabilities have been utilized more and more as the relative cost of hardware has decreased. Let us examine some of the methods for doing multiplication.

First, let us define the problem in exact terms, then select a sample problem to follow through the various methods of multiplication. What we want to find is the product, P, of two values, A and B.

$$P = A \times B$$

A and B are called the multiplicand and multiplier; let us assume that they are both 5-bit numbers: $A_4A_3A_2A_1A_0$ and $B_4B_3B_2B_1B_0$. We know from Chapter 2 that these can assume values from 0 to $2^5 - 1 = 31$. So, the largest product would be $31 \times 31 = 961$. To represent the number 961 requires $\lceil \log_2 (961) \rceil = 10$ bits; hence, we say that the product of two N-bit numbers requires $2 \times N$ bits to represent. With our assumption of a positional notation system, the product can be represented as:

$$P = A \times B$$

$$= A \times B_4 \, B_3 \, B_2 \, B_1 \, B_0$$

$$= A \times B_4 \times 2^4 + A \times B_3 \times 2^3 +$$

$$A \times B_2 \times 2^2 + A \times B_1 \times 2^1 +$$

$$A \times B_0 \times 2^0$$

In practice, we write this as follows:

					A_4	A_3	A_2	A_1	A_0
				$\times$	B_4	B_3	B_2	B_1	B_0
$PP_0 \rightarrow$					$A_4{\cdot}B_0$	$A_3{\cdot}B_0$	$A_2{\cdot}B_0$	$A_1{\cdot}B_0$	$A_0{\cdot}B_0$
$PP_1 \rightarrow$				$A_4{\cdot}B_1$	$A_3{\cdot}B_1$	$A_2{\cdot}B_1$	$A_1{\cdot}B_1$	$A_0{\cdot}B_1$	
$PP_2 \rightarrow$			$A_4{\cdot}B_2$	$A_3{\cdot}B_2$	$A_2{\cdot}B_2$	$A_1{\cdot}B_2$	$A_0{\cdot}B_2$		
$PP_3 \rightarrow$		$A_4{\cdot}B_3$	$A_3{\cdot}B_3$	$A_2{\cdot}B_3$	$A_1{\cdot}B_3$	$A_0{\cdot}B_3$			
$PP_4 \rightarrow$	$A_4{\cdot}B_4$	$A_3{\cdot}B_4$	$A_2{\cdot}B_4$	$A_1{\cdot}B_4$	$A_0{\cdot}B_4$				
$PR \rightarrow$				Sum of all rows					

The five rows labeled PP_0 to PP_4 are known as the partial product array. For this multiplication, the rows of the partial product array are composed of 5 bits, and each bit is an AND function of a bit from the A input and a bit from the B input. The product itself (PR) is the sum of the rows of the partial product array, when the rows have been aligned appropriately for bit significance. The effect of the multiplication by powers of two in the above equation is accounted for by the shifting of the rows in the partial product array. This is the same situation as that taught in grade school for base 10:

```
      1324
      2435
      6620
     3972
    5296
   2648
  3223940
```

In the base 10 example, each row in the partial product array is the result of the multiplication of the first number by one digit in the second number. As explained above, in the base 2 system this product is very easy to obtain, since multiplication in base 2 is accomplished on a bit-by-bit basis. Therefore, the creation of the partial product array for a base 2 example is very simple: merely AND each bit in the multiplicand with the appropriate bit in the multiplier. Then the rows of the partial product array are summed in some fashion. Let us examine some methods for accomplishing this.

The most straightforward method for doing the multiply is the traditional "shift and add" method. One implementation of this is shown in Figure 3.9. The multiplier shown in the figure is set up to do an 8×8-bit multiply. Several

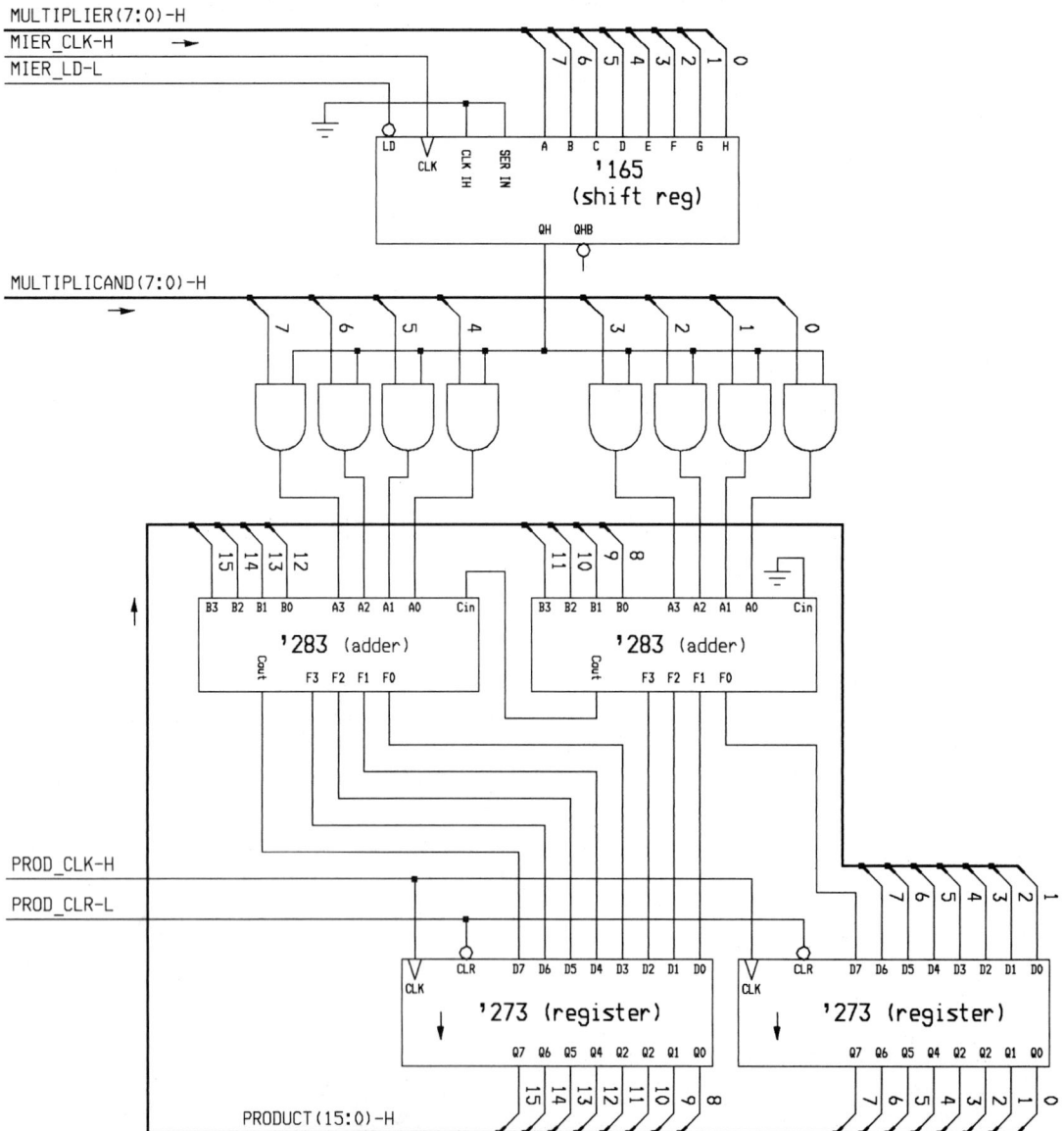

Figure 3.9. Data Path Logic Diagram for Simple Multiplier.

observations can be made concerning this system. First of all, the adder used is an 8-bit adder; this will function properly since the partial product addition is done from the least significant partial product to the most significant partial product. There is nothing magic about the order of partial product addition, so long as the bits are added in their appropriate significance. That is, for an N-bit multiply, the partial products PP_{N-1} to PP_0 could be added in the order shown (PP_0 first to PP_{N-1} last), in the reverse order (PP_{N-1} first to PP_0 last), or in any order deemed convenient because of design considerations.

In Figure 3.9, the shifting of the result is accomplished by hard wiring the accumulating sum to line up with the appropriate bit positions in the partial product. And the partial product is created exactly as shown in the above expansion of a binary multiplication: AND gates are used to generate the partial product from the multiplicand. The multiplier bit to be used is obtained from a shift register. A timing diagram that will assert the control signals in an appropriate fashion to do the work is shown in Figure 3.10. The timing diagram shows a set of control signals that will work in all cases; however, the result can be obtained faster in some circumstances if the control section is modified to look for specific conditions. One such condition is that either the multiplier or the multiplicand is zero; in such a case, the result is zero, and the answer can be given immediately. A flow diagram showing such a set of decisions is shown in Figure 3.11. The design of a control section that will create the appropriate signals is the topic of Chapter 5 and will not be covered here.

The circuit shown in Figure 3.9 is only one of a variety of implementations that will accomplish the work of multiplication. Other solutions to the problem would try to create the "best" design based on some criteria of the designer. For example, in the design shown in Figure 3.9 two chips are required for the AND function; these can be removed by using a slightly more complicated product register capable of shifting internally as well as loading from an external source. This reduces the number of chips (and hence board area required) for the function, but will necessitate a slightly more complex control. Another type of design may test for the condition that the remainder of the multiplier is all zero, hence the multiplication is essentially complete. The challenge in that type of design is to be sure that the final product bits are in the correct bit positions.

No matter what type of data path is selected, and its appropriate algorithm devised, the designer is faced with the problem of proving correctness. Several methods are available to do this, from simulation of the hardware if such a

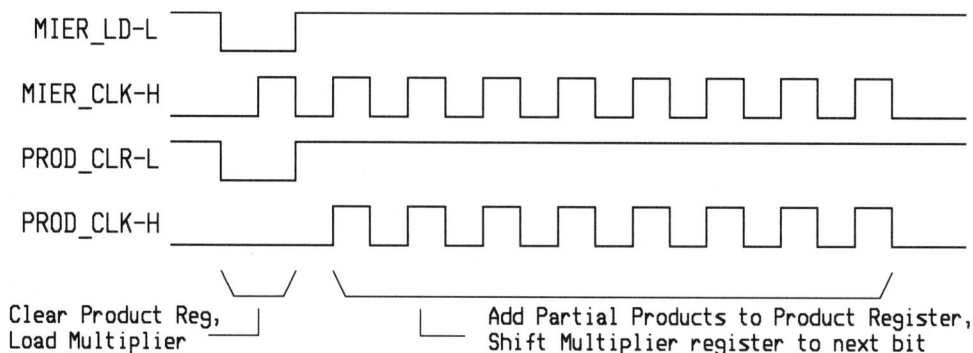

Figure 3.10. Timing of Control Signals for Simple Multiplier.

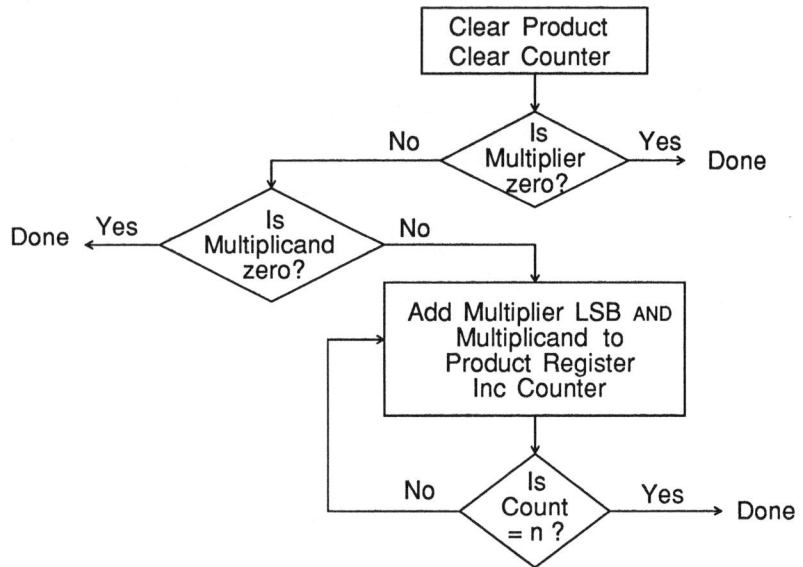

Figure 3.11. Flow Diagram for Data Dependent Multiply Algorithm.

simulation system is available, to examples worked through by hand. Before the design is fabricated, the designer should select several appropriate examples and show that the system will provide proper results.

Example 3.3: Multiplier Design: Design a data path for a multiplier that will add the partial products in "reverse" order, from the most significant to the least significant. What are some of the benefits and penalties of doing this?

This could be accomplished in a number of ways, one of which is shown in Figure 3.12. The figure shows the parts and principal interconnections needed; a more detailed schematic representation is found in Appendix B. This method requires an adder as wide as the final product. For simplicity this is shown as four '283s; faster add times could be attained by using an adder with lookahead capabilities. The product register is constructed out of '273s, which are 8-bit edge triggered registers. The bits from this register are fed back to one set of inputs on the adders. The inputs to the product registers come from the same bit positions in the adder.

The multiplier register is composed of two '195s which have been configured to be a shift register. The control section will be responsible for asserting the clock line (PLIER_CK-H) when data is available to be loaded, and also when the multiplication is proceeding. The output of the multiplier register is constantly checked to see if it is zero (PLIER_ZERO-L).

The multiplicand register is composed of two types of shift registers: '195s and a '164. The '195s provide for the load of the multiplicand value, at the same time clearing the '164 (PCAND_LD-L). Again note that the control section will be responsible for asserting the load and clock lines in the proper sequence to cause the data to be loaded at the appropriate time, and then shifted during the execution of the multiplication itself. As the multiplicand is shifted out of the '195s, it will be shifted toward lower significance in the '164. This is the method whereby the stated design

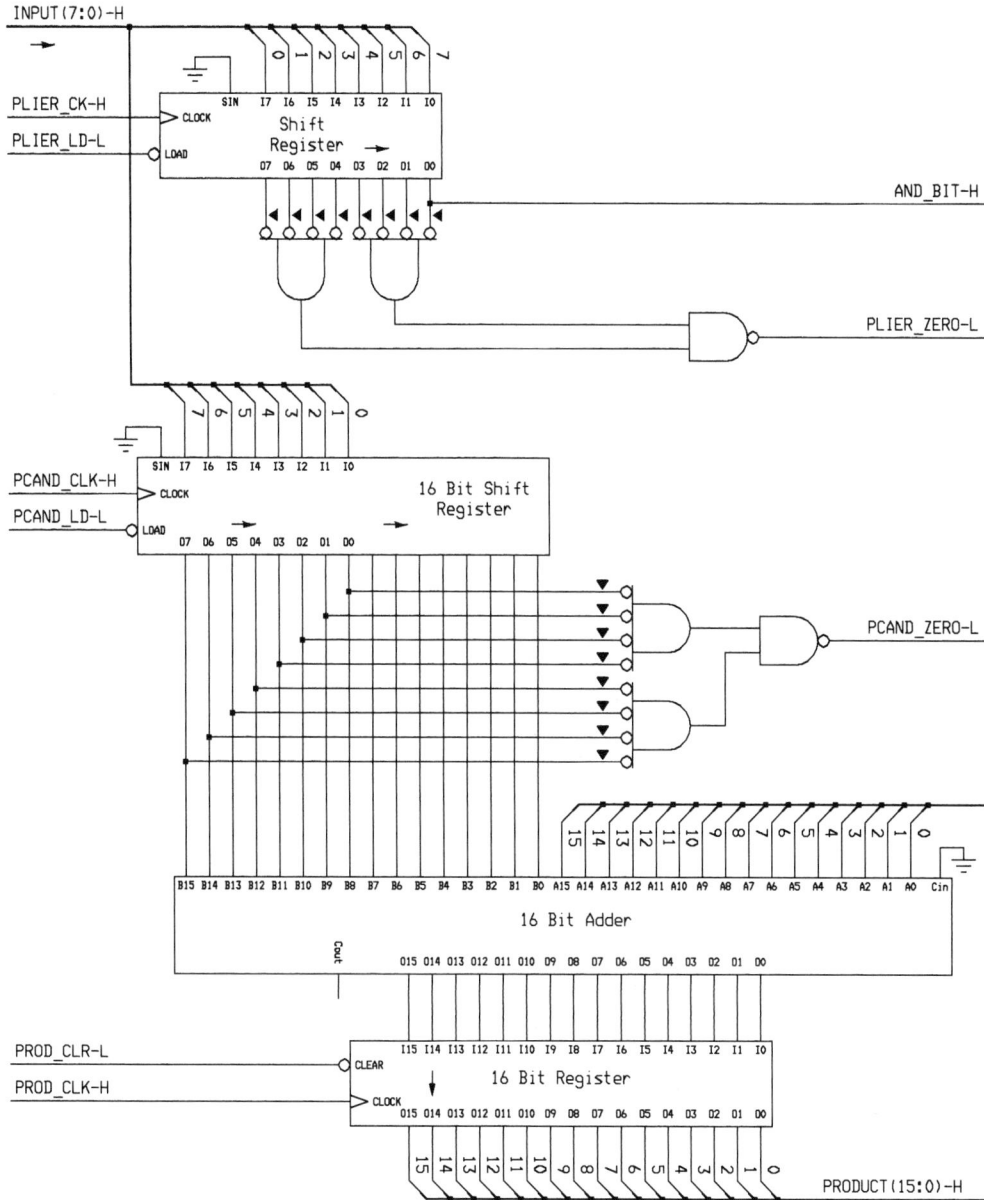

Figure 3.12. Data Path for Multiplier of Example 3.3.

objective of "reverse" order of partial products will be accomplished. The multiplicand can also be checked for a zero value (PCAND_ZERO-L) when it is loaded, but this will only be effective at the beginning of the algorithm.

A flow diagram for implementation of the multiplication algorithm is shown in Figure 3.13. This diagram indicates how the algorithm proceeds, and identifies some of the benefits of this organization. The first step is to clear the product register; this is the correct answer if the multiplicand is zero, which is checked next. It is also the correct answer if the initial value

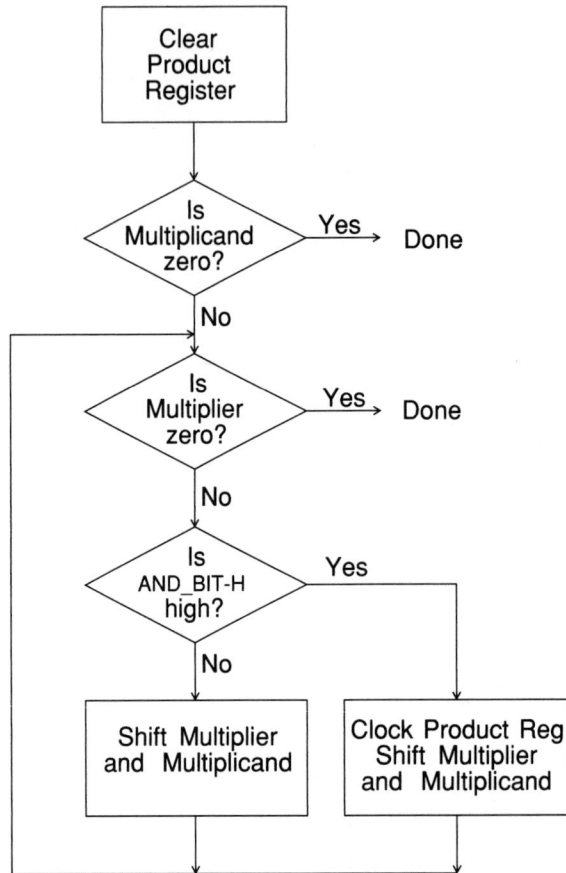

Figure 3.13. Flow Diagram for Multiplier of Example 3.3.

in the multiplier is zero, which is the next condition checked. Then the iterations begin in earnest. The value in the multiplicand register is added to the value in the product register; this result may or may not be placed into the product register. That decision is based on the most significant bit in the multiplier register (AND_BIT-H); if the bit is asserted, then the product register is loaded. In either case, the multiplier and multiplicand registers are shifted by one bit position. If the number of iterations is N (8 in this case), then we are done. If not, check the multiplier register to see if we have added in all of the appropriate values. If we have, then the algorithm is finished. As this description points out, the time required for this algorithm is data dependent. It is not necessary to check for zeros, since the algorithm would function correctly with an iteration counter and no data checks. However, by testing the values during execution of the multiply, the number of iterations will depend on the arrangement of one's and zero's in the data. By doing the additions in the "reverse" order, the product bits are in the correct position whenever all the required additions have been performed. Thus, the time to complete the instruction will vary according to the data, which will speed up the processing.

Another benefit from this method is the absence of AND gates to do the individual partial product multiplications. The partial product is always added to the accumulating product, but this value is conditionally loaded into the product register, based on the appropriate bit in the multiplier. Thus the AND function is supplied by control of the product load line, rather than an AND line on every bit.

One of the obvious tradeoffs with this method is that the speed benefits and the reduction in gating (no AND gates) have been obtained at the expense of a larger adder and multiplicand register. So, before a designer declares this method better/worse than another method, he needs to ascertain the various costs of the method and decide if the tradeoffs match his system resources.

The multiplication methods discussed to this point are iterative methods: the same adder system is used a number of times until the correct result is obtained. One of the questions to be addressed is the time required for the multiplication. The time that we worry about here does not include the time required to load the multiplier and multiplicand registers, and, in an actual implementation, those times need to be included in any timing estimates. The multiplication time, T_{MULT}, can be grouped into two contributing factors: the setup time, T_{SETUP}, and the iteration time, T_{ITER}.

$$T_{MULT} = T_{SETUP} + N \times T_{ITER}$$

The setup time includes the time required to clear the product register and perform any initial checks identified by the algorithm. This is reflected in the "is multiplicand zero" condition in the algorithm of Example 3.3. The iteration time is the time required to create the partial product (perform the AND function), to add the partial product to the running sum, and to load the resulting value into the product register. These times are reflected in the following equation:

$$T_{ITER} = T_{AND} + T_{SUM} + T_{REG}$$

The first term (T_{AND}) is the time needed by the algorithm to form the partial product. Note that in some algorithms, such as that described in Example 3.3, this time will be zero, since the same effect is obtained by conditionally loading the product register. The second term (T_{SUM}) accounts for the time required to form the sum of the partial product with the product register. This time will be determined by the adders being used and the interconnection method (carry propagate adders or carry look-ahead adders). The term should reflect the time required from all data inputs stable to all outputs stable. The last term T_{REG} is a combination of the times required for the register being used, which can be obtained from the data sheet for the device. These include the setup time (the time that the data must be stable prior to the assertion of the clock), the hold time (the time the data must be stable after the assertion of the clock), and propagation delay (the time for *stable* outputs, from the assertion of the clock). All of these times must be accounted for in deciding on the time required for the clock cycle of the unit. However, if a designer is willing to provide for nonequal clock times, then the time required by the system of Example 3.3 can be reduced. That is, if the AND_BIT-H is not asserted, then the add will not be needed, and the system can move on to the next bit (shift multiplier and multiplicand) without waiting for T_{SUM}.

These multiplication methods can be used to build multipliers out of commercially available parts, such as the system shown in Figure 3.12. Or they can be used to implement multiplications by using resources (adders, registers, and data paths) internal to a chip, such as a microprocessor. Since these methods are iterative in nature, they can be readily implemented with microcode methods. We will look more closely at microcode in Chapter 5, but an understanding of the iterative nature of the system helps to explain why some manufacturers identify the times required by multiplication instructions in numbers of cycles. And why some multiplication instructions indicate that the time for instruction completion is dependent on the data being used.

Before we move on to direct methods of multiplication, we will note that in the considerations thus far we have carefully avoided any mention of negative numbers. Without any modification, the techniques mentioned will not function for negative numbers. A number of techniques have been used to allow use of negative as well as positive numbers. The technique we will describe here is called Booth's algorithm, after a pair of British mathematicians, but similar techniques are used elsewhere. These techniques are classified as recoding techniques, since the multiplication is modified by a recoding scheme. Let us see how this is applicable to the problem of multiplication of signed numbers.

First of all, we need to remember from Chapter 2 that the bits in the number have a different meaning for signed numbers. That is, the most significant bit has a different meaning. The five bit numbers which were used earlier for an example had the form and meaning:

$$B = B_4\, B_3\, B_2\, B_1\, B_0$$

$$= B_4 \times 2^4 + B_3 \times 2^3 + B_2 \times 2^2 +$$

$$B_1 \times 2^1 + B_0 \times 2^0$$

$$= B_4 \times 16 + B_3 \times 8 + B_2 \times 4 +$$

$$B_1 \times 2 + B_0 \times 1$$

The difference for a two's complement number is shown in the following fashion:

$$B_{2\text{'s COMP}} = B_4 \times (-16) + B_3 \times 8 + B_2 \times 4 +$$

$$B_1 \times 2 + B_0 \times 1$$

As can be seen from the equation, the most significant bit is different in its weighting formulation and must be treated accordingly. The Booth's algorithm approach can be understood by first doing some algebra on the number. In a step-by-step fashion, we can express the two's complement number in a new form:

$$B_{2\text{'s COMP}} = (-16) \times B_4 + 8 \times B_3 + 4 \times B_2 +$$

$$2 \times B_1 + 1 \times B_0$$

$$= (-16) \times B_4 + (16 - 8) \times B_3 + (8 - 4) \times B_2 +$$

$$(4-2) \times B_1 + (2-1) \times B_0$$

$$= (-16) \times B_4 + 16 \times B_3 - 8 \times B_3 + 8 \times B_2 - 4 \times B_2 +$$

$$4 \times B_1 - 2 \times B_1 + 2 \times B_0 - 1 \times B_0$$

$$= -16 \times (B_4 - B_3) - 8 \times (B_3 - B_2) - 4 \times (B_2 - B_1) - 2 \times (B_1 - B_0) - 1 \times (B_0 - 0)$$

The values in parentheses in the above equation are composed of the subtraction of two bits, and can have the values +1, 0, or −1. Note that the weights are what we would expect in that all are powers of two. Therefore, multiplication by the weighting factors can be achieved by the shifting used in the first algorithm. The complexity comes in that now, instead of strictly adding, we need the ability to add, subtract, or do nothing. However, once a subtraction (addition) has been performed, the next operation will be an addition (subtraction). (This can be easily seen by examining possible bit patterns and the resulting order of operations.) This alternate nature of the operations guarantees that the size of the adder/subtractor will be limited to N bits. The easiest way to visualize this process is to work through an example:

> *Example 3.4: Signed multiplication with recoding:* Utilize the Booth's algorithm recoding scheme to perform the multiplication: $25_{10} \times -19_{10}$.
> The bit patterns for the two numbers are:

> 011001   Let $A = 25_{10}$ be the multiplicand.
> 101101   And $B = -19_{10}$ be the multiplier.

The recoding algorithm works on pairs of bits as shown below. Note that the product is sequentially formed; the steps shown below to form P_0 to P_4 correspond to the cumulation of the partial products to that point.

$$
\begin{array}{rcll}
-1 \times (b_0 - 0) & = & -1 & \text{Subtract } A \text{ from 0 to form } P_0. \\
-2 \times (b_1 - b_0) & = & +2 & \text{Add } 2 \times A \text{ to } P_0 \text{ to form } P_1. \\
-4 \times (b_2 - b_1) & = & -4 & \text{Subtract } 4 \times A \text{ from } P_1 \text{ to form } P_2. \\
-8 \times (b_3 - b_2) & = & 0 & P_3 = P_2. \\
-16 \times (b_4 - b_3) & = & +16 & \text{Add } 16 \times A \text{ to } P_3 \text{ to form } P_4. \\
-32 \times (b_5 - b_4) & = & -32 & \text{Subtract } 32 \times A \text{ from } P_4 \text{ to form } P_5. \\
\end{array}
$$

These steps can be followed as identified to ascertain that the answer is −475 as expected. The multiplication by powers of two called for here is achieved by the appropriate shift of the operand A. The hardware that would perform this kind of a multiplication can be visualized as shown in the following example.

> *Example 3.5: Hardware for recoding multiplication:* Design the data path for a multiplier that will perform multiplication according to Booth's algorithm. Assume that the input values are 8 bits each.
> One solution to the problem is shown in Figure 3.14. The multiplicand register and the product register are formed using '273s, which are 8-bit registers. The multiplier is loaded into a '165, which is a parallel-in/serial-out shift register. Note that, when the multiplier is loaded, the

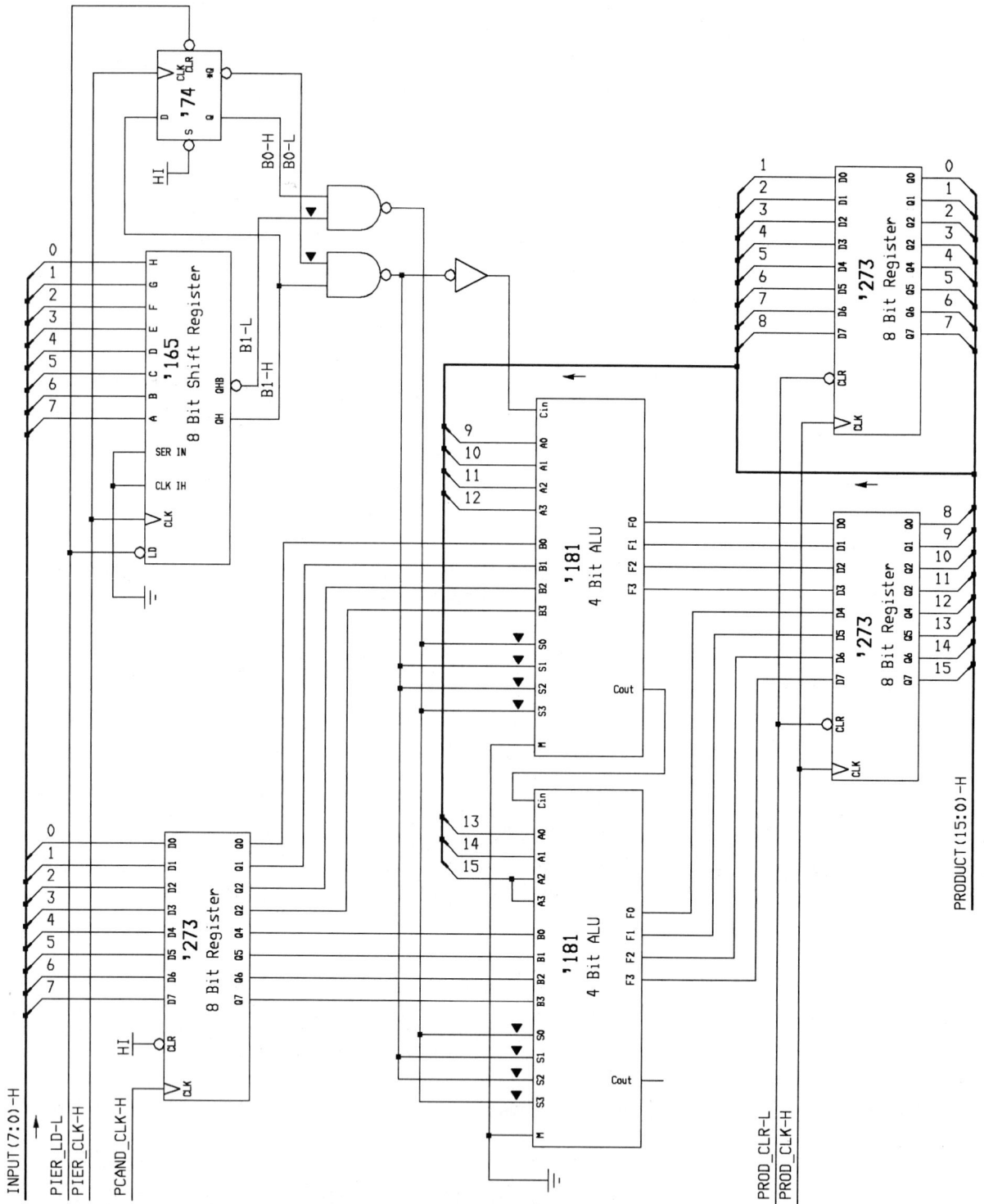

Figure 3.14. Multiplication by Booth's Algorithm.

flip-flop for storing the previous bit in sequence is cleared. The add/subtract/do–nothing requirement of the algorithm is handled by a pair of '181s, which are capable of performing all of the functions. The determination of the function of the '181s is handled by the arithmetic select lines (S3–S0), and the desired function is identified by the bits of the multiplier, as seen in the previous example. The appropriate bits are called simply B0-H and B1-H in the diagram. As the multiplier shifts through the register during the execution of the algorithm, the appropriate bits will appear on these lines. The function of the '181s should then be determined by the following table:

'Plier Bits		ALU Sel				Function
B1-H	B0-H	S3-H	S2-H	S1-H	S0-H	
0	0	0	0	0	0	Pass product value.
0	1	1	0	0	1	Product plus multiplicand.
1	0	0	1	1	0	Product minus multiplicand.
1	1	0	0	0	0	Pass product value.

This logic is implemented in the few gates in Figure 3.14. Like the first multiplication method, this one will require a fixed number of clock pulses on the control lines to complete. Of course, it would be possible to check for a zero input condition, but it will not function properly if it is stopped in the middle of a multiply.

As can be seen from the example, the logic required for multiplication of negative as well as positive numbers does not greatly increase, but more care must be taken in the design and verification of the system. Nevertheless, the iterative approach will produce the proper result if enough caution is used in its implementation. Some of the many references for design techniques and examples of iterative methods of multiplication are listed at the end of this chapter. This is by no means intended to be an exhaustive explanation of multiplication methods, but rather it should identify some practical systems that can be used to perform the needed operations. For systems requiring more speed, there are faster methods for accomplishing the multiply, as we see in the next section.

3.4. Direct Multiplication Methods

All of the above methods require that the product be formed by combining the partial product with a value that will eventually form the final result. One of the reasons that an iterative approach is desirable from a resources standpoint is that it requires a single adder to perform the entire multiplication. The tradeoff has been made to sacrifice speed in favor of minimal logic resources. But in what way could more resources be applied to the problem? That is, given the situation where a designer is willing for purposes of speed to include a great number of gates, how should those gates be configured? We have already seen that, by examining the addition problem and using a different technique, the addition time could be changed from a linear function to a logarithmic function. Now we will analyze the multiplication function and identify methods that can be used to decrease the multiplication time.

Consider the following multiplication:

$$
\begin{array}{rl}
\text{Multiplier} \rightarrow & 01101001 \\
\text{Multiplicand} \rightarrow & 01011010 \\
\hline
PP_0 \rightarrow & 00000000 \\
PP_1 \rightarrow & 01101001 \\
PP_2 \rightarrow & 00000000 \\
PP_3 \rightarrow & 01101001 \\
PP_4 \rightarrow & 01101001 \\
PP_5 \rightarrow & 00000000 \\
PP_6 \rightarrow & 01101001 \\
PP_7 \rightarrow & 00000000 \\
\hline
\text{Product} \rightarrow & 0010010011101010
\end{array}
$$

The multiplication process requires two separate functions: forming of the partial products and adding all of the partial products together. The formation of all the partial products ($PP_7 - PP_0$) can be done in a single gate delay from the time that the data is stable. The hardware cost in the above example is 64 two-input AND gates, but, with that gate investment, the partial product array can be generated in parallel. Once the partial products are available, they can be summed as before. However, our objective here is speed, so rather than have a single adder and iterate to a register, let's use multiple adders and feed the result of one adder directly into another. The system resulting from this is shown in Figure 3.15(a), and it would require $N-1$ adders for N rows of partial products.

In the previous section, T_{MULT} was a function of a setup time and a multiple number of iteration times, T_{ITER}. The system shown in Figure 3.15(a) reduces the time by changing T_{ITER} to be simply the add time, T_{SUM}. The adders shown in the figure are carry look-ahead adders, but any kind could be used. The point here is that the time for a direct method with a linear connection of adders, $T_{\text{MULT}_{\text{DIRECT-LIN}}}$, is given by:

$$
T_{\text{MULT}_{\text{DIRECT-LIN}}} = (N-1) \times T_{\text{SUM}}
$$

The time is linear in the number of rows (bits), which is a situation that will only get worse for more bits. The obvious solution is to get a time reduction to a logarithmic function by arranging the adders in a tree fashion, such as that shown in Figure 3.15(b). This would change the time from a linear function to a logarithmic function: $T_{\text{MULT}_{\text{DIRECT-TREE}}} = \lceil \log_2(N) \rceil \times T_{\text{SUM}}$ where there are N bits in the multiplier. This system will indeed obtain the product in a smaller time than the linear system, but other methods can achieve even higher speed.

The next method to consider has received several names, but we will call it row reduction. To understand what is going on, let us return to a simple example, a 4×4-bit multiplication for positive values only. The problem setup is exactly as we have seen it before, with the elements of the partial product array being formed as the AND of the appropriate bits. Here we want to emphasize the rows formed in the partial product array, so we will consider the multiplication by labeling elements in the partial product array as $R_{X,Y}$, where X gives the row number and Y is the element in the row. Thus, a 4-bit multiplication becomes:

$$
\begin{array}{rcccc}
 & A_3 & A_2 & A_1 & A_0 \\
\times & B_3 & B_2 & B_1 & B_0 \\
\hline
 & R_{0,3} & R_{0,2} & R_{0,1} & R_{0,0} \\
 R_{1,3} & R_{1,2} & R_{1,1} & R_{1,0} & \\
 R_{2,3} & R_{2,2} & R_{2,1} & R_{2,0} & \\
R_{3,3} & R_{3,2} & R_{3,1} & R_{3,0} & \\
\hline
\end{array}
$$

Sum of partial products

Each row of the partial product array forms a more significant portion of the final product, as seen by the shifting nature of the information. Now let's put together a set of full adders to do this multiplication according to the above setup. That is, we will do a multiplication in the method of $T_{\text{DIRECT-LIN}}$ above, but use full adders for this simple case. This is shown in Figure 3.16. As expected, the partial product bits ($R_{X,Y}$) are added into the product by shifting them appropriately and

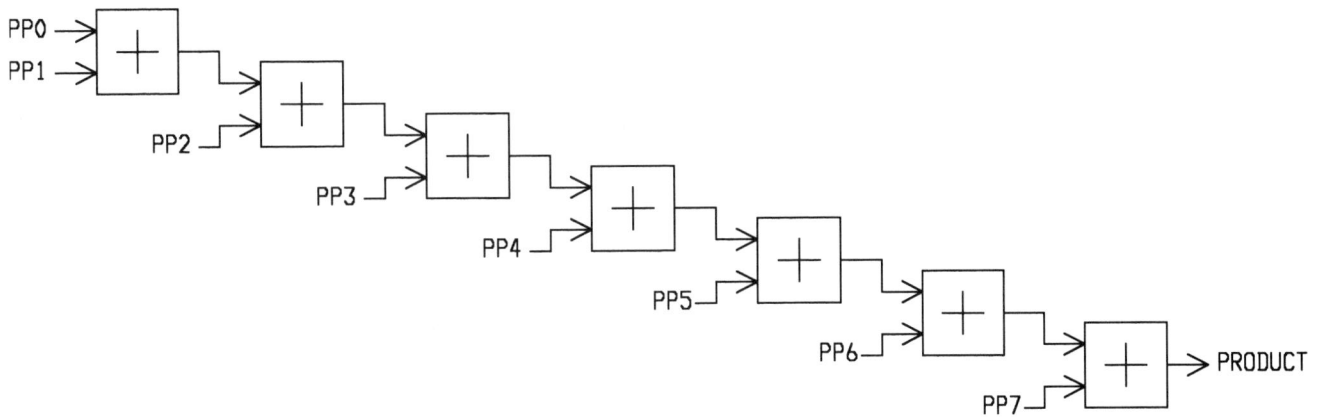

(a)

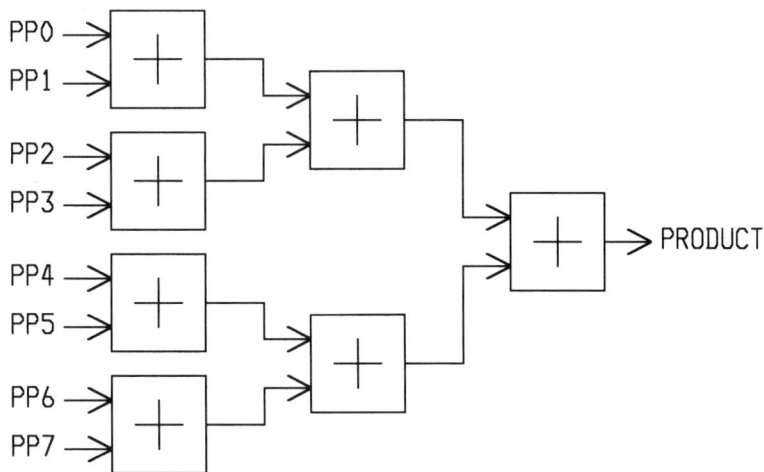

(b)

Figure 3.15. Multiplication by Direct Methods: Linear and Tree.

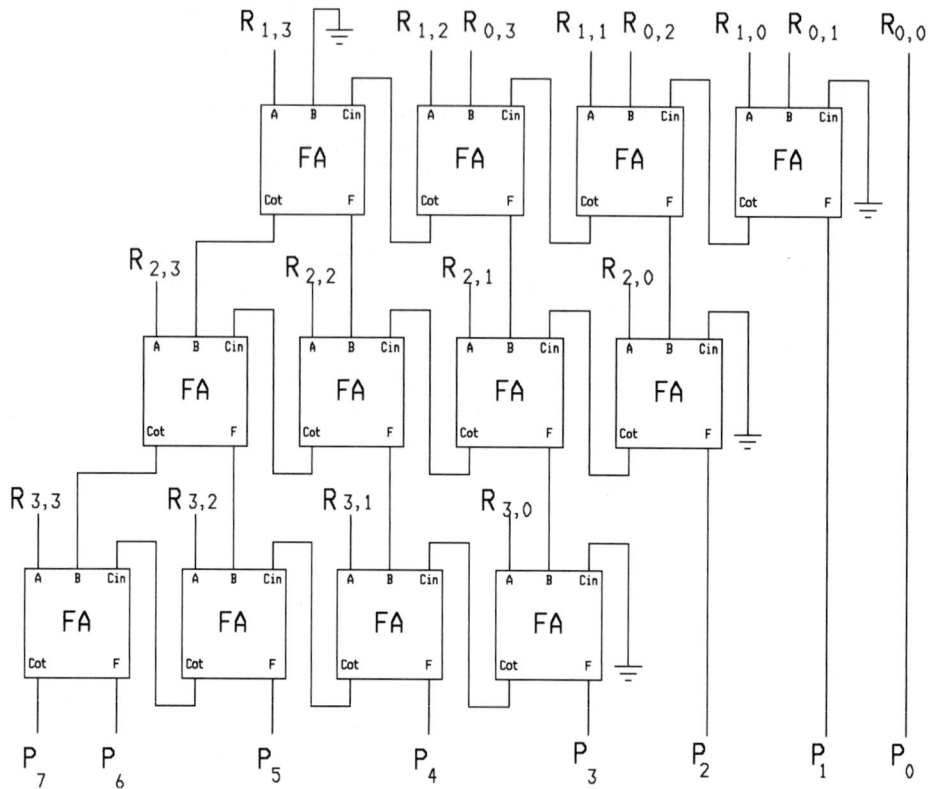

Figure 3.16. Partial Product Addition with Full Adders.

using full adders to add to the running sum. Now we ask the question, what is the function of the full adder? We often see a symbol for a full adder as shown:

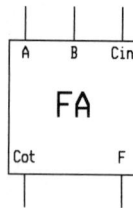

We mentioned earlier that the outputs form a 2-bit number that gives the number of one's on the input lines. The three inputs (A, B, C_{IN}) all have the same significance; the sum output has the same significance, and the carry out has a significance of one higher bit position. There is no reason that the carry needs to be added into the sum *in the same row* that it is generated; that is, the carry can be saved for the next level of adders. The benefit of passing the carry to the next set of adders is that the work accomplished by the first stage no longer requires a time based on the number of bits in the word; the time is *always* two gate delays. The policy of saving the carry to the next stage gives rise to the name "carry save adder," or CSA. The multiplier of Figure 3.16 is redone to utilize this feature, and the result is shown in Figure 3.17.

Chap. 3: Arithmetic Units: Data Manipulation

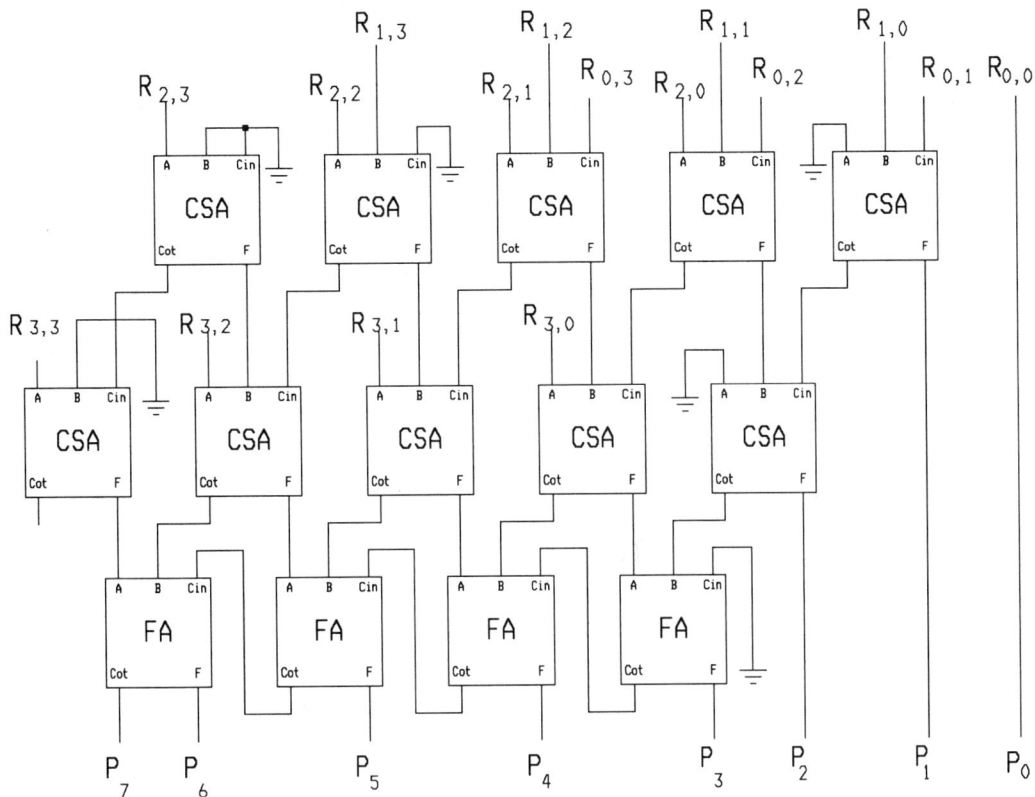

Figure 3.17. Partial Product Addition with Carry Save Adders.

The use of carry save adders to speed up the addition process reduces the time required for the intermediate steps to two gate delays, but the carry process cannot be put off forever. The final stage of such a system must be an adder that implements the carry process the width of the final result. The effect is that the intermediate stages can be designed with a relaxed resource criteria, and more design effort can be directed toward speeding up the final stage. One way of looking at what is happening is to recognize that using adders as shown above (saving the carry to the next level of addition) reduces the number of rows that need to be added. The carry save adder, then, is a 3-row-to-2-row reduction unit: 3 rows of bits are reduced to an equivalent operation that requires only 2 rows. For example, in the first level of CSAs in Figure 3.17, 3 rows of bits from the partial product array ($R_{0,x}$, $R_{1,x}$, and $R_{2,x}$) are reduced to 2 rows of bits. Then, the 2 rows of bits obtained by that process, plus the remaining row of bits from the partial product array ($R_{3,x}$) are reduced to 2 rows of bits. Finally, these 2 rows form the input to a set of full adders, which does the final addition. Thus, Figure 3.17 shows an implementation of two 3-2 (3-row-to-2-row) reduction units and a final CPA stage.

The output for any bit position of a row reduction unit contains a value that identifies the number of "ones" found in that bit position of a number of rows. Thus, a row reduction unit with k outputs will be able to represent numbers from zero to $2^k - 1$. Hence, a row reduction unit with k outputs will be able to reduce $2^k - 1$ rows; therefore, 7-3, 15-4, 31-5, and so on, are all possible configurations for row reduction units. One additional benefit of row reduction is the ability to do portions of the partial product addition in parallel. That is, since all of the partial products can be generated simultaneously, the row reduction process can begin immediately to reduce the *N* rows of bits to 2 rows, which will then be added to form the final result. And independent row reduction units can operate on different rows of the partial product array simultaneously. This is demonstrated in the following example:

Example 3.6: Multiplication with row reduction: The DEC floating point number system has a double precision configuration with a mantissa length of 56 bits (including the hidden bit). Design a high speed multiplier to do a 56×56-bit multiply. Assume that the largest row reduction unit you have to work with is a 15-4 row reduction unit. Also assume that there is an adder at the last stage organized in 8-bit units for carry generate and carry propagate. How long will the multiplication take?

The formation of the partial product results in 56 rows of bits that need to be added together. These are then fed into row reduction units to reduce the total number of rows from 56 to 2. The overall design approach for this system, using 15-4, 7-3, and 3-2 reduction units, is shown in Figure 3.18. As can be seen from the figure, this requires two stages of 15-4 row reduction units, one stage of 7-3 row reduction, and a stage of 3-2 row reduction. These steps can all be accomplished in 8 gate delays. Note,

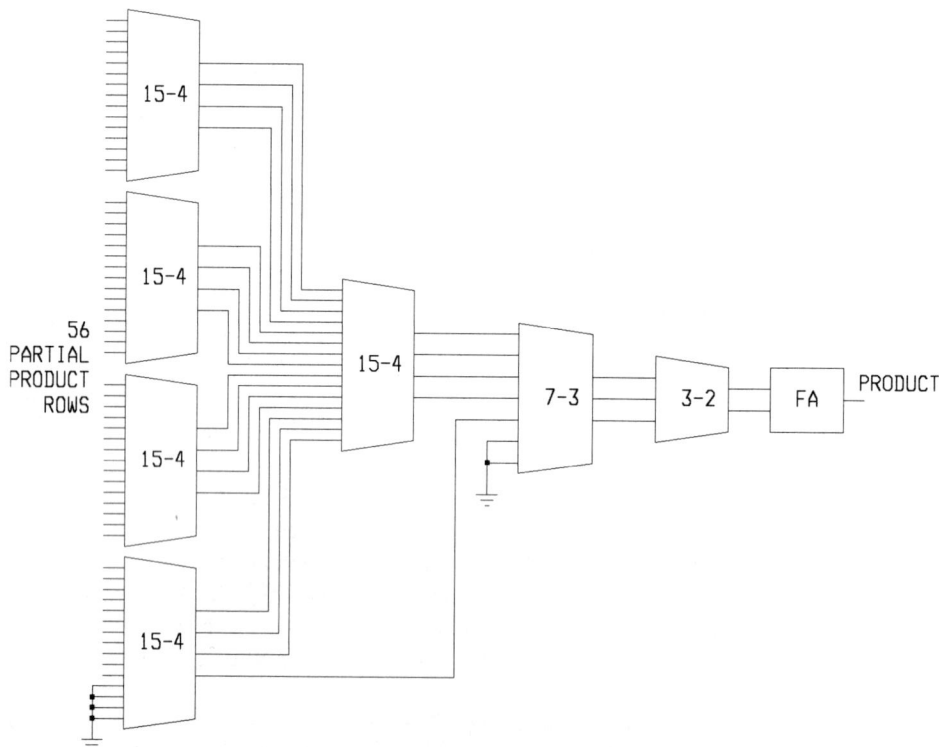

Figure 3.18. 56-Bit Multiplication Using Row Reduction.

Chap. 3: Arithmetic Units: Data Manipulation

however, that the complexity of the 15-4 reduction units will be much larger than the carry save adders, which form the 3-2 reduction stage. The final stage is a carry look-ahead adder that will produce the 112-bit result. We will assume that each row reduction unit requires only two gate delays. Thus, the time required for signals to propagate from the data inputs to the final addition stage is 9 gate delays (one for formation of partial products, two each for the four stages of row reduction units). From the equation for time required for carry look-ahead addition, the final addition process will require

$$T_{\text{LACA}} = 2 + 4 \times (\lceil \log_8(112) \rceil - 1)$$

$$= 2 + 4 \times (3-1)$$

$$= 10 \text{ gate delays}$$

So, the final result will require 19 gate delays. The cost of doing this is an enormous amount of hardware. This is not really practical in systems made of individual gates; however, this could be done in a reasonable fashion internal to an integrated circuit.

To better understand the multiplication mechanism, let us consider what is happening at each stage of the above process. The action being performed is to group portions of the partial product array together, and to then provide a number that is a count of the number of "1"s in the appropriate columns. This sectioning of the partial product array can be done in any manner that will produce the same results as the lengthy "normal" process. Thus, portions of the partial product array can be formed and summed, and then these intermediate sums combined to produce the final result. Any consistent mechanism can be used to identify portions of the multiply process for sectioning. The simplest example of this is the 3-2 reduction unit (CSA), which provides a count on the two output lines of the number of "1"s on the input lines. Other types of sectioning can be performed by using special purpose ICs, or by using similar techniques in multipliers that are internal to processor chips.

An example of the concept of subdividing the partial product array into sections can be found in the stepwise creation of the final result by considering only portions of the original problem. That is, using special purpose integrated circuits, portions of the partial product array are formed (the ANDing is done inside the chips) and the resulting elements combined in the fashion described above. The output of these chips is a number that is a sum of parts of the partial product array. Conceptually, this is shown in Figure 3.19. The figure indicates that some of the bits of the partial product array are formed, and then summed in an initial step in the multiplication process. These partial sums are then combined together to produce the final result. Using these techniques, large multipliers can be built using multipliers that work only on portions of the input values, as shown by the following example.

Example 3.7: Multiplication with sectioning: Design an 8×8 multiplier, using 74284 and 74285 4×4-bit multipliers.

These devices jointly form the 8-bit product of two 4-bit numbers: the '285 produces the four least significant bits; the '284 produces the four most

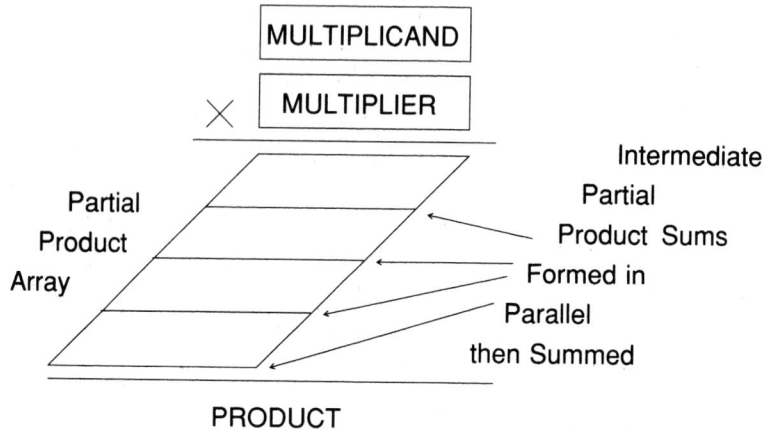

Figure 3.19. Partial Product Reduction by Sectioning.

significant bits. Therefore, an 8×8 multiply will be able to effectively use four pairs of devices. First, let's look at what one pair will produce:

$$
\begin{array}{ccccccccc}
 & & & & X_3 & X_2 & X_1 & X_0 \\
 & & \times & & Y_3 & Y_2 & Y_1 & Y_0 \\
\hline
 & & & & R_{0,3} & R_{0,2} & R_{0,1} & R_{0,0} \\
 & & & R_{1,3} & R_{1,2} & R_{1,1} & R_{1,0} \\
 & & R_{2,3} & R_{2,2} & R_{2,1} & R_{2,0} \\
 & R_{3,3} & R_{3,2} & R_{3,1} & R_{3,0} \\
\hline
P_7 & P_6 & P_5 & P_4 & P_3 & P_2 & P_1 & P_0
\end{array}
$$

So, the organization of an 8×8 multiply will be exemplified by the following configuration:

```
                    0  1  0  1  1  1  0  1
                    0  1  1  1  0  0  1  1
                    0  1  0  1  1  1  0  1
                 0  1  0  1  1  1  0  1
              0  0  0  0  0  0  0  0
           0  0  0  0  0  0  0  0
        0  1  0  1  1  1  0  1
     0  1  0  1  1  1  0  1
  0  1  0  1  1  1  0  1
0  0  0  0  0  0  0  0
─────────────────────────────────────────
0  1  0  1  0  0  1  1  1  0  0  0  1  1  1
```

Note that the pattern established above is utilized four times, and that the various portions of the partial product overlap. So some type of an adder tree would be needed to do the summation of the partial products. This is accomplished with a carry save adder stage (3-2 reduction) and an adder. The schematic for this is shown in Figure 3.20. This works rather well, but doesn't handle large multiplications without a corresponding large number of chips. Texas Instruments is no longer making this part; however, this same method of building portions of the partial product array can be utilized using larger multipliers. For example, several manufacturers make a 16×16

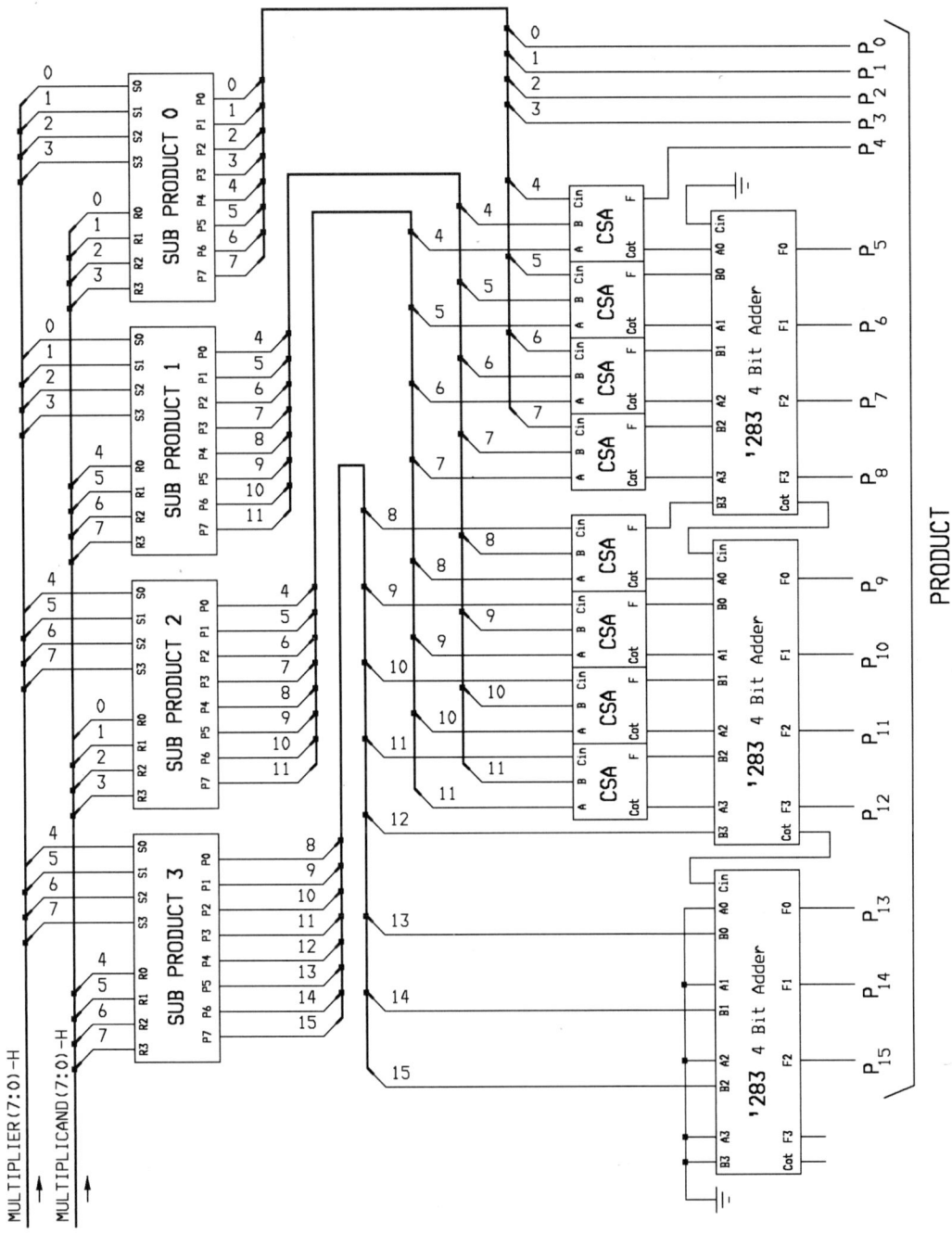

Figure 3.20. Logic diagram for a Fast Multiplier Using 74284 and 74285.

multiplier (like TDC1010), which could be cascaded in exactly this fashion to create a 32×32-bit multiply.

This example works on the basis of a "normal" partial product array; the respective portions of the array are generated internal to the multiplier chips, and partial sums formed. Then these sums can be combined to form the appropriate result. This same type of organization, forming portions of the partial product array from multiplicand and multiplier bits, can also use the recoding ideas introduced with Booth's algorithm. Indeed, the 74261 is a 2×4-bit multiplier that requires three bits of the multiplier in order to do the recoding necessary. But the system handles both positive and negative numbers, and the results are correct two's complement numbers. Like the system of Example 3.7, several sections of the parts can be combined to handle larger numbers.

All of these algorithms for high speed multiplies attempt to form the appropriate portions of the partial product array in parallel, then do as much of the partial product addition in parallel as possible. This includes delaying the final stage of the addition, where the carry will need to propagate all of the way across the output, as long as possible. Therefore, much of the design emphasis can be placed on this stage, which will be the speed bottleneck.

The multiplication process, then, adds into the final result the appropriate number of copies of the multiplicand. This can be accomplished by using a single adder and a register, and iterating through the necessary calculations. This type of system consumes considerable time resources (takes a relatively long time), but few hardware resources. One advantage to this approach is that it can be easily incorporated into a microprogrammed machine. Another multiplication method is to organize the calculation to use parallel application of partial product generation hardware, and then sum the final result with row reduction elements and high speed adders. This design consumes little time, but requires many hardware devices. The type of design selected will be dictated by the intended application, and the relative cost of system resources.

3.5. Direct Division: Basic Division Algorithms

Whereas multiplication finds the sum of multiple copies of an operand, division is concerned with finding out how many times one value can be found in another value. The numbers involved are the divisor, D_S, the dividend, D_D, the quotient, Q, and the remainder R. Mathematically, these elements are easily related to one another:

$$D_D = Q \times D_S + R$$

The division operation determines the quotient and the remainder. One of the assumed requirements on R is that it has a smaller magnitude than D_S. In the process of designing a system to do division, care must be taken to provide hardware that will do the work required by the system. That is, magnitudes should be considered, the number of bits to be provided in the operands, the bits required in the answers, and the placement of the radix point. All of this information must be considered in the design process.

One of the most straightforward methods to use in the approach to the design of the system is to mimic the operations of paper-and-pencil long division for positive numbers. Consider, for example, the steps required for dividing 58 by 5:

$$
\begin{array}{r}
1011 \\
101 \overline{)111010} \\
101 \\
\hline
10010 \\
000 \\
\hline
10010 \\
101 \\
\hline
1000 \\
101 \\
\hline
11
\end{array}
\qquad
\begin{array}{l}
\text{Quotient, } Q \\
\leftarrow \text{ dividend, } D_D \\
Q_3 \times D_S \\
R > D_S, \text{ continue} \\
Q_2 \times D_S, \text{ shifted} \\
R > D_S, \text{ continue} \\
Q_1 \times D_S, \text{ shifted} \\
R > D_S, \text{ continue} \\
Q_0 \times D_S, \text{ shifted} \\
R < D_S, \text{ done}
\end{array}
$$

Divisor, $D_S \rightarrow$

This operation proceeds in the same fashion as paper-and-pencil, long division. The base 10 algorithm with which we are familiar will produce a new base 10 digit at each iteration; the base 2 equivalent exemplified here will produce a new base 2 digit (bit) at each iteration. This is accomplished by subtracting the appropriate shifted divisor from the remainder value. The result of the subtraction determines the value of the bit in the quotient. A block diagram of such a divider is shown in Figure 3.21. The division process involves repetitive shifts and arithmetic operations, so the hardware is organized to accomplish that. The operation begins by placing the divisor in the register marked D_S, the dividend in the Q register, clearing the R register. In each iteration another bit of the answer is created, and this bit is shifted into the Q register as the dividend is shifted into the R register to be used in the calculations. As seen in the above example, the most significant bits are used in the first comparisons, so the shifting is configured to do least-to-most significant shifts. And this is exactly what is needed for the final result, since the quotient is generated most significant bit first and shifted into Q one bit at a time. At the completion of the process, the remainder will be found in R, and the quotient will be in Q.

The basic algorithm for the direct divide is very simple. After the operands are in place, the division process begins by subtracting the divisor from the value in R, which is the accumulating remainder. If the subtraction would result in a positive number, that number is loaded back into the R register and conditions are set up to introduce a "1" into the Q register. Otherwise, the R register is not changed and a "0" is readied for the Q register. Then the Q and R registers are shifted left, and the process is continued. We make the observation that since we

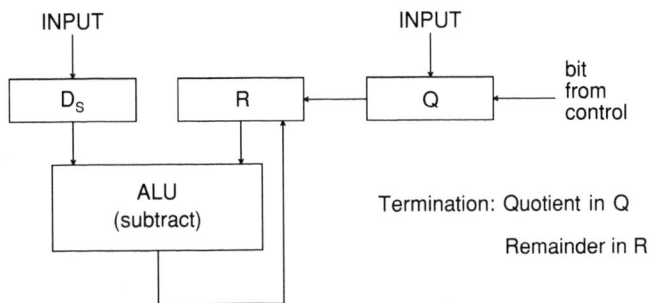

Figure 3.21. Block Diagram for Basic Division.

are working with positive numbers in this system, the subtraction will not change the bits in the lesser significant places. This observation indicates why the results of the subtraction are loaded only into the R register, and do not affect the Q register. Thus, the only information loaded into the Q register, once the process has begun, are the individual bits as they are generated and shifted in.

A flow chart for the divide operation is given in Figure 3.22. As can be seen from the flow chart, two decisions need to be made in the execution of the operation. The first concerns the action at the R register: should the value available from the subtraction be loaded into the R register or not? This decision is made based on the results of the subtraction: if the result is a positive number, then it is loaded and a "1" is setup for loading into the Q register. Otherwise, the result is not loaded, and a "0" is readied for loading. Then a count is checked to see if we are done with the operation.

The algorithm shown in Figure 3.22 conditionally loads the results of the subtraction $(R - D_D \rightarrow R)$ based on the value to be loaded. This is easily accomplished if the hardware is set up specifically to accomplish the divide. However, note that the hardware to do the direct multiply is very similar to that required for the divide. Hence, some systems are so configured that the ALUs and registers can be used for either function, and the control is slightly more complicated. In

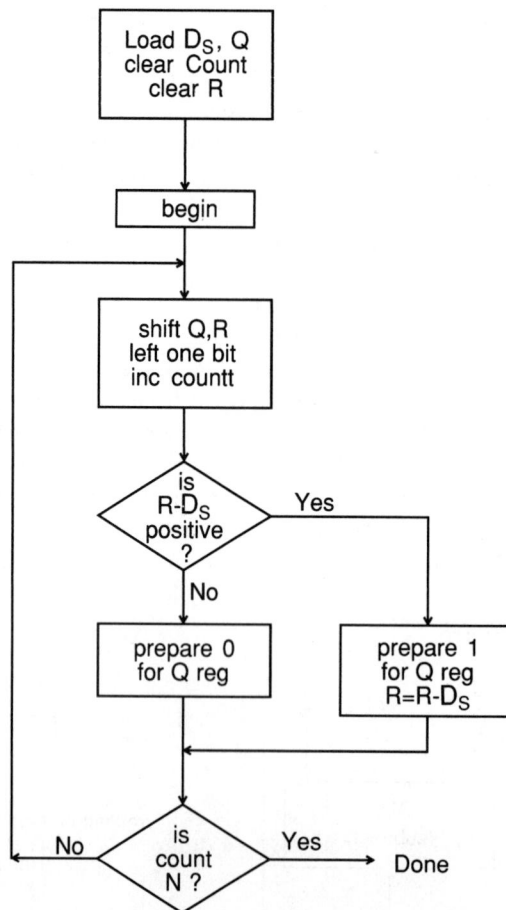

Figure 3.22. Flow Diagram for Division Operation.

Chap. 3: Arithmetic Units: Data Manipulation

such a system, it may be that the subtraction result must be stored (ALU out $\rightarrow R$) in order to set bits to be tested by microcode, or some other control mechanism. The algorithm shown in Figure 3.22 must then be changed accordingly. The net effect is that as well as setting up to put a "0" in Q, the value which was subtracted out must be restored, requiring another addition operation. This kind of an algorithm is called a restoring algorithm; another algorithm, called the nonrestoring divide, is so configured that the value is not restored, but set up to contribute the appropriate value for the next iteration of the process. The net result is fewer overall ALU operations.

> *Example 3.8: Hardware system for direct division:* Design a set of hardware that will accept data from a bus and perform a 16-bit division using the operations identified by the flow chart of Figure 3.22.
>
> The block diagram for one solution to this problem is shown in Figure 3.23. The actual logic diagram is found in Appendix B. Here the bus provides input for three registers: D_S, Q, and R. The divisor register is made of two '564s. Since the operation needed is to subtract the divisor, this is an inverting register. Two's complement subtraction can be accomplished by inverting the divisor (hence the inverting register), incrementing the result, and then adding the other operand, which in this case is the remainder. Here the remainder (R) register is made of two '198s, which can load or shift. The remainder register can be initialized to the dividend (D_D) value from the bus by using the '157s multiplexors. Finally, a pair of '198s are used for the Q register. The $R - D_S$ subtraction is accomplished by using adders; the R value comes directly from the R register, and the inverse of D_S provides the other input. And the increment part of the "complement and increment" two's complement negation is done by asserting the carry in of the adders. The result of this subtraction is returned to the R register through the MUXs, which allows the control to load the bus value of the subtraction value as required. That is, the bus provides the information for initialization, and from the adder comes any parallel load information required in the execution of the process. If the parallel load is required by the algorithm, then the control section causes the load. Then the '198s can be shifted simultaneously, with the control section providing the correct bit as input to the Q register. Missing from this diagram is the counter needed to identify the termination conditions. The control design methods required will be covered in Chapter 5.

The direct division mechanisms here can be implemented with individual adders as demonstrated by Example 3.8. Also, networks of divider cells can be constructed to produce results faster than the divide algorithms described above, since time is not required for storing and shifting operations. But the basic concepts of those division mechanisms are the same. Most high speed computers, however, do division by repeated multiplication, as shown in the next section.

3.6. High Speed Division: the Iterative Approach

We know from the definition of division that a reciprocal relationship holds for the values involved. One of the design approaches to the problem is to recognize the reciprocal relationship, and to utilize that to build a faster system. A great

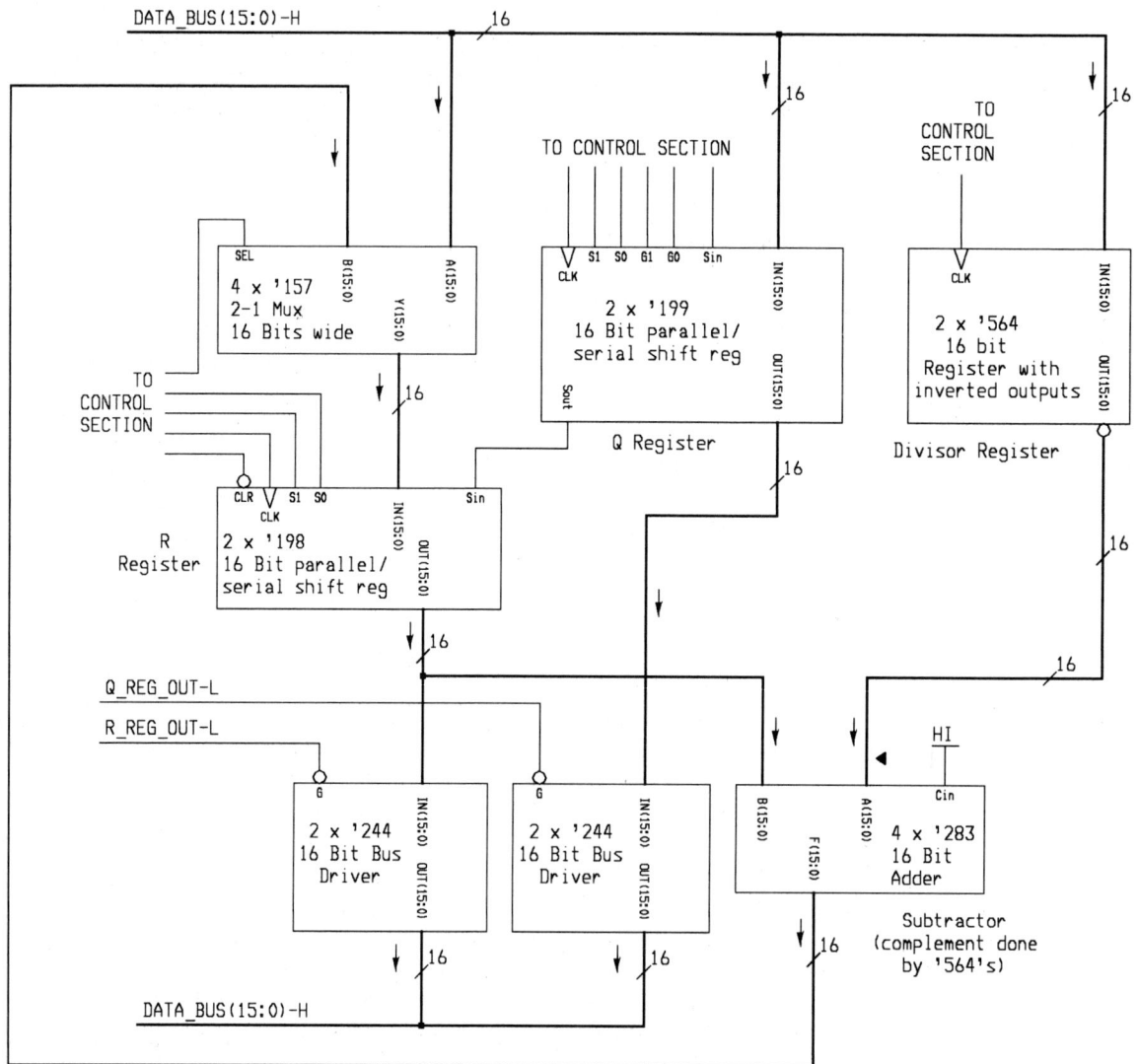

Figure 3.23. Logic for Divide Operation.

deal of effort has gone into making the multiply operation as fast as possible; is there some way that the multiplier can be utilized to do the division, so that the process benefits from the speed mechanisms available in the multiply? One way for the hardware for the multiplier to be used to do the division is to utilize the Newton-Raphson iteration:

$$x_{i+1} = x_i - \frac{f(x_i)}{f'(x_i)}$$

We know that for a well behaved function f, and an appropriate initial value x_0, this iteration system can deliver a desired result, which is the root of $f(x) = 0$. Thus, to find the reciprocal value, we first select a well behaved function which has a root at the reciprocal. We will choose to let

$$f(x) = \frac{1}{x} - w$$

The root of this equation will be $x = 1/w$. If $f(x) = (1/x) - w$, then

$$f'(x) = -\frac{1}{x^2}$$

and the iteration system will be

$$x_{i+1} = x_i - \frac{\dfrac{1}{x_i} - w}{-\dfrac{1}{x_i^{\,2}}}$$

$$= x_i + (x_i - w \times x_i^{\,2})$$

$$= 2 \times x_i - w \times x_i^{\,2}$$

$$= x_i \times (2 - w \times x_i)$$

Therefore, the operation $A \div B$ can become $A \times (1/B)$, and the system hardware can produce $1/B$ according to the above equation using only the multiplier, and a subtractor for other operation required in the iteration. The Taylor series expansion of the function shows quadratic convergence, which indicates that the number of correct bits doubles every iteration. Therefore, the desired precision can be approached by using the proper number of iterations.

Division by the above process first finds the reciprocal ($1/B$), and then using that value to multiply by the other operand to get the final result. Some commercially available devices include all of the capabilities needed to do the iteration described above, and hence can be used to perform the iterative divide algorithm. See, for example, the AM29C325 by Advanced Micro Devices.

Another similar approach to iterative division is to form the result directly, rather than specifically calculate a reciprocal. In this approach, we assume that the numbers in question are normalized floating point numbers. This means that the dividend and divisor will be expressed as a fraction (at least, the mantissa is a normalized fraction). Now we want to find the quotient Q, where

$$Q = \frac{D_D}{D_S}$$

To achieve this we will multiply both the dividend and the divisor by the same factor, f_k:

$$Q = \frac{D_D \times f_0 \times f_1 \times f_2 \times f_3 \times \cdots}{D_S \times f_0 \times f_1 \times f_2 \times f_3 \times \cdots}$$

We want the result of the various multiplications to approach the correct answer, Q, so we will choose the f_k in such a way that the denominator approaches unity. This will result in the numerator approaching the correct answer Q. Since we know that the part of D_S that we are working with is a normalized fraction, then let us represent this fraction as:

$$D_S = 1 - x$$

where the value of x is determined by the particular D_S. But since D_S is less than 1, x is also less than 1. Now, choose

$$f_0 = 1 + x$$

$$= 1 + (1 - D_S)$$

$$= 2 - D_S$$

But notice that the product of D_S and f_0 is:

$$D_S \times f_0 = (1 - x)(1 + x)$$

$$= 1 - x^2$$

which is closer to 1 than D_S is. Each iteration both numerator and denominator are multiplied by f_k, and each iteration the result gets closer to Q. With $D_S \times f_0 = 1 - x^2$, let us choose f_1 so that

$$f_1 = 1 + x^2$$

With this condition, then

$$D_S \times f_0 \times f_1 = 1 - x^4$$

which is even closer to the correct answer. And so the iterations continue, each time getting the answer closer to the correct value. One of the questions to be addressed is how to find the succeeding values of f_k. We know f_1 in terms of x, but we only know x in terms of D_S and f_0:

$$f_1 = 1 + x^2$$

$$= 1 + (1 - D_S \times f_0)$$

$$= 2 - D_S \times f_0$$

Thus, each new f_k is formed by taking the two's complement of the multiplication of the f_{k-1} and the denominator result to that point. Within a computer, then, the values are presented to the divide hardware, and the iterations carried out until the answer is at the desired precision. The number of iterations required is determined by the value of f_k; when f_k is close enough to "1," the result will be close enough to the correct answer. How close is "close enough" will be determined by the application and the number of bits in the representation. However, rather than test each f_k to determine when to stop, generally a fixed number of iterations is used. Therefore, to assure that the process converges sufficiently close to the correct answer under all conditions, rather than use $2 - D_S$ to calculate f_0, a ROM is used to find an appropriate value for f_0. Providing the initial "seed" value in this fashion guarantees that the results will be acceptable after a fixed number of iterations.

A block diagram of the hardware required to do this operation is shown in Figure 3.24. The divisor and dividend are presented to the divide hardware, and the quotient is iteratively generated, each stage getting closer to the desired value. The ROM is used to be sure that the initial precision of f_0 is close enough to complete the process in a reasonable number of iterations.

Example 3.9: Iterative divide operations: For the divider shown in Figure 3.24, show the values of the numerator, the denominator, and the f_k at each step along the way for the following calculations: $0.4 / 0.7$, $0.7 / 0.4$. $0.1 / 0.15$. Give the values for six iterations, rather than the three shown in the figure. Assume that the f_0 is calculated as $2 - D_S$ rather than to use a ROM.

The division operation begins by calculating f_0, then multiplying this value times the D_D and D_S, as shown in Figure 3.24. For the calculation $0.4 / 0.7$, the calculation proceeds in the following fashion:

D_{D_0}	0.4000000	D_{S_0}	0.7000000	f_0	1.3000000
D_{D_1}	0.5200000	D_{S_1}	0.9099999	f_1	1.0900000
D_{D_2}	0.5668000	D_{S_2}	0.9918999	f_2	1.0081000
D_{D_3}	0.5713911	D_{S_3}	0.9999344	f_3	1.0000656
D_{D_4}	0.5714286	D_{S_4}	0.9999999	f_4	1.0000000
D_{D_5}	0.5714286	D_{S_5}	1.0000000	f_5	1.0000000
D_{D_6}	0.5714286	D_{S_6}	1.0000000		

With an x value of 0.3, this calculation approaches the correct value within four iterations. The next requested calculation is $0.7 / 0.4$, which is the inverse of the calculation just done:

D_{D_0}	0.7000000	D_{S_0}	0.4000000	f_0	1.5999999
D_{D_1}	1.1199999	D_{S_1}	0.6400000	f_1	1.3599999
D_{D_2}	1.5231999	D_{S_2}	0.8704000	f_2	1.1295999
D_{D_3}	1.7206066	D_{S_3}	0.9832038	f_3	1.0167962
D_{D_4}	1.7495062	D_{S_4}	0.9997178	f_4	1.0002821
D_{D_5}	1.7499998	D_{S_5}	0.9999999	f_5	1.0000001
D_{D_6}	1.7499999	D_{S_6}	1.0000000		

This calculation takes longer to approach the correct value, since the initial x was 0.6. Note that the result in this case ended up greater than one, which

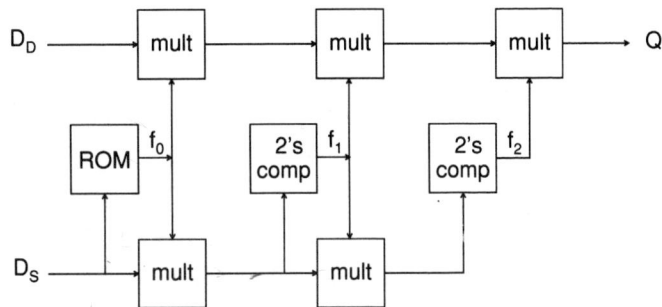

Figure 3.24. Block Diagram for Iterative Divide Operation.

is to be expected and must be handled by the hardware. That is, with normalized fractions for initial values, there is a limit that the results will not exceed, but the hardware must be able to generate numbers to that limit. The final calculation for this example is 0.1 / 0.15.

D_{D_0}	0.1000000	D_{S_0}	0.1500000	f_0	1.8499999
D_{D_1}	0.1850000	D_{S_1}	0.2775000	f_1	1.7224999
D_{D_2}	0.3186625	D_{S_2}	0.4779938	f_2	1.5220062
D_{D_3}	0.4850063	D_{S_3}	0.7275094	f_3	1.2724905
D_{D_4}	0.6171659	D_{S_4}	0.9257489	f_4	1.0742511
D_{D_5}	0.6629912	D_{S_5}	0.9944868	f_5	1.0055132
D_{D_6}	0.6666464	D_{S_6}	0.9999696		

This calculation doesn't quite get to the desired value, even with six iterations. This highlights the fact that in order to approach a desired precision within a specific number of iterations, a ROM is needed in the initial stage.

The iterative approach to the divide operation allows the hardware associated with the multiply to be used for more than one type of operation. For processors with single instruction stream capability the same hardware may be utilized for both operations. But since several steps are required for the divide operation, these instructions will generally take three to five times longer to execute than a multiply instruction.

3.7. Floating Point Arithmetic

In the previous sections we have looked at the problem of designing hardware to do the basic arithmetic operations: add/subtract, multiply, and divide. Storing information in a floating point format compounds the complexity of the problem and requires additional hardware to complete the operations. Let's first examine addition and some issues raised by addition, then look at multiplication and division. The floating point addition also includes subtraction, since the sign/magnitude method of storing information necessitates that the hardware be capable of both.

3.7.1 Floating point addition

The difficulty when adding two floating point numbers stems from the fact that the mantissas, in general, have different significance. That is, unless the exponents of the two numbers are the same, the most significant digit of one mantissa has a different magnitude associated with it than does the most significant digit of the other mantissa. Therefore, before the two numbers can be properly added together, the mantissas must be aligned. This involves determining which operand value is smaller, and then aligning the mantissa of that operand appropriately with the mantissa of the larger operand. The alignment is accomplished by shifting the mantissa of the smaller operand a number of positions to the right, hence making the digits of the smaller operand line up with the digits of the same significance in the larger operand. The amount of the alignment, the number of positions to shift, is determined by the difference in the exponents. The addition element then receives the mantissa directly from the larger operand, and the aligned mantissa from the smaller operand.

To demonstrate this process, assume that A, B, and C are floating point numbers, and find $A = B + C$. Furthermore, assume that $B < C$. (Also, for simplicity, assume B and C are positive numbers.)

$$A = B + C$$

$$= M_B \times r_s^{E_B} + M_C \times r_s^{E_C}$$

$$= (M_B \times r_s^{E_B - E_C} + M_C) \times r_s^{E_C}$$

With the assumption that $B < C$, the value of $E_B - E_C$ in the above equation is negative, and multiplying M_B by $r_s^{E_B - E_C}$ is nothing more than shifting the mantissa M_B to the right $E_B - E_C$ places. Note that we have said nothing about the radix of the system; this applies to base 10, base 2, or any other base. The shift for alignment is accomplished by moving the value the appropriate number of digit positions.

A block diagram for floating point addition is given in Figure 3.25. This diagram shows the arithmetic portion as an ADD/SUBTRACT unit, instead of strictly an add operation. The reason for this is that floating point numbers are almost always stored in sign-magnitude form; hence there is no sign associated with the mantissa itself. Therefore, if two numbers are to be added together, and one of the numbers has a negative sign, then what should actually be performed is a subtraction. Thus, the arithmetic unit associated with the floating point adder must be capable of doing both addition and subtraction.

The selection of the appropriate mantissa to be aligned (from the smaller number) is made based on a comparison of the magnitude of the two exponents. Thus, the result of this comparison directs the SELECT multiplexers to select the unaligned mantissa, and the same signal directs the ALIGN network to select the other mantissa and align it by shifting the appropriate number of positions. These two results, one unaligned mantissa and one aligned mantissa, are then fed to the

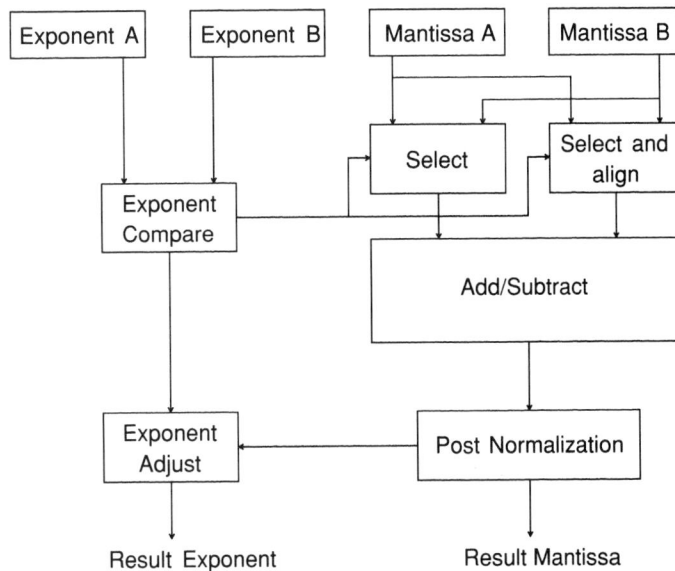

Figure 3.25. Block Diagram for Floating Point Addition.

ADD/SUBTRACT unit for the actual calculation. The resulting number is then provided to the POST NORMALIZATION unit.

The function to be provided in a post normalization step is to be sure that the final result is itself a normalized number. This unit must be capable of shifting to the right to take care of examples like the following base 10 examples (the same principles hold in any base):

$$
\begin{array}{rl}
0.8045 & \text{Input } A \text{ is normalized.} \\
+ \ \underline{0.7132} & \text{Input } B \text{ is normalized.} \\
1.5177 & \text{Result is not normalized.}
\end{array}
$$

Thus the post normalization unit must be capable of a shift of at least one position to lesser significance. The unit must also be capable of shifts of many positions to higher significance:

$$
\begin{array}{rl}
0.8045 & \text{Input } A \text{ is normalized.} \\
- \ \underline{0.8033} & \text{Input } B \text{ is normalized.} \\
0.0012 & \text{Result is not normalized.}
\end{array}
$$

The result of this example must be shifted left two positions to be properly normalized. Note that two N-digit floating point numbers, when subtracted, may result in a required post normalization alignment of $N-1$ positions. This post normalization network must then be capable of adjusting the size of the exponent to reflect any normalization. At the end of this process, the result will have been properly formed and ready for any additional operation required of it.

Floating point addition, then, requires many more operations, and hence more hardware, than its integer counterpart. The addition techniques examined earlier will apply in the arithmetic unit inside a floating point adder, but other functions are also required.

> *Example 3.10: Mantissa alignment for floating point add:* Design the network used to align the smaller mantissa to be added to the larger mantissa in Figure 3.25. Use readily available ICs, and assume that the mantissa is 24 bits, base 2.
>
> A mantissa of 24 bits is a fairly common size for 32-bit floating point number system. Since the number system is base 2, the alignment network must be capable of shifting any number of bits, from 0 to 24. Figure 3.26 shows that one way of accomplishing this is to use a number of 2-1 multiplexers. The figure shows the logic in a block diagram form; a logic diagram of the system is found in Appendix B. The assumption here is that the adders used to compare the exponents provide a binary number (size: 0 to 24; hence 5 bits) which indicates how far the number needs to be shifted in the alignment process. The MSB of this number is then used by the first level of MUXs to shift the number by 16 bits (the 1 condition), or provide no shift at all (the 0 condition). Similarly, the second MSB of the number is used by the second set of MUXs to shift the number provided by the first set of MUXs by 8 (the 1 condition) or provide no shift at all (the 0 condition). This process continues, with each level of multiplexers shifting the number by some power of 2, until all 5 bits have been utilized. The result is an

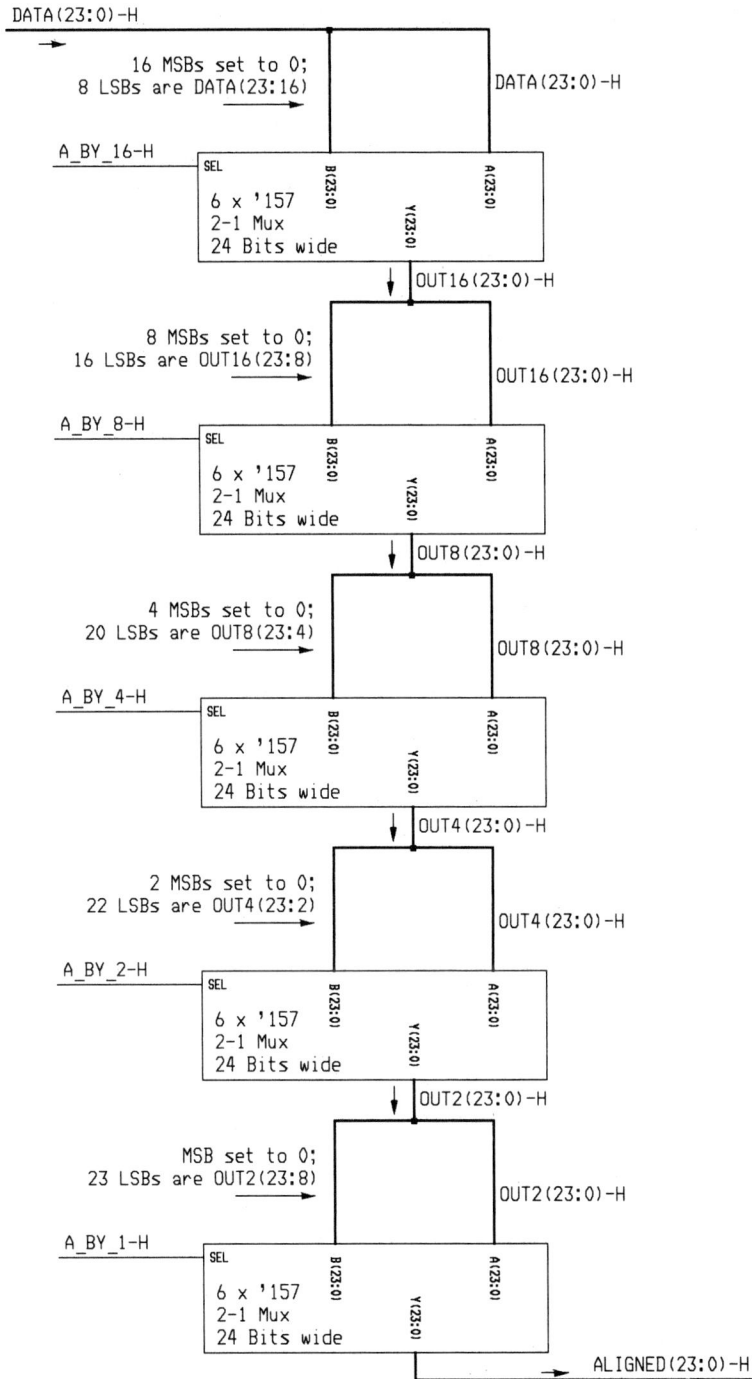

Figure 3.26. Logic for Alignment Shift Network.

output that has been shifted the number of bit positions identified by the 5-bit control number.

This network can be used to illustrate some interesting characteristics of the system. The network of Figure 3.26 has been configured to place zeros to the left of the aligned bits. This could be changed to align with sign bit (not needed here, but possible in some applications of shift networks) by asserting the unspecified inputs of the the multiplexers with the sign bit of the aligned number, rather than forcing them to zero. Another observation concerns the amount of logic needed for the alignment function. This network has been set up to do the alignment required by a base 2 number, such as the DEC or IEEE floating point system. However, if the floating point system has a different base, such as the base 16 IBM floating point system, then not all of the above levels are needed. Notice that the base 16 system does not need to align to each bit position, but rather to each digit position, which is every four bits. Thus, the last two of the five levels of logic shown in the figure would not be necessary, with a resulting in less overall logic and a speed enhancement of 40%. Thus a floating point system that does not use base 2 results in a greater range and smaller logic requirements for *some* of its constituent parts.

3.7.2 Handling the extra bits

Two problems are illustrated by the example of floating point addition, both of which deal with what to do with the extra bits. The first "extra" bit problem is identified by the following example. Assume a 6-bit mantissa for a base 2 number system, and assume that the second number has been shifted two bit positions to allow the exponents to agree. Then the mantissa addition may be something like:

$$
\begin{array}{ll}
101010 & \text{Larger mantissa.} \\
+\ \underline{110010} & \text{Smaller mantissa, aligned.} \\
11011010 & \text{Addition results in 8 bits.}
\end{array}
$$

There are more bits than can be dealt with in the result, so something must be done with the extra bits. Several ways have been proposed and used to deal with these bits. The first and most obvious method is merely to ignore them; this is called truncation, and the unwanted bits are truncated from the result. This results in an error, since the final mantissa (call it M_F) differs from the real result, M_R, by whatever bits happen to be in those bit positions. This results in a truncation error, $\text{ERR}_{\text{TRUNC}}$, which will result in an bias, or offset, after a number of operations have been performed. For purposes of comparison with other methods of handling extra bits, let us define the error as the difference between the real result and the final mantissa:

$$\text{ERR}_{\text{TRUNC}} = M_R - M_F$$

We will also define the bias as the sum of the $\text{ERR}_{\text{TRUNC}}$ over a span of possible results. The span we will use is all possible combinations of 2 bits, for two iterations. Thus the bias for truncation would be calculated as follows (let the decimal point mark the number of bits storable/usable by the machine):

	M_R	M_F	$\text{ERR}_{\text{TRUNC}}$
a	xx0.00	xx0	0.00
b	xx0.01	xx0	+0.01
c	xx0.10	xx0	+0.10
d	xx0.11	xx0	+0.11
e	xx1.00	xx1	0.00
f	xx1.01	xx1	+0.01
g	xx1.10	xx1	+0.10
h	xx1.11	xx1	+0.11

The bias is the sum of all the errors over this span. Adding all of the elements in the $\text{ERR}_{\text{TRUNC}}$ column results in a bias of $+11.0_2$, or $+3_{10}$. Obviously, if we chose fewer elements within a span, such as only one extra bit instead of two, the bias would be less. Or if more points were selected the bias would be greater. Note that, if we included three extra bits instead of two, there would be twice as many values in the above table, all contributing to the error. But as we compare truncation with other methods we will be careful to utilize the same set of M_R so that the comparison will be valid. Truncation always throws away information, which results in a positive bias: the number stored is smaller than the actual number to be represented. Thus, over many calculations results will tend to be smaller than the true value.

Another method of handling the extra bits is to try to reduce the bias by adding half the value of the least significant bit position to the number before truncation. This method is exemplified by the following operation:

	101010	Larger mantissa.
+	110010	Smaller mantissa, aligned.
	11011010	Addition results in 8 bits.
+	00000010	Now add half of the LSB position.
	11011100	Final result, now truncate.

This method is called rounding, and the answers result in errors that have both positive and negative values:

	M_R	$M_R + \frac{1}{2}$ LSB	M_F	$\text{ERR}_{\text{ROUND}}$
a	xx0.00	xx0.10	xx0	0.00
b	xx0.01	xx0.11	xx0	+0.01
c	xx0.10	xx1.00	xx1	−0.10
d	xx0.11	xx1.01	xx1	−0.01
e	xx1.00	xx1.10	xx1	0.00
f	xx1.01	xx1.11	xx1	+0.01
g	xx1.10	xy0.00	xy0	−0.10
h	xx1.11	xy0.01	xy0	−0.01

Note here that the last entries g and h above have had a carry propagate into the word, a fact that is indicated by the xy in lieu of xx for the value in the table. Whatever value was represented by xx is incremented to be xy, and any carry which results continues to propagate into the word. The bias here is −1.0. The error in this method is always smaller than truncation, but the bias does not disappear.

One of the methods utilized to minimize the error of calculations is to create a rounding scheme that will result in a zero bias solution. These schemes have different names, such as round-to-zero or R^* rounding. One such method operates according to the following rule: whenever the value to be truncated has a "1" in the most significant bit, and "0" in all other bits, that a "1" is forced into the least significant bit of M_F. This scheme results in a bias which is zero over many calculations:

	M_R	$M_R + 1/2$ LSB	M_F	ERR$_{\text{ZERO BIAS RND}}$
a	$xx0.00$	$xx0.10$	$xx0$	0.00
b	$xx0.01$	$xx0.11$	$xx0$	+0.01
c	$xx0.10$	$xx1...$	$xx1$	−0.10
d	$xx0.11$	$xx1.01$	$xx1$	−0.01
e	$xx1.00$	$xx1.10$	$xx1$	0.00
f	$xx1.01$	$xx1.11$	$xx1$	+0.01
g	$xx1.10$	$xx1...$	$xx1$	+0.10
h	$xx1.11$	$xx1.11$	$xy0$	−0.01

The two values in the above set that are handled differently from "normal" rounding are entries c and g. In both cases, a "1" is forced into the least significant bit position of the value saved. Although both entry c and entry g are handled in this way, only entry g ends up with a value different from the "normal" rounding system. The bias with this method totals zero, and over many calculations will tend to smaller errors than other techniques.

At this point, we will mention two other techniques. The first is called jamming, and was proposed by von Neumann as a good method to reduce overall errors; that is, it is better than truncation. The method is to "jam" a 1 into the least significant bit of the result, regardless of the values of the extra bits. This method results in larger errors than other methods, but over time it has the same bias as rounding. Thus, it is as fast as truncation (no time required for rounding step, since LSB is always forced to 1), but has a smaller bias.

Another method centers on the ability to look at the extra bits and the least significant bits to be retained, and using this information make an educated decision as to the value to be added. This step is carried out by using a ROM or other method of looking at several bits for the decision process. The reason for doing this is to construct the value added in the rounding step in such a way that there is no carry to propagate into the higher bit positions. This will speed the rounding step, since the method guarantees no carry beyond the least significant bits. But since the choice of the value to add in this step is made judiciously, the bias is controlled, and again over time the bias should be zero.

The errors resulting from the various methods of handling extra bits are graphically depicted in Figure 3.27. Note that the shape of the envelope of error is the same for truncation and rounding, one being offset from the other. However, the rounding process has made the overall bias smaller. Note also that jamming has the same shape, but that the variations are greater. The zero bias schemes, round-to-zero and ROM rounding, have shapes that reflect their approaches to achieving their results. In both cases, the bias is minimized by intelligent handling of the extra bits involved in the action.

The second "extra bit" problem deals with the number of bits that need to be retained in the alignment process. That is, if the resulting mantissa is going to be 24 bits, must we construct adders and alignment networks capable of 48 bits or more? If the difference in the exponents is greater than 24, what should happen

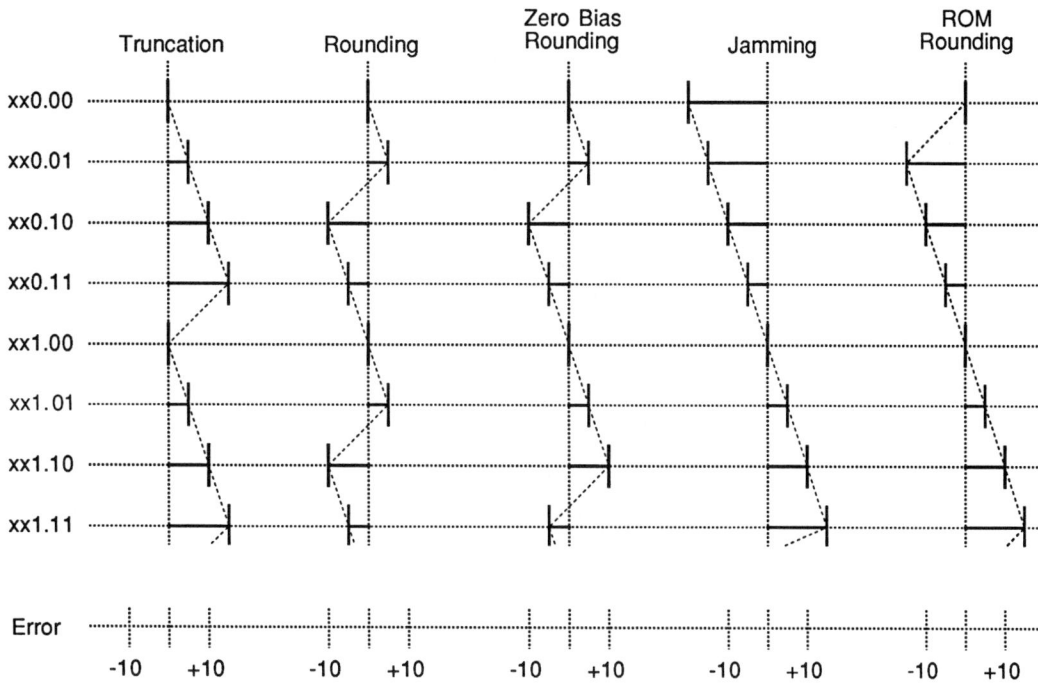

Figure 3.27. Errors in Handling Extra Bits.

to the aligned operand? These questions must be addressed by the designer to create a properly functioning system. Let us look at the problem with some examples.

As we have noted before, the alignment process takes the mantissa of smaller significance and shifts (aligns) it the proper number of places, which is the difference in exponents. Let the amount the alignment be represented by a, and then consider some cases. We will use mantissas which consist of 5 bits. First of all, if $a = 0$, then no alignment is necessary in the problem setup, but post normalization may be necessary, such as:

$$\begin{array}{r} 0.10000 \\ -\ 0.10001 \\ \hline -\ 0.00001 \end{array}$$ Post normalization
necessary of 4 places left.

Now consider some examples where alignment is necessary. We will consider subtracting an aligned version of the largest mantissa representable from the smallest mantissa. The smallest mantissa for this system is just 0.10000, while the largest mantissa has a value of 0.11111. Thus for the problem $0.10000 \times 2^1 - 0.11111 \times 2^0$, the value of a will be 1, and the addition problem can be represented:

$$\begin{array}{r} 0.10000\ 0 \\ -\ 0.01111\ 1 \\ \hline 0.00000\ 1 \end{array}$$ Post normalization
necessary of 5 places left.

This is perhaps the worst case for post normalization. However, note that the problem required a single bit wider than the 5 bits of the normal mantissa. The situation when $a = 2$ is depicted in Figure 3.28, as is the situation with other values of a. First we point out that in each of the situations depicted in Figure 3.28 there is a leading zero in the result, which will need to be removed in post normalization. The next observation concerns the bits retained by the system in the computation. These bits are underlined in the figure. Note that, for any rounding scheme (except jamming) to work properly, at least one more bit than the (end of the) underlined bits must be retained. For example, if truncation is to be used, which is the simplest of the methods mentioned above, the answer would be different if that one additional bit is not included in the calculation. Finally, we observe that the answers would all be the same if only one 1 bit were retained to the right of the vertical lines in the figure. We call this bit a "sticky" bit, and it has the characteristic that if any 1 bit were to be shifted through that position in the process of alignment, then the bit is set to a 1. This allows the results to turn out as expected.

Thus, three digits are needed beyond the number required by the number system. (This has been shown in binary, but is true in any radix.) One digit is needed for post normalization, at least one digit is needed for the rounding method, and one digit is used as the "sticky bit."

Handling the additional bits involves making reasonable decisions about the bits that result when operations generate more bits than can be retained in a result. This involves bits generated in multiplication and division, since both of these operations generate more bits than can be retained in a floating point number with the same characteristics as the input values. For example, multiplication of two 24-bit mantissas will result in a 48-bit value, which must then be reduced to 24 bits by an appropriate algorithm. Additional bits to be concerned about in the design process include the bits in the alignment process for floating point addition. In each case, the system architect and designer need to identify the goals of the system, and based on those goals make appropriate decisions on the number of bits to retain and the rounding algorithm to produce a desired result.

With the adoption of the IEEE floating point number system, many of these decisions have been dealt with by the specification. That is, different types of rounding schemes are available, and the user has the option of specifying the mechanism that will be most appropriate for the calculations to be done.

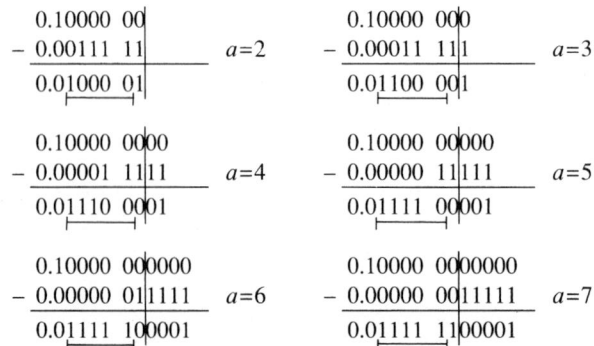

Figure 3.28. Subtraction with Alignment of Operands. (Alignment is done by a shift of a bits.)

Chap. 3: Arithmetic Units: Data Manipulation

3.7.3 Floating Point Multiplication

Floating point multiplication is perhaps the simplest floating point operation in terms of the required operations. That is, there is no alignment of operands required before initiating the operation, and minimal normalization is required at the end of the transaction. The required operations are simply stated:

$$A = B \times C$$

$$= M_B \times r_s^{E_B} \times M_C \times r_s^{E_C}$$

$$= (M_B \times M_C) \times r_s^{E_B + E_C}$$

That is, the mantissa of the result is the product of the mantissas of the two input operands, and the exponent of the result is the sum of the exponents of the input operands. A block diagram of this operation is shown in Figure 3.29. The basic operations shown in the block diagram are identical to those indicated in the above equations: the operands are separated into their constituent parts, the exponents are added, and the mantissas are multiplied. The only difficulties are implementation specific, once the floating point representation has been selected. For example, the IEEE 32-bit floating point system calls for representing the exponent in an excess 127 code; therefore, the exponent adder must be so designed to correctly present the result in excess 127 code. The other block in Figure 3.29 that is not obvious from the above equations is the post normalization block. This block has the responsibility of checking the output of the multiplier to ascertain if the result is a normalized number. If it is not, then it must be adjusted accordingly, and the exponent modified. To identify the number of digit positions that can be involved in this process, let's look at the two extremes: the

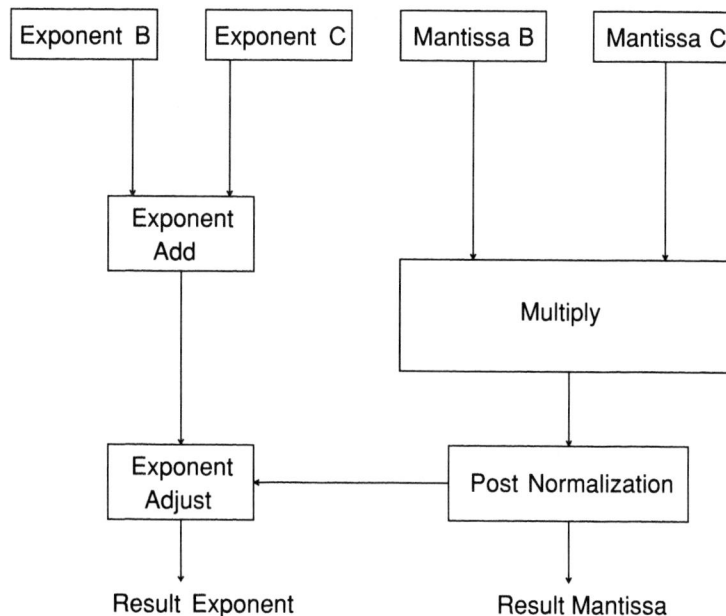

Figure 3.29. Block Diagram for a Floating Point Multiply.

product of the largest legal mantissas, and the product of the smallest legal mantissas.

Largest × largest

Base 2	Base 10	
0.1111	0.9999	
× 0.1111	× 0.9999	
0.1110	0.9998	Aligned properly, no postnormalization.

Smallest × smallest

Base 2	Base 10	
0.1000	0.1000	
× 0.1000	× 0.1000	
0.0100	0.0100	Not aligned properly, postnormalization of one digit position.

For many of the multiplications performed, no alignment will be needed in the post normalization stage. The worst case will be a post normalization of one digit position. If this occurs, then the exponent must be decremented by one before the operation is complete. It is interesting to note that the base 10 and base 2 problems are exactly the same for the smallest case (this would be true of any radix), but that the number of bits required to represent these values is not the same.

The above calculations also point out the fact that the final mantissa is composed of only portions of the result out of the multiplier. For example, the complete bit pattern resulting from the largest base two multiplication above is 11100001. But since the result is handled in the same number of bits as the original operands, the same questions arise as those discussed in connection with floating point addition: should the result be rounded? Truncated? Or what? Also, need all of the partial product array be created in the process of generating the result, or only portions of it? These questions must be addressed by the system designer in the creation of an appropriate multiplication unit.

3.7.4 Floating point division

The division operation in floating point contains almost the same steps as the multiplication operation:

$$A = B \ / \ C$$

$$= (M_B \times r_s^{E_B}) \ / \ (M_C \times r_s^{E_C})$$

$$= (M_B \ / \ M_C) \times r_s^{E_B - E_C}$$

A block diagram of the hardware required to accomplish this would look very similar to the multiplication system of Figure 3.29. The only differences are that the exponent addition would actually be subtraction, and that the multiplication block would be replaced by a divider. This division could be handled by either direct or iterative methods. The result of the mantissa division may then require post normalization in the opposite direction of the multiplier:

| Largest / smallest | | |
Base 2	Base 10	
0.1111	0.9999	
÷ 0.1000	÷ 0.1000	
1.1110	9.9990	Not aligned properly, postnormalization of digit position.

| Smallest / largest | | |
Base 2	Base 10	
0.1000	0.1000	
÷ 0.1111	÷ 0.9999	
0.1000	0.1000	Aligned properly, no postnormalization.

Again the questions of rounding methods and number of places to calculate are raised, and the system decisions made will reflect the resource constraints placed on the system.

3.7.5 Floating point status

We discussed earlier the various status bits normally found in the status register of a computer. In general, these bits are controlled by the "normal" instructions in a computer; floating point instructions have their own conditions that add additional system status information. That is, the bits discussed previously do not form a sufficient set to reflect the conditions associated with floating point arithmetic. Thus, floating point systems often provide for indication of the following conditions:

- *Overflow.* This is similar to the overflow discussed earlier: the result has exceeded the ability of the system to represent information, because the result to be represented is too large. This can result from adding two numbers already at the maximum representable by the system, or, more generally, by multiplying two numbers whose exponents add to an exponent not representable in the system. Division can also cause overflow, dividing a very large number by a very small one.
- *Underflow.* This results when a number is too small to represent in the number system. This will occur when two very small numbers are multiplied, and the resulting exponent cannot be represented in the system. Similarly, division of a small number by a large one can cause the same condition to exist.
- *Zero.* Like the integer counterpart, this condition indicates that the specified operation resulted in a value of zero.
- *Sign.* The sign of the result can be the MSB of the word, like the integer case, or accessed by whatever method is indicated by the number system. This can then be used in the same fashion as the sign of an integer number.

Some manufacturers also provide additional information when building a floating point arithmetic unit:

- *NAN (not a number)*. After the hardware performs the operation requested by the instruction, the result is not a legal number in the floating point number system. This could be an operand reserved by the manufacturer, or the IEEE Not-a-Number value.

- *Inexact*. This condition arises when the operation specified results in a value not infinitely precise, due to rounding. This can be used as an indication of truncation or roundoff error.

- *Invalid*. The IEEE floating point system utilizes specific patterns for representation of $+\infty$ and $-\infty$. The invalid flag of a system indicates that an operation has been performed which was invalid, such as $\infty \times 0$.

These status conditions can be incorporated in a register with the "normal" status bits, or they can form a separate status register accessible in a different manner. The implementation details will differ with design constraints and system definition.

3.8. Summary

Many books and articles have been written about performing arithmetic on computers, and designing hardware to do the actual arithmetic. What we have looked at are some of the basic concepts utilized in the design of arithmetic units. Addition is perhaps the most basic, since it is used in the other types of operations. We found that addition can be done in a time linear in the number of bits to be added (with full adders) or in a time that is logarithmic in the number of bits to be added (with carry look-ahead). Thus, the addition process can be made faster at the expense of additional gates or integrated circuit real estate.

Multiplication is a simple operation that can be done in a fashion similar to paper and pencil methods, using a single adder and a register to maintain the sum of the partial products. However, if speed is a major consideration, then other methods can be utilized to reduce the time required at the expense of additional hardware. We looked at methods using carry-save adders and row reduction techniques, as well as methods that would reduce the number of rows actually needed in the partial product array. This latter method utilized parts that not only performed the generation of partial product bits, but combined those bits into partial results. The amount of useful parallelism will be decided by the system designer as he or she considers the relative cost of system resources.

Division is another operation that can be done with direct methods, such as paper and pencil methods or with iterative techniques. We have looked at some of each of these techniques. One feature of the iterative methods is the ability to use the multiplication hardware in performing the division. This justifies some of the additional design effort and hardware costs of a high speed multiplier.

Finally, we looked at some of the considerations introduced by combining the adders, multipliers, and dividers into systems for floating point arithmetic. The floating point systems introduced a number of issues related to the storage and manipulation of information. The manner in which a designer addresses these issues will have an impact in the complexity of the hardware constructed, and it will also have an impact in the complexity of any software required to effectively utilize the hardware.

3.9. Problems

3.1 Design a circuit that will accept as input a BCD digit and produce a 7-bit output that is the square of the input digit.

3.2 Design a circuit that accepts as input two 2-bit numbers, A and B. The output is a 3-bit number, which is the sum of the two input values, modulo 5.

3.3 Design a 2-bit adder that functions in no more than 3 gate delays. Inputs include two 2-bit numbers and a carry in. Outputs are the 2-bit sum, a carry generate, and a carry propagate.

3.4 Design a 2-bit subtractor. Inputs are two 2-bit numbers and a borrow. Outputs include the 2-bit difference out and the borrow output.

3.5 Create the logic equations that demonstrate the look-ahead process for subtraction. That is, show (with logic equations) how a subtractor could be built so that it uses a "look-ahead borrow" technique.

3.6 Design a circuit that accepts as input two 2-bit numbers, A and B, and produces three outputs: $A>B$, $A=B$, and $A<B$. Assume an unsigned binary representation for the numbers.

3.7 Repeat Problem 3.6, but include $A>B$, $A=B$, and $A<B$ inputs. How should these devices cascade? Show how these devices could be used to compare 8-bit numbers.

3.8 Prove that the overflow bit for a two's complement addition is the exclusive OR of the carry in and the carry out of the most significant stage of the addition.

3.9 Design a carry look-ahead generator circuit for 4 bits. Inputs include a carry in, as well as propagate and generate signals from four adders. Outputs are three carries, a propagate out, and a generate out. Compare your solution with the 74S182. How are they the same? How are they different? Why?

3.10 Design the logic necessary to create the status bits for a system that requires the following bits in the status register: zero, overflow, carry, sign. Assume that the carry bit out of the ALU is available.

3.11 Row reduction can be used to speed up the multiplication process. A 3-2 row reduction unit for a single bit position is a carry-save-adder, which has the same logic equation as a full adder. A 7-3 row reduction unit can be created from 3-2 row reduction units, or from random logic. Design a 7-3 row reduction unit using both methods and compare the result from the aspect of gate count and speed of operation.

3.12 Give a logic diagram for the data path of a multiplier that will produce the product of two 24-bit numbers. Use the standard shift-and-add algorithm (partial products added least significant to most significant). Use a shift register for the product register and no AND gates. Also, create a flow chart that specifies the action of the system. Be sure you know which lines go where and why.

3.13 Give a logic diagram for a multiplier system that uses the shift-and-add algorithm for partial products added in the reverse order (from most significant partial product to least significant). Use '283s for adders; use

'198s for the register functions needed. Identify the control signals on the individual parts that must be asserted to do the work, and the levels (or edges) that cause the action to occur. Include a flow chart for the action of the system.

3.14 Create a logic diagram for a 16×16 multiplier using Booths algorithm. Use '382s for the arithmetic element, and whatever registers and shift registers are needed. Include the logic required to control the function lines for the addition/subtraction/do nothing performed by the '382s.

3.15 Create a logic design for the data path to divide a 16-bit number by an 8-bit number to give an 8-bit result and an 8-bit remainder. Be sure you know why the connections are made as you specify in your design. Use '382s to perform the arithmetic. Give a flow chart that identifies the work to be done and the assertion levels of the signals required to do the work.

3.16 Design a 2×4-bit multiplier with a maximum delay from input to output of 3 gate delays.

3.17 Create an 8×8-bit multiplier system using 2×4-bit multipliers, carry save adders, and adder systems as needed.

3.18 Give a block diagram for a 32×32-bit multiply system using 7-3 row reduction units, 3-2 row reduction units, with the final stage being a carry propagate add system. Estimate the speed of the system in gate delays.

3.19 Design a floating point adder system for the floating point format given in Problem 2.10.

3.20 Obtain a data sheet for the Am29C325 floating point multiplier, and identify the steps which can be used to perform a divide operation.

3.21 **Create the logic diagrams needed for the data path of a 32-bit floating point multiplication system. Assume that the inputs have been loaded into two 32-bit registers, and that the output will be loaded into a third 32-bit register. Assume that the floating point format is a normalized format with the radix of the system equal to 2, the mantissa stored in fractional form using the hidden bit technique, and the 8-bit exponent stored in excess 128. The multiplier must use a shift-and-add algorithm. In addition, provide a status register with bits for the sign of the result, underflow, overflow, and result equal to zero. Identify the control points, and the levels of the control signals to do the work. Give a flow chart that identifies the proper levels for the signal assertions.

3.22 Multiply problem. Design a multiplier for a 24×24-bit multiply. You have three types of parts to work with: 3-2 row reduction elements, 4-bit carry look-ahead adders, and 4-bit carry look-ahead generators. Construct a data path block diagram of the multiply process, starting with rows of the partial product array. Show all of the interconnections necessary at the row reduction stage, but not at the CLAA stage. Assuming two gate delays for all of the functions (that is, assume that the row reduction elements, the CLAAs, and the CLAGs all take two gate delays to do their work), how much time is required for the multiply? How many individual CSAs are needed for this function?

3.23 One method for performing the iterative divide operation is described as follows:

$$Q = \frac{D_D}{D_S}$$

can be calculated by:

$$Q = \frac{D_D \times f_0 \times f_1 \times f_2 \times f_3 \times \cdots}{D_S \times f_0 \times f_1 \times f_2 \times f_3 \times \cdots}$$

if the successive f_k's are chosen so that the denominator approaches one. The numerator iteration for this method is $D_{D_{n+1}} = D_{D_n} \times f_n$. The denominator iteration is used to calculate the f's, and is $f_{n+1} = 2 - D_S \times f_n$. Assume that a ROM is provided to choose an appropriate f_0, which is correct to 8 bits. Create a block diagram of a system that will follow the iteration system. Assume that you have *one* multiplier available, and *one* two's complement unit available, as well as the initial value ROM and whatever registers you need. With the block diagram include a description of how a divide will proceed. How many steps to get a result correct to 56 bits?

3.10. References and Readings

[AMD85] Advanced Micro Devices, *Bipolar Microprocessor Logic and Interface Data Book*. Sunnyvale, CA: Advanced Micro Devices, 1985.

[AnLe81] Anderson, T., and P. A. Lee, *Fault Tolerance, Principles and Practice*. Englewood Cliffs, NJ: Prentice Hall International, 1981.

[Arms81] Armstrong, R. A., "Applying CAD to Gate Arrays Speeds 32 bit Minicomputer Design," *Electronics*. Vol. 54, No. 1, January 13, 1981, pp. 167–173.

[Baer84] Baer, J. L., "Computer Architecture," *Computer*. Vol. 17, No. 10, October 1984, pp. 77–87.

[Baer80] Baer, J. L., *Computer Systems Architecture*. Rockville, MD: Computer Science Press, 1980.

[Bart85] Bartee, T. C., *Digital Computer Fundamentals, 6th edition*. New York: McGraw-Hill Book Company, 1985.

[Boot84] Booth, T. L., *Introduction to Computer Engineering: Hardware and Software Design*. New York: John Wiley & Sons, 1984.

[BoTj78] Borgerson, B. R., G. S. Tjaden, and M. L. Hanson, "Mainframe Implementation with Off-the-Shelf LSI Modules," *Computer*. Vol. 11, No. 7, July 1978, pp. 42–48.

[Bree89] Breeding, K. J., *Digital Design Fundamentals*. Englewood Cliffs, NJ: Prentice Hall, 1989.

[BuCa84] Burger, R. M., R. K. Calvin, W. C. Holton, et al., "The Impact of ICs on Computer Technology," *Computer*. Vol. 17, No. 10, October 1984, pp. 88–96.

[Cava84] Cavanagh, J. J. F., *Digital Computer Arithmetic: Design and Implementation*. New York: McGraw-Hill Book Company, 1984.

[ErLa85] Ercegovac, M. D., and T. Lang, *Digital Systems and Hardware/Firmware Algorithms.* New York: John Wiley & Sons, 1985.

[Flet80] Fletcher, W. I., *An Engineering Approach to Digital Design.* Englewood Cliffs, NJ: Prentice Hall, 1980.

[Gosl80] Gosling, J. B., *Design of Arithmetic Units for Digital Computers.* Springer-Verlag, 1980.

[Haye88] Hayes, J. P., *Computer Architecture and Organization,* 2nd Edition. New York: McGraw-Hill Book Company, 1988.

[JaSm85] James, M. L., G. M. Smith, and J. C. Welford, *Applied Numerical Methods for Digital Computers.* New York: Harper & Row, 1985.

[Knut73] Knuth, D. E., *The Art of Computer Programming: Volume 1, Fundamental Algorithms.* Reading, MA: Addison-Wesley, 1973.

[Knut69] Knuth, D. E., *The Art of Computer Programming: Volume 2, Seminumerical Algorithms.* Reading, MA: Addison-Wesley, 1969.

[KuLa77] Kuck, D. J., D. H. Lawrie, and A. H. Sameh (Eds.), *High Speed Computer and Algorithm Organization.* New York: Academic Press, Inc., 1977.

[Kuck78] Kuck, D. J., *The Structure of Computers and Computations.* New York: John Wiley & Sons, 1978.

[KuMi81] Kulisch, U., and W. L. Miranker, *Computer Arithmetic in Theory and Practice.* New York: Academic Press, 1981.

[Lang82] Langdon, G. G., Jr., *Computer Design.* San Jose, CA: Computeach Press Inc, 1982.

[Leis83] Leiserson, C. E., *Area-Efficient VLSI Computation.* Cambridge, MA: MIT Press, 1983.

[Mano79] Mano, M. M., *Digital Logic and Computer Design.* Englewood Cliffs, NJ: Prentice Hall, 1979.

[Mano88] Mano, M. M., *Computer Engineering: Hardware Design.* Englewood Cliffs, NJ: Prentice Hall, 1988.

[McCl86] McCluskey, E. J., *Logic Design Principles, with Emphasis on Testable Semicustom Circuits.* Englewood Cliffs, NJ: Prentice Hall, 1986.

[MeCo80] Mead, C. A., and L. Conway, *Introduction to VLSI Systems.* Reading, MA: Addison-Wesley, 1980.

[Prad86] Pradham, D. K. (Ed.), *Fault Tolerant Computing: Theory and Techniques.* Englewood Cliffs, NJ: Prentice Hall, 1986.

[Prep85] Preparata, F. P., *Introduction to Computer Engineering.* New York: Harper & Row, 1985.

[Schm74] Schmid, H., *Decimal Computation.* New York: John Wiley & Sons, 1974.

[Shiv85] Shiva, S. G., *Computer Design and Architecture.* Boston, MA: Little, Brown, 1985.

[Stal87] Stallings, W., *Computer Organization and Architecture.* New York: Macmillan Publishing Co., 1987.

[Swar80] Swartzlander, E. E., Jr. (Ed.), *Computer Arithmetic.* Dowden, Hutchinson & Ross, 1980.

[Tane84] Tanenbaum, A. S., *Structured Computer Organization.* Englewood Cliffs, NJ: Prentice Hall, 1984.

[TI85] Texas Instruments, *The TTL Data Book, Volume 2.* Dallas, TX: Texas Instruments, 1988.

[WaFl82] Waser, S., and M. J. Flynn, *Introduction to Arithmetic for Digital Systems Designers.* New York: CBS College Pub., 1982.

[Wilk87] Wilkinson, B., *Digital System Design.* Englewood Cliffs, NJ: Prentice Hall International, 1987.

4

Instruction Set Processing

Thus far we have been dealing with the blocks from which computers are built. Chapter 2 described some of the decisions involved with choosing a method for representing the information within the computer. Chapter 3 is a discussion of the issues involved in doing some of the arithmetic operations required of a machine. In both cases, tradeoffs must be made to assure that the system resources are utilized in an efficacious manner. Representation ranges of number systems must be effectively weighed against the cost of those representations, and the targeted applications of the machine. Similarly, the methods used for doing the arithmetic must be balanced in such a way that the speed and complexity match the intended uses of the system.

In this chapter, we will look at how the arithmetic building blocks can be combined with other functional units, such as registers and memories, to create computing systems. Here we seek to address some of the basic questions concerning data manipulation methods. What are some of the issues involved in choosing an instruction set? What basic operations should be included? How do we specify the operations to be performed, and identify the operands to be used in that operation? What are the steps required to accomplish the specified work? What are the costs associated with the specification and execution of these instructions?

Let us first look at some of the basic tools used to describe machine structure and data manipulation methods. The tools are very simple: diagrams to identify structure and a register transfer language to specify data movement within that structure. Then we will identify some of the methods utilized by different machines to accomplish their work. Often what is considered "good" depends on several factors, and good design practices using one set of constraints will not be considered good design practices using a different set of constraints. Like the other ideas explored in the previous chapters, engineering choices are made after a careful examination of the alternative methods of doing the work. The key is to choose appropriate metrics or measurement methods and to apply the metrics uniformly to the various alternatives.

The first area of interest concerns the data manipulation instructions and related topics: single address machines, two address machines, operand specification methods, and so on. Then we will look at program flow instructions: jumps, branches, subroutine calls, and the like. In a related area we will look at the machine reactions when exception conditions occur: interrupts and traps. This will necessitate some discussion of I/O programming methods as well. Finally, we will identify some of the issues in the ongoing RISC/CISC debate, and explore reasons that the two methods are alternately considered good and bad.

4.1. Basic Building Blocks for Instruction Specification

As the computers space expands, the distinction between the responsibilities of the individual parts becomes more and more blurred. So, we will begin by looking at some of the concepts utilized in the early machines, and then as the operations and methods become more complex, we can recognize the parentage of the ideas, and see possible applications and design methods.

The building blocks used by the earliest machines comprised a very small set: registers, ALUs, memory, and data paths. In this discussion we will assume that the ALU model is as shown at the beginning of Chapter 3: two different inputs and an output. The ALU is assumed to be as wide as the machine; the word width is a decision based on what needs to be represented. We will assume that the ALU is capable of all of the arithmetic and logic operations which are required by the instructions.

Figure 4.1 shows the basic building blocks we will use in consideration of machine operation. The ALU we have already mentioned; it is used for data manipulation. Missing from the diagram are some very necessary lines, and in that sense the representation is incomplete. The missing lines include the control lines, which specify the action of the ALU (add, subtract, AND, etc.), and the data lines that do not form part of the designated inputs and output. These additional data lines often connect directly to a status register and include such things as the carry (in and out), the sign bit, overflow bit, and the like. Thus, for operations needing this additional interaction, we will assume that the connections do indeed exist and that the bits are transferred appropriately.

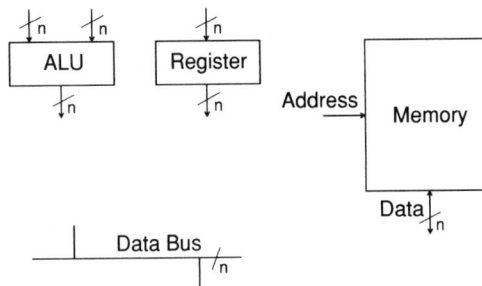

Figure 4.1. Basic Building Blocks for Instruction Set Processing: ALU, Register, Memory, and Communication Paths.

The data to be manipulated by an ALU is first stored in a memory, and such an element is shown in the figure. For our purposes we will say that the memory is as wide as the data path, but we will see later how this may be altered as part of the machine design. Our model for the memory element is simply that there are M memory locations, and these are arranged in such a way that they can be accessed by an address supplied on $\lceil \log_2(M) \rceil$ address lines. The data path allows reading and writing of data in these locations. As with the ALU, some lines are missing from the memory block as shown in Figure 4.1. These lines are the control lines used to cause the actual write or read of data from the memory devices. These lines are system-specific, and we will assume that the designer is aware of the required lines and handles them in an appropriate fashion.

Much of our current practice of memory system design and utilization is the result of the ideas explored by Von Neumann and his colleagues in the late 1940s [BuGo46]. Some of the earliest memory systems were organized such that the instructions could be held in one memory, and the data in another, and that these two memories were disjoint in function and fabrication. However, Von Neumann observed that the memories organized in that manner were not always effectively used; some tasks would leave the data memory practically empty while crowding the program memory, or vice versa. So he reasoned that since both instructions and data were basically information, both could be stored in the same memory space. Organizing the memory system in this manner brought a number of benefits, since programs could be treated as data. Instructions could be selectively altered to allow different functions or addresses as required, or data values could act as instructions if the conditions permitted. By organizing the memory in this fashion, only one memory element was needed, with its associated addressing and data retrieval capabilities. The two types of information, data and instructions, were combined into the same memory. The principal drawback to the arrangement was that interaction with the memory element was now needed for both types of information, and hence the path between computational functions and storage functions became a primary impediment to the effective processing speed. This has become known as the Von Neumann bottleneck, and we will present some of the suggestions made to minimize its effect. However, we will still treat memory as a linear array of storage locations, accessed by an appropriate address.

Another element shown in the figure is the data path. The width of the data path is assumed to be the same as the machine, but, as with most generalizations, exceptions can be found. We will use that width as a natural value, and later we will discuss ways to use widths other than the basic machine width for transferring information. These interconnections can be point-to-point wires from one element to another (containing the appropriate number of individual wires), or they can be buses, which are capable of transferring information between several distinct elements. Direct connections allow for high speed, but have low versatility. With tri-state logic readily available, a number of alternative busing arrangements can be made. We will discuss various types of buses in Chapter 6.

The final element shown in Figure 4.1 is the register. For our purposes, this is an element that is as wide as needed to match the buses, memories, and ALUs, used for storing information. This is another basic device that needs additional control lines not included in the figure. A register will require a clock line identifying when data is stable on the input line, and the register should load that data into its collection of storage elements. Other control lines may also be needed, such as output control lines for tri-state devices, or shift/load control lines for multifunction registers. Again, we will assume that the designer of the system is aware of the capabilities of the registers being used, and that appropriate control lines are included in the machine.

Registers are used for a variety of applications, and generally receive names that denote their function. Figure 4.2 shows a block diagram that will serve as a vehicle for describing how the various registers and other elements function together to accomplish work. By work we mean the information transfers required to do some task. The registers shown in the figure form a fairly minimal set:

- *Memory Address Register (MAR)*. This collection of storage elements has the responsibility of identifying the memory location of the information to be transferred. The transfer could be either into or out of memory.

- *Memory Buffer Register (MBR)*. The memory buffer register is used to store information moved into and out of memory. With destructive readout devices, such as core memory, it is a requirement; reading the value of a memory location destroys the contents of that location, and to preserve what was there it must be written back. The value to be restored is obtained from the MBR as the value is being used by the other parts of the circuit. With most semiconductor memories, the storage of the data going into and out of the memory is not required, and this register is optional, and used only in systems where there is a specific requirement to maintain the data after it is read.

- *Program Counter (PC)*. The program counter is used to identify the location of the instruction to execute next. For machines that store one instruction per memory location, this register will increment by 1 during the execution of an instruction, which is why it has become known as a program "counter." Other organizations will have differing requirements for updating the PC value. For now, we will assume that the program counter will increment as needed to specify the next value needed from the instruction stream.

- *Instruction Register (IR)*. The instruction register is used to store the instruction currently being executed. This allows the control portion of the machine to assert the control lines of the registers, memories, and arithmetic elements in an appropriate manner to cause the action needed. The design of the control section will be the subject of the next chapter. The IR may only be as wide as

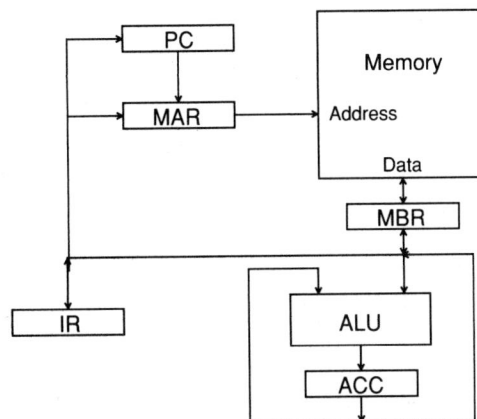

Figure 4.2. Block Diagram of Simple Machine.

needed to store the operation code of the instruction, or it may be wide enough to keep a temporary copy of all of the information associated with an instruction.

- *Accumulator (ACC).* The accumulator is shown here as the receptacle of the action of all of the data manipulation instructions. In the next section we will discuss the implications of the use of an accumulator for doing arithmetic.

This collection of resources (registers, ALUs, memory, and data paths) provides a sketchy view of the system, but it is sufficient to represent transactions that occur within the machine. We also need some method of describing those transactions. To do useful work we will need to specify the work to be done, and this work will be directed by the control section. The user of a computer system has a view of what the capabilities of the computer system are, and this view results directly from the instructions that the machine can execute. This view of the machine, or the appearance of the machine as seen by the assembly language programmer, is sometimes called the instruction set architecture of the system. By the use of the instructions included in this set, the user specifies the action which should occur on the data.

This work of an instruction is accomplished by a fetch-decode-execute mechanism: the instruction is fetched from memory and placed in a register specifically designated for that purpose (the IR), the required decoding is performed, and then the data transfers required by that instruction are executed. At the completion of this action, the machine starts over again, requesting another instruction, decoding it, and performing the needed action. The process continues until the machine has completed all of the designated instructions.

The action of an instruction can be described by identifying the data transfers needed to do the requested work. The specification of this work is done by a register transfer language (RTL); the transfers occur along the permissible data paths in the machine from one major component to another. Only transfers that can actually occur, given an accurate block diagram of the system, are permissible components of the specification for an instruction. For example, transfers from the PC or MAR to the MBR of the system shown in Figure 4.2 would not be possible, since the data paths between those elements do not permit data transfer in that direction. Thus, RTL descriptions specify the order of register transfers and arithmetic action required to carry out the work of an instruction. This information can then be utilized by the designer of the control system to identify the order of activation of control lines to actually cause the desired transfers. This points out one of the basic divisions of the computer design process: the data path (with its appropriate arithmetic capabilities) is specified, and then in a quite separate process the control section for the data path is designed. The design of the data path section is done in such a way that data manipulation goals are met. The design of the control section is then carried out so that the timing requirements of the system are met.

A register transfer language can become as simple or as complex as needed to specify the transfers required in the system. Since we will be using an RTL to describe the action of systems in this chapter and in the remainder of the book, we will describe the few primitives which will follow. The basic operation is the transfer of the contents of one register to another:

$$PC \rightarrow MAR$$

specifies that the contents of the program counter are transferred to the memory address register. If the data paths of the system are rich enough to allow multiple operations in the same time period, these can be represented by specifically linking the transfers together:

$$PC + 1 \rightarrow PC$$
$$MBR \rightarrow IR$$

identifies that in the same time period the value of the program counter is incremented and the contents of the MBR are transferred to the IR. Normally, all of the information is involved in the transfer. However, if a subset of the information is to be transferred, then the specific bits are identified by the use of pointed brackets:

$$IR<3:0> \rightarrow ALU$$

specifies that bits 3 to 0 of the instruction register are directed to the ALU. Similarly, locations of memory or a set of registers are specified with square brackets:

$$REG[2] \rightarrow MEM[MAR]$$

indicates that the contents of register 2 in a general register set (REG) is transferred to the location in memory identified by the memory address register. Finally, for operations that are conditional in nature, we include an "if" facility patterned after the C language if construct:

$$\text{if (carry == 1)} \quad PC - 24 \rightarrow PC$$
$$\text{else} \quad PC + 1 \rightarrow PC$$

identifies that if the carry is equal to 1, the program counter is adjusted by a factor of –24; otherwise the program counter is incremented.

Using the above constructs, a wide variety of instructions can be specified. For example, consider the following add instruction:

fetch:	These register transfers get the instruction.	
	$PC \rightarrow MAR$	Instruction location to MAR.
	$M[MAR] \rightarrow MBR$	Put instruction in MBR.
	$MBR \rightarrow IR$	And then put it in the IR.
	$PC + Ilen \rightarrow PC$	Bump the program counter to next instruction.
decode	The decode process identifies the instruction.	
execute:	and the execute portion performs the needed work.	
	$IR<adr> \rightarrow MAR$	Address of operand to MAR.
	$M[MAR] \rightarrow MBR$	This is value to add to ACC.
	$ACC + MBR \rightarrow ACC$	Do the actual work of instruction.

At this point we will pause to consider briefly some of the timing considerations. All of the operations identified by the RTL require some finite time to accomplish. Exactly how much time is required depends on the technology of implementation and the electrical characteristics of the system. A simple register transfer in a tri-state bus system requires time for the source register to be enabled, time for the data to become stable on the bus, and a setup time and a hold time for the data at the destination register. These times become very important to the designer of the control system, as all of the appropriate timing requirements must be met. In this chapter, we will assign times for the operations specified by the RTL for some of the instructions. These times, when added together, identify the total time required for the execution of the instruction. The times required for operations specified in RTL statements will be identified by a number in parentheses with the statement, and that number represents the execution time in nanoseconds.

By identifying the times required for the actions specified by the RTL statements, time can be used as a metric for the comparisons that need to be made in system evaluations. The overall instruction rate is then the inverse of the average instruction time. It is possible to increase the instruction rate (decrease the instruction time) by increasing the complexity of the system. For example, concurrent register transfers can be possible if multiple data paths exist within the system. Note, however, that the increased complexity may also result in longer machine cycle times, and this must be considered in the process of creating a system. As before, the tradeoffs involving complexity and speed must be made by the system architect using reasonable engineering judgements based on metrics that demonstrate the effective use of system resources.

Another piece of information used in the RTL descriptions included here is a statement number, which allows identification of the steps of an instruction. This identification is often needed in the description of the process.

With the ability to represent the machines at the register level, the data paths connecting the registers and the transfers of data between the major components, let us examine some of the methods used to organize machines and perform useful work.

4.2. Single Address Machines

The first machines constructed made very judicious use of registers since registers required a nontrivial amount of system resources. One of the registers was designated as the one that would be utilized in arithmetic and logic operations; others were also involved as needed. The register involved in these operations was most often called the accumulator, as we have indicated in Figure 4.2. This same technique has been used in many different machines, and provides insight when compared to techniques more prevalent in newer architectures.

On machines that operate in this manner, operations requiring only one operand, such as complement, increment, clear, and the like, find the operand in the accumulator. And the result remains in the accumulator. Functions requiring two operands also use the value in the accumulator as one of the operands. The other operand is identified by a single address in the instruction; hence the name single address machine. To demonstrate how these machines might perform each kind of instruction, let us use the block diagram shown in Figure 4.2 and identify the transfers needed for a negate instruction and a subtract instruction. We are assuming that the machine in question uses the two's complement number system, so forming the negative of a given value can be accomplished by complementing and incrementing. The following RTL description implements the negate instruction:

fetch:

1	PC → MAR	Instruction location to MAR.
2	M [MAR] → MBR	Put instruction in MBR.
3	MBR → IR	And then put it in the IR.
4	PC + Ilen → PC	Bump the program counter to next instruction.

decode

execute:

5	$\overline{ACC}$ → ACC	Complement value in ACC.
6	ACC + 1 → ACC	And then increment it.

All instructions start as does this one, with the fetch cycle. The address from the program counter, which identifies the location of the next instruction to execute, is placed in the memory address register (step 1). The value pointed to by this address is fetched from memory (step 2), and placed in the instruction register (step 3). The machine then readjusts the program counter to point to the next instruction (step 4). To correctly do this, the machine must be aware of the length of the instruction. That is, it is possible that machines have instructions of different length, and when the program counter is adjusted to identify the next instruction, the amount of that adjustment (Ilen) is information which is associated with the instruction. For example, the 68020 has instructions ranging in length from 2 to 14 bytes.

The actual work of the instruction is accomplished by steps 5 and 6 above: the value in the accumulator register is fed to the arithmetic/logic unit, where it is first complemented and that result is then incremented. In general, the exact steps utilized to do the work of an instruction depend on the capabilities of the ALU in the system. (Alternatively, the capabilities of the ALU can be based on the requirements of the instruction set.) Usually two iterations through the unit will not be needed. However, this is a good example of some of the possible methods that can be used to accomplish work: the system resources are used as required to complete the tasks of an instruction. These transfers are coordinated by the control unit in agreement with the technology demands of the system.

The subtract instruction requires two operands. One question is the order of operands: which should be the subtracted value? We will assume that the instruction SUB X means, subtract the value stored in the location X from the value currently in the accumulator and store the result in the accumulator. We will further assume that the address X is adequately contained in the instruction itself, so no additional information beyond the instruction will be required. With those assumptions, a set of data transfers that will perform the work of the subtract instruction follows:

fetch:

1	PC → MAR	Instruction location to MAR.
2	M [MAR] → MBR	Put instruction in MBR.
3	MBR → IR	And then put it in the IR.
4	PC + Ilen → PC	Bump the program counter to next instruction.

decode

execute:

5	X → MAR	Put address X in the MAR.
6	M [MAR] → MBR	Value at memory address X to MBR.
7	ACC − MBR → ACC	Subtract it from value currently in ACC.

The fetch cycle of this instruction is identical to the other fetch cycles: get the instruction and bring it into the instruction register, then bump the program counter. The real work begins in step 5, where the address of the operand is transferred to the MAR. The intended operand of the instruction, the value stored at location X, is then transferred (step 6) to the memory buffer register. Since the address is contained in the instruction, the value of X needed for step 5 can come from either the instruction register or the MBR. Finally, the value is subtracted (step 7) from the value currently in the accumulator, and the result left there. This mechanism for doing the subtraction assumes a more capable ALU than did the negate instruction above. If the ALU needed to form the negative of the value in the MBR by a complement and increment fashion, then additional operand storage facilities would be required.

A number of variations of this method have been made, while the machines have remained basically single address machines. The IAS, Von Neumann's machine built in 1946-7, utilized a word length of 40 bits. The word length was capable of storing more information than required for a single instruction and a single address, so two 20-bit instructions were placed in a single 40-bit word. Each instruction was composed of an 8-bit op code and a 12-bit address; up to 256 operations could be specified, and, if needed, the single address could identify one of 4,096 data locations. But although each word of storage was capable of handling two addresses, the instruction format was limited to a single address per instruction. The restriction of 12 bits for an address in the single address machine of IAS was not restrictive since the total addressable memory was only 4,096 words. However, this limit is generally not acceptable, so different mechanisms have been implemented to extend the permissible range of the operands.

One of the mechanisms utilized for storing addresses needed to identify the location of operands is to place them directly after the operation code (op code) that identifies the work to be done. This method has several advantages that make it an attractive alternative. If there is no need for an address (such as the negate instruction above), then no room is taken up in the instruction itself for a value (address), which will not be used. If multiple length addresses are permitted, that is, addresses of 1, 2, or more bytes depending on addressing mechanism, then only the requisite number of bytes after the op code are utilized to identify the address. And after the fetch portion of the instruction the program counter identifies the location of the address itself. An RTL implementation of this type of subtract instruction is shown in Figure 4.3. Notice the change that results if the assumption is made that the operand address is located in the instruction stream directly following the bits specifying the instruction.

The RTL included in Figure 4.3 indicates that the program counter is used twice, once for the address of the instruction to be executed, and once for the address of the operand. In the first instance, it was incremented by the length of the instruction; in the second, it was incremented by the length of the address. We are making the assumption here that the decoding of the instruction/address identified the appropriate lengths and treated the program counter appropriately. By separating the op code fetch from the address fetch in this manner, the number of bits needed to specify the operation is allowed to expand to meet the appropriate requirements.

Example 4.1: RTL and timing calculations for ADD: How much time is required to execute an ADD instruction for a machine organized as demonstrated above?

The time required for execution of the instruction will include the time necessary to obtain the instruction from memory, decode it, and exe-

fetch:

1	PC → MAR		Instruction location to MAR.
2	M [MAR] → MBR		Put instruction in MBR.
3	MBR → IR		And then put it in the IR.
4	PC + Ilen → PC		Bump the program counter to next value the PC will then point to memory location holding the address of the operand.

decode

execute:

5	PC → MAR		PC is needed again.
6	M [MAR] → MBR		Address at this location to MBR.
7	MBR → MAR		This is address of operand.
8	M [MAR] → MBR		And this is operand.
9	PC + Alen → PC		Now bump PC by length of address.
10	ACC − MBR → ACC		Subtract it from value currently in ACC.

Figure 4.3. RTL Implementation of a Subtract Instruction for a Single Address Machine.

cute the necessary steps. To determine the time required for instruction execution, we must first develop an appropriate RTL implementation of the operations. One such implementation is shown in Figure 4.4.

Each of the items involved in Figure 4.4 will take time to accomplish, and the time for the operation will be implementation dependent. We will assume for the purposes of this example that the accesses to memory cost 300 nsec, the access to a register cost 50 nsec, and that the add itself can be done in 100 nsec, not including the register time. The amount of time for each of the operations identified above is given in the RTL itself. Note that we have assumed that the bumping of the PC can be done in the time it takes to load the register. Also note that step 10 accounts for both the add time and the register delay time. With these figures, we can see that the total time is 1.1 μsec. The instruction fetch itself requires 450 nsec, which is almost half of the total time. If we look only at the time metric, we can draw some conclusions concerning the efficient use of time to accomplish

fetch:

1	PC → MAR	(50)	Start by loading MAR.
2	M [MAR] → MBR	(300)	And get instruction
3	MBR → IR	(50)	into the IR.
4	PC + Ilen → PC	(50)	Bump the program counter. PC now points to address of operand.

decode

execute:

5	PC → MAR	(50)	PC is needed again.
6	M [MAR] → MBR	(300)	This is really address of operand.
7	MBR → MAR	(50)	So put in MAR.
8	M [MAR] → MBR	(50)	And get operand to MBR.
9	PC + Alen → PC	(50)	Now bump PC by length of address.
10	ACC + MBR → ACC	(150)	ADD value in MBR to value in ACC.
		(1100)	

Figure 4.4. RTL Implementation and Timing Considerations an ADD Instruction.

the work of the system. If we now ask how many bits are required, and what are the costs involved in storing and moving data, a different type of conclusion may be available. However, this demonstrates that the fetch of an instruction from memory is definitely not free. It also demonstrates one of the mechanisms that can be used to obtain information about the execution time for instructions.

One of the single address machines built in the mid-1960s that enjoyed wide popularity was the PDP 8, made by Digital Equipment Corporation. This was a 12-bit machine, a block diagram of which is shown in Figure 4.5.

The instruction format called for a 3-bit op code, which left 9 bits of the 12-bit instruction for the address. With 3 bits for specifying the action of the instruction, the possible operations were limited to 8, and these 8 were chosen with care. One of them was an ADD instruction, which added to the accumulator the value identified by the single address included in the instruction. The 9 bits of address specification in the instruction limited the number of addressable operands, so different operand specification mechanisms, such as indirect addressing, were used to increase the number of accessible values. We will discuss alternative addressing methods in Section 4.4. The instructions that required an address for operand identification, such as DCA (deposit value currently located in the ACC to the memory location identified and clear accumulator), TAD (two's complement add), and ISZ (increment and skip if zero), used the 9 address bits to specify the location of the operand. Instructions that did not require an address, such as CLA (clear accumulator), INA (increment accumulator), and CLE (complement accumulator), expanded on one of the eight available op codes to specify the action to take place.

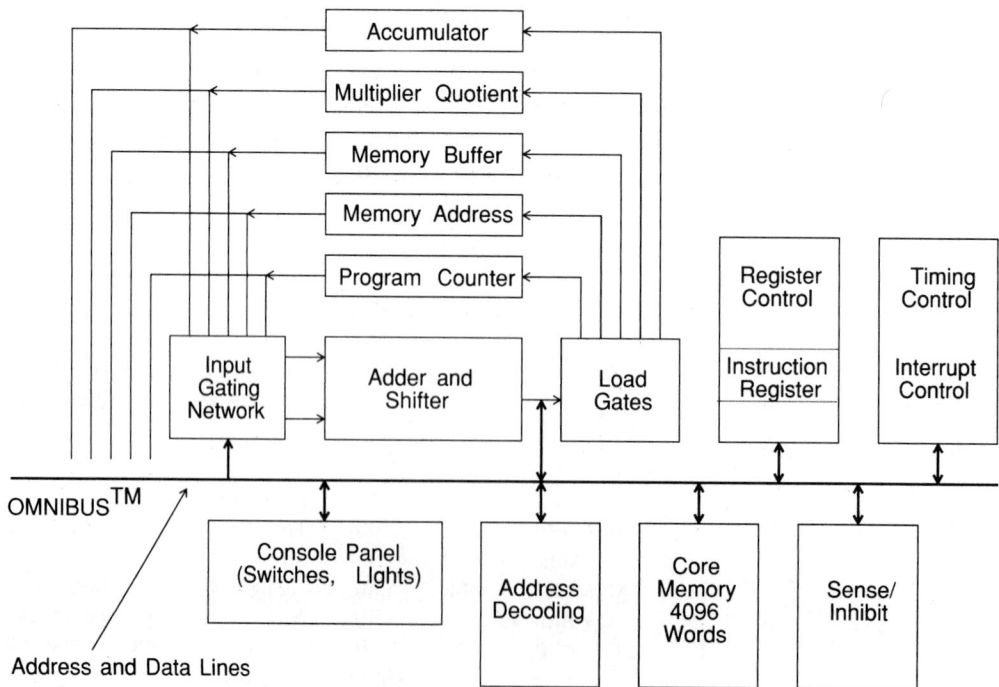

Figure 4.5. Block diagram of the PDP 8 Computer.

The format of the PDP 8 instruction set is given in Figure 4.6. At the time of the creation of the system, memory was a very expensive system resource, and hence the word length was limited to 12 bits. As the relative costs of memory and other system components change and diminish, uses of those system resources will also be appropriately change. The designers of the PDP 8 system, with a limited number of bits to work with, chose the operations of the system with care. A 3-bit op code limited the number of instruction patterns to 8. Six of the possible instructions required an address, and this address was determined by the 9 LSBs of the instruction. These six instructions were logical AND, add, increment-and-skip-if-zero, deposit-and-clear-accumulator, subroutine jump, and unconditional jump. Another of the eight patterns identified an I/O instruction, and the remaining 9 bits specified one of 64 I/O devices, and one of eight operations. The operations were defined by the design of the I/O device itself. The final pattern identified instructions that needed no address, and hence could all share a common instruction code in the op code bits. This allowed a number of operations to be specified, such as clear the accumulator, or increment the accumulator, and so on. One of the most challenging tasks facing a computer architect is to identify the instructions to be incorporated into a new machine, and then encode the specification of those instructions in a format acceptable for the new system. We will examine some more examples of instruction formats later in this chapter, each of which demonstrates a different view of the optimal utilization of system resources.

All of the above examples have a common operational mode: the instruction stream provides a single address, and this address is utilized to identify the location of an operand. For data operations, that operand is used in conjunction with whatever is needed in an assumed location (the accumulator), and the result is left in a predefined place, usually the accumulator. With this type of a machine all of the operations needed by a system can be performed, but the result may not be as efficient as desired. With the fetch utilizing a large fraction of the instruction time, one approach would be to try to utilize more effectively the information fetched from memory. One method proposed for this is to make the system more

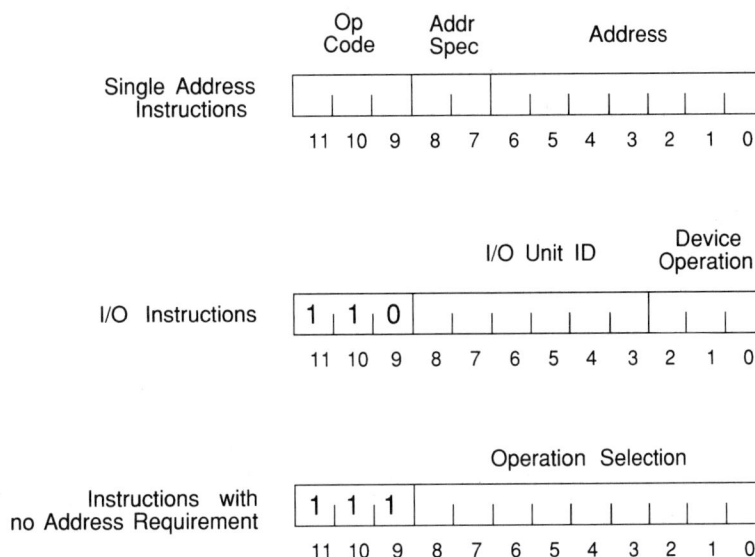

Figure 4.6. Instruction Formats for the PDP 8 Computer.

efficient by using more than one address in a single instruction to specify a greater variety of operations and operands.

4.3. Multiple Address Instructions

Multiple address instruction formats carry with them both benefits and added specification requirements. With a single instruction more operations are identified, so fewer instructions are required to implement a string of arithmetic. At the same time, the instructions must identify all of the work to do, since no assumptions will be made concerning the location of the data. Thus, multiple address instructions will identify both source and destination of the information. The myriad possibilities are exemplified by the following formats:

$$\text{ADD2} \quad \text{A,B}$$
$$\text{ADD3} \quad \text{A,B,C}$$

Although the system architect can choose any reasonable specification mechanism, the assumption we will make concerning the syntax of these instructions is that the final address specified is the destination of the function. With this assumption, the ADD2 instruction adds the value in the location identified with the A address to the value in the location identified by the B address, and the result is returned to the location specified by the B address. Thus, this instruction changes the value identified by the B address. The ADD3 instruction obtains the operand identified by address A, adds to it the value stored at the location specified by address B, and places the result at the location identified by address C. In a machine that utilizes this type of capability, the op codes must differentiate between the various types of operations.

That is, a separate code must be available for each instruction; ADD2 and ADD3 will be specified by different patterns. This results in a larger operation code field, since many different codes must be representable. And it also results in different length instructions, since some instructions will require three addresses, while others will require only two. Consider the following example, in which we compare two and three address add instructions.

Example 4.2: Two and three address instructions: Compare the operation of the ADD2 and ADD3 instructions, using the times identified in Example 4.1. Assume that the operation codes require the same number of bits to represent as the addresses. (Is this a valid assumption?) What is the execution time required for each of the instructions?

In order to address these questions, we need to identify some of the details of the system. That is, before the RTL of implementation can be determined, we need to understand what mechanisms are being utilized. Let us assume that the first value obtained from memory at the location identified by the PC is the appropriate op code, and that the next values are the respective addresses. This is somewhat simplistic, as we shall see a little later. But it will help to identify some of the underlying issues. The next problem to be dealt with needs a little more detailed consideration. This consideration is the mechanism for the addition: how is it to be carried out. In order to visualize the transfers necessary and the order of events, we need to know the available registers and their interconnection. The basic elements required for this example are given in Figure 4.7. The figure has

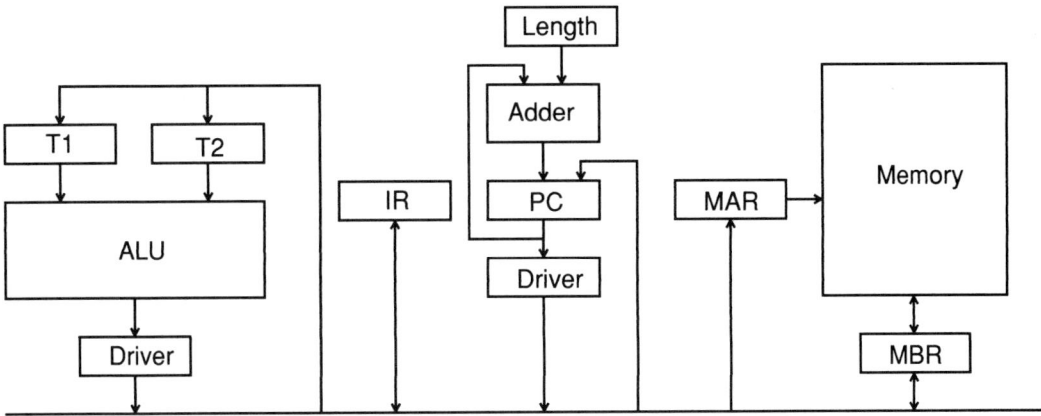

Figure 4.7. Block Diagram of System for Example 4.2.

two registers, T1 and T2, which are not part of the instruction set architecture. That is, the system as defined by the instruction set does not include these storage elements. However, they are very useful when doing instructions that require holding information to be utilized by the system. Armed with this knowledge about the underlying structure, let us examine RTL representations of the instructions.

The RTL statements describing one implementation of the two address ADD instruction is found in Figure 4.8. The figure also contains timing information with the RTL statements, indicating the time required to complete the task.

The RTL for the three address case is included in Figure 4.9. Note the similarity with the two address version in the initial stages of the instruction

fetch:

1	PC → MAR	(50)	Address of instruction to MAR.
2	M [MAR] → MBR	(300)	Instruction to MBR.
3	PC + Ilen → PC	(50)	Bump the PC to point at address.
4	MBR → IR	(50)	Instruction finally to IR.

decode
execute:

5	PC → MAR	(50)	Go get address of operand.
6	PC + Alen → PC	(50)	Bump PC to point at next address.
7	M [MAR] → MBR	(300)	This is address of first operand.
8	MBR → MAR	(50)	So put in MAR.
9	M [MAR] → MBR	(300)	And get the value there, first to MBR,
10	MBR → T1	(50)	And then to T1.
11	PC → MAR	(50)	This is to get address of second operand.
12	PC + Alen → PC	(50)	Bump PC to next instruction.
13	M [MAR] → MBR	(300)	Address of second operand to MBR.
14	MBR → MAR	(50)	And then to MAR.
15	M [MAR] → MBR	(300)	The second operand goes to MBR.
16	MBR → T2	(50)	And then to T2.
17	T1 + T2 → MBR	(150)	Do the add, results to MBR.
18	MBR → M [MAR]	(300)	Put results where operand two used to be.
		(2500)	Total time: 2.5 μsec

Figure 4.8. RTL Implementation of a Two Address ADD Instruction.

fetch:

1	PC → MAR	(50)	Address of instruction to MAR.
2	M[MAR] → MBR	(300)	Instruction to MBR.
3	PC + Ilen → PC	(50)	Bump the PC to point at address.
4	MBR → IR	(50)	Now, instruction to IR.

decode

execute:

5	PC → MAR	(50)	This is to get first address.
6	PC + Alen → PC	(50)	And bump PC by address length.
7	M[MAR] → MBR	(300)	Now the address to the MBR.
8	MBR → MAR	(50)	And then to the MAR.
9	M[MAR] → MBR	(300)	This is the first operand.
10	MBR → T1	(50)	So put it in T1.
11	PC → MAR	(50)	Now, go get the second address.
12	PC + Alen → PC	(50)	Bump the PC appropriately.
13	M[MAR] → MBR	(300)	This is the address itself.
14	MBR → MAR	(50)	So, put it in the MAR.
15	M[MAR] → MBR	(300)	Now, get the second operand.
16	MBR → T2	(50)	And put it in T2.
17	PC → MAR	(50)	Gotta go get the final address.
18	PC + Alen → PC	(50)	Bump PC to point to next instruction.
19	M[MAR] → MBR	(300)	Get the address of the result.
20	MBR → MAR	(50)	And put in the MAR.
21	T1 + T2 → MBR	(150)	This is actual work of the instruction.
22	MBR → M[MAR]	(300)	Put in location specified by third address.
		(2950)	Total time: 2.95 μsec

Figure 4.9. RTL Implementation of a Three Address ADD Instruction.

implementation. Then, when fetch has been completed and the actual work of the instruction begins, the statements in the RTL reflect the different action of the two instructions.

Since the addresses of the operands are stored in the instruction stream, obtaining and storing information requires two memory references for each value: one to obtain the appropriate address, and another to utilize that address for a fetch or store. Each of these interactions requires time to complete, resulting in seemingly long instruction times, 2.5 μsec for the ADD2 instruction and 2.95 μsec for the ADD3 instruction. As would be expected, the ADD3 instruction takes longer than the ADD2 instruction, since one more address is involved in the operand specification. This requires modifying the PC to point at the address, and an additional memory access to fetch to get the appropriate address. The resource utilization of these instructions can be viewed in number of ways. If one simply looks at the time required for the instruction, then the ADD2 instruction is more attractive than the ADD3 instruction. However, if one looks at the time required to implement a set of operations, such as

$$X = Y \cdot Z + W \cdot V$$

then the differences become more apparent:

With ADD2	With ADD3
MOVE Y,X	AND3 Y,Z,T
AND2 Z,X	AND3 W,V,Y
MOVE W,Y	ADD3 T,Y,X
AND2 V,Y	
ADD2 Y,X	

The stream of instructions that utilize the ADD2 method require 15 memory locations to store and 12.5 μsec to execute; the ADD3 method requires 12 memory locations, and executes in 8.55 μsec. In contrast to the above methods, a single address implementation of the equation would require 14 memory locations to store, and be executed in 8.95 μsec, making similar assumptions about the address storage and execution mechanisms. To more appropriately evaluate the merits of one, two, and three address instruction mechanisms, a more complete set of example instructions and system usage is required.

It is possible to generate examples in which each of the mechanisms discussed thus far — single address machines, two address machines, and three address machines — has a better time characteristic than the other two. Among other things, this indicates that the metric we have chosen for comparison, combined with the underlying assumptions, is not a sufficient test. To make a more realistic comparison, further analysis and additional criteria are required. Nevertheless, the above example illustrates a viable method: when a choice between different alternatives is to be made, a metric is chosen that demonstrates the use of the appropriate system resources, and the associated costs are determined. Caution must be exercised to ascertain that the costs not included in the metrics will not undermine the effectiveness of the comparison.

One observation that could be made concerning the system is that a great deal of the execution time for the ADD2 and ADD3 instructions, as shown above, is consumed in fetching addresses of operands and the operands themselves. A similar comment can be made concerning the number of bits required to store the addresses: if the range of addresses can be limited in some fashion, the number of bits required for addresses (and hence the entire instruction) can be greatly reduced. For both of these reasons — the time required for operand access and the number of bits needed for address specification — register sets have been included in machines.

The use of a register set reduces the time required for instruction performance. One demonstration of this is to rework Example 4.2, this time assuming that the add instructions deal with values in registers, rather than values that reside anywhere within the memory space of the machine. The block diagram for this example is given in Figure 4.10. Note the similarities and differences with Figure 4.7. The main difference is the inclusion of a set of registers, shown here to contain 8 different storage locations. Thus, to represent the operand location requires only 3 bits, and this field can be incorporated into the instruction format. The net result is a reduction in the number of memory references required by each instruction to get information.

Example 4.3: ADD2 and ADD3 instructions with registers: Again compare the operation of the ADD2 and ADD3 instructions, but this time assume that the operands reside in registers, and that the register specification is con-

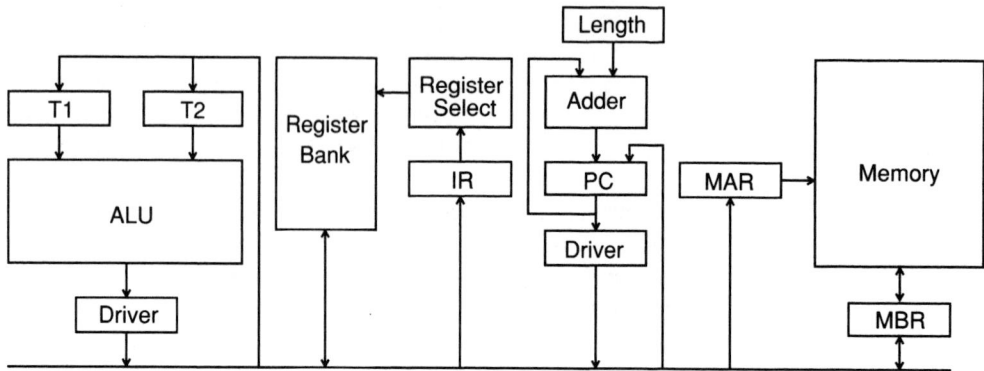

Figure 4.10. Block Diagram of System for Example 4.3.

tained within the instruction itself. That is, an additional memory cycle to obtain addresses is not required, since the identification of the appropriate register is accomplished by using a multiplexer (register select MUX) to select the appropriate bits from the instruction register, as shown in Figure 4.10.

The RTL required for this example follows the RTL for the previous example, with the obvious differences:

ADD2 R_A, R_B			ADD3 R_A, R_B, R_C		
PC $\rightarrow$ MAR	(50)		PC $\rightarrow$ MAR	(50)	
M[MAR] $\rightarrow$ MBR	(300)		M[MAR] $\rightarrow$ MBR	(300)	
PC + Ilen $\rightarrow$ PC	(50)		PC + Ilen $\rightarrow$ PC	(50)	
MBR $\rightarrow$ IR	(50)		MBR $\rightarrow$ IR	(50)	
$R_A \rightarrow$ T1	(50)		$R_A \rightarrow$ T1	(50)	
$R_B \rightarrow$ T2	(50)		$R_B \rightarrow$ T2	(50)	
T1 + T2 $\rightarrow$ R_B	(150)		T1 + T2 $\rightarrow$ R_C	(150)	
	(700)			(700)	

Note that the operands are in the registers, and the resulting instruction times reflect the reduced requirements for operand access. Both instructions now require 700 nsec, but we must recognize that the storage requirements are different for both instructions. That is, the ADD2 instruction must be wide enough to include two addresses, while the ADD3 instruction must be even wider, sufficient for three addresses. If all instructions are to be the same width, it must be the wider of the two formats. That is, if instructions are to be a common width (to match a memory constraint, for example), then the word width must match the widest instruction. For a system utilizing this technique, an instruction that requires fewer than three addresses will waste some of the capabilities of the storage mechanisms. The point is that tradeoffs must be applied to each situation to determine their relative merits, and the choice of the metric will directly impact the comparisons. The metrics may include the number of bits (or bytes) required to store a program segment, the time required to execute, the complexity of the algorithms required to implement the instructions, or any of a number of other appropriate metrics.

The above example demonstrates that the use of registers greatly reduces the time requirements for instructions. As mentioned above, the main reasons for this are the reduced time requirements for interacting with the operands and reduced memory requirements for storing the instruction itself. The reduced time requirements for operand access result from the fact that register access is faster than main store access. The reduced memory requirements are a function of operand identification, since identification of an appropriate register requires a few bits, while identification of a main store address requires a great many more bits. We have used the example of the IAS, which used 12 bits to identify a location in memory; more recent systems, such as the 68030 microprocessor, require as many as 32 bits to specify a location in memory.

A number of existing machines utilize multiple address formats, and we can benefit from an examination of the instruction set architecture of those systems. However, before we consider those machines, we will need to examine a "feature" that we have ignored to this point. The very mechanism that saves time by reducing the memory requirements also reduces to a very small number the allowable locations for operands to reside. However, in general, we would like to be able to access any operand, and operands should be able to reside anywhere in main store. Thus, some mechanisms must exist that will allow operand access to arbitrary locations. Let us examine some of the mechanisms used for operand access.

4.4. Operand Addressing Mechanisms

When an instruction requires an operand for execution, the location of the operand can be assumed, as in the CLA (clear accumulator) instruction, or the operand location can be identified in the instruction itself. In this section we will examine different mechanisms for the specification of the location of the operand. First we will look at direct and indirect addressing, and some variations of indirection that have proved useful in different machines. Then we will look at some of the indexed and register relative modes. Combinations of these mechanisms will provide the versatility needed to identify locations in main store for all types of machine instructions. A visual representation of the addressing mechanisms is included in Figure 4.15 (page 154), and it may be useful to refer to that figure throughout the section.

In our discussion of addressing modes, we are concerned with the manner of specification of the effective address of the operand. That is, how is the location of the operand identified. Thus, we are concerned with the generation mechanism or formula for the effective address (EA).

The term "direct addressing" refers to the situation where the effective address of the operand is supplied directly by the instruction. Thus, for direct addressing

$$EA = A$$

That is, for the ADD2 X,Y instruction, with direct addressing,

$$EA_{OPERAND\ 1} = X$$

$$EA_{OPERAND\ 2} = Y$$

The actual address is contained within the instruction. This is the situation that was assumed for the instructions considered in Example 4.3. As we have mentioned, various costs associated with this method diminish its effectiveness, so other approachs to operand identification are used. One useful mechanism is to use the information contained in an instruction to identify not the operand, but rather the address of the operand.

The term indirect addressing is applied when the instruction identifies not the operand, but rather the location of the operand. That is, for an ADD2 X,Y instruction with indirect addressing,

$$EA_{OPERAND\,1} = M[X]$$

$$EA_{OPERAND\,2} = M[Y]$$

The information in the instruction tells the machine where to find the address of the appropriate operand. Different manufacturers have different mechanisms for specifying that a value identified by the instruction is not an operand, but rather the address of an operand. The mechanism we will use is to include an asterisk (*) before the operand specifier. Thus,

$$ADD2\ X,Y$$

specifies an instruction that adds a value stored at location X to a value stored at location Y. However,

$$ADD2\ *X,\ *Y$$

specifies an instruction that adds two values: the address of the first value is found at location X, and the address of the second value (as well as the result) is found at location Y. These mechanisms can be combined in instructions, so that

$$ADD2\ *X,\ Y$$

adds the value found in main store at the address found in location X to the value at location Y, and the result is placed in location Y.

The usefulness of indirect addressing is best demonstrated by example. Then a variety of uses becomes apparent, such as accessing arrays in a regular fashion or accessing information in a data dependent fashion.

Example 4.4: Indirect addressing: Using indirect addressing and two address instructions, demonstrate a method for adding the elements of three single dimensional arrays together. These arrays are located in main store, and their starting locations are also found in main store at the locations named $ARRAY_1$, $ARRAY_2$, and $ARRAY_3$. The result is to be placed in an array in main store, the starting location of which is in a location named $ARRAY_4$.

We have not yet considered the branching instructions needed for this problem, so those functions will be identified but not specified. Also, we will make the assumption that the information is stored one value per location (instead of double precision or other considerations), so that incrementing an address by one automatically points to the next value. This addition could be performed in a number of ways, but one way is demonstrated by the following instructions.

Set up problem first, then enter this loop:

over:	MOVE *ARRAY$_1$, TEMP	Get value from first array.
	ADD2 *ARRAY$_2$, TEMP	And add value from second array.
	ADD2 *ARRAY$_3$, TEMP	And third array.
	MOVE TEMP, *ARRAY$_4$	Now move answer to right spot.
		With the arithmetic over, adjust
		the addresses appropriately.
	INC ARRAY$_1$	These increment instructions
	INC ARRAY$_2$	bump each address to point
	INC ARRAY$_3$	to the next value.
	INC ARRAY$_4$	
	if not done, go to over	End of loop.

Note that the MOVE and ADD2 instructions access the information in the arrays indirectly. Thus, the location identified in the instruction is not the location of the operand, but rather the location where the address of the operand is found. Then the increment instructions, which access their appropriate locations directly, cause the addresses to point to the next elements of the appropriate array. The way in which the above section of code was written modifies the locations ARRAY$_{1-4}$, which is in general not a good idea. A better solution would have been to place these addresses in temporary locations and operate on them in those locations. Another comment that can be made concerns the use of the temporary location. The location would not be needed if the MOVE instruction placed the value in the location identified by ARRAY$_4$, and the subsequent ADD2 instructions used that location to sum the value. Thus, the number of memory locations needed for the execution of the program would be reduced. However, indirect references require one more memory reference than direct references, so the required time to complete the code would be increased. Thus, the "best" solution will be determined by which metric is the critical one for the application.

Including both direct and indirect addressing mechanisms in an instruction set allows a wide variety of operand access capabilities. These concepts are directly applicable to systems with register sets, where the identification bits in the address refer to a specific register. Direct addressing in this fashion is sometimes referred to as register direct addressing. An indirect reference occurs when the value contained in the register is an address identifying the location in main store of an operand. This would then be register indirect addressing, and operates in the same fashion as the indirect addressing mentioned above. The benefits of this mechanism have already been identified: the number of bits required to specify the address are reduced, and the time required for register access is much less than that required for main store access.

Example 4.5: Cost of direct and indirect addressing: Determine the times for the ADD2 instruction using direct and indirect addressing. Compare the system of Figure 4.7, which doesn't have a register set, with the system of Figure 4.10, which includes a general register set.

The times required for these instructions can be obtained only if we know the set of register transfers required to accomplish the work of the additions. So, the first step is to obtain the RTL of instruction implementation. First we will look at the system without registers, then observe the effect when a register set is available. The direct addressing implementation of the ADD2 instruction is shown in Figure 4.11. The transfers required to perform the work consume a total of 2.5 μsec. Of that time, 0.450 μsec is required for fetching the instruction, the other 2.05 μsec is used in execution. Another view of the time requirements comes from examining the time used by the memory interaction. There are six memory transfers, one for the instruction and five for addresses and operands; these total 1.8 μsec. We would expect the indirect addressing example to take even more time, and this is confirmed by examining the RTL of the indirect addressing version contained in Figure 4.12. The indirect addressing system is longer, but only by 0.7 μsec. The instruction fetch again took 0.45 μsec, while the eight memory transfers consumed 2.4 μsec, or 75% of the total instruction time. This gives an indication of one of the reasons that computer architects have attempted to reduce the memory interaction as much as possible. The times involved in the register implementations of the ADD2 instruction indicate how well that can be accomplished.

The work required for register-oriented ADD2 instructions, both for direct and indirect addressing, is demonstrated by the RTL implementations in Figure 4.13.

An examination of the implementations of Figure 4.13 indicates that indeed time is saved when the operands (and/or addresses) are contained in the registers. When the operands are located directly in the registers, then the ADD2 instruction requires only 0.7 μsec, 28% of the time required for the memory implementation. The principal contributor is the fact that this implementation requires only one memory transfer, compared to six transfers for the ADD2 X, Y instruction.

ADD2 X, Y (*Direct Addressing*)

fetch:

PC	→	MAR	(50)	First, address of instruction to MAR.
PC + Ilen	→	PC	(50)	Now bump PC.
M[MAR]	→	MBR	(300)	Retrieve instruction.
MBR	→	IR	(50)	And move to IR.

decode

execute:

PC	→	MAR	(50)	This to get address of X.
PC + Alen	→	PC	(50)	Bump PC by length of address.
M[MAR]	→	MBR	(300)	MBR now contains address of X.
MBR	→	MAR	(50)	So put in MAR.
M[MAR]	→	MBR	(300)	And retrieve X.
MBR	→	T1	(50)	Move operand to T1.
PC	→	MAR	(50)	Do same thing for Y.
PC + Alen	→	PC	(50)	
M[MAR]	→	MBR	(300)	
MBR	→	MAR	(50)	
M[MAR]	→	MBR	(300)	
MBR	→	T2	(50)	Move Y to T2.
T1 + T2	→	MBR	(150)	Do the ADD.
MBR	→	M[MAR]	(300)	And store back where Y was.
			(2500)	

Figure 4.11. RTL Implementation of a Two Address ADD Instruction with Direct Addressing.

fetch:				
PC	→	MAR	(50)	As before, address of instruction to MAR.
PC + Ilen	→	PC	(50)	Bump PC.
M[MAR]	→	MBR	(300)	Retrieve instruction.
MBR	→	IR	(50)	And move to IR.
decode				
execute:				
PC	→	MAR	(50)	This to get address of address X.
PC + Alen	→	PC	(50)	Bump PC by length of address.
M[MAR]	→	MBR	(300)	MBR now contains address of address X.
MBR	→	MAR	(50)	So, put in MAR.
M[MAR]	→	MBR	(300)	And retrieve address of X.
MBR	→	MAR	(50)	Put address of X in MAR.
M[MAR]	→	MBR	(300)	And retrieve X.
MBR	→	T1	(50)	Move X to T1.
PC	→	MAR	(50)	Do same thing for Y.
PC + Alen	→	PC	(50)	
M[MAR]	→	MBR	(300)	
MBR	→	MAR	(50)	
M[MAR]	→	MBR	(300)	
MBR	→	MAR	(50)	
M[MAR]	→	MBR	(300)	
MBR	→	T2	(50)	Move Y to T2.
T1 + T2	→	MBR	(150)	Do the ADD.
MBR	→	M[MAR]	(300)	And store back where Y was.
			(3200)	

Figure 4.12. RTL Implementation of a Two Address ADD Instruction with Indirect Addressing.

A similar savings is obtained with the register indirect method, also shown in Figure 4.13. The speedup of the register indirect implementation is not as dramatic as the register direct method, but 1.7 μsec is 53% of the time required by the system when no registers are present. Again the difference reflects the extent to which memory is utilized: with registers the instruction required only four memory transfers, while the system without registers required eight memory transfers. The following table summarizes this information:

Addressing Technique	Memory References	Fetch Time	Execute Time	Total Time
Direct	6	450	2,050	2,500
Indirect	8	450	2,750	3,200
Register Direct	1	450	250	700
Register Indirect	4	450	1,250	1,700

Note from the table that the instruction fetch time of all of these instructions is identical. For the ADD2 *X, *Y instruction, this is only 17% of the instruction time, while for the ADD2 R_X, R_Y instruction, this is 64% of the instruction time. This will form a portion of an interesting observation later in the chapter.

ADD2 R_X, R_Y (*Register Direct Addressing*)

fetch:

PC → MAR	(50)	Once again, address of instruction to MAR.
PC + Ilen → PC	(50)	Bump PC.
M[MAR] → MBR	(300)	Retrieve instruction.
MBR → IR	(50)	And move to IR.

decode

execute:

R_X → T1	(50)	Get first operand to T1.
R_Y → T2	(50)	Get second operand to T2.
T1 + T2 → R_Y	(150)	And result back to R_Y.
	(700)	

ADD2 *R_X, *R_Y (*Register Indirect Addressing*)

fetch:

PC → MAR	(50)	Address of instruction to MAR.
PC + Ilen → PC	(50)	Bump PC.
M[MAR] → MBR	(300)	Retrieve instruction.
MBR → IR	(50)	And move to IR.

decode

execute:

R_X → MAR	(50)	R_X holds address of first operand.
M[MAR] → MBR	(300)	Retrieve operand.
MBR → T1	(50)	And put in T1.
R_Y → MAR	(50)	R_Y holds address of second operand.
M[MAR] → MBR	(300)	Retrieve operand.
MBR → T2	(50)	And put in T2.
T1 + T2 → MBR	(150)	Do the work.
MBR → M[MAR]	(300)	And store results.
	(1700)	

Figure 4.13. RTL Implementation of a Two Address ADD Instruction with Register Direct and Register Indirect Addressing.

The inclusion of registers in the system reduces the time required to perform most functions, as shown in the above example. The register indirect method is a very useful mechanism for identifying the location of operands in main store. In a previous example, we considered the use of indirect instructions to access every element in an array. This type of mechanism is used often enough to justify including a specific addressing mode which handles the incrementing of the address automatically. This is called an autoincrement capability, and is included in many instruction sets. We will indicate that an address is to be incremented after it is used by including a plus sign (+) after the indirect specification. That is, an ADD instruction that uses the indirect autoincrement mechanism for its first operand and register direct access for the second operand would be specified as

$$\text{ADD2} \quad *R_X+, R_Y$$

The increment amount used in the instruction is generally tied to the size of the operand. That is, an instruction set may have three different integer add instructions: one for byte, one for word (two bytes), and one for double word (four bytes) operands. The process of autoincrement for these instructions would increase the address by one, two, or four, respectively, for the different situations.

The autoincrement mechanism is very useful for dealing with data in data structures within the computer. For example, one data structure utilized extensively in some types of processing is the stack. Stacks can be created in main store by allocating space for the structure and associating a "stack pointer" address with it. Conceptually, information is placed on a stack and then removed as needed. That is, it is a last-in, first-out mechanism for storing information. We will identify some of the uses of this type of information storage later in this chapter.

Stacks can be constructed by means of a number of methods, but perhaps the most prevalent mechanism is to allow the stack to grow downwards in memory. A POP operation for such a stack is included in Figure 4.14. The address provided by $R_{STACK\ POINTER}$ indicates where the current top of the stack (TOS) is located. This address can identify either the next available location for storing information, or it can specify the location containing the information on top of the stack. For a stack that grows downward in memory, the common mechanism is to utilize an address that points to the value currently on the top of the stack. Notice that the action of extracting information from the stack can be achieved with the register indirect autoincrement addressing mode:

$$\text{MOVE} \quad *R_{STACK\ POINTER}+, R_X$$

The above instruction moves information from the stack to R_X. Since $R_{STACK\ POINTER}$ points to the value currently on the top of the stack, the read action transfers that value from the memory at that location. Then the system automatically increments the stack pointer by the appropriate amount, and at the end of the instruction the stack pointer identifies the next element to be on the top of the stack.

POP Operation for Stack which Grows Downward in Memory

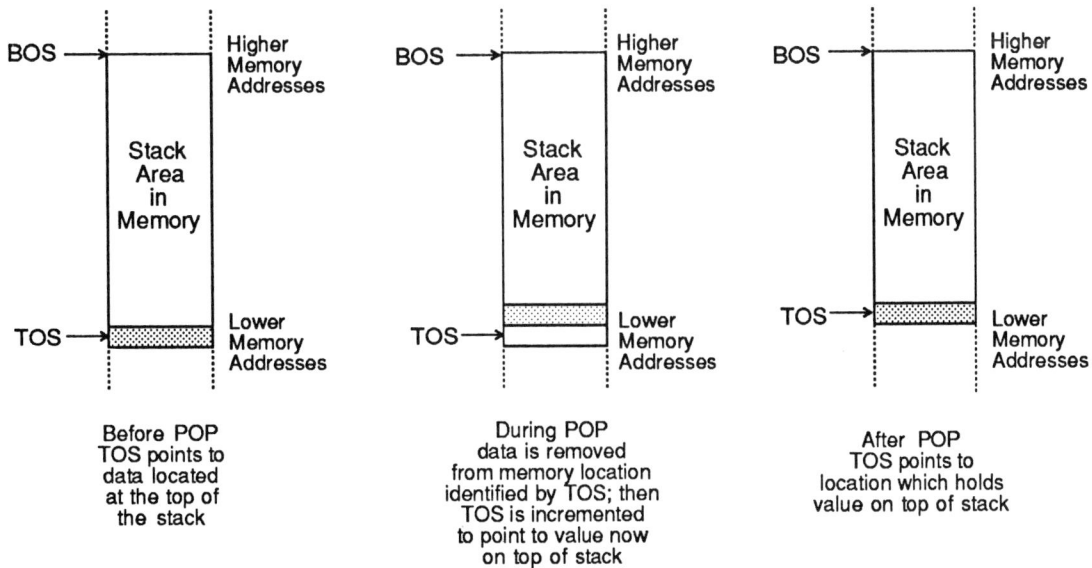

Figure 4.14. Stack Mechanisms in Main Store.

To complete the data transfers needed for stack implementation, we must consider the action required to place information on the stack. Obviously, we will need the ability to decrement the address in $R_{STACK\ POINTER}$. To do this, many instruction sets also include an autodecrement facility. This works in exactly the same fashion as the autoincrement mechanism, except that generally the decrement is done before the address is used, rather than after. In this text we will assume that all autoincrement operations are postincrement operations, and that all autodecrement operations are performed in a predecrement manner. This permits the following pair of operations to be used for stack manipulation:

$$\text{MOVE } R_X, \ ^*R_{STACK\ POINTER}^- \qquad \text{Push value in } R_X \text{ onto stack.}$$
$$\text{MOVE } ^*R_{STACK\ POINTER}^+, \ R_X \qquad \text{Pop value from stack to } R_X.$$

The first instruction does a push: the address in $R_{STACK\ POINTER}$ is first decremented and then used as an address by the system, and the information in R_X is written to that address in main store. The second instruction is used to pop information from the stack: the address in $R_{STACK\ POINTER}$ is used to access the information, and then incremented to point to the next element on the stack. Both the push action and the pop action leave the address pointing at the value on the top of the stack, as expected.

Thus far we have identified direct and indirect addressing, with and without registers, and the idea of autoincrementing (autodecrementing) a value being used as an address. Before we look at some real machines to see in what way these mechanisms are specified and used, three other addressing schemes need to be mentioned.

One mechanism that can be used to access information which is known when a program is created is instruction stream addressing. This mechanism uses the PC to identify data and addresses in the same manner that instructions are identified. As an instruction executes, the information is retrieved from the instruction stream, the location of which is identified by the PC. This method is sometimes called the immediate mode, since data and addresses are "immediately" available for use. In this way, constants (or predetermined addresses) can be included in the instruction stream.

Another method has several names, but we will call it register relative addressing. The basic idea is that a location in main store is specified by identifying an offset from a value in a register. Thus, the effective address of the location will be obtained by adding the two values:

$$\text{Effective address} = \text{Address in register} + \text{Offset amount}$$

A common use of this type of addressing is to identify locations in a program relative to the current position of the program counter. This is often called PC relative addressing, and is used extensively for identifying the destinations of branches or jumps in programs. The offset amount is generally included in the instruction itself.

Another use of register relative addressing is to locate information based on the mode of execution of the program combined with the instruction. Some systems have registers that are given specific operating system responsibilities, and references to information are automatically made relative to these registers. An example of this is the 80X86 series of processors made by Intel, which contain four segment registers. The addresses in these registers identify the location in main store of data, program, stack, and extra segments. Thus, any access to memory is automatically made relative to the appropriate segment register.

Finally, another mechanism for addressing information is indexing. Here, the address of the desired information is the sum of at least two values. One of these values is considered the base value, and can be supplied by the instruction stream or be stored in a register. The second value is usually in a general purpose register. The sum of these two values provides the effective address of the desired location. Thus the base value is "indexed" by the value in the register. One example of the use of this mechanism is to provide the base address of an array in the instruction stream, and then to identify the desired element of the array by a value in a register. Indexed references provide an effective way to reference structured data.

It is helpful to visualize the relationship of the various components making up the various addressing modes. A visual summary of the addressing mechanisms described above is shown in Figure 4.15. Additional addressing mechanisms can be constructed by combining the different basic mechanisms to extend the total number of possibilities. We will use many of these addressing mechanisms in examples throughout the text, and a summary of the nomenclature used in the assembly language level examples is included in Table 4.1.

These basic methods are combined in a variety of ways to accomplish the task of identifying in main store a desired location. One of the remaining tasks, which we have not yet discussed, is representing these different choices in a manner that they will be acted upon in a reasonable fashion by the CPU. We know from Chapter 2 that with N bits we can represent 2^N different entities. The problem is to use N bits to specify the operation code (op code) or instruction to perform, the register(s) needed for operand identification, if any, and the appropriate addressing mode. Let us consider two examples of how this has been accomplished by system architects in real machines. First, we will look at some of the mechanisms used by DEC, then the NS32032 processor.

> *Example 4.6: Encoding of addressing modes:* The PDP 11 series of computers utilizes a number of different addressing schemes to identify locations. How are the single and double operand instructions encoded?
>
> The PDP 11 has been one of the most popular 16-bit computers ever built. One of the features of the PDP 11 instruction encoding scheme is that all of the op codes for the instructions fit into 16-bit words, with whatever additional information (addresses, for example) needed occupying additional 16-bit words. To accomplish this, different formats are utilized for those 16-bit instructions. The two of interest to us are those used for single address and double address functions, the formats of which are shown in Figure 4.16. The PDP 11 utilizes eight general purpose registers, which are numbered from 0 to 7. Register 7 is also the program counter, and there are some special modifications to the addressing mechanisms when this register is specified. To identify one of the eight registers requires 3 bits, and locations for these bits are reserved in both representations. An additional 3 bits are used to specify how the register is to be used. Note that using both register and mode bits for the two address format leaves only 4 bits for identification of the instruction. These 4 bits are coded as shown in Table 4.2.
>
> As can be seen from the table, certain patterns in the 4 most significant bits (MSB) expand to consume the bits used for the source

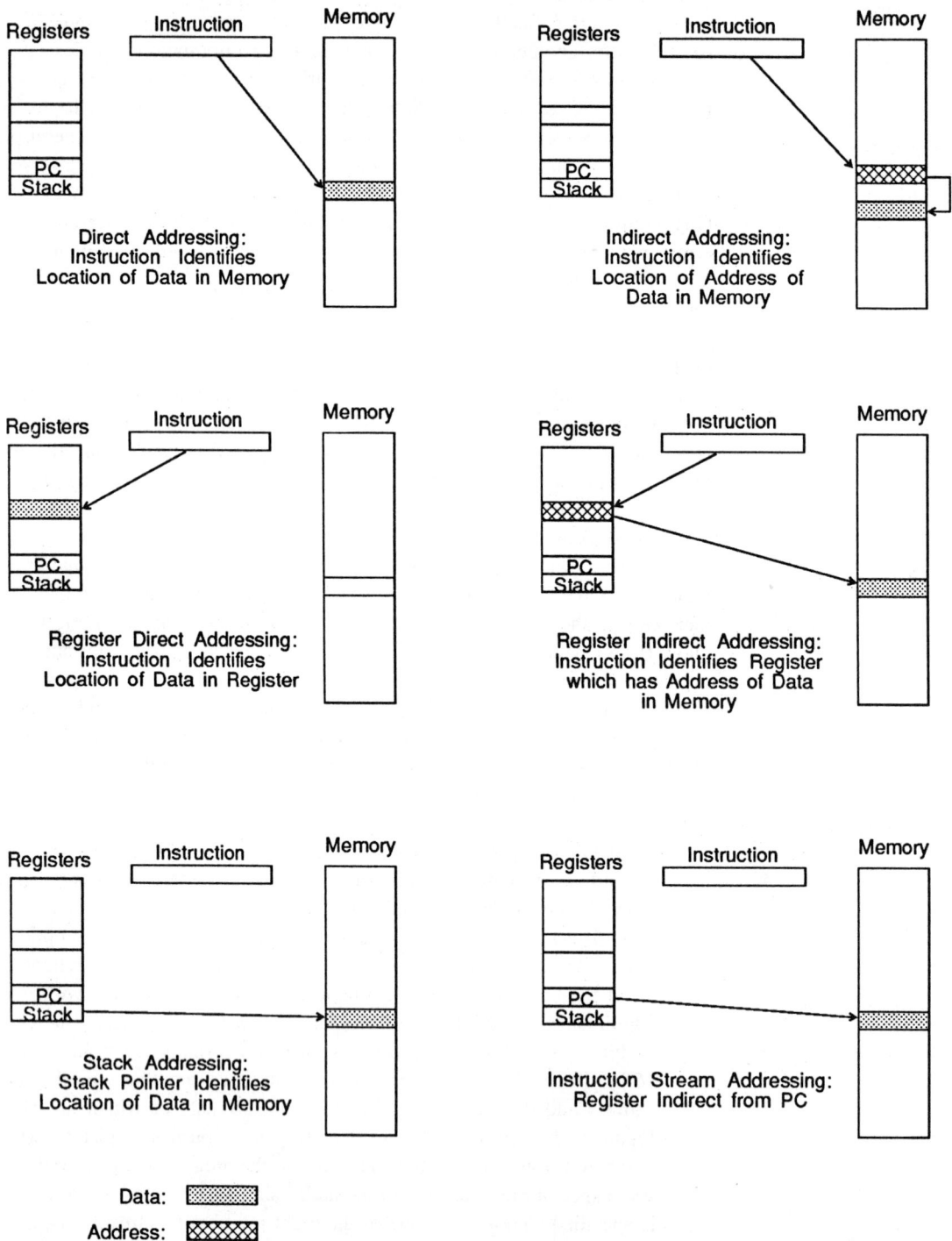

Figure 4.15. Addressing Mechanisms for Accessing Information in Main Store.

register (R_S) mode and register identification bits. This allows a few patterns in the MSBs to be utilized to represent many different single address and program control instructions. The bits used to specify the addressing mechanism are coded as shown in Table 4.3.

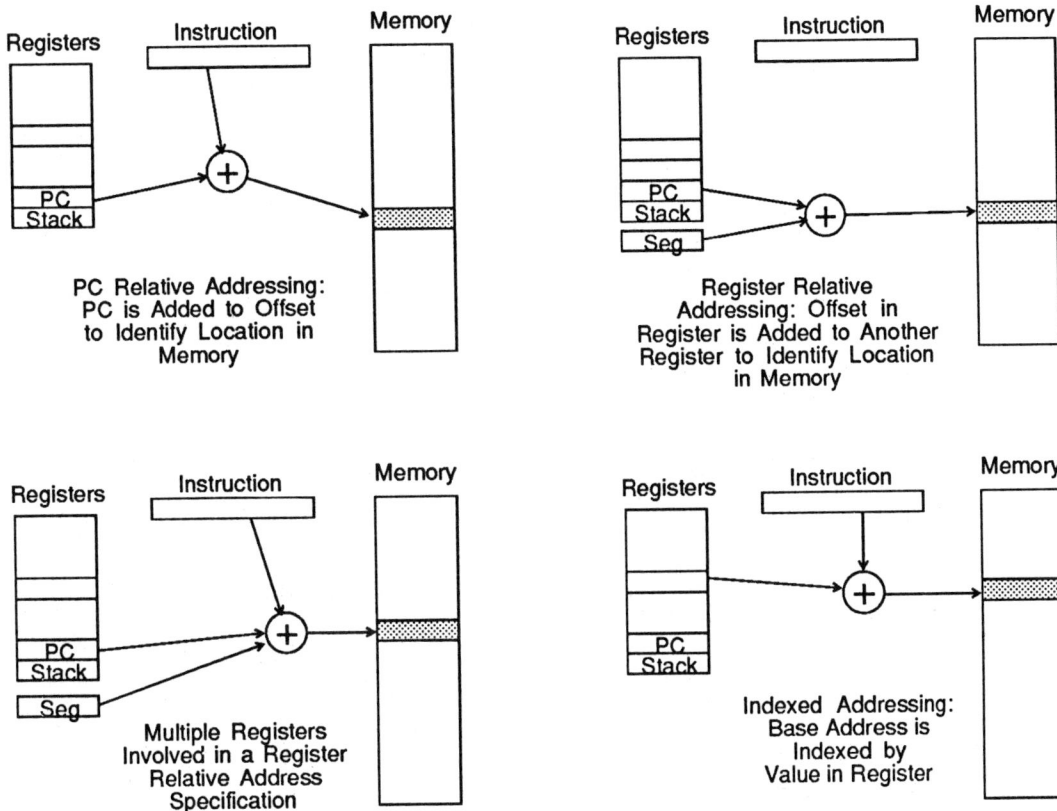

Figure 4.15. *(cont)* Addressing Mechanisms for Accessing Information in Main Store.

The addressing mechanisms detailed in Table 4.3 indicate one approach to operand addressing, an approach that can be extended or modified to meet the needs of a system. The instruction set architecture, as well as the structure of the machine, will reflect the intended use of the

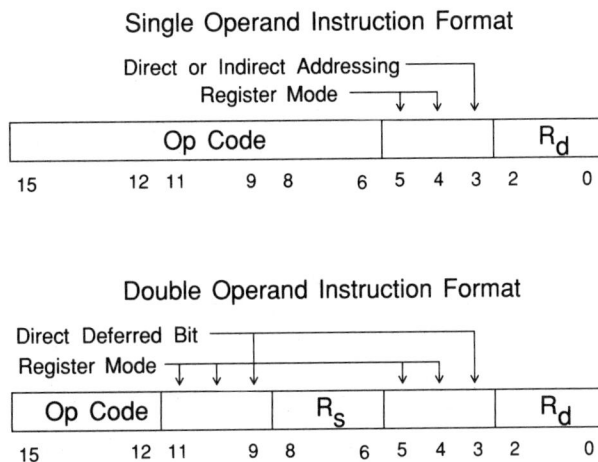

Figure 4.16. PDP 11 Instruction Formats for Single and Double Operand Instructions.

Table 4.1. Addressing Modes and their Nomenclatures.

Addressing Mode	Represented By	Comment
Direct	@<address>	Address is part of instruction.
Register Direct	Rn	Operand in found in register.
Indirect	*(<address>)	Address is part of instruction; operand is located in memory at that address.
Register Indirect	*Rn	Address found in register; operand in memory at that address.
Instruction Stream	#<value>	Value is stored in instruction stream.
Register Indirect Autoincrement	*Rn+	Register used as address; value in register incremented at end of instruction.
Stack Addressing	Push Pop	Stack pointer indentifies location in main store for transfers; value in stack pointer adjusted as necessary.
PC Relative	$<offset>	Offset identifies target address relative to current location identified by program counter.
Memory-Based Index	(<address> i Rm)	Operand is located in memory at address which is sum of <address> and Rm.
Register-Based Index	(Rn i Rm)	Operand is located in memory at address which is sum of Rn and Rm.

system and the relative importance of system resources: the number of registers, the amount of memory, and the times required for arithmetic, register, and memory interaction. The register direct addressing referred to in Table 4.3 is as we expect: the operand is located in the specified register. And the register indirect uses the specified register as an address pointing to the desired location. The register indirect autoincrement is as described above, the value in the register being used as an address and incremented as part of the instruction. Mode 3 is a multiple use of indirection, with the register being incremented after use; that is, the value in the specified register is used as an address and then incremented. But the address extracted from the register points not to the operand, but rather to the address of the operand. DEC refers to this additional level of indirection as "deferred" addressing. The same thing happens on the autodecrement and two level indirect with autodecrement. The decrementing of the register value is done first, and then the address used, in the first case as the address of the operand, and in the second case as the address of the address of the operand.

Table 4.2. Encoding of Instructions for the PDP 11
Architecture.

Op Code	Function Performed
0 0 0 0	Single address and special function instructions
0 0 0 1	Move instruction
0 0 1 0	Compare instruction
0 0 1 1	Bit test instruction
0 1 0 0	Bit clear instruction
0 1 0 1	Bit set instruction
0 1 1 0	ADD2 instruction
0 1 1 1	Single address instructions
1 0 0 0	Single address and special function instructions
1 0 0 1	Move instruction (byte)
1 0 1 0	Compare instruction (byte)
1 0 1 1	Bit test instruction (byte)
1 1 0 0	Bit clear instruction (byte)
1 1 0 1	Bit set instruction (byte)
1 1 1 0	Subtract instruction
1 1 1 1	Special purpose instructions

Table 4.3. Encoding of Addressing Information
in the PDP 11 Architecture.

Addressing modes for PDP 11 operands

Addr bits		Addressing mode
0	0 0	Register direct
0	0 1	Register indirect
0	1 0	Register indirect — autoincrement
0	1 1	Two level indirect, autoincrement register
1	0 0	Register indirect — autodecrement
1	0 1	Two level indirect, autodecrement register
1	1 0	Indexed
1	1 1	Indexed indirect

Addressing modes when PC is target register

Addr bits		Addressing mode
0	1 0	Immediate mode
0	1 1	PC absolute mode
1	1 0	PC relative
1	1 1	PC relative, indirect

The index mode uses the specified register as an index, and a value from the instruction stream as the base. This information is coded as follows:

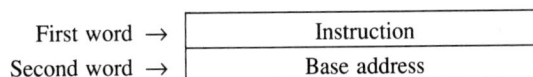

First word →	Instruction
Second word →	Base address

The address of the operand is the sum of the base address and the amount in the register. For the indexed indirect mode, the address resulting from the sum points not to the operand, but to the address of the operand.

Finally, the PC specific addressing modes all require a second value in the instruction stream. The first value is the instruction that identifies the appropriate PC addressing mode. The immediate mode is used to supply an operand directly from the instruction stream:

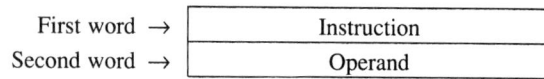

First word →	Instruction
Second word →	Operand

The PC absolute mode is used to specify an address directly in the instruction stream:

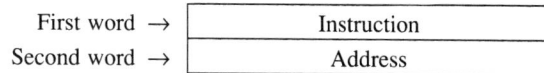

First word →	Instruction
Second word →	Address

The PC relative mode is also coded as above, but the address is relative to the PC (actual address is sum of PC and supplied address). The PC relative, indirect mode uses the same mechanism to identify the address of an operand, rather than the operand itself.

When DEC expanded on the ideas and concepts of the PDP 11 to create the VAX11 architecture, the capabilities of the address mechanism were also expanded. However, the same basic elements are utilized: direct and indirect addressing, indexing, and relative addresses. The number of registers was expanded to 16, and the bits identifying the different addressing modes expanded to 4, so specifying an address required 8 bits. The number of instructions has also been expanded, so that the list includes not only one and two address instructions, but three address instructions as well.

Example 4.7: Expanding op codes: The advances in semiconductor technology have allowed microprocessors to become more and more powerful. One of the 32-bit microprocessors is the NS32032, by National Semiconductor. Although the instruction set does not include three address instructions, it does have some interesting capabilities in the addressing mechanisms. How are the one and two address instructions encoded?

Some of the addressing formats for the NS32032 are shown in Figure 4.17. The processor has several different addressing modes, but the ones that concern us are one and two address formats. An interesting feature of the instruction set is that many of the instructions which are usually associated with a single address are two address instructions for the 32032. The single address instructions are used for functions like JUMP and JSR. The target location is identified by the use of the five address specifier bits. These allow 32 different addressing combinations, some of which use the eight general purpose registers in the processor. Included in the mechanisms are register direct, register relative, register indirect, two level indirect, immediate, absolute, stack, and indexed references. When a displacement or other constant is needed (constant for immediate values, addresses for memory locations), this value directly follows the instruction bits in the instruction stream. The size of an immediate value is determined by the instruction (byte, word, longword). However, an address displacement is composed of 1, 2, or 4 bytes, as shown in Figure 4.17. This allows storing in the instruction stream only the bits needed to identify the target address.

Single Address Format

15   11 10   7 6   2 1 0

| | | 1 1 1 1 1 | |

Address Specifier — Op Code — Oper Type

Double Address Format 1

15   11 10   7 6   2 1 0

Address Specifier 1 — Address Specifier 2 — Op Code — Oper Type

23   19 18   14 13   10 9 8 7   0

| | | | - 1 0 0 1 1 1 0 |

Address Specifier 1 — Address Specifier 2 — Op Code — Oper Type

Double Address Format 2

One Byte Displacement; Range: -64 to 63

7 6   0

| 0 | Displacement |

Two Byte Displacment; Range: -8192 to 8191

7 6 5   0

| 1 0 | MSB Displacement |
| LSB Displacement |

Four Byte Displacement; Range: as an Address: Entire Address Space; as a value: $+/- 2^{29}-1$

7 6 5   0

| 1 1 | MSB Displacement |
| |
| |
| LSB Displacement |

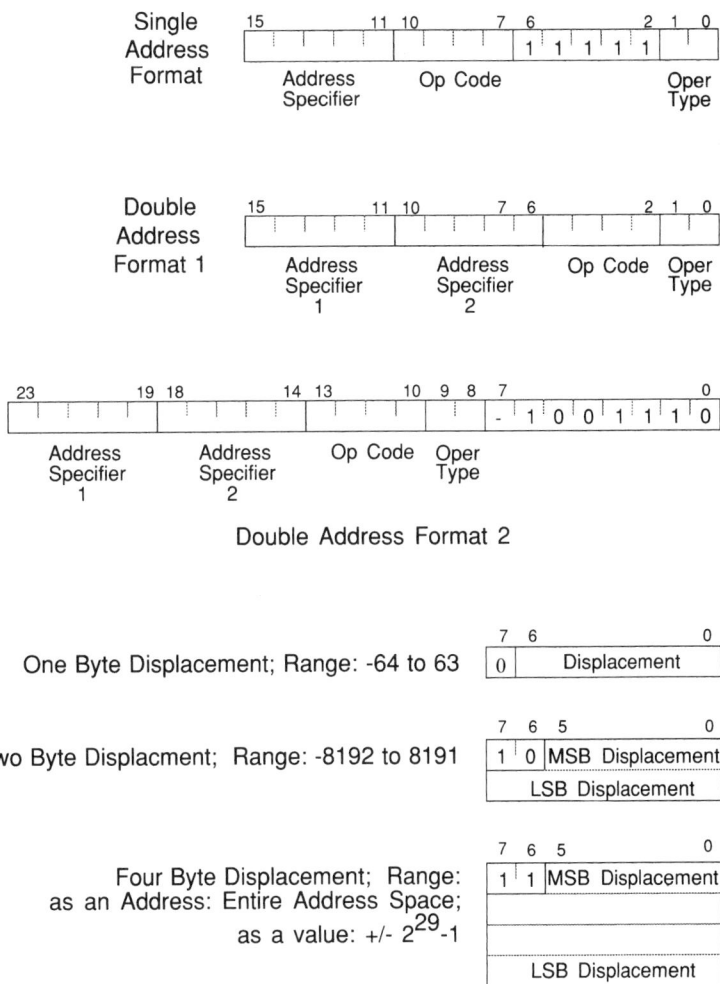

Figure 4.17. NS32032 Formats for Single and Double Operand Instructions.

As mentioned above, the two address format is used not only for adds and subtracts, but also for instructions traditionally considered single address instructions. Thus, the negate instruction extracts a value from one location, forms the negative value by subtracting it from zero, and then places the result, not back in the original location, but rather in a location identified by the destination address. Figure 4.17 includes two of the two address formats; the more often used instructions make use of the shorter format. These include add, subtract, compare, move, and others. The longer formats are used by instructions that do not occur as often, such as divide, test bit, shift, and absolute value. In the two address formats, all of the addressing modes are possible, allowing location of operands in both registers and memory.

The 32032 instruction set is a good example of the concept of the expanding op code. That is, the bits required to specify interaction expand to provide the necessary information. The shortest instructions occupy a single byte; more complex instructions can consume 3 bytes in instruction specification, then more bytes for index, address, and constant specifications.

Both the PDP 11 and the NS32032 provide examples of one and two address instruction sets, as well as providing real examples of a variety of addressing modes. The specification of a target address, whether for operand identification or for program control, can utilize a combination of the basic modes, as we have seen. The decisions involved in selecting the modes to include in an instruction set reflect the design philosophy of the system architects. The basis for those decisions is formed by the intended application, the resources available (time, power, chip area, etc.), and the targeted system goals. Before we examine some of those issues let us look at another approach: machines that use instructions with no address specification.

4.5. Zero Address Machines: the Use of Stacks

A stack is a last-in, first-out storage mechanism, where information is stacked up much like pieces of paper. The stack mechanisms described in the previous section are built in main store with appropriate instructions. However, it is also possible to do arithmetic with stacked values: an arithmetic operation is specified, and any needed operands are extracted from the stack. The result of the arithmetic operation is then placed on top of the stack. Because the operands are assumed to be located on the stack, no addresses are needed in the instruction to identify operand location. Hence, this type of system is called a zero address machine.

In addition to the arithmetic or logic instructions that actually cause work to occur, additional instructions are needed to push information onto the stack, and then to pop it off the stack when the arithmetic is finished. The operation of a stack system to do work is demonstrated by a simple example.

Example 4.8: Arithmetic with a stack: Consider the expression

$$F = A + (B \times C + D \times (E / F))$$

Give a set of stack-oriented instructions that will calculate the expression.

This could be done in several ways; we will mention two. These are listed below, assuming that the machine can perform push, pop, add, divide, and multiply operations.

PUSH A	PUSH E
PUSH B	PUSH F
PUSH C	DIV
MULT	PUSH D
PUSH D	MULT
PUSH E	PUSH B
PUSH F	PUSH C
DIV	MULT
MULT	ADD
ADD	PUSH A
ADD	ADD
POP F	POP F

Notice that the only instructions that require addresses are the push and pop instructions. All of the other instructions merely indicate the action to take place. In fact, some stack systems use push and pop instructions that do not require addresses, but rather use the value located on the top of the stack as the address of the target location of the instruction. The ADD instruction, for example, pops two values off of the stack and places on the top of the stack the sum of the two values. Another thing that needs to be pointed out is the depth of the stack. The major difference between the two solutions above is that the stack depth of the first solution (the maximum number of items on the stack) is 5, whereas the stack depth of the second solution is 3. The depth of the stack will have a direct impact on the speed of execution, depending on the implementation of the hardware.

Another thing that needs to be pointed out is that the instructions here will be best implemented if they are of variable length. Note that the push and pop instructions will need to be long enough to include the appropriate address bits, but the arithmetic instructions can be very short, since only action specification is required.

The use of a stack for implementing a variety of functions is very attractive in certain circumstances. The most obvious drawback is that the time required can be great because of moving data to and from the stack, especially since the stacks we have mentioned to this point have been constructed in main store. One solution to this is to construct a special hardware module that places the top elements of the stack in hardware registers. A block diagram of such a module is shown in Figure 4.18. The figure shows four hardware registers forming the top of the stack. Information to be placed on top of the stack (by instructions) comes from the memory, and information popped off of the stack flows to the memory through the memory interface. This module has the responsibility for maintaining the stack pointer and the transfer of information from the appropriate hardware register to/from memory. Organization of a hardware stack control system is an attempt to minimize the interaction with memory, since stack depths of up to four (for the system shown in Figure 4.18) needn't require interaction with memory (except as called for by the instructions being executed). The ALU is shown receiving input from the top two registers. This arrangement allows the ALU to perform needed arithmetic and place the result back on top of the stack, all in a single clock period. The stack control circuitry is then responsible for handling the flow of information within the stack, and between the hardware registers and the memory.

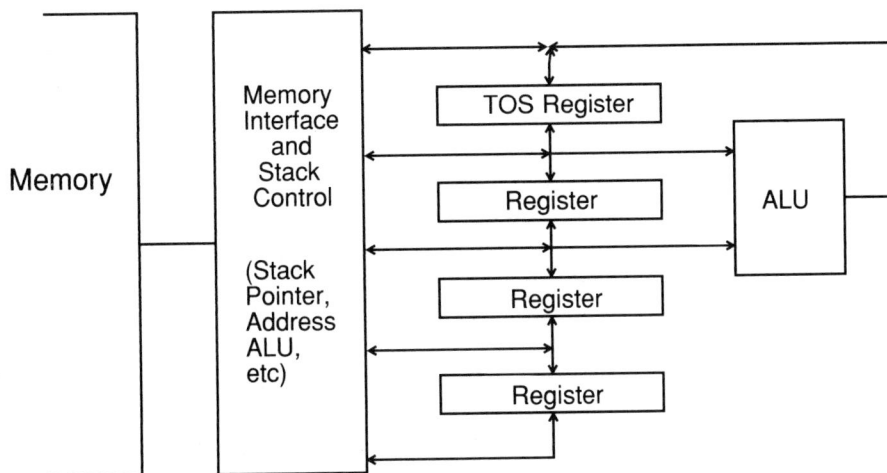

Figure 4.18. Block Diagram for a Hardware-Oriented Stack System.

The use of a stack system within a machine organization allows for some very useful capabilities. Stacks can be effectively utilized for some arithmetic capabilities and also for specific algorithms, such as optimization algorithms in compilers and other software systems. Another example of effective stack usage is parameter passing between routines, since operands needed for a subroutine can be placed on the stack, and then the subroutine is called. The code of the subroutine knows that the operands are located on the stack, so it performs the needed operations and places the results on the stack before returning control to the calling program.

However, there are some drawbacks to the use of the stack, such as saving results for further use. For example, consider the following expression:

$$A = B \times (C + D + E) - F \times (C + D)$$

The C + D portion of this statement can be used twice, and in a register machine this would be straightforward to accomplish. The method of doing this on a stack machine is not so obvious, since only items on the top of the stack can be used for calculations. However, this type of operation is very prevalent in most calculations that a machine will perform. Another operation used extensively in computations involves structured data (arrays, queues, etc.). A calculation like

$$ARRAY\_1[\,I\,] = ARRAY\_2[\,J\,] + ARRAY\_3[\,J + I\,]$$

which involves references into several arrays and address on array subscripts, is handled very naturally on a register machine with the various addressing modes already discussed. These manipulations are not easily accomplished on a pure stack machine. Because of the need to access information in situations such as this, most practical stack machines include capabilities not available in a pure stack machine. These include additional registers for addressing, such as index registers, as well as operand referencing with respect to the top of the stack. The ability to reference information held in the stack (but not at the top of the stack) adds capabilities that can be effectively utilized by a computer system. These various capabilities can allow stack machines to be used for many types of computations.

4.6. Program Control Instructions

The instructions dealt with thus far are instructions required to do work in machines, where work is defined as arithmetic or logic operations. These concepts will also apply to operations that are often not considered as part of the "computing" realm, such as editing or control processing. However, this is not a broad enough definition to cover all of the types of operations that of a machine. Calculation of values covers only one type of operation that computers must provide. In addition to computing, a machine must be able to make decisions, transfer information, and control devices. The instructions oriented toward input/output operations (I/O) will be dealt with in a later section; we now turn our attention to instructions used to control the program flow.

The area of program flow instructions can be divided into two general groups: instructions that change the flow of the program without side effects, and instructions that modify the program counter and also cause additional operations to occur. Examples of the first type of instruction are conditional and unconditional branches, while the second type of instruction is exemplified by a subroutine call.

The simplest instructions to deal with are those that change the program flow without any side effects. As we have indicated by the RTL representations of instruction execution, the assumed address for the next instruction to execute identifies the location immediately following the current instruction. That is, normal program behavior calls for the program counter to be incremented from one instruction to the next. When the next instruction to execute is not the next one in the memory, then the program counter must be modified accordingly. The program counter must be changed to identify to the appropriate instruction to be fetched. We will follow the terminology used by many manufacturers that a program counter change that uses direct addressing mechanisms is called a jump, and a program counter change that identifies its target address as an offset from the current location (PC relative) is a branch.

The jump/branch instruction is very straightforward: the target address is identified, and the program counter is changed accordingly. The target address can be specified by combinations of the various addressing modes that we have already identified. The system operation changes somewhat when the branch is made conditional. In this situation, the contents of the PC at the completion of the branch instruction is dependent upon some system status condition or on some comparison identified by the instruction. The conditions may include the status bits contained within the status register of the machine; some arithmetic possibilities were identified in Sections 3.2 and 3.7. Other conditions found in status registers reflect the status, not of the arithmetic operations, but rather of the entire system. These include such information as interrupt information, errors and traps that have occurred, semaphores used in synchronizing system resources, and any other information that details the state of the system.

In the definition of the system architecture, the designers of the system must determine the information to be included in the status register, as well as the possible conditions that will be testable with the instructions defined in the instruction set. Two different examples of the approaches that can be taken are available in the VAX architecture (from Digital Equipment Corporation), and the MIPS architecture (from MIPS Computer Systems). Both systems include a 32-bit system status word; however, the information contained within the status word is different for both systems. The VAX status word contains bits that reflect arithmetic conditions, while the status register of the MIPS system does not contain results of arithmetic operations. The VAX system, which is an architecture based on a complex instruction set philosophy, has over 35 instructions to test various combinations of bits in the status register. The MIPS system, on the other hand, has eight conditional branch instructions, two of which compare two general purpose registers (equal, not equal), and the rest of which check conditions of a single register (equal to zero, not equal to zero, positive, etc.). The MIPS system is an example of the reduced instruction set approach to machine design, which we will discuss in Section 4.8.

Regardless of the type of instruction set architecture chosen for a particular system, if the proper conditions are satisfied, the PC contents are modified to allow the program to continue at an address identified by the instruction. If the conditions are not satisfied for modifying the program flow, then the program counter is incremented in the normal fashion and execution of the program continues with the next instruction in the normal order of execution. These program counter modification mechanisms are demonstrated by the following example.

Example 4.9: Jump and branch instructions in a PDP 11 type architecture:
In the PDP 11 architecture, jumps can use any of the appropriate addressing modes to identify the target address. Assuming that the target address is included in the instruction stream, give the RTL for a jump instruction. Also, give the RTL for an instruction that branches if the carry is set. The branch instruction on the PDP 11 encodes the target address as an offset from the PC, and 8 bits are included in the instruction to specify the offset. Since PDP 11 instructions must be on even word boundaries, the offset is multiplied by two before it is added to the PC.

The jump instruction required by the example must retrieve the target address from the instruction stream and move it to the PC. This can be accomplished as follows:

fetch:		*Go get the instruction*
	$PC \rightarrow MAR$	Address of instruction to MAR.
	$PC + 2 \rightarrow PC$	Bump PC to point to address.
	$M[MAR] \rightarrow MBR$	Retrieve instruction.
	$MBR \rightarrow IR$	And move to IR.
decode		*Control system figures out what to do*
execute:		*And begins the proper action:*
	$PC \rightarrow MAR$	Go get the target address.
	$M[MAR] \rightarrow MBR$	And put in MBR.
	$MBR \rightarrow PC$	This is actual modification of PC.

As seen by the RTL, this is a very simple instruction, and because of its simplicity it can be done relatively fast. Nevertheless, time is required for each of the steps. For the instruction mechanism shown in the example, two memory fetches are required, one for the instruction and one for the address. For that reason, the branch instruction is often a desirable alternative, since the target address is identified with respect to the PC, and the offset is included in the instruction. Consider the RTL for the instruction that branches if the carry is set:

fetch:		
	$PC \rightarrow MAR$	Address of branch instruction to MAR.
	$M[MAR] \rightarrow MBR$	Retrieve instruction.
	$MBR \rightarrow IR$	And move to IR.
decode		
execute:		
	if (carry == 1) {	Check the condition; if satisfied, then . . .
	$PC + (2 \times IR < 7:0 >) \rightarrow PC$	Next instruction is at target address.
	} else {	Also, $IR < 7:0 >$ is sign extended to 16 bits.
	$PC + 2 \rightarrow PC$	Change PC address if condition not true.
	}	

To perform the work of the instruction it is necessary to be able to selective execute the appropriate transfers. That is, the control section sets the PC to PC + 2 or to PC + offset depending on the appropriate condition, which in this case is the contents of the carry bit. The manner in which the arithmetic is done will be system-dependent; however, the logic required to increment the program counter will be available to be utilized as needed. See Figure 4.10 for an example of a system where a separate adder is used to add the appropriate length to the PC. Including a multiplexer to select either the instruction length of the offset, based on the selected condition, would permit the necessary decision to be made.

As the above example indicates, the instructions that modify the program counter do so in a manner that reflects the capabilities of the machine and the instruction set. The target address is identified, by whatever combinations of addressing modes are available, and the specified address is placed in the program counter. In the case of conditional execution, the necessary condition is tested, and then the appropriate action is taken. We have indicated a simple choice, where the program counter goes to the next instruction or to a different target address. However, more complicated mechanisms can be set up in a system. For example, one minicomputer used a three-way branch for its arithmetic tests: three target addresses followed an arithmetic conditional branch instruction. A different target address was used for the greater than, equal to, and less than arithmetic conditions.

The above example also contains an anomaly when compared to other RTL descriptions of instructions included in this chapter. The fetch portion of the conditional branch did not include incrementing the program counter to point to the next instruction. Historically, the modification of the program counter to identify the location of the next instruction has been done in the fetch portion of the instruction. For example, many 16-bit computers configure all instructions to occupy one 16-bit word. Then, in the fetch portion of an instruction the program counter is incremented by two bytes. If the instruction needs an immediate value or an address in its execution, the PC then points to this value, and the execution portion of the instruction will obtain this value and increment the PC accordingly. Thus, by the end of the instruction execution, the PC does indeed point to the next instruction to execute.

The conditional mechanisms provided in instruction sets reflect the intended use of the systems. For example, some instruction sets will contain a dedicated CASE instruction (see the NS32000 system) that facilitates decisions requiring a multiway branch capability. Other systems will use combinations of instructions to perform this function. Another example is the use of a special LOOP instruction, such as used in the I80X86 system, to simplify implementation of loops. This instruction decrements a register and branches to a target address unless the result of the decrement is zero.

In the definition of a computer system, the system architect must decide the mechanism for PC relative references, and then maintain consistency in the application of the methods to all instructions. One of the most natural mechanisms is to identify the offset from the address of the instruction itself for all PC relative references, both references for additional values obtained from the instruction stream and references for other locations with an address that is specified with respect to the PC. One mechanism used to implement this technique (address specification from instruction address) is to delay updating the PC until the end of the instruction. Otherwise, some other method must be utilized to adjust the references made during instruction execution to account for the continued incrementing of the PC. A different approach is to make all PC-relative references made with respect to the contents of the PC as it adjusts itself during the execution of the instruction. The two approaches result in different hardware requirements, with a corresponding difference in programming techniques. Whatever mechanism is selected, the resources of the system (address adders, registers, data paths, etc.) must be used in a reasonable fashion to obtain the desired results.

While the PC modification instructions are relatively simple, the extension of the ideas to linkage instructions brings additional complications. The basic requirement is that the program flow is changed in such a way that control transfers to another routine, a subroutine, in such a way that program flow can return to the point of departure having accomplished some useful function. The machine then executes the code that follows the subroutine call. The method of accomplishing the subroutine linkage can be very simple or quite complicated. To transfer control in a reasonable fashion, we must create a mechanism that will cause the program counter to change so that instructions are fetched from the subroutine. At the same time, the linkage mechanism must provide a way to return to the calling routine. There are a number of methods which are used to provide this facility; we will describe three.

One subroutine calling sequence used by a few machines in the mid-1960s is to have the subroutine itself remember from which address it was called. The PDP 8, a 12-bit machine, used the first location of the subroutine to store the return address. The action would then proceed somewhat like:

fetch:

$PC \to MAR$	Start instruction.
$PC + 1 \to PC$	Bump PC to point at next instruction.
$M[MAR] \to MBR$	Get instruction from memory.
$MBR \to IR$	And transfer to IR.

decode

execute:

$IR \to MAR$	This assumes address contained in instruction.
$PC \to M[MAR]$	Put return address in first location of subroutine.
$IR \to PC$	Now put same address in PC.
$PC + 1 \to PC$	And bump it to point to next location, which is actually the first instruction of the subroutine.

At the completion of the transfers outlined above, program execution proceeds in the new routine. The address required to return to the original (calling) code has been stored in memory with the subroutine. The return from this subroutine mechanism is accomplished with an indirect jump. That is, the target of the jump is the address stored at the beginning of the subroutine. The last instruction of the subroutine identifies the first location of the subroutine, fetches the address stored there, and jumps to that address. The RTL for this action would be:

fetch:

$PC \to MAR$	Get the instruction.
$PC + 1 \to PC$	Bump PC; this value not actually used.
$M[MAR] \to MBR$	Get instruction (which is a jump) from memory.
$MBR \to IR$	And transfer to IR.

decode

execute:

$IR \to MAR$	This assumes address contained in instruction. Address identifies first location of subroutine.
$M[MAR] \to MAR$	Get return address from first location of subroutine.
$M[MAR] \to PC$	Which is actually address to return to; put in PC and program continues at instruction after subroutine call.

This type of subroutine linkage does indeed work, but it has some inherent problems. One problem is the implementation of reentrant code, or subroutines with recursion. Since the return address is stored in a specific location in memory, only one calling routine can utilize the subroutine at any one time.

Thus, a system with more than one user (such as a time-sharing system) would be unable to share code between users. Likewise, a subroutine could not call itself, since in the process of doing so the return address to the original call would be destroyed. Another problem encountered with this mechanism is that the technique does not work in systems that store the programs in read only memory (ROM). And since microprocessors make extensive use of ROM for storing programs this method is particularly unattractive for those systems.

A second type of subroutine linkage involves storing the return address in a general purpose register. Instead of copying the updated program counter (which identifies the instruction after the subroutine call) to a location in memory, it is saved in a general purpose register. This solves the memory and reentrant problems, but not the recursion problem. It does provide a more rapid linkage mechanism. That is, since references to memory are not required to store and retrieve the address, the time required for both the call and the return will be proportionately less. This is the mechanism used by the Texas Instruments 9900 architecture, where the branch and link instruction (BL) places the return address into general register 11. A similar mechanism is used by some instructions in the IBM 370 system.

Perhaps the most extensively utilized method for subroutine linkage is the use of a subroutine stack. Systems that use this method will have a register designated as the stack pointer, which will control a stack in the memory of the machine. A subroutine call will push the return address onto this stack. The return reverses the process, popping the address from the stack to the program counter. This method is very attractive from several aspects, since it provides a solution to the problems identified earlier. The stack is built in memory, which need not be shared with the program, so the program can be in ROM while the stack is in RAM. When multiple users are executing programs on a single computer, then each user will have a private stack space and can share a single copy of the code. Since each call to a routine will push a new return address onto the stack, recursive routines can be utilized as well. For these reasons, the stack method for establishing subroutine linkage is used by many systems.

Example 4.10: Subroutine linkage: The 68020 instruction set architecture has eight data registers $(D_0 - D_7)$ and eight address registers $(A_0 - A_7)$, to which users have access, one of which (A_7) is considered the stack pointer. In addition, there is a program counter. Give an appropriate RTL for the JSR (jump subroutine) instruction, assuming an address register indirect, relative addressing mode to identify the location of the subroutine. Also give an RTL for the RTS (return from subroutine) instruction.

This subroutine linkage instruction mechanism is very straightforward. Note that the following RTL is not necessarily accurate if the 68020 is considered in detail, since that processor has a pipelined implementation that increases the complexity of the system. However, as far as the user is concerned, the action of the JSR instruction can be considered as shown in the RTL included in Figure 4.19.

Notice that since the 68000 series processors utilize a stack that grows down in memory, the adjusting of the stack pointer to put information on the stack is to decrement it; the proper value is then placed at this address. At the end of the operation the SP is pointing at the value at the top of the stack. The address register on the 68020 is 32 bits long, so the SP must be decremented by 4 since the addresses of the system are byte addresses. To pop information off of the stack, the value is first removed, then the stack

RTL for JSR (Jump to Subroutine) Instruction

fetch:		
PC	→ MAR	Start fetch of instruction.
PC + 2	→ PC	All 68000 instructions start with 2 bytes. So point to next value to be fetched.
M [MAR]	→ MBR	Get the JSR instruction from memory.
MBR	→ IR	And transfer to IR.
decode		*This must identify addressing mode, etc.*
execute:		
PC	→ MAR	Since addressing mode needs value from instruction stream.
M [MAR]	→ Temp	Get the value and store temporarily.
PC + 2	→ PC	Bump PC by 2 to identify return address.
SP – 4	→ SP	Get stack pointer ready for new addition to stack.
SP	→ MAR	Set up MAR to identify memory location for return address.
PC	→ M [MAR]	And push PC, which has return address, onto stack.
Temp + A_N	→ PC	Now put address of subroutine in PC. Note that A_N is specified by instruction.

RTL for RTS (Return from Subroutine) Instruction

fetch:		
PC	→ MAR	Start fetch of the return instruction.
PC + 2	→ PC	All 68000 instructions start with 2 bytes.
M [MAR]	→ MBR	Get the RTS instruction from memory.
MBR	→ IR	Transfer to IR.
decode		
execute:		
SP	→ MAR	Identify memory location where return address is stored.
M [MAR]	→ PC	This will be a 4-byte transfer.
SP + 4	→ SP	Increment stack pointer to point at next value on stack and the action is completed.

Figure 4.19. RTL Implementations of Subroutine Linkage for a 68020 System.

pointer adjusted accordingly. One such implementation is also included in Figure 4.19. The call and the return, as demonstrated by the RTL of this example, implement a very simple but effective mechanism for linking calling routines with subroutines.

The mechanisms above for providing subroutine linkage control the flow of the instructions from one routine to another. But what has been ignored in the above discussion is the treatment of parameters being passed to and from a subroutine. Several techniques are used in different circumstances, each of which has its relative merits. Rather than discuss the implementation techniques and how they may be used by different language systems, let us discuss some of the instructions included in different machines to help with the problem.

The most obvious methods require no special instructions: leave the operand in a known place, like a register, and call the subroutine. When the subroutine has completed its work, leave the result in a known location and return to the calling routine. The complexities arise when the called routine wants to use general resources, such as registers, but leave those resources unchanged when control is returned to the calling routine. The subroutine can then copy the registers that it will use, do the work, then restore the registers and return. For this reason some instruction sets include special features to simplify this process. One example is the SAVE instruction of the NS32000 system, which pushes onto the stack copies of the selected registers. These can then be restored at the proper time with a RESTORE instruction that works in the reverse manner, popping values from the stack and placing them in the registers.

Another facility is provided by the LINK facility in the 68000 instruction set. Often when a routine is accessed, it is desirable to provide for it an area in memory for local variables. One way to accomplish this is to use some of the system stack for this purpose. The LINK instruction allocates space on the stack for the routine to use as needed. This stack space can be used not only for local variables, but also for parameter passing between the two routines. The values are accessed by indexing into the stack (with the indexing mechanism provided by the addressing modes) from the current stack pointer.

One of the more complicated mechanisms for linking routines is demonstrated by the CALLS instruction in the VAX architecture. This instruction uses the stack to pass arguments to a routine, with the assumption that the stack has already been modified to contain those arguments. The instruction then needs to know the number of arguments and the address of the target routine. The action of the CALLS instruction begins by pushing a number of arguments onto the stack. The location of the routine being accessed is identified; this could involve combinations of the addressing mechanisms already mentioned. The first 16 bits of the routine being called form an entry mask, which identifies the registers to be saved before the routine can be entered. The stack pointer (SP) is aligned to a 32-bit boundary, and those registers are pushed onto the stack, as well as the program counter (for return address), the frame pointer, and the argument pointer. Then two 32-bit values containing status and mask information are also placed on the stack. Finally, the new frame pointer and argument pointer are set up, and the program counter is set to the location after the entry mask, and control passed to that point. This mechanism performs the work of transferring control to the new routine and providing, via the stack, a parameter passing mechanism.

4.7. I/O, Interrupts, and Traps

The instructions investigated thus far have included mechanisms for doing work (arithmetic and logic instructions), mechanisms for passing information (moves, etc.), and mechanisms for controlling the work (program control instructions). One of the areas not mentioned is the transfer of information to and from external devices. This is generally called input/output processing (I/O), but involves more than transfer of data. Additional requirements include such things as testing of conditions and initiating action in an external device. Some of the I/O programming is in response to an external event signaling the processor that a device needs to be serviced. This signaling process is called an interrupt, and the processor responds to the interrupt in a predetermined fashion. Finally, traps serve much the same purpose as interrupts, but result from conditions detected internal to the processor.

I/O processing has evolved from the very simple capabilities of the first machines to sophisticated mechanisms used in some machines available today. In its simplest form, I/O transfers data to or from an addressed device under the direct control of the processor. This is called programmed I/O. In single address machines, the data is moved from/to the accumulator. For example, the PDP 8 instruction set has input and output instructions that identify one of 64 devices.

Having selected the appropriate device, the system can transfer information in the ACC to the device, information from the device to the ACC, or test a condition in the device. The conditional instruction is similar to the conditional branches already discussed: the order of instruction execution is modified if the proper conditions are met.

This concept of having specific instructions for input and output has continued, and some microprocessors include an additional control signal to indicate that the address appearing on the address lines is to identify an I/O device address, rather than a memory address. However, another technique, called memory mapped I/O, is perhaps more widely utilized. With this method, I/O devices are assigned specific locations in the address space of the processor, and any access to that address actually results in an I/O transfer of some kind. The memory mapped I/O scheme has the advantage that no special I/O instructions are required in the instruction set, and this reduces the complexity of the instruction decode mechanism. In addition, devices attached to the processor need not decode special signals to differentiate between memory and I/O requests. However, the fact that I/O instructions are included in an instruction set does not prevent the use of memory mapped I/O techniques in a system. The user of the system can decide which technique would be most appropriate for the goals of that particular implementation.

We will identify specific I/O functions and methods in Chapter 6. But as far as the instruction set architecture is concerned, the important point is that the system be capable of transferring information to and from devices attached to the processor. This can be data or status information, and can be used in calculations and decisions in the same manner as other data/status information within the system. Consider the following simple example of a transfer method.

Example 4.11: Memory mapped I/O: A 16-bit computer system that uses the memory mapped I/O scheme has been configured so that the addresses $FFE0_{16}$ and $FFE1_{16}$, are assigned to a simple I/O device. The status of this device is obtained by reading $FFE0_{16}$. The least significant bit is set whenever the device is ready to accept a value, which can be written to the address $FFE1_{16}$. The second bit is set whenever the device has data that the processor can read. This data is obtained by reading address $FFE1_{16}$. Create an appropriate code segment to move data from the array DATA_OUT to the device, at the same time accepting data from the device and putting it in the array DATA_IN. Assume that the operation will finish when the last value of DATA_OUT has been transferred.

The actual code for this example would depend on the instructions in the system, but the point here is to use the memory mapped capabilities to do the desired work. The code must check to see what data transfers are possible and perform them:

```
        MOVE #length, R0       Put the number of transfers in R0.
        MOVE #FFE0, R1         Move the status address to a register.
        MOVE #FFE1, R2         And the data address.
        MOVE #<datain>, R3     Fill R3 with address of input area.
        MOVE #<dataout>, R4    Fill R4 with address of output area.
loop:   MOVE *R1,R5            The MOVE sets status bits according to value
        JZERO loop                transferred; back to loop if it's zero.
        AND #1,R5             If it's not zero, is the LSB set?
```

	JZERO output	If LSB not 1, must be ready for output.
	MOVE *R2, *R3+	This is input function.
	BRANCH loop	Now go back and check again.
output:	MOVE *R4+, *R2	This outputs one value (and inc's address).
	DECREMENT R0	Now are we done? Decrement R0, and if the
	JNZERO loop	result is not zero, go back and try again.
	instruction	Otherwise, we this is the next instruction.

This code will cause the machine to poll the I/O device until either the device has information for the system, or the I/O device can accept data from the system. The polling is done by reading the status register of the I/O device, which is available at address $FFE0_{16}$. When the status register indicates that transfers can occur, they are performed by writing/reading the appropriate memory location.

The above example identifies one method by which information can be transferred between a processor and a peripheral device. However, the polling mechanism demonstrated by the code is extremely inefficient in many circumstances. For example, if the processor issued a command to a tape drive to seek a particular file on a tape, a very long time will pass between issuing the request and having the device respond with the desired results. With the polling technique, the capabilities of the system are not available for anything else during the seek time. Therefore, it is more efficient to have the I/O device send a signal to the system when the action of a command (in this case the seek action) has been completed. This signal is an interrupt, and it signals the processor to interrupt its current action and do something. What the system should do when it responds to an interrupt is defined in a routine called an interrupt service routine. The behavior of the system when responding to an interrupt is identical in many respects with the action of calling a subroutine. Thus, the instructions dealing with interrupts mimic the instructions involved in subroutine linkage.

One of the most basic requirements of the system with respect to the interrupt facility is the ability to enable or disable interrupts. This action is provided in some systems by including two specific instructions: one to turn on the interrupt facility, and one to turn it off. This function can also be handled by a bit (often called the interrupt enable bit) in the status/control register of the system. This bit is set and cleared by the logic instructions of the system.

If the interrupt capability of the system is enabled, the interrupt facility is checked at the end of each instruction. If an interrupt is pending, the appropriate action is taken. If the conditions are such that the interrupt should be recognized, then the system responds by causing execution of the interrupt sequence. If the interrupt conditions are not met, then the request is ignored. The "conditions" range from the simple to the complex. In some extremely simple systems, all interrupting devices activate the same control line, so there is no way of differentiating (in hardware) what caused the interrupt. Hence, any interrupt will cause the interrupt sequence to be initiated. Another method is to group interrupting devices into levels, and to prevent interrupts below a specified level from being recognized. A system with this ability may prevent interrupts from devices of a lower priority from being handled until the action required by a higher priority device has been completed. Another method is to individually control the interrupt ability of I/O devices. Thus, before an interrupt can be recognized, both the system level interrupt and the device level interrupt facilities must be enabled.

The interrupt acknowledge sequence is identified by the system architect when the design is specified. One interrupt sequence is to do an automatic subroutine call with a predefined target address. The subroutine, which is the interrupt handling routine, is then responsible for disabling further interrupts, saving whatever information is needed, and then doing the work. When the interrupt service routine has completed the action needed by the interrupting device, then the system reenables the interrupt, and returns to the program where the execution was active when the interrupt occurred.

The desired behavior is for the interrupt action to be invisible, except for the time required by the interrupt service routine. That is, the state of the machine should be the same directly after the interrupt has been serviced as it was before the interrupt occurred. The state of the machine refers to the contents of all of the appropriate registers, both general purpose and special registers. For this reason, the information saved by the interrupt action must include all registers altered by the interrupt service routine. These will be restored in the process of returning to the interrupted program. For example, when the 6800 microprocessor recognizes an interrupt, the accumulators (there are two), the program counter, and the status register are all pushed to the stack. The RET instruction restores all of these values and continues execution. Other systems respond in a similar fashion, storing a sufficient amount of state information to return to normal programming at the end of the interrupt service routine.

If one address is specified for all interrupts in the system, then the interrupt service routine does not have a sufficient amount of information to identify which of the possible interrupting devices actually is requesting attention. Therefore, the routine must poll all appropriate devices to ascertain which one needs service. A more time-efficient mechanism is to ask the devices to identify themselves so that a specific routine can be accessed. This is called a vectored interrupt, and is implemented in a variety of ways. One is to have an interrupting device supply the address at which the interrupt service routine will be located. This is the method used in UNIBUS devices: a special interrupt acknowledge bus cycle requests the address from the applicable device, and obtains from that address the address of the interrupt service routine (one level of indirection) and a new status word.

A similar mechanism for vectored interrupts is used by a variety of microprocessors. The technique calls for a number of interrupt levels, and to each level is assigned a device or number of devices. Within the memory of the processor is created a table containing the address of the interrupt service routine for each level. An interrupt is requested by asserting the lines to indicate the appropriate level, and the processor automatically extracts the corresponding address from the table. With this technique, if several devices have the same priority level, then the interrupt service routine must use an additional information mechanism, such as polling, to find the device that actually requested the service.

The interrupt mechanism is very useful for handling any event that needs service. The above discussion deals with external interrupts, such as a disk or tape drive interacting with the processor. But the same kinds of information are needed for exception conditions that occur during the execution of a program. For example, if an overflow or similar arithmetic problem occurred during the execution of a program, the system must deal with it in a reasonable fashion. One way is to ignore it, which requires no additional facilities. Another way is to allow the system hardware to cause an interrupt in the same manner as a disk drive. This is called a trap or exception, and is used for a variety of functions, as demonstrated by the following example.

Example 4.12: Interrupt mechanisms: The instruction set architecture for the 68020 is given in Figure 4.20. What is the interrupt mechanism for this device? What traps are established in the system that also use this mechanism?

The figure indicates that the system can function at two levels, the user level and the system level. The user is prevented from accessing some of the registers of the device, whereas the system does have access to all the user registers and those that have a direct impact on the system operation. Of particular interest for this example is the treatment of the status register. The user has access to the condition codes (extend, negative, zero, overflow, carry), but not the other portions of the status register. The user cannot influence the 3 bits comprising the interrupt mask. The system establishes the interrupt level by setting the 3 bits to the desired level. At the end of each instruction the three interrupt lines of the processor are checked to see if they form a number that indicates a high enough priority level to request an interrupt. If no interrupt is pending, or if the pending interrupt is not of sufficient priority to request attention, then the next instruction is fetched and processing continues. However, if an interrupt of sufficiently high priority is pending, then several things happen to begin the appropriate processing. The status register is copied so that it can be restored when the interrupt processing is complete. The system state is changed to supervisor mode. The interrupt mask level is set to the level that caused the interrupt, so that interrupt requests of the same (or lower) priority are ignored until the current one is completed. The processor requests a vector number from the interrupting device; the vector number is obtained on the data bus. This will be used to obtain the address of the interrupt service routine from the exception vector table shown in Table 4.4. After obtaining the interrupt number, the current processor context is saved. This is done by pushing onto the active supervisor stack an exception stack frame, whose format is shown in Figure 4.21. The figure shows the information in a 16-bit configuration, but the processor, which is capable of 32-bit transfers, will use the wider data transfers as much as possible to speed up the process. The status register used is the copy of the status register made at the initiation of interrupt processing. The program counter is the 32-bit address of the next instruction to execute. The vector offset is the offset value (interrupt number $\times$ 4) that will be used to identify the address of the interrupt service routine. And the additional state information contains other system registers and information. This will vary from 0 to 42 words, depending on the interrupt that initiated the action. (For further details, refer to the device specification.) Under certain circumstances, an additional exception stack frame will be created on the interrupt stack. Finally, the address of the interrupt service routine will be obtained by adding the offset value to the contents of the vector base register. At that location is the address of the interrupt service routine. Processing continues at that location.

As can be seen from Table 4.4, addresses are maintained in the exception vector table for both user-defined interrupts and system traps. If the floating point unit detects an underflow, for example, the interrupt sequence for interrupt number 51 is initiated. Regardless of the source of the interrupt, when the service routine has completed the necessary processing, control is returned to the controlling program by the RTE (Return from exception) instruction, which pops the appropriate information off of the stack and restores it to the appropriate registers. The format bits shown in

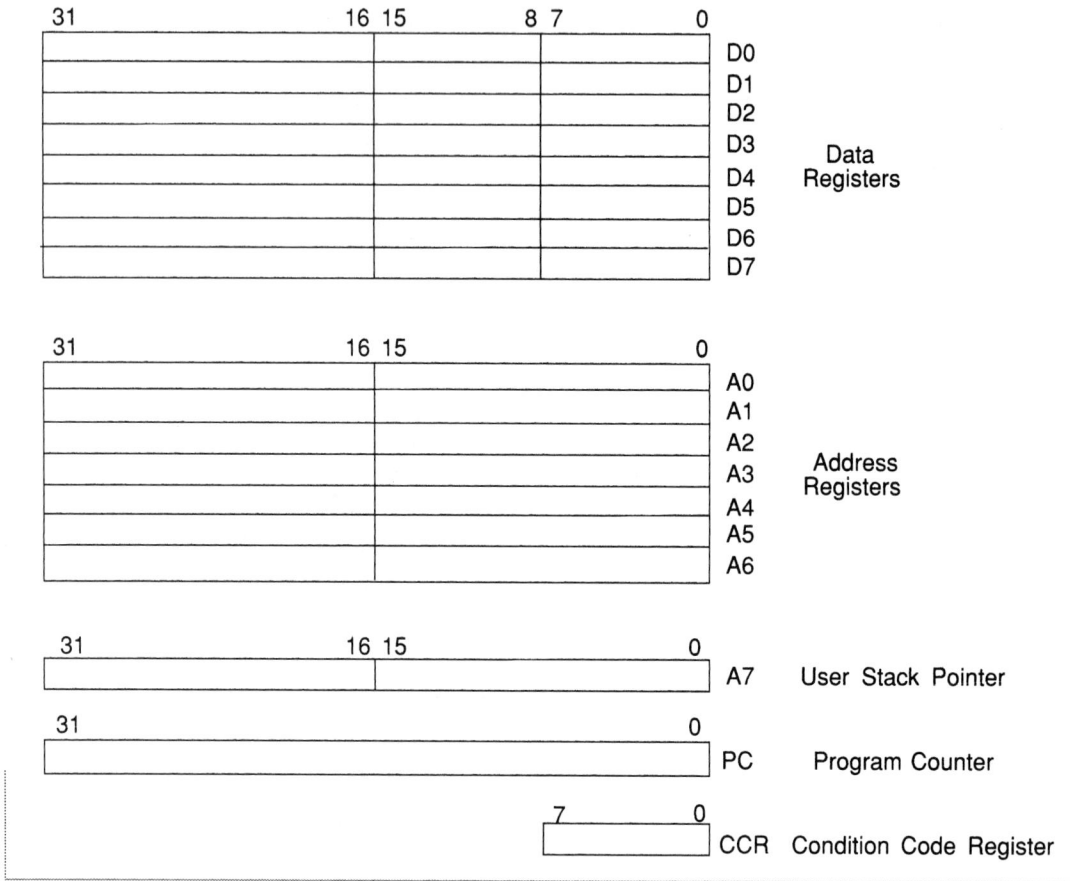

User Accessible Registers

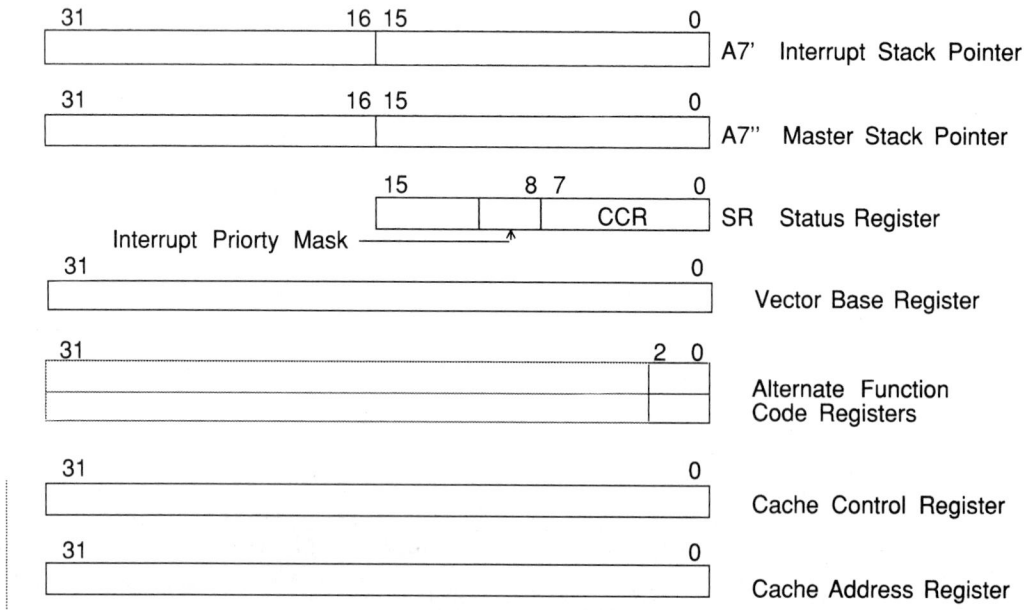

System Accessible Registers

Figure 4.20. Instruction Set Architecture for the 68020.

Table 4.4. Exception Vector Assignments for the 68020.

Vector Number	Vector Offset		Assignment
	Hex	Space	
0	000	SP	Reset: initial interrupt stack pointer
1	004	SP	Reset: initial program counter
2	008	SD	Bus error
3	00C	SD	Address error
4	010	SD	Illegal instruction
5	014	SD	Zero divide
6	018	SD	CHK, CHK2 instruction
7	01C	SD	ccTRAPcc, TRAPcc, TRAPV instructions
8	020	SD	Privilege violation
9	024	SD	Trace
10	028	SD	Line 1010 emulator
11	02C	SD	Line 1111 emulator
12	030	SD	Unassigned, reserved
13	034	SD	Coprocessor protocol violation
14	038	SD	Format error
15	03C	SD	Uninitialized interrupt
16-23	040-05C		Unassigned, reserved
24	060	SD	Spurious interrupt
25	064	SD	Level 1 interrupt auto vector
26	068	SD	Level 2 interrupt auto vector
27	06C	SD	Level 3 interrupt auto vector
28	070	SD	Level 4 interrupt auto vector
29	074	SD	Level 5 interrupt auto vector
30	078	SD	Level 6 interrupt auto vector
31	07C	SD	Level 7 interrupt auto vector
32-47	080-0BC		TRAP #0-15 instruction vectors
48	0C0	SD	FPCP Branch or set on unordered condition
49	0C4	SD	FPCP Inexact result
50	0C8	SD	FPCP Divide by zero
51	0CC	SD	FPCP Underflow
52	0D0	SD	FPCP Operand error
53	0D4	SD	FPCP Overflow
54	0D8	SD	FPCP Signaling NAN
55	0DC	SD	Unassigned, reserved
56	0E0	SD	PMMU Configuration
57	0E4	SD	PMMU Illegal operation
58	0E8	SD	PMMU Access level violation
59-63	0EC-0FC	SD	Unassigned, reserved
64-255	100-3FC	SD	User-defined vectors

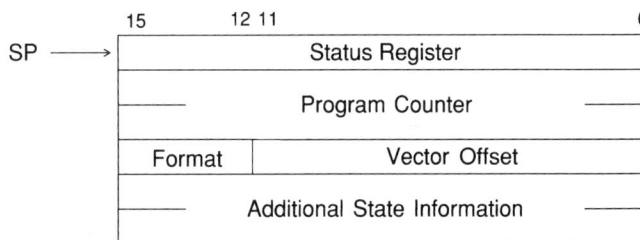

Figure 4.21. Exception Stack Frame of the 68020.

Figure 4.21 will indicate to the system the number of words in the additional state information, and the system can then restore them appropriately.

An important time in determining the efficiency of an interrupt system is the amount of time required to recognize an interrupt and return, without performing any work. The actual times will depend on the processor speed, the memory speed, and the state of the cache memory. However, a "normal" interrupt will require four 16-bit words, or at least two 32-bit transfers onto the stack, to save the state, then a memory transfer to obtain the address of the interrupt service routine, and a memory transfer to obtain the first instruction to execute. Thus, a minimum of four memory transactions are required to initiate an interrupt service routine. A minimum of two transfers (from the stack) is required to restore the system to functioning order, plus one to obtain the next instruction to execute. Additional times would be required for the other, nonmemory activities as well.

In this section we have seen that a processor requires the ability to communicate with external devices. This can be accomplished by using dedicated I/O instructions or by using the memory mapped I/O technique. In either case, the system hardware has the ability to transfer information to and from the external device. This can be data, or it can contain status and control information. However, for transfers involving large amounts of data, programmed I/O techniques are not always applicable, and some form of automatic transfers are used. These techniques, such as direct memory access (DMA), will be discussed in Chapter 6. When an I/O device has completed its assigned task, it often has the ability to signal the CPU that it needs attention, and this interrupt facility allows the processor to be doing other tasks while the I/O device is busy.

When interrupts are recognized by the processor, the CPU will save a sufficient amount of information to be able to return to what it was doing, and then transfer control to an interrupt service routine. This routine identifies the device that requested the service, and performs the necessary processing. The identification process can be taken care of by polling, by a vector mechanism, or by appropriate combinations of these techniques. When the interrupt processing is complete, the CPU can return to the original processing in much the same way that a subroutine is performed.

4.8. RISC vs. CISC: Instruction Set Strategies

To this point in this chapter we have identified different types of instructions and addressing mechanisms. One of the questions that must be addressed by a system architect concerns the number and type of instructions to be included in a specific computer system. One strategy is to include a large number of instruction types and addressing modes. A system of this type is called a complex instruction set computer (CISC). An alternative method is to reduce the complexity of the instruction set, and hence the reduce the logic required for the implementation of the system, including only the instructions needed for the desired application. A system of this type is called a reduced instruction set computer (RISC). In this section, we will examine some of the issues involved in the decision process, and some of the techniques that have evolved with the RISC machines.

The earliest machines were very simple in their architecture and implementation, both because experience with computing systems was nonexistent and because the technology of implementation mandated a simple machine. Thus, the language of the machine was correspondingly simple. However, users of the computers wanted to solve relatively complex problems, and these users described their problems in a language that treated variables and arithmetic at a higher level than the language of the machine. This resulted in what has become known as the semantic gap, which is the gap between the language of the machine and the language of the user. The languages of users (FORTRAN, Pascal, LISP, C, etc.) became more complex to represent increasingly more complex problems. In response to this trend, computers themselves became more complex, changing with the available technology and user demands for speed and versatility. The attempt was to reduce the semantic gap by creating more complex computing systems. This would enable users of computers to more effectively utilize the computational capabilities of the system.

Effective utilization of a computing system is accomplished by creating a suitable bridge for the semantic gap. The most common bridge is a compiler, which accepts as input a problem written in the language of a user, and creates as output a corresponding solution in the language of the machine. Complex instruction set computers seek to reduce the difficulty of the task of the compiler by making the instructions of the machine more closely conform to the instructions of the higher level language. Some systems [RiSm71, Ditz81] have been created in which a high level language is the native language of the processor, but this is not a general practice.

Observations of the behavior of programs executing on real machines provided some interesting insight into the operation of computers. These observations indicated that most of the time the computer was utilizing a small subset of all available instructions. Carrying this observation to the next logical step, system architects concluded that the system speed could be enhanced by including only the often used instructions, and by making them as fast as possible. This simplification of the instruction set and the implementation hardware results in a unit that can run faster. However, the more complex functions of a programming language must be accomplished with subroutines or with longer instruction sequences than corresponding CISC instruction sequences. The result is that a program may require more instructions to complete on a RISC machine than on a CISC machine, but the RISC instructions will, in general, have a higher execution rate.

The RISC approach, then, is to create a system that is simpler in architecture and faster in implementation than a CISC machine. With the simplicity comes the promise of speed, and with many implementations this promise is realized. However, care must be taken when comparing machines based on a rate of instructions per second, since the work accomplished by a RISC instruction will, in general, not be as great as the work accomplished by a CISC instruction.

The basic issue, which is treated differently by the RISC and CISC approaches, is one of resource utilization. How can the system resources be used most effectively? Different answers to this question are possible, based on the relative costs associated with the resources by the system architect.

The tenets of RISC architectures strive to maximize the speed and minimize the complexity of the implementation. Simplicity is the basis of both the architectural definition and the implementations. Some of the basic policies which are the result of this type of an architecture are a minimal number of instructions and addressing modes, fixed instruction formats, hardwired instruction decoding, single cycle execution of most instructions, and the use of a load/store type of organization.

Minimal number of instructions and addressing modes. By including only the instructions that are executed often, the system need not include seldom used features. The result is a smaller, faster system, that is capable of doing more instructions in a given amount of time than a CISC machine. The CISC machine, on the other hand, will specify more work in a single instruction. Thus, while the CISC instruction will take longer to complete, fewer such instructions are required to do the work of a high level task.

Fixed instruction formats. By restricting the format of the instructions, the tasks of the control system are simplified. In the *fetch-decode-execute* mechanism of stored program computers, the decode function must identify the work to be done. By causing all of the instructions to use the same format, then the decisions required of a decoder are minimized. For more complicated instructions, such as those of a CISC system, the decoder must first ascertain the length of the instruction, extract the necessary information from the instruction stream, and then finally specify the tasks needed to do the work. With fewer available choices and a restricted location for the specification information, the speed of the system is enhanced.

Hardwired instruction decoding. This characteristic accompanies the fixed instruction format idea, and can be useful for two different reasons. The first is that hardwared instruction decoding (using random logic to implement the decoding function) can, in general, be done more rapidly than the alternative mechanisms, such as microcoding. We will discuss different alternatives for the control system in the next chapter. Hardwired logic has traditionally been faster than memory based techniques, such as microcode. The early machines used this technique simply because the memory technology was not sufficiently fast to be attractive. However, the development time was longer because of the difficulty of generating correct logic for all conditions. When small, high speed memories became a reasonable alternative, then microcoded systems became attractive because of their regularity and versatility. The speed ratio of data memory and microcode memory has been steadily decreasing in recent years, so the use of microcode for speed is not as beneficial now as it was previously, although the use of microcode for versatility is still attractive. Thus, to enhance the speed of the control function, hardwired logic for instruction decode is a reasonable alternative. The increased use of computers as tools to aid in the design process has made this alternative viable, since the correctness of the design can be tested before the design is committed to hardware or silicon.

Single cycle execution of instructions. If a computer system can be so organized that one instruction is executed in each cycle, then by some standards maximum utilization of all system resources can be approached. Again, the technology plays a part in the decision process, limiting and shaping the types of things that can be done in a cycle time. As VLSI technology evolves, functions that once took many cycle times, such as floating point arithmetic, can now be done in a very short time. Thus, organizing the system to take advantage of this can be very beneficial. However, this limits some of the action of a system, since certain types of operations cannot be accomplished in a single cycle. For example, incrementing a value located in memory cannot be done in a single cycle, since the value must be obtained from memory, then updated, and then rewritten to memory. Hence, the instructions included in the system are all restricted to what can be accomplished in a single cycle. Some RISC systems deviate from this to allow certain instructions to take two (or more) cycles, which permits reuse of certain system resources, or allows for delays through logic that require more time than allowed in a single cycle.

Load/store memory organization. With a load/store memory system, the only instructions that deal with memory are those that load information into registers from memory or that store information from registers to memory. All arithmetic/logic instructions work with values in registers. By placing the operands of arithmetic/logic instructions in registers, the above stated objective of an instruction per cycle can be met. With this organization, the operands are readily available, and can be extracted as needed from the registers. No time is lost waiting for operands to be obtained from the data memory. However, separate instructions are required to move the information to the registers to be used. The RISC technique relies on the observation that in general information will be used several times before results are written to memory. The CISC technique, which does not restrict the location of the operands for the instructions, allows either the register intensive technique or memory-to-memory operations to be used.

In addition to the tenets listed above, the RISC architectures rely on effective utilization of additional architectural techniques such as pipelining, multiple data paths, and large register sets. These techniques are not strictly associated with RISC machines, but combining the techniques with the reduced instruction set ideas often results in a higher speed system. At this point we should hasten to add that not all RISC systems adhere to all of the tenets listed above, and that most available RISC systems violate at least one of them.

The basic concepts and ideas of pipelining are discussed in Chapter 8, so we will not elaborate on the RISC use of pipelines here. But one of the reasons that pipelining functions well for RISC machines is that the restricted operand placement for arithmetic/logic instructions minimizes pipeline delays for operand fetches. An operand required for execution of an instruction must be obtained by a pipeline before the operation can continue. If these operands are always restricted to fast registers, such as in the RISC case, then the delays associated with operand access are minimized. If the operand is in general purpose memory, such as in a CISC machine, then a relatively long time is required to obtain the information, which reduces apparent system speed.

The use of multiple data paths allows a greater amount of parallelism and concurrency to be used in the implementation of systems. This is evident in two areas, as seen by the block diagram for the Motorola 88000 RISC system, shown in Figure 4.22. The two areas identified in the figure are the multiple buses contained within the 88100 processor chip and the distinct instruction and data paths to memory.

The use of multiple buses internal to a processor allows transfer of multiple operands in any given cycle. In particular, two source operands can be provided to a functional unit, and a destination operand from a functional unit provided to the register file within a single cycle. This requires buffer registers within the functional units to hold the values while the buses are released to be used elsewhere. And the multiplicity of functional units increases the opportunities for parallel activity within the processor itself.

Providing different paths for both the instruction and data transfers allows those two functions to proceed simultaneously. This is necessary if the goal of one instruction per cycle is to be achieved. But by using this technique a new instruction can be made available in each cycle, regardless of the data transfers needed by the system. For arithmetic instructions, the data path to memory would not be needed. But for instructions that transfer information to and from memory, both ports would be used very efficiently.

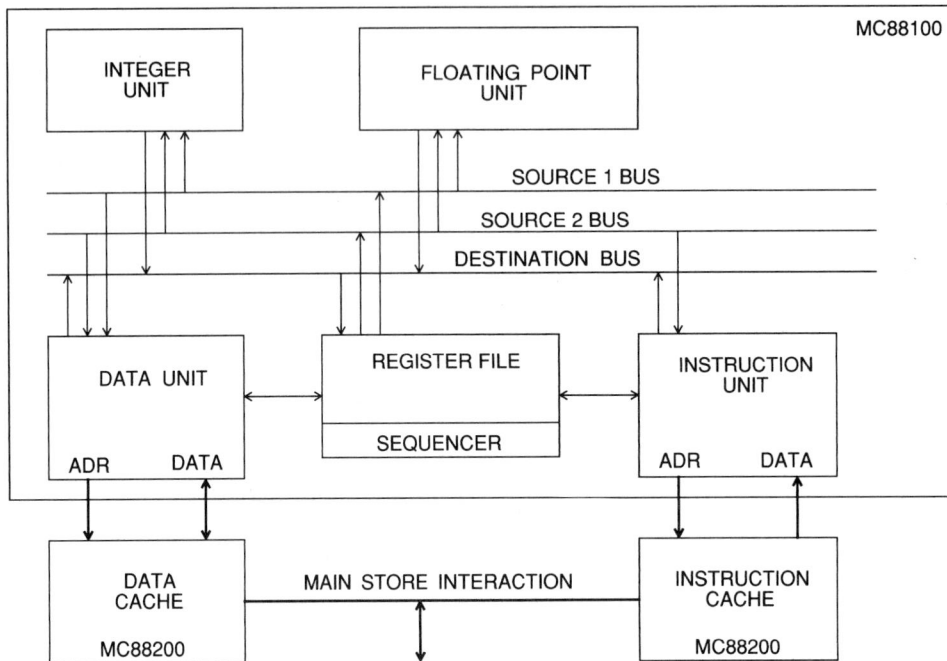

Figure 4.22. Motorola 88000 RISC system.

Like pipelining, the concept of multiple paths for information transfer is not limited to use in RISC systems. However, a system that follows the RISC concepts will be able to optimize the use of multiple information paths for enhanced system speed. The same is true of large register sets. This technique can be used in systems of any type. However, one of the techniques that has been linked with RISC systems, and that utilizes a large register set, is the use of register windows for parameter passing in subroutines.

By measuring the frequency of instruction execution, it has been observed that the process of calling and returning from subroutines consumes a large amount of processor time. In an effort to minimize this, the idea of using register windows on a large register set has been proposed. The basic idea is that many registers are included in the system, but that only a limited number of them are accessible by the system at any one time. This limited number of registers is identified as the "window" into the set of all registers. To change the window, a pointer that identifies the active registers is modified to specify a new set of active registers. When the windows overlap between routines, then parameters can be passed by placing them in the registers that are accessible by both routines. In this way, the memory transactions required for pushing parameters onto a stack, and then popping them off, are minimized. As long as the number of parameters is less than the register overlap, no memory transactions are required for passing of the parameters.

This technique was utilized by the architects of the RISC I system at the University of California at Berkeley, and their use of registers is shown in Figure 4.23. The instruction set uses 5 bits to specify registers to be used in an instruction. Thus, 32 different locations can be accessed. The first ten registers (R0–R9) are global registers, and are accessed by any routine, regardless of the number of subroutine calls. The remaining 22 registers are broken into three groups: the

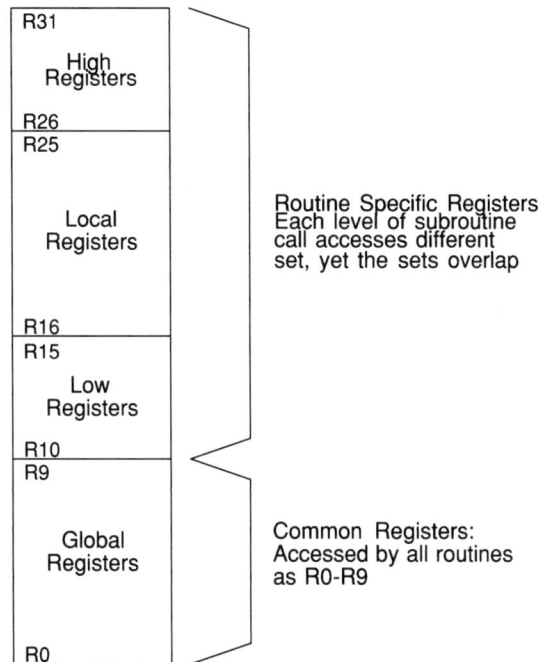

Figure 4.23. Register Use in RISC I.

high registers, the local registers, and the low registers. The high and low groups each contain six registers, while the local group contains 10 registers. Together these three groups form a routine specific set of registers. Thus, when a routine is accessing register storage, it will identify a value in either the global registers or the routine specific registers. It is then the responsibility of the system/user to use the registers in a coherent manner.

As mentioned above, one of the primary reasons for using register windows is for parameter passing in subroutines. When returning from or calling a subroutine, a pointer that identifies the location of the routine specific registers within the set of all registers is modified to point to the next set of routine specific registers. This modification is an increment/decrement by 16, which causes six of the registers to be shared between routines. With 22 registers in the routine specific set, this causes an overlap of six registers between the two routines. Any data to be exchanged between the two is merely left in an agreed-upon register by one routine, and the other routine knows where to obtain the information when it is needed.

This process of information exchange is graphically depicted in Figure 4.24. Only a portion of the overall register set is shown. If a program is executing Routine A, then the 32 registers to which it has access are the global register set (R0–R9) and the routine specific set which begins at location 90 in the register set. The routine specific registers for Routine A are referred to as R10 to R31 by instructions within the routine, but the system actually utilizes registers R90 to R111. Now assume that Routine A is going to call Routine B, and that it needs to pass two values. Routine A places the values in R10 and R11 (which are physically R90 and R91) and calls Routine B. The subroutine call identifies the address of Routine B; execution of the instruction changes the program counter, creates the appropriate return linkage, and decrements by 16 the pointer identifying the

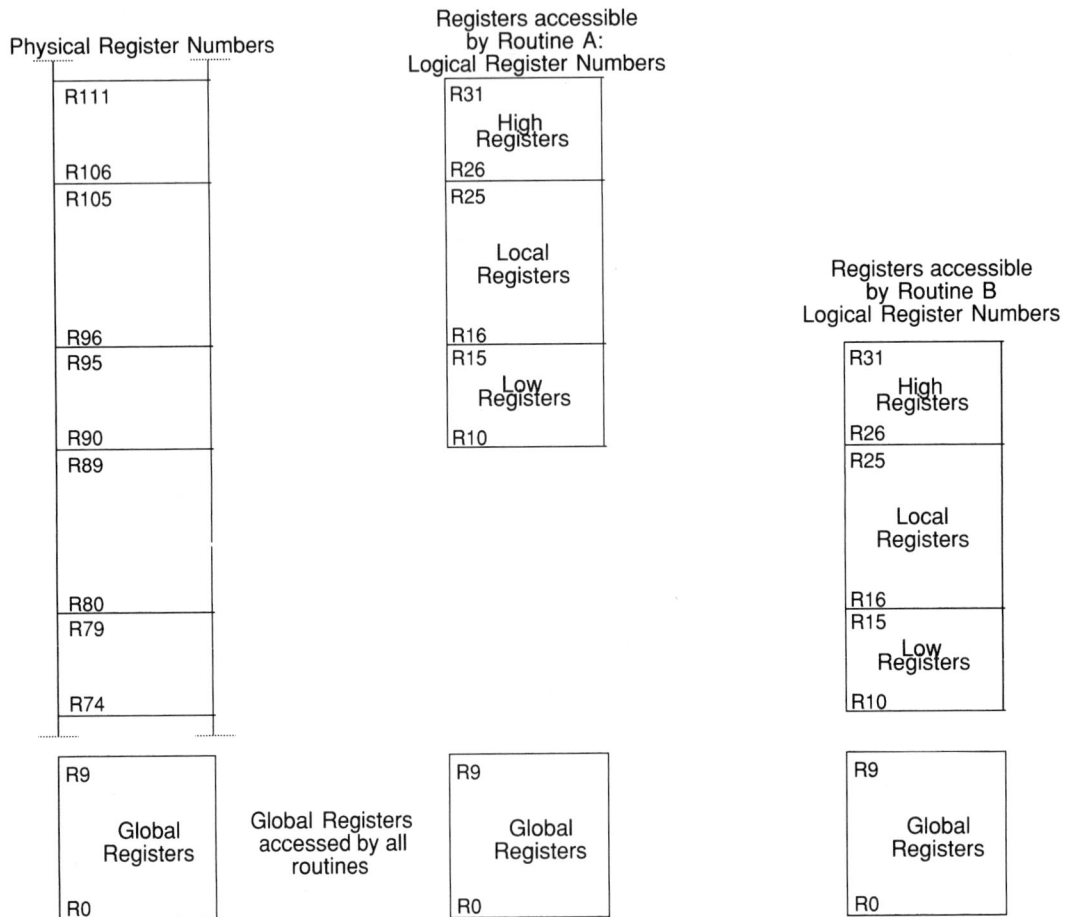

Physical Register Numbers

R111	
R106	
R105	
R96	
R95	
R90	
R89	
R80	
R79	
R74	

R9
Global Registers
R0

Registers accessible by Routine A: Logical Register Numbers

R31
High Registers
R26
R25
Local Registers
R16
R15
Low Registers
R10

Global Registers accessed by all routines

R9
Global Registers
R0

Registers accessible by Routine B Logical Register Numbers

R31
High Registers
R26
R25
Local Registers
R16
R15
Low Registers
R10

R9
Global Registers
R0

Figure 4.24. Parameter Passing with Register Windows.

routine specific set of registers. When Routine B needs the information passed to it, it will access R26 and R27 (which are physically R90 and R91). Parameters passed back to a calling routine will utilize the same technique, with Routine B leaving results in, say, R31 (physically R95) and returning control to Routine A. And Routine A obtains the value by accessing R15 (which is physically R95). Note that no special stack operations were involved to pass parameters; the parameter passing was accomplished by merely organizing the processing in such a way that, when the subroutine was called, the information to be passed was found in the overlapped register area.

The use of register windows allows parameters to be passed without memory intensive stack operations. A second benefit is that a subroutine need not save state before beginning actual work. In a "normal" machine, if a subroutine is going to modify eight of the general purpose registers, it will first save the contents of those registers (probably on the stack). Then, before returning to the calling routine, the registers can be restored to their previous value. These operations are not needed if register windows are used, since different physical registers are used for each routine specific set of registers. However, care must be taken to be sure that overlapped registers are used in a reasonable fashion.

The above technique will minimize the memory interactions needed for parameter passing and subroutine use of registers, but the technique incurs some different costs. One of the costs is the number of registers needed to store the information. Obviously, it would be ideal to have an infinite number of registers, but that is not a reasonable solution. The number of registers included is based upon the expected depth of subroutine calls. Studies of actual programs have shown that, for most applications, the nesting level of subroutines is on the order of eight. Including 144 registers would allow the above technique to have a subroutine call depth of eight before additional transfers would be needed. Obviously, if the nesting level exceeds eight, then a great many memory transfers would be required to save either the entire set of registers or some designated portion of it. As with other techniques, the idea of including register windows in a system is not solely a RISC concept, but rather a mechanism that can be utilized wherever it will result in an improved system.

The use of memory is another of the interesting aspects of RISC architectures that needs to be considered in a system. Memory technology has made rapid advances in both speed and size of available memory systems. In a time when memory systems were quite small by today's standards, the size of a program was a critical measure of the effectiveness of the system. However, as memories have become faster and larger, the need for having small programs has been reduced. In general, programs on a RISC machine will occupy a somewhat larger section of memory than similar programs on CISC machines, since more instructions are required to do the work. However, since memories are becoming increasingly larger, this is often not considered a drawback. Also, since the architecture attempts to minimize delays due to memory interaction (separate data/instruction paths, and register only arithmetic, for example), overall effect is to create a system that can do work faster.

The term RISC refers to an approach rather than to a specific system or set of requirements. For example, one of the tenets listed above is that a RISC system will use hardwired control, yet some computer systems advertise themselves to be RISC computers that utilize microcoded control systems. Real computer systems will range from units that adhere strictly to the RISC approach and simplify all aspects of the system, to units that follow the CISC approach and include highly complex capabilities. The "best" system will be the one that makes the most judicious use of system resources to solve the problem for which it is intended. And whether a RISC approach or a CISC approach is a better choice cannot be determined without applying appropriate metrics, and perhaps trying the systems in a real application.

4.9. Summary

We have discussed a number of mechanisms for doing work in computers, where work is defined as directing a CPU to perform a specific task. The work that a computer is capable of doing is defined by the set of instructions controlling the operation of the machine. The set of instructions of the system also identifies the apparent architecture of the system or the instruction set architecture. Implementations of the architecture may or may not contain all of the registers, functional units, and data paths alluded to in the instruction set architecture.

The structural aspect of the system — the functional units, data paths, and storage elements included in the machine — will determine the mechanisms needed to implement the instruction set architecture. When the structure of the system is known, then the internal transfers required to carry out the work of the instructions can be represented in a register transfer language.

Instructions that control the arithmetic and logic operations of a system can have a varying number of addresses, from zero address stack machines to three address systems capable of identifying both sources and destination of an operation. The choice of the instructions to be included in the system is made by the system architect after careful consideration of the application area of the machine and the utilization of available system resources to accomplish the required system objectives.

The use of registers for operand storage reduces the number of bits required to identify the location of information as well as the time required to obtain the information. Registers can also be used to effectively identify the location of values in a memory system.

Operands for instructions can be located in general purpose memory or in registers. The instruction set may contain multiple addressing modes to identify the location of the information. These include combinations of direct and indirect addressing, indexing, stack operations, and instruction stream accesses.

Program control instructions allow changing the flow of control in a program executing on the system. This change of flow can be unconditional or based on some status of the system. Also, routines can be called from within a program, and a return linkage established.

Interaction with devices external to the system is accomplished with I/O instructions, or I/O techniques like memory mapped I/O. These devices have the ability to signal the computer system, or "interrupt" the program flow, when interaction is needed. In addition, internal conditions, such as arithmetic overflows, can cause interrupts within the system.

The RISC approach to computer architecture is to simplify actions to a minimal set, and use high speed hardware and optimizing software techniques to create a system that will execute programs at a high speed.

The functional units of a computer system, the interconnection system, and the instruction set that controls the action of the system must be created with all of the above ideas in mind. The architecture that is most effective in a given application will make the most efficient use of system resources, where resources can be time, power, memory, or any of a number of other measurable quantities.

4.10. Problems

4.1 A general purpose computer system must have the ability to perform certain basic functions in order to do useful work. Three of the basic functions are store, load, and add.

a. Name four other basic functions that the computer must do.

b. Name four additional instructions that would be nice to have.

4.2 Consider a machine with the following characteristics:

It is a two address machine.

Subroutine linkage is through a stack mechanism, in main memory.

There are eight general purpose registers, plus other special purpose registers.

The machine is capable of absolute, indirect, base plus displacement, and general indexed addressing modes.

a. Give a block diagram showing the major components of the system and their interconnection. Include arrows indicating flow direction of the data.

b. Using the block diagram, give the RTL necessary for

ADD R1, R2
    Add the contents of register 1 to register 2
MOV *R1, *R2+
    Move the contents of memory stored at the location identified by R1 to the location identified by R2; then increment R2
CALL #A0F4
    Go to the subroutine located at address A04F; this address is stored in the location following the CALL instruction in the instruction stream.
RETURN
    Return to the calling routine from a subroutine.

4.3 One of the methods of evaluation for a machine is to determine its behavior for a program or program segment. Two of the basic computer methods discussed in this chapter are single address machines with a general purpose accumulator, and two address machines with a general register set. Create block diagrams for a single address machine and a machine with a general purpose register set. Then create assembly level code to implement the following statements:

$$\text{for (i = 0 ; i < 100 ; i++)}$$

$$\text{A[i] = B[i] * C[i];}$$

Use the code generated and contrast the two methods. In particular, identify the number of instructions executed, the number of memory references required, and the number of arithmetic operations. Which of the figures of merit is the most crucial? Why?

4.4 Use the technique of Problem 4.3 to compare a CISC machine approach to a RISC machine approach. That is, create block diagram representations for a CISC architecture and a RISC architecture. Then create code to implement the loop of Problem 4.3. Use the number of memory references, the number of register references, and the number of arithmetic operations to contrast the two methods.

4.5 You have been given the task of developing a single address computer to be utilized in general purpose applications. This machine is to be a 16-bit single address computer capable of direct and indirect addressing. Operands obtained via the direct addressing mode are identified by their position with respect to the PC, so the access method could be called PC relative. This permits programs to be located anywhere in the memory. The machine will have more than eight but less than 16 instructions requiring memory access.

a. Give a block diagram of a computer that will fit these requirements. Show all major registers, and all data paths, including the direction(s) of data flow on the data paths.

b. Propose a method for encoding the instruction information for the system. That is, what should the instruction format be in the 16 bits stored in the computer's memory.

c. Give the register transfer language steps required for the following instructions:

ADD (indirect addressing)

CLEAR

JUMP TO SUBROUTINE (direct addressing)

RETURN FROM SUBROUTINE

4.6 Computer Designers, Inc., has been contracted to design a special purpose computer with the following requirements (not a complete list): The machine will operate with a two address, register-oriented instruction set, with 16 general purpose registers. These registers are denoted R0–R15. The subroutine linkage is accomplished with a stack, R15 being the stack pointer. The program counter is R14. Operands (results) are obtained (deposited) either directly from (to) the registers or indirectly through the registers from (to) fast semiconductor memory. The memory space is 65,536 bytes. The indirect references can leave the pointer-register unchanged, increment it, or decrement it. The instruction set is composed of over 16 instructions, including ADD, SUBTRACT, INVERT, AND, OR, EX-OR, NEGATE, JUMP, JUMP-SUBROUTINE, RETURN, and INCREMENT.

a. Give a block diagram of the data path of the machine.

b. Give sufficient formats to accomplish the instructions (that is, however many formats are necessary: 1, 2, or more...).

c. Give an RTL description of ADD (with direct addressing of the operands), INVERT (use indirect, autoincrement mode to identify operand), JUMP-SUBROUTINE (use indirect addressing to identify location of subroutine), and RETURN.

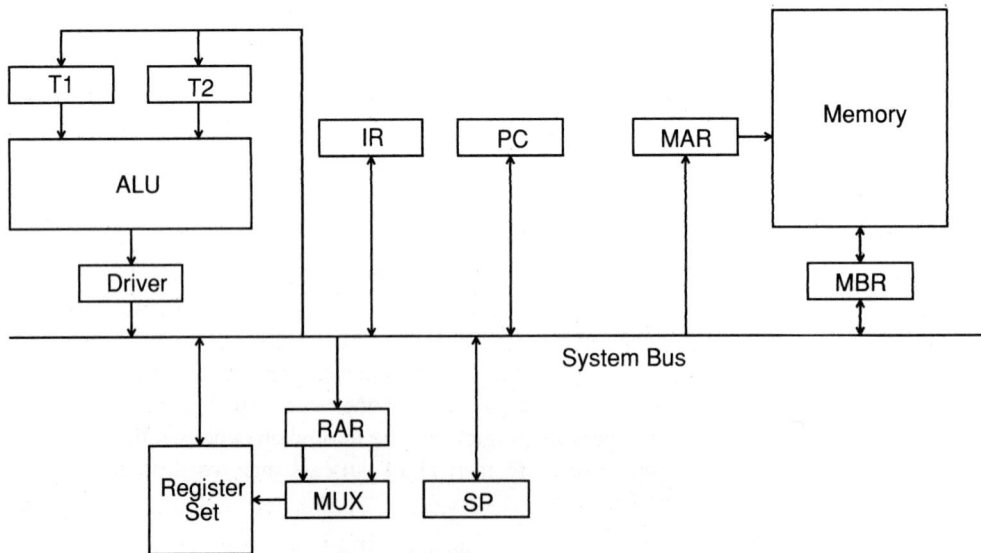

4.7 Consider the above block diagram of a 16-bit single bus system. The program counter (PC), stack pointer (SP), and instruction register (IR) are 16-bit registers capable of receiving information from and sourcing information to the general bus; the temporary registers (T1 & T2), the register address register (RAR), and the memory address register (MAR) are only capable of receiving information. The ALU can increment, decrement, invert, and add. The stack pointer identifies the next available location; stack grows to lower addresses in memory. The register memory contains 16 registers, and the main memory has 65,536 locations. The MUX on the RAR is to select either the source or destination register identification bits out of the 16-bit word loaded into the RAR. The machine has a two address instruction set with the following address modes: register, register indirect, register indirect autoincrement, immediate/absolute (absolute address is stored in next word of instruction), and program counter relative (used for jumps only; 8-bit displacement is stored in instruction word). Give the register transfer language statements for the following instructions: (operand order is Source, Destination)

a. ADD R1, *R2

b. SUBTRACT *R5+, #2A48

c. CLEAR R9

d. JUMP $-9

e. GOSUB #9BA4

4.8 For the block diagram of Figure 4.10, give the RTL representation for

a. JUMP INDIRECT <52>

52 is stored in location following jump in instruction stream. Use contents of memory location 52 as target of jump.

b. ADD R1, *R3

Add the contents of register 1 to the location in memory identified by register 3

c. JUMP TO SUBROUTINE 145

Transfer control to a subroutine located at address 145. This address is stored in the memory location following the instruction in the instruction stream.

d. INCREMENT R7

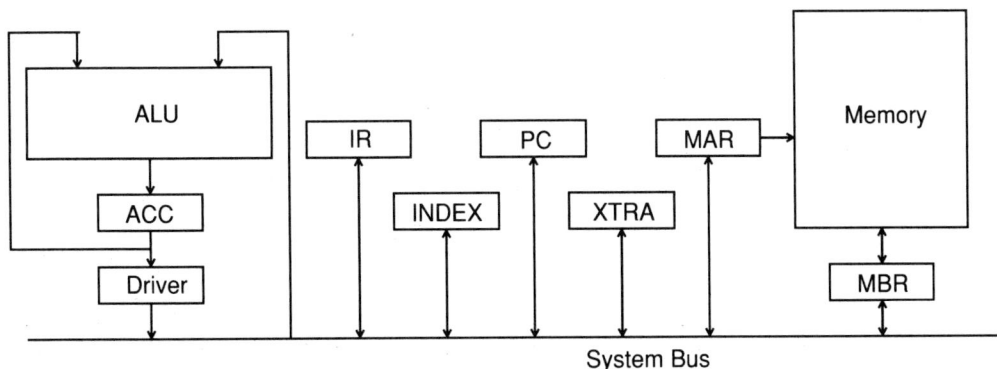

System Bus

4.9 Consider the above block diagram of a computer. ACC, XTRA, IR, INDEX, PC, MAR, and MBR are registers that can be filled from the system bus or gated to the system bus. The ALU can do add, subtract, increment, decrement, and all of the logic operations. Give a register transfer representation of the complete instruction cycle for

a. indirect addition

b. indexed AND

c. unconditional jump

4.10 Consider a microcomputer that is a single address machine, with a general purpose accumulator (ACC) and a number of special registers. These registers include a 16-bit program counter (PC), a 16-bit stack pointer (SP), and a 16-bit index register (X). The address space is 16 bits, and the system is an 8-bit system. The system has four interrupt lines (0, 1, 2, 3, with line 0 assigned highest priority), which devices can assert to cause a vectored interrupt. The numbers associated with the vector lines refer to address allocations starting from the last location of memory (FFFF). A software system has been created that contains interrupt handlers for a floppy disk (routine starts at EF36), a cassette tape recorder interface (routine starts at F340), a line printer (routine starts at D45A), and a terminal (routine starts at C344).

a. Give the allocation for the upper part of memory (give memory map for vector locations).

b. Give a register transfer language representation of the action that occurs when the cassette recorder asserts its interrupt line (which one is it?)

4.11 For the block diagram of Figure 4.2, give the register transfers required to implement an ADD instruction, and a NEGATE instruction. Assume that the number system involved is the two's complement number system. The ALU can do the following: feed MBB through, add ACC and MBR, increment ACC, and NAND ACC and MBR. Also, ACC can be cleared.

4.12 Consider the block diagram given for a Problem 4.7. The ALU is capable of addition (T1 + T2), subtraction (T1 − T2), increment (T1 + 1), decrement (T1 − 1), and logical operations (T1 op T2). All registers are registers only, not counters too. Data paths, addresses, data are all 16 bits. Give the RTL for the following instructions:

a. ADD *R1, *{*R2}
Add the contents of memory whose address is in R1 to the contents of another memory location, and store the results back in this second memory location. The second memory location is identified by an address which itself is located in memory, and the address of the address is found in R2.

b. JMS addr
Transfer program control to the subroutine located at "addr," which is an address stored at the location following the instruction in the instruction stream.

c. MOV address I R3, R5
Move the contents of a memory location to register 5. The address of the memory location is found by indexing "address" by the contents of register 3. That is, "address," which is found in the location following the instruction, is added to the value in register 3, and the result is used as an address at which to find the operand.

4.13 One of the mechanisms discussed for parameter passing was the concept of register windows. Contrast a "standard" system and a system with register windows by doing the following:

a. Prepare a block diagram of a "standard" system with 32 registers. Include as many time saving mechanisms as possible to help the execution time of instructions.

b. Specify instructions needed in this architecture to do a subroutine call.

Include not only the JMS itself, but also whatever other instructions are needed to pass parameters.

c. Prepare RTL implementations for these instructions to identify execution times. Then create a table of execution times for subroutine calls, since calling routines with a different number of parameters will result in different effective times for the subroutine calls.

d-f. Repeat steps a-c for an architecture that uses the concept of register windows. Use the same number of registers for the architecture as for the nonregister window system. Assume that the system has a sufficient number of registers to allow subroutine nesting to a depth of eight.

g. Suggest a mechanism to be utilized when the subroutine nesting level exceeds eight. How much time will be required to handle that situation?

4.14 Obtain instruction set specifications and instruction set architecture descriptions for the VAX architectcure, the MIPS architecture, and the 32000 architecture. Compare the contents of the status registers for the three systems, and the conditional branch instructions available. Defend one of the approaches as better than the other two, using system resource requirements and reasonable metrics to explain your position.

4.11. References and Readings

[AgDa78] Aguero, U., and S. Dasgupta, "A Plausibility-Driven Approach to Computer Architecture Design," *Communications of the ACM.* Vol. 30, No. 11, November 1987, pp. 922–932.

[AlWo75] Alexander, W. G., and D. B. Wortman, "Static and Dynamic Characteristic of XPL Programs," *IEEE Computer.* Vol. 8, No. 11, November 1975, pp. 41–46.

[AmBl64] Amdahl, G. M., G. A. Blaauw, and F. P. Brooks, Jr., "Architecture of the IBM System/360," *IBM Journal of Research and Development.* Vol. 8, No. 2, April 1964, pp. 87–101.

[Baer84] Baer, J. L., "Computer Architecture," *Computer.* Vol. 17, No. 10, October 1984, pp. 77–87.

[Baer80] Baer, J. L., *Computer Systems Architecture.* Rockville, MD: Computer Science Press, 1980.

[Barb81] Barbacci, M. R., "Instruction Set Processor Specification (ISPS): The Notation and its Application," *IEEE Transactions on Computers.* Vol. C-30, No. 1, January 1981, pp. 24–40.

[BaSi82] Barbacci, M. R., and D. P. Siewiorek, *The Design and Analysis of Instruction Set Processors.* New York: McGraw-Hill Book Company, 1982.

[BaNo80] Barbacci, M. R., and J. D. Northcutt, "Application of ISPS, An Architecture Description Language," *Journal of Digital Systems.* Vol. 4, No. 3, Fall 1980, pp. 221–239.

[Bart85] Bartee, T. C., *Digital Computer Fundamentals, 6th edition.* New York: McGraw Hill Book Company, 1985.

[Basa85] Basart, E., "RISC Design Streamlines High Power CPUs," *Computer Design.* Vol. 24, No. 7, July 1, 1985, pp. 119–122.

[BeNe71] Bell, C. G. and A. Newell, *Computer Structures: Readings and Examples.* New York: McGraw-Hill Book Company, 1971.

[Blak77] Blake, R. P., "Exploring a Stack Architecture," *Computer.* Vol. 10, No. 5, May 1977, pp. 30–41.

[Boot84] Booth, T. L., *Introduction to Computer Engineering: Hardware and Software Design.* New York: John Wiley & Sons, Inc., 1984.

[Bulm77] Bulman, D. M., "Stack Computers: An Introduction," *Computer.* Vol. 10, No. 5, May 1977, pp. 18–29.

[BuGo46] Burks, A. W., H. H. Goldstine, and J. von Neumann, "Preliminary Discussion of the Logical Design of an Electronic Computing Instrument," Institute for Advanced Studies, 1946, reprinted in [Swar76].

[Case85] Case, B., "Building Blocks Yield Fast 32-Bit RISC Machines," *Computer Design.* Vol. 24, No. 7, July 1, 1985, pp. 111–117.

[CoHi85] Colwell, R. P., C. Y. Hitchcock, E. D. Jensen, et al., "Computers, Complexity, and Controversy," *Computer.* Vol. 18, No. 9, September 1985, pp. 8–20.

[Dasg89] Dasgupta, S., *Computer Architecture: A Modern Synthesis.* New York: John Wiley & Sons, Inc., 1989.

[Dasg84] Dasgupta, S., *The Design and Description of Computer Architectures.* New York: John Wiley & Sons, Inc., 1984.

[DECC77] Digital Equipment Corporation, *PDP 8/e Small Computer Handbook.* Maynard, MA: Digital Equipment Corporation, 1970.

[DECC77] Digital Equipment Corporation, *VAX11-780 Architecture Handbook,* Vol 1. Maynard, MA: Digital Equipment Corporation, 1977.

[Ditz81] Ditzel, D. R., "Reflections on the High-Level Language Symbol Computer System," *Computer.* Vol. 14, No.7, July 1981, pp. 55–66.

[FlWa86] Fleming, P. J., and J. J. Wallace, "How Not to Lie with Statistics: The Correct way to Summarize Benchmark Results," *Communications of the ACM.* Vol. 29, No. 3, March 1986, pp. 218–221.

[FoDy82] Foderaro, J., K. van Dyke, and D. A. Patterson, "Running RISCs," *VLSI Design.* Vol. 3, No. 5, 1982, pp. 27–32.

[FoIb85] Foster, C. C., and T. Iberall, *Computer Architecture,* 3rd. Edition. New York: Van Nostrand Reinhold Co., 1985.

[FuBu77] Fuller, S. H., and W. E. Burr, "Measurement and Evaluation of Alternative Computer Architectures," *Computer.* Vol. 10, No. 10, October 1977, pp. 24–35.

[HaVr78] Hamacher, V. C., Z. G. Vranesic, and S. G. Zaky, *Computer Organization.* New York: McGraw-Hill Book Company, 1984.

[HaDe68] Hauck, E. A., and B. A. Dent, "Burroughs' B6500/B6700 Stack Mechanisms," *Proceedings Spring Joint Computer Conference,* 1968, pp. 245–251.

[HeJo82] Hennessy, J. L., N. Jouppi, S. Przybylski, et al., "MIPS: A Microprocessor Architecture," *Proceedings of the 15th Annual Workshop on Microprogramming.* Los Angeles: IEEE Computer Society Press, 1982, pp. 17–22.

[Hirs84] Hirsch, A., "Tagged Architecture Supports Symbolic Processing," *Computer Design.* Vol. 23, No. 6, June 1, 1984, pp. 75–80.

[HiSp85] Hitchcock, C. Y., and H. M. B. Sprunt, "Analyzing Multiple Register Sets," *Proceedings of the 12th Annual International Symposium on Computer Architecture.* Silver Spring, MD: IEEE Computer Society Press, 1985, pp. 55–63.

[HuLa85] Hugnet, M., and T. Lang, "A Reduced Register File for RISC Architectures," *SIGARCH Computer Architecture News.* Vol. 13, No. 4, September 1985, pp. 22–31.

[Kain89] Kain, R. Y., *Computer Architecture, Software and Hardware.* Englewood Cliffs, NJ: Prentice Hall, 1989.

[Kane87] Kane, Gerry, *MIPS R2000 RISC Architecture.* Englewood Cliffs, NJ: Prentice Hall, 1987.

[Kate85] Katevenis, M. G. H., *Reduced Instruction Set Computer Architectures for VLSI.* Cambridge, MA: MIT Press, 1985.

[Kee78a] Keedy, J. L., "On the Use of Stacks in the Evaluation of Expressions," *SIGARCH Computer Architecture News.* Vol. 6, No. 6, February 1978, pp. 22–28.

[Kee78b] Keedy, J. L., "On the the Evaluation of Expressions Using Accumulators, Stacks, and Store-Store Instructions," *SIGARCH Computer Architecture News,* Vol. 7, No. 4, December 1978, pp. 24–27.

[Keed79] Keedy, J. L., "More on the Use of Stacks in the Evaluation of Expressions," *SIGARCH Computer Architecture News.* Vol. 7, No. 8, June 1979, pp. 18–22.

[Lang82] Langdon, G. G., Jr., *Computer Design* San Jose, CA: Computeach Press, Inc, 1982.

[LoKi61] Lonergan, W., and P. King, "Design of the B 5000 system," *Datamation.* Vol. 7, No. 5, May 1961, pp. 28–32.

[Lund77] Lunde, A., "Empirical Evaluation of Some Features of Instruction Set Processor Architectures," *Communications of the ACM.* Vol. 20, No. 3, March 1977, pp. 143–152.

[Mano82] Mano, M. M., *Computer System Architecture.* Englewood Cliffs, NJ: Prentice Hall, 1982.

[Myer77] Myers, G. J., "The Case Against Stack-Oriented Instruction Sets," *SIGARCH Computer Architecture News.* Vol. 6, No. 3, August 1977, pp. 7–10.

[Myer78] Myers, G. J., "The Evaluation of Expressions in a Storage-Storage Architecture," *SIGARCH Computer Architecture News.* Vol. 6, No. 9, June 1978, pp. 20–23.

[Myer82] Myers, G. J., *Advances in Computer Architecture.* New York: John Wiley & Sons, Inc., 1982.

[Patt85] Patterson, D. A., "Reduced Instruction Set Computers," *Communications of the ACM.* Vol. 28, No. 1, January 1985, pp. 8–21.

[PaSe82] Patterson, D. A., and C. Sequin, "A VLSI RISC," *Computer.* Vol. 15, No. 9, September, 1982, pp. 8–21.

[PaSe81] Patterson, D. A., and C. Sequin, "RISC 1: A Reduced Instruction VLSI Set Computer," *Proceedings of the 8th Annual International Symposium on Computer Architecture.* New York: IEEE Computer Society Press, 1981, pp. 443–458.

[PaDi80] Patterson, D. A., and D. Dietzel, "The Case for the Reduced Instruction Set Computer," *SIGARCH Computer Architecture News (SIGARCH).* Vol. 8, No. 6, 1980, pp. 25–33.

[PaPi82] Patterson, D. A., and R. Piepho, "RISC Assessment: A High Level Language Experiment," *Proceedings of the 9th Annual Symposium on Computer Architecture.* New York: IEEE Computer Society Press, 1982, pp. 3–8.

[PeSh77] Peuto, B. L., and L. J. Shustek, "An Instruction Timing Model of CPU Performance," *Proceedings of the 4th Annual Symposium on Computer Architecture.* New York: ACM/IEEE, March 1977, pp. 165–178.

[Radi82] Radin, G., "The 801 Minicomputer," *Proceedings of the ACM Symposium on Architectural Support for Programming Languages and Operating Systems.* New York: ACM, 1982, pp. 39–47.

[RiSm71] Rice, R., and W. R. Smith, "SYMBOL-A Major Departure from Classic Software Dominated von Neumann Computing Systems," AFIPS Conference Proceedings, 1971 SJCC, Vol. 38. Montvale, NJ: AFIPS Press, 1971, pp. 575–587.

[SaCh81] Saur, C. H., and K. M. Chandy, *Computer Systems Performance Modeling.* Englewood Cliffs, NJ: Prentice Hall, 1981.

[Schn85] Schneider, G. M., *The Principles of Computer Organization.* New York: John Wiley & Sons, Inc., 1985.

[ShKa84] Sherburne, R. W., Jr, M. G. H. Katevenis, D. A. Patterson, and C. H. Sequin, "A 32-Bit NMOS Processor with a Large Register File," *IEEE Journal of Solid State Circuits.* Vol. SC-19, No. 5, October 1984, pp. 682–689.

[Shus78] Shustek, L. J., "Analysis and Performance of Computer Instruction Sets," Ph.D. Dissertation, Stanford, CA: Computer Systems Laboratory, Stanford University, 1978.

[SiBe82] Siewiorek, D. P., C. G. Bell, and A. Newell, *Computer Structures: Principles and Examples.* New York: McGraw-Hill Book Company, 1982.

[Ston80] Stone, H. S. (Ed.), *Introduction to Computer Architecture.* Chicago, IL: Science Research Associates, 1980.

[Swar76] Swartzlander, E. E., Jr. (Ed.), *Computer Design Development: Principal Papers.* Rochelle Park, NJ: Hayden Book Company, 1976.

[Tibe84] Tiberghien, J. (Ed.), *New Computer Architectures.* San Diego, CA: Academic Press, 1984.

[Wall85] Wallich, P., "Toward Simpler, Faster Computers," *IEEE Spectrum.* August 1985, pp. 38–45.

[Wilk83] Wilkes, M. V., "Size, Power, and Speed," *Proceedings of the 10th Annual International Symposium on Computer Architecture.* Silver Spring, MD: IEEE Computer Society Press, 1983, pp. 2–4.

5

Control System Design

The design of a computer system, like that of all digital systems, requires both data manipulation capabilities (logical units, adders, multipliers, etc.) and control capabilities. The data manipulation elements form the data path of the machine, while controlling the flow of data on that data path is the responsibility of the control section. The design of the data path elements and the instructions that identify the work to be done on the data paths have been the subjects of the preceding chapters. In this chapter we will deal with methods used to control the flow of information within a computer. Our intention is not to provide an in-depth discussion of sequential design techniques; a number of excellent texts provide that material [Mano79, Flet80, McCl86, Bree89]. Our intention is to provide some insights into different ways in which those methods can be applied in the design of a control section of a computer.

The control system of a computer is basically a sequential system that implements the fetch-decode-execute function of instruction execution. Since it is a sequential system, it can be designed using the same techniques used to design counters, controllers, or any of a wide variety of digital systems. In this chapter, we examine different techniques for implementing sequential systems, and apply those techniques to the control of computational elements. Thus, our first task is to review some of the concepts used in sequential design.

The application of sequential design techniques will result in a control system that activates the appropriate clock lines, enables, and interface signals to accomplish the work of the computer system. However, before the control system can be specified and implemented, it is necessary to identify the appropriate clocks, enables, and other signals used in the system. Therefore, the first requirement of a computer system design is to develop a detailed data path block diagram. This diagram must identify the control lines that can be used to manipulate data in the system. And with this diagram and the definition of the instructions to perform, RTL descriptions of the data transfers needed can be developed.

Thus, we will look again at the problem of data path definition and RTL specifications, and see how they are used in the process of control system design.

The designer of a control system must know what signals are available for the control and manipulation of the data in the system; these control lines are identified by the detailed block diagram. In addition, the order of operations must be specified, and this information comes from the RTL descriptions of the work to be done. With this global view of the system, a designer can select the most appropriate sequential design technique and create a system that will assert the control lines to do the work. We will look at different methods for implementing the control systems, providing examples of each.

5.1. Elements of Sequential Design: A Review

The circuits of the preceding chapters are all classified as combinational circuits: the outputs are functions only of the inputs. These can be modeled as shown in Figure 5.1; the outputs will change whenever the inputs change. This model applies to a variety of devices and circuits: random logic, ALUs ('181, '381), multiplexers ('151, '157), decoders ('138, '154), memories, PLAs, and the like. Normally we like to think that these circuits are perfect, that the outputs will change instantaneously to their new value whenever the inputs change. However, associated with real devices are real delays, and the outputs will follow the inputs after some finite time delay. Some outputs may change during the finite time delay, and resume their former values after the delay period has passed. This results in glitches that can cause problems in circuits, and care must be taken to prevent the glitches from occurring or to ascertain that, if glitches do occur, they will not cause problems. Thus, a designer must be aware of the timing restrictions in the process of creating the data path and the transfers represented by the RTL statements.

If a system is to have outputs that reflect not only the current set of inputs, but the history of the system as well, then a different model is necessary. An addition to the model of Figure 5.1 is shown in the model of Figure 5.2. Here the outputs are not only a function of the current inputs, but also the past history of the system as well. This history is reflected in the "state" of the machine, which is the value stored in the collection of memory elements within the system. If there are N memory elements, then there are 2^N possible states that the system can assume. Hence, systems with more than a few flip-flops are intractable; a system with 20 bits of memory arranged in registers or other flip-flops would have more than a million possible states.

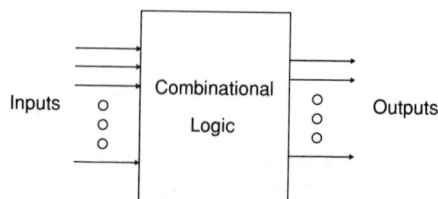

Figure 5.1. Block Diagram of Simple Combinational Circuit.

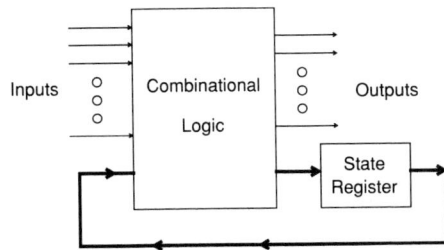

Figure 5.2. Simple Block Diagram of
Sequential Circuit.

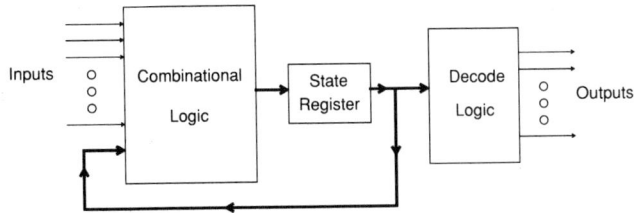

Figure 5.3. Sequential Circuit: A Moore Machine.

The system depicted in Figure 5.2, where the outputs are functions of both
the current state and the inputs, is called a Mealy machine. This kind of machine
is useful in certain circumstances, but can cause problems because of the lack of
synchronization between inputs and states. That is, the outputs may be of varying
lengths, since the inputs change asynchronously with respect to the states of the
machine. A different, slightly more restricted, model for a sequential system is
shown in Figure 5.3. This type of system is called a Moore machine. Here the
outputs are functions of the present state only. Inputs then influence the outputs
only in that they can affect the next state of the sequential machine, but the outputs are not directly functions of the inputs. This model, and variations of it,
represent the controllers that we will consider for the control sections of computers and other digital systems. The outputs of the sequential machine will be the
control signals needed to manipulate data and move it within the system. The
inputs required to specify the desired sequence of steps consist of synchronization
flags, status bits, test conditions, and other information that influences the
behavior of the system. The designer's challenge, then, is to design a sequential
system that will assert the outputs in an appropriate manner to accomplish the
work of the system. However, before the control system can be defined and the
sequence of outputs specified, the data path must be specified and the control signals on the data path identified.

5.2. Data Path Formulation

The formulation of the data path for a computer or other digital system is a complex task that is influenced by many factors. The foremost requirement is that the
system be able to perform the action required by the underlying task. Just how
that task is accomplished is a designer's choice; the decisions made by the
designer reflect his understanding of the task and the requirements imposed by

system constraints. Consider, for example, the IBM System 360/370 family of computer systems. This was one of the first families of computers in which the different models were identified in the beginning, rather than having different models announced as permitted by customer demand and marketing strategy. The 360 family was set up to cover a variety of performance capabilities and economic ranges. Nevertheless, a program executed on different members of this family should arrive at the same answer on each machine. The instruction set architecture of the system appears the same to a programmer regardless of the model on which the program runs. However, the techniques used to implement the operations vary from model to model. The number of data paths, the arithmetic units, the memory interactions, and the control system for each model are configured to match different sets of economic and performance constraints. The same idea will be true for all digital systems: the parts used, the data paths provided, and the interfacing methods will be dictated by the intended use of the system. Some of the constraints and their implications are listed below:

- *Economic:* How expensive are the components used to build the system? This includes not only the integrated circuits, but other components as well, such as sockets, connectors, display elements, wire, printed circuit boards, and so on, as well as manufacturing costs.

- *Interface requirements:* Many devices are specifically designed to interface to TTL components. However, other technologies can require a different set of voltages and currents for information exchange. This also applies to the protocols required for the exchange.

- *Speed:* A variety of questions must be addressed. One of the first is to choose the technology in which the system will be implemented. Lower speed requirements can utilize some MOS technologies that conserve energy and do not have fast cycle times. Higher speed technologies, such as ECL and GaAs, require careful adherence to design constraints. However, another speed issue is the extent of the use of concurrency within the system, from pipeline techniques to multiple data paths. Each of these options carries with it a set of constraints that identify its range of usefulness.

- *Power:* The amount of power that a system utilizes may be a factor in the system. If the unit is to operate on battery power for extended periods of time, or be limited in the amount of available power, then the designer must select components and techniques accordingly.

- *Dynamic range:* Arithmetic requirements are often mandated by the intended applications of the system and the allowable signal to noise ratio. A system may be able to satisfy the data representation requirements with integer or fixed point arithmetic of a certain number of bits; or the required dynamic range may indicate that floating point operations are necessary. The data paths and arithmetic capabilities must match system needs.

- *Flexibility:* Many digital systems are created not to solve a single problem, but to provide a device that can be used in a variety of applications to achieve a reasonable solution. Therefore, the system must be flexible enough to be used easily in any of a number of target areas.

- *Maintainability:* Building a computer system, or other digital device, to satisfy a particular need is only part of the overall problem. Because of device failures, power surges, or other problems the system will at some time cease to function properly. One of the desirable characteristics for digital systems is that they be maintainable. That is, the design and the implementation be done in such a way that devices and subsystems that are not functioning properly can be identified and easily replaced.

- *Environment:* This nebulous heading is used here to include a variety of other types of restrictions. If the system is satellite-based, it must not only conserve power used, but it also may have a radiation hardening requirement. If the unit is to operate in an airplane, it may have vibration tolerance requirements, extended temperature requirements, or other restrictions.

Acceptable limits for these and other requirements are identified by the specifications for the system to be designed. The designer must utilize the ingenuity that he has to propose a design that will meet the specifications of the system. There are many different approaches to solving a given problem; indeed, vastly different data path solutions may be proposed which satisfy the requirements of the system. These approaches may use single bus implementations, multiple bus implementations, point to point techniques, or any of a variety of approaches. In any case, the system must satisfy the requirements placed upon it by its application area and intended use.

The designer must select the data path components from the pool of available parts in the target technology, arrange the components and the interconnections so as to meet the system requirements, and identify the basic transfers and manipulations required to perform the necessary work. We wish to make two points. First, the design of the data path is basically independent of the control design. There may be factors in the intended control design that influence the data path formation, and there may be elements of the data path that bear on the control design, but basically they are two different problems. Second, having identified the elements in the data path, a designer must then identify the signals that will control the flow of information within the data path. It is the responsibility of the control section to assert the signals in such a way that the appropriate work is accomplished, and, once the signals are identified, the design of the control section can proceed to achieve that objective.

To reiterate the points made above, the designer must:

- First select an appropriate technology and a set of components in that technology to provide for the needs of the system.
- Interconnect the components in such a way that the work of the system can be accomplished.
- Then, using a register transfer language or other means of specifying the action to take place, identify the data transfers and arithmetic required by the system.
- Identify the control signals required to accomplish the work of the system.

When the data path has been defined to this level, the design of the control portion of the circuitry can proceed.

This process is best illustrated by an example. The example chosen here, and the other examples in this chapter, are contrived to illustrate specific points, and do not necessarily reflect the "trickiest" way to accomplish some work. But once the principles have been identified, the designer can then proceed to apply them to other designs. The following example, like the other examples in this chapter, is more extensive than those in earlier chapters; for instance, Section 5.7 consists entirely of two different implementation techniques applied to the same machine. Therefore, the examples here are interwoven with the text, not separated as a short example to illustrate a single point.

Our first example of a digital system is the calculation of an inner dot product. This is used repeatedly in mathematics for doing matrix manipulations; it is also used in digital signal processing for transversal filters. The example is to design a finite impulse response (FIR) digital filter with 25 coefficients. The equation for this calculation is:

$$\text{output} = \sum_{i=0}^{24} S_i \times C_i$$

where S_i represents samples of an input stream and C_i represents constant coefficients. We will assume that the system is to stand alone; that is, that the system will contain an A/D converter to provide samples and a D/A converter to accept outputs. We will also assume that the coefficients are known and constant. The data manipulations involved in the FIR process are shown in Figure 5.4. The input is sent to a delay network, which saves 25 values of the data stream. Each of the delayed values forms one of the S_i of the above equation. Each sample is multiplied by its corresponding coefficient (C_i), and all of the resulting values are summed to form the final result. The system architect/designer has the task of implementing the data manipulations represented by the FIR equation in real hardware.

The network shown in Figure 5.4 could be implemented directly in hardware. However, that would require 25 separate multipliers and some mechanism for summing 25 results in parallel. A more conservative solution is to build a system around a multiply/accumulator (MAC), a device that will perform a multiply and an add in each clock cycle. These modules have been available for several years and are applicable to a variety of different calculations; the FIR example is an ideal use for this module, since the chip performs all of the arithmetic needed to obtain the result. To present the appropriate values to the MAC, we will utilize memories to store the data and the coefficients. Thus, our problem will be to design a system that will accept a sample, store it in a memory, and then perform the calculations identified by the above equation using the current sample and the previous 24 samples.

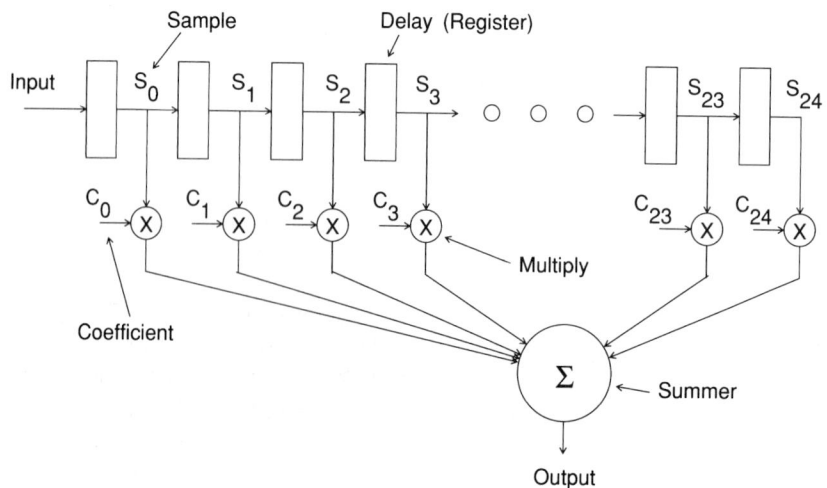

Figure 5.4. Data Manipulations Involved in Inner Dot Product.

A simple block diagram of a piece of hardware to do this is shown in Figure 5.5. The MAC can be connected to the other elements of the system in a variety of ways to satisfy different system requirements. The solution shown is capable of a fairly high computation rate, and yet is simple in its implementation. The elements of the system, their names and their responsibilities are as follows:

- *Coefficient memory:* (C_MEM[k]) This memory contains the constants (C_i) needed by the algorithm. The memory chosen here is a small PROM (programmable read only memory).

- *Coefficient memory address register:* (C_ADR) This is a counter used to identify the current coefficient. It must start at zero for each iteration and increment through the coefficient numbers, which are used directly as coefficient addresses.

- *Sample memory:* (S_MEM[k]) The sample memory is used to store the current sample and the previous 24; actually the memory is made of a number of RAMs, so 32 values are stored, but only 25 used for any single calculation.

- *Sample memory address register:* (S_ADR) This counter is initialized to the address of the current sample; it is then incremented to point at the preceding samples in order.

- *Initial sample address register:* (I_ADR) This register identifies the starting point of the algorithm for each pass. The correct starting point for the current iteration is one less than the starting point for the previous iteration. Thus, this counter will decrement once each pass.

- *A/D converter:* (ADIN) This module provides the new data for each iteration. We assume that the time at which conversion begins is controlled by an

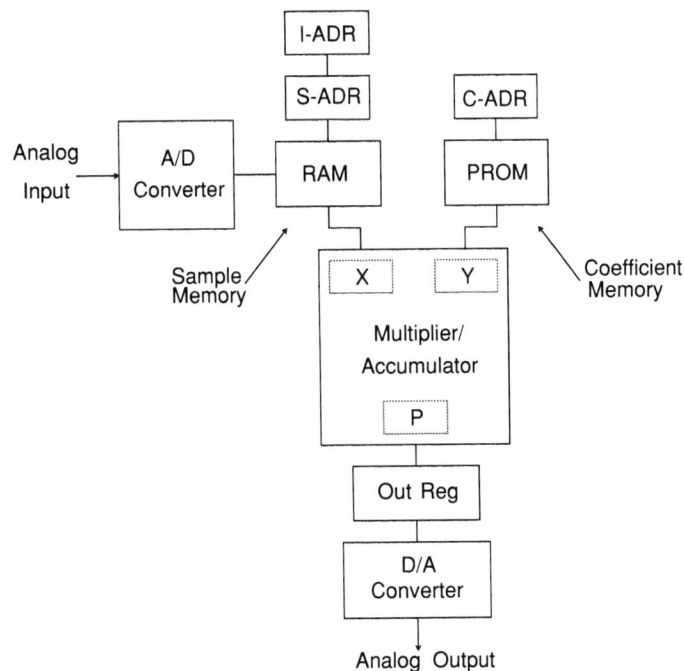

Figure 5.5. Simple Data Path Block Diagram for Finite Impulse Response System.

external source. When new data is available, a ready flag will be asserted. Thus, testing this ready flag will identify when the algorithm should be performed.

- *D/A converter:* (DAOUT) This module accepts the output of each interaction and converts it to an appropriate analog value.

- *Output register:* (OUT) This is a register that isolates the D/A converter from the values on the output of the MAC during the calculation process.

- *Multiplier/accumulator module:* This module has the responsibility for doing the arithmetic needed by the algorithm. It will do each multiply, then add the value to a running sum. There are three registers internal to the system, two input registers (X, Y) and an output register (P).

When the designer has arrived at a data path representation such as that shown in Figure 5.5, the next step is to identify the work to take place. As identified in the formula defining the calculation, 25 coefficients will be multiplied by 25 data values, and the results of the multiplies summed to the result. Assuming that the RAM and PROM (for the data and coefficient storage) both contain 32 locations, these memories can be visualized as shown in Figure 5.6. Part a shows the coefficient storage. These values are always used in order, from location 0 to location 24. Thus, at the beginning of each iteration the address register for the coefficients will be set to zero. Figure 5.6(b) indicates that the first value received will be placed in location 0 of the RAM, and then the initial sample address register will be decremented. Thus, the next location to be filled by a sample value will be location 31. Figure 5.6(c) shows the contents of the RAM after 33 samples have been received. The 33rd sample (Sample 32) overwrites the first sample (Sample 0). The output of the FIR calculation uses the 25 most recent samples, also identified in part c. The 25 most recent samples utilize a different portion of the RAM for each iteration. The samples used for the 41st iteration (Sample 40 through Sample 16) are identified in of Figure 5.6(d). Once the basic algorithm is understood, we can specify the work to be done with RTL statements:

start: if (ADIN not ready)		goto *start*	Check input data.
0	⌐→	C_ADR	Clear coefficient address.
I_ADR	⌙→	S_ADR	Load sample address.
ADIN	⌐→	S_MEM [S_ADR]	Data to sample memory.
I_ADR	⌙→	I_ADR	Decrement initial address.
S_MEM [S_ADR]	⌐→	X	Load sample to X reg.
C_MEM [C_ADR]	→	Y	Load coefficient to Y reg.
S_ADR + 1	→	S_ADR	Increment sample address.
C_ADR + 1	⌙→	C_ADR	Increment coefficient address.
X × Y	⌐→	P	Load product register.
S_MEM [S_ADR]	→	X	Load sample to X reg.
C_MEM [C_ADR]	→	Y	Load coefficient to Y reg.
S_ADR + 1	→	S_ADR	Increment sample address.
C_ADR + 1	⌙→	C_ADR	Increment coefficient address.

over:	$P + X \times Y$	$\rightarrow$	P	Add product into P register.
	$S\_MEM[S\_ADR]$	$\rightarrow$	X	Load sample to X reg.
	$C\_MEM[C\_ADR]$	$\rightarrow$	Y	Load coefficient to Y reg.
	$S\_ADR + 1$	$\rightarrow$	S_ADR	Increment sample address.
	$C\_ADR + 1$	$\rightarrow$	C_ADR	Increment coefficient address.

if (not done)   goto *over*   Repeat for all samples.
                                   Work is done when C_ADDR is 25.

$P \rightarrow OUT$ Update output value.

goto *start*   Start over.

(a)

Coefficients stored in first 25 locations of PROM

(b)

Samples start at location 0 of RAM

First sample stored at location 0 (0th sample)

Initial Sample Address Register decrements to point to location 31

(c)

Each new sample stored at location numbered one lower than previous sample

32nd Sample 31st Sample 8th Sample 2nd Sample 1st Sample

25 values used in summation after accepting Sample 32

(d)

Summation calculation done with 25 most recent samples

32nd Sample 31st Sample   25 values used in summation after accepting Sample 40 40th Sample 34th Sample 33^{rdt} Sample

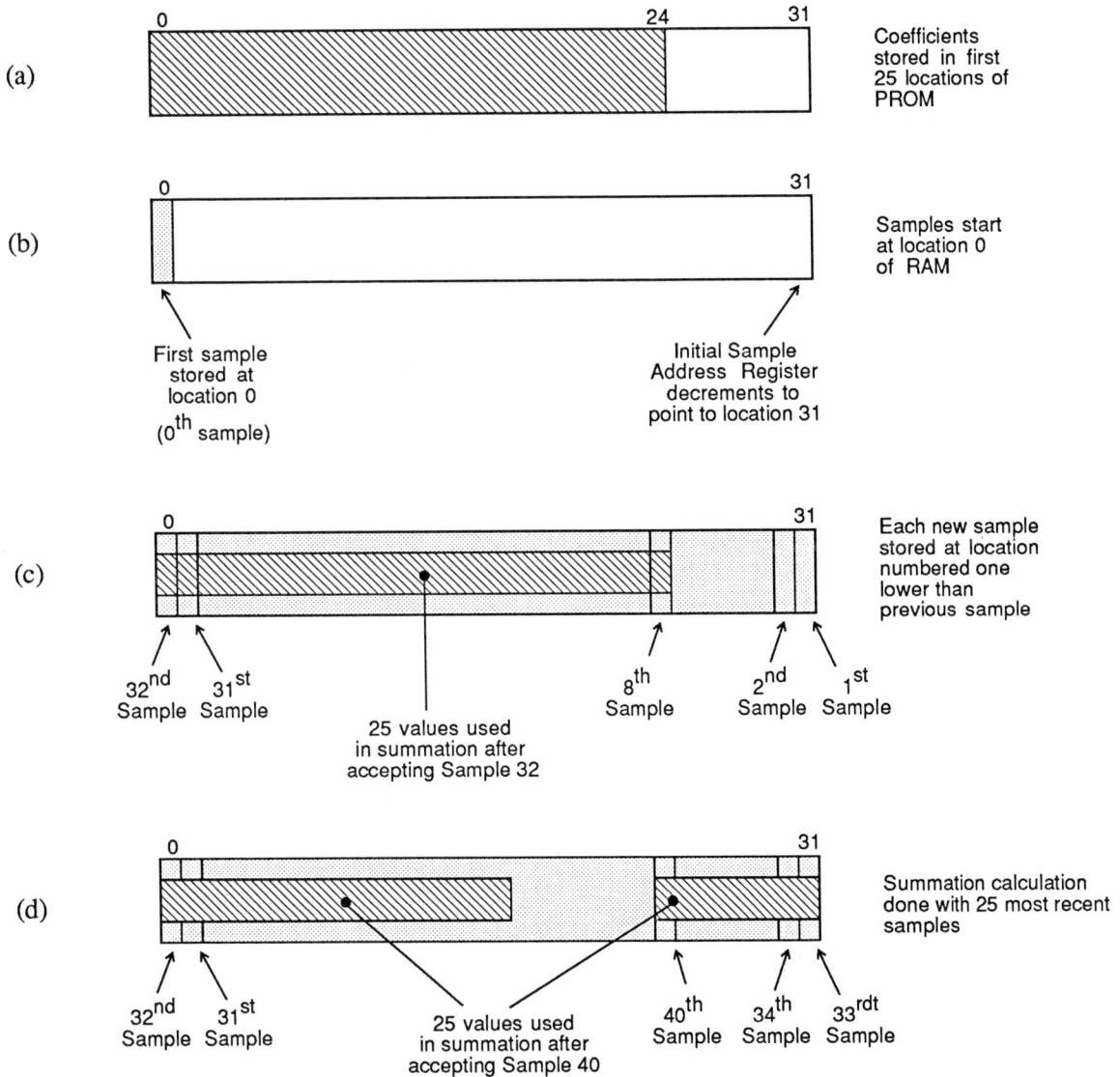

Figure 5.6. Coefficient and Data Storage for FIR Example.

This identifies the work needed to perform the appropriate calculations, as well as the possible parallelism of simultaneous events. The system waits for new data to become available (ADIN ready), at which point the data processing begins. The first step is to clear the coefficient address and load the sample address register from the initial sample address register. These two events can happen simultaneously. Then, the input value is loaded into the sample memory (at the address just loaded into C_ADDR from I_ADDR), and the initial sample address is decremented. Again, these two events can occur at the same time. The next step is to load the first sample and the first coefficient into the X and Y registers of the MAC, as well as increment the sample address register and the coefficient address register. The next group of transfers specify loading a product into P, a new sample into X, a new coefficient into Y, and incrementing the address registers. At this point a loop is entered, which adds the new product to the running sum, loads a new sample and a new coefficient, and increments the address registers. This continues until the process is done, which will occur when the final sample-coefficient product has been added to the running sum and is available at the inputs of the output register. This condition is checked simply by counting the number of operations, and when the result is ready moving on to the next transaction. The final transfer moves the newly calculated value to the output register (OUT), at which point control returns to the beginning to start over again.

If all of the transfers in the RTL occur instantaneously, then there is no problem with the system. However, in real systems each of the actions identified in the RTL takes a nonzero amount of time to accomplish. One of the challenges of the designer is to create a control section that will manipulate the signals in such a way that the transfers maintain the appearance of the simultaneity specified in the RTL. To prepare to design such a control section, we will create a state diagram that identifies the action of the RTL. We will see that this state diagram can be used to directly implement an appropriate control section. This state diagram is shown in Figure 5.7. It is called a preliminary state diagram, because it will be modified slightly before the actual implementation of the control section. The states that do not specify any work are added for timing purposes, and we will discuss them in connection with the actual implementation.

When the RTL description of operations and the state diagram are ready, the designer must complete the details of the data path block diagram by choosing the exact parts to be used in the system and identifying the control signals required on those parts to perform the work. Figure 5.8 shows the system of Figure 5.5 with the parts specified and the control signals identified. Note that, although the same parts are used both for the coefficient memory address register and the sample memory address register, the control lines needed are not the same. Both address registers need clocks, so that signal is shown for both blocks. However, the coefficient MAR needs to be cleared but not loaded, and the sample MAR needs to be loaded but not cleared. These differences are evident in the control signals included in Figure 5.8. Note also that control lines of the components that do not need to be manipulated during the computation are not identified in the diagram. It is assumed that the designer has studied the specifications of the components and made provisions for the other signals. Some of these will be grounded, others tied to a high level, and so on.

To summarize, the creation of the data path can be done in a manner that is relatively independent from the choice of a control mechanism for a digital system. The designer must first become familiar with the work required of the system. This includes the operations needed, the limitations of the data representation and manipulation methods, the order of events, and other considerations.

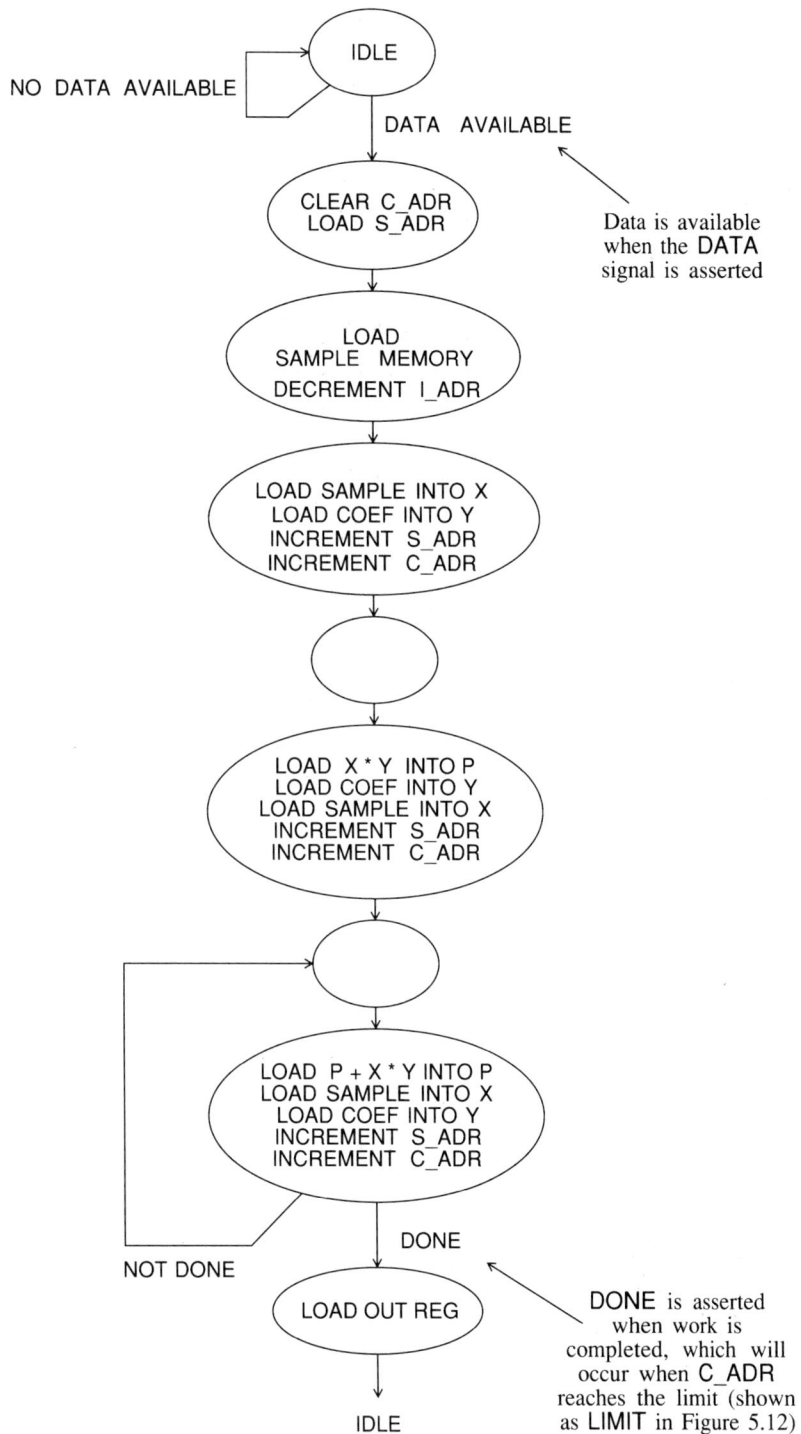

Figure 5.7. Preliminary State Diagram for Finite Impulse Response System.

With the system and device specifications in mind, the designer then organizes appropriate devices in such a way that the necessary data manipulations can be performed and the system constraints can be satisfied. The flow of information

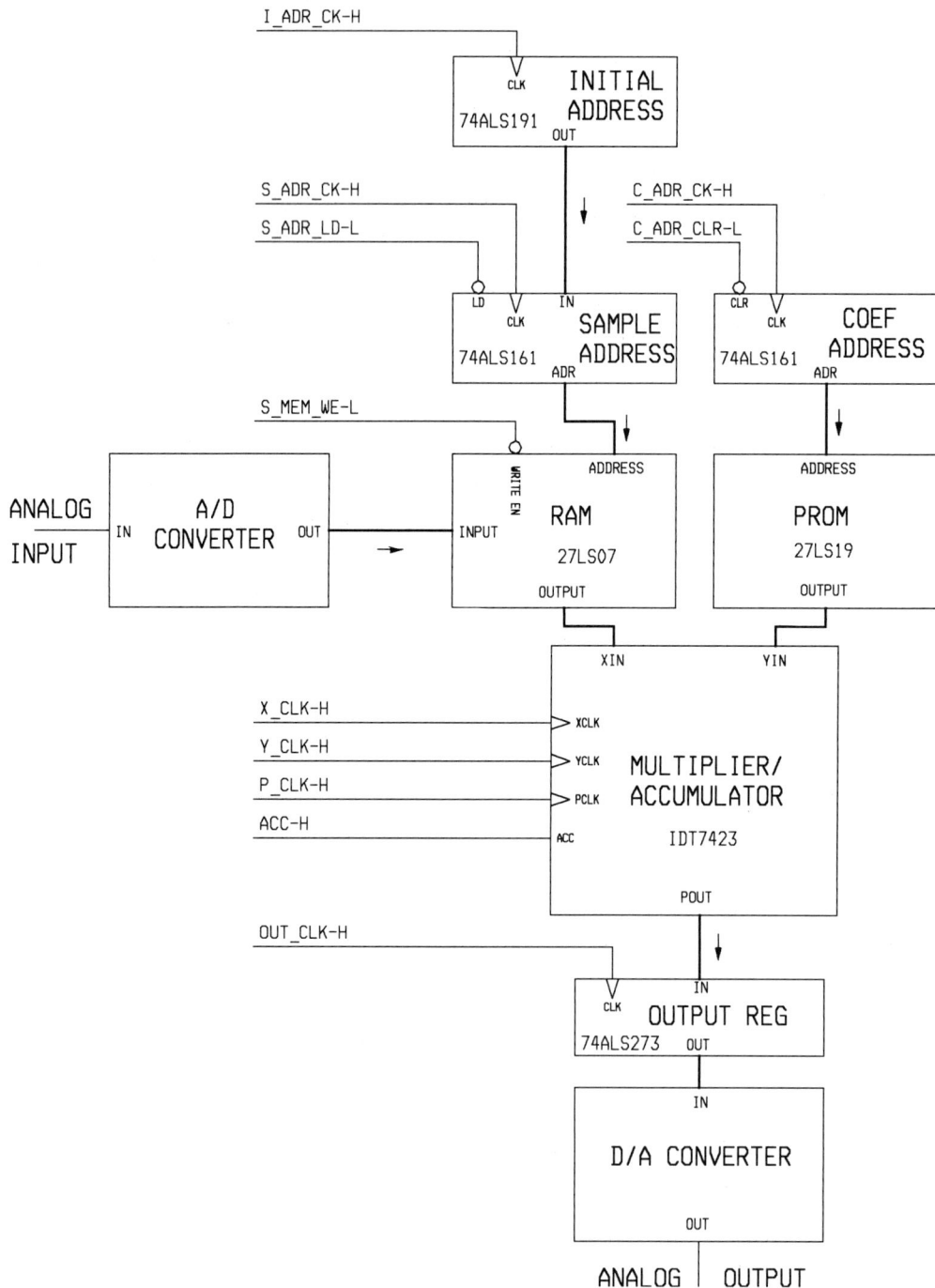

Figure 5.8. Detailed Data Path Block Diagram for Finite Impulse Response System.

within the system is then identified with register transfer specifications, state diagrams, and any other design aid that can provide insight into the operation of the system. Finally, the components are identified and the control lines of those components identified so that the detailed design of the control section can be performed.

5.3. A Simple State Machine Controller

Once the problem is understood to the point that a detailed data path block diagram and a preliminary state diagram are available, then the design of the control section can proceed. The classical approach would begin by creating a detailed state diagram, then a detailed enumeration of all possible state and input combinations. This would be translated into flip-flop excitation tables, state tables, next state and output truth tables, and logical equations for the appropriate signals. These would then be implemented with random logic, and, if all of the steps were correctly followed, the circuit should do the necessary control work. We present here a method that follows the same basic steps as the classical approach, but that is relatively simple to understand and implement. First, the state diagram is expanded as necessary to include the appropriate assertion levels for the control lines of the detailed data path block diagram. Then the system is mapped directly onto the Moore model of Figure 5.3. The simplicity of the implementation has some advantages and disadvantages, as we shall see.

A state diagram as shown in Figure 5.7 indicates the order in which events should occur to produce the desired results, but the details necessary for the control signals are missing. The designer must be sufficiently familiar with the parts being used so that the assertion of the control lines will be handled correctly. We now examine the primitive state diagram and the detailed data path block diagram in order to derive a correct and complete state diagram.

One observation concerning the state diagram of Figure 5.7 is that there are nine states in it, and to represent all of the states would require 4 bits of state information. One of the first steps of a design procedure is to attempt to reduce the number of states, if feasible, so that the number of bits required to represent the state is at a minimum. Two states in the state diagram appear to be unused, since no work is called out in these states. These states are useful, however, since they play a part in forming the control signals. Asserting signals in some states and not in others results in levels and edges that do the actual work of the system. A designer must visualize the desired behavior of the signals and create state sequences to produce that behavior.

In state diagrams we will identify signals to be asserted by naming them in the states in which they are active. The asserted level of the signal is identified by the use of polarized mnemonics included with the signal name. This is demonstrated by the segment of a state diagram shown in Figure 5.9. Five different states are indicated in the figure, and the system moves from state to state without any branching. Each state time corresponds to a single cycle of the system clock (SYS_CLK-H). In this fragment of a state diagram a single signal is called for in three different states (C_ADR_CK-H), and in each of those states it will be asserted, as shown by the waveform included in the figure. This signal is included on the detailed block diagram of the FIR filter implementation for clocking (incrementing) the coefficient address register. However, even though this signal is asserted in three different states in Figure 5.9, the register would only be incremented by two. The implementation calls for a counter that is activated by a rising edge on the clock line, and as seen by the waveform of the figure, there are only two rising edges on C_ADR_CK-H. Thus, a designer must be aware of the shape of signal waveforms which will result from specifying assertion of the signals in a state diagram. A signal can be asserted for a single state time (C_ADR_CK-H in State 2), or a signal can last for many clock cycles (C_ADR_CK-H in States 4 and 5). We will later examine additional methods for creating control signals with state machines.

As shown by the signal waveform of Figure 5.9, removing the "empty" states in the preliminary state diagram would result in an incorrect function for the system. The states cause the signals that control the clocking of the address registers and the loading of the registers of the DAC to become unasserted, so that the proper edges are created when the signals are asserted in the following states. Thus, these states are needed, and another method must be used to try to reduce the total number of states in the state diagram.

The observation we now make is that there is some redundancy in the state diagram: if there is a method of accomplishing "LOAD PRODUCT INTO Z" and "ADD PRODUCT INTO Z" with the same signal, then two of the states can be combined. A careful examination of the specifications for the multiplier/ accumulator indicates that the function of the PCLK pin is determined by the level of the ACC line at the time that the X and Y registers are loaded. Thus, the desired behavior of the circuit will be obtained if the ACC line is low for the loading of the first values into X and Y, and high thereafter. This will allow combining of the appropriate states from the initial state diagram.

A detailed state diagram can now be created by identifying the desired behavior from the initial state diagram and specifying the signal assertions which

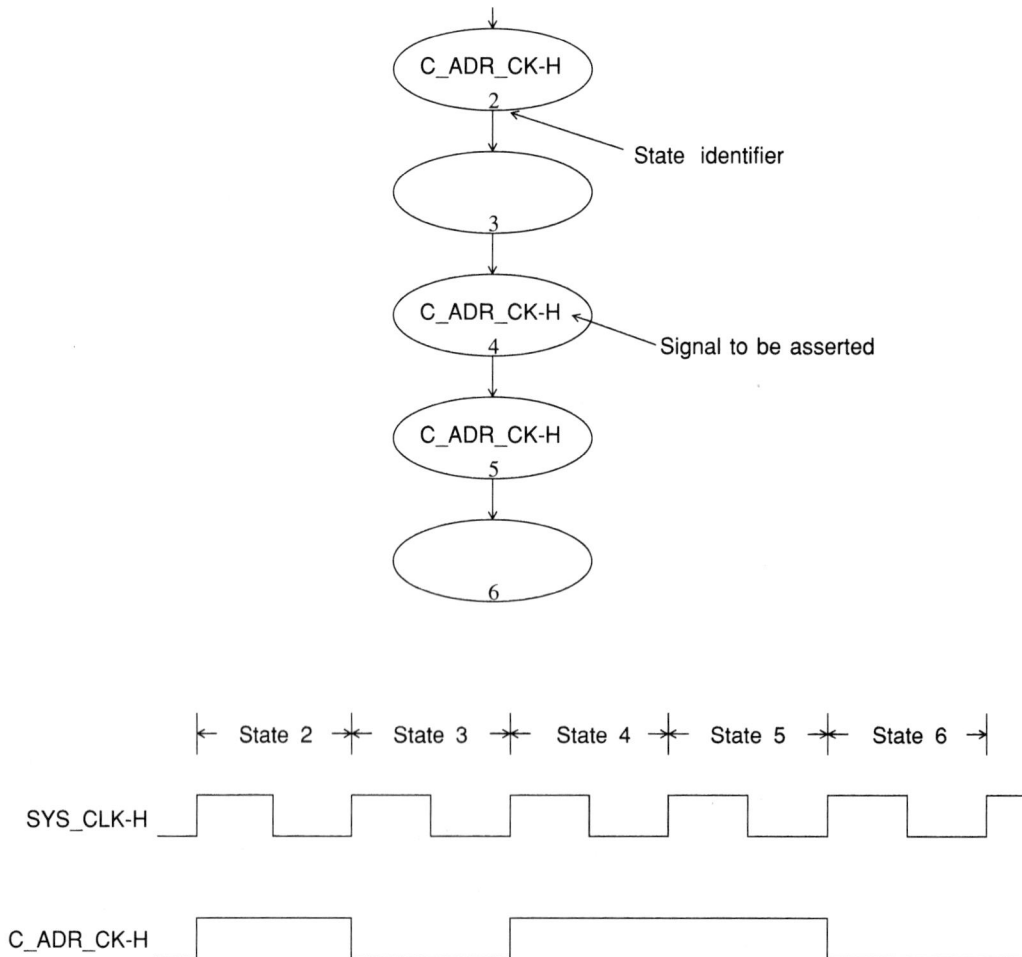

Figure 5.9. State Diagram Segment with Signal Assertion.

will cause that behavior. The new state diagram is given in Figure 5.10, and we will now explain in detail the signal assertions identified there. Two signals identified in Figure 5.10 are controlled by SET-RESET flip-flops to allow one behavior in one portion of the state diagram and another in a different portion of the state diagram. These signals are the S_ADR_LD-L line and the ACC-H line. The S_ADR_LD-L line is asserted by a signal in State 0 (SET_SA_LD-L) to allow

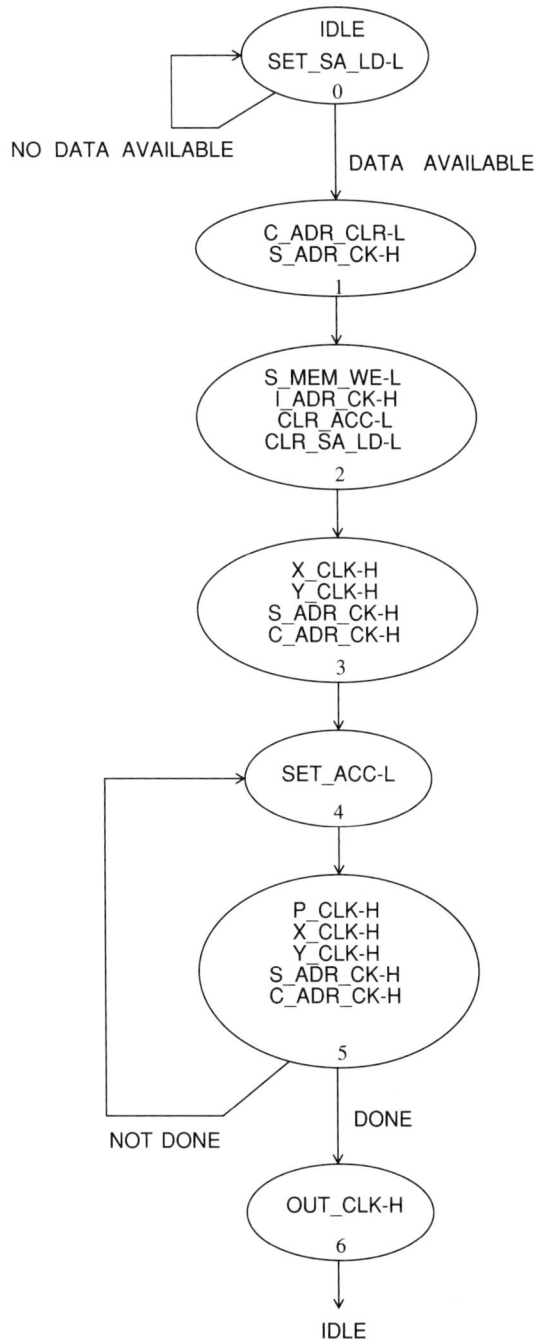

Figure 5.10. Detailed State Diagram for FIR Filter.

loading of the sample address register when its clock line is asserted in State 1. It is reset in State 2 (by CLR_SA_LD-L) to allow the address to increment when the clock line is asserted later. The ACC-H line is cleared in State 2 (by CLR_ACC-L) to set up the load of the product register. It is set in State 4 (by SET_ACC-L) to allow accumulation of results after the initial product load. We now consider each of the states, and the signal assertions needed for the process:

- *State 0* is the idle state; the SET_SA_LD-L signal is asserted to set up conditions for loading the sample address register, which will be accomplished in State 1.

- *State 1* should clear the coefficient address register and load the sample address register from the initial address register. The clear of the coefficient address register is accomplished by asserting C_ADR_CLR-L. The loading of the sample address register requires that the sample address load line be asserted, and then the clock line is asserted. The load was asserted in State 0; the clock is asserted in this state.

- *State 2* causes three things to happen. The S_MEM_WE-L line is asserted to write the sample into the sample memory (the appropriate address was loaded in State 1). The initial address register is decremented by asserting I_ADR_CK-H. And the product load condition is set up by asserting CLR_ACC-L.

- *State 3* causes load of the sample (X_CLK-H) and the coefficient (Y_CLK-H) into the MAC, then increments the two addresses (S_ADR_CK-H, C_ADR_CK-H).

- *State 4* sets up the accumulate condition for the product register in the multiplier/accumulator chip by asserting SET_ACC-L.

- *State 5* is where all of the work is done in steady state. The first time the state is entered, the assertion of P_CLK-H causes the product register to be loaded with $X \times Y$. Subsequent assertions of P_CLK-H load the product register with $X \times Y + P$. Samples and coefficients are loaded by asserting X_CLK-H and Y_CLK-H. The addresses are incremented by asserting S_ADR_CK-H and C_ADR_CK-H. The net result is that values are loaded and addresses incremented to look at the next values. The use of positive edge triggered devices assures that the current values are loaded before they change; the change will occur some time later because of propagation delays in the address registers and the memories themselves.

- *State 6* causes the output register to be filled by asserting OUT_CLK-H.

When the state numbers have been assigned to the state diagram, we are ready to map the controller onto the Moore machine. We will do this as shown in Figure 5.11. The present state register holds the current state of the system. The next state logic looks at the present state and the inputs and selects the next state. As shown in the figure, the logic blocks in the next state logic are multiplexers; the inputs to the multiplexers are chosen to select the correct next state from the current state. So the outputs of the multiplexers can be specified as shown in Table 5.1. The two signals included in the table have not yet been identified. The first is DATA-H, which is a flag from the A/D converter identifying that we have new data to process. A possible arrangement for this flag is shown in Figure 5.12(a). Here the end of conversion signal from the A/D converter causes a flip-flop to be set; the flip-flop is cleared by the same signal that clears the coefficient address. The second signal is DONE-H, which is asserted when the required number of iterations have been completed. We could create a new counter for

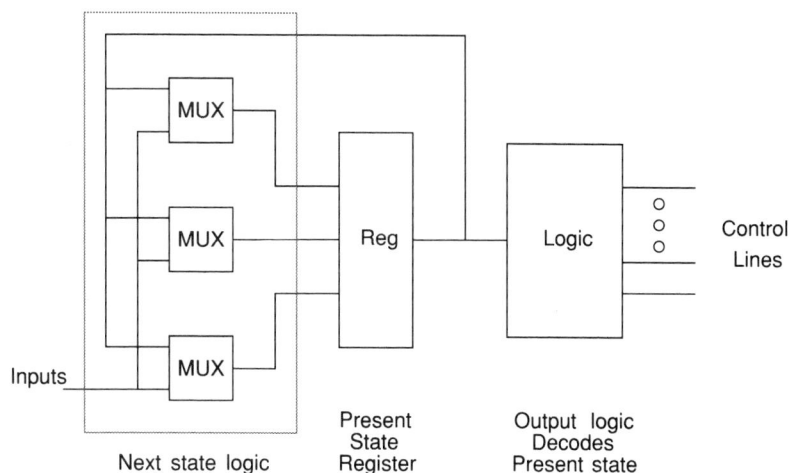

Figure 5.11. Implementation of Control System for FIR Filter.

Table 5.1. Next State Multiplexer Specifications.

	MUX 2	MUX 1	MUX 0
State 0	0	0	DATA-H
State 1	0	1	0
State 2	0	1	1
State 3	1	0	0
State 4	1	0	1
State 5	1	DONE-H	0
State 6	0	0	0

this, but that counter would duplicate the numbers used as the coefficient addresses. Therefore, Figure 5.12(b) shows a comparator connected to generate a DONE-H signal using the numbers available from the coefficient address.

The entries in Table 5.1 specify the inputs needed for the multiplexers for the state machine. The resulting circuit is shown in Figure 5.13. Figure 5.13(a) shows the present state register and the next state circuitry; Figure 5.13(b) shows the decode of the present state register to generate the necessary control signals.

Several observations should be made at this point. The first is that the method described above is simple and direct, and easily applicable to state machines with up to 32 states. Larger state machines have been constructed using this method, but the number of parts involved becomes unwieldy. The simplicity of the technique allows ideas to be tested quickly; changes are easily made by moving a few wires on the inputs of the multiplexers. The basic feedback mechanism need not be disturbed. This ease of modification allows the circuit to be quickly changed to conform to the needs of the system. This basic system allows different design ideas to be implemented and and tried with a minimal investment of time and effort.

One of the tasks required when the implementation has been completed is to check out the system to verify that the unit functions correctly and that the signals are controlled in an appropriate manner. The checkout process must identify and

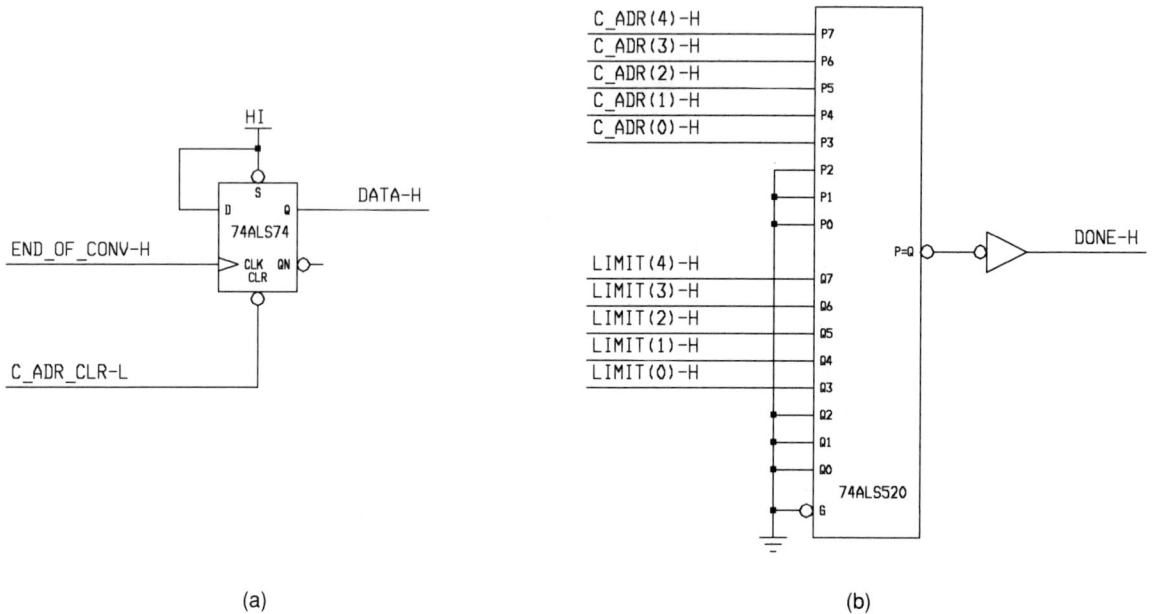

Figure 5.12. Control Signals for the State Machine.

remedy any errors which cause improper assertion sequences for the control signals. Generally errors will fall into one of two categories: either the system has wiring errors and the behavior does not follow the state diagram, or the implementation is correct but the state diagram is flawed because the designer did not thoroughly understand the system requirements. In either of these cases, modifications to a system designed in the method described above can be made easily, and the system can then be completed.

A second observation concerns the synchronization of input signals with the state machine. Figure 5.13(a) shows that the DATA-H signal is not directly fed into the multiplexers, but that it is first synchronized with the system by sending it through a buffer register that is clocked with the system clock. In the example, the buffer register is the same device used as the present state register, since the device is not entirely utilized. But what is required is keeping the input synchronous with the system clock. If this provision is not made, then the inputs may change in a manner such that, when the system clock does occur, that the next state is changing and the result is an illegal state transition. If the inputs are not synchronized, the system will fail when changes on the input lines occur at the same time that the present state register is being clocked. Note also that the DONE-H signal is not buffered by a register. The reason for this is that the DONE signal changes synchronously with the system clock, and hence does not need the effect of the register.

Another observation deals with the generation of the output signals. As shown in Figure 5.13(b), the present state is decoded to generate the appropriate signals for the system. Generally our concept is that as the system proceeds through the states identified by the state diagram, the lines of the decoder will become asserted at precisely the right time. However, since real devices contain real delays, and the delays can cause glitches, provisions must be made for the correct operation of the system. If the signals being activated are level sensitive,

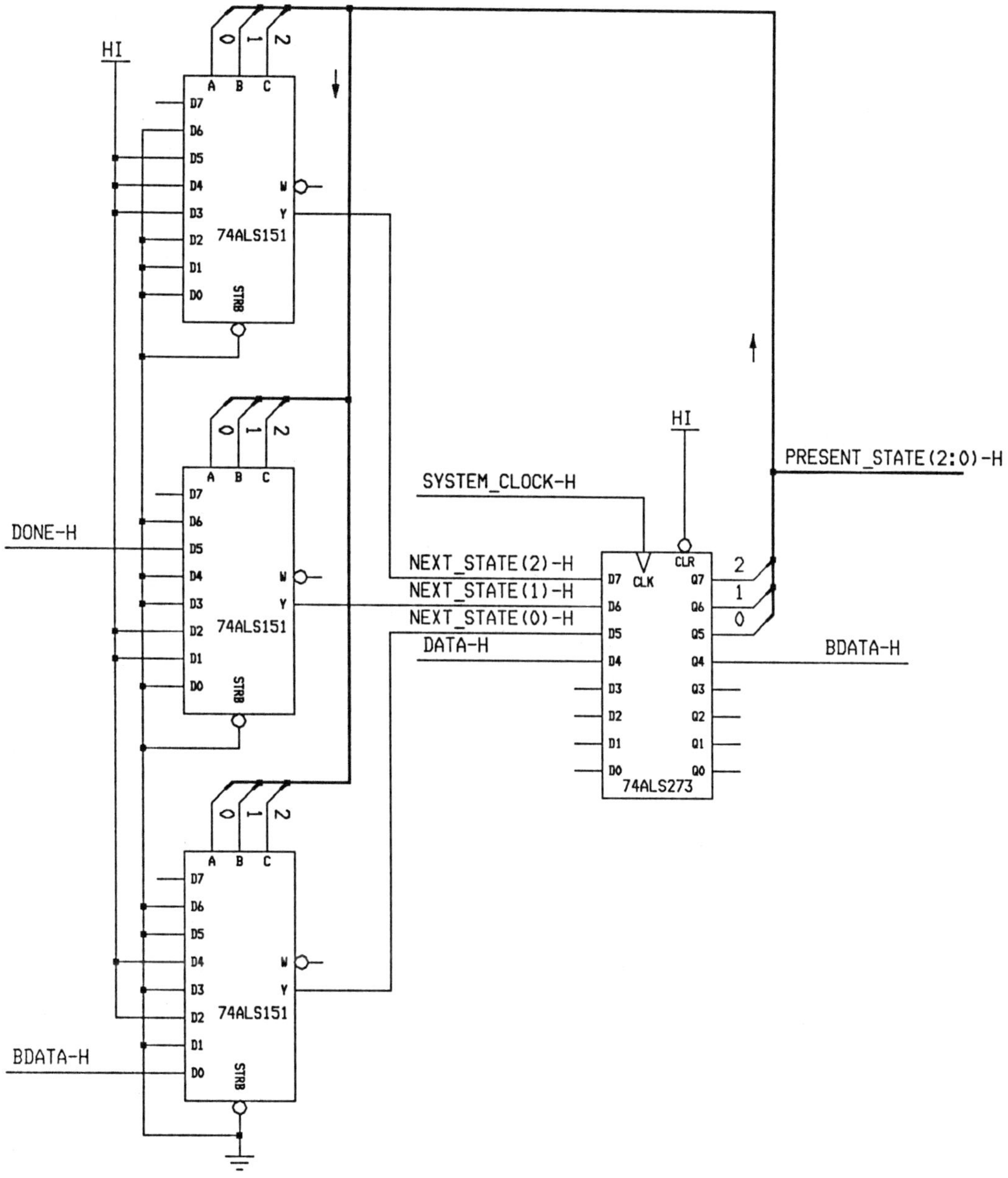

Figure 5.13(a). Present and Next State Logic for Control System.

then a glitch will not cause problems. However, if the signals are edge sensitive, as all of the clocks in our example are, then glitches on the control lines can cause problems. Figure 5.14(a) shows a decoder set up to demonstrate a number of possible combinations.

The problem of glitches on output lines is illustrated in Figure 5.14. The control line which is used in different ways in the example is the enable line of the decoder. If the decoder behaves as a perfect decoder, and no glitches occur on the output lines, then behavior similar to the waveform of Figure 5.7 can be obtained by always enabling the decoder. Figure 5.14(b) shows the results when

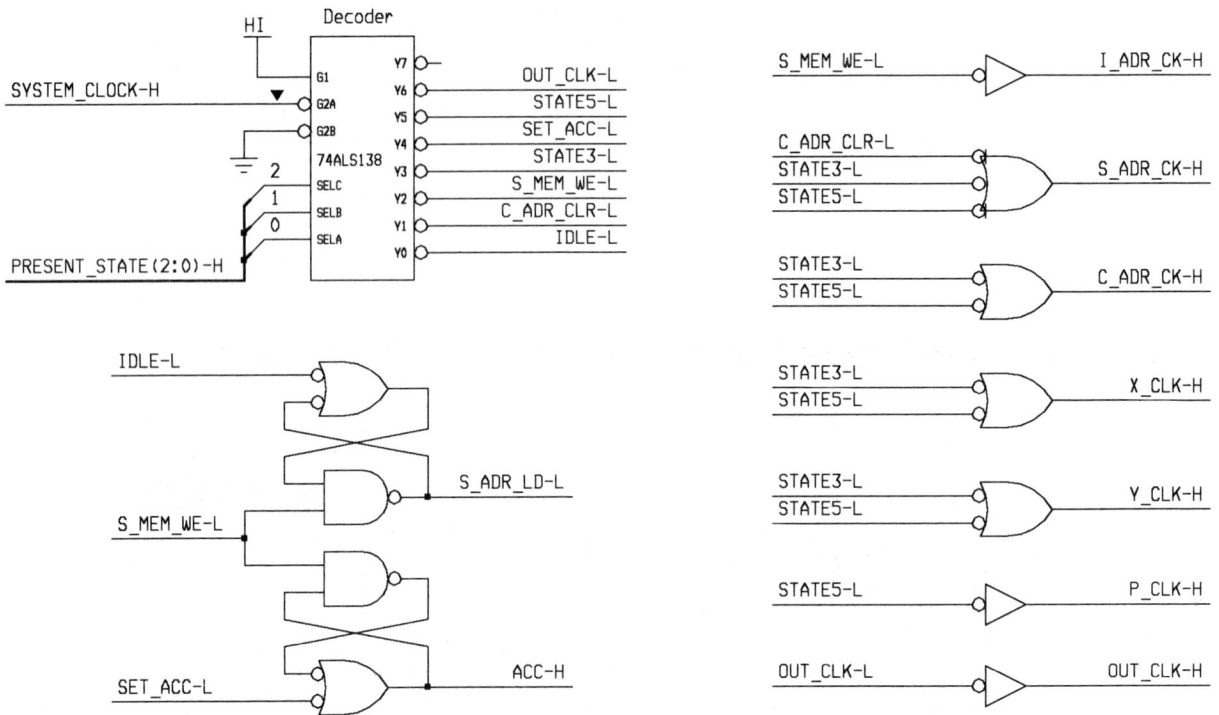

Figure 5.13(b). Generation of Control Signals from Present State.

the enable line is always asserted: glitches occur on the output lines of the decoders. In Figure 5.14(c) the enable has been tied to SYSTEM_CLOCK-H. The result is that the appropriate decoder output will be asserted only during the time that the system clock is low, which is the last half of the cycle. As can be seen from the figure, the assertion occurs half way through the cycle. This is the method utilized in the finite impulse response filter example. This is the reason that the ACC-H and S_ADR_LD-L lines are driven from flip-flops, since the decoder outputs are only asserted for half of the cycle.

The success of obtaining the last half of the cycle may prompt one to attempt to obtain the first half of the cycle by using the other phase of the clock.

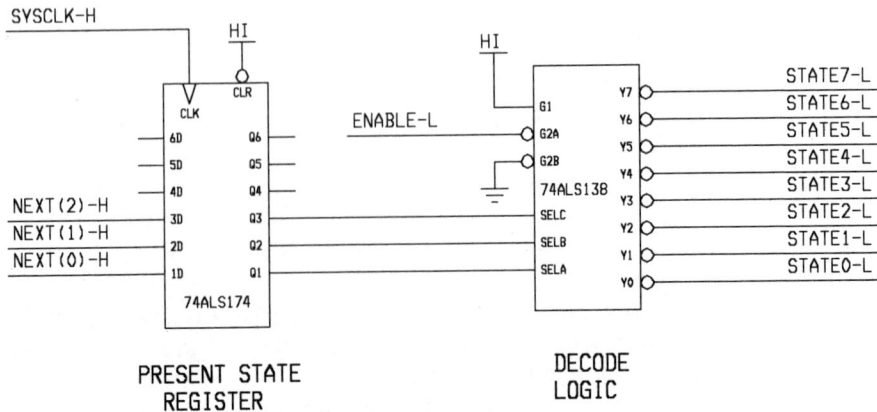

Figure 5.14(a). Test Setup for Using State Decoder.

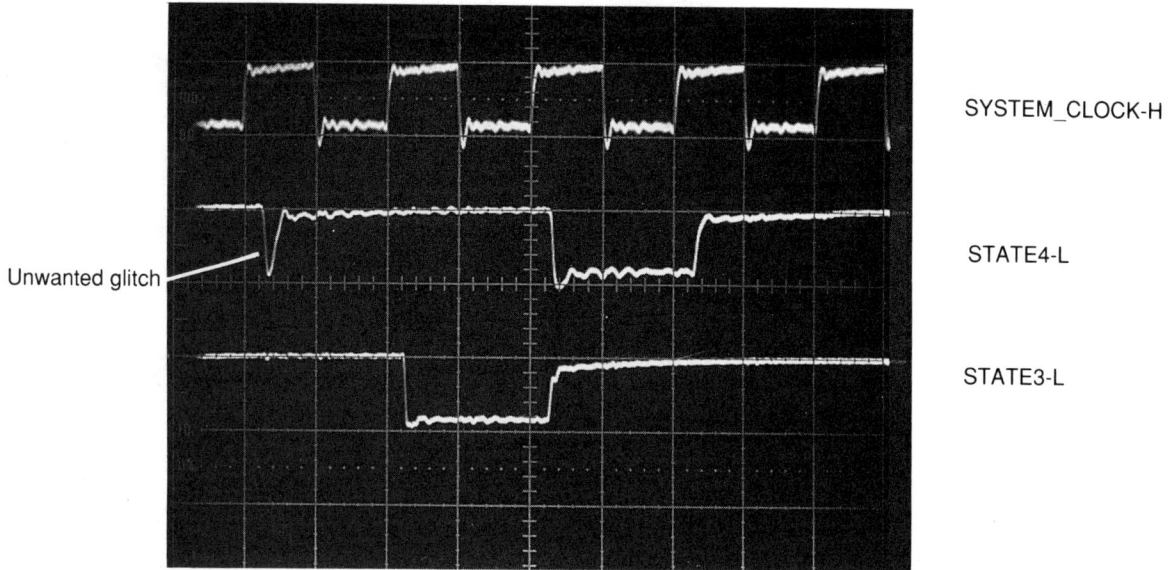

Figure 5.14(b). Waveform for Decoder with Enable Always Asserted.

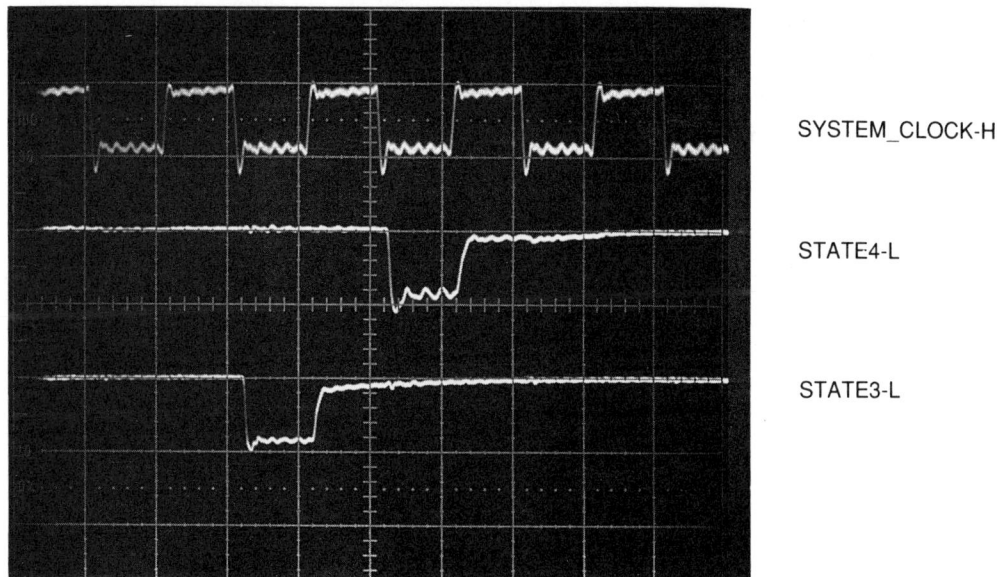

Figure 5.14(c). Waveform for Decoder with Enable Tied to SYSTEM_CLOCK-H.

The result is shown in Figure 5.14(d), which indicates that unwanted pulses occur; this is a result of the propagation delay from clock assertion to change of decoder output. As can be seen from the waveforms of Figure 5.14, a number of options are available to a designer, and the merits of each option must be considered before selecting a design method.

The FIR filter example demonstrates some of the basic principles of controller design. It is imperative that the designer first understand the system specifications; this includes aspects often neglected, such as the implications of

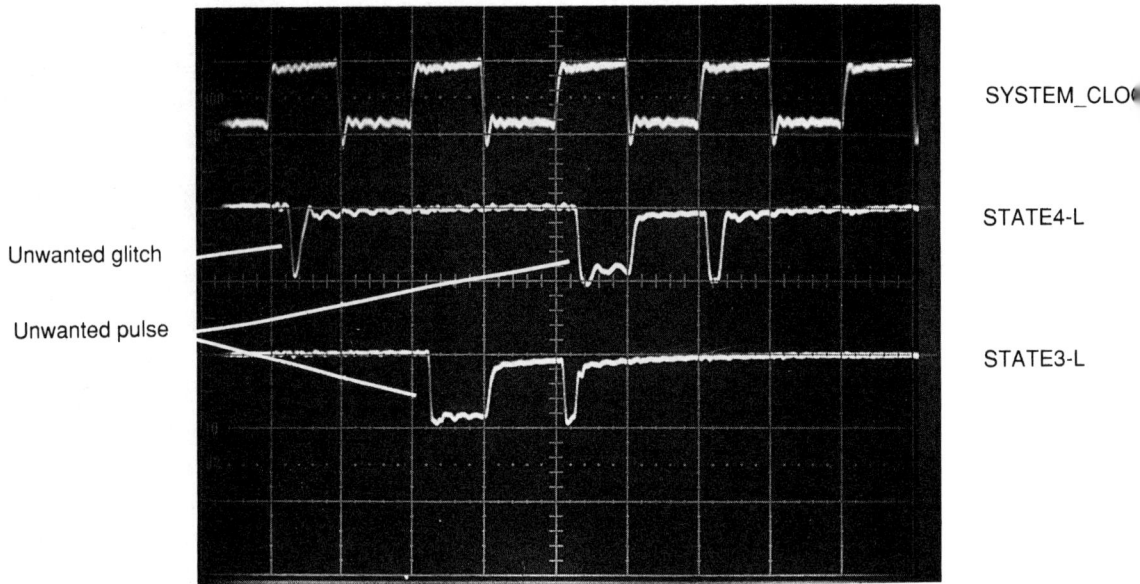

Figure 5.14(d). Waveform for Decoder with Enable Tied to
SYSTEM_CLOCK-L.

the arithmetic methods, number of bits on the data path, and interaction protocols.
The designer then generates a data path block diagram, an RTL description of the
desired system behavior, and a preliminary state diagram. These tools assure the
designer that the system specifications will be satisfied, and that the necessary
data transfers can be made. When the block diagram is defined, the control signals of the components of the system are identified and labeled with appropriate
polarized mnemonics. The state diagram can now be refined to specify the assertion of the control signals that will cause the desired work to be accomplished.
The state diagram can then be mapped onto the Moore model to provide a working control system. The result is a system that will activate the control signals in
the proper sequence to achieve the necessary results.

The state diagram approach is easy to understand, and it is also fairly easy
to implement for small systems. We have shown the next state decode logic to be
multiplexers; classical methods dictate the use of random logic. Manufacturers
now provide registered PLAs (programmable logic arrays) that allow the designer
to put both the present state register and the next state logic inside a single chip,
which is then programmed to follow some specified state diagram. Outputs are
handled in much the same way. One use of these controllers will be used in Section 5.6. However, historically other methods have been applied to the control
systems of computers. We now look at some of these methods.

5.4. Sequential Systems with Individual Delays

As we have seen, the first step in any control design is to derive a block diagram
that meets the system specifications, and then to identify on that block diagram
the control lines needed. In this section we will look at an extremely simple computer, and use that machine to exemplify the delay method of sequential control

systems. The principles here are similar to those used in the state machine control of the previous section, but the application methods are slightly different. Rather than have the state of a system stored in a single register, and the state changes reflected by changes in the state number, the action of the delay type system is governed by a control pulse that traverses the elements of the control system.

The technique of individual delays described here has been used in the past for a number of computer systems, but is not widely used in new systems. However, in some systems constructed entirely within an integrated circuit chip, delay lines play a prominent part in generating control signals.

The block diagram for our example is given in Figure 5.15. The diagram shows a simple single address machine, with enough detail represented to illustrate the principles of this section. The diagram does not by any means represent a complete system, since a diagram of that complexity would be overwhelming. The data paths are patterned after some of the first computers: the connections are

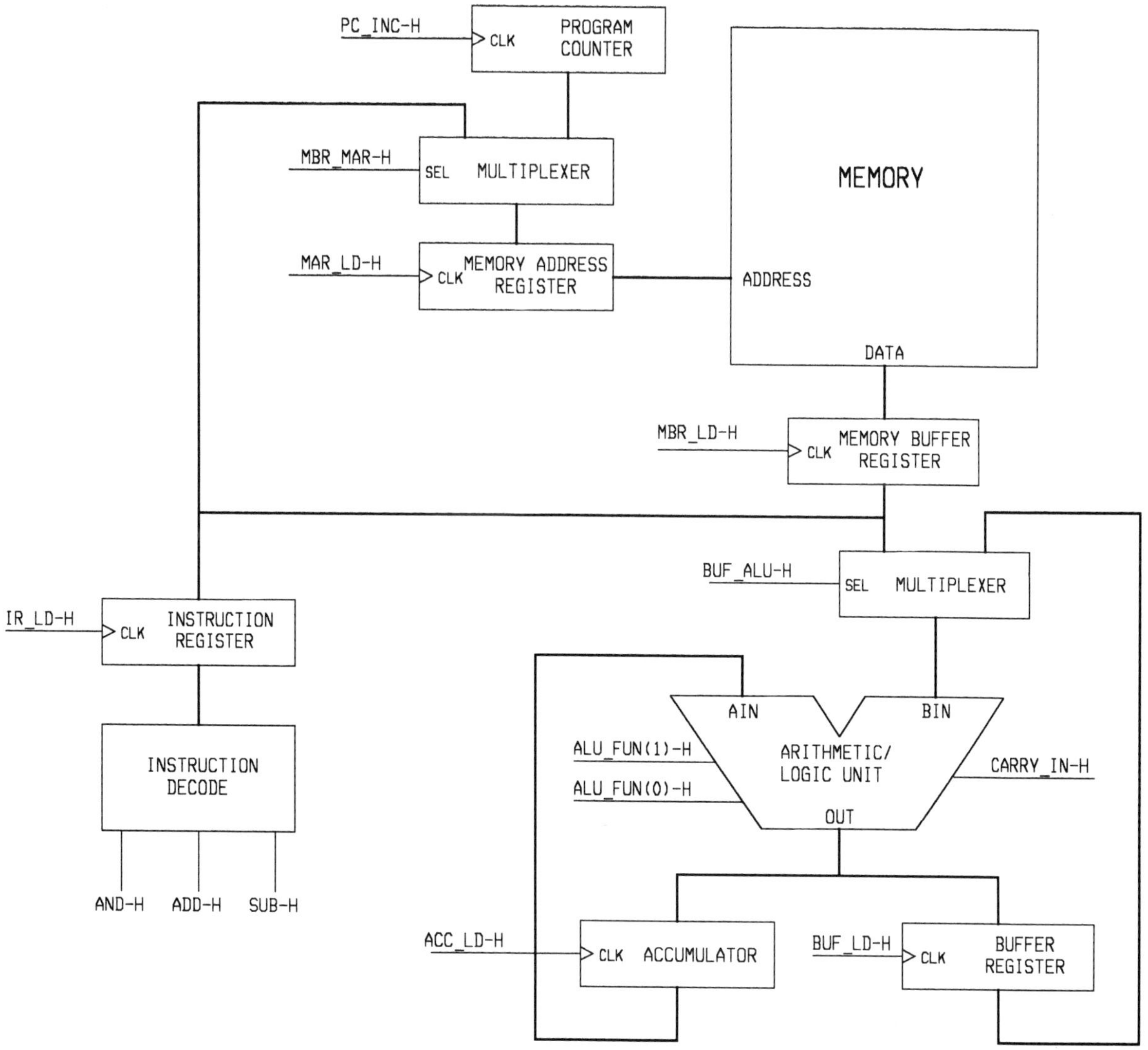

Figure 5.15. Block Diagram for a Simple Computer.

basically point to point rather than bused. Note that the data paths are not complete, as exemplified by the fact that there is no path to the program counter.

The desired behavior for this example is to implement three simple instructions: ADD, SUBTRACT, and AND. All three of these instructions require two operands. Since this is a single address machine, one operand is found in the accumulator, and the other is found in memory at a location specified by the instruction. The task required of the control section is to cause the requested action on the data and leave the result in the accumulator.

As in the previous example, the first task is to create a suitable data path block diagram, which was given as part of the definition of the example. The designer then must arrange for the required action, utilizing the capabilities of the data path hardware. The hardware capabilities of this example include:

- *Program counter:* The content of this register identifies a location in memory where the instruction to be executed can be found. The process of instruction execution should increment this register to point at the next instruction. This can be accomplished by asserting PC_INC-H.

- *Memory address register:* This register holds an address to identify a location in the memory.

- *MAR multiplexer:* The multiplexer selects the source of information for the MAR. Normal operation is for the PC to be output to the MAR. However, when MBR_MAR-H is asserted, the address is obtained from the memory buffer register.

- *Memory:* The memory will provide to the memory buffer register the contents of the address specified by the memory address register within some specified delay. For this example we will assume that the delay is 200 nsec.

- *Memory buffer register:* For destructive readout memory technologies this register remembers the data just read so that it can be restored to the memory. In general, modern semiconductor memories do not need this capability.

- *ALU multiplexer:* This device selects the BIN operand of the arithmetic/logic unit. Normal operation selects the contents of the memory buffer register; when BUF_ALU-H is asserted, the ALU receives the contents of the buffer register.

- *Buffer register:* This register is used for internal operations that need a temporary storage location. It is not visible to assembly level programmers.

- *Accumulator:* This is the known register of the machine. All instructions that manipulate data will find information in this register, and instructions that produce data results will leave their information in this register.

- *Arithmetic/logic unit:* This functional unit is capable of some rudimentary actions, as specified by the following table:

ALU_FUN		OUT Function
0	0	Bitwise AND of AIN, BIN
0	1	Bitwise OR of AIN, BIN
1	0	Inverse of BIN
1	1	Binary ADD of AIN, BIN

This ALU has the characteristic that logical operations (AND, OR, INVERT) take 40 nsec to complete; the arithmetic operation (ADD) takes 80 nsec to complete.

- *Instruction register:* This register is used to hold the instruction during its execution.

- *Instruction decode:* The decode circuitry identifies the type of instruction to be performed. In this example there are only three, but generally there will be many instructions. The appropriate output line will be asserted to identify which of the instructions has been decoded.

In addition to the times specified for the ALU and memory functions, we will assume that register to register transfers require 40 nsec.

The designer utilizes knowledge of the data path connections and the capabilities of the components used on the data path to specify the required action of the control system. The first step is to identify the required register transfers, and for this example these transfers are given in RTL form in Table 5.2. The table specifies the order in which the transfers are to be accomplished. Our task is now to take these transfers and implement them in hardware. The first step in this process is to generate a flow chart that identifies the required steps. The flow chart for these three instructions is given in Figure 5.16. Note that the flow chart identifies the signal assertions required to accomplish the transfers specified by Table 5.2, as well as the delays necessary between the assertion of those signals. Also note that there is a one to one correspondence between the operations identified in Table 5.2 and the operations caused by the signal assertions identified in the flow chart.

To illustrate the process of instruction execution, we will examine the subtract instruction. A timing diagram showing the control lines involved in this instruction is shown in Figure 5.17. The process begins by transferring the address of the instruction from the program counter into the memory address register with MAR_LD-H. Note that the multiplexer normally supplies this information to the MAR, so no action is required on the control lines of the multiplexer. The memory has a 200 nsec delay, so the MBR_LD-H signal is delayed by that amount after loading the MAR. The program counter is also incremented at the same time. The instruction register is loaded from the MBR 40 nsec later, since 40 nsec is required for register transfers; after a period of time for instruction decode, the MBR_MAR line is asserted so that the MAR receives its information from the MBR. A delay time later the MAR_LD-H line is asserted again, loading the address of the operand required for the operation. After the memory

Table 5.2. Register Transfers for Three Instructions.

Register Transfers for Example

AND *Instruction*	ADD *Instruction*	SUBTRACT *Instruction*
PC $\rightarrow$ MAR	PC $\rightarrow$ MAR	PC $\rightarrow$ MAR
M [MAR] $\rightarrow$ MBR	M [MAR] $\rightarrow$ MBR	M [MAR] $\rightarrow$ MBR
PC + 1 $\rightarrow$ PC	PC + 1 $\rightarrow$ PC	PC + 1 $\rightarrow$ PC
MBR $\rightarrow$ IR	MBR $\rightarrow$ IR	MBR $\rightarrow$ IR
MBR $\rightarrow$ MAR	MBR $\rightarrow$ MAR	MBR $\rightarrow$ MAR
M [MAR] $\rightarrow$ MBR	M [MAR] $\rightarrow$ MBR	M [MAR] $\rightarrow$ MBR
MBR $\bullet$ ACC $\rightarrow$ ACC	MBR + ACC $\rightarrow$ ACC	$\neg$ MBR $\rightarrow$ BUF
		BUF + ACC + 1 $\rightarrow$ ACC

```
                          START
                            │
                            ▼
                  ┌───────────────────┐
                  │      MAR_LD-H      │
                  └───────────────────┘
                            │
                            ▼
                  ╭───────────────────╮
                  │  200 NSEC DELAY   │
                  ╰───────────────────╯
                            │
                            ▼
                  ┌───────────────────┐
                  │      PC_INC-H      │
                  │      MBR_LD-H      │
                  └───────────────────┘
                            │
                            ▼
                  ╭───────────────────╮
                  │   40 NSEC DELAY   │
                  ╰───────────────────╯
                            │
                            ▼
                  ┌───────────────────┐
                  │      IR_LD-H       │
                  └───────────────────┘
                            │
                            ▼
                  ╭───────────────────╮
                  │   80 NSEC DELAY   │
                  ╰───────────────────╯
            ┌───────────────┼───────────────┐
            ▼               ▼               ▼
          AND             ADD             SUB
```

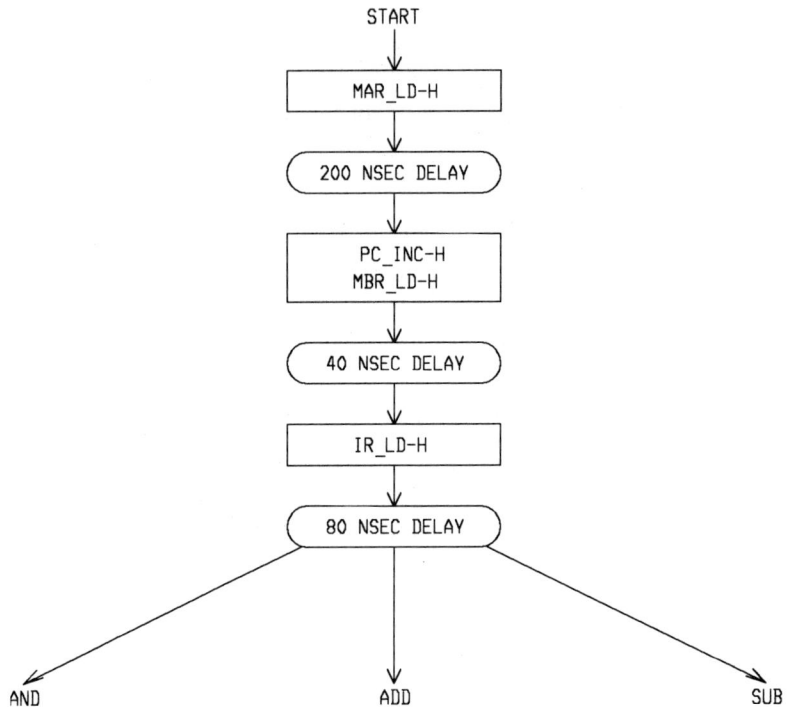

Figure 5.16(a). Flow Chart for Delay Implementation of Three Instructions.

delay the MBR is loaded and the MBR_MAR-H line reset. Since the subtraction method specified calls for inversion of the MBR, the ALU_FUN(1)-H line is set high to present to the input of the buffer register the inverse of the MBR. This information is then loaded into the buffer register, and the ALU prepared for an addition operation. By also forcing the carry input to be a "1," the final operation is the desired subtraction, and after the required delay the ACC_LD-H line is asserted to load the information into the accumulator. The *fetch-execute* cycle then repeats itself, beginning with the assertion of the MAR_LD-H signal.

The flow diagram and timing diagram together specify the action to occur and the timing relationship between control signals. The individual delay method of sequencer design consists of directly implementing the flow diagram with delay elements. A delay element consists of either a semiconductor device or an analog equivalent that will accept a signal, usually a pulse, and delay the signal by a preset amount. In this example we need delays of 40 nsec for the register accesses — 80 nsec, 120 nsec, and 200 nsec. With these available, a designer matches the flow diagram with timing elements, and then uses logic gates and flip-flops to create the appropriate control signals. The delay elements for this example are shown in Figure 5.18(a), and the additional logic required is shown in Figure 5.18(b) and Figure 5.18(c).

The system would begin action by injecting into the delay network a single pulse at RUN-H. This would assert START-H, which in turn asserts MAR_LD-H. After a delay of 200 nsec, I_FETCHED-H is asserted. This causes the assertion of both PC_INC-H and MBR_LD-H. Another delay element is used to place the required time between the load of the MBR and the assertion of IR_LOAD-H. The AND gates then direct the pulse down the appropriate set of delays, depending on the instruction decoded. And so the process continues, with the pulse traversing

```
        AND                        ADD                        SUB

         │                          │                          │
         ▼                          ▼                          ▼
┌──────────────────┐      ┌──────────────────┐      ┌──────────────────┐
│  set MBR_MAR-H   │      │  set MBR_MAR-H   │      │  set MBR_MAR-H   │
└──────────────────┘      └──────────────────┘      └──────────────────┘
         │                          │                          │
         ▼                          ▼                          ▼
╭──────────────────╮      ╭──────────────────╮      ╭──────────────────╮
│  40 NSEC DELAY   │      │  40 NSEC DELAY   │      │  40 NSEC DELAY   │
╰──────────────────╯      ╰──────────────────╯      ╰──────────────────╯
         │                          │                          │
         ▼                          ▼                          ▼
┌──────────────────┐      ┌──────────────────┐      ┌──────────────────┐
│     MAR_LD-H     │      │     MAR_LD-H     │      │     MAR_LD-H     │
└──────────────────┘      └──────────────────┘      └──────────────────┘
         │                          │                          │
         ▼                          ▼                          ▼
╭──────────────────╮      ╭──────────────────╮      ╭──────────────────╮
│  200 NSEC DELAY  │      │  200 NSEC DELAY  │      │  200 NSEC DELAY  │
╰──────────────────╯      ╰──────────────────╯      ╰──────────────────╯
         │                          │                          │
         ▼                          ▼                          ▼
┌──────────────────┐      ┌──────────────────┐      ┌──────────────────┐
│     MBR_LD-H     │      │     MBR_LD-H     │      │     MBR_LD-H     │
│  reset MBR_MAR-H │      │  reset MBR_MAR-H │      │  reset MBR_MAR-H │
└──────────────────┘      │  set ALU_FUN(1)-H│      │  set ALU_FUN(1)-H│
         │                │  set ALU_FUN(0)-H│      └──────────────────┘
         ▼                └──────────────────┘               │
╭──────────────────╮               │                          ▼
│  80 NSEC DELAY   │               ▼                ╭──────────────────╮
╰──────────────────╯      ╭──────────────────╮      │  80 NSEC DELAY   │
         │                │  120 NSEC DELAY  │      ╰──────────────────╯
         ▼                ╰──────────────────╯               │
┌──────────────────┐               │                          ▼
│     ACC_LD-H     │               ▼                ┌──────────────────┐
└──────────────────┘      ┌──────────────────┐      │     BUF_LD-H     │
         │                │     ACC_LD-H     │      │  set ALU_FUN(0)-H│
         ▼                │ reset ALU_FUN(1)-H│     │  set CARRY_IN-H  │
      START               │ reset ALU_FUN(0)-H│     │   set BUF_ALU-H  │
                          └──────────────────┘      └──────────────────┘
                                   │                          │
                                   ▼                          ▼
                                START               ╭──────────────────╮
                                                    │  120 NSEC DELAY  │
                                                    ╰──────────────────╯
                                                             │
                                                             ▼
                                                    ┌──────────────────┐
                                                    │     ACC_LD-H     │
                                                    │  reset BUF_ALU-H │
                                                    │ reset ALU_FUN(1)-H│
                                                    │ reset ALU_FUN(0)-H│
                                                    │ reset CARRY_IN-H │
                                                    └──────────────────┘
                                                             │
                                                             ▼
                                                          START
```

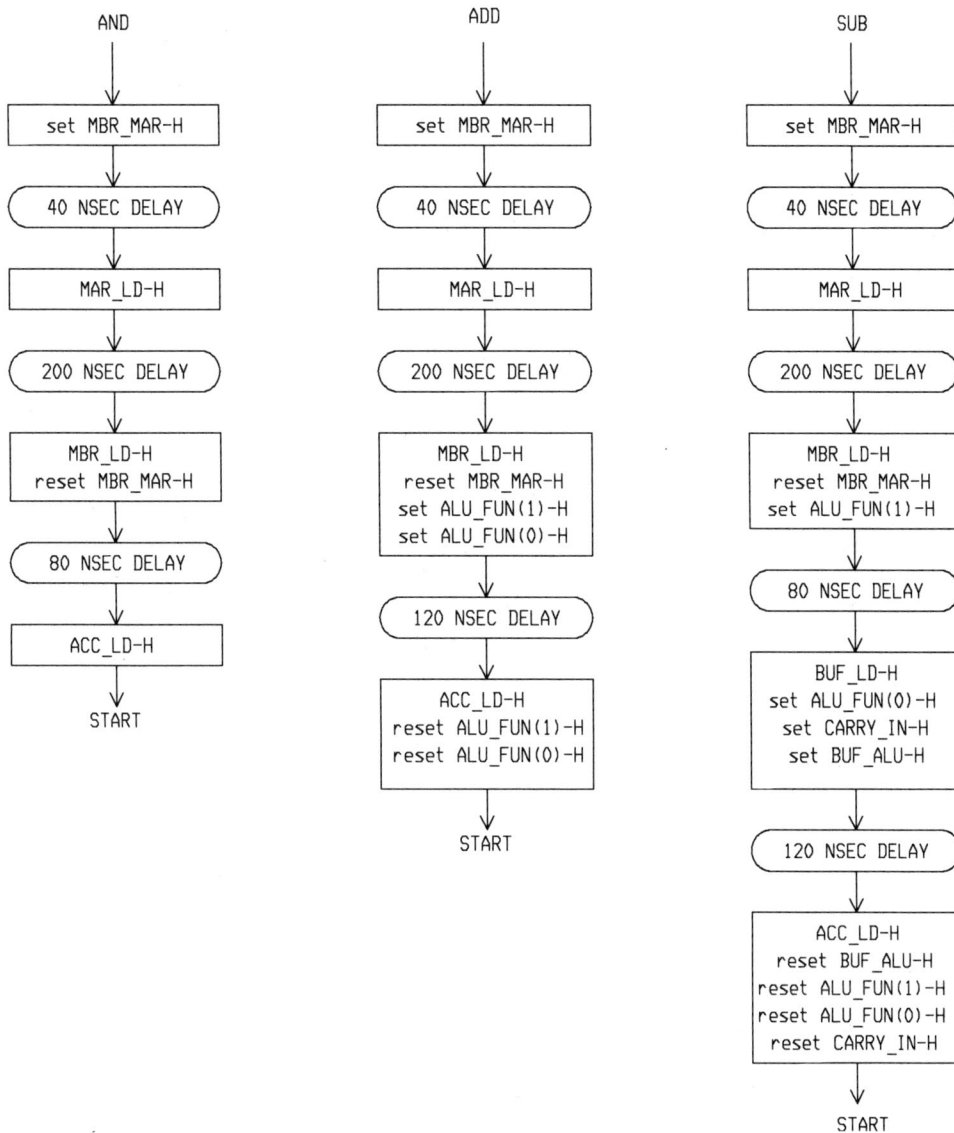

Figure 5.16(b). *(cont)* Flow Chart for Delay Implementation of Three Instructions.

the delay network and doing work as required. The control signals are created by tapping the appropriate spots in the delay network, as specified by the flow diagram. For example, ACC_LD-H is created by ORing the signals from the AND, ADD, or SUB delay sections together. For signals that need to remain set for lengths of time, the flip-flop arrangement shown for MAR_MBR-H can be used. The signal is set when it is first needed, and then reset when it is no longer needed. This allows both pulses and levels to be used in the system.

The preceding example has shown that systems can be designed in a straightforward manner using delay elements and gates to cause the appropriate action. The data path block diagram identifies the control points that need to be activated, and the flow diagram and timing diagram specify the actions and delays to take place to accomplish the appropriate tasks. This example can easily be extrapolated to include other instructions: the flow diagram will require additional

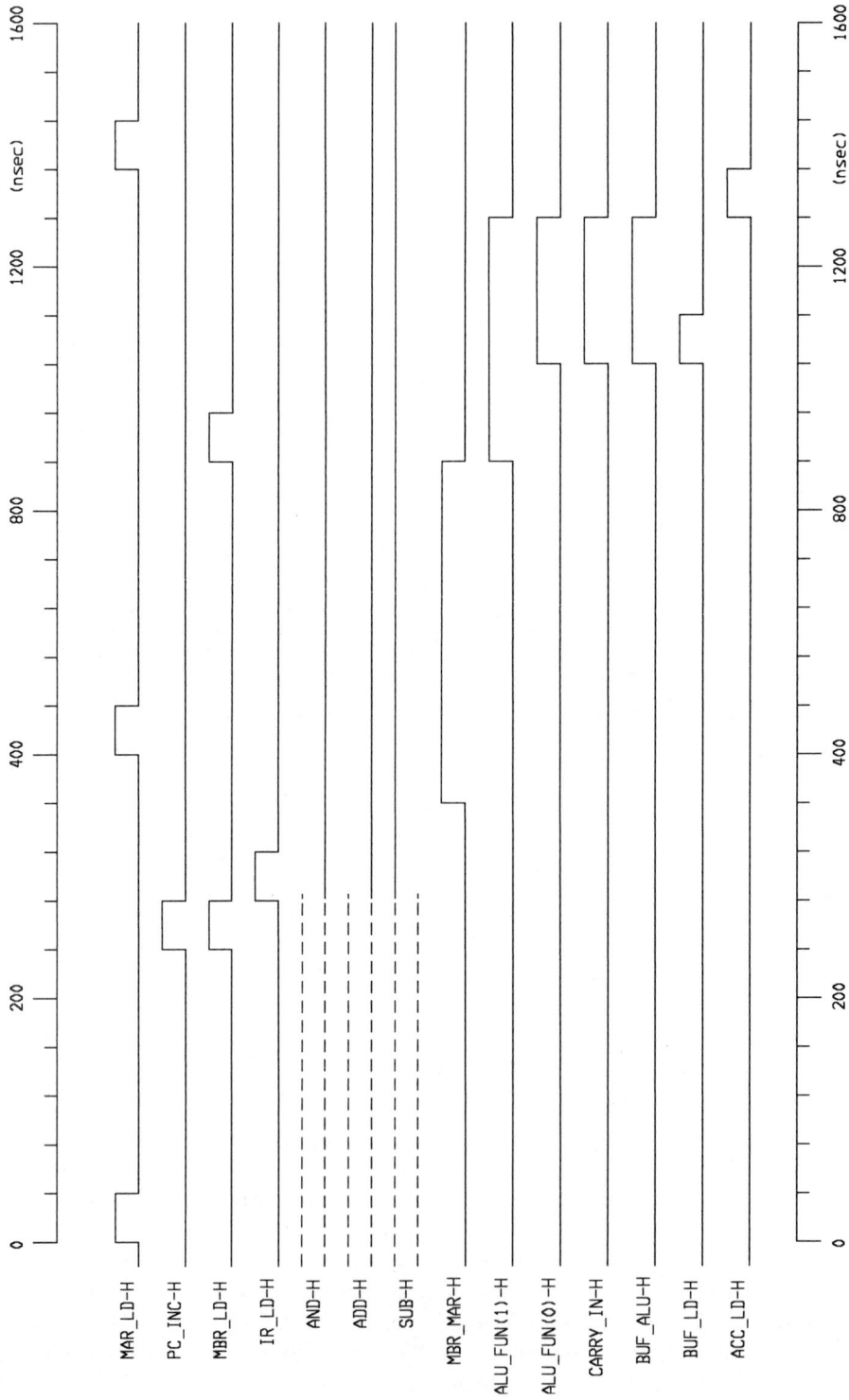

Figure 5.17. Timing Diagram for Control Signals: Subtract Instruction.

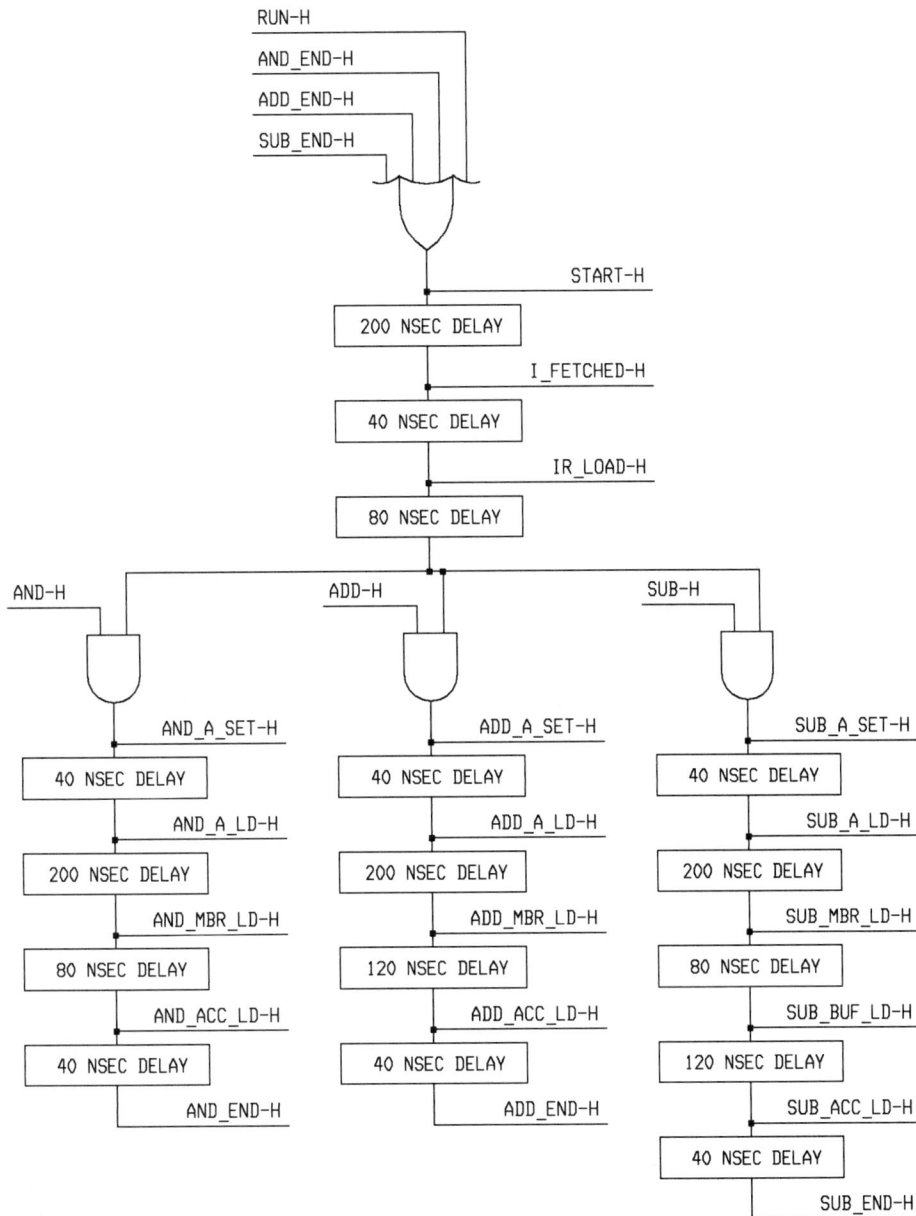

Figure 5.18(a). Delay Elements Needed for Simple Machine.

branches in the decode section, and additional register transfer level specifications will identify the work required for arithmetic or procedural instructions. For example, not all instructions will require action from the ALU, and other data paths will be required for jumps and other activity.

This method of design has an advantage in that the control can be tuned to provide the fastest action possible. That is, if it is known that the ALU will do an AND action in 38 nsec, then the 38 nsec delay can be placed in the appropriate spot in the system, and the AND instruction will take 2 nsec less than an OR instruction. But offsetting the speed advantages are some of the practical problems. The fidelity of the pulse as it travels through the system must be carefully

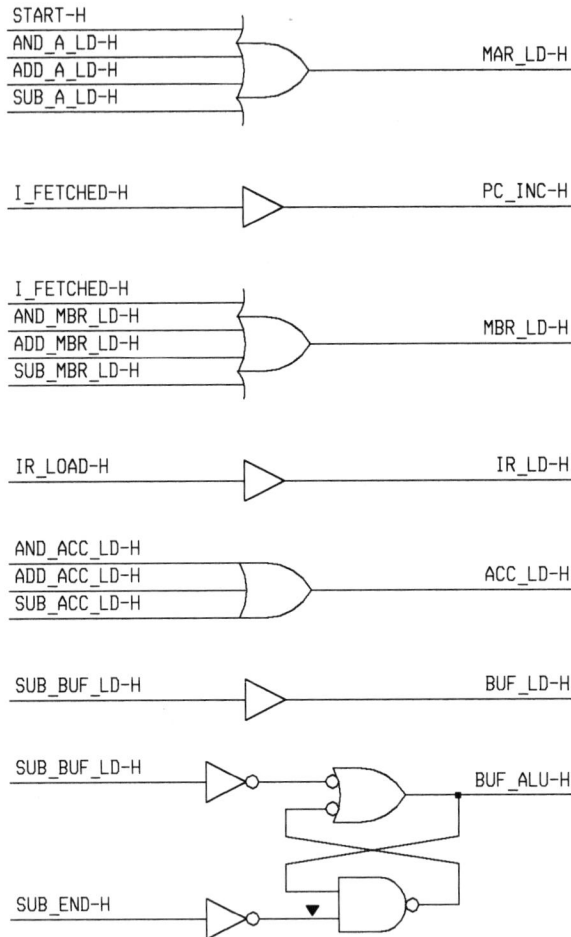

Figure 5.18(b). Creation of Control Signals for Delay Method.

maintained, and this can cause additional problems. The system must be carefully designed to prevent spurious pulses from entering the network; an interesting error mode is when two pulses are traversing the system simultaneously.

This method allows a straightforward combination of data path block diagram, flow diagram, and timing information to result in a tunable, high performance control system. The control system provides both pulse and level capabilities, and can be easily modified either by changing the delays or by including other points in the delay network in the creation of control signals. Many of these characteristics are also evident in the shift register method of control design.

5.5. Sequential Systems Using Shift Register Timing

The concepts of the shift register timing method for control design follow closely those of the individual delay method. The data path block diagram is used to identify the control signals, the flow diagram identifies the register transfers and other work that need to be done, and the timing diagram specifies the interaction of the control signals required to accomplish the work. However, the timing

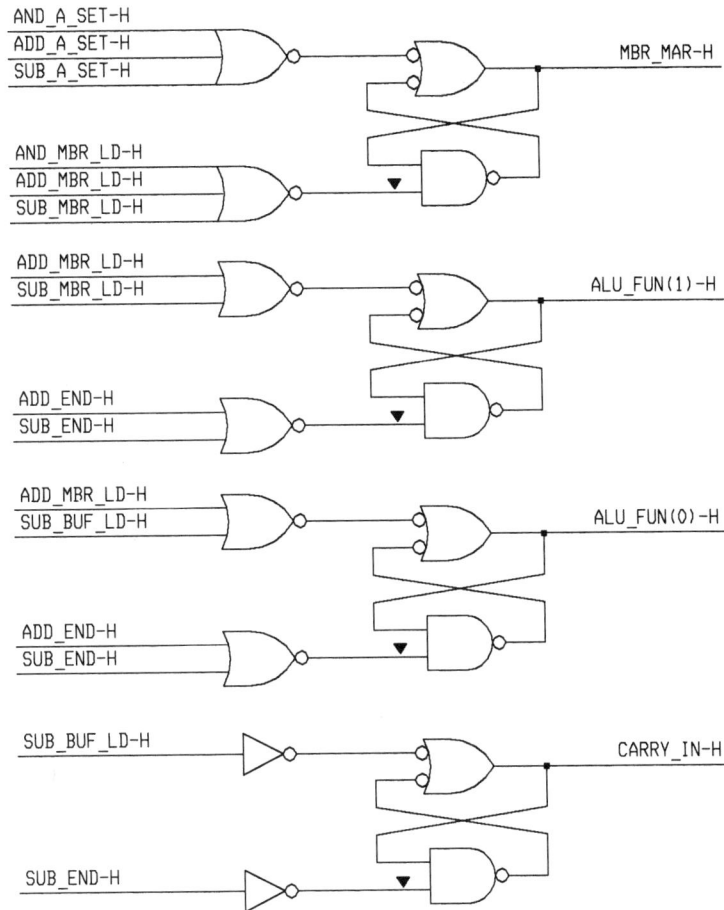

Figure 5.18(c). *(cont)* Creation of Control Signals for Delay Method.

diagram must now represent events that occur at multiples of the system clock. That is, the delays of a flow chart such as Figure 5.16 must all be multiples of the system clock. The preceding example was chosen so that all of the delays were multiples of 40 nsec — so that will be the assumed system clock rate for this section. The concept for the shift register method is to identify the work to be done, and then to create the proper waveforms by using gates to harness a pulse proceeding down a shift register.

The creation of the timing action is accomplished by the action of a shift register. One such arrangement is shown in Figure 5.19. The desired pulse action is initiated by asserting START_PULSE-L. On the next clock pulse the signal PULSE_0-H will be asserted. If a pulse duration of one cycle is desired, the STOP_PULSE-L control line can be created by inverting PULSE_0-H. Thereafter, on each leading edge of the system clock the pulse "moves" down the shift register. The resulting pattern is shown in Figure 5.20, called Method One. The pulses depicted for Method One form a precise timing capability for the system. If an event is to occur 80 nsec after initiation of the instruction, then PULSE_2-H can be used to cause the event. However, if a control line needs to be asserted for more than one clock period, then more than one time period is needed. That is, if a signal is to be asserted from 80 to 160 nsec after initiation of the instruction,

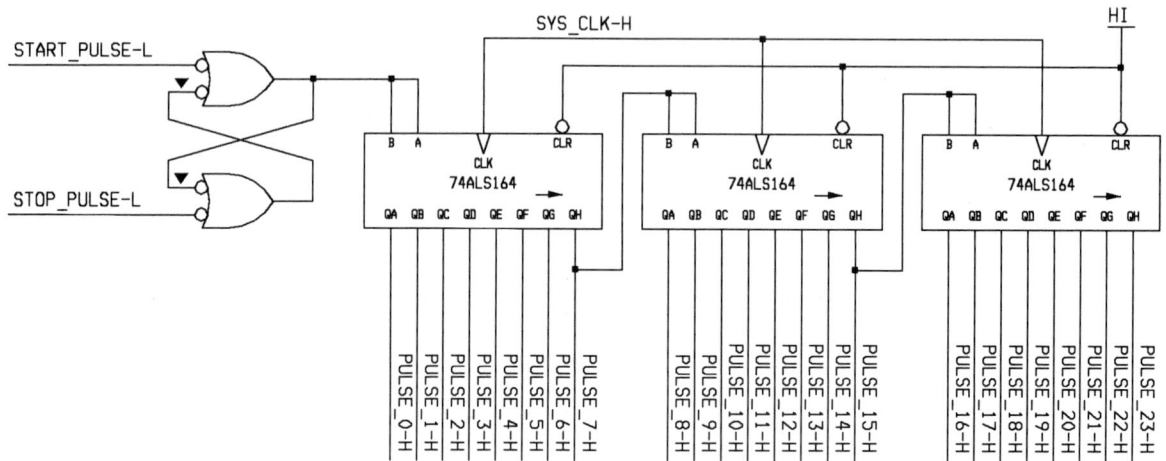

Figure 5.19. Pulse Creation with Shift Registers.

then the signal can be created by ORing PULSE_2-H and PULSE_3-H. This will indeed result in a signal of duration 80 nsec; however, there may be a glitch in the signal caused by the timing difference of deasserting PULSE_2-H and asserting PULSE_3-H.

One way to get around the problem of glitches on the control lines is to use set-reset flip-flops as we did with the delay line method. Another solution to the problem is to use overlapping pulses, as shown in Method Two of Figure 5.20. Pulses with a length of two system clock periods can easily be created by using the inverse of PULSE_1-H to be STOP_PULSE-L. When these signals are ORed together, the resulting signal is free of glitches caused by the hazards associated with pulse assertion.

The similarities between this method and the individual delay method are apparent from the approaches both take in implementing the control signals. The principal difference is that one method uses individual delays and a pulse that traverses a control network to accomplish work, while the other method achieves the correct timing relationships by the use of measured delays in a shift register. Both methods create the control signals by gating appropriate delayed values with the necessary enable conditions. The result is a system that asserts the control signals needed to accomplish the necessary work.

An example of gating for the shift register method for the system of the previous section is given in Figure 5.21. The gates shown are derived directly from the timing and flow diagrams. The MAR_LD-H signal is always asserted at PULSE_0 time, or it is asserted at PULSE_10 if the instruction is an AND, ADD, or SUBtract instruction. For this example, this is the entire collection of instructions, so the AND and OR gates are superfluous. However, if a number of other instructions were included in the system, then the gates would be needed. The PC_INC-H instruction always occurs at PULSE_6 time, so no additional gating is needed. The ALU_FUN(1)-H signal is asserted during PULSE_16, PULSE_17, or PULSE_18, if the instruction is an ADD instruction, or during PULSE_16, PULSE_17, PULSE_18, PULSE_19, or PULSE_20, if the instruction is a SUBtract instruction. It is not asserted during an AND instruction. The other control signals are created in a similar fashion. Note that the STOP_PULSE-L signal occurs at PULSE_1 time, resulting in overlapped pulse operation. Also note that the START_PULSE-L

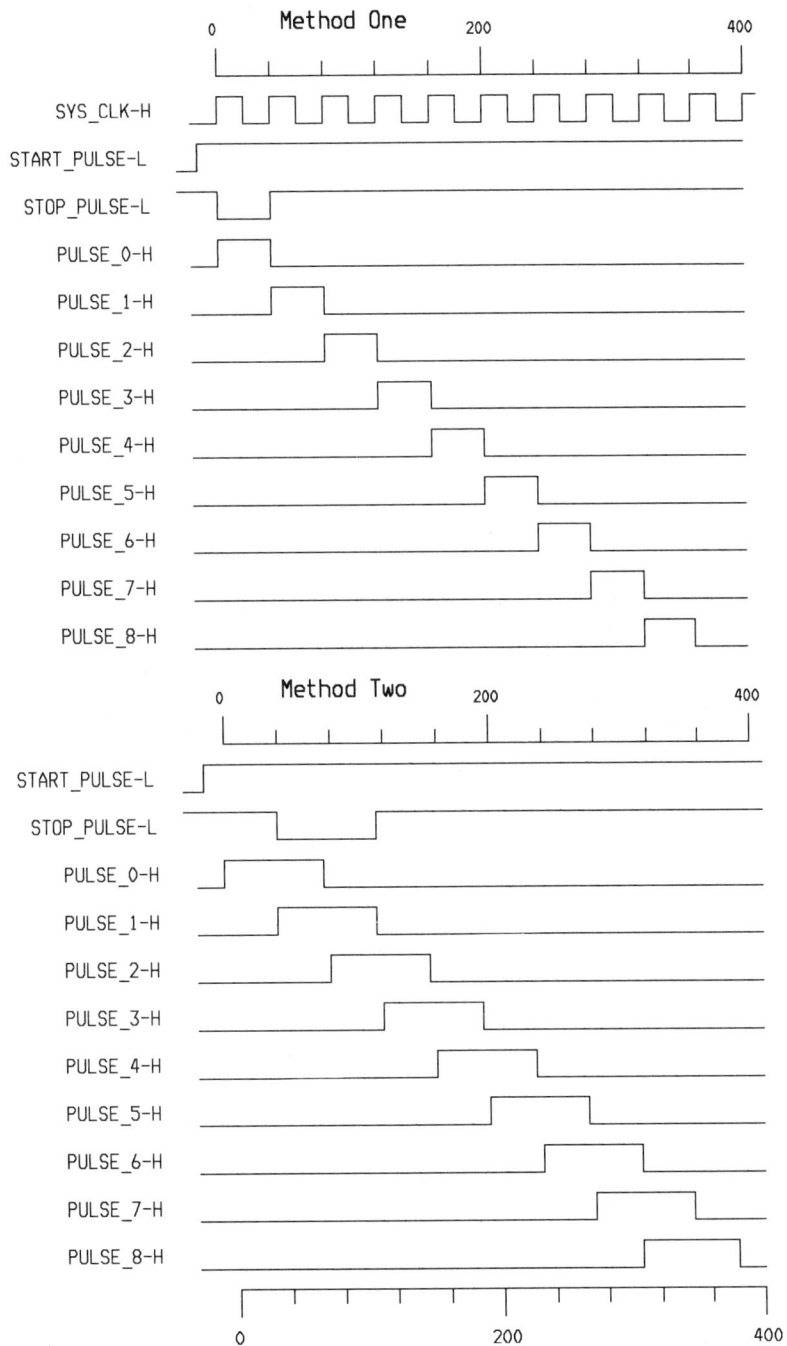

Figure 5.20. Timing Diagrams for the Shift Register Method.

signal occurs at different times for the different instructions, and that initialization comes from some external circuitry.

Both the delay method and the shift register method provide straightforward approaches of building control circuitry, mapping the information from the flow and timing diagrams directly into hardware. Both methods allow the designer flexibility to implement the necessary signals to match the constraints of

START-H

PULSE_19-H
AND-H

PULSE_20-H
ADD-H

PULSE_22-H
SUB-H

START_PULSE-L

PULSE_0-H

STOP_PULSE-L

PULSE_0-H

PULSE_10-H

AND-H
ADD-H
SUB-H

MAR_LD-H

PULSE_6-H

PC_INC-H

PULSE_6-H

PULSE_16-H

AND-H
ADD-H
SUB-H

MBR_LD-H

PULSE_7-H

IR_LD-H

PULSE_18-H
AND-H

PULSE_19-H
ADD-H

PULSE_21-H
SUB-H

ACC_LD-H

PULSE_18-H
SUB-H

BUF_LD-H

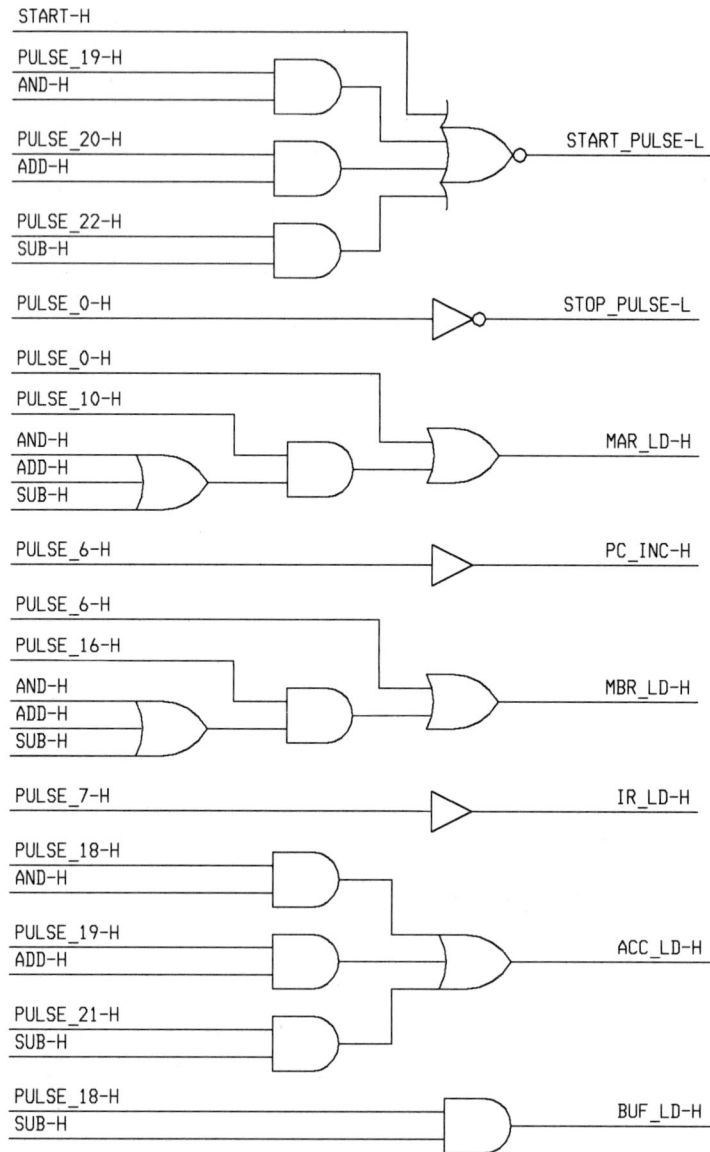

Figure 5.21(a). Control Signal Generation with the Shift Register Method.

technology and application. And both methods have interesting error modes when more than one signal enters the delay network/shift register. Nonetheless, both of these methods have been utilized in the design of many types of digital equipment. However, perhaps the most extensively utilized control design method in recent years is microcode.

5.6. Microcode Controllers: A Regular Control Structure

In 1951 Wilkes presented a paper in which he suggested that the design of control systems was entirely too complicated. He went on to suggest that the process could be greatly simplified by the use of a regular method for making decisions

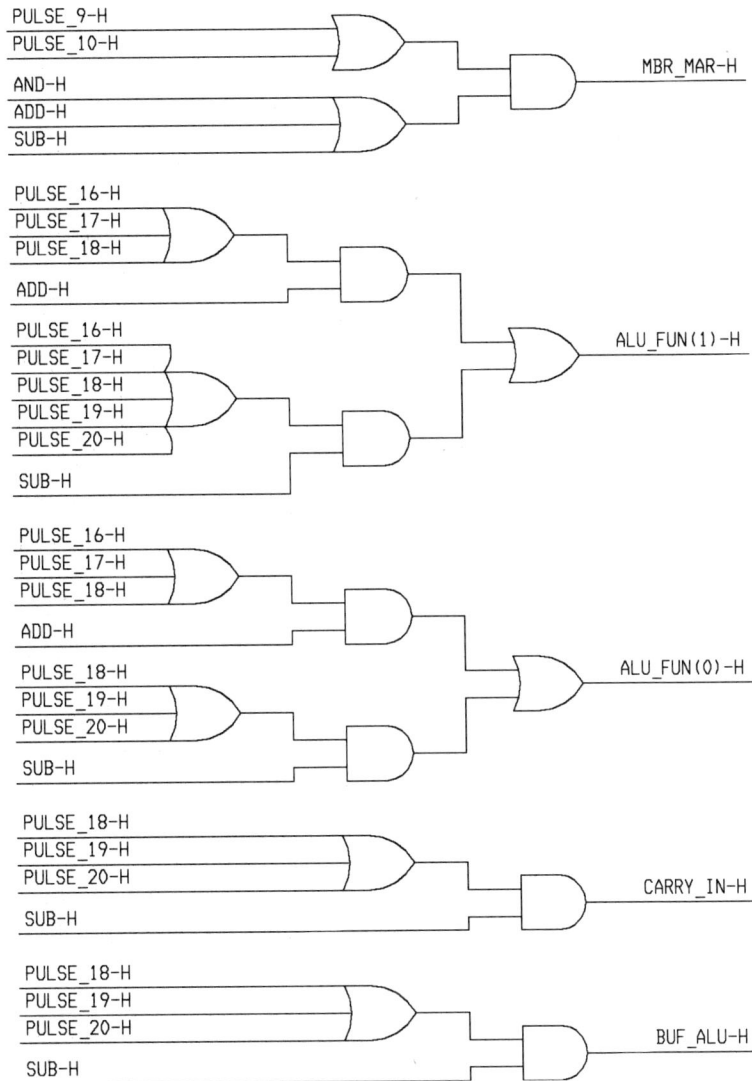

Figure 5.21(b). *(cont)* Control Signal Generation with the Shift Register Method.

concerning the next thing to do and what control signals to assert. The heart of this method was a high speed memory element needed to remember the appropriate sequence of information. However, at that time the memory technology was not as fast as random logic, nor as readily available. Hence, for many years Wilkes' suggestions went unheeded. Instead, designers utilized classical techniques, as well as the delay line and shift register methods, to implement sequential controllers. However, in the mid-1960s memory technology advanced to the point that it was an attractive alternative to use high speed memory to govern the action of a control system. We will introduce the method by taking another look at state machine control, and transfer the state machine ideas to the use of microcode.

We begin our examination of memory-based control methods by reorganizing the block diagram of Figure 5.15. The same basic components are utilized, but the organization is changed. The reason for changing the block diagram will become apparent as we discuss the implementation methods of this section. The main organizational change is the inclusion of a single data path that is utilized by all of the components. This single bus organization is very useful in systems where universal communication is desirable. Each component can transfer information to any other component; however, only one value can be transferred in a clock period. The component required to accomplish this is a bus driver, which isolates the register outputs from the bus except when the information in that particular register is required. At that time, the bus driver is enabled and information from the register is made available to the other elements on the bus.

Transferring the contents of the program counter to the memory address register is achieved by asserting PC_BUS-L to place the contents of the program counter on the bus, and then after a time required for propagation delay, settling time, and setup time, MAR_LD-H is asserted to load the information into the MAR. One method of implementation is to make the various registers from simple register devices such as the '273, and the drivers from tri-state drivers, such as '244. For situations where the data is not necessary except to drive the bus, such as the buffer register, it is possible to obtain both register and driver in a single package, such as the '574. However, not all registers can take advantage of this capability, since the output of the accumulator is always needed at AIN of the ALU, and the value in the memory address register is required at the memory.

As with the other control implementations, our first requirement is a complete data path block diagram, with control points identified. This is given in Figure 5.22. We can now generate a state diagram that identifies the assertions required in order to accomplish the desired results. These results have already been identified by the flow chart given in Figure 5.16; we can now generate a state diagram to do the same work. One such state diagram is given in Figure 5.23. This state diagram illustrates some interesting points, and represents a fairly conservative approach to system design. Let us consider the methods illustrated by Figure 5.23, and then consider some alternatives.

The method used for transferring information across the bus is illustrated in the first two states, which cause the MAR to be loaded with the contents of the PC. In State A the signal PC_BUS-L is asserted, which causes the contents of the program counter to be placed on the bus. This same signal is asserted in State B, which guarantees that the value will be present during that state also. The loading of the MAR is caused by the assertion of MAR_LD-H in State B; this signal causes the register to accept the information while the bus is held steady by the PC_BUS line. The relationship between these signals is shown in Figure 5.24. The method described in the state diagram, and shown pictorially in Figure 5.24, requires two states, and guarantees that the data is loaded into the MAR at the beginning of State B. The same work can be accomplished by generating both the MAR signal and the PC_BUS signal simultaneously, as shown in the alternative method. The key to success of this method is that the register is loaded on the rising edge of the MAR_LD line. Thus, for the duration of State X the PC_BUS signal is causing the data to be placed on the bus, and sufficient time is allotted for the delay in that process, as well as the setup time on the inputs to the MAR. Then when the low-to-high edge occurs on the MAR_LD line at the end of the state, the data available is loaded into the register. For most logic families (LS, ALS, AS, etc.), the delay in turning off the driver is sufficient to guarantee that the data is stable long enough to be correctly loaded into the MAR. This alternative method requires only one state to transfer the information, instead of the two states shown for

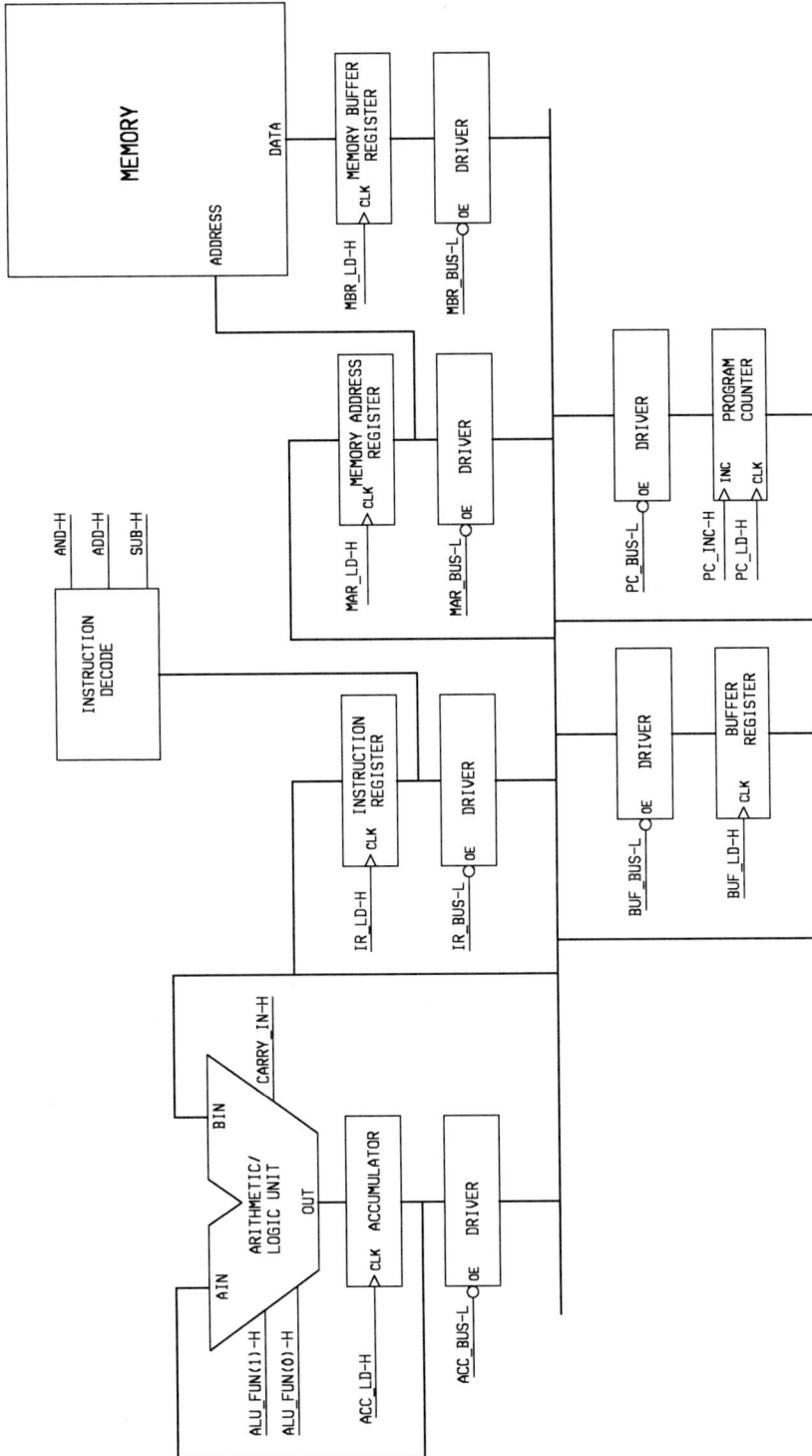

Figure 5.22. Block Diagram of Processor with Single Bus Organization.

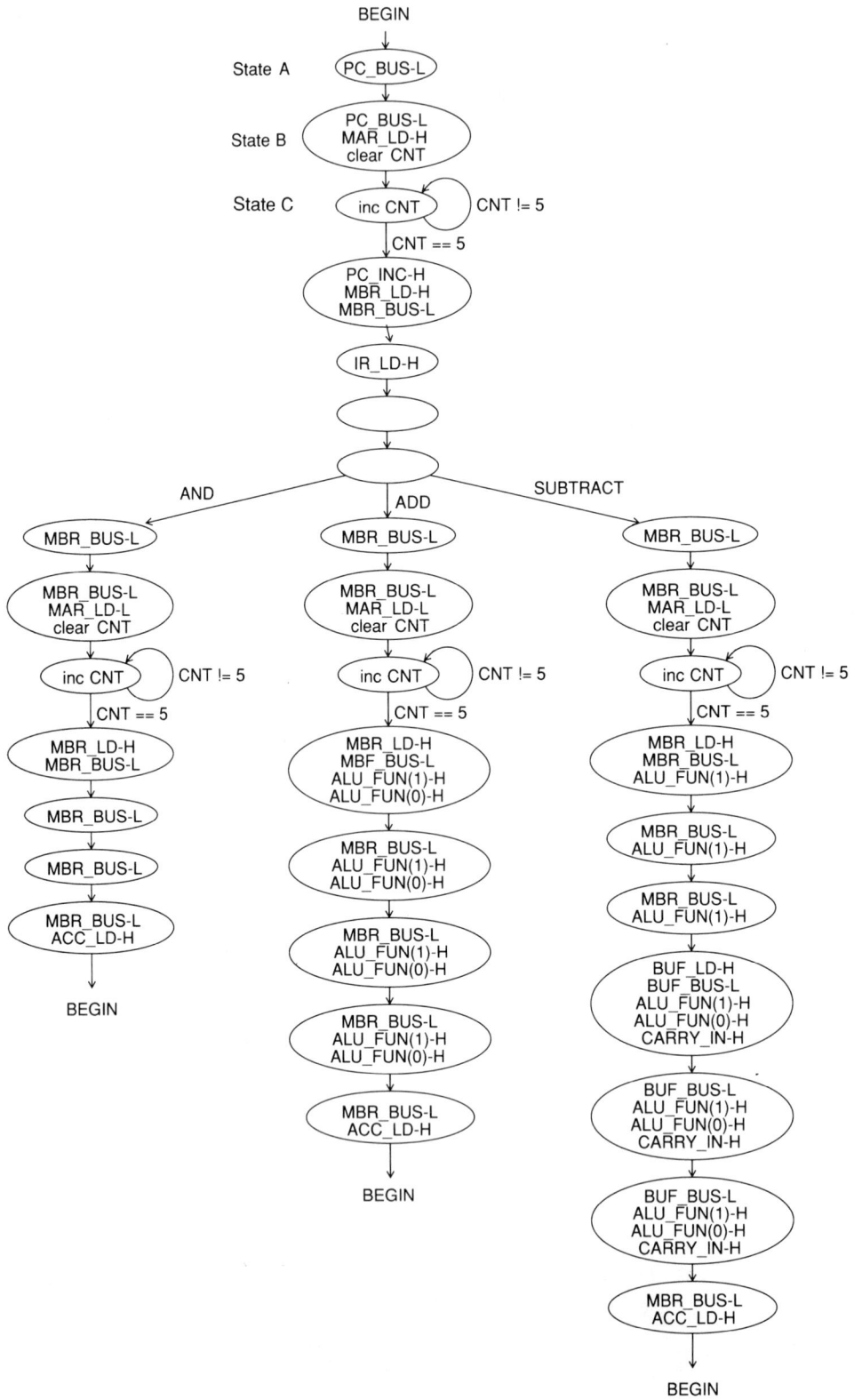

Figure 5.23. State Diagram for Single Bus Processor.

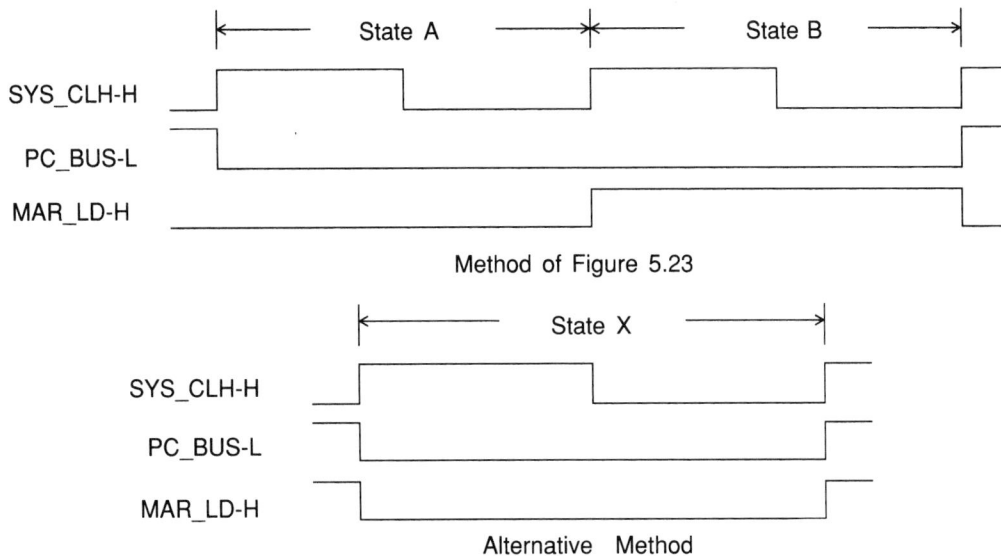

Figure 5.24. Timing for Loading MAR from PC.

Figure 5.23. One caution with this method of information transfer is that the designer must ascertain that the data has been stable in the loaded register for a sufficiently long period to guarantee desired results for the next operation. That is, the propagation delay, from clock assertion to data available, must be accounted for in any subsequent data manipulation.

This method is applicable to registers and other edge-triggered devices whose clock lines are driven directly from signals generated by the state machine. Another method to achieve this result is to use devices with separate clock and enable lines. One such device is the 74F550, shown in Figure 5.25. This register

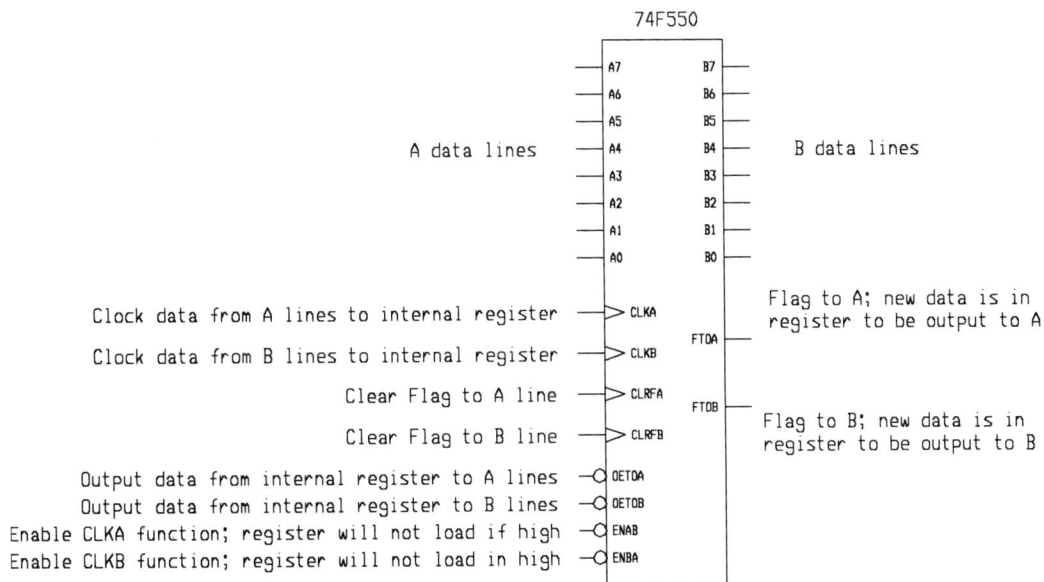

Figure 5.25. Register with Separate Clock and Enable Lines.

has a clock enable control line, which controls the effect of the clock. This allows the clock line to be connected directly to the system clock, and then the line that needs to be asserted by the control section is the enable line. This is particularly useful for systems in which all events are to happen at precisely the same time, and that time is defined by the rising edge of the system clock. A number of devices utilize this strategy for their operation, including registers (2950, 2952, '550, etc), arithmetic units (2903), and controllers.

Another example of the separate clock/enable function is demonstrated by the use of counters in this system. The 200 nsec delay required by the memory is obtained by waiting for five state times before proceeding. This wait time is governed by a counter similar to those used in the example of Section 5.2. The control design used in that section caused control signals (specifically, clock lines of counters) to be asserted when the action was needed. Another method to achieve the same result is to use counters which will increment only when enabled, even though a clock signal is present at the clock input. The counters will increment only when the enable line is asserted, and the enable line is controlled by the state machine. This is the method which is illustrated in State B and State C of Figure 5.23. The counter is cleared in State B, and then State C calls for incrementing the counter. This cannot be accomplished if the clock signal is fed directly from the decode of the state, since the state does not change. (As pointed out earlier, ANDing the clock signal with the system clock would result in a pulsating clock line.) However, if the State C signal is utilized to enable a counter, then the desired result is obtained. For the '161 of Section 5.2, the action can be obtained by using a signal generated in State C to assert the Enable P line of the counters.

Other delays are implemented by repeating the action of one state in another state. The 40, 80 and 120 nsec delays can be obtained by using one, two, or three states. Thus, delays can either be obtained by staying in one state for a predetermined number of system clock times, or by using multiple states, assuring that the required signals are asserted within those states.

The state diagram of Figure 5.23 is specifically constructed to follow the flow diagram of Figure 5.16. No attempt has been made to try to save on the number of states utilized. An examination of the state diagram reveals that there are some duplications, specifically in the area of obtaining the operand of the instruction. One method of reducing the number of states would be to delay decoding of the instruction until the operand has been obtained. This results in a system that partially decodes instructions at appropriate times to attempt to minimize the number of states. For example, the system under consideration always requires an operand for each instruction, but in a real system instructions such as "increment" or "clear" affect only the accumulator, and do not need to obtain another operand. Thus, the organization of the system hardware, the complexity of the instruction set, and the goals of the system all influence the designer in the creation of the state diagram that describes the control algorithms of the system.

Using classical methods, or those described in Section 5.2, we can implement a control section that operates as described by the state diagram of Figure 5.23. A block diagram of such an implementation is shown in Figure 5.26. The current state of the system is stored in a register labeled "Present State Register." The next state logic uses the current state, the instruction, and the start signal to select the appropriate next state. In the direct implementation method of Section 5.2, this logic consists of multiplexers and perhaps some minimal logic. With classical methods, this would be some type of random logic implementation.

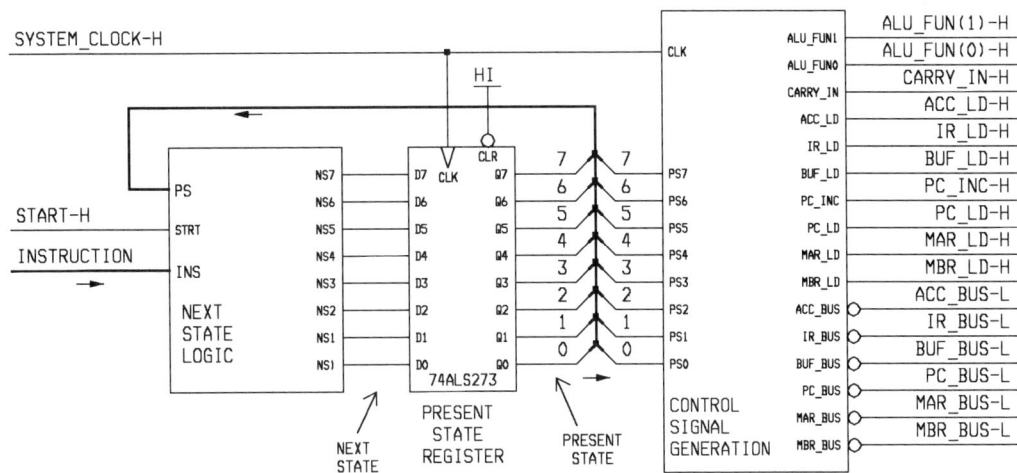

Figure 5.26. Block Diagram of State Machine Controller for Simple Computer.

Regardless of the implementation method, every clock period a new determination is made as to the next state, and if the implementation is correct, the state diagram of Figure 5.23 will be followed. The control signals are generated by decoding the present state; these signals may or may not include the system clock in their implementation. The following observation can be made concerning the control signal generation: the signals asserted at any given time are functions only of the present state (and clock), and the signals to be asserted in any given state are determined during the design process. Since the signal assertions are set up at design time, the same information used to select the appropriate next state (present state and inputs) can also be used to determine the signals that will be asserted at that time. Therefore, during the same period that the next state is determined, the appropriate signal assertions for that state can also be determined. This leads to the implementation shown in Figure 5.27.

The block diagram of a system controller as shown in Figure 5.27 is extremely simple. The next state logic determines the state to which the system will proceed from the present state, based on the present state and the external inputs. At the same time, this same information will be used by the next state control logic block to determine the control signals to be asserted in the next state. As stated earlier, this information is available at design time, and will not change during the useful life of the product. Both the state information and the control lines will be held in registers, so that transitions on control signals will occur at the same time that the state changes. If it is deemed desirable to do so, some control signals can be conditioned with the clock to create appropriate timing pulses. This arrangement eliminates the use of a present state decoder for generation of control signals, since all of the signal generation is determined prior to the active edge of the clock.

The logic utilized by a system for the next state logic and next state control logic blocks can be created by any appropriate means open to a designer. But it is instructive to note that it need not be random logic nor the multiplexer arrangement presented earlier. Some manufacturers build devices specifically designed to do this function, and they provide means to create the appropriate logic, depending on the mechanism used for implementation of the device. Figure 5.28 shows a block diagram representation of the 82S105, which is called a "Field

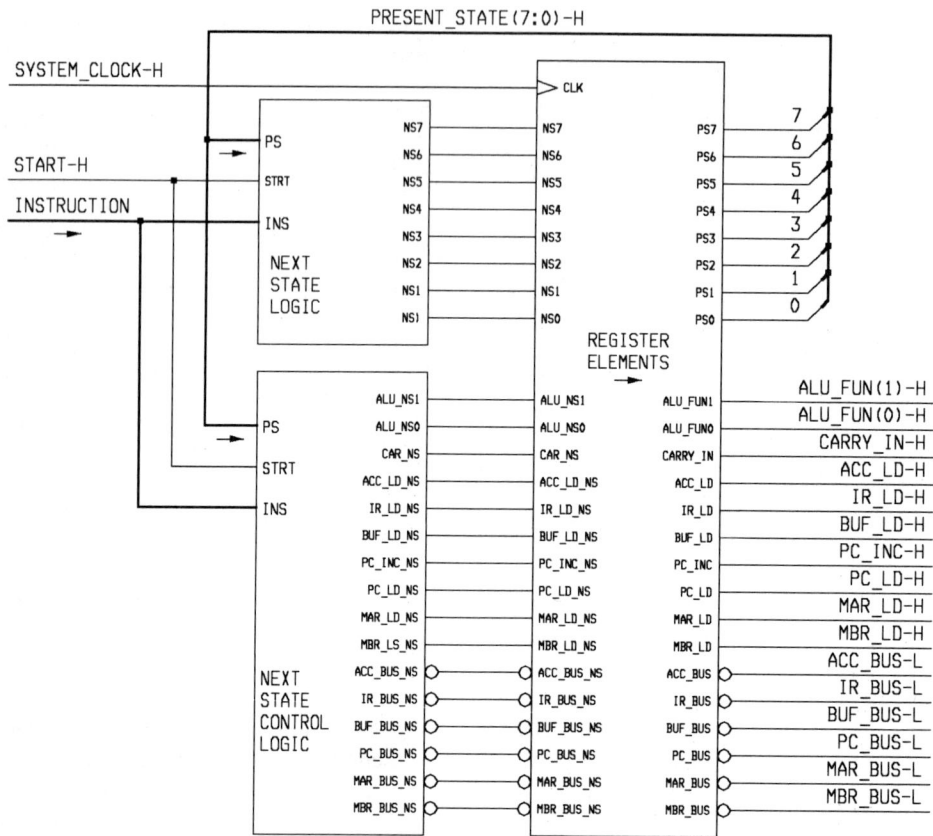

Figure 5.27. Block Diagram of State Machine Controller Combining Generation of Next State and Control Signals.

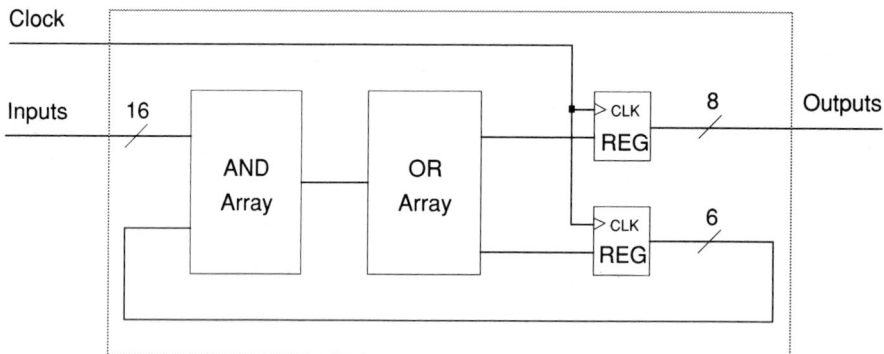

Figure 5.28. Internal Makeup of a Field Programmable Logic Sequencer.

Programmable Logic Sequencer." This device allows 16 external inputs; in addition there is a reset/output enable line (function is defined at time of programming). The device has eight outputs, all of which are registered so that the outputs will change only after a clock transition. Internal to the device are six feedback lines; this allows creation of a state machine with up to 64 states. The determination of the next state and the output levels is accomplished by a programmable AND/OR array; the limitation is that the device is capable of only 48

AND terms and 14 OR terms. This places some limits to the complexity of the state machines that can be implemented by the device, but a variety of very useful controllers is feasible. A large number of similar devices can be utilized to implement sequencers, such as registered PALs, state machine controllers, and registered PLAs.

One "feature" of this type of unit is that the feedback variables are internal to the device. This is a benefit in that the speed is not hampered by going off chip, which leads to a higher clock rate. Note that the inputs will need to be synchronized to the system in some way. The drawback to this feature is that the state variables are not available to the user to aid in the debug process. Thus, the only way to ascertain the state of the machine is to observe the output pins. The designer must be careful about his assumptions concerning the correctness of the machine during checkout. Nevertheless, programming aids, available from both manufacturers and third party vendors, greatly enhance the ability of the designer to create a correct system.

As a result of making state machine devices compact and easy to generate, many of the designs utilized in recent digital systems are created with a number of individual state machines. In these systems, each state machine is a single IC created to perform its own task, and the units function together to control the system. Thus, rather than have a single controller to control all of the action of the system, the control is divided between smaller units, and these units each activate a subset of the control lines. An example of this is described in Section 6.5, where one state machine controls the action of an interface module, while different state machine controls the signals used to interface to the bus.

The use of logic arrays for the next state and output generation allows creation of a variety of useful devices, but does not permit arbitrarily complex systems. Also, since the feedback is internal to the device, the number of outputs is limited to those available from that chip. One way to expand the use of this technique is to use memory instead of AND/OR arrays for the logic blocks. That is, if we consider the correct next state/output information as a pattern of ones and zeros stored in a memory, and the address of the correct pattern is formed by the feedback variables and inputs, then all combinations of states and input variables are possible. The memory utilized in this arrangement can be ROM or PROM, and the number of input variables and feedback variables can be increased by adding more memory chips. For example, one such device is the 27S55, a PROM with eight registered outputs and 4,096 locations, which requires 12 address lines. Three of these devices clocked together would give 24 outputs, and these could be used in any combination required by a design. A system implementing the state diagram of Figure 5.23 would require six feedback variables; these would form six of the 12 address lines on each device. That allows six other lines to be used for the start signal and instruction lines, as well as any other inputs required in the system. The 24 outputs would then be utilized for six feedback variables and 18 control lines; we have identified 16 lines in the block diagram of Figure 5.22.

This arrangement has several practical advantages. The controller is completely contained in three 24 pin devices, requiring about 1.4 square inches of board space. The fact that it is programmable allows a designer to try different state diagrams or implementation ideas by merely changing the devices, not physically changing any wires. The net result is a very versatile system controller of arbitrary complexity. No limitations have been made concerning the complexity of the state diagram, nor concerning the number of states in which control signals can be asserted.

At this point we will pause in our discussion of control system construction to identify a technique that can be beneficial in the checkout and maintenance of sequential machines. One basic model for a sequential system was given in Figure 5.2, and this basic model is reflected in the diagram of the sequencer shown in Figure 5.28. One of the basic problems facing system designers is the checkout of equipment that has been constructed. For simple designs made from individual gates, or for any system in which access to major system components is readily available, a brute force method of checkout is often utilized. With this method, the outputs of the system are observed under the necessary conditions of input and history to check for correctness. If improper behavior of output signals is observed, then the logic required to generate those signals is meticulously checked for correctness. The problem may lie in improper implementation of the logic, or the problem may concern an improper design based on flawed assumptions about the problem to be solved and the available inputs. Thus, not only the logic network, but also the design of the logic, must be checked for errors.

If the system to be checked is a sequential IC, such as that shown in Figure 5.28, then it is difficult, if not impossible, to test the actual logic. Access is needed for controllability and observability: we need to control the inputs to the system, and we need to be able to observe the outputs of the system. Control over the external inputs of Figure 5.28 is easily obtained, but control over the feedback variables is not readily available, since they exist solely internal to the device. Similarly, the outputs of the chip can be readily observed, but the contents of the internal state register is not available to the external to the device. One of the techniques used to provide both controllability and observability is called the scan technique, which is used to provide access to the internal registers of a system.

The basic idea of the scan technique is to provide a method for controlling and observing the contents of the registers internal to a system. Rather than providing additional pins for all of the desired points, the internal registers are configured as either a normal register or as a shift register. In normal operation, the registers behave as we have discussed to this point: at the active edge of the clock, the register is loaded with either the output information or the next state information. In diagnostic mode, the registers are reconfigured as a single serial shift register, and activating the clock shifts out the bits in a serial fashion. Thus, all of the internal register bits can be observed. Similarly, as the bits are shifted out, new bits can be input to the system to allow external control of the levels inside the device.

The application of the idea requires some modifications to a system. This is indicated by modifying the organization of the device shown in Figure 5.28 to include the elements shown in Figure 5.29. The additional lines required are minimal: a control line to normal or diagnostic operation, a serial input, and a serial output. A good description of the technique and its application is available in [McCl86]. Some manufacturers provide integrated circuits with this capability built into the register elements. Advanced Micro Devices refers the additional registers in their devices as "shadow registers," but the idea remains the same: provide ability to control and observe needed points in a system [see AMD88, Lee87, and Schm87]. This need not apply only to integrated circuits, but can be used in any sequential module. IBM utilizes this technique in a number of systems, where it is known as level sensitive scan design (LSSD) [TeSw82].

The state machines implemented to this point have been created to match a timing constraint given in the problem statement. One of the questions to be

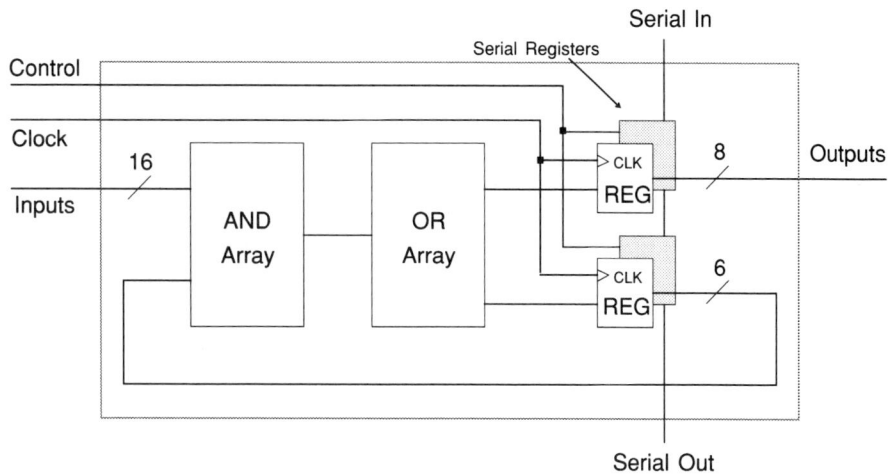

Figure 5.29. Internal Makeup of a Field Programmable Logic Sequencer with Registers for Scan Technique.

addressed concerns the speed of a state machine: how fast can it run, or how fast should it run? These two questions, in general, have different answers. One answer comes from the speed at which the controller can operate. The other answer comes from the speed at which the elements of the data path can operate.

All of the examples included in this chapter use edge-triggered registers, in which the outputs change to coincide with the values at the inputs when the active edge of the clock occurs. Thus, the timing requirements of the system must satisfy the constraints of edge triggered devices. Another design approach is to use devices that operate on a latching principle, in which the level of the outputs (of the latch) follow the level of the inputs so long as the clock (or enable) of the latch is asserted. A description of the differences in designing with edge-triggered devices and latched devices is found in Section 7.2.

A state machine controller of the type shown in Figure 5.27 consists of a register and some logic for generation of control signals and next state determination. The minimum cycle time for the system clock (SYSTEM_CLOCK-H) must include times sufficient for each of these functions. This time can be broken down into three basic components, as shown in Figure 5.30. When the active

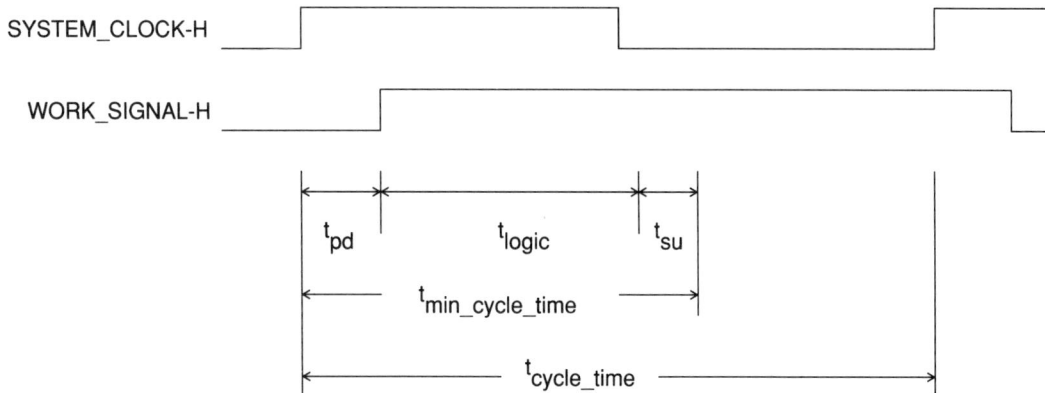

Figure 5.30. Component Times for Controller Cycle Time.

edge of the clock occurs, there is a propagation delay time (t_{pd}) after which signals become asserted, both in the present state register and in the signals that cause work in the data path. Once the present state is stable (and also the register holding the synchronized inputs), there is a time required for the choice of a next state to become stable. This is labeled in the figure as t_{logic}, but the decision could be made by random logic, PLAs, or memory. Whatever mechanism is utilized to determine the next state and the correct levels for the control lines in that state, t_{logic} must be sufficient to allow the these signals to become stable. When these values are stable, another time must be accounted for, which is the setup time of the register being used as the present state register (and the registers for the work signals). This is shown as t_{su} in the figure. The setup time is the amount of time prior to the active edge of the clock that a signal must be present at the input of a device to guarantee that the output stays at the required level after the clock occurs. Any time after the setup time requirement has been satisfied, the next active edge of the clock can occur. The sum of these three times provides a minimum cycle time that must be met by the system. For some high speed TTL parts, t_{pd} = 8 nsec, t_{logic} = 19 nsec, and t_{su} = 3 nsec, and the minimum cycle time would be 30 nsec, which gives a system clock frequency of 33.3 MHz.

As can be seen from Figure 5.30, the actual cycle time is often much longer than the minimum cycle time. The reason for the longer cycle time is not that the controller is incapable of running faster, but rather that the functions occurring on data path require a longer time to complete. Consider the timing relationships shown in Figure 5.31, which shows some of the signals required to add a value from the MBR to the accumulator. After the active edge of the clock, time is required for the work signals to become asserted, as shown in both Figure 5.30 and 5.31. Once the work signal becomes asserted, another propagation delay time is required; in this instance, it is for the driver to assert the value contained in the memory buffer register onto the bus. Once the value on the bus is stable, another time is required, which is the addition time of the ALU. It is assumed that the function lines and the carry input line of the ALU for the addition function became stable at the same time that the MBR_BUS-L signal became asserted; hence, these

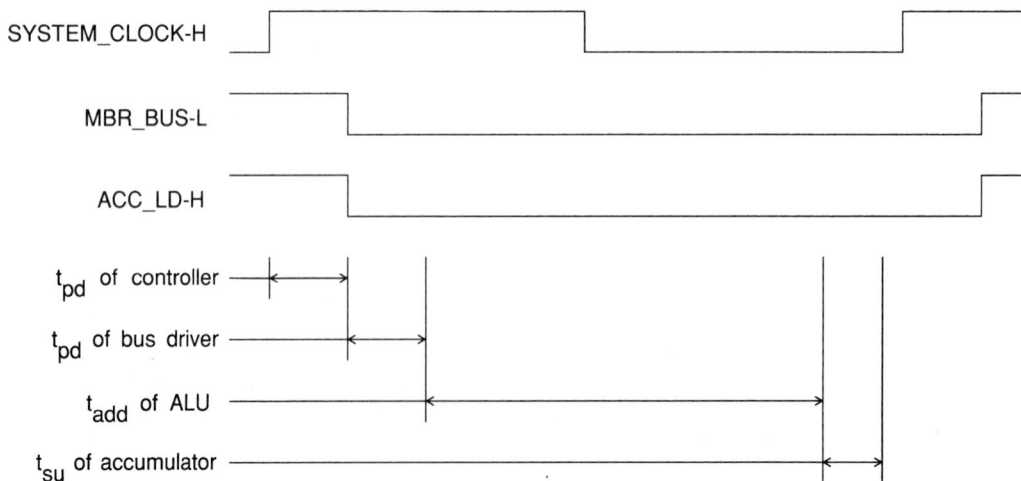

Figure 5.31. Component Times for Data Path Cycle Time.

lines are not shown in the figure. If for some reason these lines were not stable until after the data at the input to the ALU became stable, then the t_{add} of the ALU must be adjusted to reflect the delay time from the last stable signal. Once the correct results are stable on the outputs of the ALU, a t_{su} is required before the clock line of the accumulator can be asserted. The sum of the times required for the longest sequence of events in a single cycle establishes the minimum allowable cycle time for the data path, which is usually longer than the minimum cycle time for the controller. So the controller time is adjusted to match the cycle time requirements for the data path in the operation of the system.

Two basic functions are provided by the systems shown in Figure 5.26 and Figure 5.27. These are the choice of a next state, and the assertion levels of the control signals for each state. As we have seen, the next state logic and the next state control logic of Figure 5.27 can be implemented with memory devices. We now formulate a different view of the function provided by Figure 5.27, and present this view in Figure 5.32. The same functionality is shown: part of the system is used to control the function of the device by sequencing through the proper states, and the other part of the system controls the flow of data in the system by asserting the appropriate signals on the data path devices. The only addition to the process included in Figure 5.32 is the address selection portion of the system. The function provided by this section is to determine the address in the logic memory that contains the correct next state and control line assertion information. This address is a function of the present state and the external inputs. When the memory address is provided, the memory responds with the location of that address, and this information (the new state and new levels for the control signal assertions) is available for the control registers. The number of states, the complexity of the state diagram, and the number of inputs to the system determine the amount of logic memory needed for the selection of a next state. In addition to the complexity of function and number of inputs, the number of control signals generated by the unit determines the amount of logic memory needed for control signal generation.

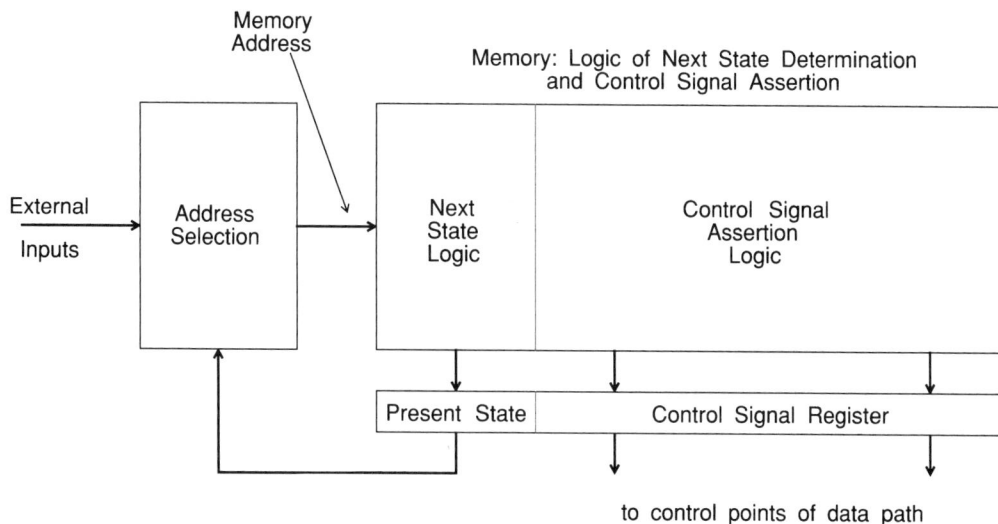

Figure 5.32. State Machine Implementation with Memory Implementing Logic Functions.

The diagrams in Figure 5.27 and Figure 5.32 represent the same function, and the difference is basically cosmetic. Figure 5.32 shows the elements of Figure 5.27 rotated by 90°. However, the diagram shown in Figure 5.32 matches most of the diagrams shown for another control technique which is called microcode. We expand the detail of Figure 5.32 slightly to obtain the system shown in Figure 5.33.

The present state register function and the registered control lines are combined in a register called the Microinstruction Register. All of the logic for control signal generation and next state selection is combined into one functional unit called Microcode Memory. Instead of a location in the microcode memory being strictly a function of the current state and all inputs, a functional unit labeled Microcode Address Generation performs the function shown as Address Selection in Figure 5.32. This unit selects the appropriate address for the next set of control lines; this forms the next microinstruction to execute. The complexity of the microcode address generation unit reflects the designer's tradeoff choices for speed versus complexity. We will describe different approaches in our next design example. Just like the present state register identified the state of a state machine controller, the registers and memory elements included in the microcode address generation module identify the state of a microcode machine. The address issued by the microcode address generation module identifies the next microinstruction to execute; the address is then analogous to the information contained in a present state register. However, the analogy is not exact, since the functions of the microcode address generation module can include things like subroutine linkage capabilities and loop control. However, the analogy does demonstrate the close conceptual relationship between microcode systems and systems designed with a state machine approach. The microinstruction register provides

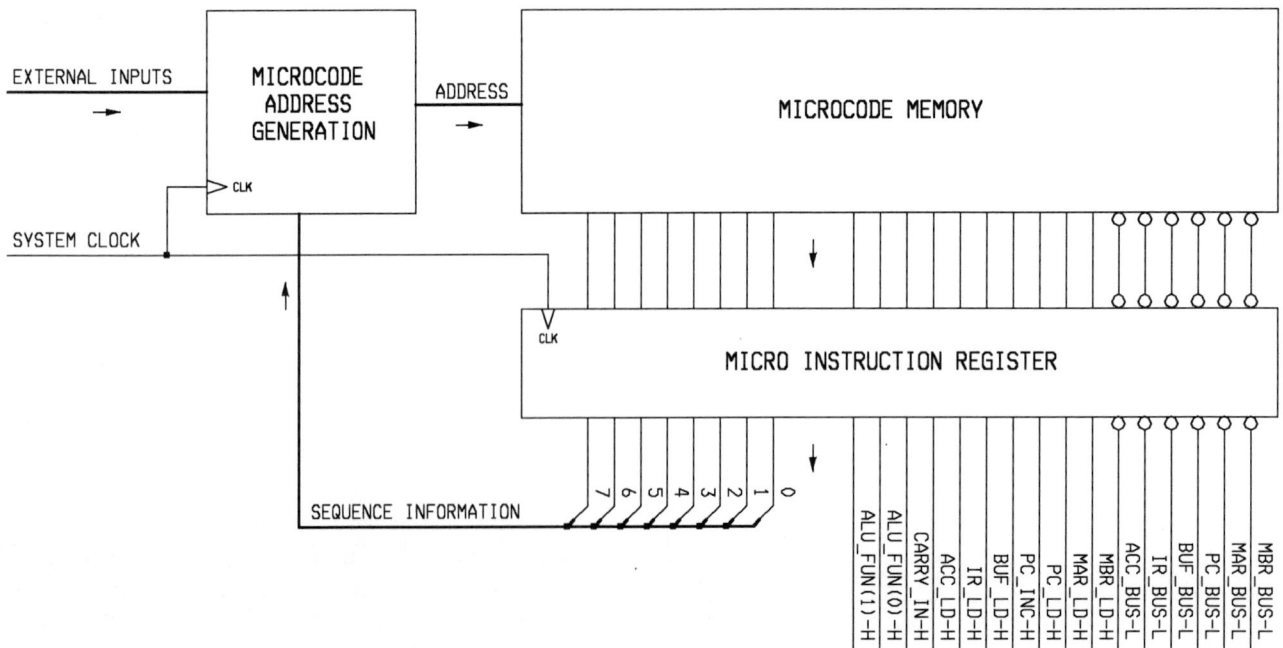

Figure 5.33. Implementation of Microcode Control.

the sequential control functions of the present state register, and it also specifies the assertion of the control lines of the data path.

This model is in agreement with the intuitive concept that work is accomplished by activating control signals in a sequential fashion. The sequential action of the control signals is specified by the sequence of microinstructions, and the address selection of the next microinstruction is derived during the execution of the current microinstruction. Thus, if the microinstructions were strictly sequential, the address could be provided by a simple counter, which would increment from one address to the next. The counter would be reset when the process needed to start again. The next address selection process can become arbitrarily complex; the address of the next microinstruction to execute can be one of many determined by a complex algorithm. In any case, a number of bits are used to control the selection of the next address; the remainder of the bits in the microinstruction register are used to control the data flow through the data path section of the device.

Let us begin our discussion of the contents of the microinstruction register by including whatever bits are required to specify selection of the address of the next microinstruction. In Figure 5.33 these bits are merely labeled "Sequence Information." The next bits to include in the microinstruction register are the control lines identified on the data path block diagram; we include one bit for each control line needed. The result is an extremely wide microinstruction register; the number of bits is the same as the number of control lines required to select the next address and control the data path. This style of microcode has received the name of "horizontal microcode," because the microcode grows wider as more functions are added.

The horizontal microcode technique results in the fastest microcode controllers for two separate reasons. The first is that, since all of the bits are independent, multiple operations can be specified in the same microcode word. For example, assume that the value in the program counter is to be loaded into the memory address register and into the accumulator. In a horizontal scheme the clocks of both registers could be activated simultaneously, resulting in the transfer of information to two destinations in one cycle. This concurrent operation is not limited to information transfers over a bus, but can be observed in any independent operations. The second reason for enhanced speed is that no decoding is required for the control signals. This reduces to a minimum the cycle time required for operation of the system.

In contrast to the horizontal microcode method is a technique called "vertical microcode." This method emphasises not speed, but rather conserving system resources — power and microcode bits. The method calls for combining the bits required for basically independent functions. For example, in Figure 5.33 there are six lines which, when activated, assert the data lines on the bus. These functions are not totally independent: we do not want more than one of these asserted at any time. Therefore, we can specify a single line to be asserted by encoding this information in fewer bits. In this case, we can specify one of the six lines with 3 bits; for example, a decoder such as a '138 could be used.

The encoding of information in this manner has two effects, both of which tend to slow down the operation of the system. The first is that the decoding of the bits is not free; more time is required in each cycle to allow for the decode function. This increases the time required for each cycle. The second cause of slowdown is that the system has a reduced capability of performing operations in parallel. Consider, for example, encoding the choice of N bus destination lines in

$\log_2 N$ bits. Combining bits in this manner precludes sending information to two destinations simultaneously; such an operation would require two cycles with the encoded scheme. Thus, the time required for accomplishment of work is increased because the individual cycle time is increased, and because more microinstructions are required. This increase in the number of microinstructions causes the required microcode memory to increase "vertically," which leads to the name of this technique.

The horizontal and vertical microcode methods both control the action of a system by sequencing through a set of microinstructions. However, each approach uses the system resources in a different way. The horizontal approach chooses to consume resources (power, number of bits in microcode word, etc.) to make the system run faster, both from concurrency of many simultaneous operations and from the minimal cycle times available. The vertical approach chooses to conserve the resources, limit concurrent operations, and accept a slower overall system speed. However, both mechanisms share many common characteristics, as demonstrated by the microcoded system in the following section.

5.7. A Microcode Controller

To demonstrate both the vertical and horizontal concepts of microcoded control, we will design two different microcode controllers for a computer system. The computer we will use for this example is patterned after the Data General Nova, which has been used for many years. This is not as exotic a machine as many newer machines. In fact, in many real aspects this system has been superseded by the 16- and 32-bit microprocessors available today. This system has been chosen to illustrate the ideas presented because it is simple enough to present in the confined space of a this section, and at the same it is complex enough to provide an fairly comprehensive example. A block diagram of the system is shown in Figure 5.34. Note that the diagram identifies the registers known to a

16-Bit Computer System

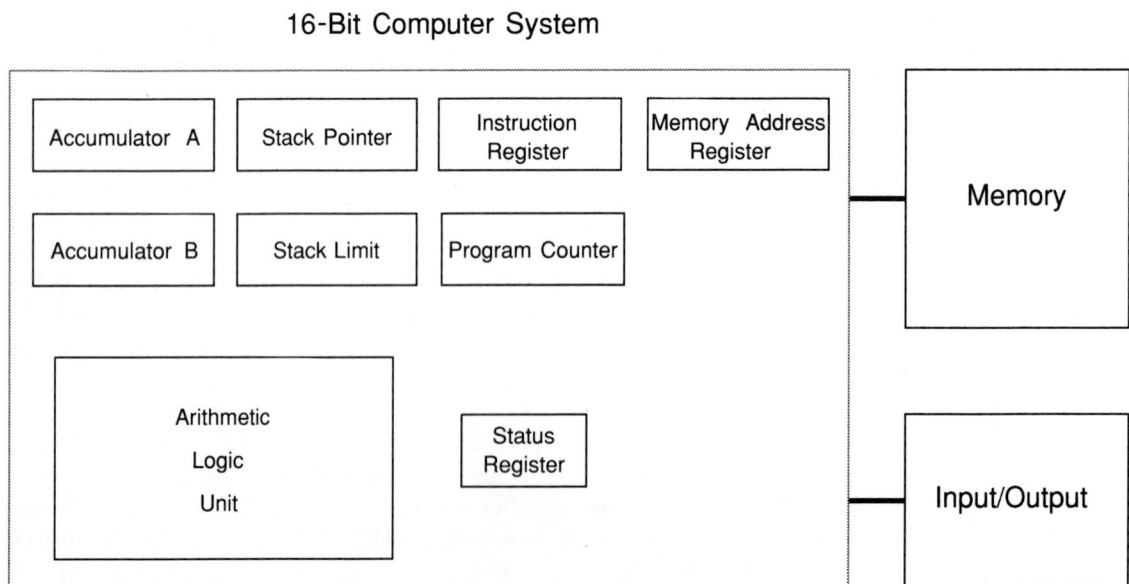

Figure 5.34. Block Diagram of 16-Bit Computer System.

programmer, without attempting to identify the physical links that connect the registers. The possible data transfers and arithmetic operations are defined by the instruction set. We will not describe the entire instruction set of such a machine; rather, we will select a few instructions and examine the rudimentary operations required to accomplish those instructions. If our instruction set matches the Nova exactly, we would like our module to execute the instructions in such a fashion that an observer would not be able to differentiate between our machine and a Nova: the "macro" machine behavior would be equivalent. We would then accomplish the work of the "macro" machine with our "micro" machine.

The machine depicted in Figure 5.34 has two 16-bit accumulators. In the Nova architecture these accumulators are also the first two locations of memory. Thus, actual registers are not required for this information; it will reside in the first two locations of main store. The memory address register, program counter, stack pointer, and stack limit register provide 24 bits of address information. The instruction register holds 16 bits, not all of which are needed by all instructions. The status register is composed of 4 bits that are both controlled and utilized by many of the instructions of the computer. The Nova instruction set utilizes I/O instructions instead of having strictly memory mapped I/O. Thus, to allow for these instructions we will need some interface lines as well. These will be described in more detail as we discuss the implementation.

The concepts of microcoded control can be applied at different levels. The address control, the microcode memory, and the microinstruction register can be composed of individual registers and memories, or the entire system can be part of a single integrated circuit. Many microprocessors utilize a microcoded control section internal to the chip. However, one family of components, called bit sliced processors, has been specifically designed to utilize microcoded control. The members of this family are so constructed that they can be put together in systems to satisfy a variety of constraints. In order to implement a microcoded system to perform the action of the system of Figure 5.34, we will use two of the most common microcoded devices. These are the 2901 Four Bit Microprocessor Slice and the 2910 Microprogram Controller. These units are available from several manufacturers, as well as newer units with extended capabilities.

A simplified block diagram of the 2901 is shown in Figure 5.35. This diagram shows the main data paths, but the control lines are merely suggested, and some of the data paths are not shown. What the diagram does indicate is that internal to the 2901 are a 4-bit ALU, a register bank holding 16 registers, a Q register, and multiplexers to control the flow of data. The registers (implemented in RAM) have two sets of addresses; the value of the register identified by the A address is loaded into the A latch, and the value of the register identified by the B address is loaded into the B latch. These loads occur at the beginning of a cycle, so that the values are available to the operand select function. The operand select portion of the device selects one of eight available combinations of the Data In, A, B, Q, and zero values. The two values chosen are fed into an ALU capable of AND, OR, EXCLUSIVE-OR, ADD, and SUBTRACT, as well as some variations of these operations. The output of the ALU can then be used as an output of the chip, as well as providing information to the registers. Writing can occur to the Q register, or to a register specified by the B address lines. In addition, there are data lines that allow cascading the modules to form units of higher numbers of bits, as well as lines that can provide status information. A data sheet should be referenced for a complete specification, but for the purposes of our example we need to know the data and control lines to be concerned with for the data path and

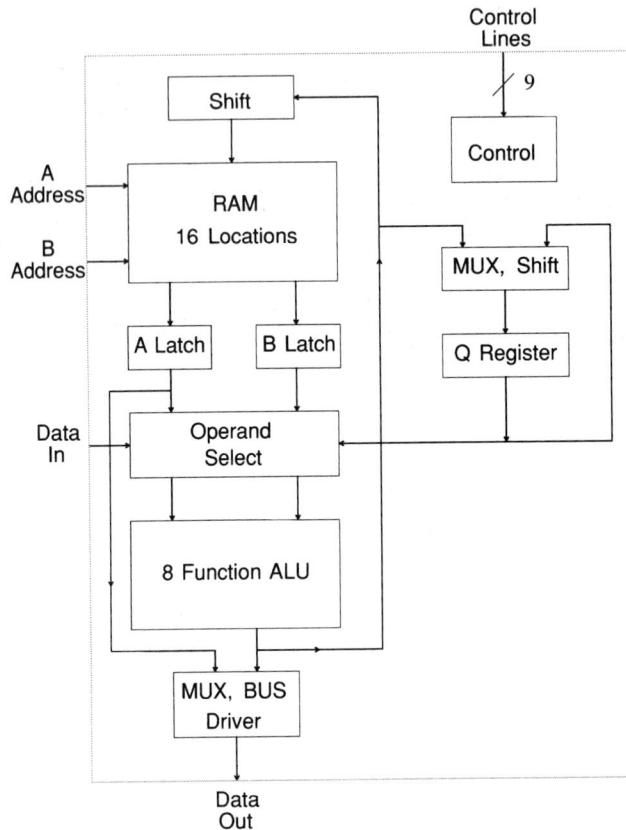

Figure 5.35. Simplified Block Diagram of a 2901 Bit Slice
Microprocessor.

microcode sections. The data path is basically taken care of by the data in and data out lines; in addition some status lines need to be utilized. The control lines include the A and B addresses, which are each 4 bits, and the nine control lines. These we will need to include in the microinstruction register.

The address selection portion of our microcoded machine will be handled by a 2910, a simplified diagram of which is shown in Figure 5.36. Like the 2901, this diagram does not show all of the features of the 2910, but points out the major capabilities. The unit is capable of handling a 12-bit address, which will address up to 4,096 words of microcode memory. This is sufficient for most applications; however, similar units are available that will control more address bits. The multiplexer in the unit selects one of four sources:

- The *data path* allows for an external source to specify what the next microinstruction address will be. This is useful for jumps, subroutine calls, and similar activities.

- The *register path* allows the functional unit to specify at some previous time an address used to specify a microinstruction.

- The *stack path* is used for returning from subroutines, and for providing an address during special function operations.

- The *microprogram counter-register path* is used to proceed to the next instruction.

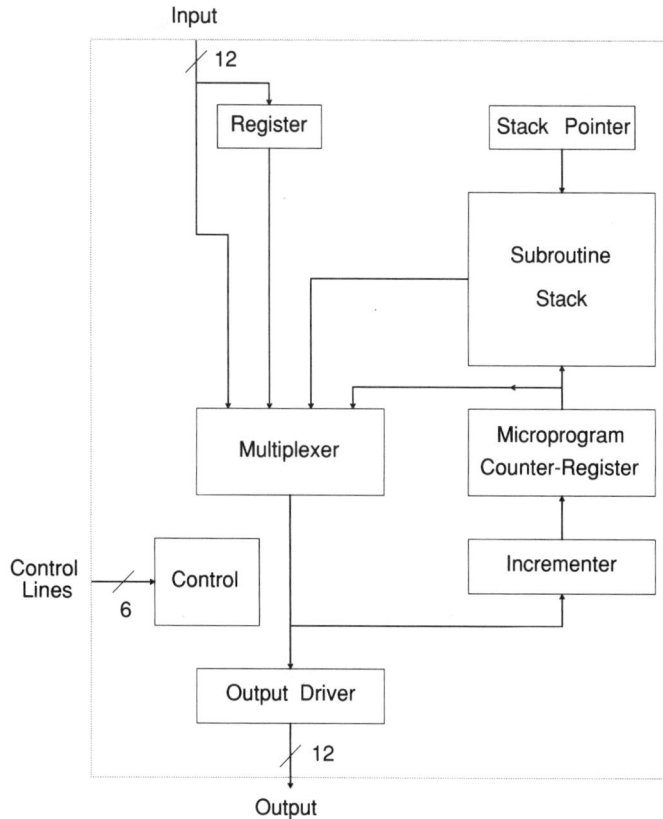

Figure 5.36. Simplified Block Diagram of a 2910 Sequencer.

The incrementer is not built into the microprogram counter-register, a situation that seems unreasonable. However, consider the desired action when a subroutine address is provided via the data path. In this situation, the microprogram counter-register contains the address of the next instruction in sequence (after the currently executing microinstruction), and this address is to be placed on the stack as a return address. The output lines contain the address of the subroutine (supplied as an input on the data lines), and the microinstruction at that address will be fetched for execution. The address of the microinstruction that should be obtained next is the second instruction in the subroutine; therefore, the value presented to the microprogram counter-register is one more than the subroutine address, not one more than the current address. Hence, the incrementer is connected to the output lines of the multiplexer, not to the microprogram counter-register containing the current address.

The control lines of the sequencer select one of sixteen instructions, many of which have a conditional nature associated with them. The conditional mechanism allows the address at the output to be one of the four values available at the input to the multiplexer, the selection of which depends upon the conditional inputs. Not shown on the block diagram are three output lines, which can be used to control the source of information presented to the input lines: PL-L, MAP-L, and VEC-L. For most of the instructions PL-L is asserted; this can be used to enable information from the microinstruction register to provide the necessary data. One of the instructions causes the MAP-L line to be asserted; another instruction causes the VEC-L to be asserted. These signals are provided so that when some external information, such as the op code of an instruction, is to cause the system to jump to an externally supplied address, that address can be made available to the sequencer. In this case, the normal source of address information is disabled (PL-L is deasserted), and the alternate source of address information is enabled (MAP-L or VEC-L is asserted). The mapping between opcodes and the address of their respective microcode implementations can be easily stored in a PROM. The output enable of the PROM can be directly connected to the MAP-L signal, and when the system requires the mapping function to be performed, the appropriate address is supplied to the inputs of the sequencer. The VEC-L line is utilized in the same fashion: an external address, such as a vector supplied by the user, is enabled onto the input lines at the appropriate time.

Like the 2901, the 2910 contains both control lines and data lines. However, in this implementation the data lines of the 2910 are all concerned with microcode addresses in the control section, and do not have a direct bearing on the data path section of the system. The data path for our example is shown in Figure 5.37. This diagram indicates that we are going to simulate the action of the 16-bit machine with an 8-bit system; 16-bit transactions will then require two transfers. The 8-bit system is composed of two 2901 processing elements that have been combined to provide 8-bit arithmetic and logic capabilities. The address and instruction information needed by the processor section are provided by the microinstruction register (MIR). In addition, the MIR supplies 8 bits of data to provide a constant load capability. Often a system designer will need the capability to place a known value in a register, or provide a constant for comparison or masking purposes. The other modules of the processor shown in Figure 5.37 are for the data and address paths. The data path is composed of bidirectional registers; this allows our system to load information in 8-bit quantities, and these quantities are then available on a 16-bit bus. The reverse path is also available, allowing our module to accept 16-bit values 8 bits at a time. The DATA HIGH and DATA LOW blocks of Figure 5.37 can be constructed from individual registers and tri-state drivers as shown in Figure 5.38(a). The address path is broken into three 8-bit quantities, which together form a 24-bit address. These registers can be read individually by the 8-bit system, or they can provide an address under the control of an arbitration module, which is not considered here. The address modules of Figure 5.37 can be created with the register and driver configurations shown in Figure 5.38(b).

Not shown on the diagram are the control signals used to interact with the memory and the I/O. This system is patterned after the Nova, but many of the features are different. We will assume that there is a separate memory address space and I/O address space; this will require a method to identify the address currently on the address bus. That is, the control lines must establish a different protocol (either different physical lines or a different accessing mechanism) for the I/O devices than that used for the memory locations. The Nova I/O structure calls for three functions/registers at each interface address, and these are labeled A, B, and C. In this implementation, there are write and read control lines to each of these elements. In addition, there are some other control signals for testing conditions and causing action at the interface. Table 5.3 identifies the various control signals that we will include in our design, in addition to those found in Figure 5.37.

With the detailed data path block diagram available, the signals needed to control the flow of information in the system have been identified. In addition,

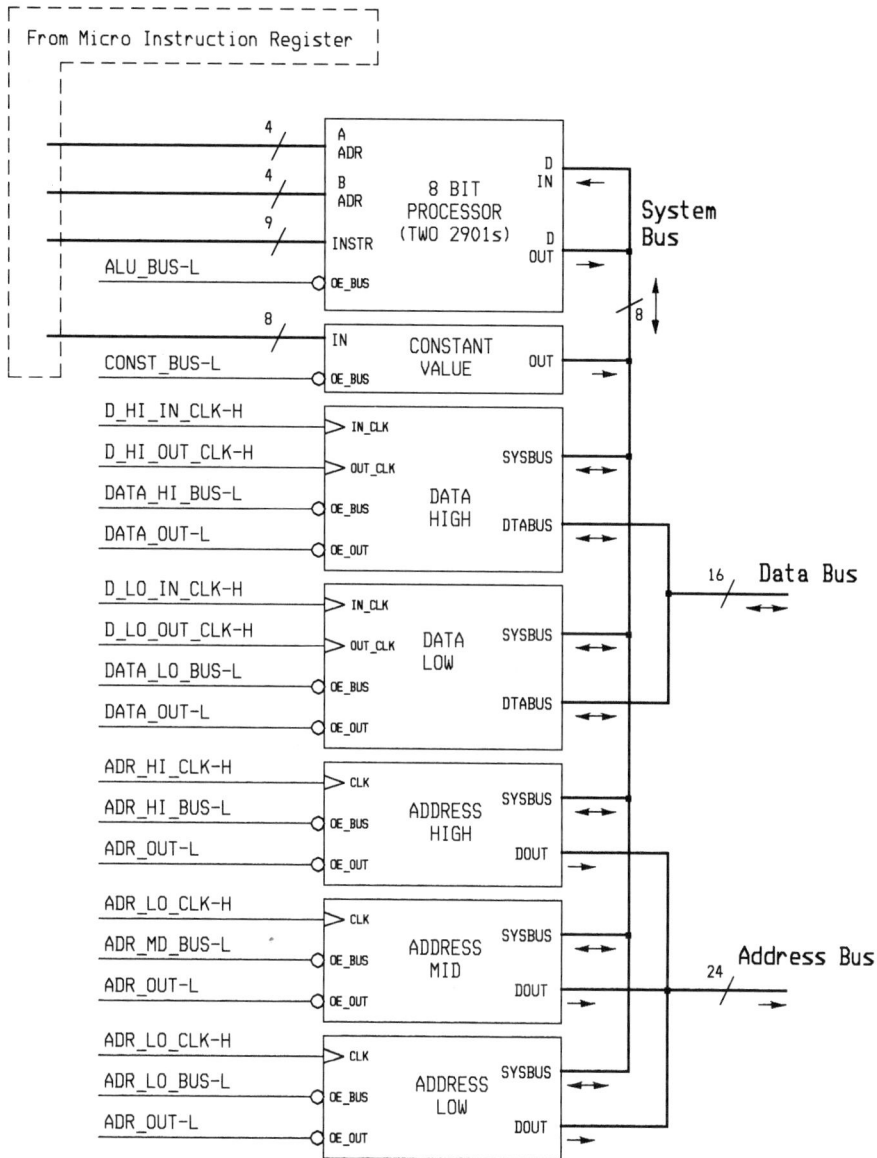

Figure 5.37. Data Path Block Diagram of Implementation of the 16-Bit Computer System.

the other control signals needed in the system have been specified. We are ready to set up the microcode control section of the computer. Before doing that, however, we will consider one more portion of the circuitry. This system is using an 8-bit processor to simulate the action of a 16 bit-processor, and hence must be able to do 16-bit arithmetic. In fact, to increment the program counter, a 24-bit addition must be possible. To accomplish that we have included the circuitry shown in Figure 5.39 to control the carry into the processor. As seen by the logic, under the control of the MIR the carry into the ALU (ALU_C_IN-H) can be forced to zero, forced to one, set to the carry out of the previous cycle (uCRY-H), or set to MCRY-H. MCRY-H is the carry bit from the status register of the 16-bit machine, which is not shown. This control of the carry input allows the designer

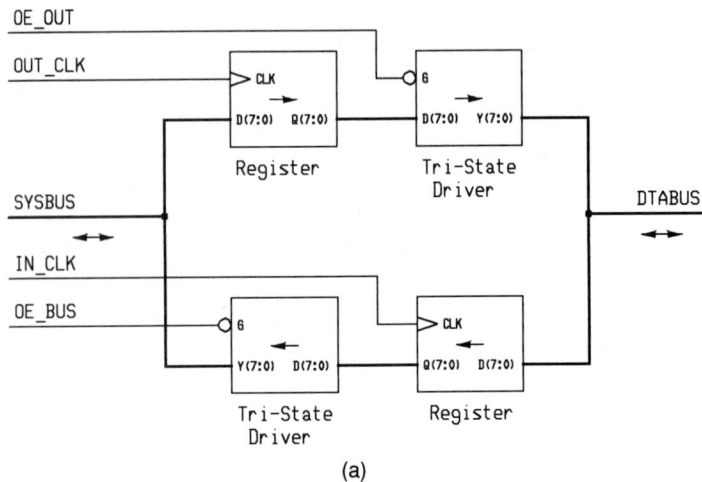

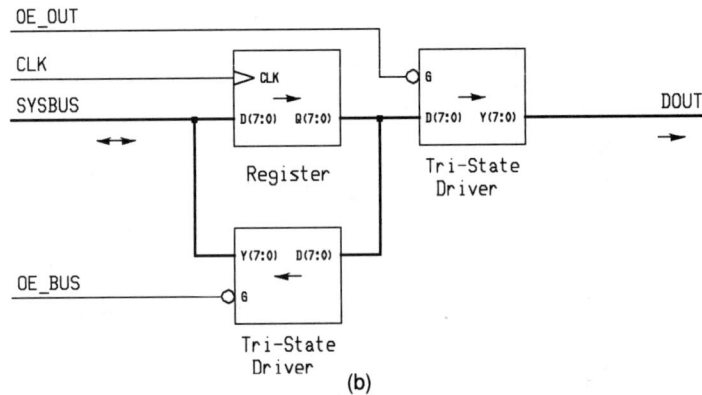

Figure 5.38. Components of the Data and Address Portions of Microcoded System; (a) Bidirectional Data Register for Microcode Example, (b) Address Driver for Microcode Example.

total flexibility; multiprecision adds can be achieved by doing 8 bits at a time and feeding the carry to the next cycle through uCRY-H. Adds of 32-bit words can be done at the assembly language level, and the microcode would then select MCRY-H as the carry in the appropriate cycle.

With this set of control bits identified, we will proceed with the design process. It should be noted that the design is not complete, and more control lines would be required for the entire system. In the horizontal microcode approach there will be 1 bit in the MIR for each control line. This results in a very wide word, but the clock cycle time is as small as possible, and the available parallelism is at a maximum. Figure 5.40 shows a diagram of the resulting system. A more detailed schematic diagram is found in Appendix B.

The diagram shows a system with the same general organization as seen in Figure 5.33. The 2910 provides the address information, and the microcode memory modules supply the microinstruction to the MIR. The bits comprising the

Table 5.3. Additional Control Lines for 16-Bit Computer.

Signal Name	Definition
MEM-H	Asserted when the transfer is for memory.
READ-H	Asserted when the transfer is a read (to CPU).
ADR_VALID-H	Asserted when address valid; deasserted at end of cycle.
DATA_VALID-H	Asserted (by CPU for write, by device for read) when data valid.
DATOA-H	A control line; asserted on output.
DATOB-H	B control line; asserted on output.
DATOC-H	C control line; asserted on output.
DATIA-H	A control line; asserted on input.
DATIB-H	B control line; asserted on input.
DATIC-H	C control line; asserted on input.
STRT-H	Start control line; asserted when needed by I/O instruction.
CLR-H	Clear control line; asserted when needed by I/O instruction.
IOPLS-H	I/O pulse; asserted when needed by I/O instruction.
MSKO-H	Mask out; asserted during MSKO instruction.
INTA-H	Interrupt acknowledge; asserted during INTA instruction.
DCHA-H	Data channel acknowledge; asserted at beginning of data channel cycle.
DCHI-H	Data channel input; asserted for channel input.
DCHO-H	Data channel output; asserted for channel output.
IORST-H	I/O reset; asserted during IORST instruction, console reset.

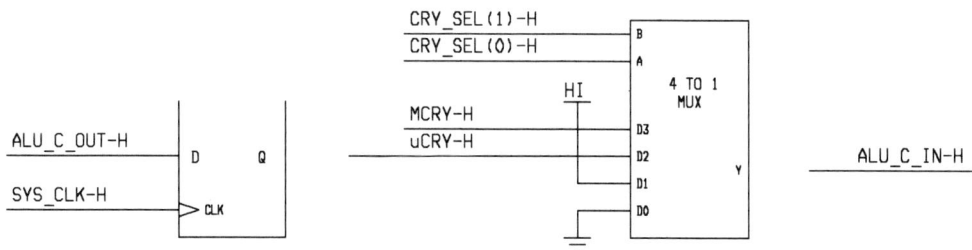

Figure 5.39. Carry Control Circuitry for 16-Bit Computer System.

MIR can be loosely grouped into three categories: bits controlling the microcode address system, bits controlling data flow on the data path, and bits controlling interaction with other machines. We will briefly discuss some points concerning each of these sections.

The address control section has four lines (SEQ_INSTR) to control the function of the 2910. When these lines identify a conditional type of instruction, the action of the module is further specified by the condition code and condition code

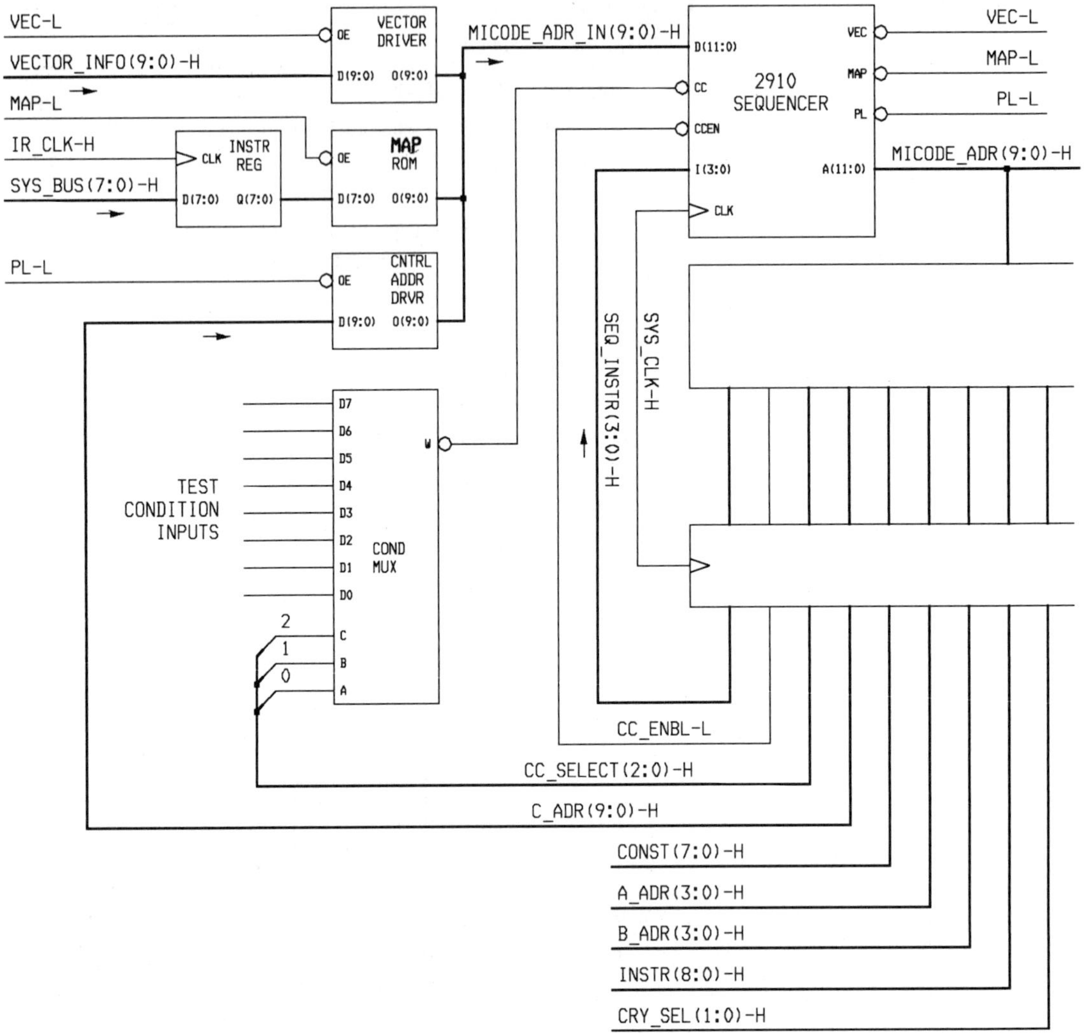

Figure 5.40. Logic Diagram for Horizontal Microcode Control.

enable (CC_ENBL) lines. The condition code is actually selected from a number of available possibilities by CC_SELECT. We have shown eight possible inputs; additional inputs could be considered by allowing a larger multiplexer and another select line. These lines control the function of the 2910, but occasionally additional information is required by the sequencer. For example, if the instruction to execute is a jump or jump subroutine, then the target address must be supplied, which is the function of the MICODE_ADR_IN lines.

There are three sources of information into the sequencer, each of which has responsibility for a different kind of information.

- The control address driver (CNTRL ADR DRVR) is the selected source when PL is asserted, and provides information from the MIR. This allows address information to be directed to the sequencer directly from the microcode.

- The second source, the map ROM (MAP ROM), is selected when the MAP signal is asserted. This allows a designer to map bit patterns loaded into the

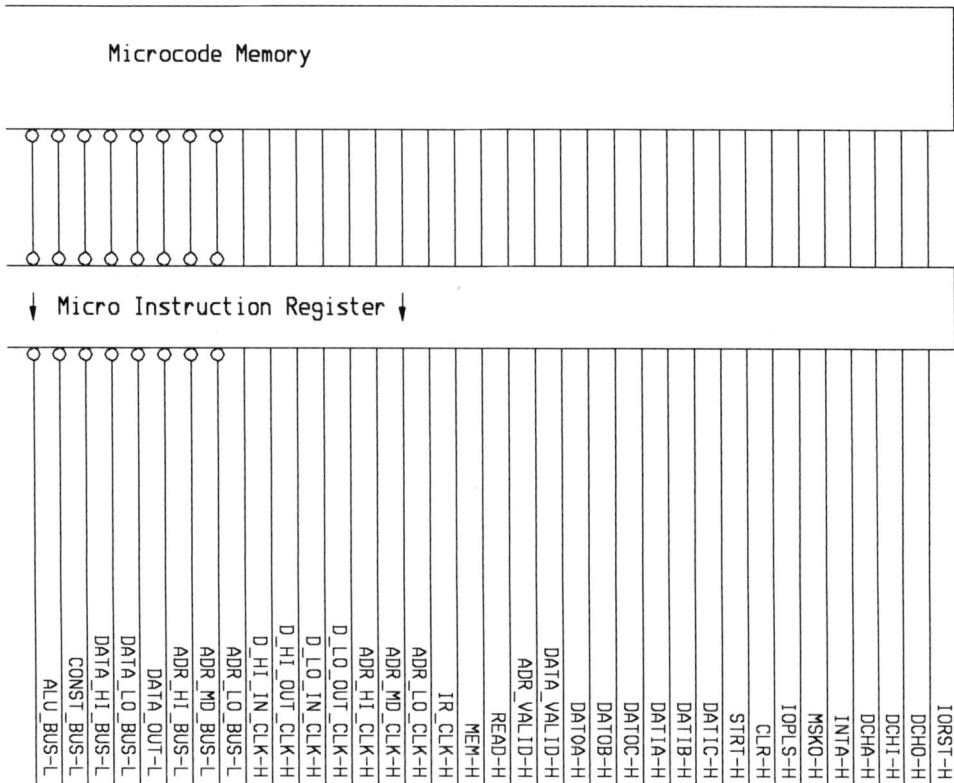

Figure 5.40. *(cont.)* Logic Diagram for Horizontal Microcode Control.

instruction register (INSTR REG) to specific addresses in microcode memory at which the necessary instruction sequence is found.

- The final source for address information is the vector driver, which accepts an address from an external source and supplies that address when the VEC signal is asserted. This allows an address to be supplied directly from a user-defined source.

As can be seen from the diagram, the sequencer requires 18 lines to control these functions, and these lines form the first part of the MIR.

The control and data lines of the data path elements are the next to be included in the MIR. The CONST lines allow a known value to be injected into the system. This is very useful for providing values to be used as constants, masks, and match values. The A and B address lines (A_ADR, B_ADR) are required by the 2901 ALU to specify the addresses needed for register identification. The instruction lines (INSTR) specify the action to be taken by the

Table 5.4. Bit Fields for Microcode of Table 5.5.

Label	Number of bits	Radix of Representation	Function
ADR		16	Address; number of bits depends on implementation (10 bits in this example).
SEQ INS	4	16	Sequencer instruction; bits to I lines on 2910.
CC EN	1	2	Condition code enable.
CC SEL	3	8	Condition code select; address of condition to test.
SEQ ADDR	10	16	Sequencer address; lines to provide address for jumps.
DATA CONS	8	16	Data constant; for constants to bus.
A ADR	4	16	A address lines of 2901.
B ADR	4	16	B address lines of 2901.
ALU INS	9	8	Instruction lines of 2901.
CRY SEL	2	2	Carry select lines.
BUS SRC	8	2	Bus source lines.
BUS DEST	8	2	Bus destination lines.
MEM I/O BITS	19	2	Bits for memory and I/O interaction.

ALU. If the instruction to be executed requires a carry input, then the CRY_SEL lines specify the appropriate carry information. These 27 lines control the processing accomplished by the processing section of the system, in addition to providing constants as needed.

The remainder of the bits are those required to control the individual elements of the system. By allowing total control of the lines (since each control line is independent of the others) the maximum parallelism is possible. For example, all of the external registers can be cleared by creating a zero value on the bus (all bits zero in constant field, assert CONST_BUS-L) and assert all of the appropriate clock lines. This would allow loading of six registers simultaneously. The bits in the microcode word also contain the control bits identified in Table 5.3 for interaction with external units. This last section of the MIR, which contains the control lines for the data path and the interaction with external devices, contains 35 bits.

One of the best ways to become familiar with the system and its capabilities and weaknesses is to prepare microcode for it. To this end we will look at a few lines of code that do two simple functions: simulate the action of an ADD A, B instruction and a JUMP instruction. These instructions are broken into separate fetch and execute portions, and the following assumptions are made: the 24-bit stack limit register comprises registers 5, 6, and 7 in the 2901s; the 24-bit stack pointer comprises registers 8, 9, and 10 in the 2901s; the 24-bit program counter is contained in registers 11, 12, and 13; 16 bits of instruction are located in registers 14 and 15 in the 2901s; the A and B registers are coincident with memory locations 000_{16} and 002_{16} (byte addresses), and are stored in memory.

The microcode is contained in Table 5.5, which can be confusing if not approached in a regular fashion. Each of the headings in Table 5.5 identifies a group of bits, and their definitions representations are given in Table 5.4. Each microcode word identifies a single operation, but since there are a large number of bits, a correspondingly large number of things can happen during each microcode cycle. Each group of bits identifies an action to be performed by the system. Required macro operations are accomplished stepwise by a succession of micro operations. Table 5.5 contains three sections of micro operations.

- The first section (addresses 0A0 to 0A8) is the code for the fetch portion. Note that the function of this code is to do PC → MAR, which takes three 8-bit transfers, at the same time that it does PC + 2 → PC. Note also that the bus destination lines are normally high in this implementation, so that (see the instruction at 0A1) when a value is available on the bus (a bus source line is asserted), that value can be loaded into the appropriate register at the end of the cycle. This occurs because the 0 becomes a 1 at the next clock pulse, creating a rising edge that causes the required load of information. Another thing to note is that the memory interaction is started by the instruction at location 0A4, and the instruction at location 0A5 waits for the memory to respond before continuing. Instructions located at 0A6 and 0A7 move 16 bits of instruction into the internal IR, as well as the 8 most significant bits to the IR that addresses the MAP ROM. The instruction at location 0A8 causes the sequencer to jump to the address specified by the MAP ROM, which will be the beginning of the code for the appropriate macro instruction. For this example, that address will either be 0F2 or 121; in general, the address can map to any appropriate location.

- The second section of code (addresses 0F2 to 100) performs the ADD A, B instruction. The address zero is forced into the MAR, and that value (the A value) is copied to temporary locations in the 2901s (registers 2 and 3). Then the address two is placed in the MAR, and that value is added to the temporary already in the 2901s. Then the result is written back, and control moves to the fetch portion to continue execution. Again note the memory interaction: the action is initialized by the microcode, and the microcode continues when the memory responds.

- The final section of code (addresses 121 to 129) is for the JUMP instruction. The assumption here is that the instruction is actually 32 bits long — 8 bits of op code and 24 bits for the target address. The fetch section has placed 8 of the 24 address bits in the internal IR, in register 15. So, the first part of this code duplicates the fetch action to obtain the next 2 bytes. These bytes are then transferred from the data registers to the address registers, along with the value contained in register 15. The microcode then moves back to the fetch portion to proceed with the program. Note here that the maximum speed is not attained, since the work done by the instruction at location 127 could be done with the work done by the instruction at location 125, and the time required for the execution of the instruction would be reduced by one cycle.

Other observations can be made concerning the microcode in Table 5.5. Some of the fields are not used much of the time, and some of the fields have only a small number of legal patterns. This is one of the observations that gives rise to the use of vertical microcode. We wish to reduce the number of bits required in a microcode word, but we still wish to be able to do all of the necessary functions. The resulting system uses single fields for multiple functions, and combines patterns into decoded information. For our example, we will combine the functions of the 2910 address, the data constant, the A and B addresses for the 2901s, and the ALU carry select into a single field. In addition, we will combine the bits required for bus source into one field, bus destination into another, and further encode the bits required for the memory-I/O interaction. The resulting system is shown in Figure 5.41. A schematic showing the detailed connections of the components is included in Appendix B.

This system is very much like the system shown in Figure 5.40. The control signals are identical; however, there are limitations on how many control

Table 5.5. Horizontal Microcode for Fetch, ADD A,B, and JUMP.

ADR ddd_{16}	SEQ INS 4 bits d_{16}	CC EN 1 bit d_2	CC SEL 3 bits d_8	SEQ ADR 10 bits ddd_{16}	DATA CONS 8 bits dd_{16}	A ADR 4 bits d_{16}	B ADR 4 bits d_{16}	ALU INS 9 bits ddd_8	CRY SEL 2 bits dd_2	BUS SRC 8 bits $d \cdots d_2$	BUS DEST 8 bits $d \cdots d_2$
0A0	E	x	x	xxx	02	x	x	037	xx	10111111	11111111
0A1	E	x	x	xxx	xx	B	B	200	00	01111111	11111101
0A2	E	x	x	xxx	xx	C	C	203	10	01111111	11111011
0A3	E	x	x	xxx	xx	D	D	203	10	01111111	11110111
0A4	E	x	x	xxx	xx	x	x	144	xx	11111111	11111111
0A5	3	0	1	0A5	xx	x	x	144	xx	11111111	01011111
0A6	E	x	x	xxx	xx	x	E	337	xx	11101111	11111111
0A7	E	x	x	xxx	xx	x	F	337	xx	11011111	11111110
0A8	2	x	x	xxx	xx	x	x	144	xx	11111111	11111111
0F2	E	x	x	xxx	00	x	x	144	xx	10111111	11110001
0F3	E	x	x	xxx	xx	x	x	144	xx	11111111	11111111
0F4	3	0	1	0F4	xx	x	x	144	xx	11111111	01011111
0F5	E	x	x	xxx	xx	x	2	337	xx	11101111	11111111
0F6	E	x	x	xxx	xx	x	3	337	xx	11011111	11111111
0F7	E	x	x	xxx	02	x	x	144	xx	10111111	11111101
0F8	E	x	x	xxx	xx	x	x	144	xx	11111111	11111111
0F9	3	0	1	0F9	xx	x	x	144	xx	11111111	01011111
0FA	E	x	x	xxx	xx	2	2	305	00	11101111	11111111
0FB	E	x	x	xxx	xx	3	3	305	10	11011111	11111111
0FC	E	x	x	xxx	xx	2	x	134	xx	01111111	11101111
0FD	E	x	x	xxx	xx	3	x	134	xx	01111111	10111111
0FE	E	x	x	xxx	xx	x	x	144	xx	11110111	11111111
0FF	3	0	1	0FF	xx	x	x	144	xx	11110111	11111111
100	3	1	x	0A0	xx	x	x	144	xx	11111111	11111111
121	E	x	x	xxx	02	x	x	037	xx	10111111	11111111
122	E	x	x	xxx	xx	B	B	200	00	01111111	11111101
123	E	x	x	xxx	xx	C	C	203	10	01111111	11111011
124	E	x	x	xxx	xx	D	D	203	10	01111111	11110111
125	E	x	x	xxx	xx	x	x	144	xx	11111111	11111111
126	3	0	1	126	xx	x	x	144	xx	11111111	01011111
127	E	x	x	xxx	xx	F	B	334	xx	11111111	11111111
128	E	x	x	xxx	xx	x	C	337	xx	11101111	11111111
129	3	1	x	0A0	xx	x	D	337	xx	11011111	11111111

signals can be asserted at any given time. For example, one of the functions of the horizontal microcode example was to load a zero value into three registers simultaneously; in this implementation that would require three separate instructions, since only one destination line can be asserted at any time. Also, the horizontal microcode method has independent address and data fields in the code; it would be possible to jump to one address and load a constant in the same cycle. With the vertical microcode implementation one field is used for both these functions; hence, one could not load an arbitrary constant and perform a microcode jump at the same time. This type of system is, in general, slower than the horizontal microcode system, since more instructions are required, and the cycle time is longer. However, the number of bits required in the microcode word is smaller, and the total number of bits (number of words × number of bits/word) is, in

Table 5.5. *(cont.)* Horizontal Microcode for Fetch, ADD A,B, and JUMP.

MEM I/O BITS 19 bits $d \cdots d_2$	ADR ddd_{16}	Comment
		PC → MAR; increment PC (PC = R11, R12, R13)
0000000000000000000	0A0	Move constant 02_{16} to Q reg of 2901.
0000000000000000000	0A1	R11 → MAR$_{7-0}$; increment R11.
0000000000000000000	0A2	R12 → MAR$_{15-8}$; inc R12 with previous carry.
0000000000000000000	0A3	R13 → MAR$_{23-16}$; inc R13 with previous carry.
1110000000000000000	0A4	MEM bits initiate memory read action.
1110000000000000000	0A5	Stay here till memory ready; 0 → 1 on destination lines loads result.
0000000000000000000	0A6	Move LSB to R14.
0000000000000000000	0A7	Move MSB to R15 and IR.
0000000000000000000	0A8	Jump to address provided by MAP ROM.
0000000000000000000	0F2	0 → MAR
1110000000000000000	0F3	MEM bits initiate memory read action.
1110000000000000000	0F4	Stay here till memory ready; 0 → 1 on destination lines loads result.
0000000000000000000	0F5	LSB of mem value to R2.
0000000000000000000	0F6	MSB of mem value to R3.
0000000000000000000	0F7	02_{16} → MAR$_{7-0}$
1110000000000000000	0F8	MEM bits initiate memory read action.
1110000000000000000	0F9	Stay here till memory ready; 0 → 1 on destination lines loads result.
0000000000000000000	0FA	Add LSB of memory to R2.
0000000000000000000	0FB	Add MSB of memory to R3 with previous carry.
0000000000000000000	0FC	R2 → MEM$_{7-0}$
0000000000000000000	0FD	R3 → MEM$_{15-8}$
1010000000000000000	0FE	MEM bits initiate memory write action.
1010000000000000000	0FF	Wait here till memory done.
0000000000000000000	100	Jump back to address $0A0_{16}$ for next fetch.
0000000000000000000	121	Move constant 02_{16} to Q register of 2901.
0000000000000000000	122	R11 → MAR$_{7-0}$; increment R11.
0000000000000000000	123	R12 → MAR$_{15-8}$; inc R12 with previous carry.
0000000000000000000	124	R13 → MAR$_{23-16}$; inc R13 with previous carry.
1110000000000000000	125	MEM bits initiate memory read action.
1110000000000000000	126	Stay here till memory ready; 0 → 1 on destination lines loads result.
0000000000000000000	127	Move first byte to PC from R15.
0000000000000000000	128	Move second byte to PC from MBR.
0000000000000000000	129	Move third byte to PC from MBR; jump to fetch.

general, smaller. For this example, the number of bits in the microcode word decreased from 80 bits (horizontal) to 45 bits (vertical), a decrease of over 40 percent in the number of lines required.

The method a designer uses to combine functions and lines into groups, and the amount of overlap used in a system, reflect the design choices made in the design process. If a designer is using 8-bit parts, he may attempt to end up with a system that uses a multiple of 8 bits. If a designer is constrained by power requirements, he may combine as many fields as possible into one. Any of a number of different requirements will influence the choices made in the process. This example brings out several techniques that can be used, which we point out here. The constant lines, the address lines, and the A and B addresses from the ALU have been combined into a single field. This constrains what can be done at

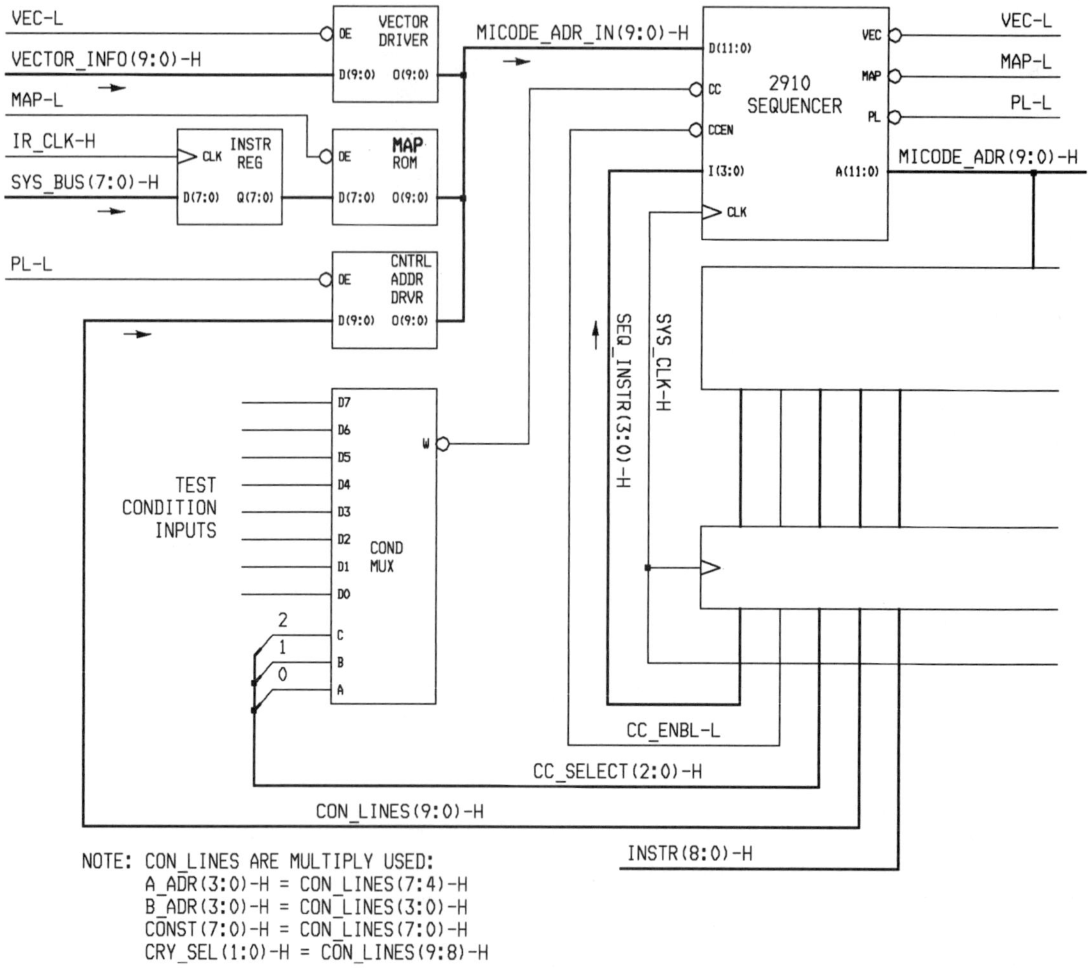

Figure 5.41. Logic Diagram for Vertical Microcode Control.

one time, since only one function can be performed by the CON_LINES at any one time. One example is the jump/load conflict. Another example is loading constants into the ALU: since the B address lines specify the destination of a write function, information that is to go to an arbitrary register in the ALU is first placed in the Q register, then moved to the appropriate register. Thus, what was accomplished in a single cycle in the previous system requires two cycles in this system.

In general, it is not a good idea to permit more than one driver to place a value on a bus at any one time. Thus, there is danger in the scheme of the horizontal microcode implementation, since it is possible to enable more than one source to the bus simultaneously. This possibility has been removed in the vertical microcode example by the use of a decoder; now only one line can be asserted at any one time. A decoder has also been used to identify the destination, which removes the possibility of sending information to two or more destinations simultaneously. Since there were eight destinations in the original system, a three to eight decoder has been used to do this decoding; however, since we want the ability to select none of the destinations, an additional line has been added to enable the entire destination function. A different technique for not asserting any line

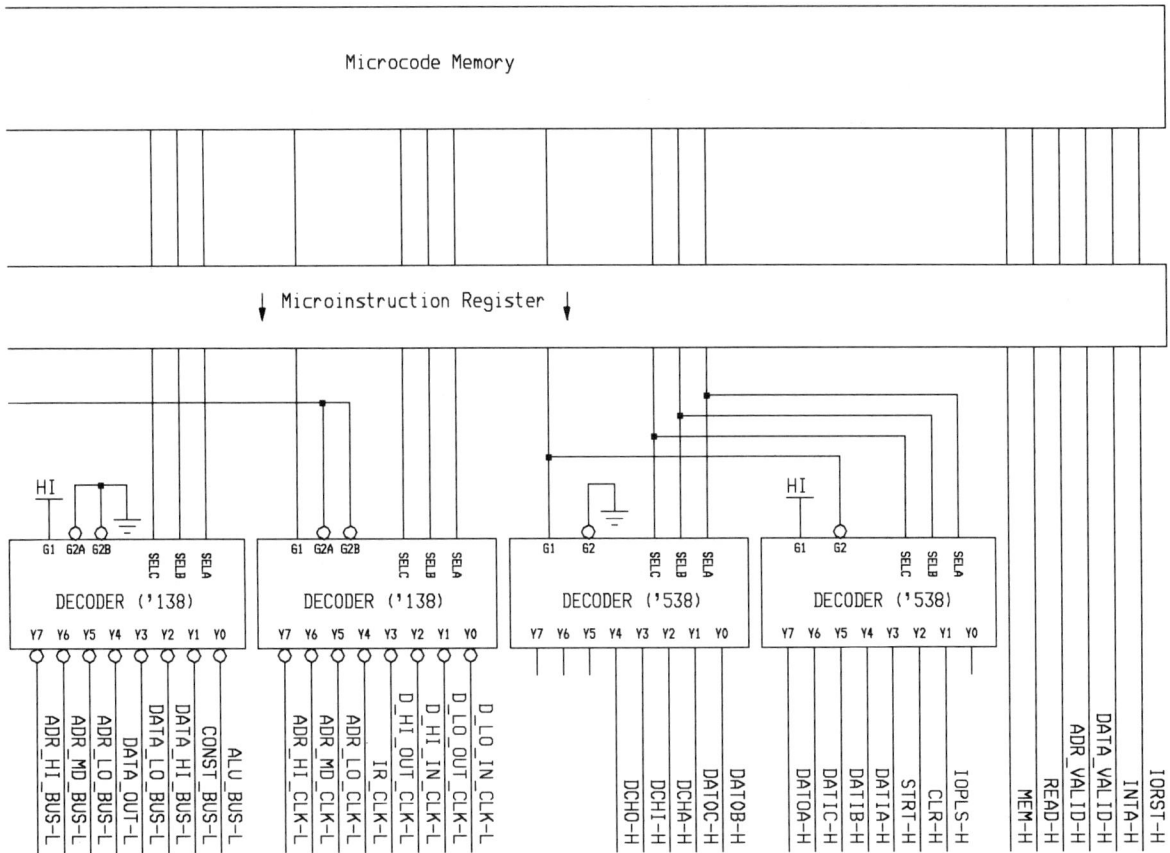

Figure 5.41. *(cont)* Logic Diagram for Vertical Microcode Control.

has been used for the I/O bits: the zero line is left unused. Thus a value of zero on the I/O bit lines will result in no action. Finally, those lines that cannot be independently asserted, such as READ, MEM, and the like, are not combined, but left to be asserted as needed by the system.

Some care must be taken to guarantee correct system function with respect to the nonideal nature of the decoders. The decoder used for the bus source is always enabled, and the microcode system can control only the address lines. This will result in glitches on the decoder output lines as the internal logic changes to agree with changes of the address lines. The outputs of this decoder are connected to tri-state enable lines of devices that can assert information onto the data bus. These glitches will not cause problems with the data being enabled onto the bus, since the glitches always occur at the beginning of the cycle when the bus lines have not assumed the correct assertion level.

Table 5.6.

ADR ddd_{16}	SEQ INST 4 bits d_{16}	CC EN 1 bit d_2	CC SEL 3 bits d_8	CON LINES 10 bits ddd_{16}	ALU INST 9 bits ddd_8	BUS SRC 3 bits d_8	BUS DEST 4 bits d_{16}	I/O BITS 4 bits d_{16}	MEM BITS 6 bits $d \cdots d_2$	ADR ddd_{16}	Comment
0A0	E	x	x	002	037	1	0	0	000000	0A0	PC → MAR; PC is stored in R11, R12, R13; first, 02_{16} to Q reg.
0A1	E	x	x	0BB	200	0	D	0	000000	0A1	R11 → MAR_{7-0}; increment R11.
0A2	E	x	x	2CC	203	0	E	0	000000	0A2	R12 → MAR_{15-8}; increment R12 with last carry.
0A3	E	x	x	2DD	203	0	F	0	000000	0A3	R13 → MAR_{23-16}; increment R13 with last carry.
0A4	E	x	x	xxx	144	0	0	0	111000	0A4	MEM lines initiate read action.
0A5	3	0	1	0A5	144	0	0	0	111000	0A5	Wait for memory to respond.
0A6	E	x	x	xxx	144	0	8	0	111000	0A6	Strobe MEM LSB to accept info.
0A7	E	x	x	xxE	337	3	A	0	111000	0A7	Strobe MEM MSB to accept info; transfer LSB to R14.
0A8	E	x	x	xxF	337	2	C	0	000000	0A8	Transfer MEM MSB to R15 and IR.
0A9	2	x	x	xxx	144	0	0	0	000000	0A9	Jump to address provided by MAP ROM.
0F2	E	x	x	000	144	1	D	0	000000	0F2	Set MAR_{7-0} to zero.
0F3	E	x	x	000	144	1	E	0	000000	0F3	Set MAR_{15-8} to zero.
0F4	E	x	x	000	144	1	F	0	000000	0F4	Set MAR_{23-16} to zero.
0F5	E	x	x	xxx	144	0	0	0	111000	0F5	MEM lines initiate read action.
0F6	3	0	1	0F6	144	0	0	0	111000	0F6	Wait for memory to respond.
0F7	E	x	x	xxx	144	0	8	0	111000	0F7	Strobe MEM LSB to accept info.
0F8	E	x	x	xx2	337	3	A	0	111000	0F8	Strobe MEM MSB to accept info; transfer LSB to R2.
0F9	E	x	x	xx3	337	2	0	0	111000	0F9	Transfer MEM MSB to R3.
0FA	E	x	x	002	144	1	D	0	000000	0FA	Load MAR_{7-0} with 02_{16}.
0FB	E	x	x	xxx	144	0	0	0	111000	0FB	MEM lines initiate read action.
0FC	3	0	1	0FC	144	0	0	0	111000	0FC	Wait for memory to respond.
0FD	E	x	x	xxx	144	0	8	0	111000	0FD	Strobe MEM LSB to accept info.
0FE	E	x	x	022	305	3	A	0	111000	0FE	Strobe MEM MSB to accept info; add LSB to R2.
0FF	E	x	x	233	305	2	0	0	111000	0FF	Add MEM MSB to R3 with last carry.
100	E	x	x	x2x	134	0	9	0	000000	100	Transfer contents of R2 to MEM LSB.
101	E	x	x	x3x	134	0	B	0	000000	101	Transfer contents of R3 to MEM MSB.
102	E	x	x	xxx	144	0	0	0	101000	102	MEM lines initiate write action.
103	3	0	1	103	144	0	0	0	101000	103	Wait for memory to respond.
104	3	1	0	0A0	144	0	0	0	000000	104	Jump back to fetch microcode (address 0A0).
121	E	x	x	002	037	1	0	0	000000	121	PC → MAR; 02_{16} to Q reg.
122	E	x	x	0BB	200	0	D	0	000000	122	R11 → MAR_{7-0}; increment R11.
123	E	x	x	2CC	203	0	E	0	000000	123	R12 → MAR_{15-8}; increment R12 with last carry.
124	E	x	x	2DD	203	0	F	0	000000	124	R13 → MAR_{23-16}; increment R13 with last carry.
125	E	x	x	xxx	144	0	0	0	111000	1254	MEM lines initiate read action.
126	3	0	1	126	144	0	0	0	111000	126	Wait for memory to respond.
127	E	x	x	xFB	334	0	8	0	111000	127	Strobe MEM LSB to accept info; also copy R15 to R11.
128	E	x	x	xxC	337	3	A	0	111000	128	Strobe MEM MSB to accept info; transfer LSB to R12.
129	E	x	x	xxD	337	2	0	0	000000	129	Transfer MEM MSB to R13.
12A	3	1	0	0A0	144	0	0	0	000000	12A	Jump back to fetch microcode (address 0A0).

The decoder associated with the bus destination control is connected in a different fashion. Note that the system clock has been connected to the low true enable of this decoder. Connecting the clock to the decoder enable in this fashion will assert the designated signal only during the last half of the cycle, which will prevent glitches from occurring on the decoder output lines. This prevents unwanted action to occur since these lines activate edge triggered functions. The I/O and memory bits do not have this enabling function, which indicates that the system designer was willing to live with the glitches which would occur on these lines. If this is unacceptable, then steps must be taken to be sure that glitches do not cause unwanted results.

As with the horizontal microcode example, one of the best ways to get a feel for the system capabilities is to prepare microcode for it. Table 5.6 contains the microcode for the same instructions, ADD A, B and JUMP. The fields of Table 5.6 are similar to the fields of Table 5.5. The two differences are that the CON lines in Table 5.6 (10 bits, base 16 representation) combine the function of the SEQ ADR, DATA CONS, A ADR, and B ADR, fields of Table 5.5, and the bus and I/O lines are encoded in the vertical example, and hence represented in base 16. The code in Table 5.6 performs the same functions as that in Table 5.5, but more instructions are required. For example, at 0F2 of the horizontal code is an instruction that loads zero into three registers simultaneously. With the vertical example this requires the three instructions located at 0F2, 0F3, and 0F4. This is an example of the way that code will "grow" in the vertical dimension to perform a function, when compared to a horizontal implementation.

The above examples demonstrate that microcode is a technique that enables a designer to perform work with a state machine type of controller, and have the action dictated by the contents of a memory. The microinstruction register of the microcode machine serves the function of the present state register to follow the progress of the work to be performed, and the MIR and microcode memory combine do the work of the decode portion of a state machine. The net result is to allow assertion of control signals using techniques of low level programming. This permits nested subroutines and conditional jumps to be part of a hardware designer's collection of usable techniques. The designer can then make design choices based on the constraints of his particular design to accomplish the goals of his system, using whatever combination of horizontal and vertical techniques may be most beneficial.

One final comment is in order concerning the design examples used in this chapter. The examples have become increasingly complex, starting with the simple, seven state controller for the FIR filter function, and ending with a controller capable of implementing the necessary control for an entire computer system. Thus, the microcode mechanisms can appear to be much more complex than the state machine or delay methods of control, when the principles on which all of the controllers are based are the same. The apparent complexity stems from the complexity of the data path being controlled, not from an inherently complex technique.

5.8. Microcode Machine Example: VAX 11/780

The microcoded method of control implementation has been used by many machines since the appropriate memory technology became available. Each of these machines has a unique blend of techniques to generate its control signals. One of theese examples was introduced by Digital Equipment Corporation in the 1970s. This system, the VAX 11/780, is a 32-bit machine with general purpose computing capabilities. The system has been utilized for scientific, business, and office applications, and a variety of models with different speeds and complexity are now available.

The VAX 11/780 itself has a microcoded engine to control about 2,600 integrated circuits on 19 circuit boards. The clock cycle time of the system is 200 nsec, applicable to both the internal modules and the bus that allows connection of memory modules and peripherals. The organization of the system is shown in Figure 5.42. The diagram is done to reflect the physical division of the system as well as the logical connections available. As can be seen from the figure, a number of data paths are used to transfer information between system components. The synchronous backplane interconnect (SBI) is the mechanism used to transfer information from memory and peripheral devices into the CPU itself. This bus is time shared between address and data, and the highest data rate will occur when an address is transferred, followed by two 32-bit data words. This results in a data rate of 8 bytes in 3 cycles (600 nsec), or 13.3 Mbytes per second. The SBI control interacts with devices on the SBI to perform whatever transfers are required by the system.

The internal data bus is used to move information between any of the major system components as required by the system. This is in contrast to the other buses with a more specific purpose. The control store bus is composed of the microcode bits, and is used to control the action of all of the system components. The memory data bus is used to transfer information to and from memory. This includes the cache memory as well as the memory accessible via the SBI. The virtual address provides the address of information requested by the program in the virtual address space; this must be converted to an appropriate physical address, which will be placed on the physical address bus. Finally, the microprogram control bus is used to address the appropriate microcode word, which will be extracted from the control store and used to specify the appropriate action.

Some of the blocks connected by these buses are self-explanatory. The SBI control is used to control the interaction with devices that transfer information via the SBI. The data cache is a small cache used to store the most recently used pieces of information. The translation buffer and decode, which ascertains the

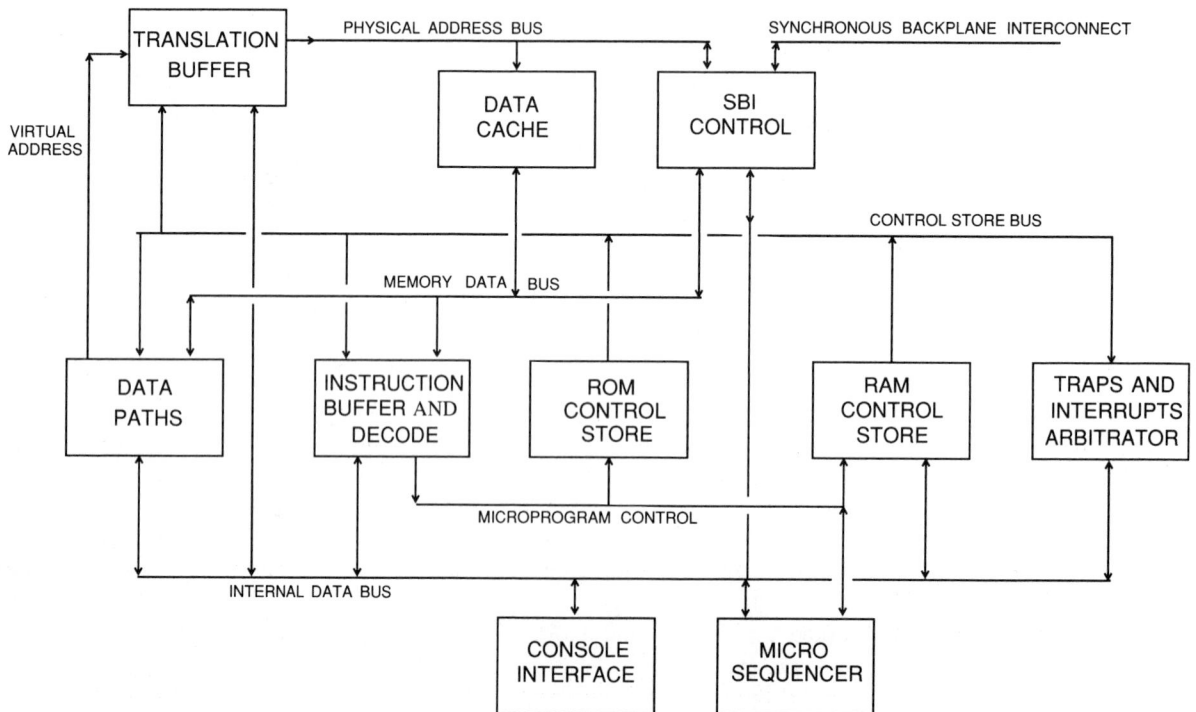

Figure 5.42. Block Diagram of the VAX 11/780 Computer.

machine instruction to be performed, provides the appropriate control to the microcode machine.

The microcode machine itself is contained in the micro sequencer, the ROM control store, and the RAM control store. The ROM control store contains the microcode for the basic instructions of the system; this includes a comprehensive set of variable length instructions for general computing, and some other functions needed by the system. The ROM control store provides storage for 4,096 microinstructions. The RAM control store serves the same basic function, storing microinstructions for system use. However, the content of the RAM control store must be provided by the user at an appropriate time, usually when the system is initialized. This capability of writing new information to the control memory is often called writable control store (WCS). The WCS can be used to provide corrections to faulty operations in permanent control store, or to speed up certain often executed sequences, such as operating system primatives. Having these functions in WCS allows changing them to grow with system needs or to correct faulty operation. It also allows users to tailor their system to enhance its operation in a specific environment. In any case, the system operates by having the micro sequencer supply a microcode address, and the ROM or RAM control store supplying the microinstruction.

The microinstruction is a 96-bit word whose format is given in Figure 5.43. The 96 bits are broken into 30 different fields, each of which controls part of the function of the machine. Table 5.7 identifies the various fields and the elements they control. Each microinstruction is capable of controlling the hardware of the system to do the work required. The techniques used are the same techniques we have already identified. Some fields provide an address to a multiplexer function (SMX, EBMX, RMX, KMX, etc.) to select one operand or source of data for a

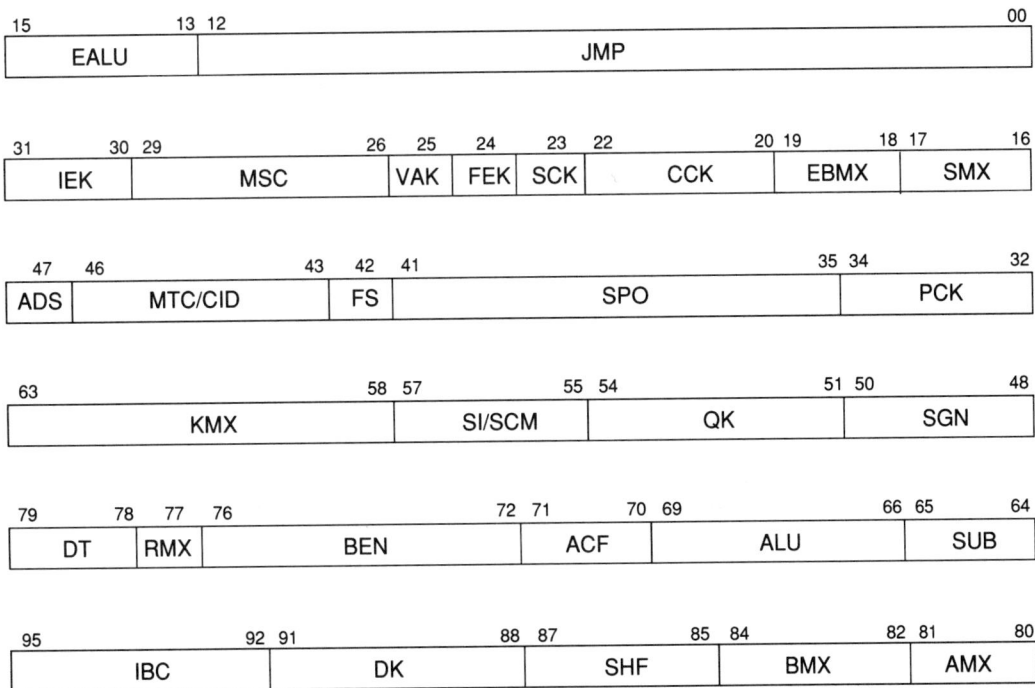

Figure 5.43. Fields of VAX 11/780 Microinstructions.

Table 5.7. Microcode Fields in VAX 11/780.

Mnemonic	Name	Function
JMP	Jump Address	Address of next microinstruction.
EALU	Exponent ALU	Control ALU for exponent arithmetic.
SMX	SMX Select	Control selection of value for S operand.
EBMX	EBMX Select	Control selection of value for EB operand.
CCK	Condition Code	Identify bit for condition code test.
SCK		
FEK		
VA		
MSC	Miscellaneous	Control various functions not included elsewhere.
IEK	Interrupt and Exception	Control function of interrupt logic.
PCK	Address Count Control	Control program counter and address specification.
SPO	Scratch Pad Operation	Control function of scratch pad area.
FS	Function Select	Identify function of MCT/CID bits.
MCT/CID	Memory and Control Bus	Control bus transfers.
ADS	Address Select	Identify source of effective address.
SGN	Sign Control	Identify source of sign bit.
QK	Q Reg Control	Control action of Q register.
SI/SCM	Shift Input Control	Control action of shift network.
KMX	Constants Select	Select source, value of constants.
SUB	Subroutine Control	Provide control for subroutine linkage.
ALU	ALU Control	Specify function performed by ALU.
ACF	Accelerator Control	Identify function of accelerator.
BEN	Branch Enable	Control branching function.
RMX	Reg Mux Control	Specify source of operand in reg mux.
DT	Data Type	Identify type of data being operated on.
AMX	A Mux Select	Control value supplied by A Mux.
BMX	B Mux Select	Control value supplied by B Mux.
SHF	ALU Shift Control	Control action of ALU shifter.
DK	D Reg Control	Control action of operand in D register.
IBC	Instruction Buffer Control	Specify action of instruction buffer.

specific register or function. Other fields use a single bit to identify the function of another field (FS). The ALU bits directly control the function of the arithmetic element in the system. The SUB bits identify the action to be taken on a microcode subroutine. Each of the fields controls action to occur somewhere in the system in each 200 nsec clock cycle.

One of the interesting techniques exemplified by this system is the selection of the next microinstruction. The JMP field of each microinstruction, which is *not* multiplexed with any other function, identifies the next microinstruction to be executed. Thus, there is no requirement that successive microinstructions be located in successive locations in microstore. The microinstructions can be located in any available locations in memory. If some choice of next microinstruction is required — that is, if a conditional branch of some type is needed — this is controlled by the BEN field. The effect is to modify the address in the JMP field in some predetermined fashion. For example, the JMP field can provide the most significant portion of an address, and the least significant bits can be provided by sign bits, processor state indicators, or other machine information. This provides a multiway branch capability, so that the next instruction is one of 8, 16, or 32 possible instructions, based on the function selected by the BEN field. The multiway branch ability permits multiple decisions simultaneously, since more than one bit can be used in the selection of the next microinstruction. The requirement for this to be effective is that the set of instructions that are possible next instructions for a specific microinstruction be located at an appropriate address boundary in the microcode. This is one of the reasons that each microinstruction carries the address of the next microinstruction, since placing sets of next instructions on address boundaries fragments the available microcode memory.

The VAX 11/780 is a good example of a microcoded system, but certainly not the only example. The technique has been used in a host of different machines to provide a programmable control system that can be utilized in a regular system fashion.

5.9. Control System Design: Asserting Control Lines in a Timely Fashion

This chapter has dealt with the concepts and practices involved in producing a control system for a digital device. The device can be as simple as a counter or as complex as a computer, but the principles involved in the process are the same. Before the design of the control system can begin, it is imperative that the data path be defined, and that the appropriate control lines be identified. This process must not only identify the lines to be controlled, but also specify the assertion levels required to perform the work. Armed with this information the designer can then proceed to provide a control section which will assert the lines in an appropriate fashion.

Once the set of signals required for control of a system has been identified, then the order of assertion and other specific information must be determined. This process requires that the designer be familiar with the system components, their uses, and their limitations. But the action of the control section can be specified by utilizing system knowledge, design techniques, and desired behavioral characteristics. This specification may take the form of a state diagram, which is useful for direct implementation of state machines. Or it may take the form of a flow diagram, which can provide the basis for a delay line or shift register method of control signal implementation. The state diagram or flow diagram can also be useful in preparing a system that utilizes microcode techniques for asserting the control lines. Each of the techniques can be effectively utilized where the system characteristics call for behavior of one type or another. For example, RISC machines generally need extremely fast control, but being relatively simple the amount of logic required for direct implementation permits random logic in the control system. On the other hand, CISC machines often require numerous steps and decisions to perform a specific instruction, so microcode is very appropriate. The designer, then, has the responsibility of selecting the implementation technique that will maximize effective use of system resources.

5.10. Problems

5.1 Consider the block diagram given in Figure P5.1 for the data path of a computer. This data path is to be used to implement a single address machine. The following information about the machine may or may not be useful. The add is not cascadable (no double precision adds.) The memory is fast RAM. The MAR ignores bits higher than its address space, which are transferred to it. The only control lines you have access to are those listed on the diagram. No initialization is needed for any of the logic. Design a sequencer for this data path that will do SUBTRACT, LEFT-SHIFT, and NEGATE. Use microcoding techniques. Include an RTL description of the transfers necessary. Give a logic diagram (at a reasonable level) of the control section, specify the bits in the microinstruction word, and give the microcode needed. The available microcode sequencer has the following pins: address out, address in, JUMP-H (test input) and CONTROL-H. When CONTROL-H is L (normal case) the instruction obtained is the next in sequence. When CONTROL-H is H, then an conditional jump is performed, with the address input being used as the source of address if JUMP-H is asserted. The ALU is capable of the following operations:

C1	C0	Function
0	0	F = A + B
0	1	F = A nand B
1	0	F = not B
1	1	F = A or B

5.2 For the single address machine shown in Figure P5.1, design a sequencer that will do ADD or OR, using some technique other than microcoding. Include RTL description of the transfers needed and the logic of the control section.

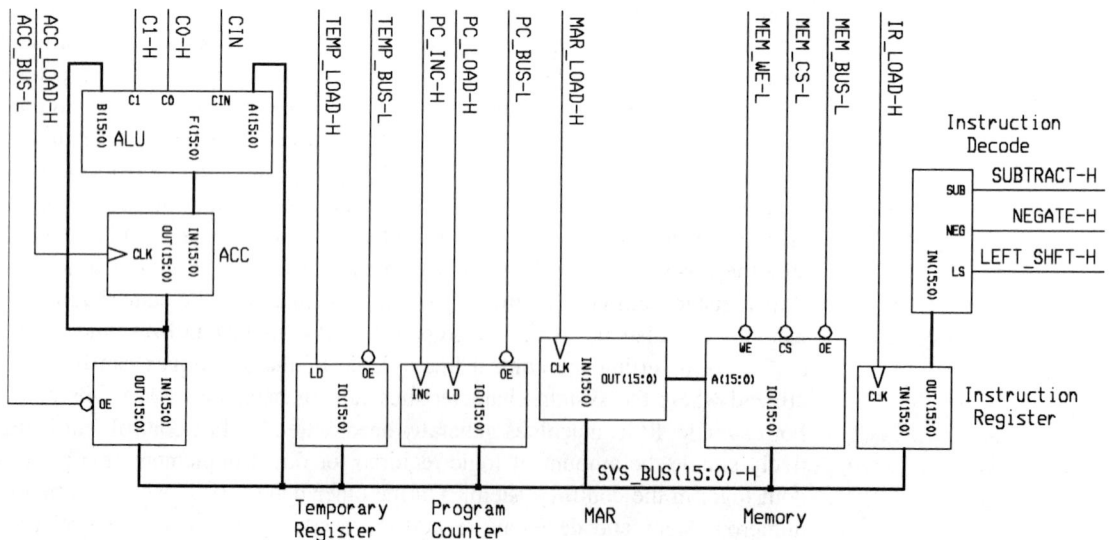

Figure P5.1. Block Diagram for Single Address Machine.

5.3 Consider the controller for the finite impulse response digital filter of Section 5.3. Implement the controller using the technique of individual delays. How can the loop be implemented?

5.4 Consider the controller for the finite impulse response digital filter of Section 5.3. Implement the controller using the shift register technique to develop the timing pulses. How can the loop be implemented?

5.5 The state machine controller shown in Figure 5.27 can be used to implement the state diagram shown in Figure 5.23. Provide the necessary additional details, and specify the contents of the memory to create the system. That is:

a. Identify which of the address lines of the memory are provided by the present state lines, and which are provided by external inputs.

b. Identify which of the memory outputs are used for next state determination and which are used for signal generation.

c. Create a table that specifies the next state patterns and the signal line patterns for each of the appropriate addresses.

A computer system can be a very valuable tool for this project, using a simple program to help develop the basic patterns, and an editor system to modify the patterns as necessary.

5.6 Design a control system using the state machine technique for the shift and add multiply system of Figure 3.9. Implement the state machine with the multiplexer method (like Figure 5.13), and then do the design with random logic for next state determination. Compare the two implementations based on board space, power consumption, and ease of implementation.

5.7 Design a controller for the Booth's algorithm multiplier of Figure 3.14. Use a state machine implementation mechanism.

5.8 Consider the block diagram of a portion of the control system for a unit that utilizes a microcoded organization. The contents of the microcode memory for the original organization are as follows:

addr	contents of addr
0	0100100011111010011101100011010
1	1011011100011010010010010001001
2	0100100011111010011101100011010
3	1101001000100100010010001000010
4	1011011100011010010010010001001
5	0010100100100101001001001001000
6	0100100011111010011101100011010
7	1101001000100100010010001000010
8	0011100100101010001010010001001
9	1011011100011010010010010001001
10	1001001001010010010100100101000
11	1101001000100100010010001000010
12	0100100011111010011101100011010
13	1011011100011010010010010001001
14	1101001000100100010010001000010

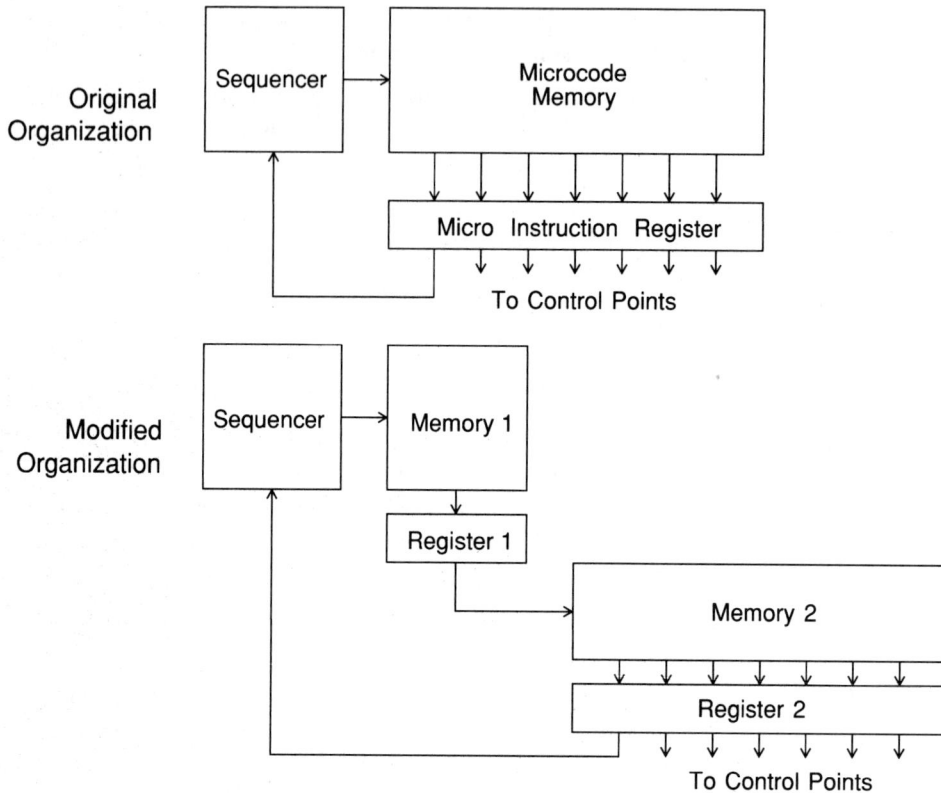

Figure P5.8. Alternative Microcode Organizations.

Give the contents of Memory 1 and Memory 2 for the modified organization. What are the advantages, if any, of the second organization?

5.9 Design a state machine controller for the divider shown in Figure 3.23. (See also Appendix B.) Use a memory for the next state logic, and specify the contents of the memory for all of the appropriate locations.

5.10 Consider the horizontally organized microcode system of Figure 5.40; details of this implementation are shown in Appendix B. Some microcode appears in Table 5.5. Write microcode to implement a JUMP instruction, a JUMP TO SUBROUTINE instruction, and a RETURN instruction. State whatever assumptions that you need to make.

5.11 Modify the microcode shown in Table 5.5 so that the fetch portion of the microcode checks for the existence of an interrupt. Include microcode to handle the interrupt. State whatever assumptions you need to make.

5.12 Consider the vertically organized microcode system of Figure 5.41. Some of the microcode appears in Table 5.6. Write microcode for a memory-to-memory add instruction with the format ADD <addr1> <addr2>. Assume that the two addresses (<addr1> and <addr2>) are stored in locations directly following the instruction in program memory.

5.13 Obtain data sheets for the devices of Figure 5.40 (see also Appendix B) and determine the minimum cycle time for the data path and the minimum cycle time for the control path.

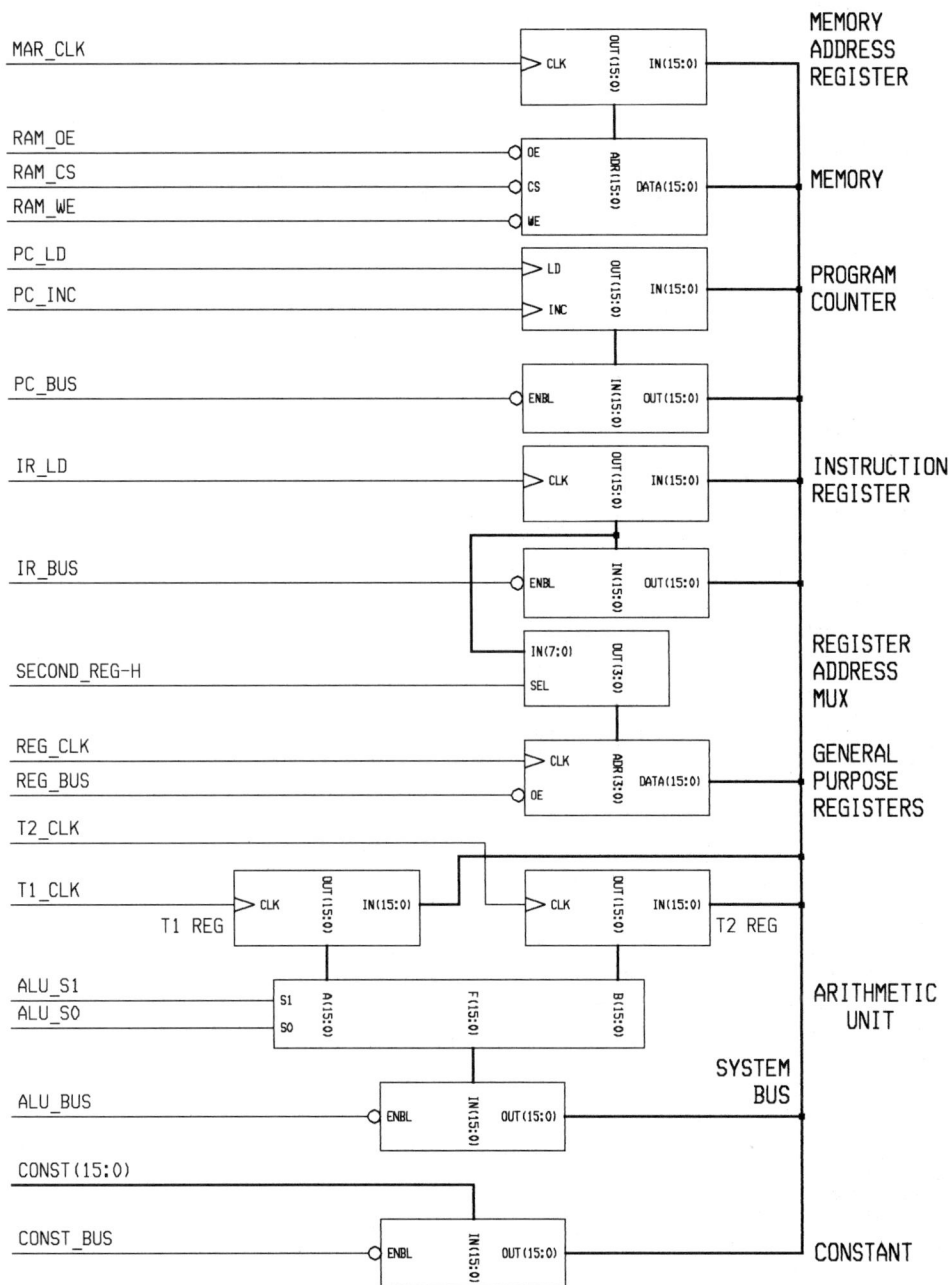

Figure P5.14. Logic for Data Path of 16-Bit Computer System.

5.14 The diagram shown in Figure P5.14 is a single bus system that can be used to implement a simple 16-bit machine. Using horizontal microcode techniques, create microcode to perform the ADD instruction with possibilities for register direct, register indirect, register indirect autoincrement (post increment), and register indirect auto-decrement (predecrement). That is:

a. determine the contents of the microinstruction register

b. complete the naming for the control signals of the system

c. identify the work needed (RTL) to perform the ADD instruction

d. give the microcode bit patterns needed to accomplish the work

State any assumptions needed to complete the specification.

5.15 The diagram shown in Figure P5.14 can be used to implement a 16-bit machine. Using vertical microcode techniques, create microcode to perform a NEGATE instruction, an INCREMENT instruction, and a CLEAR instruction. To accomplish this:

a. determine which control lines can be activated by a decoded field in a microinstruction word, and which lines can share a field

b. specify the contents of the microinstruction register

c. complete the naming for the control signals of the system

d. give the RTL needed to perform the instructions

e. give the microcode bit patterns needed to perform the work of the RTL specified

State any assumptions needed to complete the specification.

5.16 For the data path shown in Figure P5.14, implement with horizontal micro-code techniques a JUMP SUBROUTINE instruction and a RETURN (from sub-routine) instruction. Include with the answer the following information:

a. the format of the microinstruction

b. the proper naming of the control signals

c. the RTL for the instructions

d. the microcode bit patterns that will implement the instructions

Assume that R15 of the register set is designated as the stack pointer. Also assume that the memory for this problem is slow RAM, and that once the MAR has been set, three cycles are needed to write/read the memory.

5.17 Repeat Problem 5.16, using vertical microcode techniques. How can the bus destination signals be created in a manner that will prevent glitches from occurring? For the system of Figure P5.14, the following information may be useful:

The memory write enable, chip select, and output enable are all asserted low.

The program counter can be loaded or incremented; both actions occur on the low-to-high transition of the control signal.

When one register is identified by an instruction, the register address mux will feed the correct lines to the general purpose registers.

When two registers are specified by an instruction, the register address mux will feed the pattern identifying the first register to the general purpose registers unless SECOND_REG-H is asserted, at which point the pattern identifying the second register will be directed to the general purpose registers.

The arithmetic unit operates according to the following table:

S1	S0	Function
0	0	F = A plus B
0	1	F = A nand B
1	0	F = B
1	1	F = A or B

The CONST field allows the controller to place a known value into the system.

5.11. References and Readings

[AMD85] Advanced Micro Devices, *Bipolar Microprocessor Logic and Interface Data Book.* Sunnyvale, CA: Advanced Micro Devices, 1985.

[AMD88] Advanced Micro Devices, *PAL Device Handbook.* Sunnyvale, CA: Advanced Micro Devices, 1988.

[AnLe81] Anderson, T., and P. A. Lee, *Fault Tolerance, Principles and Practice.* Englewood Cliffs, NJ: Prentice Hall International, 1981.

[Andr80] Andrews, M., *Principles of Firmware Engineering in Microporgram Control.* Potomac, MD: Computer Science Press, 1980.

[Arms81] Armstrong, R. A., "Applying CAD to Gate Arrays Speeds 32-bit Minicomputer Design," *Electronics.* Vol. 54, No. 1, January 13, 1981, pp. 167–173.

[BaRa82] Banerji, D. K., and J. Raymond, *Elements of Microprogramming.* Englewood Cliffs, NJ: Prentice-Hall, 1982.

[Bart85] Bartee, T. C., *Digital Computer Fundamentals.* 6th edition, New York: McGraw Hill Book Company, 1985.

[Boot84] Booth, T. L., *Introduction to Computer Engineering: Hardware and Software Design.* New York: John Wiley & Sons, 1984.

[Bree89] Breeding, K. J., *Digital Design Fundamentals.* Englewood Cliffs, NJ: Prentice Hall, 1989.

[BuCa84] Burger, R. M., R. K. Calvin, W. C. Holton, et al., "The Impact of ICs on Computer Technology," *Computer.* Vol. 17, No. 10, October 1984, pp. 88–96.

[Damm85] Damm, W., "Design and Specification of Microprogrammed Computer Architectures," *Proceeding of the 18th Annual Workshop on Microprogramming.* Washington, DC: IEEE Computer Society Press, 1985, pp. 3–9.

[Dasg80] Dasgupta, S., "Some Aspects of High Level Microprogramming," *ACM Computing Surveys.* Vol. 12, No. 3, September 1980, pp. 295–324.

[Dasg79] Dasgupta, S., "The Organization of Microprogram Stores," *ACM Computing Surveys.* Vol. 11, No. 1, March 1979, pp. 39–65.

[Davi86] Davidson, S., "Progress in High Level Microprogramming," *IEEE Software.* Vol. 3, No. 4, July 1986, pp. 19–26.

[ErLa85] Ercegovac, M. D., and T. Lang, *Digital Systems and Hardware/Firmware Algorithms.* New York: John Wiley & Sons, 1985.

[Flet80] Fletcher, W. I., *An Engineering Approach to Digital Design.* Englewood Cliffs, NJ: Prentice Hall, 1980.

[Habi88] Habib, S., *Microprogramming and Firmware Engineering.* New York: Van Nostrand-Rheinhold, 1988.

[HaVr78] Hamacher, V. C., Z. G. Vranesic, and S. G. Zaky, *Computer Organization.* New York: McGraw-Hill Book Company, 1984.

[Haye88] Hayes, J. P., *Computer Architecture and Organization,* 2nd Edition. New York: McGraw-Hill Book Company, 1988.

[Hopk83] Hopkins, M., "A Perspective on Microcode," *Proceedings of COMPCON 83* (Spring), New York: IEEE, 1983, pp. 108–110.

[Lang82] Langdon, G. G., Jr., *Computer Design.* San Jose, CA: Computeach Press Inc, 1982.

[Lee87] Lee, F., "Designing a State Machine with a Programmable Sequencer," *Electronic Products Magazine.* Vol. 29, No. 17, February 1, 1987 pp. 29–35.

[Mano79] Mano, M. M., *Digital Logic and Computer Design.* Englewood Cliffs, NJ: Prentice Hall, 1979.

[Mano88] Mano, M. M., *Computer Engineering: Hardware Design.* Englewood Cliffs, NJ: Prentice Hall, 1988.

[McCl86] McCluskey, E. J., *Logic Design Principles, with Emphasis on Testable Semicustom Circuits.* Englewood Cliffs, NJ: Prentice Hall, 1986.

[Prad86] Pradham, D. K., (Ed.), *Fault Tolerant Computing: Theory and Techniques.* Englewood Cliffs, NJ: Prentice Hall, 1986.

[Prep85] Preparata, F. P., *Introduction to Computer Engineering.* New York: Harper & Row Book Company, 1985.

[Sali76] Salisbury, A. B., *Microprogrammable Computer Architectures.* New York: Elsevier, 1976.

[Schm87] Schmitz, N., "Prose Devices Simplify State Machine Design," *Computer Design.* Vol. 26, No. 2, April 1, 1987 pp. 97–102.

[Swar76] Swartzlander, E. E., Jr. (Ed.), *Computer Design Development: Principal Papers.* Rochelle Park, NJ: Hayden, 1976.

[Tane84] Tanenbaum, A. S., *Structured Computer Organization.* Englewood Cliffs, NJ: Prentice Hall, 1984.

[TeSw82] Tendolkar, N. N., and R. L. Swann, "Automated Diagnostic Methodology for the IBM 3081 Processor Complex," *IBM Journal of Research and Development,* Vol. 26, No. 1, January 1982, pp. 78–88.

[TI85] Texas Instruments, *The TTL Data Book,* Volume 2. Dallas, TX: Texas Instruments, 1985.

[Wilk41] Wilkes, M. V., "The Best Way to Design an Automatic Calculating Machine," *Report of the Manchester University Computer Inaugural Conference.* University of Manchester, UK, 1951. Reprinted in [Swar76], pp. 266–270.

6

Input and Output Operations

We have discussed several of the characteristics attributed to a machine, including the methods of information representation and the instruction set. We have also discused methods of designing the functional elements, such as the arithmetic unit or the control unit. But it is not sufficient to compute; the results of the computation must be made available to other systems. These systems may be other computers, computer peripherals, or similar devices. Eventually, the information may need to be presented in a form easily understood by humans; many interface systems convert information not only into readable text, but also graphic images, synthesized sound, or some other suitable form.

The term "input" is attached to the process of transferring information into the computer, and "output" to the transfer of information out of the machine. When both are possible, it is simply "I/O." In this chapter we will discuss the methods used to perform these transfers, some of which we have already alluded to in the consideration of instruction sets. This will include mechanisms used for asynchronous and synchronous bus transfers, time multiplexing of information on buses, and so on. We will also consider arbitration techniques, which decide who is the "owner" of a bus when a transfer is made. And we will include both programmed control and direct memory transfers to move information. Included with the discussions are a number of examples that illustrate the concepts and techniques. Once the ideas are understood at both the conceptual and implementation level, I/O systems and interface modules can be more easily designed and understood.

The instruction set architecture of a machine will determine the apparent organization of the I/O system. That is, the mechanisms envisioned for system I/O will be one of the factors considered in the process of the creation of the instruction set of the system. In many respects, the computer system will be judged by its ability to coordinate information transfer in a reasonable fashion. A more comprehensive view of the total system impact is obtained by considering computer system performance from a systems aspect, taking into account the characteristics of the CPU, the peripheral devices, and the transfer mechanisms. (See, for example, [LaZa84].) Our intention is to understand the principles utilized in the transfer mechanisms.

6.1. Asynchronous Bus Transfers

The block diagram of Figure 6.1 indicates that a number of functional units can exchange information over a common communication medium: the bus. The transfer of information will begin when one of the modules recognizes a need to communicate with another module. This need will result from any of a number of mechanisms, such as a processor module that must obtain the status of an interface module, or an I/O module that must transfer information into system memory. If a module has the ability to control the bus, we call it a "bus master." In general, there will be several bus masters in a bus-oriented system. When a master needs to transfer information, it will request ownership of the bus. The process of allocating control of the bus to a bus master is called arbitration, and we will discuss arbitration mechanisms in a later section. When a master has obtained control over the bus, it then initiates a bus transfer by activating the appropriate lines. The module activated by this transaction (the one that responds to the master) is called the "bus slave." The set of rules or algorithm utilized in this process is called the "bus communication protocol." This protocol will identify the sequence of events to occur in the process of transferring information, and specify the timing requirements of the transfer.

In this section we will discuss the exchange of information over the lines assuming an asynchronous protocol. That is, the modules of the bus system do not share a common clock, and the transfer proceeds in an asynchronous manner. In the communication process, the master and the slave assert signals on common communication lines in a predetermined manner so that the transfer can proceed. We will assume that the arbitration process has been completed and that the master is in control of the bus. The master is now capable of initiating the transfer, and will do so by activating the appropriate bus lines according to the defined protocol. The bus lines (except power and ground, which are also distributed along the bus) belong to one of three groups: address, data, or control, as shown in Figure 6.2.

The address lines are used to identify the target of the transaction. That is, the master places an address onto the address lines that will uniquely identify the location to be used for the transfer. The number of address lines that can be used for this function determine the number of addressable locations, since N lines are capable of selecting one of 2^N locations. This address is the only mechanism the master has to identify the target module. All of the modules that can respond to addresses to perform transfers are connected to the address bus, and they receive

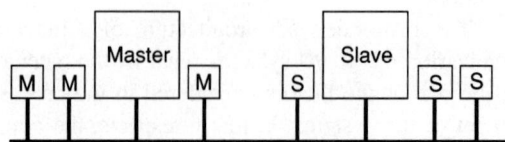

Figure 6.1. Module Organization for Bused Systems.

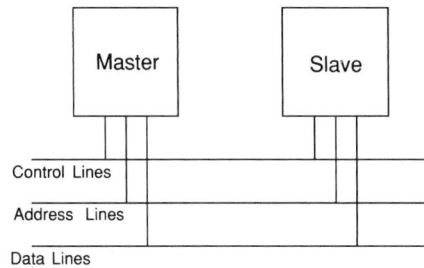

Figure 6.2. Bus Lines Connecting the
Master and the Slave.

this address and compare it to their assigned address space. The address should identify only one module; if more than one module recognizes the address, the transaction will not function properly. (As usual, there are exceptions to this rule, which we will note later.) Once a master has initiated a transfer, it will allow a predetermined amount of time for the address comparisons, then proceed with the transaction. The slave module with an assigned address matching the target address will respond to the master, and the transaction will proceed governed by the assertion of the control lines. The control lines are used to synchronize the action between the master and the slave modules. The mechanism for this is shown in Figure 6.3. This figure shows the address lines as a group, the data lines as a group, and three of the control lines. A number of other control lines will be involved with the arbitration mechanism, but for this discussion we will limit ourselves to the three control lines identified in the figure: READ-H, REQ-H, and ACK-H. The READ-H line identifies a read transaction when it is asserted. That is, when it is high, the master module is reading a location from the slave module. When the READ-H line is not asserted (when it is low), the master module is writing to the slave module. The READ-H line has the same timing requirements as the address lines, which are explained in conjunction with the other control lines.

The two lines that control the timing and sequence of the events involved in the transaction are the request line (REQ-H) and the acknowledge line (ACK-H). The write cycle proceeds as shown in Figure 6.3(a). The master, which has already obtained control of the bus, asserts the address of the desired location. This time is identified as t_0 in the figure. A finite time is required for this address to propagate to all of the slave modules and be decoded by them, so the master must wait for a specific period before asserting the request line. The amount of time required is a function of the technology in which the hardware is implemented, and the physical and electrical characteristics of the bus. When the required time period has passed, the master asserts the request line (time t_1). This is then accepted by all of the slave modules, but only the module with the matching address will respond. When the slave has performed the requested action, which in this case is to accept the data on the data lines, the slave module asserts the acknowledge line (time t_2). When the master detects the assertion of the acknowledge line, it recognizes that the work of the transaction has been completed. So it releases the request line (time t_3), and when the slave detects the release of the request line, it releases the acknowledge line (time t_4). The master must keep the address lines asserted after the release of the request line to prevent any spurious action that may occur if the address changes before the release of the request

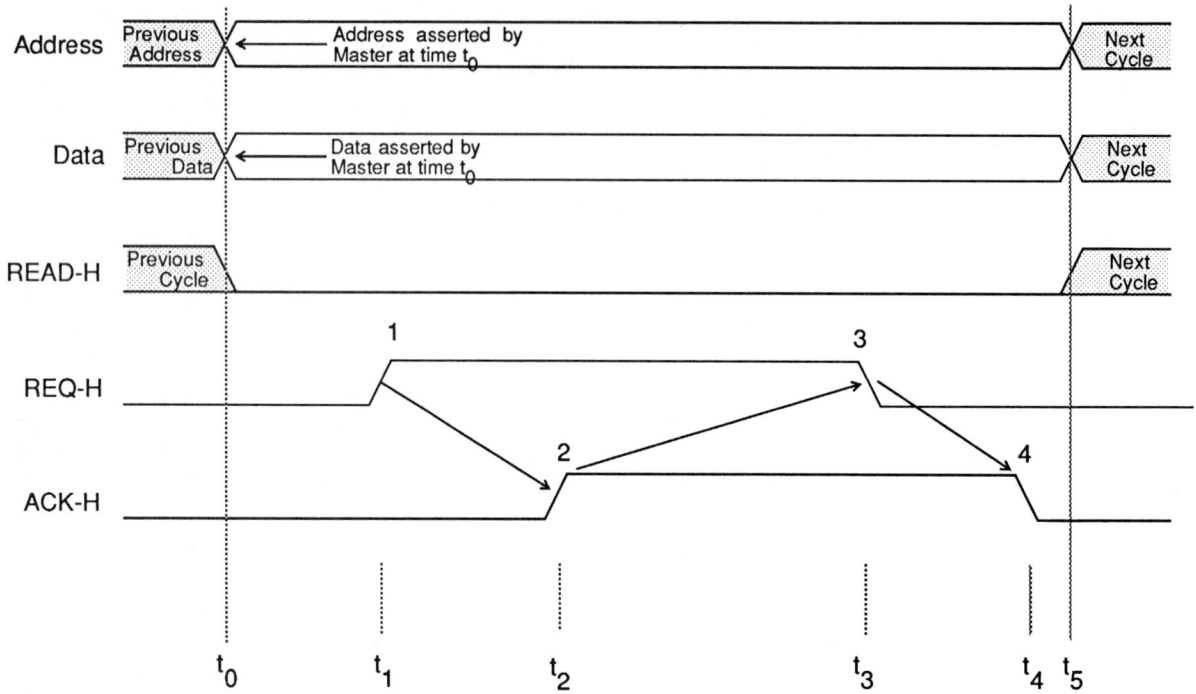

(a) Write Cycle

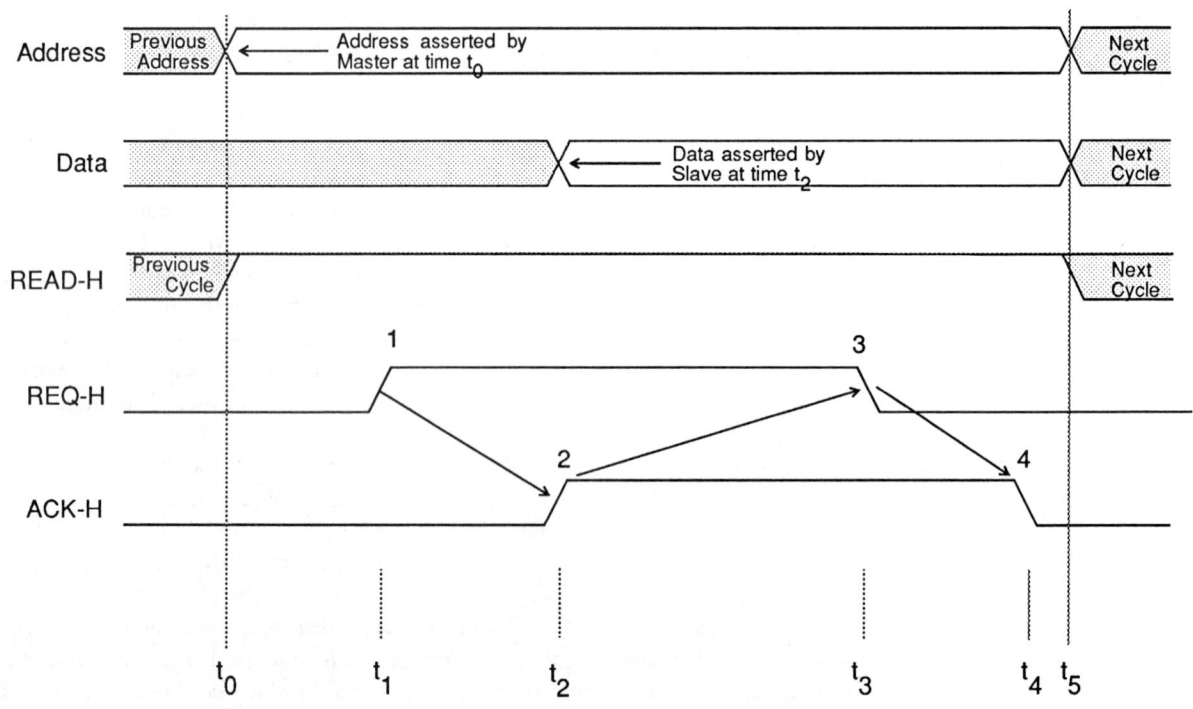

(b) Read Cycle

Figure 6.3. Read and Write Transactions for Asynchronous Handshake Protocol.

line has propagated through the decode logic of the slave modules. This may be accomplished by holding the address lines for a specific time after the release of the request signal, or until the master detects the release of the acknowledge by the slave module. This mechanism is sometimes called the four event bus transfer, since four events ($1 \rightarrow 2 \rightarrow 3 \rightarrow 4$ in Figure 6.2) are involved in performing the transfer.

The read transaction is almost identical to the write, and the appropriate lines are shown in Figure 6.3(b). The major differences are that the read control line is asserted and that the data is now asserted by the slave module. The master begins the transaction as before, by asserting the address and waiting the necessary time for propagation delay and skew. Even though the master may assert all of the address lines simultaneously, they will not all arrive at the decoder of the slave modules simultaneously, since the electrical characteristics of the bus and the propagation delays of the address lines may be different from one another. The time difference from the arrival of the first signal to the arrival of the last signal is called the skew time, and the bus protocol must include a sufficient time delay to account for the maximum expected skew time of the bus. When the master has allowed time for propagation delay and skew, it then asserts the request line (time t_1), asking the addressed slave to provide the information. The addressed slave module performs whatever action is required to obtain the data; if it is a memory device this will require a memory cycle, but if it is an interface module the information may be readily available. When the data has been obtained, the slave module asserts the data onto the data bus, as well as asserting the acknowledge line (time t_2). At this point the master must wait for a period of time to allow for skew, then it accepts the data and releases the request line (time t_3). When the slave detects the release of the request line, it releases the acknowledge line. Some time after the release of the request line, the master is free to release the address.

This basic asynchronous communication protocol is used by a number of different microprocessors and minicomputers. It has the advantage of not needing a specific clock, since the transaction proceeds according to the signals asserted by each module. Since the modules can proceed as fast as their functions allow, the transactions can proceed as fast as data is available. The drawback is that the built-in delays, needed to allow for signal skew and propagation delay, force a relatively long minimum cycle time. For the UNIBUS, which is the bus on which the Digital Equipment Corporation PDP11 series is based, a typical minimum cycle time is 400 ns. Nevertheless, because of its simplicity and ease of function, the asynchronous bus protocol is used extensively. One example is the Multibus, which originated with some products from Intel.

Example 6.1: Asynchronous protocol: The Multibus is an asynchronous protocol that fits the discussion above. What are the signal and control lines utilized by the Multibus, and the associated delays?

The asynchronous protocol, as described in the above paragraphs and in Figure 6.3, is directly applicable to the Multibus, with a few modifications in nomenclature. The signals on the Multibus are all asserted low, so the address, data, and control lines have a low voltage for a "1" and a high voltage for a "0." There are 20 address lines and 16 data lines, which gives an addressable space of one megabyte. The address lines are used for both I/O and memory addresses. After a master has asserted the address, it waits for 50 nsec before asserting the request line; this is the time allowed for skew and delay. The appropriate request line is asserted low (as opposed to the high assertion shown in Figure 6.3). Instead of having a read line to identify the direction of the transfer, the Multibus has separate request lines for memory read (MRDC-L), memory write (MWTC-L), I/O read (IORC-L), and I/O write (IOWC-L). This allows the address lines to be used by memory and I/O devices, and the appropriate interface module will respond only when the necessary control line is asserted. When a slave module responds, regardless of the request line that activated the module, it will assert a transfer acknowledge signal (XACK-L), in the manner shown in Figure 6.3.

Example 6.2: Interface to asynchronous system: Assume that a floating point multiplier is to be interfaced to the Multibus in the I/O space. This multiplier requires two 32-bit words to be available, one in Register X and one in Register Y. Design an interface module for the Multibus that will read and write to Register X and Register Y, and also cause the multiply to occur when accessed. Assume that the multiply process will take a variable amount of time depending on the data, and that the multiplier will assert a DONE signal when the answer is available.

The Multibus protocol allows 16-bit bus masters to address 4,096 different I/O locations, so we will assume that the floating point multiplier in question is to occupy the following addresses:

Address	Request Line	Action
$DF0_{16}$	IOWC-L	Write to Register X (low 16 bits).
$DF0_{16}$	IORC-L	Read from Register X (low 16 bits).
$DF1_{16}$	IOWC-L	Write to Register X (high 16 bits).
$DF1_{16}$	IORC-L	Read from Register X (high 16 bits).
$DF2_{16}$	IOWC-L	Write to Register Y (low 16 bits).
$DF2_{16}$	IORC-L	Read from Register Y (low 16 bits).
$DF3_{16}$	IOWC-L	Write to Register Y (high 16 bits).
$DF3_{16}$	IORC-L	Read from Register Y (high 16 bits).
$DF4_{16}$	IORC-L	Read from Result (low 16 bits).
$DF5_{16}$	IORC-L	Read from Result (high 16 bits).

The design of this system is relatively straightforward, since the logic is basically combinational in nature. The only timing requirements are those imposed by the bus protocol, and the sequentiality of action defined by the protocol is also enforced by the master. The data path for this interface module is shown in Figure 6.4(a). The registers are made up of positive edge triggered devices ('273s), which hold the information for the floating point multiplier. Note that for this system an inverting bus transceiver has been inserted into the data path. This has the benefit of presenting only one electrical load to the data bus, but incurs the penalty of an additional delay, which needs to be included in the design process. Many multipliers have registers built in, so in one sense the external registers are redundant. However, the specification indicates that these values should also be made available to the bus upon request, so the registers are needed to provide that capability. Tri-state drivers ('541s) are used to send the information to the internal data bus, which is enabled onto the Multibus data lines by the transceiver. This path is also used by the product from the multiplier.

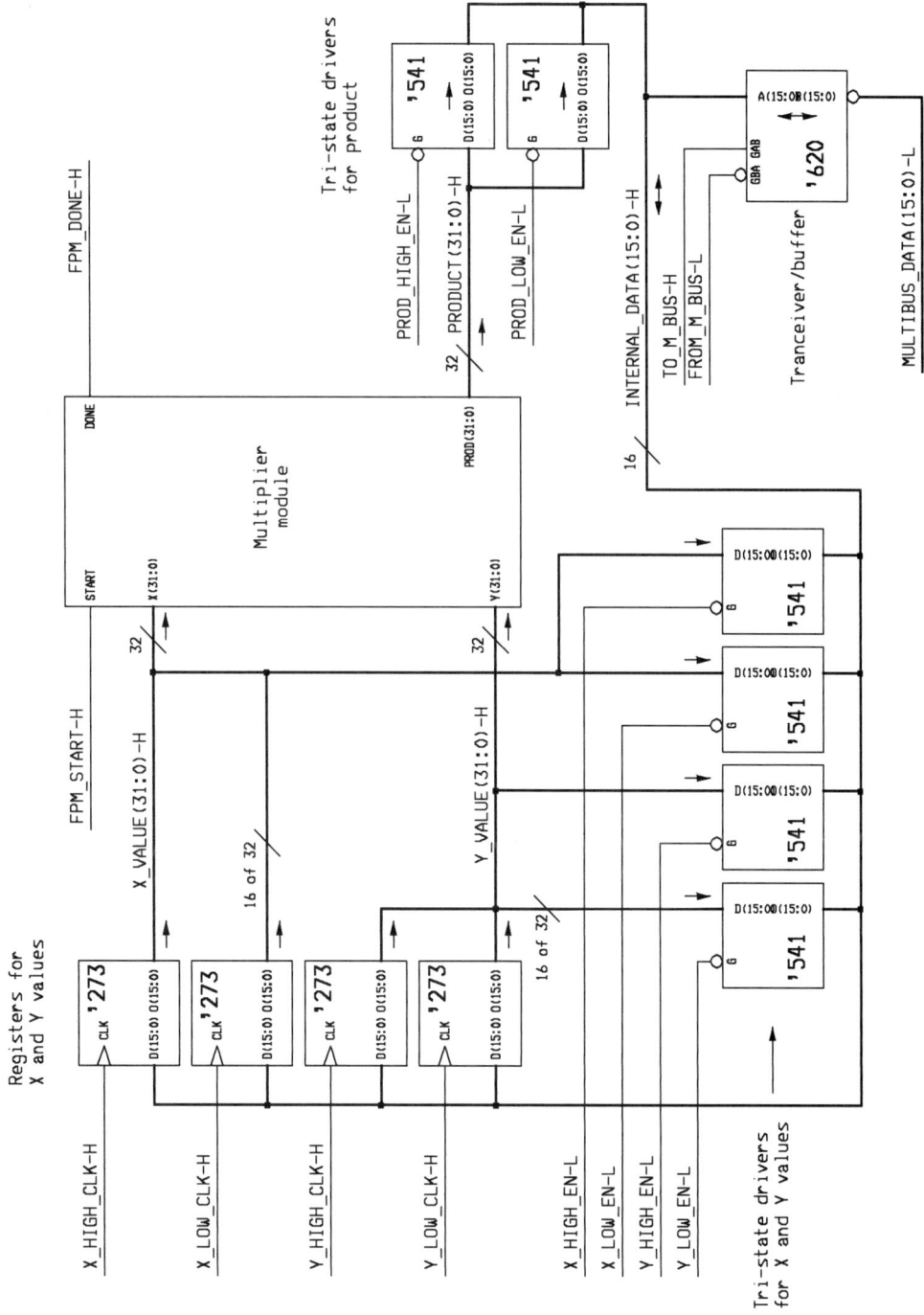

Figure 6.4(a). Data Path for Multibus Interface Module of Example 6.2.

The control signals used for this system are derived by the logic shown in Figure 6.4(b). The address lines are checked for a proper address pattern. However, since the address pattern could be asserted for memory addresses as well as the I/O addresses needed for this system, no action is

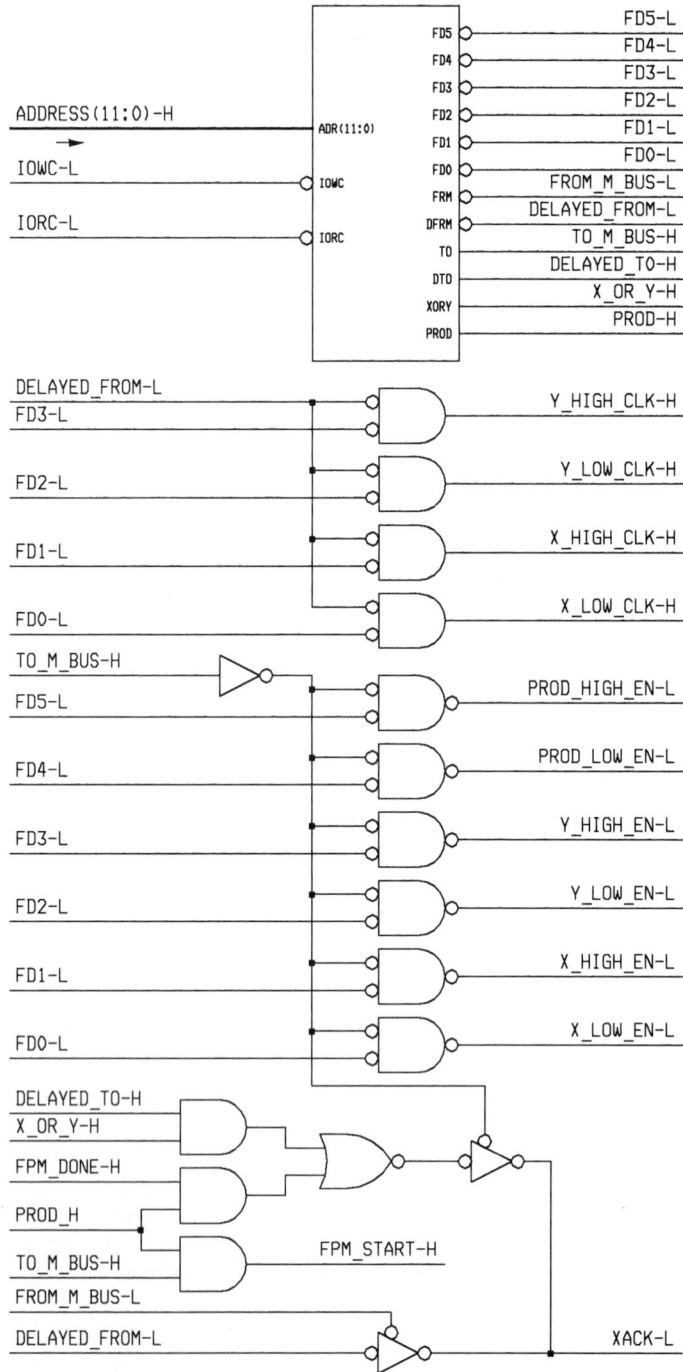

Figure 6.4(b). Control Signals for Multibus Interface Module of Example 6.2.

taken until the I/O request lines are asserted. If the transaction is a write to the X or Y register, then the Multibus data lines are enabled onto the internal data bus (with FROM_M_BUS-L), and after a delay to allow the data to propagate to the registers, the appropriate clock line is asserted. Figure 6.4(b) does not indicate how this delay is obtained, but a number of different methods could be utilized, from a tuned delay line to a synchronous method using the clock provided on the Multibus. The slave response to the I/O request lines is through the acknowledge (XACK-L), which is seized when the address is recognized, but not asserted until the transaction is complete. For filling the X and Y registers the acknowledge will be asserted when the delay has been completed. Similarly, reading the X or Y registers, or the lower bits of the product, involves a delay to allow the data to propagate onto the internal data bus and then to the Multibus data lines. When a propagation delay time has been accounted for, then the acknowledge can be asserted. Requesting the higher bits of the product causes a multiply to occur, so the acknowledge is asserted when the done signal is asserted by the multiplier. This necessitates that the most significant word of the product be requested first to achieve proper results.

The Multibus, and many other buses that use the asynchronous handshaking technique to transfer information, can be effectively utilized to pass data in a single bus environment. However, the lines required to perform this type of transfer are rather numerous. The Multibus utilizes 41 lines to perform these transfers, and the UNIBUS uses 38 lines. One of the ways to reduce the number of wires required is to time multiplex the address and data lines. That is, one set of lines contains the address for part of the time and data for another part; the information content of the lines is determined by the control signals. Thus, the total number of wires required to perform transfers is reduced. The tradeoff is between the number of wires on the bus (or pins on the integrated circuit, or on the edge of the board, or ...) and the increased time required to perform the transfer. Since the lines are utilized for two functions (address and data), then the number of control lines will increase. Nevertheless, the total number of wires is decreased, and the speed of the bus is sufficient for many applications.

Example 6.3: Time multiplexed asynchronous protocol: Digital Equipment Corporation has built a number of devices based on a protocol and physical configuration called the Q-Bus. This is a time multiplexed data/address bus with an asynchronous protocol. What is the sequence of events involved in performing a read and a write with the Q-Bus?

The waveforms for the transfers of the Q-Bus are shown in Figure 6.5. This is an abbreviated version, since there are control lines to indicate when a transfer is in the I/O page, when it is a byte transfer, and so on. But the basic principles are demonstrated by the figure. The levels indicated in the figure are logical levels only, since the assertion level of the signals on the bus itself is negative, so that on the bus a "1" is indicated by a low voltage level. The read cycle [Figure 6.5(a)] begins with the master asserting the address on the time multiplexed data/address lines (DAL), then allowing a time for propagation delay and skew. The SYNC line is then asserted (time t_1), which is used by slave devices to latch the address information as needed. The master releases the DAL lines, and at time t_2 asserts DIN, which indicates to the addressed slave that the transaction is a read. From this point the transaction follows the four event sequence, with DIN

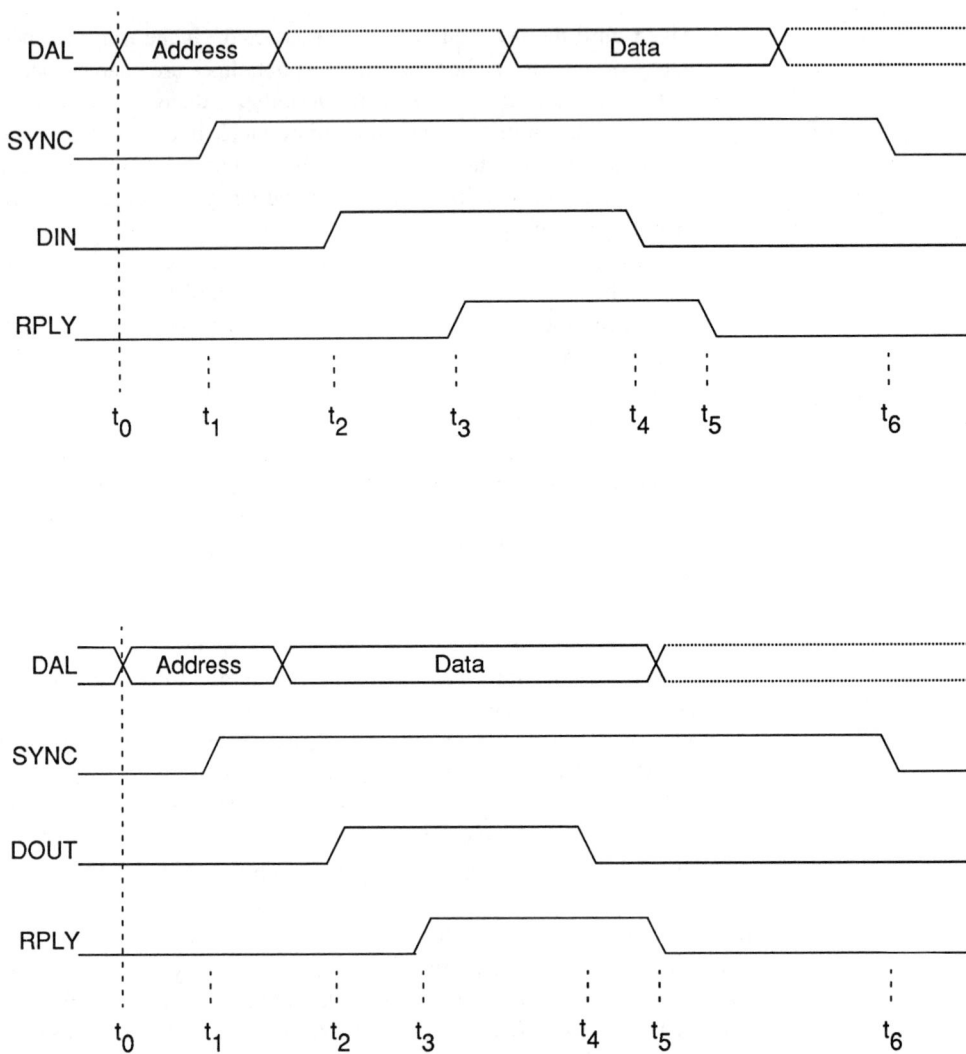

Figure 6.5. Read and Write Cycles on a Time Multiplexed Bus: (a) Read Cycle; (b) Write Cycle.

representing the request line, t_3), and then within 125 nsec asserts the data. The master responds by releasing DIN (time t_4). When the slave detects the release of DIN, it releases RPLY (time t_5), and then releases the DAL lines. The last event in the cycle is the release of the SYNC signal by the master in preparation for the next cycle.

The write cycle shown in Figure 6.5(b) is very similar to the above sequence of events. The major difference is the assertion of the data on the DAL lines by the master after the address has been issued and synchronized by the SYNC signal. Once again, the four event cycle mechanism is used. The master identifies the cycle as a write cycle by asserting DOUT. The slave accepts the data and asserts RPLY. The master then releases DOUT, which allows the slave to release RPLY. The bus protocol calls for the master to hold the data on the DAL lines for at least 175 nsec after releasing DOUT. And as before, the termination of the cycle is indicated by releasing SYNC.

The asynchronous method for information transfer can be very useful for exchanging data in time multiplexed systems and in systems with dedicated address and data lines. It is simple to comprehend, and interface modules between the bus and external devices can be designed and constructed in a relatively easy manner. The absence of a clock allows the transaction to proceed at the rate at which data (and address) information is available. Nevertheless, the data rates for this type of transfer are in general not as high as those for a synchronous protocol. Before we discuss the reasons for this, let's examine some of the arbitration mechanisms used to identify the module that will control the bus transaction.

6.2. Arbitration Mechanisms

In any system with multiple master modules, that is, modules that can assert the control lines on the bus, a mechanism must be provided for arbitration. Using some predefined priority algorithm, this mechanism must uniquely identify the module that will take charge of the bus for the next transfer. It is possible to have this decision follow each bus cycle, so that there is an arbitration between each bus transfer. But in general the arbitration process is performed in parallel with data transfers, so that during the current transfer arbitration is being performed for the next transfer. In this section we will consider arbitration mechanisms and how they can be utilized to assure that control is passed to the proper module.

Three basic mechanisms can be utilized for making the decision as to the proper module to control the bus for the next cycle. These are shown in Figure 6.6. In each case, the masters (M_1, M_2, ...) request access to the bus by asserting a bus request (BR). When the arbitration mechanism is ready to select a new master module to control the bus, it will assert the bus grant signal (BG) associated with that module. The behavior of the devices receiving the bus grant depends on the type of arbitration mechanism involved, as we shall see. When a device needs access to the bus and it detects that the bus grant line has been asserted, then it will be the next to receive control of the bus. If more than one master requests ownership of the bus at the same time, then the arbitration process selects one, and the remaining modules must wait until a later time for their respective transfers.

The fastest arbitration mechanism is the parallel system. In this system each master module has a dedicated connection to the arbitration unit, and when a master module needs control of the bus it will assert its assigned bus request line. The arbitration unit then has the responsibility of dealing with the system in some predetermined fashion. That is, the algorithm utilized in the design of the arbitration unit is not limited by the interconnection system. The arbitration can be done on the basis of first-asserted/first-served, round robin, assigned priority levels, or whatever mechanism is determined in the design process. Thus, this mechanism allows a variety of possibilities, from extremely simple to extremely complex.

In the parallel scheme, when the arbitration unit has determined that a master module has priority and should have control of the bus, it asserts the bus grant line associated with that master module. This module can then control the transfers on the bus. The data, address, and handshake lines are controlled by the selected master, and when the master no longer requires access to the bus, it will release the bus request signal. The parallel arbitration system is then free to allow other master modules to gain access to the bus.

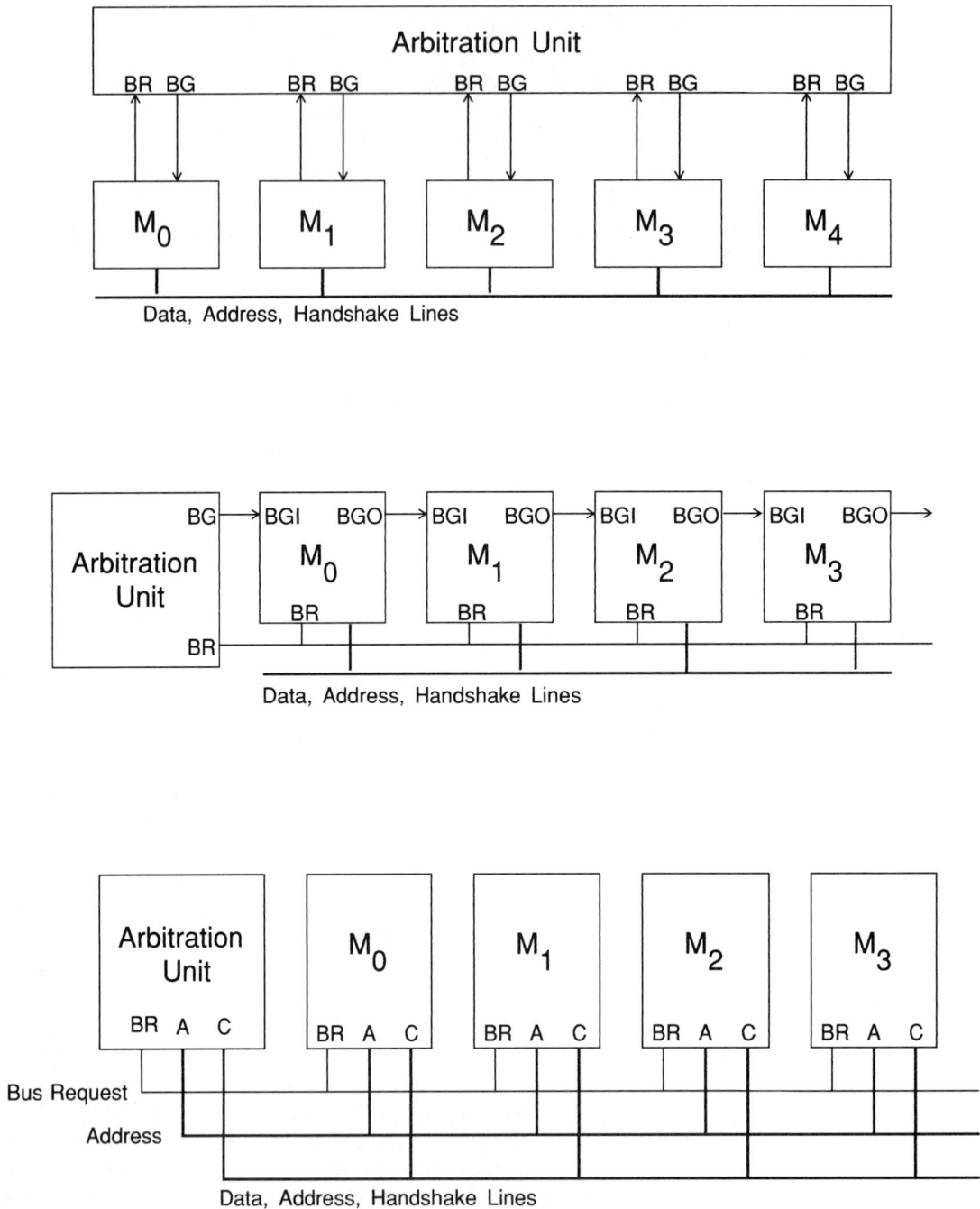

Figure 6.6. Bus Arbitration Mechanism.

The details of the transfer mechanism will vary with each implementation, but the parallel mechanism provides the highest speed of arbitration. The cost for this speed is the additional lines required to allow each possible master direct access to the arbitration unit, and the hardware costs associated with whatever arbitration algorithm is implemented. The number of lines required could be extensive, needing two lines for each module as shown in the following example.

Another mechanism would need only one line per module, as we will see later.

Example 6.4: Parallel arbitration system: Design a parallel arbitration system that will allow up to eight bus masters to access a common set of control lines. The assumed mechanism for master-slave data exchange is the four event handshake that has been discussed. If no bus master has control of the bus, then the requests are to be synchronized by an internal 10 MHz clock. If a master module has control of the common handshake lines, then the requests are synchronized on the trailing edge of REQ-H.

This type of a system can be easily constructed with a priority encoder and a decoder, such as shown in Figure 6.7. Notice that the assertion levels are low in this example. When no request is pending for the bus (no bus master requires use of the bus) the decoder is disabled, and no master has control. The requests for access are synchronized by a 10 MHz clock, and when one of the masters has made a request for the bus, the appropriate bus grant line will be asserted. If more than one module has requested the bus, then only the highest priority bus grant line will be asserted. Note that the nature of the '148 priority encoder, with its asserted low outputs, inverts the normal order on the decoder outputs.

The desired behavior, as defined above, is that the synchronization of requests take place on the trailing edge of REQ when the bus is being used by a bus master. The gates on the input of the clock of the synchronizing register multiplex between the 10 MHz clock and the bus request to allow this to happen. This simple mechanism is, in general, not sufficient, since it does not preclude the possibility of glitches occurring on the clock line. (What additional gating is required to assure that no glitches occur?)

The example demonstrates the simplicity with which parallel systems can be constructed. However, more exotic priority algorithms, such as first-asserted/first-serviced, will lead to more complex implementations. But because of the speed with which arbitration can proceed in this case, systems that need the performance will provide the lines necessary to allow parallel arbitration. Because of

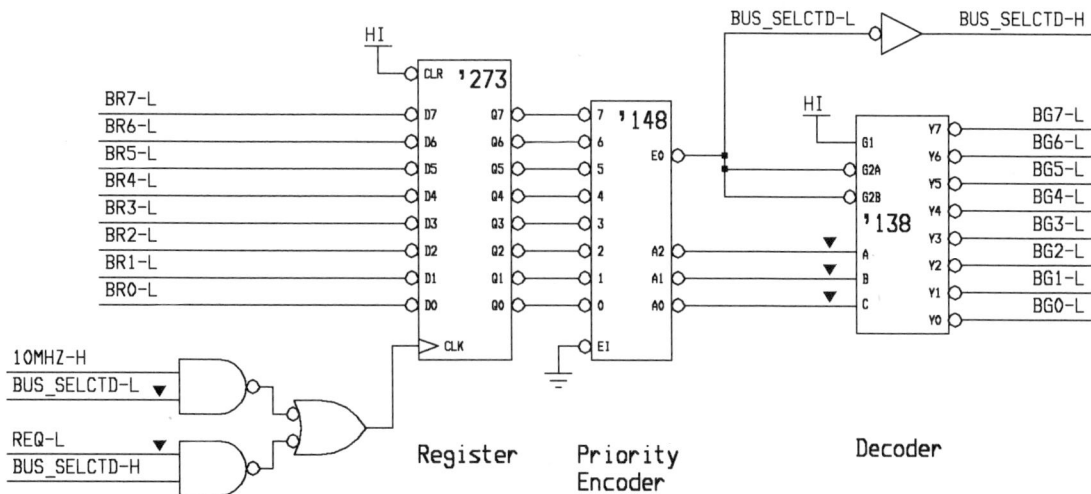

Figure 6.7. Simple Parallel Arbitration System.

the need to have dedicated lines to the master modules for parallel arbitration, the number of allowable masters on any system is fixed at the time of implementation. This places a fixed limit on the number of allowable masters, and the system cannot be expanded beyond that limit in a parallel fashion. Expansion is one of the benefits of the next type of system to be considered, the serial arbitration system.

Serial arbitration is a technique in which the bus grant lines of the bus masters are connected together in a serial fashion, as shown in Figure 6.6(b). There is a single bus request line, which is connected to all bus masters. The arbitration unit is not aware of which bus master needs access to the bus, and so the arbitration mechanism is simplified to asserting the bus grant signal at the proper time in the bus cycle. The arbitration unit is then responsible for examining the lines controlling the transfers on the bus and deciding when control of the bus can be given to a new master module. When the bus can be controlled by a new module, the arbitration unit asserts a single bus grant line connected to the first module. Since this module is the first to receive the bus grant signal, it has the highest priority: a device can receive the bus grant signal only if the modules between it and the arbitration unit do not need the bus. Because of this connection method, where one module passes the signal on to another in a serial fashion, this is referred to a "daisy chain" mechanism. And because of its serial nature, there is no limit to the number of devices that can be connected in this manner. However, each additional device results in a longer maximum arbitration time.

The serial mechanism for bus arbitration needs at least three lines to function, although more can be used, as indicated by the example below. The three lines are bus request, bus grant in, and bus grant out. A master module indicates that it needs to access the bus by asserting a common request line, as shown in the figure. This line is implemented in open collector technology, or some other method that will allow multiple units to assert the signal simultaneously. The arbitration unit uses this signal to identify when a new bus master needs access to the bus, as described above. When the arbitration unit determines that a different module can control the bus, it asserts the bus grant line. Each master receives the grant signal on its bus grant in line, and if the module does not need to access the bus, it asserts the bus grant out line. In this way the assertion of the bus grant signal is passed from one module to another, until it arrives at a module which needs access to the bus. This module does not assert the bus grant out line, but rather assumes ownership of the bus and performs the needed transfer. A master module of lower priority that needs access to the bus will continue to assert the request line, and at a later time a new bus grant signal will be asserted by the arbitration unit and passed to it.

The priority scheme of this system is strictly physical: devices of higher priority are physically (and hence electrically) closer to the arbitration unit. Devices of lower priority are farther away from the arbitration unit. The number of devices included has a direct effect on the speed of the function. Since each device must check the bus grant signal in a serial fashion, the total time for the arbitration function is proportional to the number of devices on the bus. Of course, the closer the device is to the arbitration unit (fewer modules in between), the faster the operation. But since each module requires time to complete the bus grant in to bus grant out sequence, there is a practical limit to the number of devices that can be utilized.

Because of the serial nature of the arbitration process, care must be taken to avoid the situation where two masters access the bus simultaneously. This possibility will arise in systems in which the modules operate asynchronously with respect to each other and to the transactions taking place on the bus. In this case, a module could require access to the bus directly after the bus grant out signal had been asserted to inform the next module in the chain that it can access the bus. If the first module is allowed to immediately command the bus and release the bus grant out line, then both units could be in a situation where they are accessing the bus. A practical solution to this problem is to design the units to be edge sensitive rather than level sensitive. That is, the master modules would be capable of taking ownership of the bus only when the bus grant signal is changed from its unasserted to its asserted level. Thereafter, the unit must wait until the next assertion of the signal, even though it is currently asserted. This mechanism will prevent more than one module from assuming control simultaneously.

Example 6.5: Serial arbitration system: The UNIBUS uses serial arbitration to identify bus master modules that need access to the bus. What are the lines involved in this arbitration process, and how does the protocol function? Also, what circuitry is need to connect to the arbitration lines to properly utilize the serial arbitration lines?

A number of lines in the UNIBUS are used by the master modules to control access to the bus. For the purposes of understanding the mechanism, we need consider only four signals: BR-L (bus request, asserted low), BG-H (bus grant, asserted high), SACK-L (selection acknowledge, asserted low), and BBSY-L (bus busy, asserted low). These lines and the relationship between them are shown in Figure 6.8. The sequence of events begins at t_A, when the bus arbitration unit recognizes that a new arbitration cycle can begin, since SACK is not asserted. When a master module needs to transfer information over the bus, it will signal the arbitration unit by asserting the BR line (t_B). The arbitration unit will then respond by asserting BG (t_C). Some time later (t_D), the bus grant signal will be received at the master module; there may be other master modules through which this signal has passed to reach the module that requested the transaction. When the bus grant signal is received by the module needing the bus, it will *not* pass the signal on, and it will assert SACK. This signals the arbitration unit that the arbitration process was successful, and it can now release the bus grant signal. At the same time, BR will be released by the module, but this will not necessarily mean that the line will return to its unasserted level, since another master module may also be asserting the request line. When the arbitration unit receives the assertion of SACK, it releases BG (t_E). The actual arbitration process is now complete, but the bus is still being used by a different module. When the current bus master completes its cycle, it will release BBSY (t_F), signaling the next bus master that it has completed its operation. The new bus master will wait for SSYN (not shown) to be released, indicating that the slave involved in the last transfer is idle, and BG to be released. At that time it will be able to control the transactions on the bus. The new bus master will then assert BBSY to signal the fact that it is controlling the bus, and relase SACK, to allow the arbitration process to select a new bus master.

A logic diagram of an system that does this is shown in Figure 6.9. The gates receiving bus signals (RCV) and drive bus lines (DRV) have special electrical characteristics that minimize the electrical loads placed on the bus. Otherwise, the gates have the normal NAND or NOR function shown by the shape of the gate.

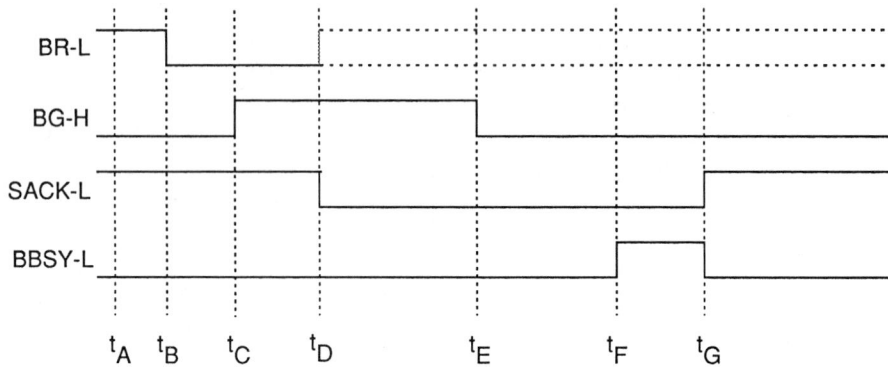

Figure 6.8. UNIBUS Bus Arbitration Lines.

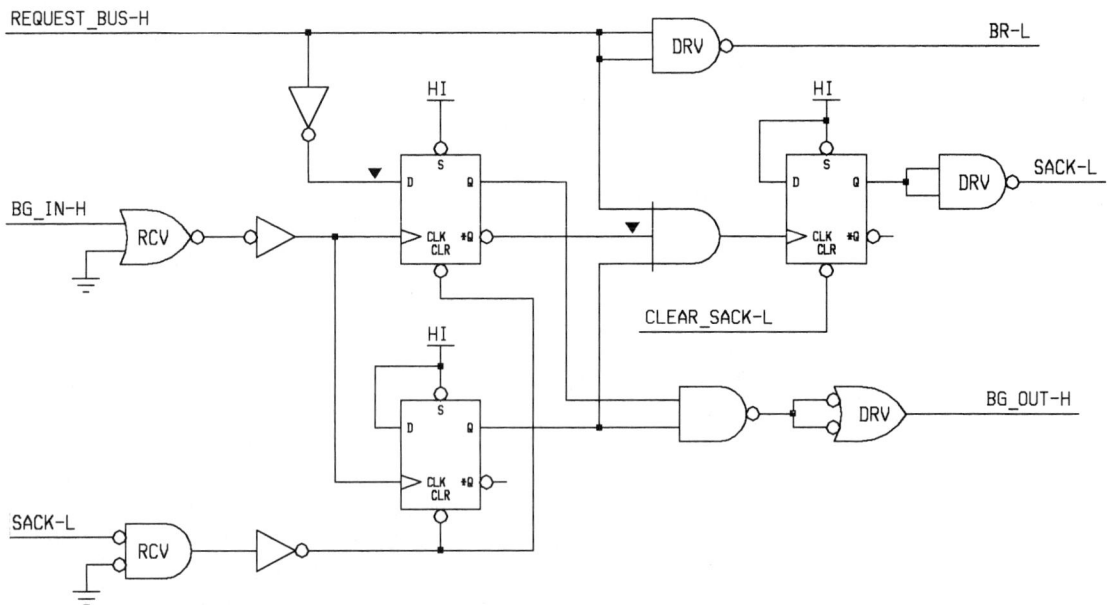

Figure 6.9. Logic for UNIBUS Bus Request-Bus Grant.

The UNIBUS protocol was chosen for this example for three reasons. First, a great number of devices have been built to interface with the UNIBUS, and so for sheer numbers this is a very prolific mechanism. Second, this example demonstrates that the arbitration process can proceed in parallel with the transfer currently in progress. Many asynchronous buses require that the current transaction terminate before arbitrating for ownership of the bus. And third, the mechanism described here is utilized in one form or another by almost all asynchronous bus arbitration systems.

The protocol described in Example 6.5 is similar to many schemes that use the daisy chain method of arbitration. One of the problems that can arise with this mechanism is the transfer of control from one master to another. Although the arbitration system can select a bus master to assume control of the bus, the actual transfer of control will not occur until the current bus master releases the

BBSY line. Therefore, a bus master may control the bus for an extended period of time, not allowing other modules access for transfers. In that sense, the protocol is not "fair," and may not be applicable in some circumstances. To prevent this type of device lockout, schemes can force the system to arbitrate for every transfer, instead of arbitrating for ownership. Or a a mechanism may be included that will force a module to relinquish ownership of the bus and allow the arbitration process to find a new bus master.

The use of one kind of bus arbitration does not exclude the use of another. The UNIBUS uses parallel arbitration in combination with serial arbitration, as does the VME bus. Parallel arbitration occurs in the UNIBUS because there are five sets of BR-BG lines, each of which has a different priority. The access to the bus between these five sets is done in a parallel fashion. Each of the five sets of BR-BG lines is a serial line, and operates as described in the example above.

The final bus arbitration technique we are going to mention is polling, which is shown in Figure 6.6(c). Here each master module has access to a common request line, which it will assert when it requires access to the common resources. The arbitration unit must then decide which of all of the possible modules made the request. It does this by placing the address of a master module on the address lines and querying each in turn, until it finds the highest priority module needing the bus. This method has the benefit that any priority scheme can be implemented — FIFO, round robin, and so on. But the cost of the mechanism is large in time requirements. For that reason it is almost never used for arbitration of bus lines, but it does find application in the arbitration of I/O requests. That is, a processor, under program control, will poll I/O devices to ascertain the module requesting an interrupt.

6.3. Synchronous Bus Protocols

The term "synchronous bus" can refer to a number of different techniques for transferring information between modules. The common characteristic of all of these mechanisms is that a clocking signal is used to synchronize all of the transfers. This restricts the length of the bus, since the signal must propagate to all bus masters and bus slaves, and be received with a reasonable degree of simultaneity at all locations. In this section we will consider some of the mechanisms that can be used for synchronous data transfers on bus systems.

One type of a synchronous bus is not a multiple master, general purpose bus. This is a bus bus system under the direct control of a central unit. This type of system fits into the model shown in Figure 6.1, but each of the units is directly connected to a master control unit. This central control unit then decides which module is to assert information onto the bus, and which element is to accept the information. That is, no general address is decoded by slave modules, but rather the central control unit selects both the source and the destination. The microprogrammed modules studied in Chapter 5 are included in this classification, since the contents of the bus are determined by the microcode word during each micro cycle.

Another bus protocol that is synchronous in some aspects is typified by the bus connections of some high performance microprocessors. The M68020 has a protocol almost identical to that described above, except that the mechanisms allow for dynamic bus sizing and other flexibility. The mode of operation is synchronous with the system clock, giving the appearance of a synchronous mechanism. If the slave (memory, for example) is not able to respond to the processor fast enough to allow continuous operation, the processor automatically inserts idle bus periods, called "wait states," until the slave responds with the desired data. Thus, the only difference in method is that the M68020 works in increments of the basic system clock, rather than using completely asynchronous signals.

Another bus protocol is used by a number of microprocessors, and works in conjunction with the system clock. One of the problems that has become prevalent as integrated circuits have increased in complexity is providing enough pins to transfer the information into and out of a device. To minimize the total number of pins required for information transfer, some devices time multiplex the bus lines to allow one set of pins to present both address and data information. Thus, a processor with a 32-bit data path and a 32-bit address requirement can use one set of 32 pins, and synchronize all requests in such a way that all bus modules know when the address is available, and when the data is required.

A sample of the NS32332 protocol is presented in Figure 6.10(a), which presents a write cycle. The 32 bits of address and data share the time multiplexed AD(31:0)-H lines; the presence of a valid address is identified by ADS-L, and the data is synchronized by WRITE-L. The DDIN-L line identifies the direction of data transfer. The minimal transaction requires four cycles; the address is presented in the first cycle, and the data is available during later cycles. If the slave cannot respond within the required time, the master can wait until the transaction is able to proceed. This may occur, for example, if a dynamic memory is performing a refresh cycle when the processor requests a transaction. Most systems that use this technique will latch the address and create the appearance of separate address and data buses. A block diagram of one such arrangement is shown in Figure 6.10(b). To a slave device attached to the separate address and data lines, this communication mechanism appears the same as those previously described: the four event transaction proceeds in exactly the same way.

The time multiplexed data/address lines provides a mechanism to efficiently utilize one scarce system resource, the number of pins on the device. But another system resource that is not effectively utilized in the protocols described above is time. The master must alert the slave that some information is needed, and then wait for the slave to respond. A more time efficient mechanism would be to identify the basic components of a transfer and so design the protocol and the bus to allow these components to occur simultaneously. This requires a greater complexity on the part of both the master and slave modules, but it does more efficiently utilize the wires used to connect the modules together.

One of the beneficial features of asynchronous protocols identified in Section 6.1 is that the transaction proceeds as fast, or slow, as both sender and receiver agree that the information can be transferred. If some event requires more time, then the protocol essentially waits for the event to complete, and then proceeds with the transfer. This provides for increased flexibility, and it also provides for fairly simple interface modules. However, the overall data rates will be higher if more capability is provided in both the sender and receiver to minimize the amount of time that the bus lines are utilized to exchange the information. This is the basic premise of synchronous protocols, and the mechanism provides for time efficient use of the bus lines.

In the protocol described in Section 6.1, the bus master was responsible for asserting the address, and then allowing time for propagation delays and signal skew before asserting the request line to initiate action. One of the reasons that a

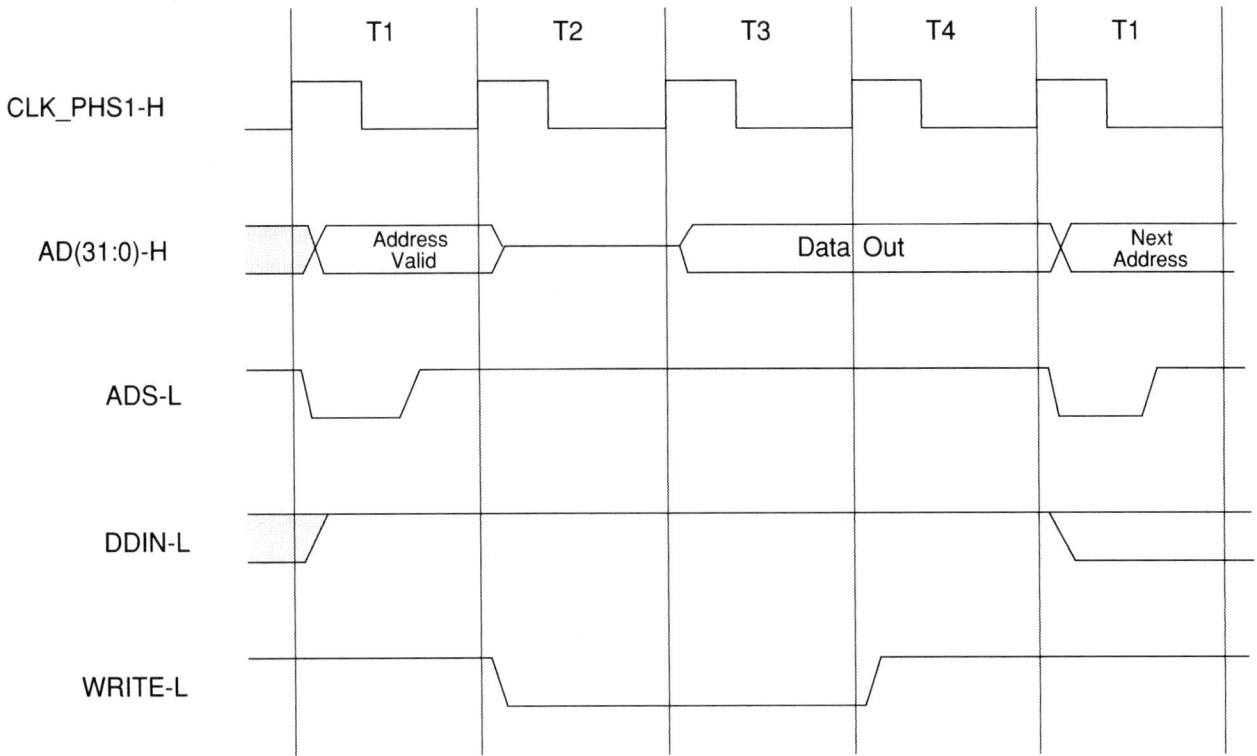

(a)

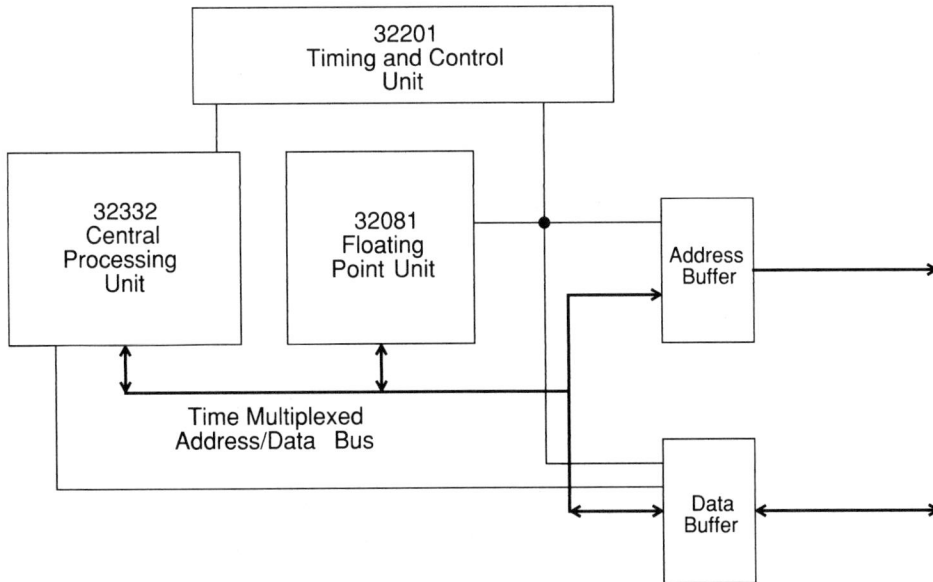

(b)

Figure 6.10. NS32332 Bus Transactions: (a) Timing Diagram for a Write Operation; (b) Block Diagram of Interface Logic.

synchronous protocol is more time efficient than the asynchronous protocol is that the action of all of the modules is coordinated by the presence of a common clock. This establishes an exact time when the information must be present on the bus, and when each module attached to the bus will know that information is available. This establishes bounds on the time required to transfer the information, and interface modules must all be designed to operate within those bounds. Thus, this mechanism calls for the interface modules to meet a time standard, rather than having the protocol adjust the time requirements to satisfy the needs of the various interface modules. The modules connecting to the bus must then be capable of transferring information at the rate determined by the bus protocol.

The mechanism of data exchange for synchronous protocols operates on a different set of principles than the asynchronous methods previously described, and this leads to a slightly different nomenclature when dealing with the units. We will call the module that initiates a transaction a commander, because it sends a command to another module. The command may or may not contain data, depending on the type of transfer. The module that fields the command we will call a responder, since it responds to the request in an appropriate manner. As with the asynchronous protocols, a number of different mechanisms will function properly. We will describe first a sample mechanism for write and read, and then examine a specific instantiation of a protocol.

There are four components of the transfer of information, and all four must be completed for a successful transfer. We discussed each of these functions in the process of describing the asynchronous protocols and arbitration mechanisms, but did not identify them as necessary constituent parts of the transfers. These components are:

1. Obtain control of the bus. This is the responsibility of the commander and the arbitration network. When a module requires a transfer, it communicates that need to the bus interface module, which initiates a request for the bus. When the arbitration process allows the commander interface module access to the bus, the transfer can proceed.

2. Initiate transfer. If this is a write, this will include data. The commander places appropriate address (and data, if needed) and control information on the bus. The responder with that address will react by accepting the request. This does not imply that the responder module will be able to handle the request, only that the request has been received.

3. Decide how to handle the request. This is the task of the responder bus interface module. This does not mean that the subsystem attached to the bus will necessarily accept (or provide) information immediately, but the bus interface module of the responder must be capable of deciding how to respond to the request. For example, if a memory is ready to accept information, it will be capable of accepting the information, and the bus interface module will decide that the information can be accepted. On the other hand, if a memory is busy with a previous request and unable to accept data, the bus interface module will decide to reject the request.

4. Inform commander of the decision of the responder. This is the feedback mechanism to allow the handshake to occur, and indicates to the commander that the request has been handled. If the request was a write, for example, the system attached to the commander bus interface module can proceed with its tasks. However, if the system attached to the responder interface module was

unable to accept the data, this decision is relayed to the commander, and the commander interface module can then initiate the request anew.

These four components are present in the asynchronous protocol, with its associated arbitration mechanism, but are not as evident as in synchronous protocols. The arbitration component can be handled in parallel, as in the UNIBUS protocol, or after a bus is available, as with most microprocessor bus systems, such as the NS32032 systems. Component 2, initiating the transfer, is handled by the bus master in an asynchronous protocol; the master module asserts the address, waits the prescribed time, and alerts the slave modules by asserting the request line. The third component, deciding how to handle the request, is an integral part of the slave module mechanism, since all requests in an asynchronous protocol are handled immediately. If a memory read is required, then the protocol awaits the response from the memory before proceeding. Thus, it is difficult to separate the act of responding from the decision to respond. However, in a synchronous protocol, these two elements are distinct, and are handled in a different manner. The decision process is handled by the bus interface module, while the response to the request is handled by the appropriate subsystem, such as a memory. The forth component, the handshaking mechanism, is handled by the request and acknowledge lines of the system.

These four events are shown in write and read sequences in Figure 6.11. The write sequence begins (period n) by the processor interface module arbitrating for use of the bus lines. When the arbitration process is settled in favor of the processor, the sequence proceeds, and the processor interface module asserts the data and address information onto the bus lines (period n+1). When the clock occurs, the memory interface module accepts data and address, and determines that the request was intended for the memory subsystem. During the next period (n+2), the memory interface module ascertains the status of the memory and determines that the data can be accepted. And finally, during the acknowledge period (n+3), the memory interface module sends an acknowledgement to the processor interface module to indicate that the transaction was successfully completed. Since the commander of the processor bus interface module started the series of events in period n, it will know that the response of the memory (accept or reject) will be found in period n+3, so it will listen to the lines at that time to find out if the write action was successful.

The read sequence is also shown in Figure 6.11. The transaction is initiated by the arbitration of the processor for the bus (period n). When the processor interface module has obtained control of the bus lines, it will then assert the address and request information on the bus (period n+1). Synchronous with the clock, the memory interface module accepts the request, and in the following period (n+2) ascertains the status of the memory and decides to accept the request. This decision is communicated to the processor interface module in the last period of this sequence (n+3). The memory subsystem is then activated in order to supply the required information. The time from period n to period m reflects the response time of the memory. When the memory provides the information, the memory interface module initiates a bus transaction, first by arbitrating for the bus (period m), and then by asserting the data onto the bus (period m+1). The processor interface module accepts the data synchronous with the clock, ascertains in the next period (m+2) that the data is in response to an earlier request, and in the last period (m+3) sends an acknowledgement to the memory interface module.

Processor

Bus Interface

Memory

Bus Interface

Synchronous Bus

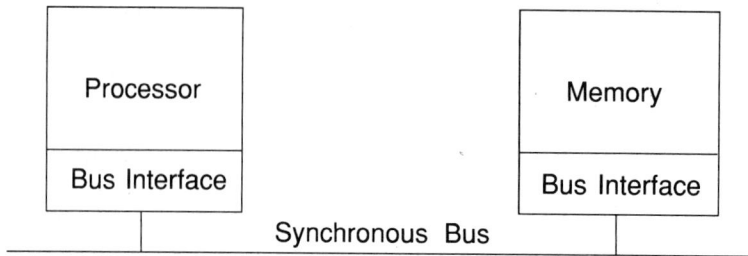

Write Sequence

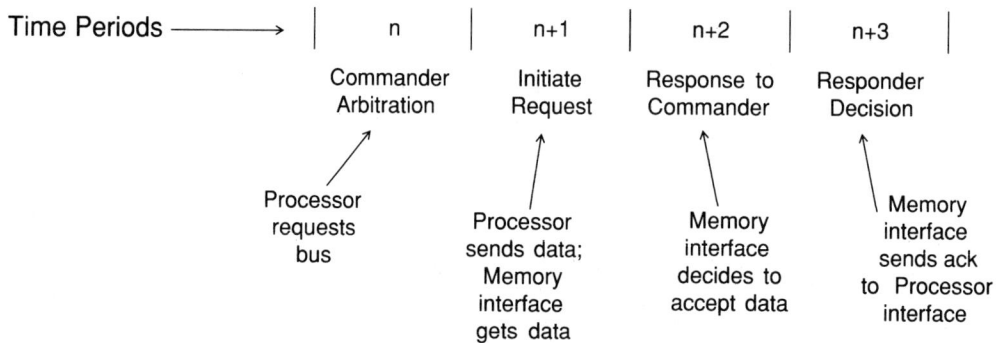

Time Periods ⟶ | n | n+1 | n+2 | n+3 |

Commander Arbitration | Initiate Request | Response to Commander | Responder Decision

Processor requests bus

Processor sends data; Memory interface gets data

Memory interface decides to accept data

Memory interface sends ack to Processor interface

Read Sequence

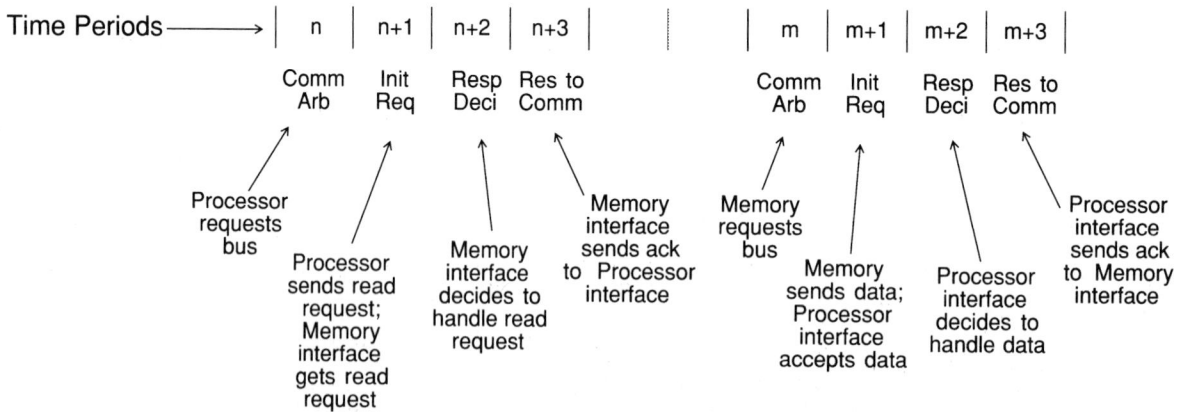

Time Periods ⟶ | n | n+1 | n+2 | n+3 | | m | m+1 | m+2 | m+3 |

Comm Arb | Init Req | Resp Deci | Res to Comm | Comm Arb | Init Req | Resp Deci | Res to Comm

Processor requests bus

Processor sends read request; Memory interface gets read request

Memory interface decides to handle read request

Memory interface sends ack to Processor interface

Memory requests bus

Memory sends data; Processor interface accepts data

Processor interface decides to handle data

Processor interface sends ack to Memory interface

Figure 6.11. Synchronous Bus Mechanisms.

As indicated in Figure 6.11, each of the four components of the exchange happens in separate cycles of the common clock, and can be pipelined. We will discuss pipelining in more detail in Chapter 8, but the basic idea is that independent events can occur in different pieces of hardware in the same period. With multiple events occurring simultaneously, a speed advantage is obtained over the same events occurring serially. With a synchronous bus protocol, the interface devices can be designed in such a manner that each of the four functions involves a different set of hardware and a different set of bus lines, so that up to four separate transactions can be in different stages of execution at any one time. Thus, the speed advantage of synchronous bus transactions stems not only from the specific windows in which information must be valid, but from the pipelining and overlapping of transactions. Note that, if not enough transactions are available to keep the different portions of the bus busy during the various clock cycles, then the speed advantage of the pipelining is lost.

Example 6.6: Synchronous bus protocol: The synchronous backplane interconnect (SBI), which is the communication mechanism for the VAX 11/780 computer, is a synchronous bus protocol. What are the methods used by the protocol, and how fast can information be transferred on the bus?

The principle lines (but not all) involved in information transfer on the SBI are shown in Figure 6.12(a). The sixteen arbitration lines [TR(15:0)] allow parallel arbitration of up to 16 different modules during a clock period. The information transfer lines include the 32 data/address lines [B(31:0)] and lines for identifying the type of transaction that is occurring. The response lines [CNF(1:0)] provide a data path for confirmation of previous transactions. The principle difference between the SBI and the protocol discussed above is that the SBI time multiplexes the data/address lines so that a write will require more than one cycle. The SBI mechanism allows for one or two words of data in a write transfer, so that up to 8 bytes of information can be written. Such a write cycle is shown in Figure 6.12(b). To demonstrate the pipelined nature of the action, the transfer is shown in a space-time manner. The lines involved in the transfers are divided into three groups: arbitration lines, information lines, and acknowledge lines. And the action of these three sets is described for each of the cycles. The DEC name for the commander and responder interface modules is the NEXUS. The first period (n) is used by the arbitration lines for the NEXUS associated with the processor to acquire control of the bus. Once this has occurred, the transfer can continue. The arbitration unit has the capability of locking out other requests for the two additional cycles needed to complete the transfer. The assertion of address and write identification information occurs in the second cycle (n+1). This information includes not only the target address of the write, but also an identifying field to specify the source of the information. The reason for this will become apparent with the read transaction. At the end of this period the NEXUS associated with the memory will receive the address and the identification information. The data/address lines are used in the next period (n+2) to send the first 4 bytes of data; at this same time, the memory NEXUS is deciding how to handle the request. At the end of the period, the acknowledgement decision has been reached, and the first bytes of data are accepted into the NEXUS. Then, during the final data cycle (n+3), the acknowledgment is returned to the originating NEXUS for the address and write identification information. In the next two cycles additional acknowledgement information is returned for the data cycles of the transfer.

The pipelined nature of possible transactions is indicated to in Figure 6.12(b) by the shaded area that indicates a possible second write cycle to be

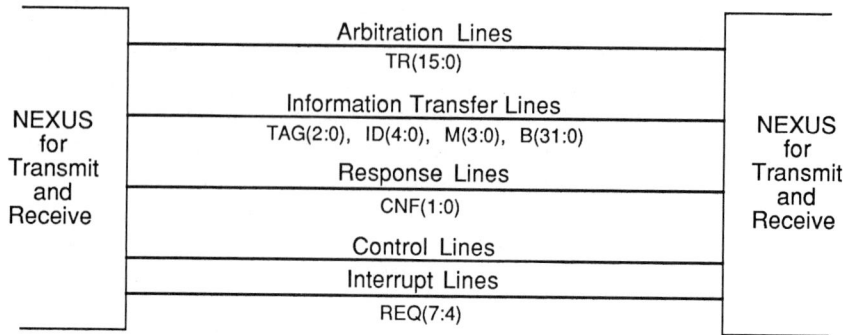

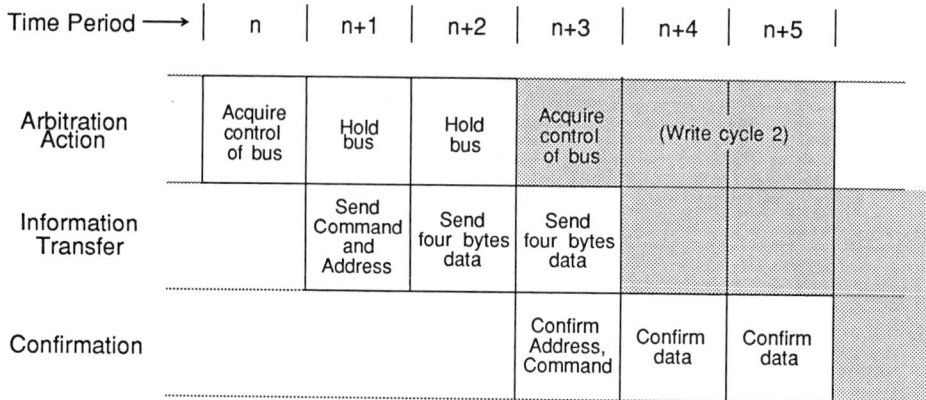

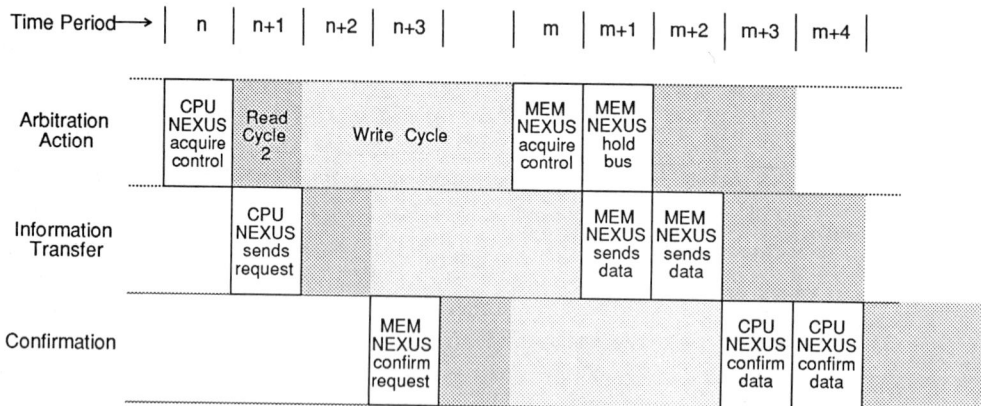

Figure 6.12. Synchronous Backplane Interconnect Protocol: (a) Control Lines Involved in SBI Information Transfer; (b) Write Transaction, 8 Bytes; (c) Read Transaction, 8 Bytes.

initiated by a second NEXUS. Note that the second cycle begins before the first cycle ends. This protocol allows meaningful data or address information to be placed on the data bus during each cycle.

The read transfer operates with a similar mechanism, except that the request and the response are separated by the response time of the memory.

This is shown in Figure 6.12(c). Here the NEXUS associated with the processor acquires control of the bus (period n), sends out a read request consisting of an address, a logical identifier, and a transfer type identification that informs the memory to supply 8 bytes. The processor receives the acknowledgement of the request in period n+3. Some time later, when the memory has the information for the processor, the NEXUS associated with the memory gains control of the bus (period m), and sends the data in two 4-byte transfers (period m+1, m+2). The destination of this information is carried by the identification lines, which will have the same logical identifier that was passed with the read request. The NEXUS associated with the processor sends its acknowledgement to the memory in periods m+3 and m+4.

Additional read and write transactions are shown in the shaded areas of Figure 6.12(c) to demonstrate the pipelining and parallel events possible with the protocol.

The clock cycle time for the SBI is 200 nsec. Thus, with the above protocol it is possible to send 8 bytes every 600 nsec. This gives an effective data rate of 13.3 MBytes/sec.

In this section we have considered some of the principles involved in transferring information with synchronous bus communication protocols. These mechanisms will, in general, lead to a higher data rate than their asynchronous counterparts for two basic reasons. First, the presence of a common clock limits the physical size of the system and synchronizes all requests for action. This synchronization establishes a time at which all action must take place. Second, the separation of the components into independent pieces of hardware, and into independent bus lines, permits pipelining of the various functions. This allows concurrent use of the available resources. The net result is that data can be transferred at higher rates than achievable with other methods.

6.4. Data Movement: Programmed I/O and Direct Memory Access

We have discussed some of the basic mechanisms involved in doing transfers of data over bus systems. Regardless of the exact protocol used, an arbitration mechanism is utilized to identify the module which controls the bus. This module then initiates a transfer, and the data is moved from one module to another. This mechanism is most often utilized to exchange information between a memory and a processor module. However, the same mechanism is used to transfer information and commands to and from I/O devices. In this section we want to explore some of the methods that can be used to control I/O devices and to transfer information to and from a computer system. For computer systems that include separate I/O instructions, generally an I/O bus is used for the communication. In some systems with I/O instructions, the system bus is used for memory and I/O transfers, but I/O transactions use a slightly different set of control lines to perform the transfers. However, one prevalent practice is to use the same address space for both memory and I/O devices. This method calls for the I/O devices to be assigned locations in the memory space, and then, when the device is to be activated and controlled, the processor does so by writing and reading the appropriate locations. This is called "memory mapped I/O," and is used extensively in minicomputer and microprocessor systems. In fact, the inclusion of I/O instructions in the processor instruction set does not preclude the use of memory mapped I/O, and the manner used for connecting I/O devices is left up to the system designer.

There are three basic mechanisms for the interaction between the processor and the I/O device. The processor responsibilities of each mechanism, the system resources required, and the complexity of the I/O interface module required by each method are all different. A block diagram showing the relationship between the processor and the I/O device is shown in Figure 6.13. The I/O interface module interacts with the system bus to provide both control signals and data to an I/O device controller. Most I/O device controllers are designed in such a way that they will control a single type of device, such as a disk or tape unit. However, the device controllers are also designed in such a way that multiple copies of I/O devices can be controlled by a single I/O device controller. If another type of I/O device is to be included in the system, then a different I/O device controller is needed, with its associated I/O interface module.

Regardless of transfer mechanism utilized, the processor must have the ability to direct action in the I/O device with instructions; this mechanism we will refer to as "programmed I/O." It is possible to control both the action and the data movement of a device with programmed I/O, as we will see in an example. It is also possible to initiate the action with programmed I/O, and then allow the interface module to interrupt the processor when data is available. This interrupt capability allows the processor to proceed with other work while the data is being obtained, and then to interact with the I/O device only when data is available. Finally, the highest speed is obtained when the interface module has the capability of exchanging data directly with the memory. This is referred to as direct memory access (DMA), and is limited in speed by the transfer rate of the bus. For

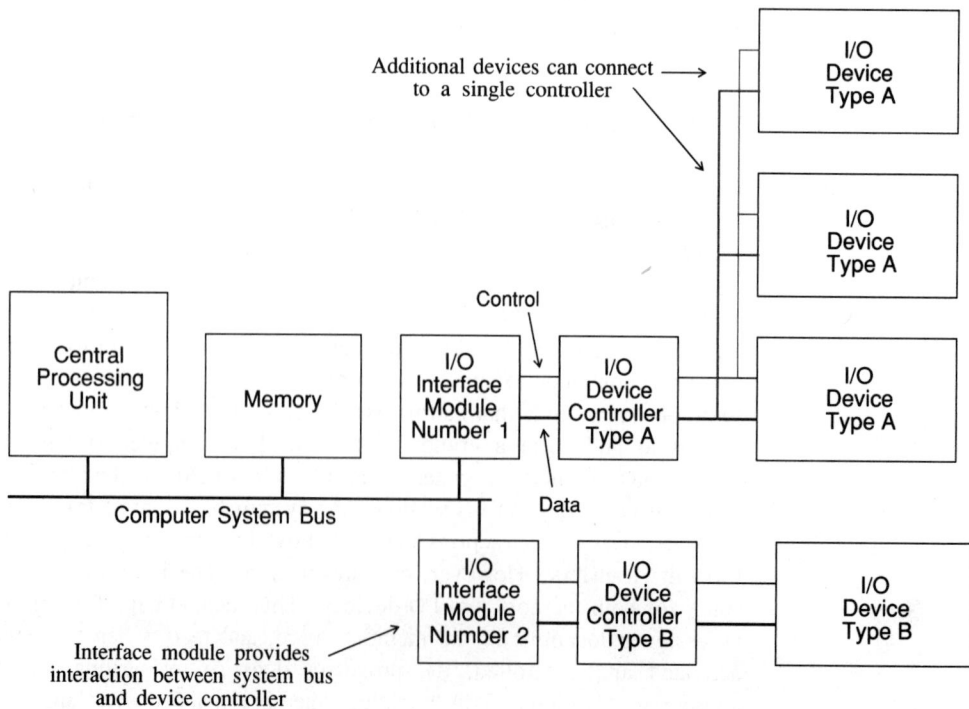

Figure 6.13. Interface System Block Diagram.

DMA transactions, programmed I/O instructions are used to set up a starting address in the system memory and the length of the transfer; and then another programmed I/O instruction initiates the action. The system is then free to perform other tasks, and the DMA interface module interacts directly with system memory to perform the transfer.

An I/O device is controlled by writing (and reading) information to (and from) specific locations. This method is independent of the type of bus protocol used, but the examples in this chapter will all be done with the asynchronous protocol, as that is the most widely used mechanism at this time. Interface module and I/O devices can be controlled by assigning a specific action to each of the addresses used by an I/O device, or by assigning an action to specific bits or bit patterns at a single address. In either case, the processor sends the command to the interface module by writing to the proper address with the necessary bit pattern. When the interface module receives a write request, it accepts the bit pattern and performs the requested work. When the interface module receives a read request, it supplies the appropriate information to the bus. In this fashion, information can be moved to and from the I/O device.

One of the most frequent inquiries made by a processor concerns the status of the interface module and I/O device, whether it is busy or not, and whether it has data available. Thus, reading a status register in the interface module must be done quickly and easily. The status register usually contains information about the device it is controlling. For example, a tape recorder interface module might have bits in its status word that indicate if the device is on line, if it is busy, if the interrupt is enabled, and so on. The processor is then capable of determining the status of the device by reading the status register.

The simplest interface mechanism results by allowing the processor to control all aspects of the transfer. This method consumes all of the time of the processor, but can be used if the need arises. Since the machine is entirely utilized with the I/O transfer, it is not capable of being used for other tasks during this time, and this is generally not an acceptable cost. Nevertheless, the interface module between the computer system and the I/O controller can be very simple, as shown by the following example.

> *Example 6.7: Interface module design:* Design an interface module that will connect a tape recorder to a 16-bit asynchronous bus for a read only operation using memory mapped I/O techniques. This mechanism is to be controlled by writing command patterns to address $FFFD80_{16}$, reading status at address $FFFD82_{16}$, and by reading the data at address $FFFD84_{16}$. What is the maximum data rate achievable by this mechanism?
>
> We will delay several of the details of the tape recorder side of the interface module, and concentrate on the interaction with the bus. Assuming that the interface method to be used is the four event protocol described in Section 6.1, the lines of interest are the address and data lines, a read line, a request line, and an acknowledge line. One design for this interface module is shown in Figure 6.14, which we will examine by function.
>
> The first function is the address decode and command line interface. The most significant lines of the address are tested with a gating network to look for the proper address ($FFFD80_{16}$ – $FFFD84_{16}$). This same function can also be accomplished by using an address decoder chip, such as the 74677, which looks for a specified bit pattern. However, if the address of the device is not known at design time, then one mechanism is to use comparators

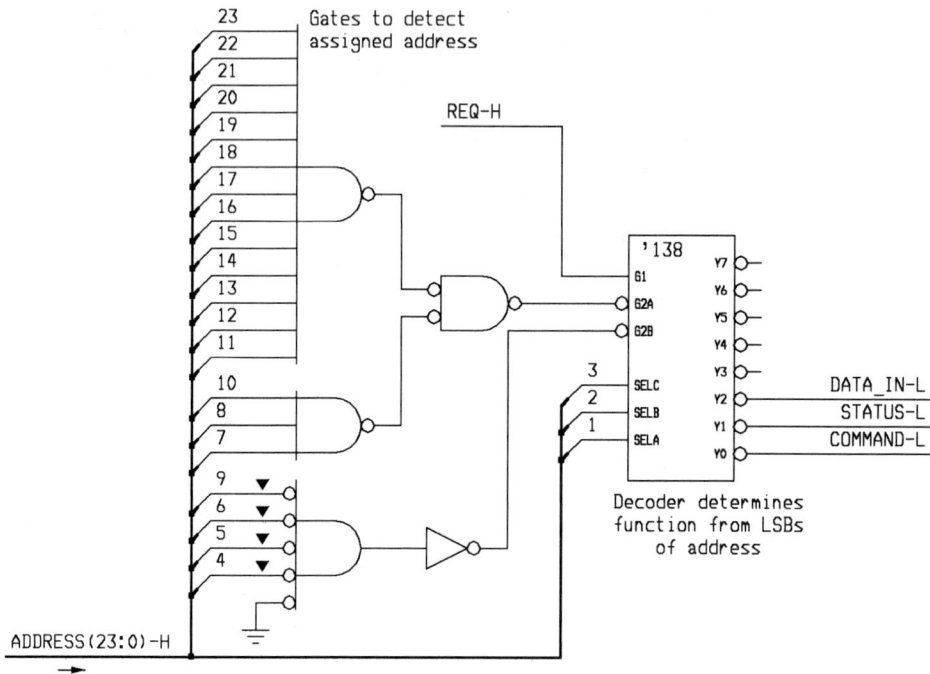

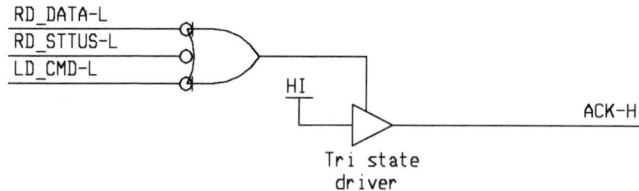

Figure 6.14(a). Tape Recorder Interface Module (Control).

configured with address specifying switches. The least significant lines are directed to a 3-line-to-8-line decoder, which asserts a line for each of the appropriate addresses. Note that the least significant line (ADDR(0)-H) is not used; we assume that the system is always going to access this information in 16-bit words, properly aligned.

If the address matches, then when the request line is asserted (REQ-H), the required action is immediately performed, and the acknowledge line asserted (ACK-H). No delay other than the gate delays of the circuitry is inserted into the system since the timing does not require it: information from the master is accepted with edge triggered devices, and the reaction time of the master will account for any hold time needed. Also, information sent to the master is asserted at the same time as the acknowledge line, and the master is responsible for any delays necessary to account for skew on the data lines. Thus, command information (and data, if it is required by the specified interaction) is accepted without delay. Likewise, as soon as a read command is received, the requested information is provided. This register interaction will result in a faster read/write time than normal memory, although it is in the same address space.

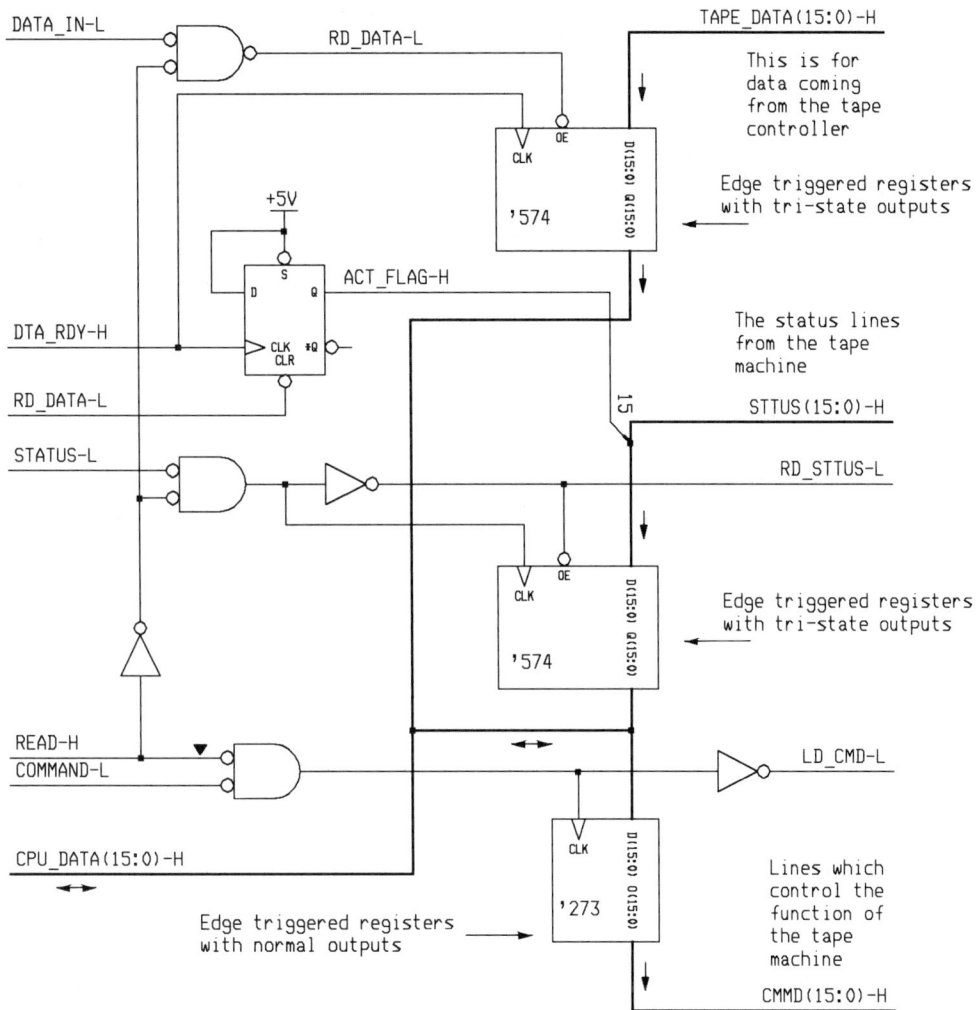

Figure 6.14(b). Tape Recorder Interface Module (Data Path).

To demonstrate the programmed I/O mechanism, consider the transactions required to cause the recorder to space forward a block, then read the next block of 512 words. Assuming that there is a simple assembly language to work with, the following code section will perform the desired work:

1		MOV #<FSF>, @FFFD80	FSF is file space forward pattern.
2	one:	TESTI #<BUSY>, @FFFD82	BUSY is pattern to test busy condition
3		JNZ one	of interface module. Loop to "one" till done.
4		MOV #<512>, R1	Set up the count.
5		MOV #<start addr>, R2	Set up the address.
6		MOV #<DAV>, R3	Set up test pattern for data available.
7		MOV #<FFFD82>, R4	Set up address of status register.
8		MOV #<FFFD84>, R5	Set up address of data register.
9		MOV #<read cmnd>, @FFFD80	Start read action.
10	two:	TEST R3, *R4	(800) Is there data?.

11	JZ two	(450) If not, go back to "two."
12	MOV *R5,*R2+	(1150) If so, move where R2 points.
13	DEC R1	(550) and bump R2; done 512 words?
14	JNZ two	(600) If not, go back to "two."
		(3550)

The first instruction writes out the pattern to indicate to the interface module that the tape recorder should move forward to the next file mark. The next two instructions merely wait until that is accomplished. Instructions 4 through 8 set up the general purpose registers to allow faster processing in the transfer section. Instruction number 9 actually starts the read action of the recorder. Instruction 10 checks to see if the data is available. It is similar in function to instruction 2, which checks to see if the recorder is busy. However, by using values in registers, rather than values in the instruction stream, the time required for the instruction is greatly reduced. In Chapter 4 we identified different instruction times for instruction types, based on the amount of work required by the instruction. Using the times identified there, instruction two requires 1,750 nsec for completion, while instruction 10 can be done in 800 nsec. Instruction 11 is to loop until data is available, when the action moves to instruction 12, which moves the data from the interface module to the designated spot in memory. And with the autoincrement feature of the destination address, the system is ready for the next iteration. Instruction 13 decrements the counter, and instruction 14 loops if the count has not reached zero. The highest data rate will occur when the instructions 10 and 11 are executed but once each iteration. When this occurs, the loop takes 3,550 nsec. Two bytes each 3,550 nsec results in a data rate of 563 Kbytes/sec. This rate cannot be sustained over time, since it does not take into account the time required to set up the transaction.

The above example indicates what can be accomplished by a machine dedicated to performing a single transfer. However, if the device being controlled is a modem or line printer, then the data rate is much lower than that attainable by programmed I/O. Most of the time the machine would be executing the wait loop, waiting for the data movement to occur. Therefore, system designers have often designed the machines in such a way that the interface module can interrupt the action of the computer when data movement is necessary. The positive effect of this is that the machine time that would be used by looping can be effectively utilized for other functions. The negative effect of this mechanism is that the transfer rate will be lower, since more work is needed for each transfer.

Example 6.8: Interface design with interrupt: Consider the system of Example 6.7, but assume that the interface module is also capable of issuing an interrupt when data is available. What is the maximum data rate for the system?

We will make the assumption that an interrupt action causes the current PC and status register to be pushed onto the system stack, and also causes the interrupt service routine to be entered with the vector mechanism discussed in Chapter 4. This mechanism will require about 1,100 nsec in our machine. We include here two sections of code, one of which is used to set up the action, and one of which is actually executed once for each word of data transferred.

```
1    setup:    MOV #<start addr>, @ADDR        Set up the initial address.
2              MOV #<512>, @COUNT             Set up the count value.
3              MOV #<read cmnd>, @FFFD80       Start the read action.
              ...

10   srvce:    MOV @FFFD84, *@ADDR+            (3650) Move the data.
11             DEC @COUNT                     (1800) Check the count.
12             JZ more                        (450) If done, do other action.
13             RTI                            (850) If not, return from interrupt.
14   more:     ...

20   ADDR:     DATA 0
21   COUNT:    DATA 0
```

The first three instructions are used to initialize the starting address and the word count, and to start the actual read action. We are neglecting here the commands necessary to position the tape at the right spot, since additional code to discern between a movement command and a data command would further slow the action of the system. For the data movement action of interest here, the instructions of note are 10 through 13. These perform essentially the same action as the code of Example 6.7; instruction 10 moves the data, instruction 11 decrements the count, and instruction 12 gets out of the loop if the count has reached zero. The count will reach zero when the appropriate number of words have been transferred, and at that point the transfer is complete. If the transfer is not complete (COUNT has not reached zero), then instruction 13 returns the program to the execution in progress when the interrupt occurred.

The difference in instruction execution times results from the fact that now the address information is contained in the instruction stream, and many more references to memory are needed to obtain and manipulate the data. One benefit of this mechanism is that no registers need to be saved upon entering the interrupt service routine. However, the overall time will be greatly increased, with a time for interrupt and interrupt service routine of 7,850 nsec. This results in a maximum data rate of 254 Kbytes/sec.

As can be seen from the example, the data rate for interrupt driven transfers is much less than that achievable strictly with programmed I/O. However, for systems where the data rate is much lower, the interrupt scheme will allow the system to be utilized in other action while the transfer is in progress. In both cases, the action of the interface module and the movement of the data were controlled with programmed I/O instructions.

To increase the data rate of the system requires a more complex interface mechanism, one in which some of the responsibilities of the transfer are moved from the processor to the interface module. The most frequent and time consuming activity is the transfer of data from the device to the memory, and this is precisely the activity committed to hardware. This requires a more complicated interface system, and a simplified diagram of such an interface module is shown in Figure 6.15. The result is a direct memory access interface module, which will interact directly with memory in the transfer of the data.

As can be seen from Figure 6.15, an interface module with DMA capability also contains the basic elements of the programmed I/O interface system: the status register reports the status of the interface module and its associated I/O

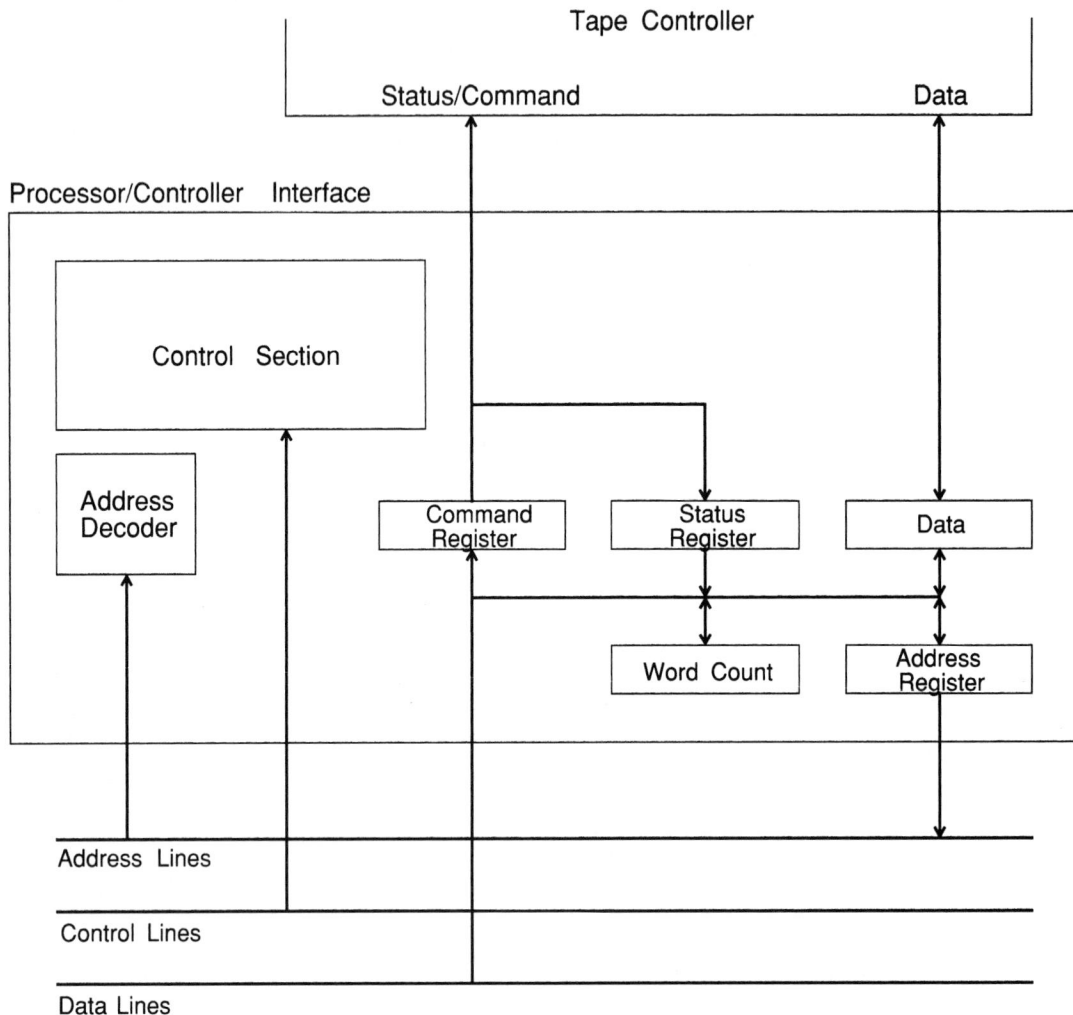

Figure 6.15. Tape Recorder Interface Module with DMA.

device, and the command register controls the action of the unit. However, two other registers have been added: the word count register (WC) and the address register (AR). These registers will be filled (and read, if required) by programmed I/O instructions. The control portion of the DMA interface module must be more complex than the previous interface modules to not only transfer control and status information, but also to control the process of automatic data movement. In general this control portion will be a sequential system designed using the concepts and ideas presented in Chapter 5.

The control of the action of the I/O device (tape movement, head positioning for a disk, etc.) proceeds as before, with programmed I/O instructions directing the appropriate movement, and the device interrupting when the specified action has been completed. However, when data movement is called for, then the code controlling the unit (commonly called the "I/O driver routine") will, with programmed I/O instructions, fill the WC register with the number of words to transfer, and the AR with the starting address in memory where this transfer is to take place. The transfer of information is then initiated with programmed I/O instructions. When the data becomes available, the interface module requests control of the bus, performs the necessary transfer, and relinquishes control of the bus. The address for the transfer is provided by the DMA interface module. After the transaction is complete, the address is changed to point to location to be used by the next transfer. In addition, the word count is decremented to keep track of the number of transfers that have occurred. Thus, the hardware handles the information transfer after data starts to flow. Using this technique, the data can be transferred at a rate limited only by the bus speed. This allows high speed devices, such as disk units, to exchange information at the data rates of the disk. A disk using an SMD protocol can transfer information in excess of 3 Mbytes/sec.

> *Example 6.9: Interface design with DMA:* Modify the tape recorder interface module developed in Example 6.8 to include DMA capability. The word count register is accessed as location $FFFD86_{16}$, and the address register is accessed as location $FFFD88_{16}$ for the least significant 16 bits, and location $FFFD8A_{16}$ for the most significant 8 bits.
>
> We will delay the design of the control system until the following section, but the other elements are shown in Figure 6.15. The use of the decoder is expanded to include the additional addresses required by the word count and address registers. Note that these registers are readable as well as writable. This does not improve the functionality of the unit, but will provide valuable help for both checkout and test.
>
> The need for action on the part of the sequential controller is indicated by a hardware flag in the control section of the interface module. This is set when the command register is filled by programmed I/O. One of the responsibilities of the controller is then to reset this flag when the action has been initiated. When the action requires tape movement, such as file space forward, then the interface module requests the movement from the tape controller and waits for the completion of the action. When data movement is required, the specified tape action is requested, and when a data transfer is necessary, the appropriate bus cycle is initiated.
>
> The transfer rate of this mechanism is limited by the bus speed of the system. For a bus system with a transaction time of 250 nsec, the maximum date rate would be 8 Mbytes/sec. This rate is somewhat inflated, since no allowance is made for other users on the bus or for the cost of bus arbitration.

This section has dealt with the transfer of information between a processor and an I/O device. There is a tradeoff in complexity of hardware and processor time to transfer information. If the complexity of the interface module is kept simple, then the responsibility of the processor to control the I/O device and the data movement increases. For transfers conducted purely with programmed I/O instructions, the processor must either continuously monitor the appropriate status lines, or it must interrogate them periodically (polling) to ascertain if any action is necessary. In either case, a large portion of the processor time is devoted to conducting the transfer.

If the concept of interrupts is utilized, then the processor is able to ignore the I/O device until action in needed, at which point the interface module will cause an interrupt, requesting interaction with the processor. The benefit of the use of interrupts is that the processor is free to do other work while the I/O device does not need supervision. The cost of this policy is the decrease in the speed of possible transfers. This policy is especially beneficial for action that does not involve data transfers, such as tape movement or positioning of disk heads.

The highest speed is achieved by direct interaction between the interface module and the memory, with the use of DMA. This method requires more complex hardware, but is capable of very high speed transfers. DMA interface modules combine the various techniques to achieve the high data rates. Programmed I/O instructions are used to communicate with the various registers that control the action of the I/O device. Interrupt techniques inform the processor that a requested action has been completed. The controller of the interface module interacts directly with the bus to transfer the data with minimal overhead, needing only the time required for successful bus cycles.

6.5. An Example of a Device Interface Module

Many of the concepts discussed in the preceding sections are more easily visualized when a specific example is utilized. For that reason, we will use the tape recorder mechanism that was the object of the previous examples, and we will design a simple DMA interface module capable of a limited amount of interaction. The interface module will control the behavior of tape drives as directed by the programmed I/O instructions issued by the CPU. Thus, the interface module should combine all of the techniques discussed: respond to instructions, assert signals going to the tape controller, cause interrupts, and control DMA transfers.

The task facing a designer is to ascertain the requirements of the system and build a device that will satisfy those requirements. In this case, we need information concerning three different facets of the design. Two of these are indicated in Figure 6.15, which shows the relationship of the interface and the tape controller. One piece of information is the bus specification, which identifies the electrical and timing requirements of interaction with a bus module. The other device specific information is the set of control and data signals used by the tape recorder. To perform the needed tape movement, read, and write operations, the device must assert these lines in the manner defined by a controller specification. The final piece of information needed is a definition of the commands to be issued and the status to be interrogated by the CPU. Thus, before the design process can begin, information about the electrical and behavioral characteristics of the interface module must be established.

The bus used for this design is the UNIBUS, but the same techniques would be applicable on a Multibus, Q-bus, VME bus, and so on. Each bus has its own characteristics, and these characteristics must be considered in the process of doing a design. The UNIBUS is relatively simple, yet it includes the salient points addressed by the previous sections. Also, because it is a 16-bit bus, the transfer techniques are not overshadowed by an enormous number of wires. To match the electrical characteristics we will use special gates, and to satisfy the timing characteristics we will use a sequential system designed with a state machine approach. Other bus systems, such as the VME bus, will use more standard gates for their interaction, but the techniques will be the same.

The tape controller that is the object of this design is capable of controlling up to four 9-track tape transports. The data path to the controller is separate from the data path coming from the controller, but both paths are 8 bits wide. Parity is used to create the ninth track for the tape, but the controller itself takes care of parity operations. In addition to the data lines, there are command signals and status indicators associated with the tape controller. The command lines are indicate in Table 6.1. Asserting these lines in the proper fashion will result in the desired control over the tape drive and the date movement. The designer must create the interface module in such a way that the signals are asserted properly. The third control is labeled SETX-L, and it used to synchronize the other commands listed. For example, when a write file mark command is required, the WRITEFM-L line is asserted, and then the SETX pulse causes the tape controller to accept the command and begin the specified work.

The control signals of Table 6.1 are used to activate the controller and perform work, but in addition to that the CPU often needs to know the status of the tape system. For this reason, a number of status lines are provided, as shown in Table 6.2. These signals are received and delivered to the CPU when the appropriate programmed I/O instruction is given.

The UNIBUS specification is used to identify the required signals on the bus side of the interface module. The controller specification provides the signals given in Table 6.1 and Table 6.2, which identify the signals of the tape drive side of the interface module. With this information a preliminary data path block diagram can be formed, and this is given in Figure 6.16.

The initial registers are identical in function to those identified in previous sections in this chapter. The command register is used to receive commands from

Table 6.1. Control Lines to Tape Controller.

Signal	Function
INIT-L	Pulse to initialize transport
SET_TRAN(3:0)-L	Level to select active transport
SETX-L	Pulse to synchronize action requests
WRITE-L	Level to identify function type
READ-L	Level to identify function type
INPUTX-L	Command for input data
OUTPUTX-L	Command for output data
FILESRCHF-L	Command for file search forward
FILESRCHR-L	Command for file search reverse
SYNCFWD-L	Command for synchronous forward action
SYNCRVS-L	Command for synchronous reverse action
WRITEFM-L	Command for write file mark
REWIND-L	Rewind command pulse

Table 6.2. Status Signals Available from Controller.

Signal	Function
TAPE_READY-L	Tape transport and controller ready
P_ERROR-L	Parity error
EOF-L	End of file mark detected
BOT-L	Tape located at beginning of tape mark
EOT-L	Tape located at end of tape mark
PROTECT-L	Tape transport senses no write ring
RWDING-L	Tape is rewinding
SEL0-L	Transport 0 selected
SEL1-L	Transport 1 selected
SEL2-L	Transport 2 selected
SEL3-L	Transport 3 selected

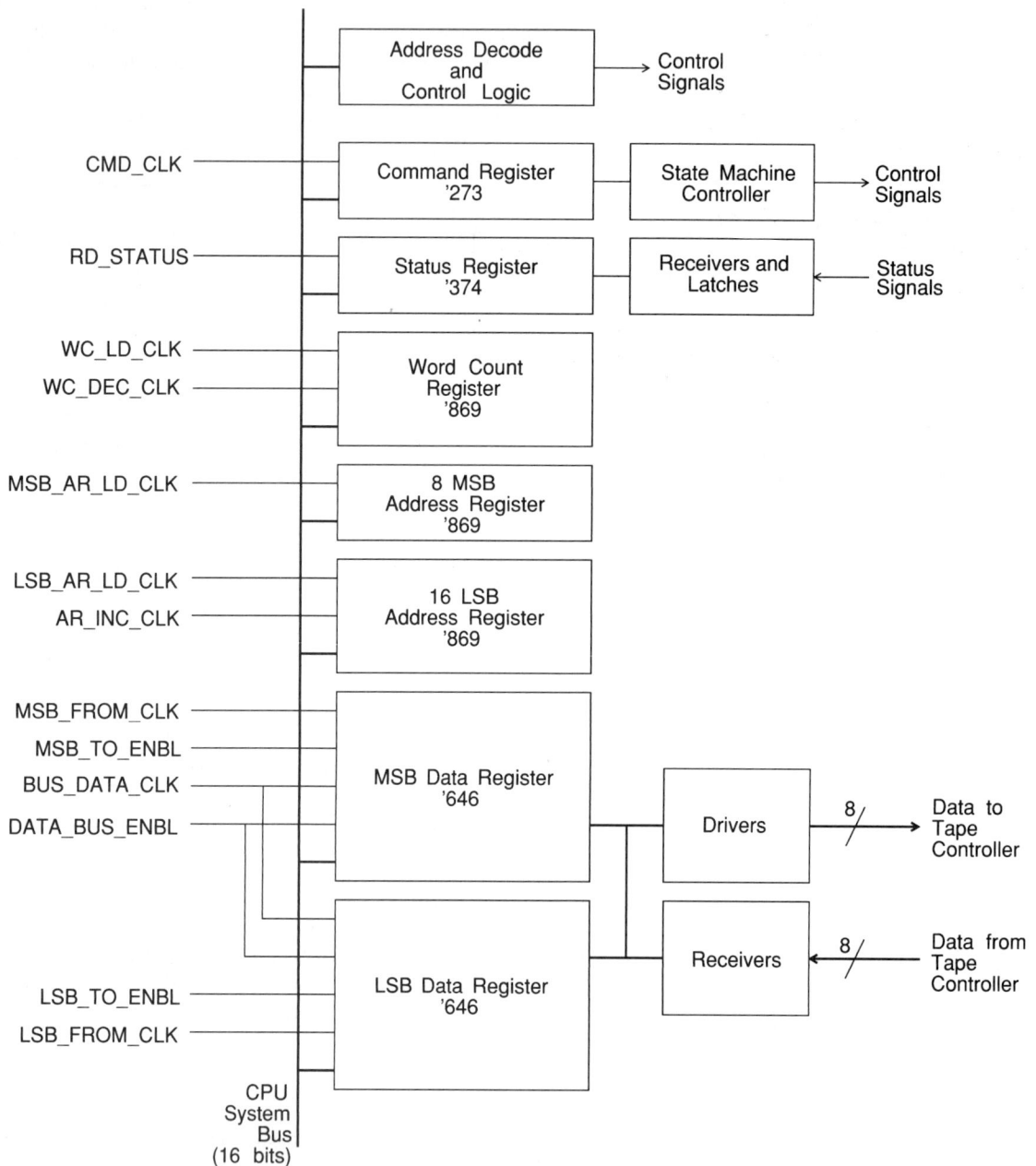

Figure 6.16. Data Path Block Diagram for Tape Recorder Interface Module.

the system; these will be acted upon by the control portion of the interface module. The status register allows the CPU to investigate the current status of the system and the selected transport. The word count and address registers operate as described in Section 6.4. The registers that have not been mentioned yet are the registers used to hold the data transferred to or from the tape transport. The output registers accept a word from the bus, and then, under control of the interface module, the bytes are alternately sent to the transport. The transport itself adds parity for the ninth bit. The path from the transport to the bus is the reverse of that described above; the bytes are accepted one at a time, then the 16-bit word is sent to the bus. If it is desirable to be able to transfer an odd number of bytes, then the interface module becomes correspondingly more complex.

Along with the initial data path, we also need a behavioral description of the interface module. We know that we want commands to cause tape movement, as well as commands for reading and writing. We will design a system capable of selecting one of the transports, and on the selected transport performing one of the following commands:

- *Read forward (R):* Tape motion is initiated by the tape controller to read data. Before this command is issued, it is imperative that the interface module be initialized with a word count indicating the number of words to transfer, and an address where the data is to be located. Data delivered from the tape controller will be placed into memory by the interface module. After the block of data has been read from the tape, the number of words read is compared to the number of words expected; if they differ, an error bit is set in the status word.

- *Write forward (W):* Tape motion is initiated by the controller, with controls configured for a write. Again, it is imperative that the word count and address registers have been properly initialized for the required transfer. DMA transfers are performed by the interface module, and the data delivered to the controller. When the word count reaches zero, the action is stopped.

- *Write file mark (WFM):* A file mark is written onto the tape by the controller.

- *File search forward (FSF):* The word count register must be filled with a number indicating how many file marks should be skipped. The interface module issues the appropriate number of file search commands, halting when the word count has been decremented to zero.

- *File search reverse (FSR):* This command positions the tape by searching in the reverse direction. It is assumed that this request will be given (with an appropriate word count) to position the tape *after* the file mark in question. That is, if the tape is positioned in the middle of a file, an FSR command with a word count of one will back up one file mark, then read over the file mark. The net result is to position the unit at the beginning of the file. An FSR command with a word count of two will position the tape at the beginning of the file before the current position of the tape.

- *Rewind (REW):* A rewind pulse is sent to the tape controller. The net result is a rewind action on the selected drive.

- *Enable interrupt (INTE):* The interrupt capability of the interface module is enabled. This will be indicated as a bit in the status register.

- *Disable interrupt (INTD):* The interrupt capability of the interface module is disabled.

Each command involving tape movement will cause an interrupt (if the interrupt facility is enabled) when the command has been completed. In addition, the system should provide various status information about the condition and configuration of the selected tape transport.

The command required of the interface module will be supplied over the bus and loaded into the command register. The commands are not ASCII words, but rather consist of bit patterns defined in advance to identify the desired action. For this project we define the following bit patterns as instructions:

Action	Bit Pattern
Read	000100
Write	001000
Write file mark	001100
File search forward	010000
File search reverse	010100
Rewind	011000
Enable interrupt facility	100101
Disable interrupt facility	100100
Select transport (xx = 0,1,2,3)	1000xx

The bit patterns identify the six LSBs of the word; the other bits are not tested in the system. Note that a pattern of all zeros is not a legal instruction. Also, the actions that do not require tape movement (transport select, interrupt enable, interrupt disable) all have a 1 in the sixth position. This will simplify some of the hardware of the system. The bit patterns used to specify the action of machine interface modules should have some correlation between the defined patterns and the hardware requirements of the interface modules. This is just one of the many examples where communication between users of computers (programmers, systems personnel, etc.) and builders of computers should communicate requirements and preferences.

The above commands are given to the interface module by writing the appropriate bit pattern to the command register. The status of the tape drive is obtained by reading the status register. This information is obtained from the signal lines identified in Table 6.2. Other signals are available, but this set will be sufficient to demonstrate the elements of our design. From those signals, as well as from signals generated by the control of the interface module, we will configure a status register as follows:

15	14	13	12	11	10	9	8	7	6	5	4	3	2	1	0
BSY	SMB	ERR			INTE	RDW	WRP	PE	BOT	EOT	EOF		Trans		

The bits are defined as follows:

- BSY: Busy bit, derived directly form the TAPE_READY signal from the tape controller.
- SMB: State machine busy, indicates when the controller of the interface module is not in the idle state.
- ERR: Record length error, which will occur when the number of words read from a block on the tape does not agree with the expected number.
- INTE: Interrupt enable bit, which is a 1 when the interrupt facility of the interface module has been enabled.
- RDW: Rewinding, set when the selected transport is in the process of rewinding.
- WRP: Write protect, which is a 1 when the selected transport does not detect the presense of a write ring on the tape.
- PE: Parity error, which is set when the last operation detected a parity error.
- BOT: Beginning of tape, indicates that the tape is located at the beginning of tape marker.

- EOT: End of tape, indicates that the tape is located at the end of tape marker.
- Trans: These 4 bits indicate which of the four transports will be controlled by the interface module.

Reading the status causes these values to be loaded into a register, so that if they should change while the instruction is being executed that change will not cause problems with the instruction itself.

The list of commands for the tape system does not have a direct correspondence with the signal lines given for the tape controller. Thus, the designer must identify the desired action and assert the control lines accordingly. For the controller used here, the functions identified above are obtained by asserting the lines according to the following table:

	Read	Write	Write File Mark	File Search Forward	File Search Reverse	Rewind
SETX-L	X	X	X	X	X	
WRITE-L		X	X			
READ-L	X			X	X	
FILESRCHF-L				X		
FILESRCHR-L					X	
SYNCFWD-L	X	X	X	X		
SYNCRVS-L					X	
WRITEFM-L			X			
REWIND-L						X

Note that the SETX line is to be asserted for all motion commands, except rewind, which requires a pulse on only the REWIND line. The INPUTX and OUTPUTX signals are pulses that activate the data transfers; that is, when the tape controller needs (or has) data for transfer, it will request this information. The interface module must respond by providing (or accepting) data on the byte-wide set of data lines to the tape drive and asserting OUTPUTX (or INPUTX). All of the other lines can be levels, and our design will treat them as such.

The interface module must be electrically compatible with both the bus with which it is working and with the tape controller. The UNIBUS requires specific set of interface chips that provide a minimal load on the bus; sample gates used by the interface module are shown in Figure 6.17(a). The assertion level on the bus is low, and these chips convert from the high assertion levels used in the interface module to the low assertion levels used on the bus. Other bus systems may use standard tri-state devices, or have other requirements, but the design process must adhere to the specification of the bus. We will not include all of the individual gates in the drawings shown in this section, but we will assume that these gates are used to match the electrical requirements needed by the signals. The drawings in this section will include the major blocks and some of the control signals involved. A more complete set of schematics can be found in Appendix B.

The tape controller also has a specification for driving and receiving the control, status, and data lines. This specifically calls for open collector drivers for the signal lines going to the controller, and resistor networks (220Ω to +5, 330Ω to ground) on the signals arriving from the controller. The effective impedance of this combination (220Ω in parallel with 330Ω) is about 130Ω, which is a

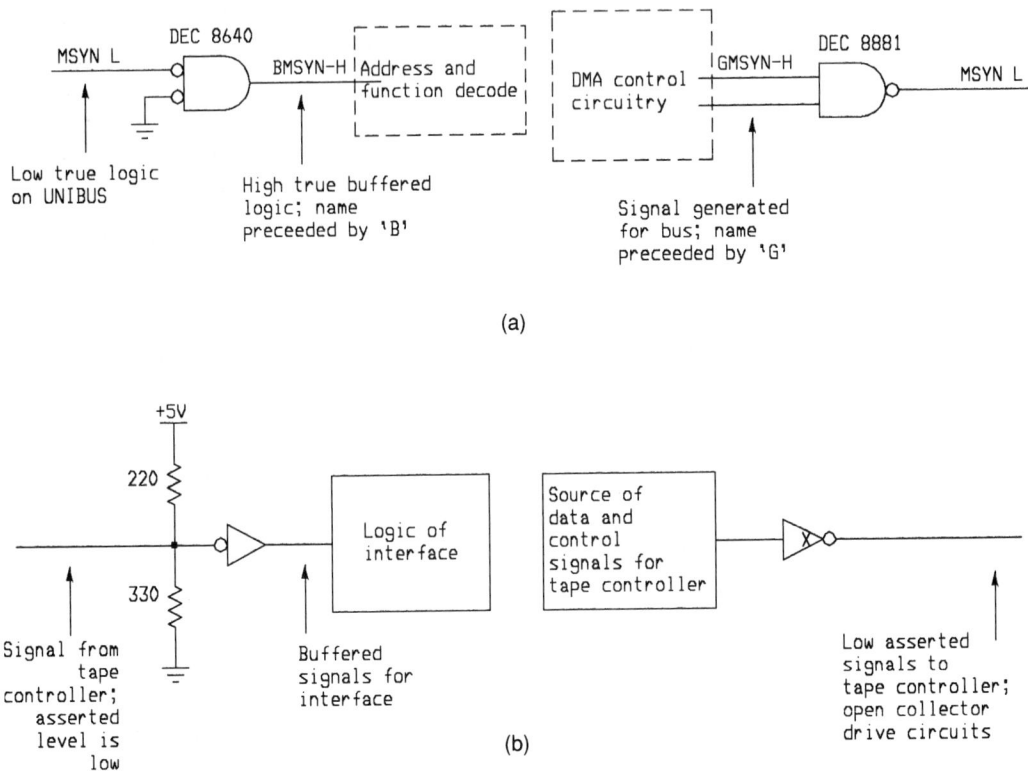

Figure 6.17. Interface Gates Used for Bus, Controller.

reasonable match for many signal transmission mechanisms. For this reason, it has been used for many years as the method for terminating signals, as shown in Figure 6.17(b).

The diagrams for the interface module are included as Figure 6.18, and we will describe the various sections and their responsibilities. The address decode and programmed I/O control signals are found in Figure 6.18(a). Gates have been provided to minimize the load presented to the address bus, and the buffered lines are labeled BADDR. These lines are used to compare the address against an addressed set up by the user. This mechanism allows the address to be determined at installation time rather than design time. The UNIBUS uses only 18 address lines, so the other lines indicated in the figure are superfluous; however, other bus systems use up to 32 bits in the address. The least significant address lines and buffered control lines from the bus are used to create signals used in the interface module. These signals allow the sequentiality of the bus protocol to provide the timing necessary to read and write registers under programmed I/O control. The request line for the UNIBUS is called MSYN, and its buffered version is shown in Figure 6.18(a). The acknowledge is identified as SSYN, and it is shown before being sent to the bus with the required bus matching gates.

Also included in Figure 6.18(a) is the command register. The action of filling the command register also sets a flag (ACTFG), which will be tested by the state machine that directs the interaction with the tape controller. The contents of the command register and the activity flag are inputs to a second register, which is labeled the buffered command register. This register, which is clocked whenever the system is in an idle state, has two purposes. The first is to synchronize the

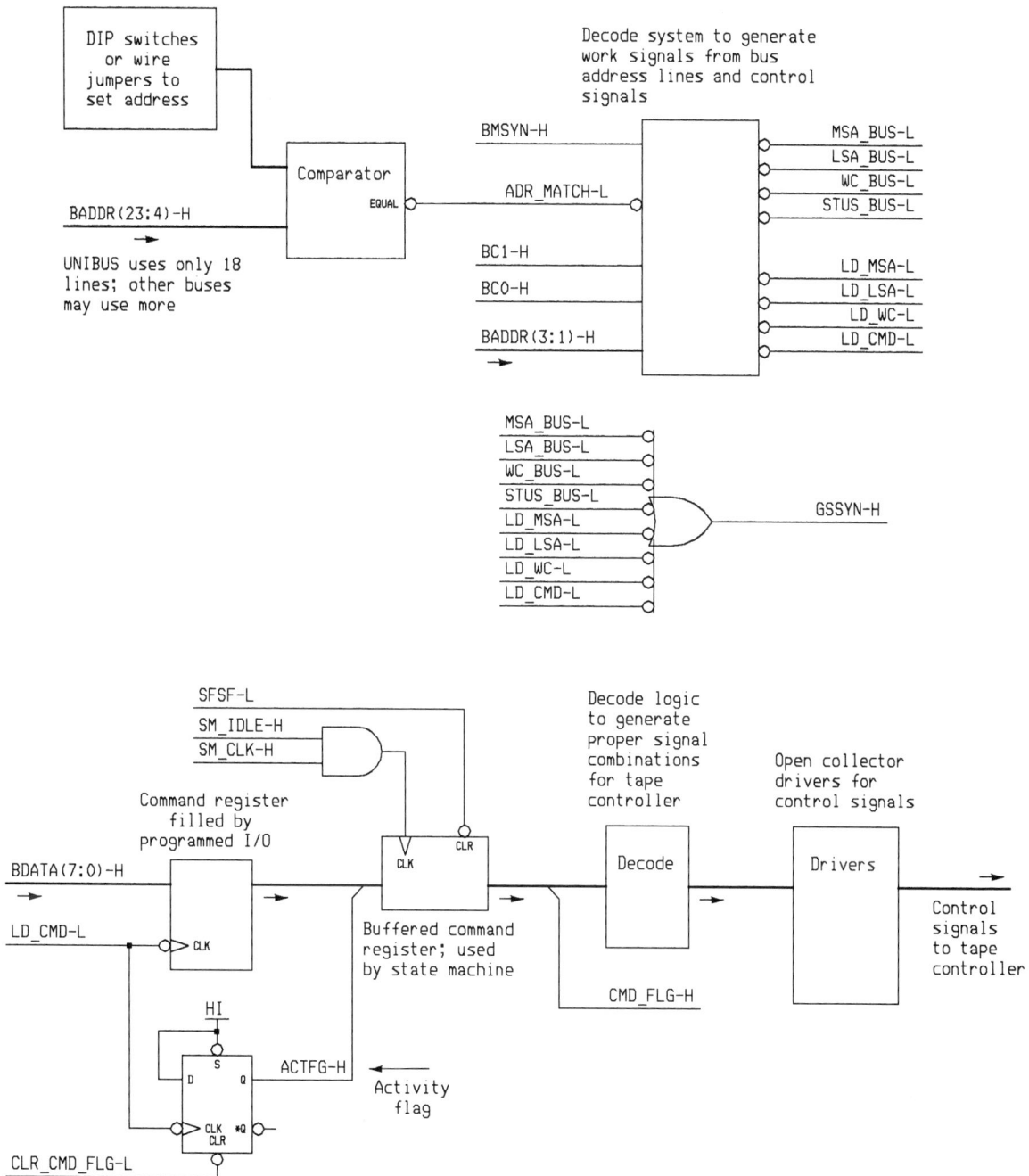

Figure 6.18(a). Programmed I/O Control and Command Registers.

filling of the command register with the clock of the state machine system. Without this mechanism the system would fail when the contents of the command register changed during the sensitive time before the active edge of the state machine clock. The second reason for the second register is to prevent any change in the command register from affecting a function in progress. The contents of the buffered command register are decoded and the appropriate control lines asserted to the tape controller. The commands and levels will be determined by this logic; the required pulses will be generated by the state machine.

The word count register and the address register are found in Figure 6.18(b). These registers must act as registers to be filled by programmed I/O instructions, and as counters to be decremented when under the control of the state machine. This is accomplished by using two clocking sources. When the state machine is idle, SM_IDLE will be asserted, and the clock is derived from the programmed I/O signals. However, when the state machine is not idle, the registers are decremented by a signal from the state machine itself (WC_DEC-L). One feature of the system that will not be used in the normal action of transfers is the ability to read the contents of the word count register. This is provided by the tri-state drivers included with the word count and address registers; when the appropriate enable

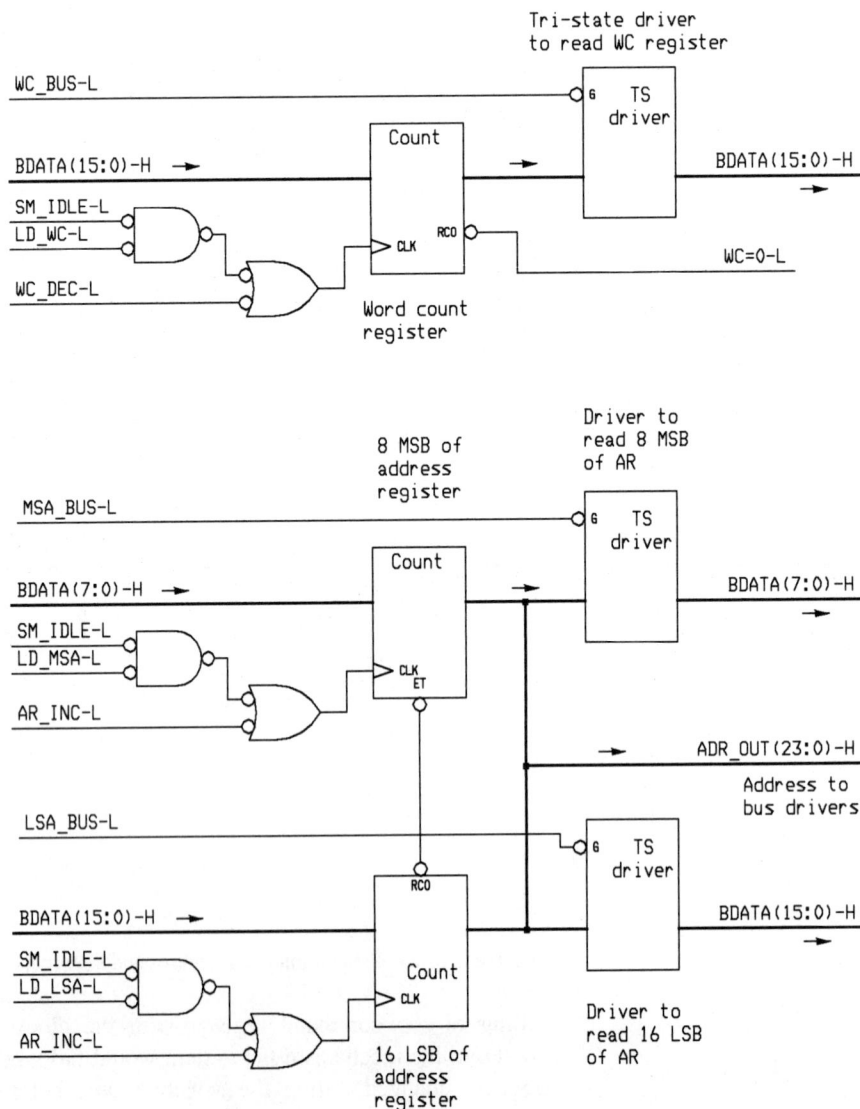

Figure 6.18(b). Word Count Register and Address Register.

Chap. 6: Input and Output Operations

signal is asserted, the information is enabled onto the internal data bus (BDATA) and then to the UNIBUS.

The data path is included in Figure 6.18(c). The path to and from the bus is provided by a pair of bidirectional registers. These devices contain two registers, one for each direction. During a write operation, information from the bus is obtained 16 bits at a time, and loaded into the register by a signal derived from the request line (DMA_OUT_CLK). This information is then fed one byte at a time to the controller, using the TAPE_DATA lines. The selection of the byte to send to the controller is handled by the enable lines (LSB_ENBL, MSB_ENBL), which are alternately enabled during a write operation. The timing signals for loading and reading the registers are generated using control signals from the tape unit and the state machine.

During a read operation, the data path is reversed. The register in the reverse direction is loaded by a signal derived from the control lines of the tape controller (TAPE_MSB, TAPE_LSB). The resulting values are enabled onto the internal data bus when needed during the DMA operation. As noted earlier, the data lines to the controller are asserted with open collector drivers, and the lines from the controller are received with resister networks. The state machine controller is responsible for asserting the appropriate information onto the TAPE_DATA lines, from one of the DMA output registers or the data in lines.

The status register is also included in Figure 6.18(c). This register monitors signals from the tape controller and from latches internal to the interface module itself, such as the interrupt enable bit. When a programmed I/O instruction requests this information, it is loaded into a register to keep it stable during the read operation. The register has tri-state outputs that directly connect to the internal data bus. This status information will be enabled onto the UNIBUS at the appropriate time by the DMA system.

The logic for controlling the interface module is shown in Figure 6.18(d). There are two state machines in this implementation. The first is for the action of the interface module itself, the second is for the DMA controller. The controller specification calls for command pulses which are a minimum of 200 nsec. For that reason, the state machine controlling the action of the interface module is clocked at 5 MHz, which provides a 200 nsec state time. We will describe the state diagrams for the system later in this section. The state machine used to control the interface module is constructed from two registered PROMs, each of which contains 2,048 words of 8 bits. This requires 11 bits of address. Five of the 11 bits are provided by the present state of the system; the remaining 6 bits are derived from the inputs to the system. Since more than 6 inputs are required to control the state machine, the 6 used at any one time are selected with a multiplexer network. The outputs of the registered PROMs provide the needed control and state information. The two devices together have 16 outputs; five of these are used for present state information, and 11 are used for control signals.

The state machine which is used for DMA and interrupt requests is also included in Figure 6.18(d). This consists of two parts: a synchronizing register and a registered PAL. These parts need to be capable of fairly high speed, since the cycle time for the unit is 50 nsec. The function of the DMA controller is to control the interaction with the bus for direct access to memory. The outputs of the PAL drive both the bus signals and the internal registers involved in the DMA transactions. Also included with the control circuitry are some flags that handle communication between the two state machines, and a timer used to create a rewind signal that is longer than 2 μsec.

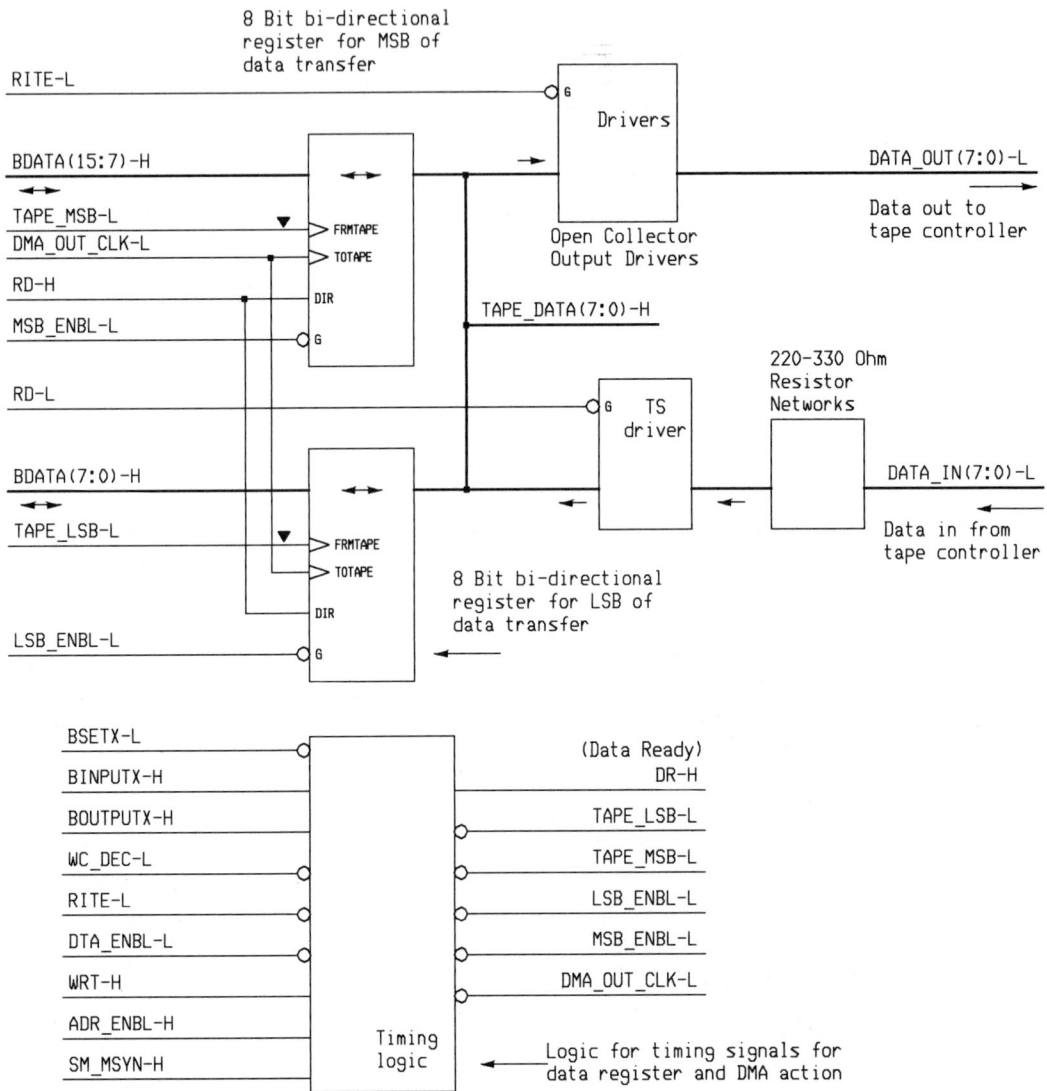

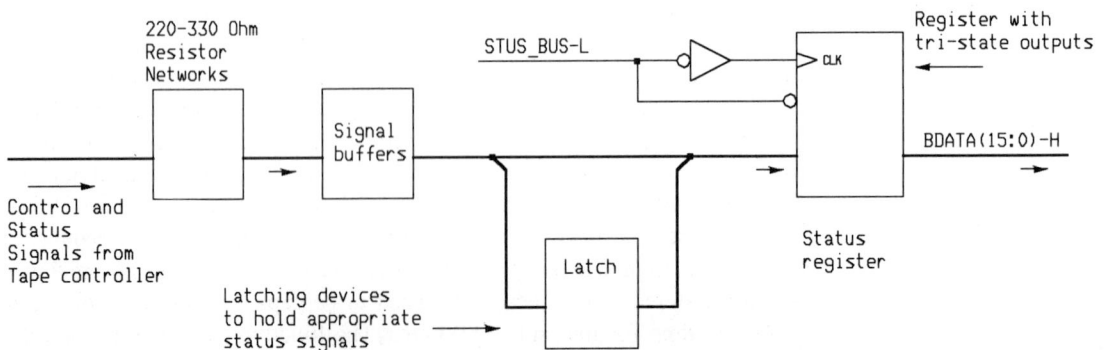

Figure 6.18(c). Data Path to and from Tape Controller and Status Register.

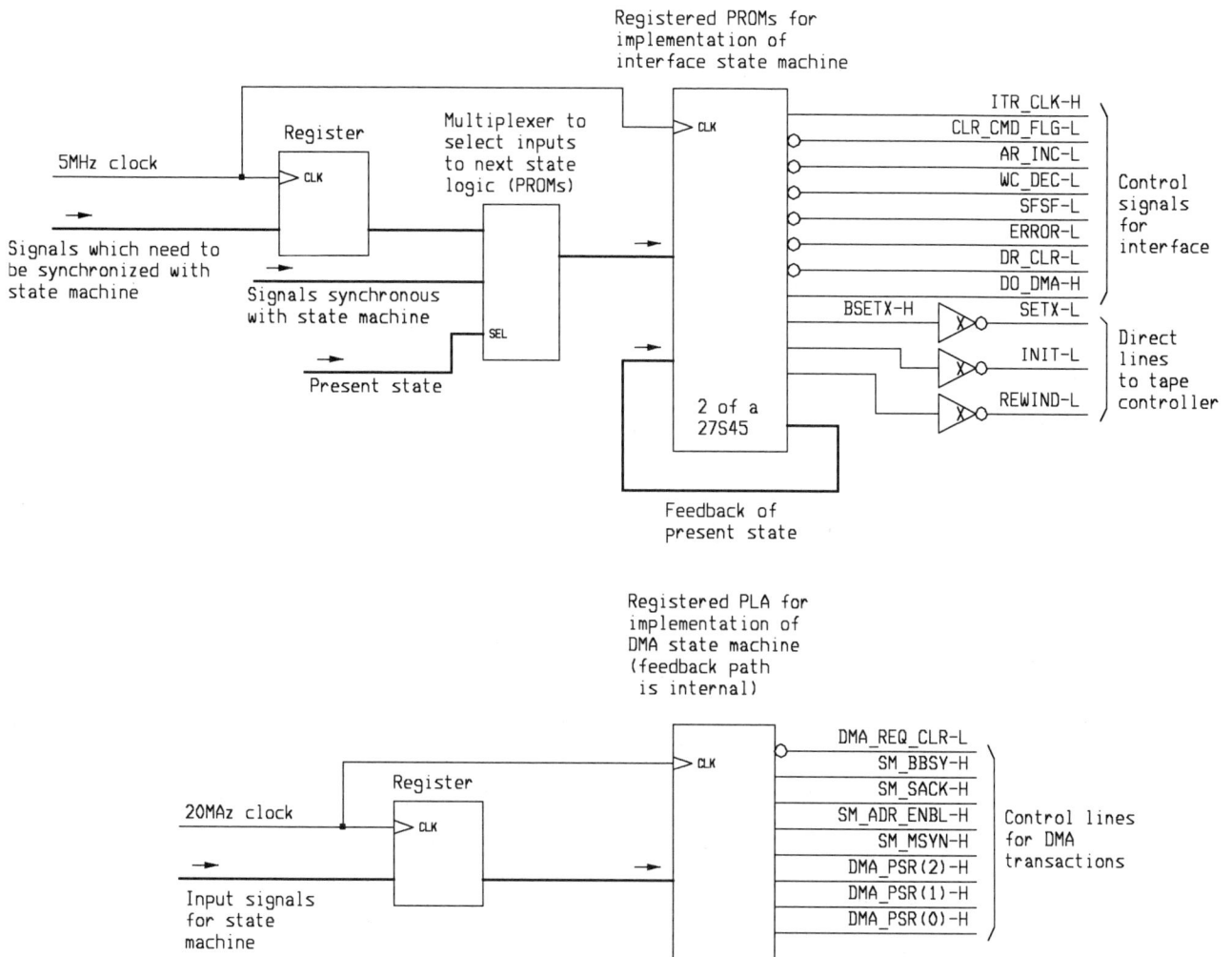

Figure 6.18(d). State Machine Controllers.

The last of the diagrams, Figure 6.18(e), contains the logic needed to connect to the bus, with the requisite gates matching the bus requirements. The address and data buses are provided with both receivers and drivers to present a minimal load to the bus as required by the bus specification. The interrupt vector address can be specified by the user, and the interface module will assert this information onto the bus at the appropriate time.

The action of the interface module is described by the state diagrams included as Figure 6.19. As mentioned above, the minimum time for the tape controller is 200 nsec, whereas the UNIBUS will be most effectively used if the state times are much less than 200 nsec. Thus, the state time for the controller of the interface module itself is 200 nsec, while the DMA controller operates with a 50 nsec clock. It would be possible to combine the two state machines, but that would result in a much larger system. Hence, the decision was made to use two different state machines.

Figure 6.19(a) deals with the behavior of the interface module itself. The states used to perform the work of directing the tape controller are identified, and the signals that need to be asserted are identified in each state. A description of

UNIBUS uses only 18 address (A)
lines; other interfaces will use
more address lines. Unused lines in this
interface need to be disabled.

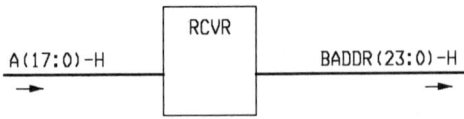

The address is supplied
to the address bus only
when needed by a DMA
transfer

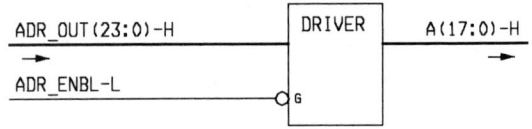

```
A(17:0)-H ──►       ┌──────┐
                    │ RCVR │ ──► BADDR(23:0)-H ──►
                    └──────┘
```

```
ADR_OUT(23:0)-H ──►      ┌────────┐
                        │ DRIVER │ ──► A(17:0)-H ──►
ADR_ENBL-L ───────────o G└────────┘
```

UNIBUS enabled to internal
data bus only when address matches
and writing to register

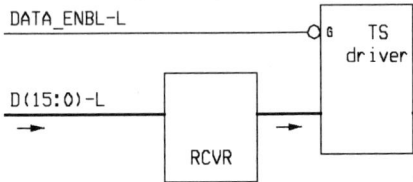

DATA_ENBL-L ──────────────o G ┌──────┐
                              │ TS │
                              │driver│

BDATA provides
bidirectional
internal data bus

The data lines of the UNIBUS
are driven only when a data
word or vector information
is needed

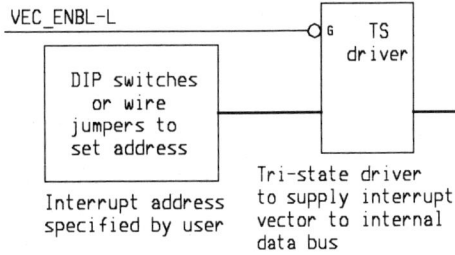

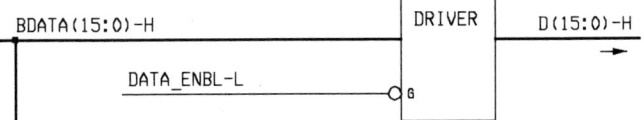

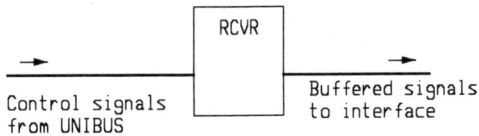

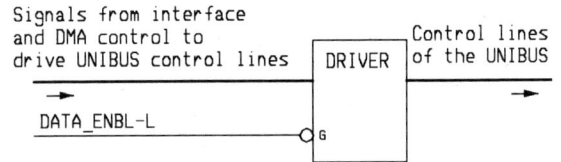

```
D(15:0)-L ──►  ┌──────┐
               │ RCVR │
               └──────┘
```

BDATA(15:0)-H

```
                    ┌────────┐
                    │ DRIVER │ ──► D(15:0)-H ──►
DATA_ENBL-L ──────o G└────────┘
```

VEC_ENBL-L ──────────o G ┌──────┐
                         │ TS │
                         │driver│

┌──────────────┐
│ DIP switches │
│   or wire   │
│ jumpers to │
│ set address │
└──────────────┘

Interrupt address
specified by user

Tri-state driver
to supply interrupt
vector to internal
data bus

Signals from interface
and DMA control to
drive UNIBUS control lines

```
              ┌────────┐ Control lines
              │ DRIVER │ of the UNIBUS
        ──►   └────────┘      ──►
DATA_ENBL-L ──────o G
```

```
        ──►  ┌──────┐   ──►
             │ RCVR │
             └──────┘
Control signals      Buffered signals
from UNIBUS          to interface
```

Figure 6.18(e). Circuitry for Bus Interaction.

the purpose of each state is included in Appendix B; here we will briefly describe
some of the action generated by the state machine.

The interface module is initialized by forcing the present state to zero, since
that is a relatively easy thing to do with the present state register. This is used to
initialize both the electronics of the interface module and the tape controller.
Once the initialization has occurred, the interface moves to the idle state, where it
will await further direction.

If the instruction which is received by the interface module does not require
tape movement, then State 3 is visited. This causes the appropriate information to
be clocked into the retaining registers and the action flag to be cleared; then the
system returns to the idle state.

If a command that requires tape movement is received, then the system
moves to State 4. If a rewind is required, then the system moves to State 20 to
issue a long enough pulse, then to State 23 to await then completion of the tape
movement. If a write file mark (WFM) command is desired, the system moves to
State 6 to create the SETX pulse, then to State 23 to await the completion of the
tape movement. Note that the appropriate command lines to the tape controller

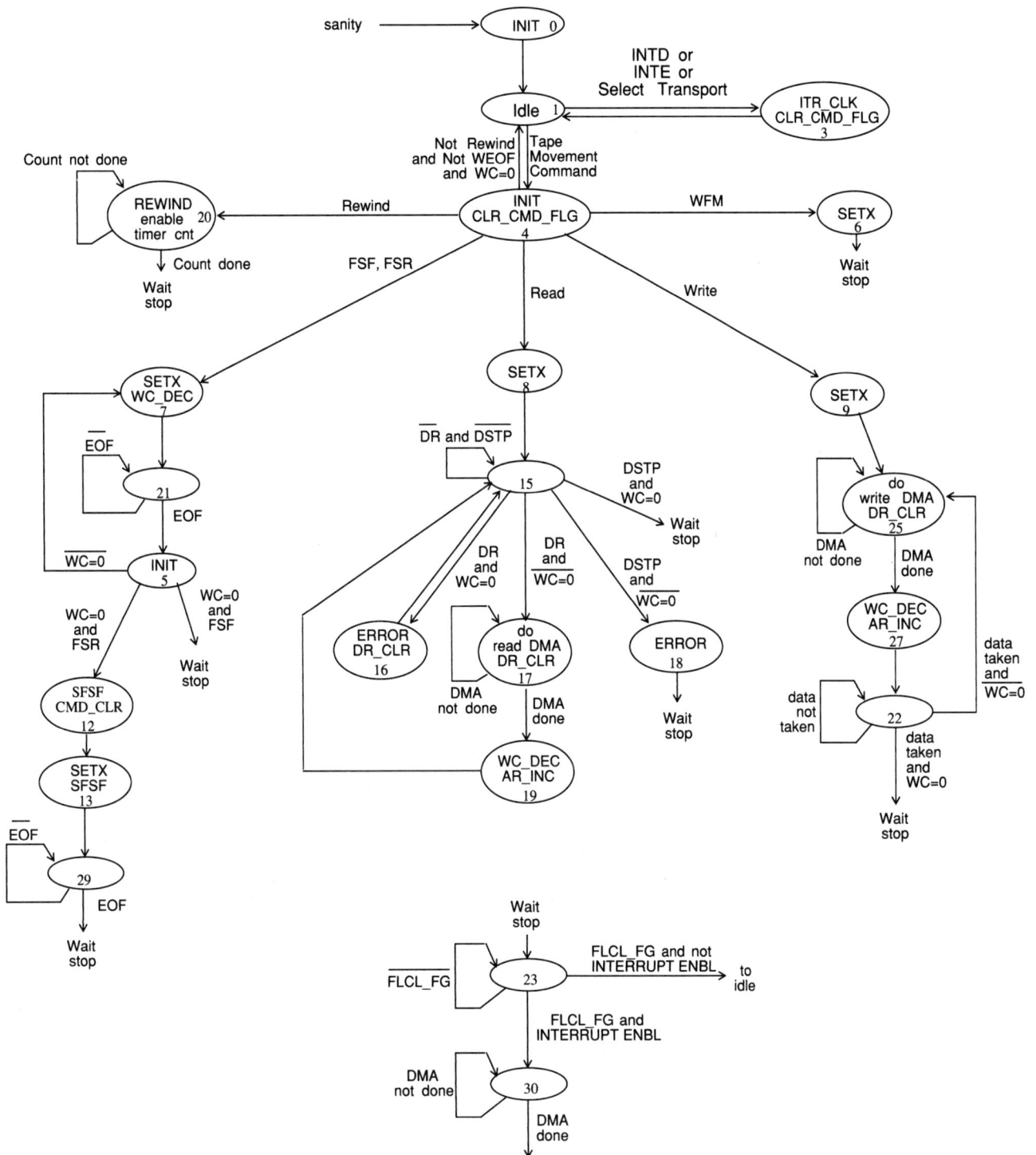

Figure 6.19(a). State Diagram for Tape Controller Interface Module.

are generated by the logic associated with the command register, and that the state machine is used only to create the pulses needed.

The remaining commands are file search forward (FSF), file search reverse (FSR), read, and write. All of these commands require a nonzero word count register, so if that condition does not exist in State 4, the state machine returns immediately to the idle state. If, however, the word count register is nonzero, then the action can begin.

The file search commands assert the SETX pulse, decrement the word count, and then wait for the controller to indicate that it has seen an end of file mark (EOF). This is repeated until the word count register is equal to zero. If the specified action was a FSF command, then the desired movement is complete, and the action of the interface module moves to state 23 to wait for the tape movement to stop. If the specified action was a FSR command, then the state machine causes one more file search command, this one in the forward direction. This action leaves the tape at the beginning of a file, rather than at the end of a file.

The write command starts the tape movement and then requests that the DMA state machine perform a DMA transfer to get the information to write onto the tape. Then the address register is incremented and the word count is decremented, and the interface module waits for the controller to take the data. The activity of the data path, while the controller takes the data, is coordinated by pulses from the controller itself, rather than from the tape machine. This maintains synchronization between the devices in the data path and the tape controller. When the information has been taken by the tape controller, the interface module checks to see if more information is needed (is WC equal to zero?). If the transfer is complete, the interface module waits for the tape movement to stop.

The action of the read command is initiated by the SETX pulse, then the interface module waits until data is ready. This condition will exist when the controller has extracted 2 bytes from the tape and placed them into the two registers on the data path. When this has occurred, then a flag is set (data ready, DR) and the appropriate action can be requested by the interface module. If the word count has not reached zero, then a DMA transfer is requested to place the information into memory. This also results in decrementing the word count and incrementing the address register. However, if the word count register has reached zero, then more data is being extracted from the tape than expected. The result here is to *not* write the information into memory; rather, an error flag is set and the data ignored. When the read action is completed, the controller will send a stop indication (DSTP). If the word count register has not reached zero at this time, then fewer words than expected were received from the tape, and this also causes the error flag to be set.

The final portion of the state machine of the interface module is used to wait for the controller to signal the completion of the tape movement, which is indicated by the FLCL_FG flag. At that time, an interrupt is requested if the interrupt flag is set in the status register. The final action of the state machine is to return to the idle state to await the next instruction from the CPU.

The interaction between the two state machines is handled with a simple flag arrangement, and when a DMA interaction is needed, the DMA_REQ flag is set. The DMA state machine is then enabled to direct the interaction with the UNIBUS. This interaction is shown in Figure 6.19(b).

The DMA state machine remains in the idle state until a DMA transfer is required. It then asserts the bus request signal (BR) to gain access to the bus. When the arbitration system grants access, then the SACK signal is asserted, and

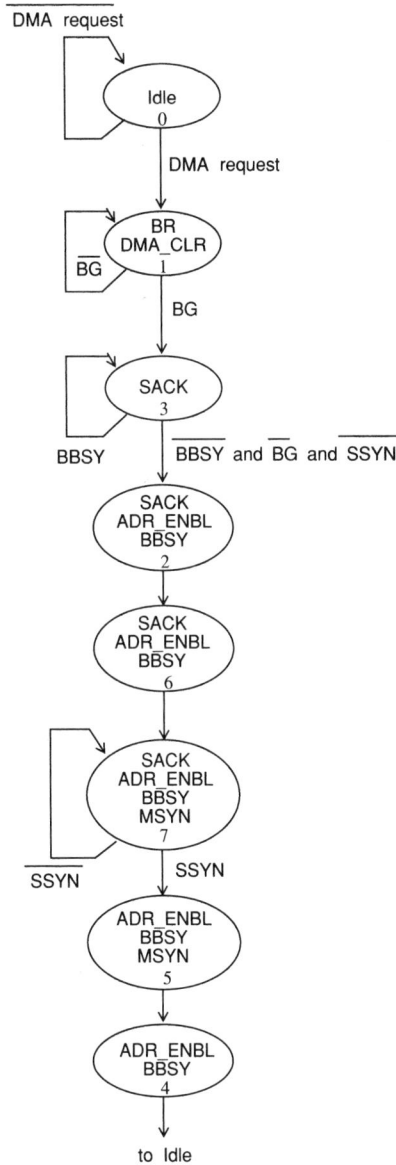

Figure 6.19(b). State Diagram for
DMA Bus Interaction.

the state machine waits for the previous bus transfer to complete. When this condition is detected, then the transfer is performed: the address is enabled onto the address lines (States 2, 6), the request line is asserted (MSYN), and the system waits for the acknowledge line to be asserted in response (SSYN). When the acknowledge is detected, the DMA state machine returns to the idle state releasing the asserted signals in the appropriate order. Also, the return to the idle state sets a flag that is detected by the state machine of the interface module to indicate that the requested transfer is complete.

If the action is an interrupt sequence rather than a data transfer, then the same action is needed, but not all of the same signals are used. Thus, the appropriate control of the gates and tranceivers in Figure 6.18(e) allows interrupt and DMA transfers to be controlled by the DMA sequencer. For example, the request signal (MSYN) is not used for the interrupt sequence, and hence the bus driver for that signal is disabled during that operation.

The interface module presented here is a relatively straightforward implementation that utilizes the concepts of bus interaction and sequential circuits. The system can be made much more complex in its interaction by including additional instructions and expanding the state diagram. For example, the controller has the capability to read and write when the tape motion is in reverse. This ability can be harnessed by including appropriate instructions in the definition of the interface system, and then including appropriate action definitions in the state machine. Other action, such as block searchs and unloading the tape, are also possible with a more complex system.

This interface system is an example of the application of the techniques discussed in earlier portions of this book. The details of the interface module were determined by a thorough examination of all of the applicable information. The electrical requirements and protocol specifications of the bus used in the system were determined. Also, the electrical requirements and protocol specifications of the tape controller were determined. And the specific action of the programmed I/O instructions of the system was determined. Once this information had been obtained, then a data path block diagram of the system could be generated, and the design of the control system performed. The design required combinational techniques to create many of the signals and conditions that were not tied to the pulses generated by the state machine. Combinational circuits were also applicable in those areas where the sequentiality of action was determined by other systems, such as filling registers from the bus. Finally, the sequential action of the interface module was defined by state machines and implemented with simple programmable logic devices.

6.6. VLSI Devices for Interface Systems

The example of Section 6.5 included individual TTL devices for every aspect of the system, from address registers to bus controller. However, newer technology has resulted in a variety of devices that place portions of an complete interface module into VLSI devices. The designer of an interface system is then required to ascertain the capabilities of the devices and apply them in a reasonable manner to the systems at hand.

The manufacturers of microprocessor systems have recognized that users of the microprocessors would almost always be desirous of interfacing the microprocessor to physical devices of one kind or another. Thus, they have provided a variety of interface devices to work with their systems. Perhaps one of the first available devices was the 8255, a block diagram of which is shown in Figure 6.20. This device was created to work with the Intel 8080, and has been used not only in 8080 systems, but many other types of systems as well. This device contains logic sufficient for 24 bidirectional lines. The control logic internal to the 8255 specifies the mode of operation for the external lines, whether they are inputs or outputs, and when to accept (supply) the information from (to) the bus. The bidirectional data bus lines allow the device to connect directly to buses of a microprocessor system, as shown in Figure 6.21. If the data bus of the microprocessor system is 8 bits wide, then the 8255s are accessed one at a time. If the data

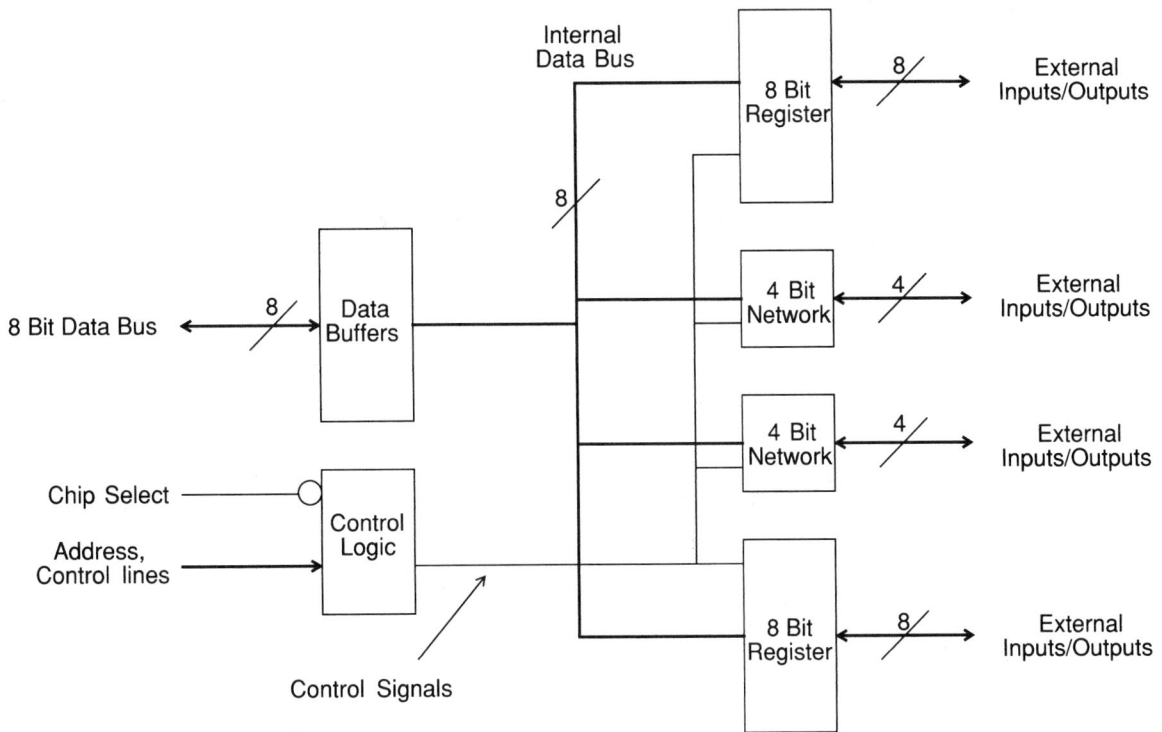

Figure 6.20. Block Diagram of the 8255.

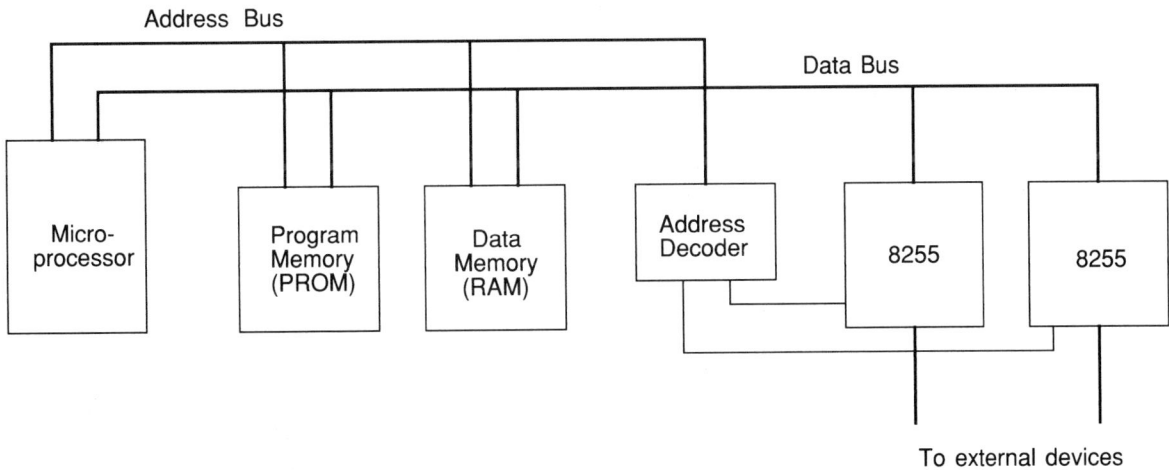

Figure 6.21. Microprocessor System with 8255 Interface Chips.

bus of the system is 16 bits wide, then both 8255s can be accessed simultaneously. Or, they could be byte-addressable and accessed uniquely. The versatility of the device, which allows using the device in any of three basic modes on each of the interface elements, permits configurations that fit the needs of many applications. However, the basic system matches the buses discussed here: the address decoder is responsible for identifying when the devices are to be accessed, and the other timing signals control the actual transfers.

One of the functions that is a prime candidate for inclusion in a single integrated circuit is the circuitry required for a DMA operation. Many manufacturers provide controllers for different types of microprocessor systems. A block diagram of the Signetics SBC68438 is shown in Figure 6.22. As indicated in the figure, the chip contains all of the logic needed to perform the DMA operations with a 68000 system bus. This includes registers for storing the word count and the address, as well as interrupt logic, daisy chain priority logic, and isolation gates for the data and address buses. The data bus is also connected to the device controlled by the SCB68430, so that when the DMA controller directs the peripheral device to do so, the data is directed to or extracted from the data bus. Thus, the connection between the DMA controller and the peripheral device allows the peripheral to signal the DMA controller when a bus transfer is needed, and the controller to indicate to the peripheral when the data transfer should take place.

The DMA controller can be used with any peripheral that needs to perform high speed transfers with a 68000 system. Such a system configuration is shown in Figure 6.23. A DMA peripheral device, such as the tape controller of the previous section, is connected to the data bus for transfers of data, and to the SCB60430 to control the data transfers. In addition, the device must be controlled by the processor, and therefore a programmed I/O connection is provided.

The use of DMA controllers in microprocessor systems greatly reduces the number of integrated circuit chips required for controlling peripherals that need the DMA capability. A number of other such devices are available from other manufacturers. Among these are the 8237A from Intel, which is designed to work with 8-bit buses and contains logic for four DMA channels. The Am9516, which is available from Advanced Micro Devices, is designed to work with 16-bit

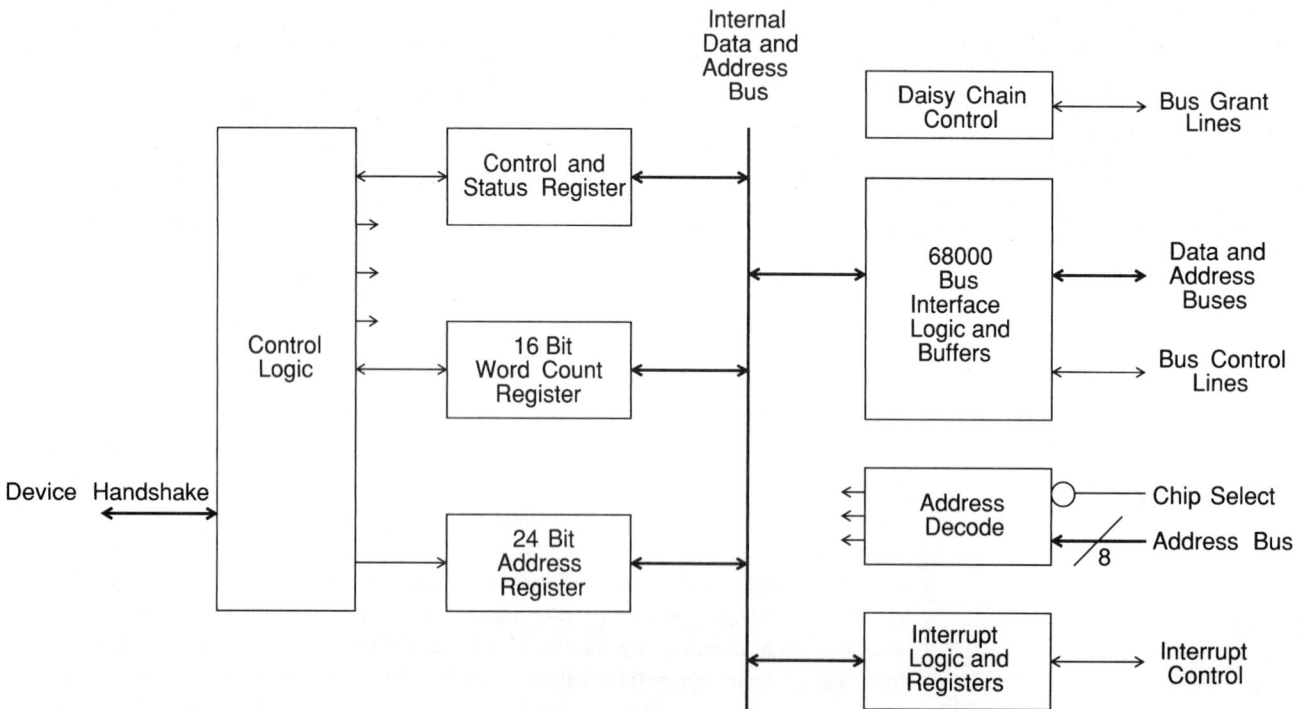

Figure 6.22. Block Diagram of the SCB68430.

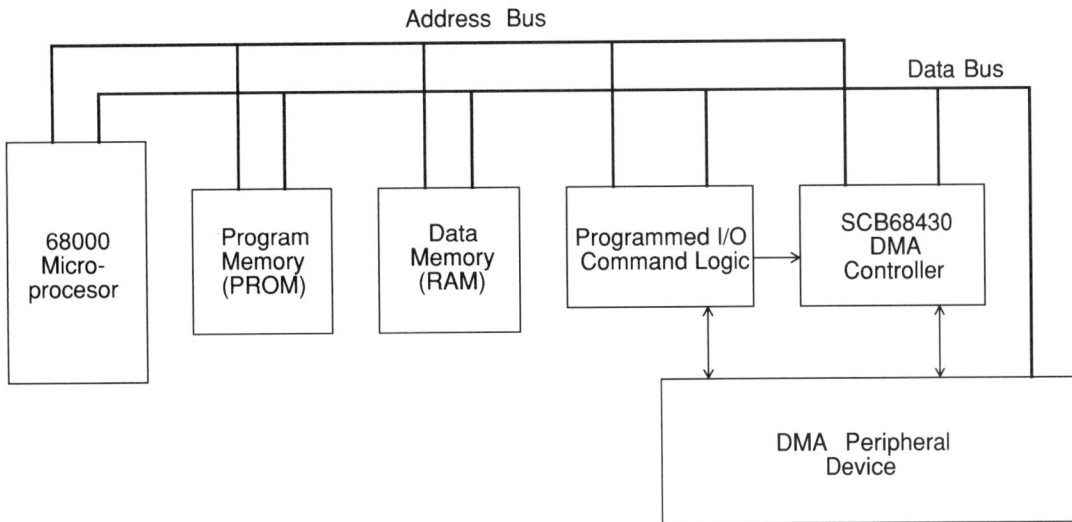

Figure 6.23. Microprocessor System with SCB68430 DMA Controller.

microprocessors, and contains two separate DMA channels. And the NS32203 from National Semiconductor is designed to work with the time multiplexed 32032 bus system, and it contains logic and registers for four separate DMA channels. In each case, the integrated circuit contains a great deal of logic to control the bus transfers needed for DMA action, but the user is required to provide the programmed I/O commands needed to control the action of the DMA peripheral.

Additional capabilities can be added to integrated circuits to further reduce the number of chips required to do particular functions. One such example is the DP8466 Disk Data Controller (DDC) from National Semiconductor Corporation. The DDC not only contains the logic needed for DMA operation, but also the logic for providing most of the interface functions to the data stream of a disk system. A basic block diagram of the device is shown in Figure 6.24. Internal to the device are registers that control the DMA action (word count, address, etc), and also registers that control the activity of the serial data stream. In this manner, different types of disk interface specifications can be handled by the same type of device. The bus connection presents a tri-state interface to the system for transfer of both data and address information. And the bus timing circuits allow transfers into the device (e.g., programmed I/O set up of registers) as well as out of the device. The FIFO permits storing of up to 32 bytes of information in the system. This allows data transfers to be performed in a burst mode: once control of the bus is obtained, data can be rapidly transferred to/from memory. The remaining logic is used to perform the functions needed to convert between the serial formats used on a disk and the parallel format of the computer system.

The DDC not only has the ability to encode and decode the information according to the serial protocols used in disk systems, but it also has capability for certain types of error detection and correction. As interface systems become more complex, one of the functions that must be provided is the ability to detect errors and, under the proper circumstances, correct them. We discussed simple error detection with parity codes in Chapter 2, as well as error correction with Hamming codes. Serial codes can use parity techniques, but often they also use polynomial codes to provide a different form of error capabilities. With the amount of

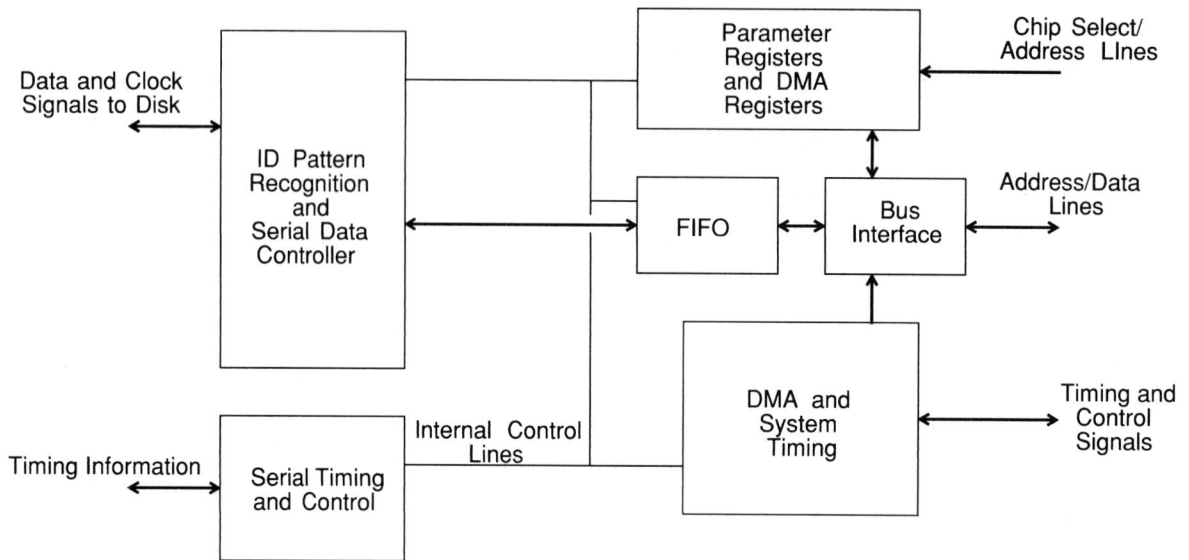

Figure 6.24. Block diagram of the DP8466.

logic available on integrated circuits, the use of these mechanisms can be included in the chips as shown by the DDC.

As with the DMA controller, the DDC can be used to control data flow in systems, but the control of the disk itself is left up to the user. Consider the block diagram shown in Figure 6.25. Much of the system is identical to the systems shown in earlier figures. The programmed I/O signals are used to control action in the DDC as well as the disk itself. The DP8466 is connected to address and data buses; some buffers, which are not shown in the figure, are required for this connection. The data and control paths to the SMD disk require differential line drivers and receivers, which minimize the effects of noise on the common data lines. For other types of interface specifications, such as the ST506, National also provides a data separator and a data synchronizer. The net effect is to have a family of integrated circuits that connect to general microprocessor bus systems and control disk systems. With this capability, a user can develop a disk system to meet a variety of needs.

We will include one final example of an integrated circuit I/O controller, which is the 7990 Local Area Network Controller for Ethernet (LANCE) of Advanced Micro Devices. Other manufacturers (Intel, National Semiconductor, etc.) have similar Ethernet devices. The LANCE chip connects to a microprocessor system in a manner similar to the other interface systems indicated in this section, as shown in Figure 6.26. The only difference here is that a second chip is required, the serial interface adapter. This chip provides the needed connection for the 7990 to connect to Ethernet systems.

Internal to the LANCE chip a number of functions are performed. A basic block diagram of the device is given in Figure 6.27. Like the other devices we have examined in this section, there is a set of isolating gates to handle the data and address lines of the bus. In addition, a number of registers are included in the system to control the action of the device. These include the normal DMA type of registers, as well as registers that control the Ethernet connection itself. However, the interaction with the memory of the LANCE is more complicated than other

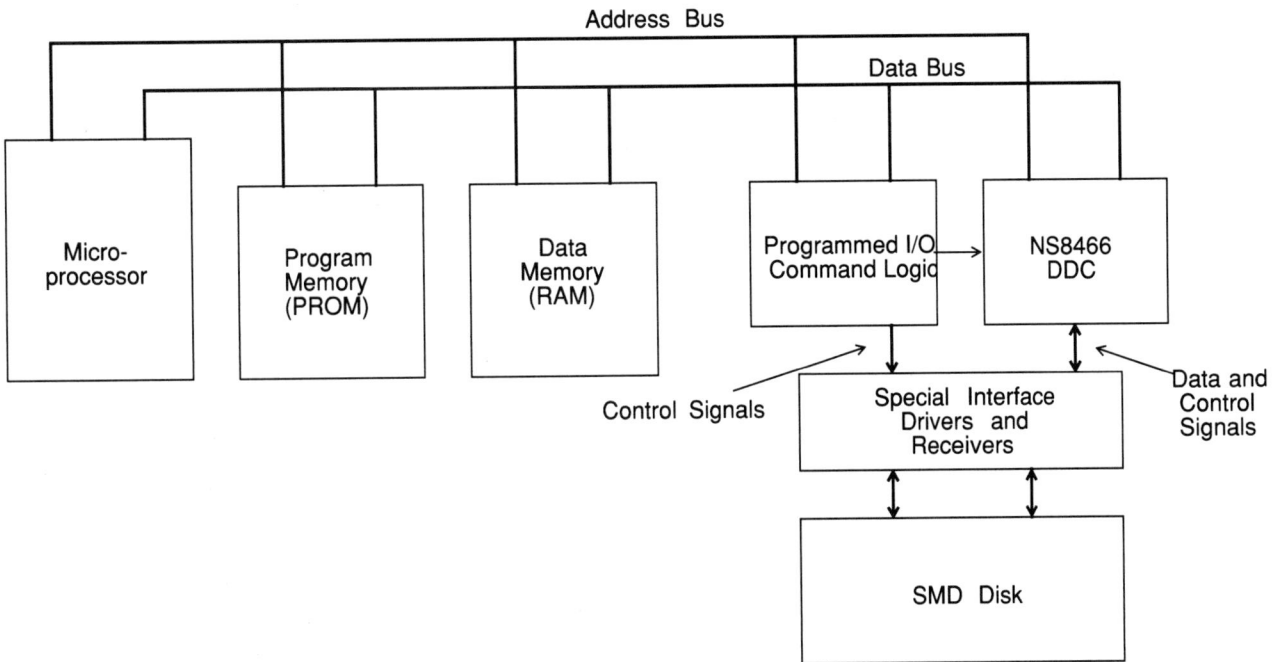

Figure 6.25. Microprocessor System with DP8466 Disk Interface.

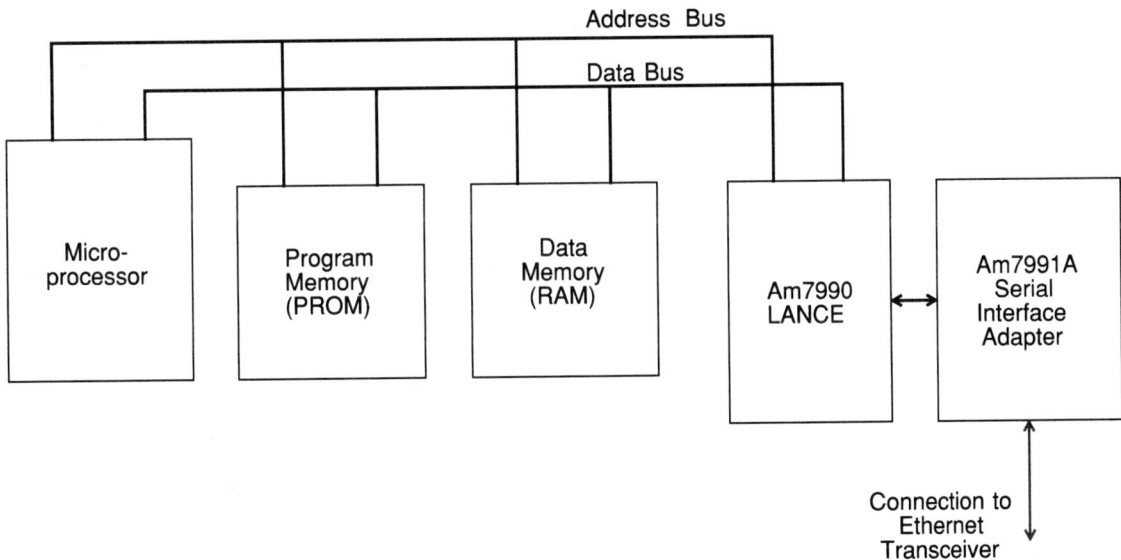

Figure 6.26. Connection of LANCE in Microprocessor System.

systems we have considered. The LANCE operates by both building and examining data structures in the memory areas of the processor. Thus, in addition to transferring data to and from memory, this unit also uses the ability to look at memory to control the activity of the Ethernet connection.

In addition to the devices described in this section, manufacturers also provide a number of other functions. These include real time clocks for keeping

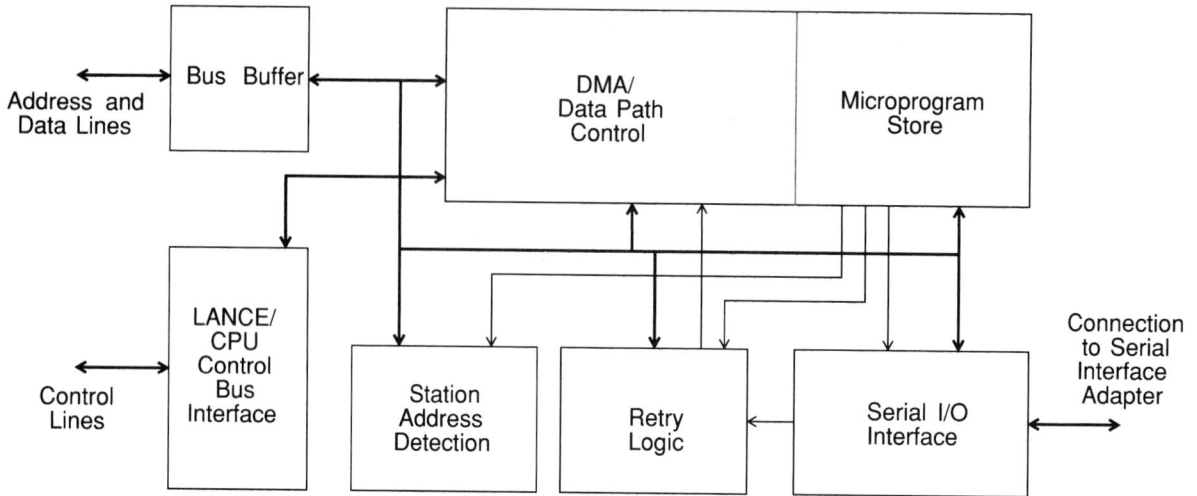

Figure 6.27. Block diagram of the Am7990.

track of the time, event timers to ascertain the time required for internal and external events, serial communications controllers, network interface systems, fiber optic interface modules, and error handling devices, to name a few. In all cases, the user must provide some programmed I/O capability to control some of the basic functions, and the interface unit handles as much of the automatic data movement as feasible. One of the challenges of system architects and designers is to use these devices in reasonable ways in useful systems.

6.7. I/O Channels and I/O Processors

The action of transferring information to and from a computer can take many forms, as we have seen. The I/O mechanisms used as examples have been limited to interaction between a processor and an I/O device connected by a common bus. Indeed, this is the normal connection mechanism for bus-oriented systems used in minicomputers, workstations, and microprocessor systems. Another method of dividing the work of the computer system is to remove from the CPU the responsibility for detailed control of I/O devices, and limit the CPU to computing and controlling. Logically, this resembles the situation depicted by Figure 6.28. The CPU operates normally, executing programs found in main store and manipulating data according to the instructions found there. However, when interaction with an I/O device is required, the CPU requests this interaction by sending a command directly to an I/O device controller. This unit is specifically designed to provide control for I/O devices, which it proceeds to do according to the instructions of the CPU. Since the I/O device controller has its own connection to main store, the data transfers occur directly to locations in memory.

The I/O device controller shown in Figure 6.28 is sometimes called a channel, and different types of channels are used in different computer systems. The channel is essentially a special purpose processing element designed to do one thing: control I/O devices. In general, the programs executed by the channel reside in main store, just as the programs executed by the CPU. The CPU indicates to the channel the work to be done by creating programs for the channel to

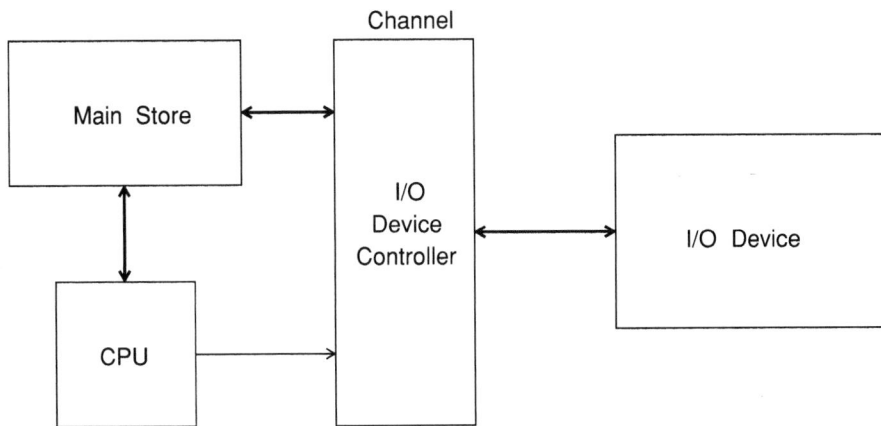

Figure 6.28. Control of I/O Devices with a Channel.

execute from the set of operations available to a channel. In some systems these I/O commands are called channel command words (CCWs). After the action is initiated by a direct command from the CPU, the channel will assert the proper signals to cause the transfer of information from the I/O device to the memory. However, the channel has more capabilities than a simple I/O interface module, such as that presented in Section 6.5. The channel may perform data conversion on data moving in the system, as well as handle error checking and correcting. Also, the channel may interrupt the CPU at any time during the transfer, if the situation requires it. Also, the CPU may request information concerning the status of the transfer at any time, and the channel will respond.

Although many different types of channels are used, channels are sometimes grouped into the classifications used by IBM. With this classification method, channels are grouped into three categories: multiplexer channels, block multiplexer channels, and selector channels. These are shown in Figure 6.29. A multiplexer channel, as its name indicates, multiplexes between a number of I/O devices. Each transfer has associated with it an I/O device address and a byte of information. Each device will have a specific address associated with it in main store, and the multiplexer channel must maintain the correlation between the physical device and its associated storage area in memory. Thus, the multiplexer channel maintains a number of addresses and other information about the physical devices over which it has control. One of the basic requirements for the devices connected to a multiplexer channel is that they are slow enough to allow the channel to switch between them as needed, since they all share the same communication path. Thus, these devices are generally of a nature conducive to the slower speeds: terminals, modems, electromechanical devices, CRTs, and so on.

The selector channel is designed to provide high speed transfers from an external device and the memory of the system. As such, it is very much like a DMA controller: once the system has designated the device to use and the location in memory of the information, the selector channel executes that transfer or control operation before initiating another. This is true even if the operation is merely a track-to-track seek of a disk or other movement command. However, because of the creation of programs consisting of channel command words in memory, the selector channel may move on to a second transfer as soon as the last data movement of the first transfer has been completed.

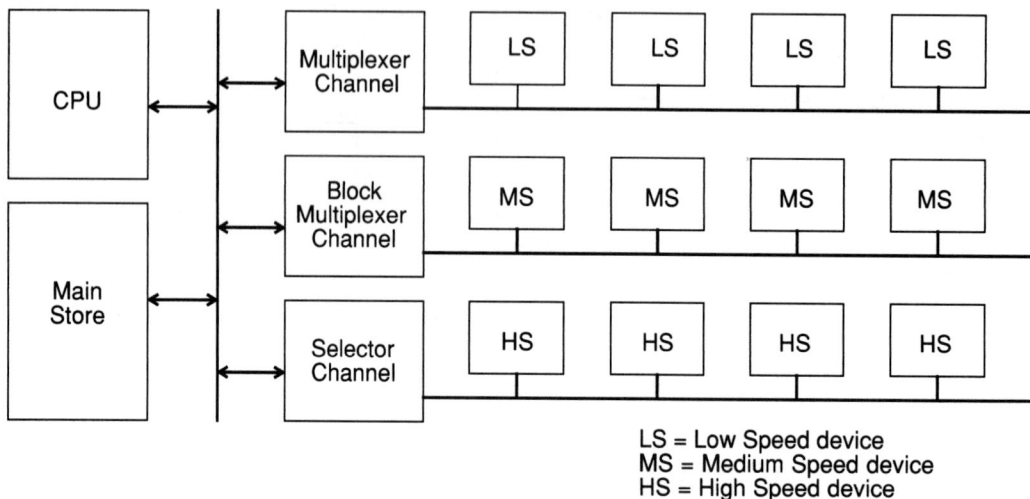

LS = Low Speed device
MS = Medium Speed device
HS = High Speed device

Figure 6.29. Computer System with Multiple Channels.

The block multiplexer channel is designed to have some of the characteristics of both the multiplexer channel and the selector channel. The block multiplexer channel is capable of multiplexing between devices, as the multiplexer channel, but the basic unit of information is no longer a byte, but rather a block of information. Thus, once the transfer of a block of information is started, the channel will maintain the logical connection between the device and its associated location in memory. When the transfer of the block has been completed, then the channel can move on to another device.

A channel provides a mechanism for the processor to off-load the burden of I/O control to a device specifically designed to handle the interaction. The channel controls the interaction with the I/O devices over the channel bus, which is an 8-bit transfer path. The devices that connect to the channel bus have the same problem examined earlier in the chapter: transfers are made over a shared data path, and the interface modules must be designed to permit this to happen in a uniform manner. However, the interface problem is somewhat simplified, since the channel is always in control of the bus. Once the channel action has been initiated, no further action is required on the part of the CPU until the transfer is complete. This leaves the processor free more of the time to do what it does best: compute.

When a computer system is configured with a number of channels, the system architect includes a sufficient number of channels to provide the I/O capability needed by the system. The transfer rate of the memory systems used in large computer systems is sufficient to allow several channel systems to operate simultaneously. Therefore, the architect is free to utilize enough channels to meet the maximum transfer rate required, or to use a small number of channels to provide capability at a minimal cost.

Channels are one example of an input/output processor (IOP). Figure 6.30 shows a system configured with a number of processing elements and IOPs. The figure indicates that the IOPs are dedicated to specific functions, such as disk or tape systems. This need not necessarily be the case. The basic requirement for an IOP is that it be capable of controlling a device and interfacing to another system. Thus, the IOPs shown in the figure each perform a designated task, and present the

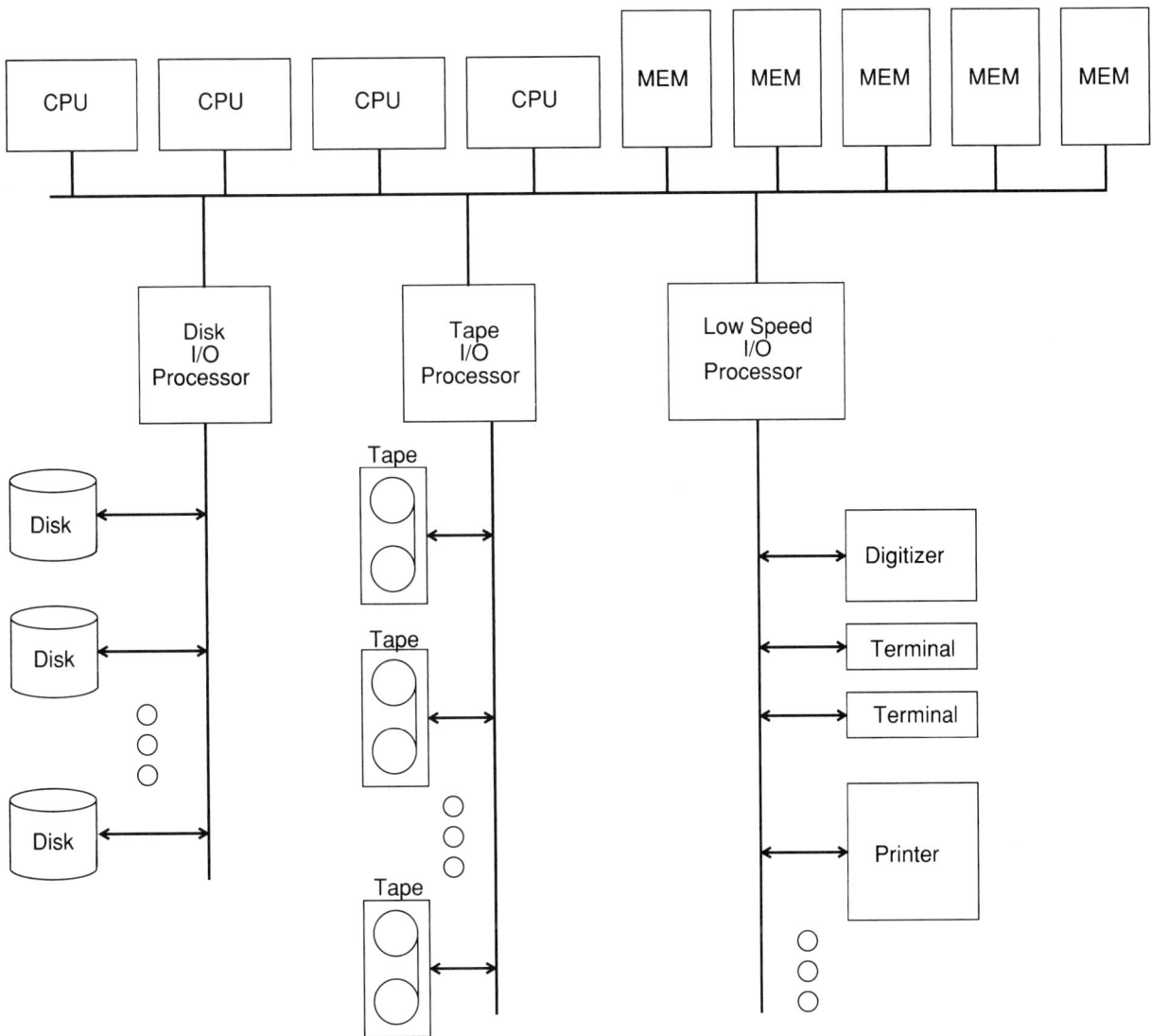

Figure 6.30. System with Multiple Processors and IOPs.

results to the larger computer system. In this context, many of the units described above have the characteristics of IOPs.

Additional systems that fall into this classification include the Am5380 SCSI (Small Computer Systems Interface) Interface Controller, made by Advanced Micro Devices, and the 8089 I/O processor, made by Intel. Block diagrams of these systems are shown in Figure 6.31. Also included in Figure 6.31 is a diagram of the 8044 remote universal peripheral interface.

The SCSI interface definition provides an 8-bit data path to peripherals, and a number of disks and tape units have been designed to be connected to computer systems by using this protocol. To the controlling CPU, the Am5380 appears as a set of eight registers; these could be located in the memory space as memory mapped I/O or in a separate I/O space. The controlling CPU monitors activity on the SCSI bus and requests appropriate action by reading or writing to these

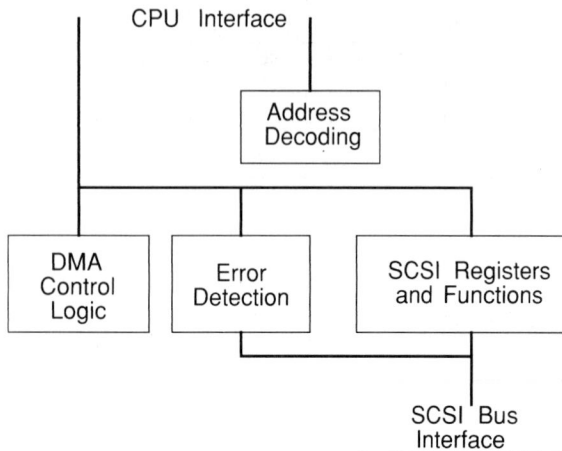

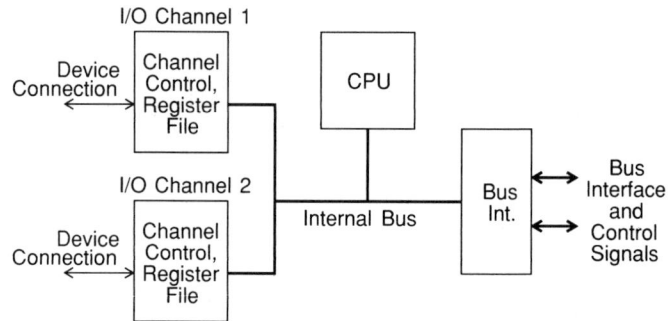

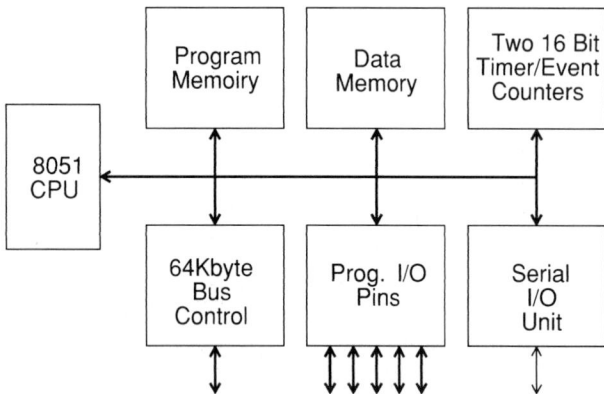

Figure 6.31. IOPs: (a) SCSI Interface Controller; (b) I/O Processor, and; (c) Remote Universal Peripheral Interface.

registers. This device must be utilized in conjunction with other devices to perform the DMA transfers required for high speed operation. In this type of a configuration, the Am5380 is used to provide the SCSI bus connection, and the other portion of the circuitry controls DMA interaction with the host. To control a number of SCSI transfers simultaneously, a system could be configured with several Am5380 devices. Each of these units would be capable of transferring information directly into the memory system under DMA control. The Am5380 can also be utilized in the design of peripheral units that connect to a SCSI bus, as it can be a target as well as an initiator on the bus.

The 8089 I/O processor is a device that contains a microprocessor capable of controlling interaction with two I/O devices. The unit is compatible with 8086- and 8088-type microprocessors, and provides high speed DMA capabilities for two separate devices. It is designed to intelligently control transceivers connecting I/O devices to a microprocessor system. The system was created to be utilized in the memory space of the host CPU; communication between host and I/O processor are accomplished by passing messages in the memory space. The instruction set of the 8089 has been created to function efficiently in its role as data mover, and the instructions include a number of load, store, and move capabilities, as well as conditional and unconditional branches, and minimal arithmetic capabilities. Devices of this nature can be used to remove from the host CPU some of the mundane action needed for I/O transfers, allowing the CPU to concentrate on the computational aspects of the system.

In addition to LSI devices, such as the Am5380 and the 8089 which control bus interaction, other devices are available to provide lines that can be connected directly to the control lines of I/O units to control the interaction. One such unit is the 8044 remote universal peripheral interface, also shown in Figure 6.31. This unit contains an 8051 CPU capable of asserting lines needed for control of I/O devices. The 8044 provides 24 programmable pins, so that a designer could create signals for controlling the action of peripheral devices, and interfacing those devices to a processor system.

Channels and IOPs provide a mechanism whereby a system can divide the tasks that are required — computation and communication — between processors that are more appropriately configured to the task. Moving I/O-oriented tasks to separate, specialized processors has two immediate benefits. First, the transfers required by I/O units are in general much slower than memory transfers, since limits are imposed by the electrical and mechanical nature of the I/O systems. This means that the IOPs can be constructed with medium speed technology and devices. The second benefit is the release of the time commitment from the CPU, since it no longer has primary responsibility for every command given to I/O devices. This allows the apparent system speed to increase.

6.8. Conclusion

The communication mechanism between the processing element and the external world is a very important part of any computer system. By this mechanism data is obtained by the CPU for use within the system, and results of the operations are made available to peripheral units, whether those units are computer systems, or disks, tapes or other peripheral devices.

The I/O mechanisms are an important part of the functionings of a computer system. To assess the impact of the I/O system, a thorough analysis of the system should be performed. This will allow evaluation of alternative utilizations of the busing schemes and other I/O mechanisms, matching the interconnection features with the characteristics of the processor(s) and peripherals.

Busing systems allow different modules to communicate with one another over the common communication medium. Asynchronous bus communication protocols allow the transfers to proceed, controlled by signals generated by both sender and receiver. This allows the transaction to seek its natural transfer rate for the bus. Asynchronous mechanisms can be used with buses that have separate address and data lines, as well as buses which time multiplex data and address on the same set of lines.

Information can also be transferred on a bus in a synchronous manner. The protocols for synchronous bus systems allow multiple operations, such as arbitration, transfer, and acknowledge, to occur simultaneously. For this reason, the data rates for synchronous bus systems is generally higher than a rate for an asynchronous bus.

The task of identifying the controller of a bus system is the responsibility of an arbitration system. The arbitration mechanism can be parallel in nature, which allows for high speed arbitration based on algorithms of arbitrary complexity. Another arbitration mechanism is serial in nature, with each module cooperating by passing a grant signal if access to the bus is not required. This method is necessarily slower than the parallel system, since decisions are made in a serial fashion. Another arbitration mechanism is polling, which is not used for bus ownership recognition, but is used in identifying active I/O devices.

Control of activity of peripheral devices is achieved by specialized I/O instructions, or by using memory mapped I/O techniques. By using instructions that control the action of peripheral devices, a processor can initiate transfers and monitor the status of the system. The complexity of the interface module between the processor and the peripheral units determines the responsibility of the CPU. If minimal capability exists within the interface module, then the CPU must monitor the status of the peripheral and cause all action with programmed I/O instructions. If the interface module is capable of interrupting the processor, then the CPU can continue processing and service the I/O device only when action is needed. Finally, if the interface module contains the ability to interact directly with the memory, then the CPU can initiate a transfer and be interrupted only when the action is complete. This direct memory access minimizes the time required by the CPU for controlling I/O functions.

Channels and I/O processors are specialized processing elements designed to remove the elemental I/O concerns from the CPU. These processors directly control peripheral elements to perform the data transfers and other functions required of I/O devices. With the byte multiplexing technique, the channel switches between I/O devices as needed and tags each byte as it is obtained. This allows many slow speed devices to be attached to a single channel. A block multiplexer channel operates on a similar principle, but the units of transfer are blocks of data rather than bytes. A selector channel selects one I/O device, and transfers data at high rates to or from that device before being switched to a different peripheral unit.

All of the techniques mentioned above — bus systems, arbitration systems, programmed I/O mechanisms, direct memory access, interrupts, channels, and IOPs — are utilized to transfer information to and from a computer system. By using the various mechanisms as called for by the peripheral devices, computer systems, and desired data rates, an effective processing system can be configured that will not only compute, but will also make available the results of the computations.

6.9. Problems

6.1 For a bus with handshake protocol shown in Figure 6.3, design a byte swap register that functions at address 776504_8. That is, writing to the specified address will fill a register, and reading from that same location will present the data in a byte swapped manner, with the data written on the most significant eight lines now available on the least significant lines, and vice versa. The system has an 18-bit address bus and a 16-bit data bus.

6.2 Design a hardware multiplier that will operate on an asynchronous bus system with a 24-bit address bus and a 16-bit data bus. The multiplier must use the shift and add algorithm shown in Figure 3.12 (and in Appendix B). The unit must respond to the following addresses on the bus (read and write are from point of view of CPU):

Address	Read Action	Write Action
777640_8	Read from multiplier register.	Write to multiplier register.
777642_8	Read from multiplicand register.	Write to multiplicand register.
777644_8	Read 16 least significant bits of result.	No action.
777646_8	Read 16 most significant bits of result.	No action.

This multiplier will function for positive numbers only. The interaction with the multiplier and multiplicand registers can be accomplished by using combinational circuits to interact with the control signals of the bus. When the location of the least significant bits is accessed, a sequential controller should perform the multiply on the data in the input registers, and present the result when the multiplication process is finished. When the most significant result location is accessed, the bits in the most significant bits of the product register should be made available, without going through another multiplication process.

6.3 One of the operations that proves to be very beneficial in the algorithm known as the fast fourier transform (FFT) is a bit reversal, where the most and least significant bits are exchanged, the second most and the second least significant bits are exchanged, and so on. Design a bit reversal register operating on a bus that uses the time multiplexed asynchronous protocol of Figure 6.5. When the address 17777605_8 is written to, a register is filled. When that same location is read, the bits in the register are presented to the bus in bit reversed order. The bus lines involved are multiplexed between a 22-bit address and a 16-bit data value. The number of bits needed for the reversal operation depends on the size of the FFT. What modifications would be needed to allow a different number of bits to be involved in the bit reversal? That is, what changes in the design would be required in the definition of the unit, and what logic complications would result?

6.4 Design a bit rotator for a time multiplexed asynchronous bus that operates according to the protocol shown in Figure 6.5. This bus multiplexes the common lines between a 22-bit address and a 16-bit data value. The rotator works at the following addresses:

Address	Read Action	Write Action
17777642_8	Read rotate value.	Write rotate value.
17777644_8	Read position value.	Write position value.
17777646_8	Read value in rotate register rotated left number of bit positions specified by position value.	No action.

The rotator has two registers: a 16-bit rotate register, which contains the value to be rotated, and a 4-bit position register, which identifies how many bits (to the left) to rotate the value located in the rotate register. The position reading and writing the rotate register and the position register simply involve the bits in the registers in question. When a rotated value is requested, then the value in the rotate register is loaded into a separate shift register, which is configured as a rotator, and this register is rotated the amount specified by the four bits of the position register. When the rotate has been completed, the value is supplied to the bus, and the transaction can terminate.

6.5 Three types of arbitration mechanisms are discussed in this chapter. Give a brief description of each of the mechanisms, along with an explanation of what are the good characteristics (and why) and bad characteristics (and why) of each mechanism.

6.6 Design a parallel arbitration mechanism for eight master modules that operates on the round robin principle. That is, once a master module has been granted access to the bus, the module with the highest priority for the next bus grant is the module with the next highest number (mod 8).

6.7 Both synchronous and asynchronous bus communication protocols are discussed in this chapter. Identify the salient characteristics of each type of protocol, and describe the good and bad features of each. Which communication mechanism is faster? Why?

6.8 An interface is to be designed to control a data logger and provide the data to a computer. The computer is organized around an asynchronous data bus, such as the UNIBUS or MULTIBUS. Give a simple block diagram of the interface, identifying the major data paths/registers and the principal control boxes. What information is transferred under program control? What is transferred on a cycle stealing basis?

6.9 Consider a computer system with the following characteristics:

> 500 nsec memory cycle time, both read and write
>
> 2 microsec instruction time for all instructions (very strange computer, since most clear instructions take less time than multiplies, or a CALL)
>
> memory mapped I/O
>
> standard instruction set

Create appropriate code segments to control I/O transfers, and determine the peak transfer rate and the average transfer rate for blocks of 512 words, for

a. interrupt driven I/O

b. straight programmed I/O

c. DMA

6.10 Consider the partial system diagram shown below, which contains two CPUs and two memories. Using the synchronous protocol of Figure 6.11, what is the shortest amount of time in which the two CPUs could write two words (each) to the memories, where CPU A is writing to MEM A, and CPU B is writing to MEM B. Plot the timing relationship of the transactions, showing

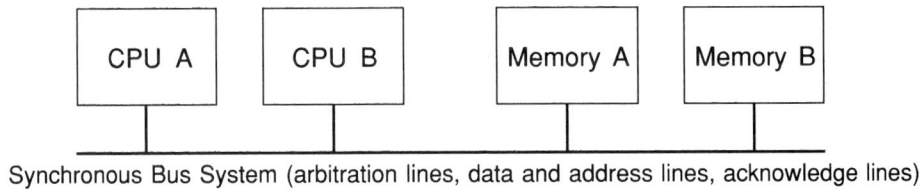

Synchronous Bus System (arbitration lines, data and address lines, acknowledge lines)

Figure P6.10. Partial System Diagram with Synchronous Bus.

the relationship between the arbitration lines, data/address lines, and the acknowledge lines. If the words are each 4 bytes, and the cycle time is 100 nsec, what is the data rate?

6.11 Repeat Problem 6.10 for read cycles, instead of write cycles. Assume that the bus cycle time is 100 nsec, and that the memory modules require five cycles to obtain the requested data.

6.12 Create a diagram similar to Figure 6.12 that explains the time relationship between commanders and responders on the SBI. Show with the diagram both reads and writes, and configure the transactions to demonstrate a maximum transfer rate. Name three different techniques that could be used to increase the bandwidth of the bus.

6.13 An A/D converter is configured as shown in Figure P6.13. Design a DMA interface that will input data to an asynchronous bus system from this A/D converter. The definition of the behavior of the interface is as follows: The interface is idle until a bit (the GO bit, which is the most significant bit of the command register) is set in the command register. When the GO bit is set, the interface will clear the DATA_AVAILABLE-H flag and wait for the A/D converter to generate a new data sample. When the sample is available, the interface will request a bus transaction by asserting a bus request line (BR-H). When the bus grant is asserted (BG-H), then the interface releases the bus request and asserts the address and data lines. After a 50 nsec delay, the interface asserts the request line (REQ-H) and awaits the assertion of the acknowledge line (ACK-H). The master then releases the request line, and when the master sees that the acknowledge line has been released, it will release the address lines and decrement a word count register. This process

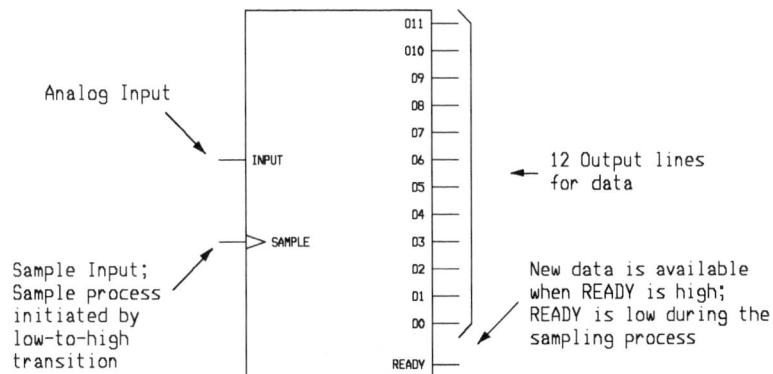

Figure P6.13. A/D Converter for Problem 6.13.

continues until the word count reaches zero. The interface contains a status register readable by the CPU, which consists simply of a busy bit (which is the most significant bit on the bus). When the interface is in the process of transferring information to the computer the bit is a one; otherwise, the bit is a zero. Thus, the busy bit will be set by the action of setting the GO bit of the command register, and reset when the word count reaches zero, and the transfer process is completed. For this system, provide:

a. a programmer's interface definition: the registers that a programmer can reach and their definitions

b. a data path block diagram that identifies all of the necessary components for the data transfers and their interconnection

c. a set of control signals that can be used to control the interface (the control signals of the data path

d. a state diagram of the interaction

e. logic diagrams for the system

6.14 The bus transactions described in Problem 6.13 are used to transfer information to a memory module. Modify the protocol description to read information from a memory. Then design a D/A converter interface with the following behavior: When a SEND_DATA flag is set, the interface extracts a value from the location identified by the address register and sends it to the D/A converter, and also resets the flag and decrements the word count. When the word count re aches zero, the word count is returned to an initial word count value and the address register is returned to an initial address value, and the process is repeated. This system could be used to draw waveforms on an oscilloscope. For this system give:

a. a programmer's interface definition: the registers that a programmer can reach and their definitions. Note that the programmer will not be able to reach all of the registers in the system.

b. a data path block diagram that identifies all of the necessary components for the data transfers and their interconnection

c. a set of control signals that can be used to control the interface (the control signals of the data path

d. a state diagram of the interaction

e. logic diagrams for the system

6.15 Obtain the data manual for a DP8466 disk data controller (DDC), and using that device design a disk interface for a 16-bit asynchronous bus. Initiate the design by identifying the possible transfers between the DDC and the bus. Then identify the additional signals required to control the action of the disk. Then, complete the design process by creating an appropriate data path block diagram, specifying the control system, and creating the appropriate logic diagrams.

6.16 Obtain a data manual for an Am9516 direct memory access controller (DMAC), and using a pair of devices design a high speed communication channel that connects two 16-bit asynchronous bus systems. These are essentially independent computer systems that are physically close together, and information is to be exchanged between the two over the DMA channels.

6.10. References and Readings

[AMD85] Advanced Micro Devices, *Bipolar Microprocessor Logic and Interface Data Book.* Sunnyvale, CA: Advanced Micro Devices, 1985.

[Baer84] Baer, J. L., "Computer Architecture," *Computer.* Vol. 17, No. 10, October 1984, pp. 77–87.

[Baer80] Baer, J. L., *Computer Systems Architecture.* Rockville, MD: Computer Science Press, 1980.

[Bart85] Bartee, T. C., *Digital Computer Fundamentals,* 6th edition, New York: McGraw Hill Book Company, 1985.

[BeNe71] Bell, C. G. and A. Newell, *Computer Structures: Readings and Examples,* New York: McGraw Hill Book Company, 1971.

[Chen74] Chen, R. C. H., "Bus Communications Systems," Ph.D. Dissertation. Pittsburg, PA: Department of Computer Science, Carnegie-Mellon University, 1974.

[Clul82] Cluley, J. C., *Minicomputer and Microprocessor Interfacing,* New York: Crane, Russak, 1982.

[DEC82] Digital Equipment Corporation, *VAX Hardware Handbook.* Maynard, MA: Digital Equipment Corporation, 1982.

[Dext86] Dexter, A. L., *Microcomputer Bus Structures and Bus Interface Design.* New York: M. Dekker, 1986.

[Egge83] Eggebrecht, L. C., *Interfacing to the IBM Personal Computer.* Indianapolis, IN: H. W. Sams, 1983.

[Flet80] Fletcher, W. I., *An Engineering Approach to Digital Design,* Englewood Cliffs, NJ: Prentice Hall, 1980.

[IEEE75] Institute of Electrical and Electronics Engineers, "IEEE Standard Digital Interface for Programmable Instrumentation," IEEE Std. 488-1975. The Institute of Electrical and Electronics Engineers, Inc., October 1975.

Intel, *Microsystem Components Handbook.* Intel Corporation, 1984.

[LaZa84] Lazowska, E. D., J. Zahorjan, G. S. Graham, and K. C. Sevcik, *Quantitative System Performance.* Englewood Cliffs, NJ: Prentice Hall, 1984.

[Lang82] Langdon, G. G., Jr., *Computer Design.* San Jose, CA: Computeach Press Inc, 1982.

[Lipo88] Lipovski, G. J., *Single- and Multiple-Chip Microcomputer Interfacing.* Englewood Cliffs, NJ: Prentice Hall, 1988.

[Mati80] Matick, R. E., "Memory and Storage," in [Ston80], pp. 205–274.

[Mati77] Matick, R. E., *Computer Storage Systems and Technology.* New York: John Wiley & Sons, 1977.

[Moto85] Motorola, *The VMEbus Specification.* 1985.

[PaWa81] Parker, A. C., and J. J. Wallace, "An I/O Hardware Descriptive Language," *IEEE Transactions on Computers.* Vol. C-30, No. 6, June 1981, pp. 423–439.

[Poll83] Pollard, L. H., "Fault Tolerant Bus Communication Protocols for Computer Systems," Ph. D. Dissertation. Champaign-Urbana, IL: University of Illinois, 1983.

[Shiv85] Shiva, S. G., *Computer Design and Architecture.* Boston, MA: Little, Brown, 1985.

[SiBe82] Siewiorek, D. P., C. G. Bell, and A. Newell, *Computer Structures: Principles and Examples*. New York: McGraw Hill Book Company, 1982.

[Stal87] Stallings, W., *Computer Organization and Architecture*. New York: Macmillan Publishing Co., 1987.

[TI85] Texas Instruments, *The TTL Data Book,* Volume 2. Dallas, TX: Texas Instruments, 1985.

[ThJe72] Thurber, K. J., E. D. Jensen, et al., "A Systematic Approach to the Design of Digital Bussing Structures," *AFIPS Conference Proceedings — Fall Joint Computer Conference*. 1972, pp. 719–740.

[ThMa79] Thurber, K. J., and G. M. Masson, "Bus Structures," in Distributed Processor Communication Architecture, Lexington, MA: Lexington Books, 1979, pp. 131–174.

[TiLa82] Titus, C. A., J. A. Titus, and D. G. Larson, *STD Bus Interfacing*. Indianapolis, IN: H. W. Sams, 1982.

[TsSi82] Tseng, C. J., and D. P. Siewiorek, "The Modeling and Synthesis of Bus Systems," Technical Report DRC-18-42-82, Design Research Center. Pittsburg, PA: Carnegie-Mellon University, 1982.

[Wilk87] Wilkinson, B., *Digital System Design*. Englewood Cliffs, NJ: Prentice Hall International, 1987.

7

Memory Systems

One of the most basic functions of a computer is the retrieval of information stored in a memory element. This action is needed to obtain the instruction to perform; it is also needed to obtain the data on which the instruction operates. One widely used model of memory is shown in Figure 7.1. In this model the memory consists of N consecutive storage locations. The size of a location is dependent on the system architecture, and the width of the data path (w) is a function of the implementation mechanisms. But the model remains the same: the address supplies the desired location, and the data is transferred to/from the memory. The number of bits needed in the address is $\lceil \log_2 N \rceil$. We will use this model to represent a memory system, and recognize that for special systems appropriate changes must be made. In many systems, the size of the memory is given in bytes, although that is not the normal width of data transfers. One reason for this is that the systems are byte-addressable, and although the width of the transfer path may not be a single byte wide, the information is obtained by giving the address of the specific byte desired. Then, if more bytes are required, they are obtained as needed by the processing unit.

The design of the memory unit is a series of tradeoffs, since a number of different factors must be considered. These include the size of the memory (N elements), the width of the data path (w), the organization method, and the speed of access. The speed of the memory depends on many factors, including technology of implementation and organizational method. Regardless of the mechanisms involved and the memory technology used, there will be a minimum time to access information, which we will call T_A. This represents the shortest time required to retrieve the information, and includes not only the access time of the memory device, but also any delay caused by additional gates needed to provide sufficient drive capability for the address or the data. Another very important time is the minimum time between accesses, or the memory cycle time, which we will call T_{CY}. For "normal" memory interaction, where information is retrieved

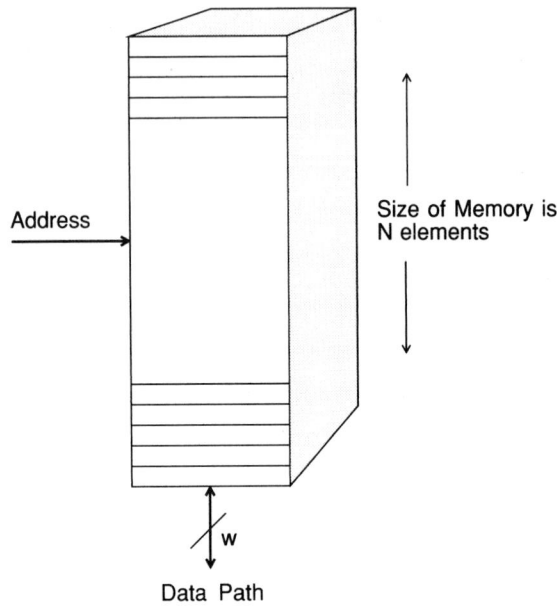

Figure 7.1. Memory Model: Linear Array of Locations.

from memory, then work is done on it, and then memory is accessed again, T_{CY} is not a limiting factor, since the action of the system will not result in memory accesses which occur faster than T_{CY}. However, for burst mode access, where several consecutive memory elements are read or written, T_{CY} is a factor that limits the rate of transfer. One simplifying assumption we will make is that the memory times are the same for the read and write cycles, which is not always true.

The memory itself is configured in such a way that all of the necessary accesses can be made to it. That is, using one or more of the communication protocols described in Chapter 6, the memory is connected to elements that need the capability of data transfer with the memory. The simple representation of Figure 7.2 shows a memory that can be accessed by a processor and I/O devices. The

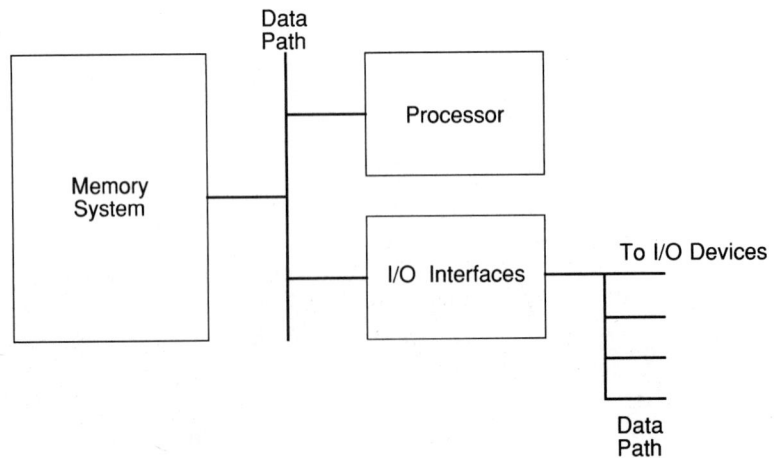

Figure 7.2. Memory System and Connections to Processor and I/O Interfaces.

data path (bus system) is also used to allow the processor to control the action of the I/O interfaces. The configuration shown in Figure 7.2 is a very simplistic representation, and the actual connections to the memory can be as simple or complex as the application requires. In general, however, we would like to create a memory with as large a size (N) as reasonable within the design constraints, with an access time (T_A) and a cycle time (T_{CY}) as short as possible. Let us look at the memory hierarchy mechanisms used to try to accomplish this, then examine details of the memory systems involved.

7.1. Memory Hierarchy: Tradeoffs in Size and Function

In the description of their 1946 IAS machine Burks, Goldstine, and von Neumann recognized that "ideally one would desire an indefinitely large memory capacity such that [information] would be immediately available ..."[BuGo46]. But the realities of the economics and the technology are such that compromises must be made. The IAS machine contained 4,096 words of 40 bits each for the main store, which "exceeds the capacities required for most problems that one deals with at present by a factor of about 10." However, they recognized that the time would come when this would not be sufficient storage for the problems to be solved in the future, and therefore looked forward to the "constructing of a hierarchy of memories, each of which has greater capacity than the preceding, but which is less quickly accessible." The machines of today indeed match this concept, and can be represented by the block diagram shown in Figure 7.3. The fastest memory elements are those closest to the processor: most systems have a small number of very high speed locations, which we call a register bank. The T_A for the registers is minimal, and in general the information stored in registers is available in the same cycle as it is needed. However, the cost of this type of storage is very high, whether the cost is measured in dollars, silicon real estate, or power dissipation. For this reason, the amount of register storage available in a system is relatively small, from eight to sixteen registers in most general purpose systems, to over a hundred in some special purpose and RISC systems.

The next element in the memory hierarchy is often a cache memory. The purpose of a cache is to enhance the operating speed of the processor by making available the most recently used information by keeping it in a high speed temporary storage. The T_A of a cache is on the order of two CPU cycle times, and we will discuss methods of approaching cache designs in Section 7.4. The amount of

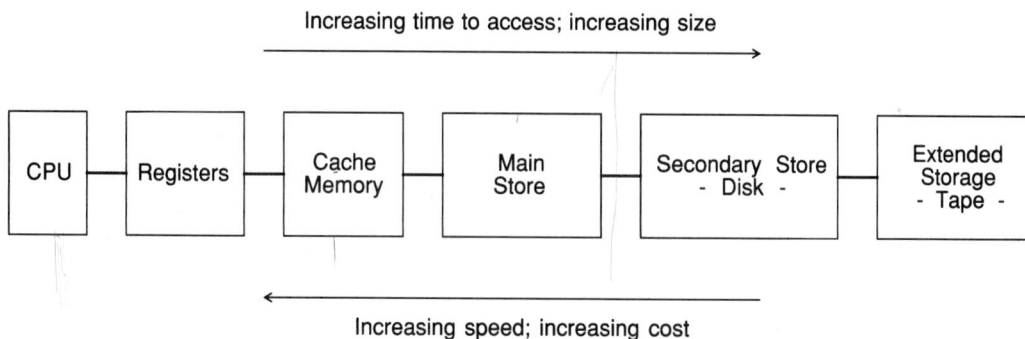

Increasing time to access; increasing size

| CPU | Registers | Cache Memory | Main Store | Secondary Store - Disk - | Extended Storage - Tape - |

Increasing speed; increasing cost

Figure 7.3. Block Diagram of Hierarchical Memory System.

memory available here is generally small in comparison to the other elements of the system. For example, the VAX 11/780 has a 2-Kbyte cache, and some other processors have even smaller caches. However, as the cost of memory decreases with respect to overall system costs, larger caches are much more common. Many newer systems have caches that contain 16 Kbytes to 64 Kbytes or more incorporated with the processing unit.

The purpose of the cache is to maintain current information for rapid retrieval. This is done in a manner that is transparent to the user. The programmer does not know of the existence of the cache, except that the speed of the system is enhanced over a system with no cache memory. Thus management of the data is done in a fashion determined at design time, in contrast to the virtual memory systems discussed below.

The information in a cache memory is a high speed copy of what is in main store, which is the "standard" memory of the computer. The amount of storage in a main store is system dependent, but it has increased with each passing year. In contrast to the 4,096 locations of the IAS system, many systems require a minimum of 8 Mbytes or more. The technology is now such that it is possible to get 8 Mbytes in eight packages, which is one of the reasons for the increased size of main store. The T_A of main store is about an order of magnitude greater than the T_A for cache. Thus, when a request is made for information, and it is determined not to be in the cache, then the system pauses until the information is retrieved from main store. At that time the processing can continue. Some of the issues involved in the design of the main store are discussed in Section 7.2.

The information resident in main store for a "standard" computer system is a sufficient amount of the operating system to maintain a continuity of action. That is, a portion of the operating system, I/O storage areas, and other basic routines are maintained in the memory of the machine. In addition, the active portions of user programs and data sets are available as well. The portions of the operating system and user programs and data that are not active are kept on the next level of the hierarchy, the secondary store.

The purpose of the secondary store of this hierarchy is to maintain copies of all of the programs and data needed by the computer. Generally this will be a disk, although it could be any block-oriented storage device with a large capacity. Such devices have been built with charge coupled devices, bubble memories, and large RAMs. This device is generally organized into files, and maintaining the files is one of the responsibilities of the operating system. In addition to the files, there is an area which is used to maintain the current copies of user program space; this area is often called "swap space." The swap space is also under the control of the operating system. The procedures and mechanisms established within the computer system to manage the use of the memory system are done so to effectively utilize the available system resources. With a combination of software/system policies and the appropriate hardware, only copies of currently active information need reside within the main store of the machine at any given time. Still, the apparent effect is that user programs execute in "virtual space," which frees up the user from being aware of the exact physical configuration of the system and the orientation of his program.

The T_A of information on the disk is much longer than the T_A for main store. Note that the cache is created from a (relatively) small amount of high speed RAM; and main store is also electrically and randomly accessible, but with lower cost, slower devices than the cache. Secondary store, on the other hand, involves electromechanical devices, and therefore requires relatively long times to find the physical location of the information and effect the transfer. The ratio for $T_{A_{\text{MAIN STORE}}} / T_{A_{\text{CACHE}}}$ is on the order of 10, but the ratio for $T_{A_{\text{SECONDARY STORE}}} / T_{A_{\text{MAIN STORE}}}$ is on the order of 100,000. For this reason, when information is needed by the processor, and it is not in main store, the operating system will request the needed information, place the current task on a queue, and get a new task to execute while waiting for the information to be retrieved from the disk. This action of "context switching" allows the processor to be shared effectively between multiple programs; such systems are often called multiprogrammed or time-shared systems. To be effective, the secondary storage system must be sufficiently large to handle the swapping functions and the necessary file system operations.

The last member of the hierarchy shown in Figure 7.3 is the extended storage. This consists of information stored on magnetic tape, which is slow in comparison to the disk storage. This storage is generally used for permanent storage of programs and data, as well as transfer of information from one computer to another. Some systems have automated tape storage capabilities, so that parts of the extended storage can be considered a random access system with capabilities similar to the disk systems, albeit much slower.

The intended operation of the memory hierarchy is to provide a very large memory capability, with the response time of a cache system and the storage capability of a disk or tape system. The mechanisms used to perform these tasks is the subject of the following sections.

7.2. "Standard" Memory Systems: Random Access Storage for Programs and Data

The storage of information in computer systems is accomplished by utilizing collections of individual storage elements, each of which is capable of maintaining a single bit. Thus, for a device to be useful as a memory element it must have two stable states, a reliable mechanism for setting the device to one state or the other, and a mechanism for interrogating the state. Memories have been built of a variety of devices that match this characteristic, including relays, individual vacuum tubes, storage tubes, and delay lines, which form a type of serial memory. In each case, information in the form of bits was entered into the memory, and then at some later time extracted for use by the system.

Storage tubes and delay lines allowed for information storage in some early machines, but the central memory technology next used by most computers utilized the magnetic properties of iron. The mechanism utilized by these memories is depicted in Figure 7.4. A ferrite material is fashioned into a circular, doughnut shape, as shown in Figure 7.4(a). The principle utilized by this device is the fact that the magnetic orientation of the ferrite material will change to coincide with a forced magnetic field, if the field is strong enough. Due to the physical nature of the material, once the magnetic orientation has been established, it will remain in that orientation until a different magnetic field is created to change it. This is shown by the flux-versus-current diagram of Figure 7.4(b), which is known as a hysteresis loop. When the current returns to zero, the orientation of the flux remains in the direction that it was established. It will remain in that orientation until a current is passed through the drive line in the opposite direction. The residual magnetic flux within the core is used to store a single bit. If the flux is aligned in one direction, the bit is a zero; alignment in the opposite direction represents a one. The use of the core for the storage of information requires at

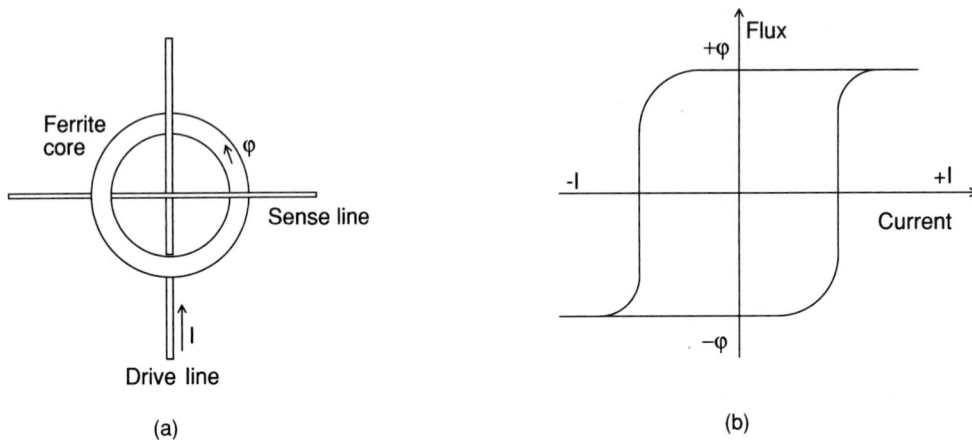

Figure 7.4. Magnetic Memory Mechanisms (a) Magnetic Core for Single Bit. (b) Hysteresis Loop.

least two wires passing through the center of the core. One line is used to write information into the core:

- Forcing current in the drive line as shown in Figure 7.4(a) will create a flux, ϕ, as shown; let this orientation represent a one.

- Forcing current in the wire in the opposite direction from that shown in the figure will reverse the orientation of ϕ; let this orientation represent a zero.

The other wire is used to sense the content of the core. Note that establishing the orientation of the magnetic flux can indeed represent binary values; but we not only need to establish the value, we also need to retrieve the value stored in the core. The sense line uses the fact that a wire in a changing magnetic field will pick up a voltage; that voltage is sensed to identify the content of the core. The process works in the following manner:

- A negative current [opposite to the direction shown in Figure 7.4(a)] is established in the drive line; the net result is to leave the core in an orientation representing a zero.

- If the sense line detects a voltage, then the magnetic field is changing, and hence the bit represented was a "one" before the process started.

- If the sense line detects no voltage, then the magnetic field is not changing, and the bit represented by the core was a "zero" before the process started.

To produce information needed by a processor, these characteristics are utilized by core memories in the following fashion:

- *Read:* To read the value stored in a bit, a current is sent through the drive line of the core for that bit. Assume that the current direction is that which establishes a "zero" in the core. If the new magnetic orientation agrees with the established orientation, no change is made and the sensed voltage is zero, which corresponds to a "zero" bit. If there is a change in the magnetic orientation, then a nonzero voltage is created on the sense line, which corresponds to a "one" bit. In either case the bit representation of the magnetic flux at the end of the read is a "zero."

The overall effect is to destroy the data stored in the core, and so core memories are destructive readout devices. This is generally an unacceptable feature, so the value read out is stored in a register and immediately returned to the core. For this reason cores generally have $T_{CY} = 2 \times T_A$ since the data must be restored to the accessed location.

- *Write:* The first step in the write sequence is to place known data in all of the cores that will be used for the write; this places a constant, known value in the core. The value could be either a "one" or a "zero," but we will assume that it is a zero. This is not absolutely necessary, but is usually combined with the electronics used for the read cycle: the first half of the read process above performs this function. Current is then directed to the drive lines on those bits which will have a "one" orientation, while current is inhibited from the cores for those bits that need to maintain a "zero" orientation. In this fashion, the correct orientation is established for the data to be written to the core.

This technology was used for many years to create the main memory for most computers. However, the cost and size of the memories, as well as their speed, became a disadvantage as semiconductor memories were developed. Each bit in the memory required a separate core, with at least two, but usually three, wires through it. The technique of storing information by the magnetic orientation of a ferrous material is now used more prevalently for other types of storage than for the central memory of a computer. The magnetic orientation of a region of ferrous material on a surface is used to store a bit, and this surface is most often on a rotating magnetic disk, or on a magnetic tape. The reading of the information still requires a moving magnetic field, but in a disk or tape unit the movement of the field is caused by physical movement between the surface and a detecting element called a head. The head is also used to create the proper fields for writing the information to the magnetic surface. Disk units are utilized to store thousands of bytes, such as floppy disks on a personal computer, to billions of bytes on larger machines. Tapes have a similar range of storage abilities, and are used on computers of all sizes.

Different types of electronic technologies have been used to store information in computers, from tubes to semiconductors. At one level we can examine the storage mechanism by looking at the gate level; another level is the device level. Figure 7.5 shows two different gating implementations for storing a single bit. These can be cascaded into several bits to store bytes or words. One method of maintaining a bit is to put it into a latch, as shown in Figure 7.5(a). The simplest gating arrangement to store a bit is cross coupled gates, and these are shown in the figure. The information placed in these gates is established by the input (D) when the enable line (ENB) is asserted. As long as the enable line is asserted, whatever information is on the data line will be passed to the storage element. When the enable line is deasserted, the last value for the data will be retained. This behavior is useful for many computer functions, and can be used to store information when needed.

The latch behavior is not the most prevalent mechanism used in storage elements in a processor. The gates shown in Figure 7.5(b) implement an edge-triggered function, the behavior generally associated with a register. The mechanism shown in the figure is used to capture the value of the data (D) on the rising edge of the clock (CLK). Analysis of the gates implementing the latch is

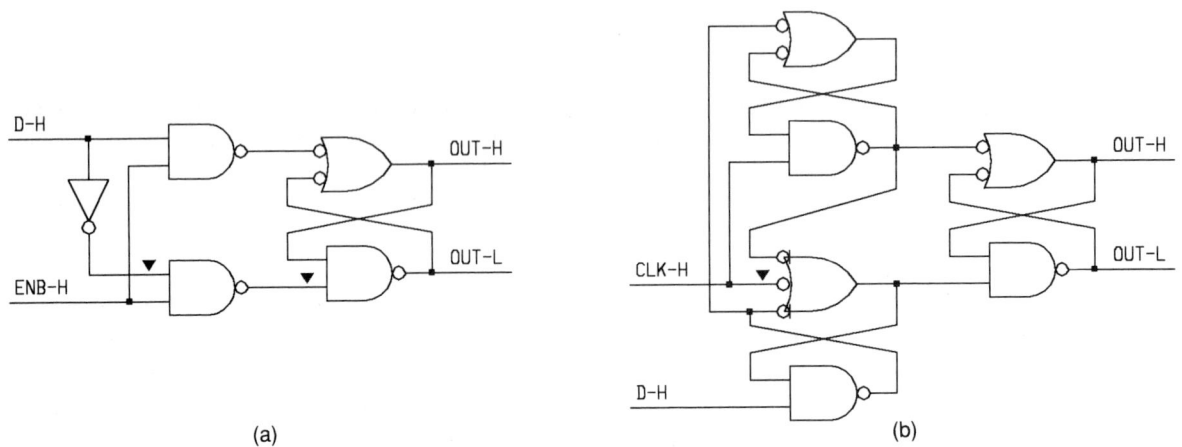

Figure 7.5. Possible Arrangements of Gates for Storing a Single Bit. (a) Latch (Single Bit). (b) Edge-Triggered Flip-Flop .

relatively straightforward, but the register function is very involved. However, in both cases the data must be stable for some window of time around the active edge of the clock (or enable). If this condition is not true, the unit can enter a metastable condition that will cause problems in high speed systems.

The circuitry shown in Figure 7.5 requires many individual transistors or other active devices to create. Therefore, they are used in small numbers in places where the storage requirements are not extensive. Creating enough register or latch type circuits in an integrated circuit to store a lot of information would not be a good use of silicon real estate. Two types of mechanisms for storing information in semiconduction memories are shown in Figure 7.6. Figure 7.6(a) shows an arrangement of parts that implements a static memory cell. As in the case of the latch, there is cross coupling between the elements, and the device has two stable states. The active action of the system makes sure that the value of the cell remains as set until an external event causes a change. Thus, a value written to this cell will be maintained until the power is lost, or until the contents is changed by the write action. In this it differs from core memories, since it is not a destructive readout mechanism.

Static memories generally have a smaller number of bits per package, and a higher power consumption, than dynamic memories. The static mechanism of Figure 7.6(a) requires six transistors in every cell; other static memory configurations utilize fewer active elements. One of the tasks of memory designers is to reduce the number of components needed in an individual storage cell, since fewer elements means that each individual cell can be smaller and require less power, which in turn leads to larger memories. The memories with the largest capacities use not a static mechanism, but rather a dynamic mechanism, as shown in Figure 7.6(b). Here the value of the bit is not determined by the current flowing through one of two different paths, but rather the bit value is determined by the amount of charge stored on a capacitor. The capacitor is created with semiconductor technology, and is extremely small. The sensing of the charge is also very difficult, and handled by circuitry on the device itself. The information is placed on the capacitor by opening an electronic gate and establishing the proper charge level. Then, the gate is closed, and the charge maintained on the node by electronically isolating it from surrounding influences. However, the time which the charge can be reliably maintained in this manner is not long,

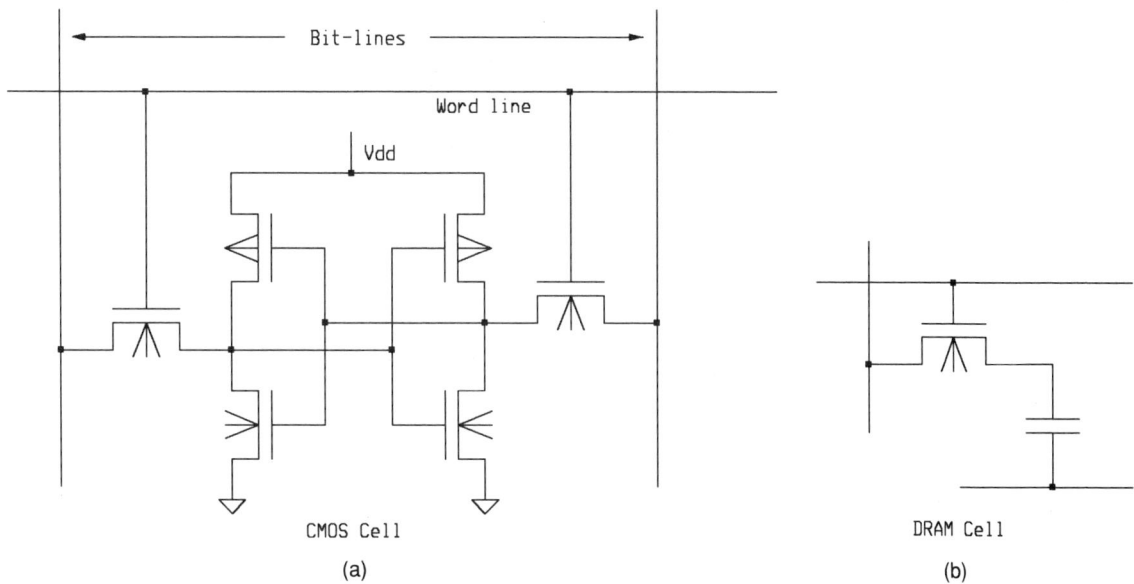

Figure 7.6. Bit Storage Elements for Semiconductor Memories. (a) Static Memory Cell. (b) Dynamic Memory Cell.

and so it must be re-established periodically. This is done by a "refresh" cycle, which detects the appropriate bit values and refreshes the bits. The length of time between refresh cycles varies from memory to memory, but a common value is 8 msec: each row must be visited at least once every 8 msec. For this reason dynamic memory controllers are designed to periodically access rows to assure that the data is maintained in the memory cells.

The storage of the information in the cells is only a part of the memory problem. The bits stored must be organized in a reasonable fashion to access the information. The two most prevalent mechanisms are random access and serial access. As the name implies, random access memories are organized such that the information can be accessed in a random fashion. That is, each location has the same access penalty, T_A, and the order of access can be entirely random. The only requirement is a mechanism to decode an address of a specific location, and a data path such that any location accessed can provide the necessary information.

On the other hand, serial access mechanisms are organized such that the data is written and accessed in a serial fashion. Thus, the T_A varies depending on the location of the information in the memory, since the data must pass a mechanism for reading each bit. Examples of serial access devices include magnetic surface systems, such as tape and disk, and serial semiconductor systems, such as shift registers and charge coupled devices.

A simplified block diagram for the random access mechanism is shown in Figure 7.7. The size of the decoding mechanism is dependent upon the size of the array of memory elements; the number of bits in memories increases each year. The mechanism used to decode the address can be designed in a variety of ways. The two most basic mechanisms are the one dimensional (1-D) and two dimensional (2-D) decoding schemes. The 1-D scheme accepts an N-bit address, and uses an N to 2^N decoder to identify one of 2^N individual elements. The location identified is then used in the read or write operation. The 2-D scheme accepts the

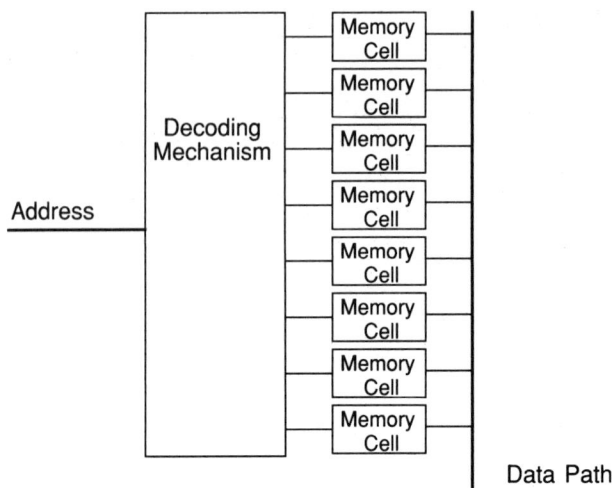

Figure 7.7. Random Access Memory Block Diagram.

N-bit address and divides it into two groups, which we will call X and Y. Thus, $X + Y = N$. These two groups of address lines control X to 2^X and Y to 2^Y decoders, which jointly specify a single element. Note that the memory cells used with the 1-D arrangement need only have a single enable line, while the memory cells used with the 2-D arrangement need two enable lines. Thus, the 1-D arrangement has a simple cell and a more complicated decoding scheme, while the 2-D arrangement has a slightly more complex cell, with less logic required in the decoding mechanism. These methods are depicted in Figure 7.8, which shows the addressing mechanism for an array of eight cells in a 1-D decoding arrangement, and sixteen cells in a 2-D decoding arrangement. Mechanisms used by manufacturers internal to memories include both the 1-D and 2-D methods, as well as other variations of the schemes. Note that there is no reason to stop at two dimensions, and higher mechanisms could be useful in some systems.

The basic ideas of the preceding paragraphs apply not only to individual bits, but also to collections of bits. That is, many memories are not organized as 1-bit entities, but rather some multiple that makes logical as well as manufacturing sense. Memories containing 4-bit words are very useful for storing BCD digits, and for use with 4-bit microprocessor systems. Memories organized 8 bits wide are useful for ASCII characters, 8-bit microprocessor systems, and byte-addressable memory systems. Combinations of 4-bit and 8-bit systems can be used as needed to meet other system needs. In dealing with the memories or other storage elements, the principles used in identifying a bit in a memory array can be applied. That is, the individual components can be organized in a one dimensional fashion, a two dimensional fashion, or in some combination of the above schemes.

Example 7.1: 1-D Design of a register set: Design a register array that contains eight registers, and that operates with an 8-bit bus. The array should have two control lines, a read line and a write line. Use individual registers in the ALS technology, and a one dimensional addressing scheme. How fast can information be made available on a read? What is the data requirement for a write?

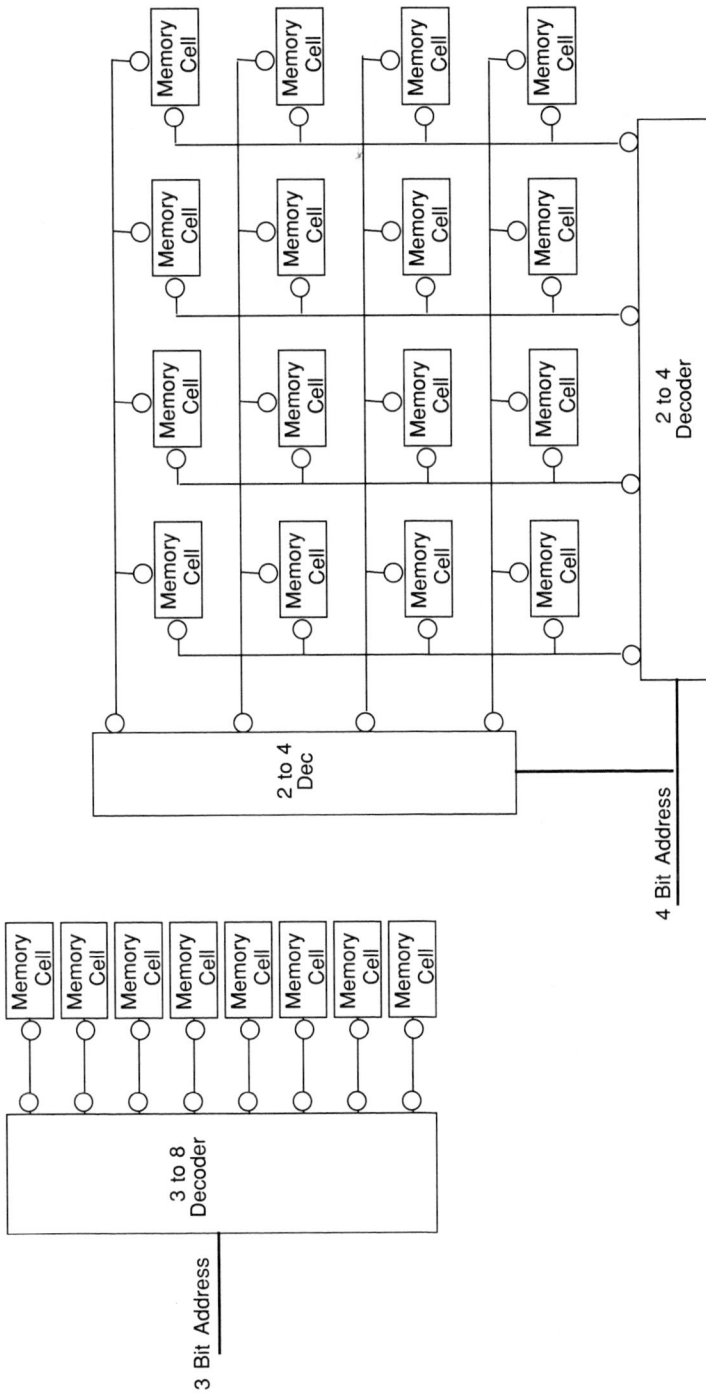

Figure 7.8. Memory Cells Organized in 1-D and 2-D Memory Arrays.

One solution to this is shown in Figure 7.9. The register selected here is the 74ALS299, which has inputs and outputs on the same pin. The inputs not shown in the figure have been appropriately disabled. With the enable lines (G1, G2) tied low, this device will output its information when the function select lines (S1, S0) are both low. When the function select lines are both high, the outputs are disabled, and a value can be accepted from the bus to the internal register. The address is decoded by two 74ALS138s. When the read line is activated, the function select lines of the appropriate register are asserted. The delay from assertion of the read line to the output data stable is the sum of the enable-to-output-stable delay of the 74ALS138 and the function-select-to-data-stable delay of the 74ALS299. The sum of the maximum times is 39 nsec; typical times would be shorter. When the write line is asserted, the clock line of the appropriate register is activated. The loading of the register occurs on the low-to-high transition of the clock at the register, which corresponds to the high-to-low transition of the clock line in the figure, since there is a change of assertion level through the 74ALS138. The maximum delay through the 74ALS138 is 17 nsec, and the

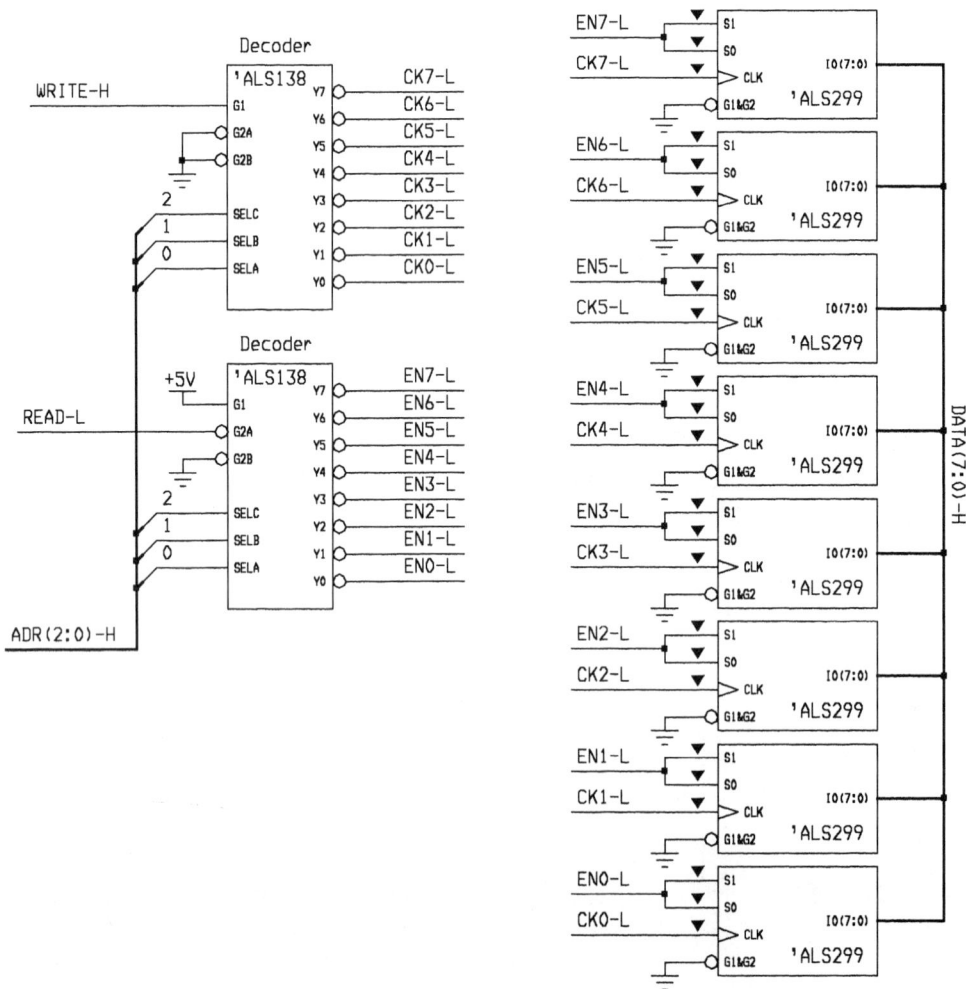

Figure 7.9. Registers with One Dimensional Addressing.

data must be stable on the bus for 16 nsec prior to the rising edge of the clock (at the register).

The arrangement of the parts as shown in the figure gives a register bank with eight registers in ten DIP packages, and a power consumption of about 1.6 watts. This is not a very efficient use of the board space or system power, but the unit can meet some requirements for special systems.

The use of individual registers as shown in Example 7.1 can be used to meet some special requirements, but the normal manner of operation is to use memory elements that contain a larger storage capacity. Nevertheless, the same principles apply, and the memories can be organized in a one dimensional or two dimensional manner.

Example 7.2: 64-Kbyte static RAM system: Design a memory system for an 8-bit microprocessor system. The memory system is to contain 64 Kbytes of static RAM memory, using 8K×8 RAMs, such as the μPD4464 from NEC Electronics Inc. Do this design in two ways, first as a one dimensional scheme, then as a two dimensional scheme. Communication lines to the memory include the address and data buses, a write line and a read line. Write and read lines are asserted low.

The 4464 is an 8K × 8 RAM with thirteen address lines, two enable lines, an output enable, and a write line. One of the enable lines is asserted high, while the other is asserted low; the write line and the output enable are both asserted low. To attain the 64K space, eight separate memories are required. Figure 7.10 shows one of the possible 1-D organizations that can be used. The lower address lines are shared by all memories; the current requirements of each input is only 1 μa, which does not cause loading problems. The upper three address lines are directed to a 3-to-8 decoder ('138), which enables only one of the memory chips. This allows sharing of all of the read and write lines, as only one memory element will be active at any one time. The burden is on the user of the system to be sure that the address lines do not change while the write line is asserted; such action will cause the data to be corrupted in the memory.

Note that this arrangement can be extended to include more memories by utilizing the unused enable lines of the 3-to-8 decoder. That is, additional decoders combined to make larger decoding systems (4-to-16; 5-to-32; etc.) can be used to make larger 1-D memory systems.

The two dimensional implementation is shown in Figure 7.11. Many of the characteristics are identical: the read and write lines are shared between all of the memories; the 13 least significant address lines are common to all memories, and the data bus is used by all chips. However, two 2-to-4 line decoders ('139s) are used to implement the decoding of the most significant address lines, instead of a single decoder. The use of the '139s allows for doubling the size of the memory (not shown) without the addition of more decoding capability. If the larger capability is not needed, then the function of the second '139 can be filled by an inverter.

The systems shown in Figures 7.10 and 7.11 demonstrate the use of decoders to make one and two dimensional systems. However, certain design criteria have not been considered in the discussion that must be taken into account in designing a specific system. For example, the time from chip enable to output valid for the μPD4464 is twice the time required for

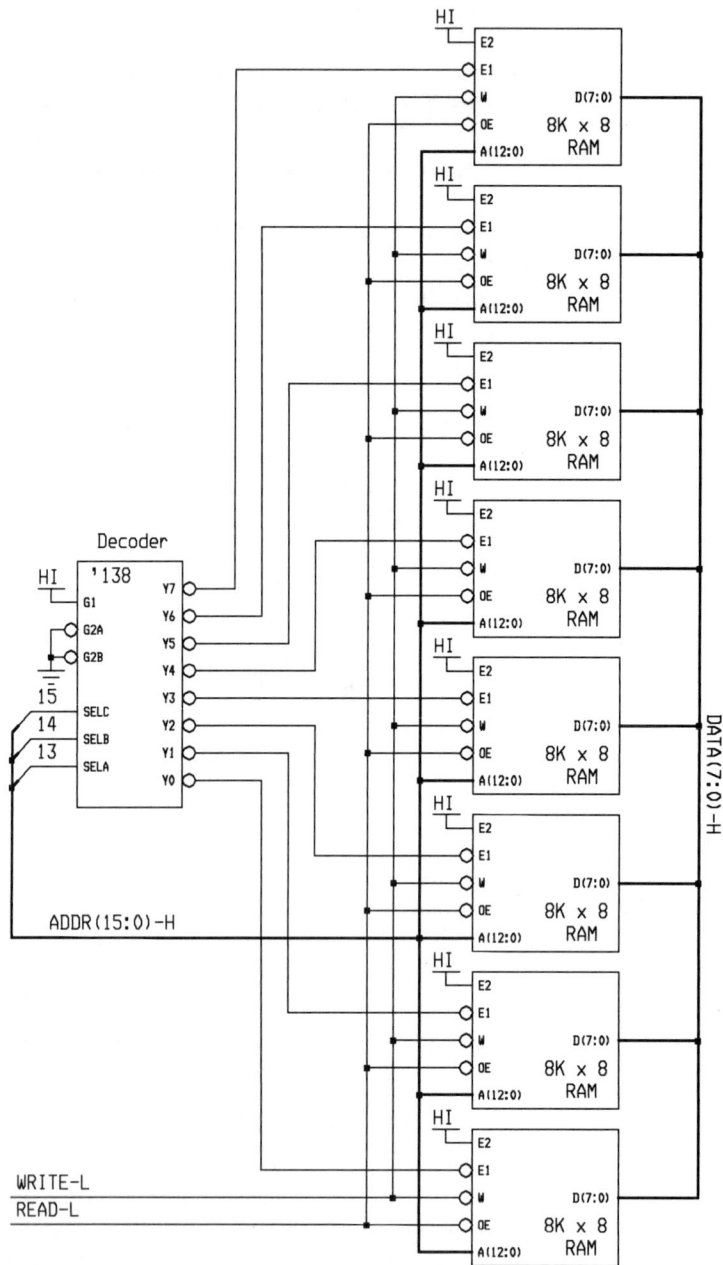

Figure 7.10. 64-Kbyte Memory Array from 8K × 8 Memories; 1-D Organization.

output enable to output valid. If the speed of the system is critical, then a different arrangement may be desired, one in which the chips are enabled all the time, and the output enable lines and write lines activated as needed to perform reads and writes. This changes the configuration of the system, since the read and write lines can no longer be common to all memory chips, but the same basic concepts are still applicable to the memory.

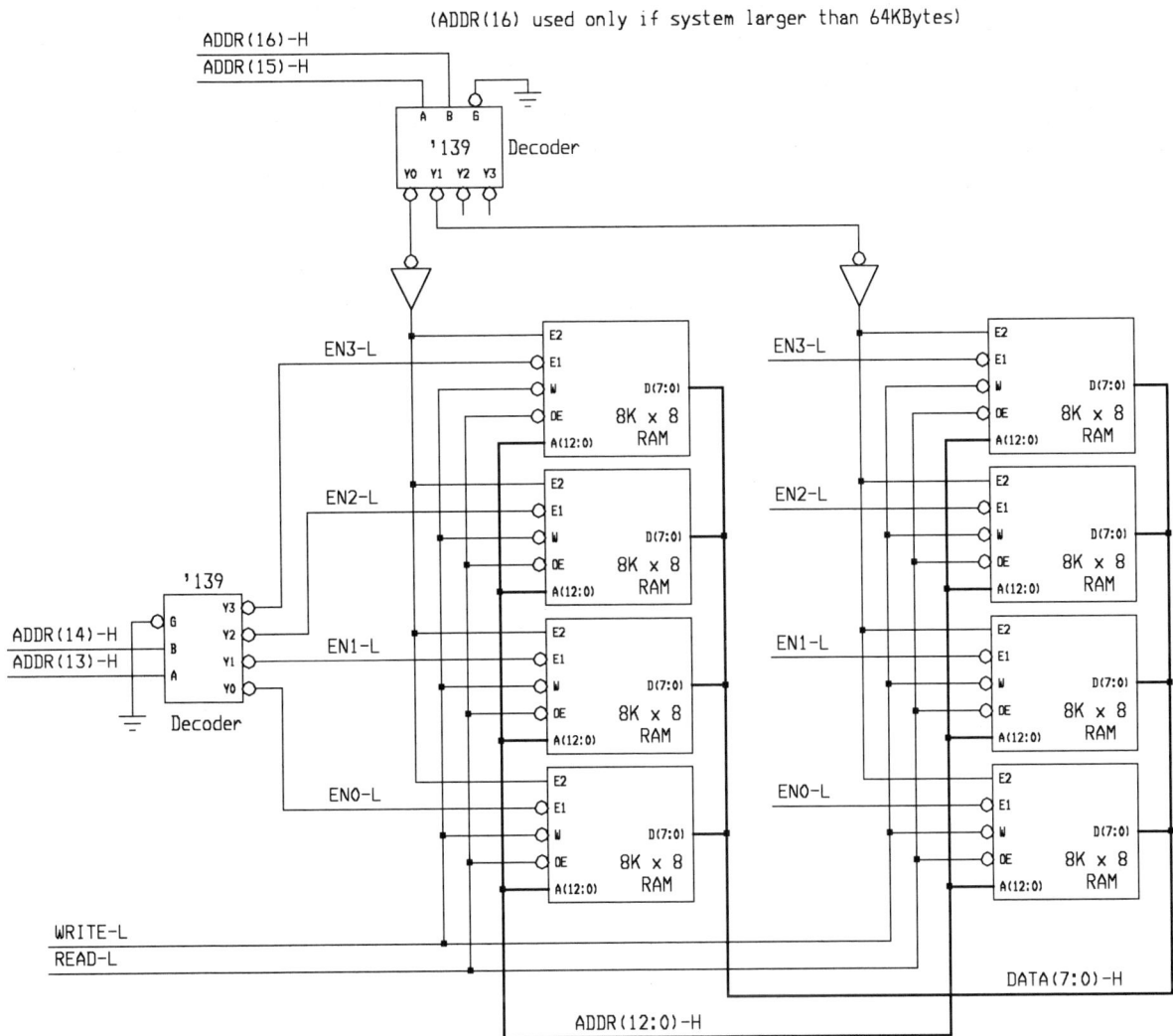

Figure 7.11. 64-Kbyte Memory Array from 8K × 8 Memories; 2-D Organization.

The concepts involved with the address mechanisms are not limited to the examples examined above. Consider the following example, in which dynamic memories are used to create a large random access memory. The addressing mechanism for identifying the appropriate memory module to activate is 1-D in nature, while the actual memories involved are selected in a 2-D fashion.

Example 7.3: Dynamic memory system: Design a memory to be used with the time multiplexed address/data bus of the NS32332 shown in Figure 6.10. The address will be supplied on the bus during T1, along with a data direction indication (DDIN). The memory should respond to the assertion of the address strobe (ADS-L) by initiating a memory request. If it is a write, the data will become available during T3; if it is a read, the data should be supplied as soon as possible, but no later than the beginning of T4. Use dynamic memories to provide as large a memory space as possible.

To discuss a system with dynamic memories, first let us examine some of the mechanisms of dealing with the memories. There are a number of device-specific characteristics, but the basic cycle for a read in a dynamic RAM is shown in Figure 7.12(b). Usually, large RAMs such as the dynamic RAMs shown here require so many address lines that the address divided into two parts and time multiplexed on a single set of address lines. These two parts of the address are called the "row address" and the "column address." After the row address is presented on the address lines for a required period, the row address strobe (RAS) is asserted. The address is held for a short time, then changed to be the column address. After a required setup time, the column address strobe is asserted (CAS), and the memory access begins. Some time later, which is the access time of the memory, the data becomes valid (T_{DATA}). When the RAS is released (T_{REL}), the output data will return to the tri-state condition. A write requires the same operation, but the write enable line is asserted during the operation,

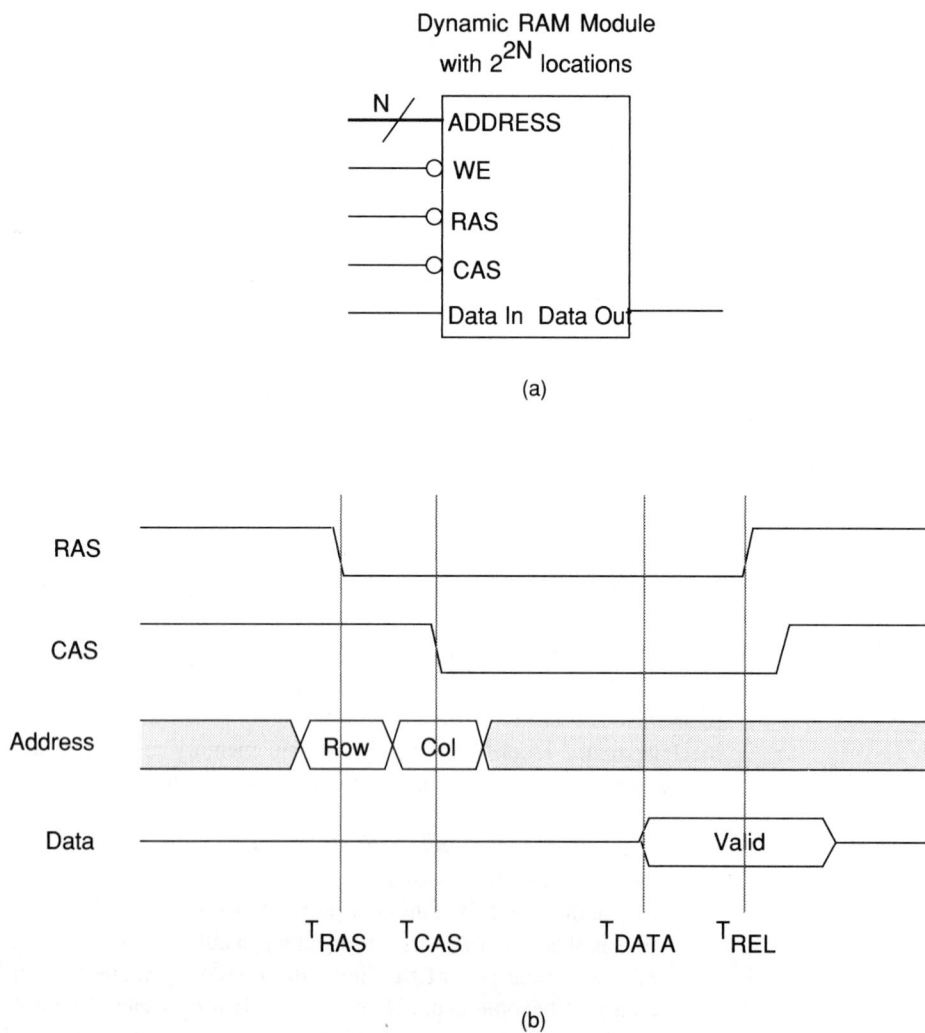

Dynamic RAM Module with 2^{2N} locations

(a)

(b)

Figure 7.12. Dynamic RAM. (a) Symbol. (b) Timing for Read Cycle.

and the data is asserted on the data lines by the module requesting the write action. As long as the rows are accessed every $T_{REFRESH}$ the information should be maintained. Thus, one of the design requirements is to access each row within the refresh time, which in many memories is 8 msec.

These individual packages can be combined in reasonable ways to be used in systems. For example, for bused systems the data in and data out pins can be tied together and connected to the system bus with transceivers. One commonly used configuration is to put nine individual memory modules on a single in line package (SIP), which is sufficient for a byte plus parity. This SIP module is used in this example; each SIP contains 256 Kbytes of information. SIP modules that contain 1 Mbyte and 4 Mbytes of information are also available.

Using modules with 256 Kbytes, an 8-Mbyte memory can be constructed with just 32 modules. Drawings of the memory are contained in Figure 7.13(a)–(c). A more complete set of drawings are found in Appendix B. Figure 7.13(a) contains the memory elements themselves and the data buffering transceivers. Note that the data lines are buffered from the bus system with a transceiver. Although the data line of each memory module does not present a large load, there are enough individual memory modules in the system to provide a nontrivial load. The buffer (transceiver) has the effect of isolating the loads from the bus and minimizing the effect of the wires required to carry the signals. Also note that the organization is such that the 4 bytes required for a 32-bit word (assuming that the word is aligned correctly) are all accessed with the same RAS and CAS line. Accesses of information not aligned on a word boundary must use the proper set of lines, and this is the responsibility of the initiator of the transaction.

The generation of row and address strobes is done by drivers capable of supplying a sufficient amount of current, and these are represented in Figure 7.13(b). The selection of the appropriate megabyte is accomplished by a decoder, which is a 1-D technique. The most significant address lines are used to identify the appropriate megabyte; expanding to a 16-Mbyte address space would require an additional decoder. The decoding is done by a '538, which is chosen for two reasons. The first is that the assertion level of the output is selectable, so that the assertion level is selected to match the gates that follow the decoder. In this case, the gates that follow are '801s which were selected for their drive capability: each RAS and CAS line has 36 individual memory modules attached to it (32 data, 4 parity). The second reason for the selection of the '538 is that, with the proper activation of the control signals, all of the outputs can be asserted simultaneously. This is very useful to allow all 8 Mbytes to perform a refresh cycle at the same time.

The address latches are also included in Figure 7.13(b). The latches accept the address during the first cycle of the transfer, and the address is then broken into three groups: nine bits for the row address, nine bits for the column address, and the most significant bits for identification of the active megabyte. The two least significant bits are not included, since the system is byte-addressable, and these bits merely identify the appropriate byte. Since all 4 bytes are accessed on every cycle, the least significant address lines are not needed here. The 9-bit row/column address bus (RC_BUS) is then presented to four sets of high current drivers, which have the capability

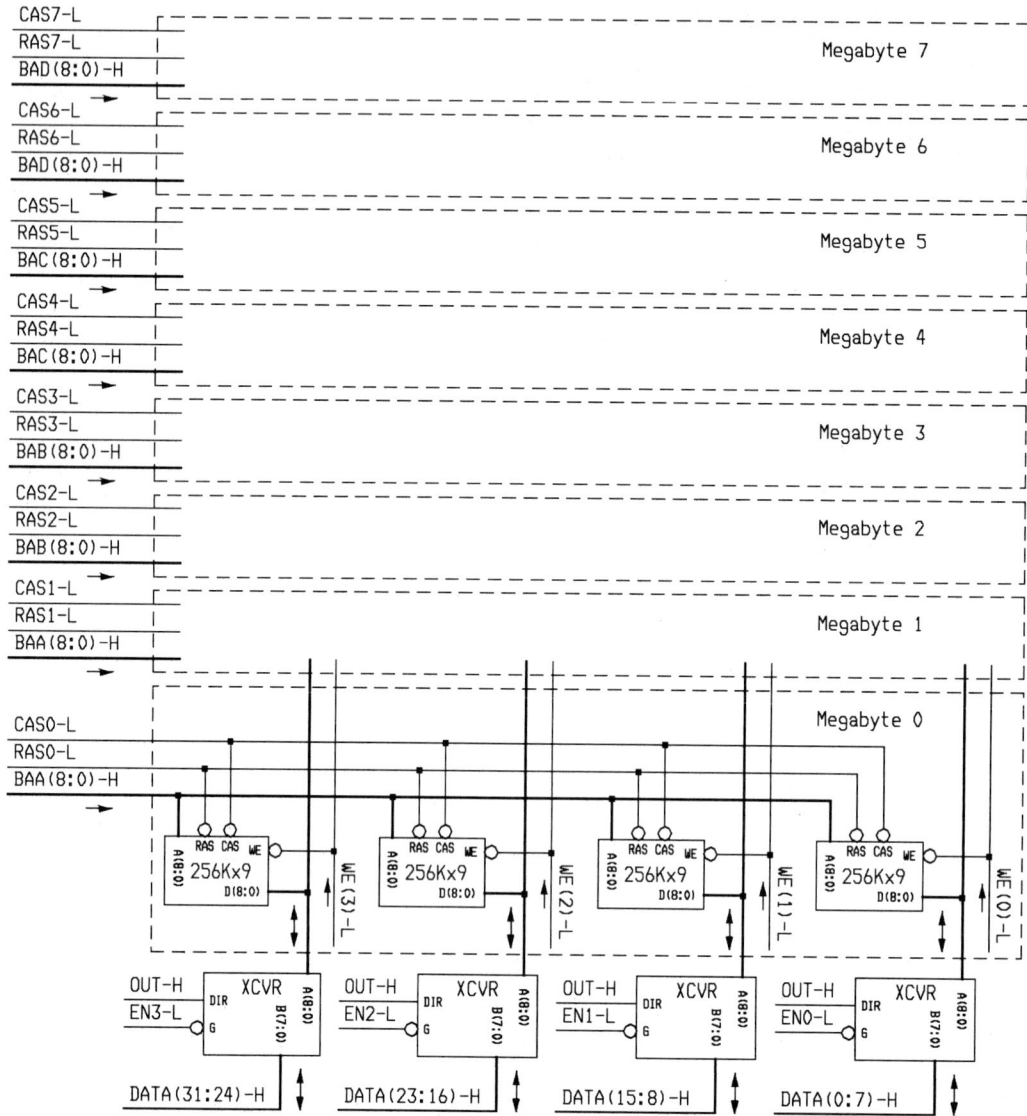

Figure 7.13(a). 8-Mbyte Memory System: Memory Array and Data Buffering Transceivers.

of providing the current needed by the collection of memories. The outputs of the high current drivers are conditioned by damping networks to minimize the undershoot and overshoot, which will occur when switching the lines between high and low logic levels. The address lines of the individual memories are supplied from the damping networks by four separate sets of lines (BAA-BAD). This buffering is required to provide sufficient drive capability, since each address line (BRA(0)-H, for example) supplies the address to 72 separate memory modules. Also included is the row counter that identifies the appropriate address for refresh. These memories refresh two rows simultaneously; so the 0 line is not involved in the count.

The control logic shown in Figure 7.13(c) coordinates the assertion of all of the signal lines. The coordinator of all of the work is a state machine

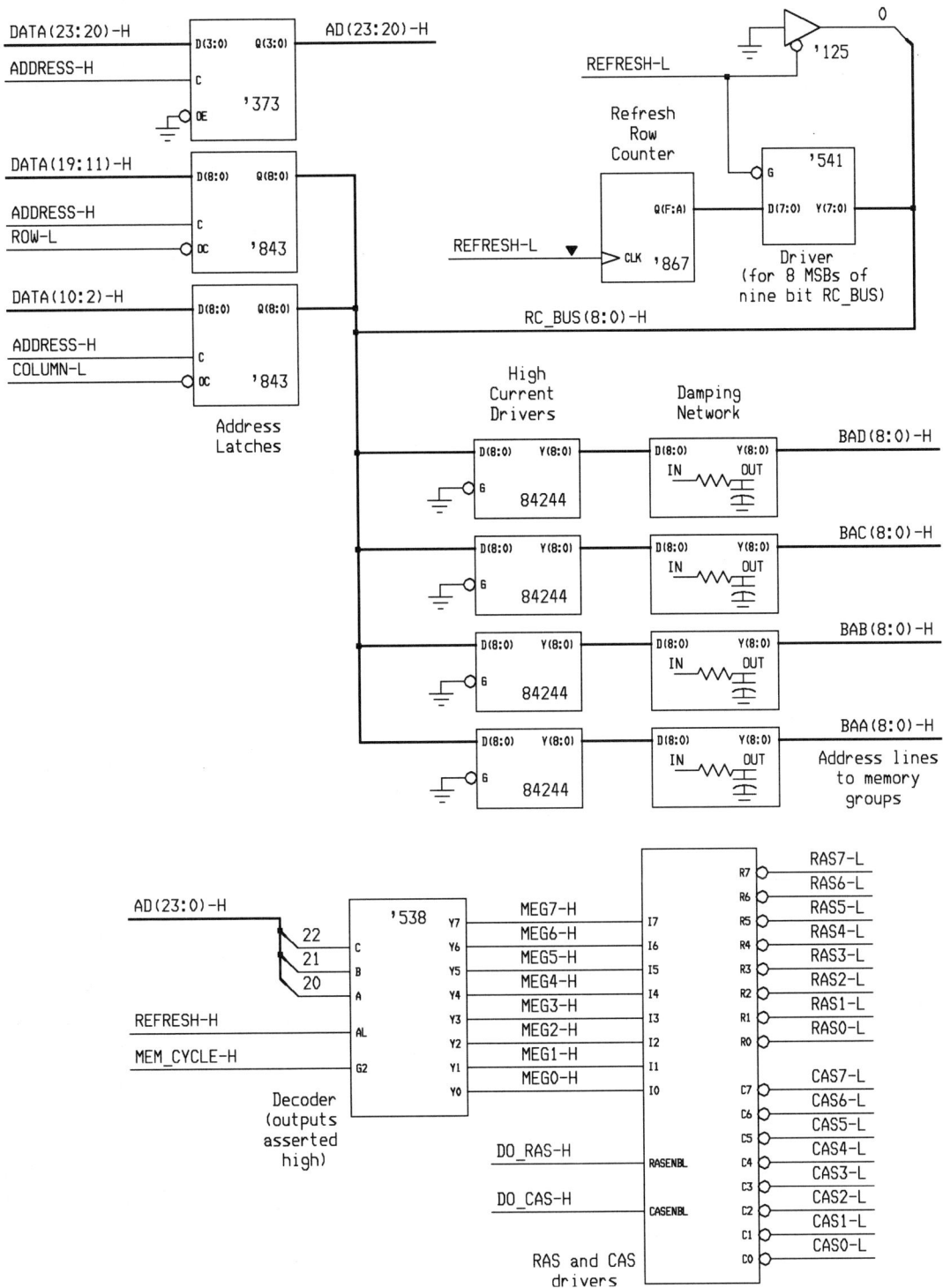

Figure 7.13(b). 8-Mbyte Memory System: RAS and CAS Logic; Address Latches and Drivers.

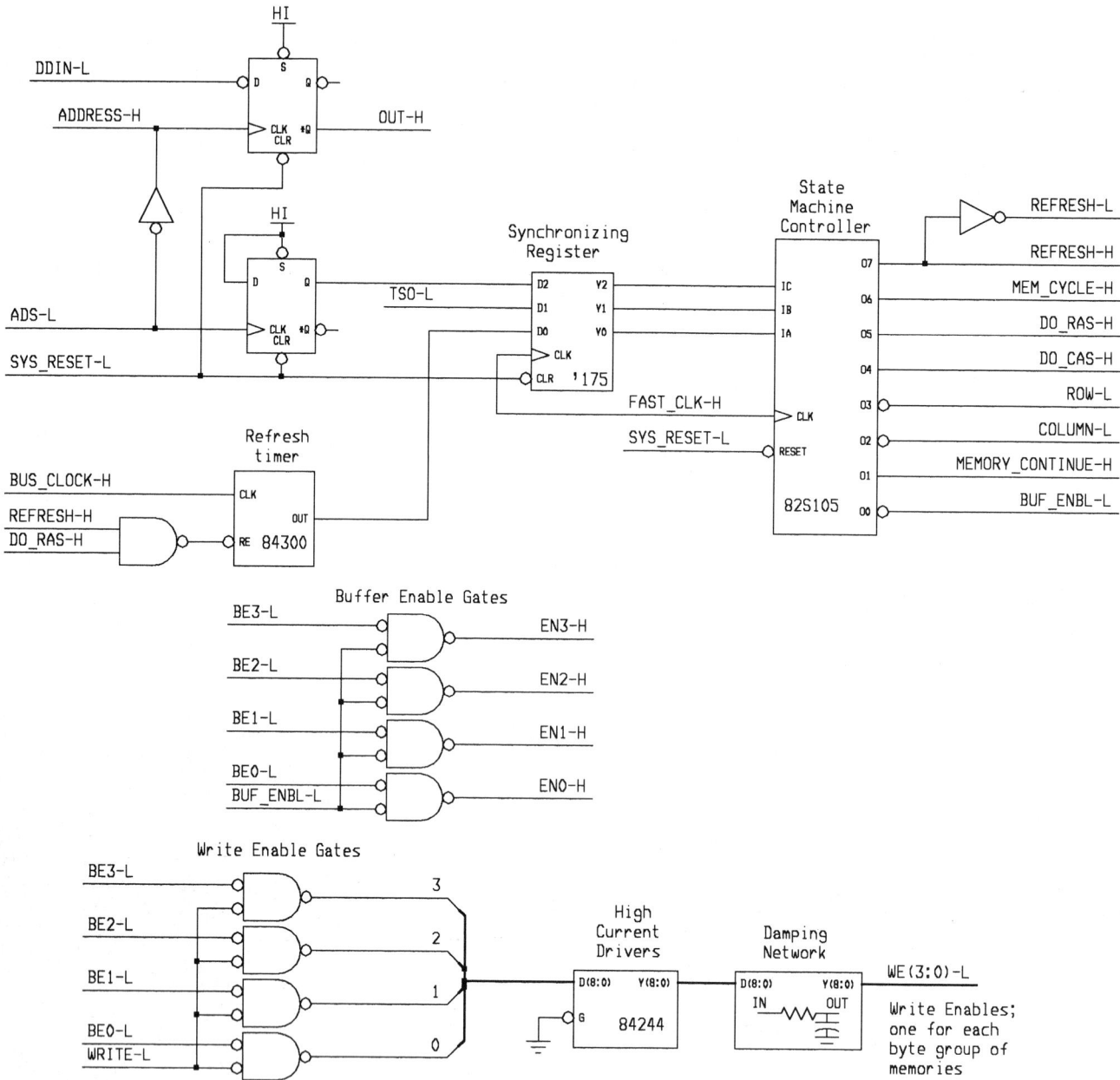

Figure 7.13(c). 8-Mbyte Memory System: Control Logic.

controller (82S105), which has the responsibility of asserting the signals in the order explained above. It is driven by a clock (FAST_CLK), which is four times faster than the bus clock (BUS_CLOCK) and synchronized with it. Thus, the bus clock and the fast clock are generated externally and supplied to the memory system. Using these two clocks in this manner allows the signals to be created in a timely fashion. The refresh counter is connected to the bus clock, which it counts down to identify the proper time to do a refresh. When the refresh is needed, it sets an internal flag that provides an input to the state machine; when the refresh is recognized the flag is reset.

The other inputs to the state machine are a flag to identify the start of a memory cycle, and the signal TSO, which comes from the timing unit of the microprocessor to identify the end of a cycle. The outputs of the state machine are used to assert RAS, CAS, and the other signals associated with the dynamic RAM. The signal MEMORY_CONTINUE is used to inform the rest of the system that the memory information is ready. This is necessary since the RAM may be in the middle of a refresh cycle when the system makes a memory request.

The two sets of gates in Figure 7.13(c) are to assert the write enable lines and the data transceiver enable lines at the appropriate time. The time is identified by the state machine controller, but the appropriate byte is identified by the byte enable signals generated by the processor. This 2-D mechanism chooses the appropriate bytes. One dimension is provided by the address; the second dimension is supplied by the processor. Thus, the processor must assume the responsibility of reading and writing information that is not aligned exactly on a 32-bit boundary.

A photograph of such a system is shown in Figure 7.13(d). This system contains 8 Mbytes of memory and a 32032 system.

The concepts discussed in this section are applicable to a wide range of memory organizations and considerations. For most processing done by general purpose computers, random access is required to the memory. This is true of core memories, semiconductor memories, and other technologies as well. Hence, the individual elements must be individually addressable and accessible through the

Figure 7.13(d). 8-Mbyte Memory System: 32032 System with 8-Mbytes Dynamic RAM.

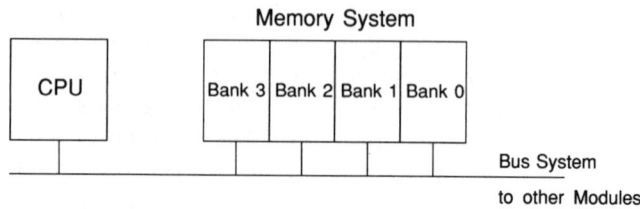

Figure 7.14. CPU with Four Bank Interleaved Memory System.

bus structure. The organization of the memory to access the addressed location can be done in a 1-D, 2-D, or related fashion, as long as only one location is actually enabled.

Creating larger memories, or memories with differing characteristics, can be accomplished by combinations of the mechanisms discussed here. For example, one of the figures of merit for a memory system is bus bandwidth, represented in bytes/sec. Since information can be transferred over a bus structure faster than it can be retrieved from a large memory, one of the ways to increase the bandwidth is to create memory in banks, and interleave the memory banks in time. Consider the system shown in Figure 7.14. The memory requests are sent to all four banks, and the response sent to the processor in different time slots. If the bus width is 4 bytes, and the memory access time is 200 nsec, and if 4 bytes can be sent every 50 nsec, then all four banks can be kept busy (assuming that there are sufficient requests). But each bank is individually organized as a random access system, and interfaces to the bus system in a manner which will allow the transfers to occur in a reasonable fashion. This requires more circuitry, but speeds up the overall data rates.

The choice of a memory organization and the technology in which it is implemented must reflect the constraints of the entire system. The choices will be based on optimizing performance for a given set of resources. If a major requirement is speed, then the designer can afford to put more resources (silicon real estate, board space, power, etc.) in the memory to provide for a minimum response time. If the critical resource is power, such as a battery operated system, then the complexity cannot be increased, and the parts and design mechanisms are optimized for minimal power consumption. Nevertheless, the system architect can choose from a variety of memory and processor organizations to create a system that will fit a particular need.

7.3. Virtual Memory Systems: The Illusion of a Memory Space

One of the principal tenets of stored program computers is that the program resides in a memory space, and the instructions are extracted from memory and executed. If the instruction calls for data manipulation, then the data is identified and utilized to perform whatever calculations are called for by the instruction. In most programs the data also resides in the memory, at least at the beginning of the program, when data is brought into the system, or at the end of the program, when data is prepared for output to the destination device. Thus, the program is loaded into the memory, started, and whatever data manipulations are called for by the program are executed. The program then terminates, and the system moves on to execute the next program.

The statements made in the previous paragraph reflect some assumptions often made about the use of the computer. Most machines used today have a collection of system facilities that we have come to call the operating system (OS). The operating system has the responsibility of doing many things, among them transferring programs and data to and from memory. When the program has been loaded, the operating system starts execution of the program at some predetermined point. However, most users of computer systems do not consider the effect of what the OS is doing; rather, they have a "model" of what the machine is, and they are operating under the assumption that the model is at least functionally correct. Such a model may appear as shown in Figure 7.15.

In multiprogrammed systems, we know that other programs will also be utilizing the machine, but generally we think of the machine as "ours," at least for the duration of our program. Knowing that a program will have a program section and a data section, we often think of the machine as shown in Figure 7.16. This simple block diagram shows only the memory and the processing capability. The possible connection between the two is identified by the instruction set, and using that instruction set we are able to perform work, where work is defined as manipulating data. The machine as seen in Figure 7.16 is what we think we have; hence, we call it a "virtual machine." In our mental model of the machine, the program starts at location zero and executes through the instructions in order. In the physical machine, the program was not loaded at location zero; rather, the operating system placed the information at a location which, for some reason, was available to be used. The operating system, then, is responsible for ascertaining what parts of memory are available; if no memory is available, then the OS makes some memory available. In a location known to the operating system there is kept a correspondence between the virtual space, which the program has the illusion of controlling, and the physical space, which contains the actual information being manipulated.

The mechanism used to define the relationship between the memory space that the program thinks it is controlling, and the actual memory locations being utilized, is called a "virtual memory mapping." The memory mapping mechanism

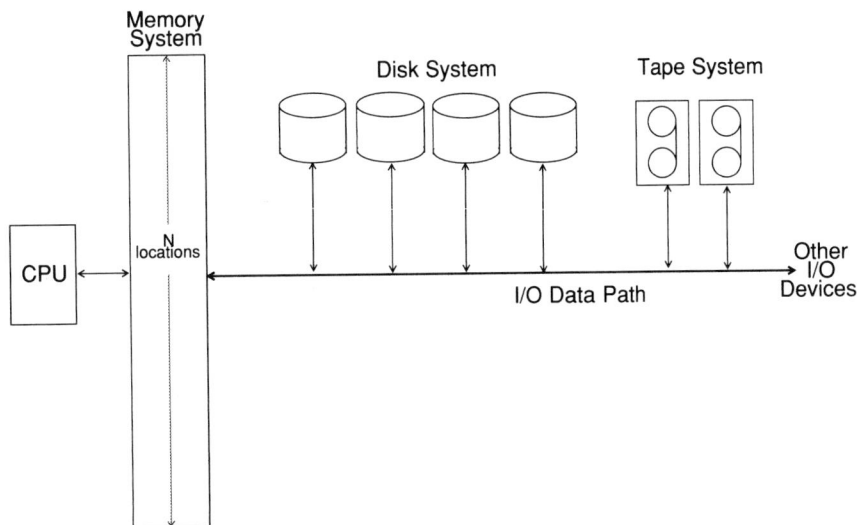

Figure 7.15. Block Diagram of a "Model" Computer.

Memory

| Main Program |
| Subroutines |
| Global Data |
| Local Data |
| Stack |

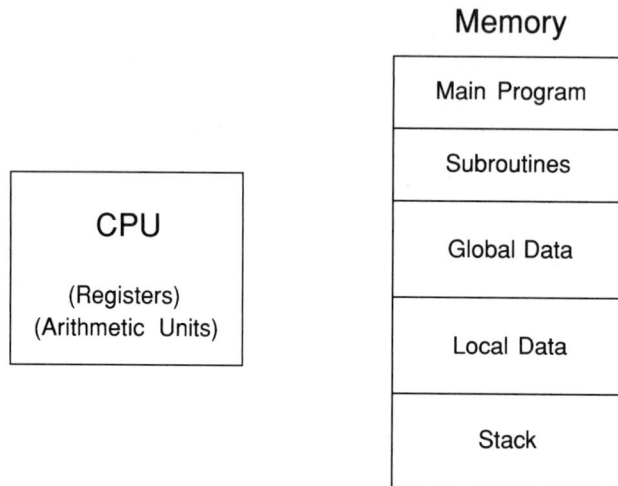

Figure 7.16. User Model for a Computer and Program.

is therefore responsible for converting an address issued by the program (the virtual address) to an address that will be used by the memory system to access the information (the real address). Two common mechanisms often considered are segmentation and paging, and some systems utilize both concepts in their implementation. It is not our intention to discuss the pros and cons of one mechanism over another. That can be dealt with more effectively in a discussion of operating systems themselves [BrHa73, PeSi83, Deit84, BiSh88]. Rather, our interest is in the low level operations required to make virtual memory work.

Information is stored in real, physical memory, and, as such, it must be referenced with a valid memory address. However, within the executing program, references are made by the program in any one of a number of different ways. The addressing mechanism, be it a program counter reference, an indirect data reference, or any other method to specify a location in memory, identifies the target location in the virtual space of the program — where the program thinks the information is located. The memory mapping mechanism manipulates this (virtual) address in such a way that the proper location in memory (the real address) is accessed.

One simple mechanism that can be used to allow multiple programs to coexist in a memory, each executing in its own address space, is depicted in Figure 7.17. In this case the operating system has placed the various programs into a large memory, and it will keep a record of the base address for each of the programs. In addition, it will keep a record of the sections of memory not used, in order to accommodate other programs as needed. Then when Program 2 is to be executed, as in the figure, the OS will place the base address of the program into the base address register, so that all references made by the CPU to memory are made relative to the base location of the program. This is an example of register relative addressing, except that *all* references to memory are made relative to the base register. In this way, the virtual address of the program (the address the program thinks it is using) is translated to a physical address, the actual location of the information, by a simple addition. This mechanism will allow a large memory to be used by a system limited in some other way. For example, the instruction set architecture of the PDP 11 family of computers limits the size of a single

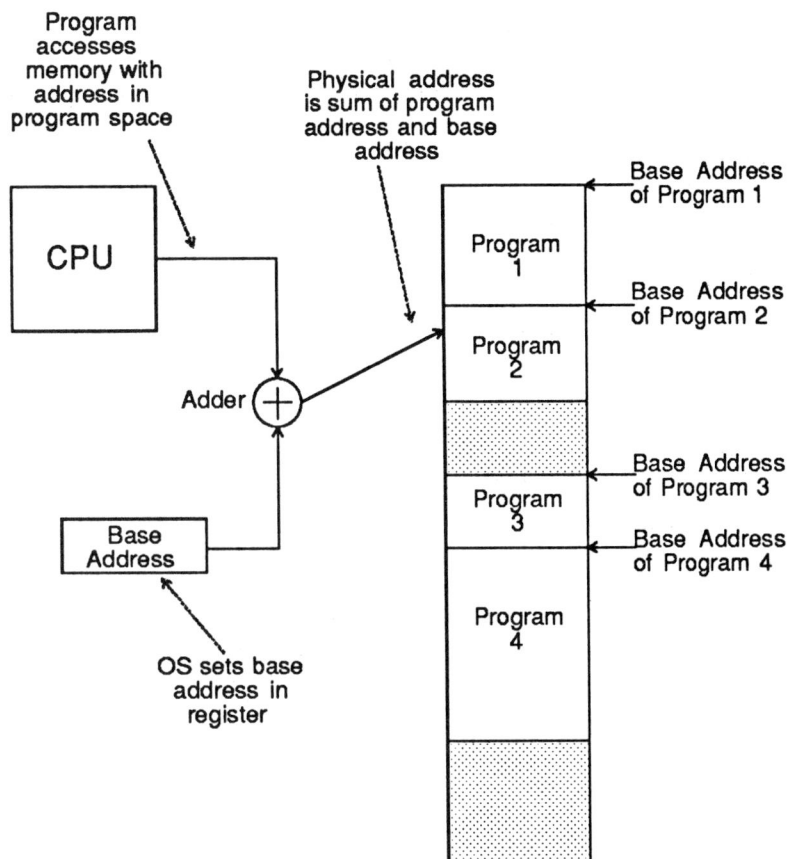

Figure 7.17. Multiple Programs in a Single Memory.

process to 64 Kbytes, the amount of byte-addressable memory that can be reached with a 16-bit address. Yet using the scheme depicted in Figure 7.17, several such programs can exist in a memory that is much larger than 64 Kbytes. The operating system can share the resources of the system between the programs in a reasonable way. In this way, a multiprogrammed environment can be created, allowing programs to share processor and I/O capabilities of the system.

The above scheme considers each program an indivisible block, and must deal with the programs in that manner. However, an extension of the scheme is to divide each program into logical segments, and load the segments into their own sections of memory. This would correspond to the program model shown in Figure 7.16. Then, as the address was created by the system to access a particular piece of information, the address generated by the program would be offset by the value in the appropriate segment register, and the resulting address would be sent to the memory.

The above process can be visualized by considering a program which has been broken into segments, such as shown in Figure 7.18. The program represented in the figure consists of four segments: a main program segment, a subroutine segment, a data segment consisting of read only data, and a data segment with locations that can be both read and modified. For this system, the processor will generate addresses consisting of a segment number and an offset within that segment. The memory management mechanism must then translate

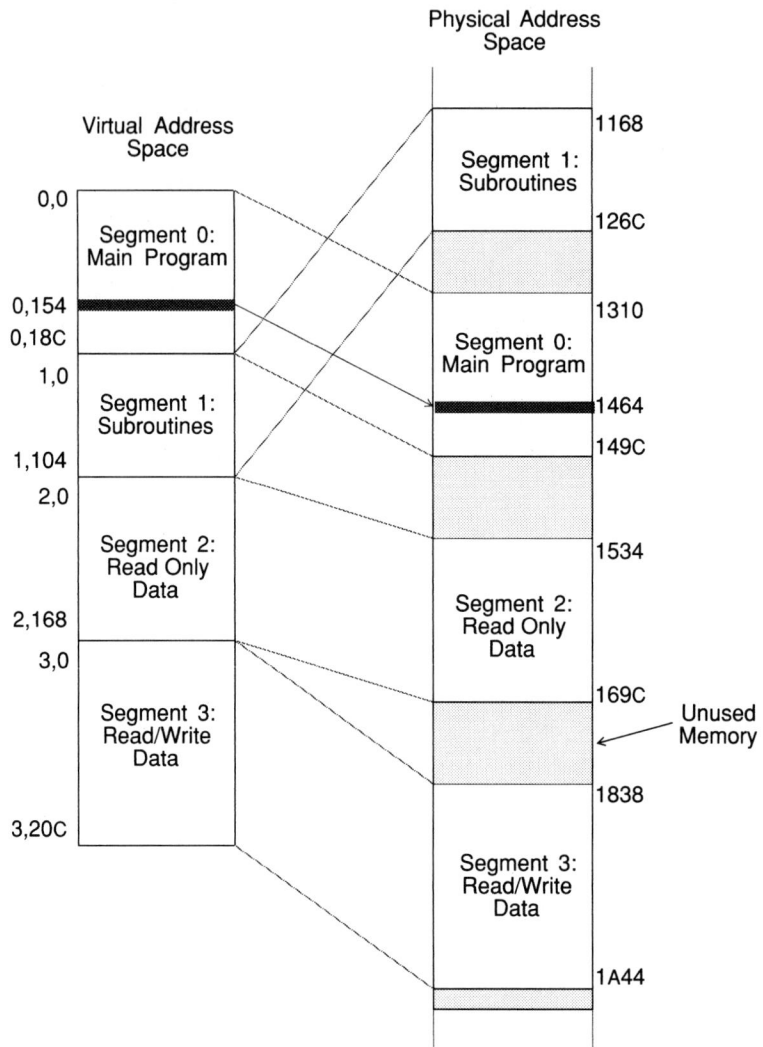

Figure 7.18. Virtual Address Mechanism with Segmentation.

Program Segment Table

Segment	Length	Address	Access
0	190	1310	Read, Execute
1	108	1168	Read, Execute
2	16C	1534	Read
3	210	1838	Read, Write

this into the proper real address. The real address, $ADDR_{REAL}$, can be represented as the sum of the base of the segment and the offset within the segment:

$$ADDR_{REAL} = ADDR_{SEGMENT\ BASE} + ADDR_{SEGMENT\ OFFSET}$$

Thus the creation of the correct address in the system involves identifying the correct segment base and adding to it the segment offset. Part of the addressing mechanism is then to consult the program segment table (PST) for each access: the segment number identifies the element of the PST that refers to the desired segment and, using that information, generates the correct physical address. The example shown in Figure 7.18 indicates that address 154 in the main program segment is converted to physical address 1464. The hardware of the system should make this conversion as quickly as possible, and at the same time check the legality of the reference. That is, does the address exceed the length of the segment? Or is the reference a write request into a read only segment? A number of systems include segmentation capability in the processor, the most prolific of which is the 80x86 family of microprocessors. Figure 7.19 gives a register level diagram of the microprocessor, in which the segment registers play a prominent part. Note that the segment descriptor registers work in conjunction with the virtual address generation hardwdare, and that jointly they can generate the required address. Thus, the mechanisms discussed are built into the hardware of the system.

If a virtual memory system is implemented by using segments, then the OS has the responsibility of maintaining the segments, and loading the segment registers with the addresses for the currently executing program. If another program is

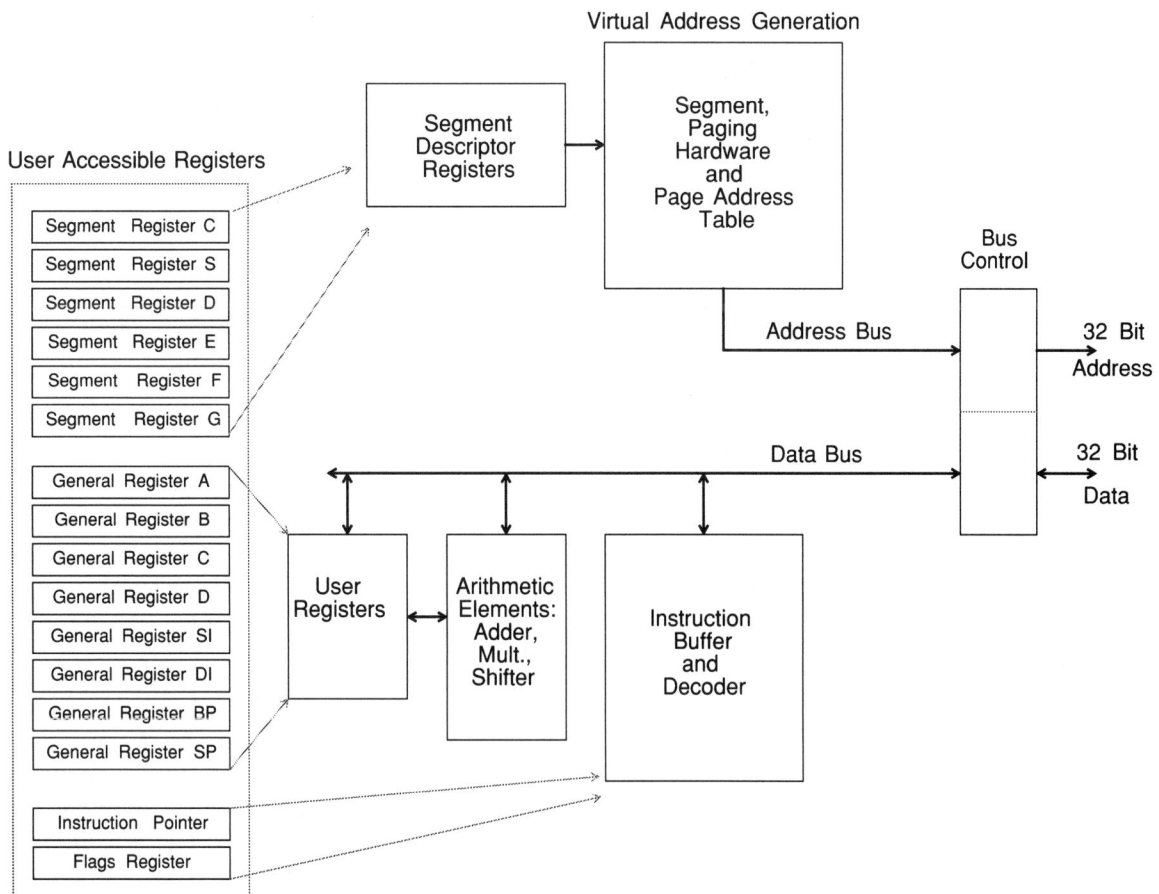

Figure 7.19. Block Diagram of a 80386 Processor.

needed, then all of the segment registers are changed appropriately. Note that this does not exclude the operating system from using the same physical segment for more than one program. For example, the program section of an editor may be needed by several users, and the operating system can be aware of this and set up the segment registers accordingly.

One of the mechanisms alluded to but not actually described has to do with the location of the programs when they are not in the memory executing. The secondary storage medium is used to hold the programs, or portions of the programs, until they are needed. This secondary storage is usually disk, but could be any storage area large enough to hold the entire program, or collection of program segments. One of the tasks of the OS is to control the use of the memory; that is, the programs or program segments that reside in the memory at any given time is determined by the OS. If a segment is needed during the execution of a program, and that segment is not in memory, then the OS brings in the information from secondary memory. In the process of doing so, it may be necessary for another segment, which is not currently active, to be returned to secondary storage. In this way the OS brings into memory the active programs and data, and those that are not currently active will migrate out of main store as the programs currently running need more memory space.

A segment is a logical entity, such as a program segment or data segment. There is no inherent size of such an entity, so there is no standard size of segments involved in a computer system. Thus, the operating system must keep track of the starting address of the segment, its length, and other information that deals with access privileges. This information is shown as part of the program segment table in Figure 7.18. One of the protection issues to be addressed in a system is the containment of programs: a program must not be able to access memory, except as that specific privilege has been granted to the program. As a program requests information in a segment, the OS must make sure that the program should have access to that segment. When accessing the information in a segment, the program should be prevented from addressing information beyond the length of the segment. One way to enforce this is to include in the system bounds checking capabilities that compare the requested address against a given maximum. This will allow the system to protect the segments against unauthorized access.

Example 7.4: Memory mapping with segments: Give a block diagram level representation of an address translation mechanism involving segments. The address supplied by the processor consists of two values, the segment number and the offset within the segment. If an out of bounds request is made, the unit should issue an interrupt. The mechanism should be capable of keeping track of 16 programs, each capable of accessing 16 segments.

A block diagram of one solution to this problem is shown in Figure 7.20. The hardware logically sits between the generation of the addresses and the actual memory. The addresses are generated in pairs, consisting of a segment number and an offset within the segment. Before the program can run, the OS loads the appropriate segments into the actual memory, then sets up the addresses and lengths in the two memories shown in the figure. Then the OS sets the correct pattern in the Program ID register and initiates the program. The address to be used for the information access in the actual memory is obtained by adding the base address of the segment to the address within the segment. However, the address within the segment is

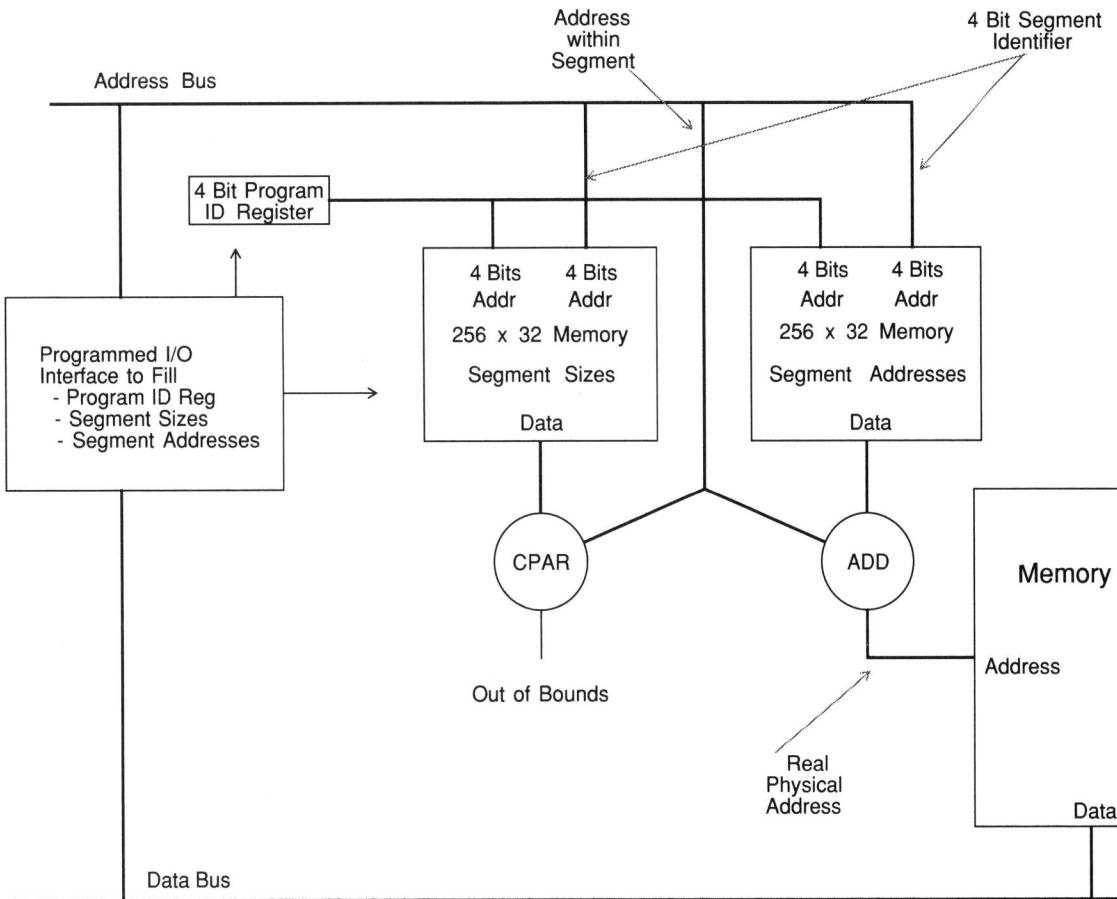

Figure 7.20. Hardware for Address Translation with Segments.

also directed to a comparator that checks the address against a maximum. If the address is too large, then the out of bounds signal will be asserted, and the system will be informed of the problem. The 256 locations in the segment sizes and segment addresses memories allow up to 16 different programs to reside in memory at the same time, and switching between them is accomplished by placing a different pattern in the program ID register. Note that some data paths are not shown, such as the path from the data bus to the segment information memories. Note also that the memories are 32 bits wide, which would allow for alignment on any byte boundary (for a system with 32 address lines). Since most memories are organized (at least) 4 bytes wide, these memories could be 28 bits wide, with the understanding that all segments must be aligned on a doubleword boundary.

As demonstrated by the preceding example, the virtual to real translation is not free; some time is required to generate the real address from the information supplied by the processor. The times involved are the time to access the segment addresses and segment sizes information, and the time to add that information to the address within the segment. This overhead is imposed on all references to virtual memory in this scheme. In addition to the overhead on a per reference basis, there is also the overhead of managing the memory space, allocating segments in the available space, collecting the empty space, and so on. All of these operations add to the overhead of the system, and lead to a discussion of different approaches to memory address mechanisms.

Another mechanism for mapping virtual addresses to physical address is to divide the original program and data space into pieces based not on logical boundaries, but rather physical boundaries. Thus the program model shown in Figure 7.16 can be modified as shown in Figure 7.21. The pages have the characteristic that they all have exactly the same size, as compared with the segments mentioned above, where the size is not a standard value. This organization allows for the individual elements (in this case pages) to fit in any location in a page frame, since all pages have exactly the same size. The pages all begin on a page boundary. The process of address generation is basically the same as that for segmentation:

$$ADDR_{REAL} = ADDR_{PAGE\ BASE} + ADDR_{PAGE\ OFFSET}$$

The principal difference is that the addition called for in the above equation is a concatenation, not a full addition. That is, since the pages are forced to begin on page boundaries, the least significant address bits (for the first location of a page) are all zero. The address bits that identify the location within the page will not extend into the nonzero bits of the address for the page boundary. Hence, no addition time is required.

The difference between the paging scheme and the segmentation scheme presented above can be visualized by a different view of the program of Figure 7.18. The addressing scheme is modified to a paging scheme as shown in Figure 7.22. As far as the program is concerned, the only difference is that the accesses are made by specifying the page number and offset within the page, not the segment number and offset within the segment. As before, the correlation between the virtual and physical addresses can be represented in tabular form, shown in the figure as the page table. As shown in the figure, the instruction located at location 344 of page 2 has a physical address of 2F44. Note that the addition is merely a

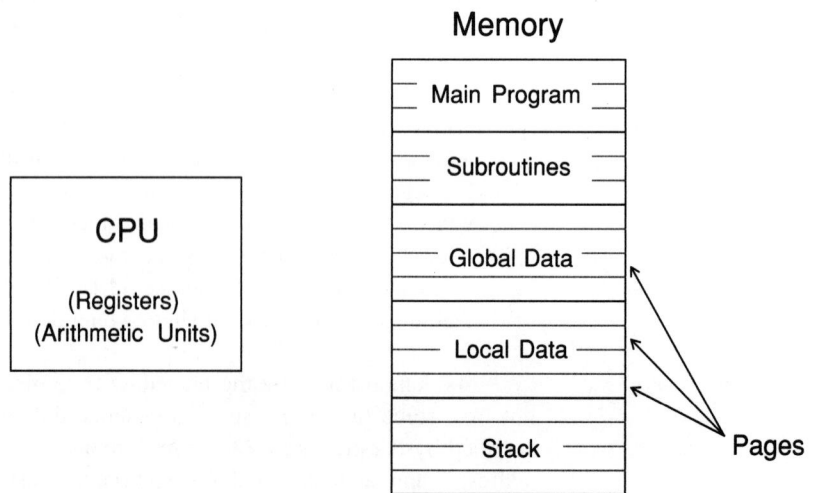

Figure 7.21. User Model for a Computer and Program, Using Pages.

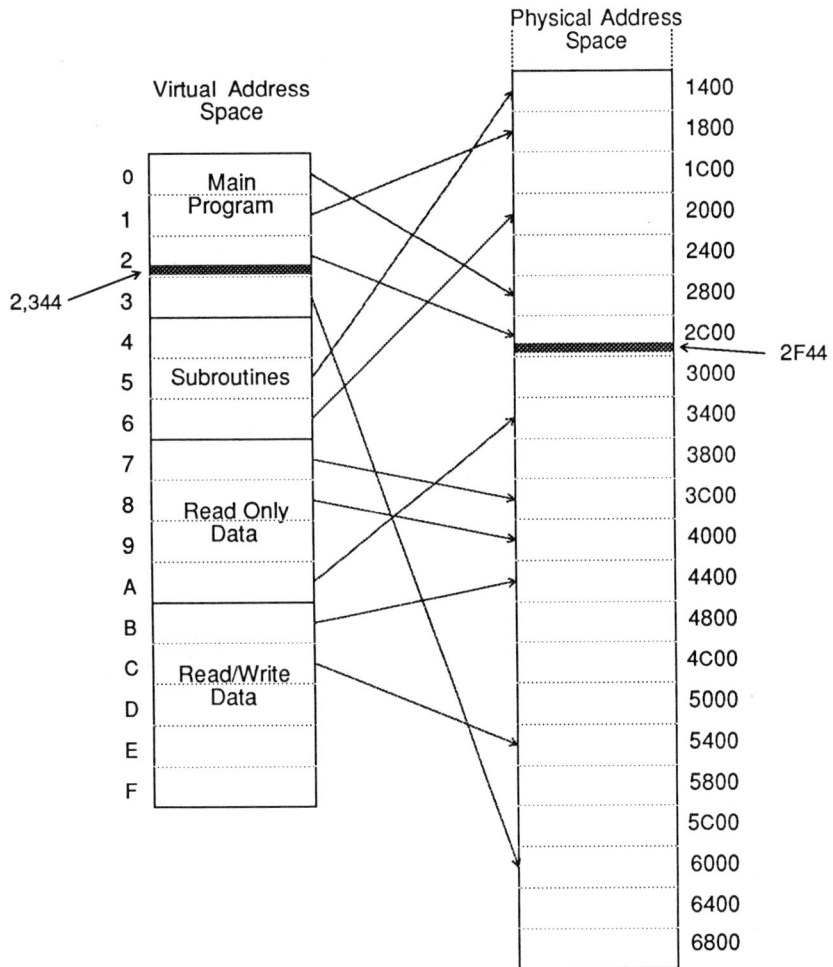

Virtual Address Space

0	Main Program
1	
2	
3	
4	Subroutines
5	
6	
7	
8	Read Only Data
9	
A	
B	
C	Read/Write Data
D	
E	
F	

2,344

Physical Address Space

1400
1800
1C00
2000
2400
2800
2C00
3000
3400
3800
3C00
4000
4400
4800
4C00
5000
5400
5800
5C00
6000
6400
6800

2F44

Page Table

Page	Address	Access
0	2800	Read, Execute
1	1800	Read, Execute
2	2C00	Read, Execute
3	6000	Read, Execute
4	Not in Memory	Read, Execute
5	1400	Read, Execute
6	2000	Read, Execute
7	3C00	Read, Execute
8	4000	Read
9	Not in Memory	Read
A	3400	Read
B	4400	Read
C	5400	Read/Write
D	Not in Memory	Read/Write
E	Not in Memory	Read/Write
F	Not in Memory	Read/Write

Figure 7.22. Virtual Address Mechanism with Paging.

concatenation, since 2C00 + 344 does not have any nonzero overlap (0010 1100 0000 0000 + 0011 0100 0100 = 0010 1111 0100 0100).

The OS burden changes under this scheme, since the question asked is not if a page will fit, but rather, where should the page be placed. This decision is a function of the method utilized by the operating system to maintain the memory space in the machine, and how much information is dealt with with each page operation. Some systems bring in only those immediately requested by the program. Other systems load into memory not only the requested page, but some surrounding pages as well. For a discussion of the various decisions and their impact on overall system performance see [PeSi83, Deit84, BiSh88].

Pages are generally much smaller than segments, ranging from 256 bytes to 1,024 bytes or more. Since the page size is smaller than a segment size, there will be, in general, many pages in a system. Thus, the table of entries cannot be limited to 16. However, the overall organization of the memory mapping scheme will be very similar. Consider the following example that proposes some hardware to provide a virtual address to real address translation.

Example 7.5: Memory mapping with pages: Design a virtual memory mapper that uses pages of 512 bytes. The page table must be capable of supporting 2,048 pages. The mechanism should function as indicated by Figure 7.22. What is the speed of the address translation mechanism?

One solution to the stated problem is shown in Figure 7.23. The address received from the processor is dealt with in two sections: the page identifier and the offset within the page. Thus, with 512 bytes per page, the 9 least significant bits (ADDRESS(8:0)-H) are used to identify the location within the page, and the remaining bits of the address are used to specify the appropriate page. Also note that with 2,048 pages, each with 512 bytes, the addressable memory is only a megabyte. This is not a large enough memory space for general usage, but will be large enough for some applications. The stated requirement of 2,048 pages necessitates 11 bits of address to identify the appropriate page. The width of the page table memory for this design is 17 bits, which allows 15 bits of address and 2 bits to indicate the status of the addressed page. One bit is used to indicate if the addressed page is in main store or not; the other bit is used to identify whether the page has been modified since it was loaded. If the page has not been modified, then, when the time arrives for it to be removed to make room for a new page, the old page need not be returned to the mass storage device.

Three basic modes of operation of the mechanism are shown. In one mode the page table can be filled with information. In this mode, the address of the page table is provided by the PIO_DATA path, and data can be loaded into the table with the chip select (CS) and write enable (WE) lines from the control logic. The information to place in the page table is loaded from the data bus, via the transceiver. The second mode of operation is normal behavior for the system. In this mode, the 9 least significant lines of the address are obtained directly from the address bus. Since there are 24 address lines total, the remaining 15 lines must come from the page table. The applicable location of the page table is identified by the 11 address lines of higher significance than the lines that identify the location of the address within the page (ADDRESS(19:9)). These lines are fed to the address of the page table, and also the output enable (OE) is asserted. Under these conditions, the page table will output the base address of the

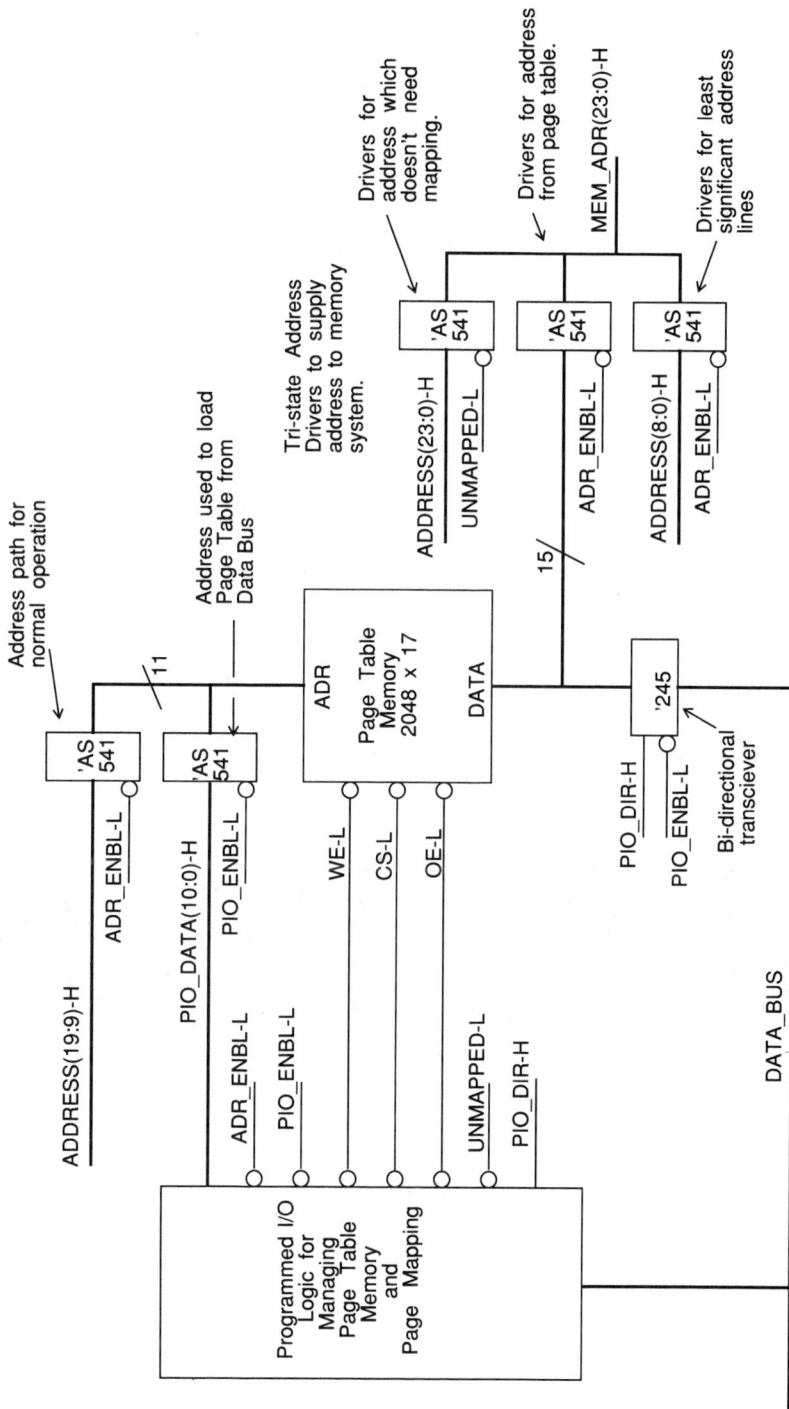

Figure 7.23. Block Diagram of Logic for Paged Memory Address Translation.

selected page, which will then be concatenated with the 9 least significant lines to form the physical address of the desired virtual location.

The third mode of operation is for addresses that do not need virtual-to-real translation. This could be used, for example, by the OS when it interrogates tables at known physical locations in memory, or activates memory mapped I/O.

Not shown in the logic diagram is any method for keeping track of the order of use of the pages. When a new page needs to be loaded into main store, a number of algorithms may be used to identify the page to be replaced. The algorithm that feels most intuitively correct is to replace the least recently used page. But the hardware required to keep track of the pages in the order of their use is nontrivial and not shown. Other algorithms are also available that optimize the behavior of the system under specific circumstances [PeSi83, Deit84, BiSh88].

As stated earlier, the addition process is one of concatenating the bits in the proper order, and no real addition is required. Thus the time required for the circuit shown in Figure 7.23 is the sum of the delay times in the respective elements:

$$T_{\text{TRANSLATE}} = T_{541} + T_{\text{MEM}} + T_{541}$$

$$= 2 \times T_{541} + T_{\text{MEM}}$$

For 74AS541s and 30 nsec memory, this totals about 42 nsec.

The paging scheme has many advantages that make it very attractive for systems. Since all pages are the same size, any page can be placed in any page frame in memory. The system is able to more effectively utilize all space, and memory does not tend to fragment as it does in systems utilizing segmentation only. The creation of the address utilizes a concatenation process, which saves time over a system that requires an addition. Nevertheless, some problems need to be addressed in real systems. One of the problems is illustrated by the preceding example. Even with a page table memory of 2,048 entries, the maximum size of the memory available to a program in this system is $2,048 \times 512 = 1$ Mbyte. Since the amount of space used by programs has increased drastically as the relative cost of memory has decreased, this is not large enough for most programs. The 24-bit address space provided by many processors allows for 16 Mbytes of memory, and this is not enough for many programs today. In a simple program used in a university environment for some research problems, the virtual memory space needed by the system exceeded 50 Mbytes. Thus, it is necessary to provide a sufficiently large page table to allow programs to grow to the necessary size.

Any limit on the number of pages that can be accessed by a program will eventually limit the usability of the system. Thus, the approach suggested by Example 7.5 is not sufficient, and the system needs to be modified to allow a larger page capability. This can be accomplished by keeping the page table, not in hardware, but in the memory of the system itself. However, if all accesses needed to obtain page addresses by going to main store, the performance penalty would be very large. One solution is to keep in hardware not all of the page table entries, but rather the most active page entries. In this manner the hardware requirements can be reduced, and still maintain critical page information to speed up the processing.

This is the approach taken in the NS32082, which is the memory management unit (MMU) for the NS32000 processor series. A block diagram of the NS32082 is given in Figure 7.24. This unit has been designed to work in conjunction with the time multiplexed bus of the NS32000 series processors, an example of which is given in Figure 6.10. When the processor generates the ADS signal, the MMU accepts the address and examines a 32 entry page table to see if it is an active page. If the match is successful, then the correct physical address is made available in the next bus cycle, and the bus transactions continue as expected. Thus, the overall effect of the virtual to real translations carried on by the MMU is to add one additional cycle to the four cycles needed for a bus transfer. This increases by 25% the time required to fetch information from memory. Studies indicate that for most programs the needed page information will immediately be found in the 32 element page table for around 98% of all accesses. When the address provided by the processor does not match one of the entries in the hardware page table, this does not mean that the page is not in memory. Rather, the information must be sought from the real page table, which is kept in main store. The NS32082 automatically generates memory requests to fetch this information from main store, whereupon it updates its hardware page table and continues the interrupted processing. This should occur for about 2% of the memory requests. A system block diagram of a NS32032 CPU with a NS32082 MMU and other support chips is shown in Figure 7.25. Note that the ADS signal is directed only to the MMU, which then creates the correct physical address and asserts PAV, physical address valid.

Like segmentation, the paging mechanism allows the system to create a "virtual" memory, which is the appearance of a memory space as it is accessed by a program. This allows the program to access more memory than is resident in the computer, since nonactive portions of the information are maintained on

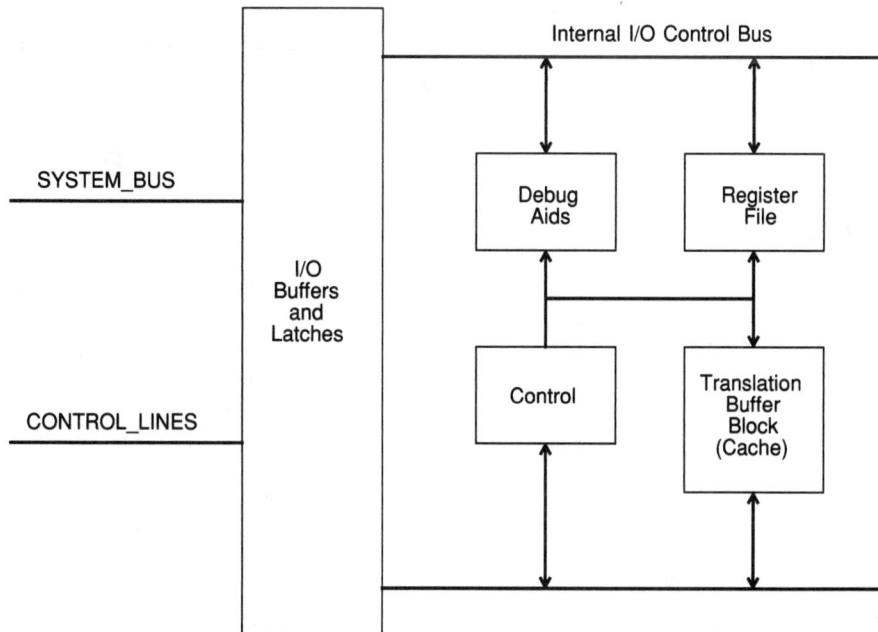

Figure 7.24. Block Diagram of NS32082 Memory Management Unit.

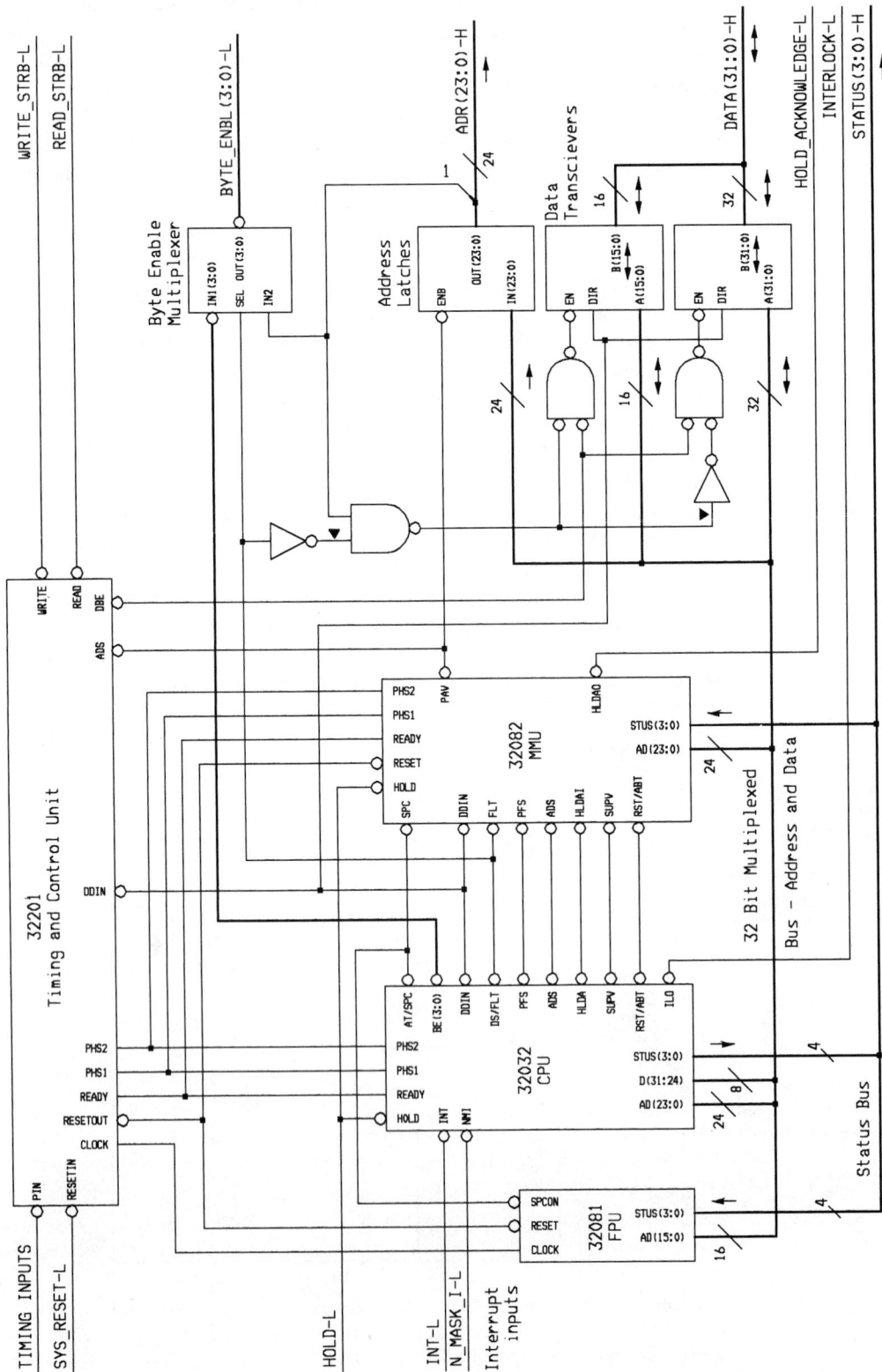

Figure 7.25. NS32032 System with NS32082 Memory Management Unit.

secondary storage. However, this is not the only application of the concept of paging. A number of instruction sets can access a limited range of memory, and paging can be used effectively in these systems as well. For example, the 8080 system has been used for many years, and it has an addressable range of 64 Kbytes. The same can be said for the PDP 11 architecture or the TI9900. However, with newer memories we can get 256 Kbytes to 1 Mbyte or more in a single SIP, which is far more that a single program can address. One way to effectively utilize the memory is a multiprogramming environment. In this fashion, each of the programs can have its own portions of memory, and accesses can be made with the paging mechanisms explained above.

The use of paging to effectively utilize a large memory for systems that limit the memory addressable by a single program allows several programs to reside simultaneously in a memory. Then, as the addresses are created by the program, a translation is performed to access the proper page. Texas Instruments, Inc., manufactures an LSI device used to perform the mapping for the case a large memory and a small inherent address capability. The block diagram of the device, which is the 74LS612, is shown in Figure 7.26(a). The assumption made by system designers utilizing this device is that the address space is broken into pages of 4,096 bytes. Thus, the 12 LSBs of the address are not touched by the paging mechanism. The 4 MSBs of the address are used to identify one of 16 locations of a page table memory inside the device. Each of these locations contains 12 bits, which identify one of 4,096 pages in the real memory space. With this device mapping can be implemented to a real memory space of 16 Mbytes.

The operating system is responsible for loading the proper page addresses into the page table, which it does by using the programmed I/O instructions and addressing the appropriate register with the RS lines. Once the system has prepared the table, the processor can access up to 16 pages by mapping the addresses into the real memory system. That way, 16 complete programs could reside in a 1 Mbyte memory, and be accessed through the 74LS612. A diagram showing its use with an 6800 system is given in Figure 7.26(b). Logically, the device resides between the processor and the memory. And the operation of the system creates a virtual space that is smaller than the physical space available, and yet uses the concepts presented above.

The use of virtual memory techniques allow effective use of the real memory, whether the available memory is larger or smaller than that needed by a specific program. The program operates under the illusion that it has access to its own memory, independent of other events that may occur in the system. With large processor systems, this results in the use of less real memory than called for by a single program. The use of a large memory with processors that cannot access all of the available storage results in systems that can load several complete programs into the available physical memory. But the basic reason that the systems are effective comes from the observed behavior of programs in execution.

Programs generally exhibit locality when they are running. That is, at any given time, or during a short period, a program will tend to use information in a small number of locales. While a program is executing a loop, the instruction fetches are confined to the memory area where the loop is located. The loop may access an array, and, while the array accesses are going on, the data references are limited to the area where the array is located. But the net result is that the amount of memory needed by a program during any small period will not be the entire addressable space, but rather a portion of it. Thus, a program may require a small number of all of its pages during any particular time slice. This behavior allows

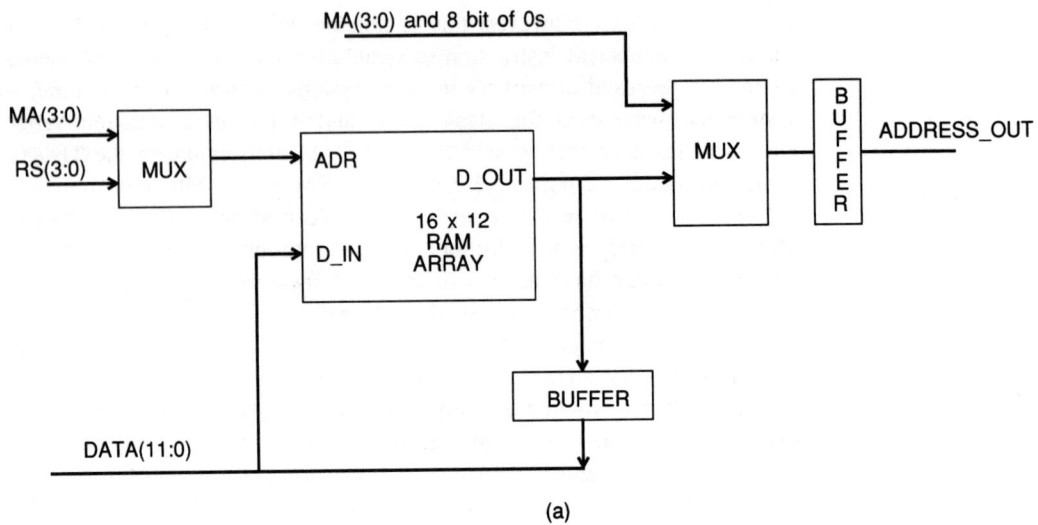

(a)

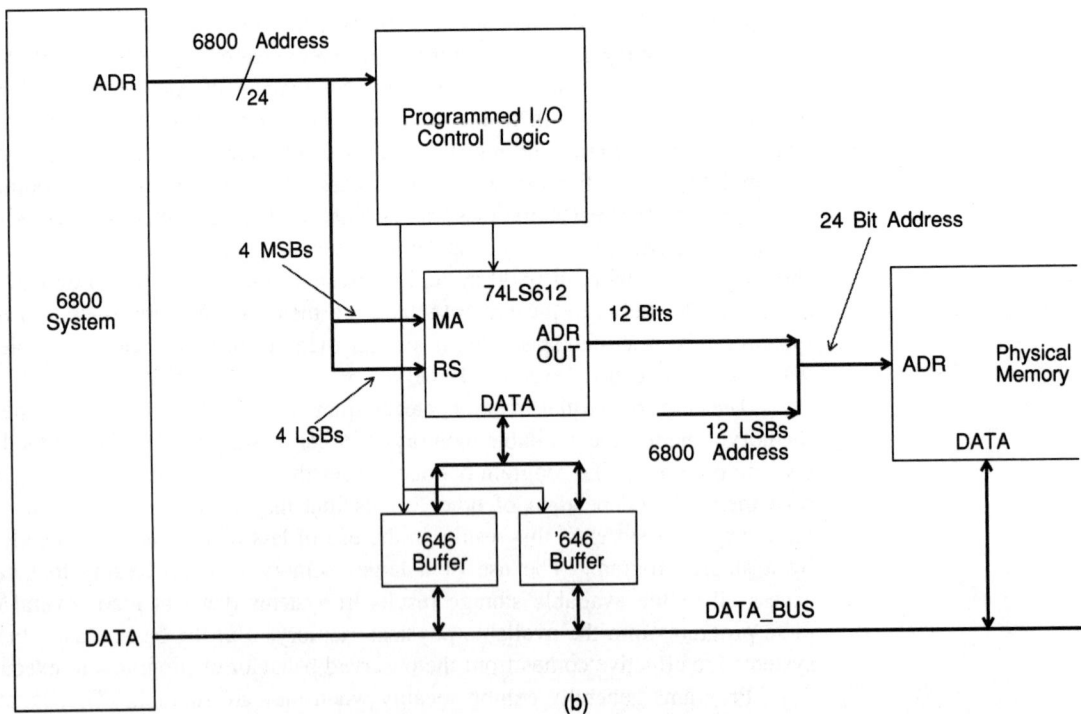

(b)

Figure 7.26. Memory Mapper for Small Virtual Space to Large Physical Space. (a) Block Diagram of 74LS612. (b) System Incorporating the 74LS612.

the virtual memory systems to be effective. The migrating action of pages in and out of main store keeps in memory the parts of the program which are needed.

The element not discussed to this point is the secondary storage. In general, the secondary storage mechanisms will be disks, although other mediums are possible. The virtual memory system must work with the secondary storage element and the main store to coordinate the transfer of information between the two. The interface mechanism will be a data transfer protocol as was discussed in Chapter 6: the controllers are activated by the processor and perform whatever tasks they are given, moving information from the secondary storage area to main store. The OS is responsible for requesting these transfers in a reasonable fashion, and maintaining page tables as needed to reflect the contents of system memory. The more pages that exist in main store, the greater the probability that a program will find the information that it needs. Nevertheless, eventually the program will access information on a page not in main store. The virtual address translation mechanism recognizes a request for data that is not in main store and interrupts the processor. The OS then must deal with the program in a reasonable way. Most often, the program is temporarily halted and the system requests that the unavailable information be brought into memory. Meanwhile, the current state of the program is saved, and the information for another program is loaded into the registers of the CPU. The system can then continue execution on another program while awaiting the arrival of data from secondary storage.

Example 7.6: Secondary storage access: Consider the block diagram for a virtual memory system as shown in Figure 7.27. As long as the processor is requesting information from main store, the system will continue executing. When the processor detects a page fault, the OS will need to bring in the appropriate page. On the average, how much time will transpire before the requested information is brought into main store? Assume that the access time to main store is 250 nsec. Also assume that the disk rotates at 3600 RPM, that there are 48 sectors per track, and that a sector and a page have the same size — 512 bytes.

The time required for the transfer will break down into three different times:

- The seek time for the disk, which is the time for the disk to find the desired track.
- The rotational latency, which is the time for the disk to rotate until the desired sector is under the read head.
- The transfer time, which is the actual time to transfer the information to the memory.

Thus the time will be:

$$T_{\text{ACCESS}} = T_{\text{SEEK}} + T_{\text{ROT\_LAT}} + T_{\text{TRANSFER}}$$

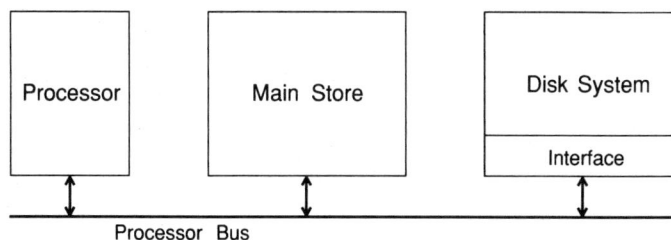

Figure 7.27. Simplified Block Diagram of Memory System.

The seek time is a characteristic of the individual disk being used. The time to seek to the next track is much smaller than the time to seek to a distant track, but an reasonable time is approximately 20 msec. The rotational latency, on the average, will be half the time for one revolution. At 3,600 RPM, the disk makes 60 revolutions per second, or one every 16.67 msec, and half of that is 8.3 msec. Since there are 48 sectors per track, the minimum transfer time is 1/48 of a revolution time, or about 347 μsec. Thus, the time for the transfer is dwarfed by the other times involved. So,

$$T_{\text{ACCESS}} = T_{\text{SEEK}} + T_{\text{ROT\_LAT}} + T_{\text{TRANSFER}}$$

$$= 20 \text{ msec} + 8.3 \text{ msec} + 0.347 \text{ msec}$$

$$= 28.647 \text{ msec}$$

Note that we have not included in this figure all of the times involved, since some time will be required by the processor to identify the appropriate page and issue the request to have the page transferred to main store. This time is not negligible, and should be accounted for in identifying the detailed costs of the transaction.

Some observations can be made at this point regarding the relative times of the transactions. One interesting piece of information is the ratio of the access time of the disk to the access time of the main store, which we will call R_{VM}, since this is the storage ratio involved with virtual memory. Thus,

$$R_{\text{VM}} = \frac{T_{\text{ACCESS}}}{T_{A_{\text{MAIN STORE}}}}$$

$$= \frac{28.647 \text{ msec}}{250 \text{ nsec}}$$

$$\approx 114,500$$

This indicates that over 110,000 transfers could take place while the disk is accessing the information not in memory. Another observation is that, during that period of time a 2 MIP machine (a machine capable of 2 million instructions per second) could execute almost 60,000 instructions. Since a significant amount of work can be done in the time required to obtain the information from secondary storage, an operating system will suspend the process that incurred the page fault, and allow another process to utilize the computational resources of the system.

Another observation is that the principal time involved in T_{ACCESS} is the seek time. Thus, systems that strive for high speed can benefit from a device that does not need a physical seek to obtain the information. Two such devices are drums and head-per-track disks. These devices have a much higher cost per bit for storage, but can be used if the circumstances warrant.

As we have seen, virtual memory can be used to more effectively utilize the resources available to a system, and in particular to use memory in an efficacious manner. Segmentation approaches the task by accessing information in logical units, such as programs, subroutines, and data areas. Note also that a system can organize the information that it needs to access as segments, so that individual data entities can be organized as individual segments. Paging accesses information by organizing information into pages, using a standard physical unit as the common denominator in all transactions. Both concepts allow the program to divorce itself from the placement of the information in physical memory, and allow the instructions to identify the location of information within a virtual memory framework. It is not necessary to use only one or the other method, and some systems combine the two together to form a paged system that also understands segments. This type of an addressing scheme allows the creation of segments, which have unique characteristics, and the further benefits of paging, which allows a regular placement policy.

7.4. Cache Memory: Speed-Up for Main Store

Cache memories are (relatively) small, high-speed memories inserted into the system between the processor and the main store. The purpose of cache memory is to speed up the processing rate by allowing the processor to execute at a higher rate than that possible by using main store alone. It utilizes many of the same concepts used with virtual memories, but in a slightly different fashion. One of the first machines to utilize this mechanism was the IBM 360/85 [Lipt68], but the concept has become widely implemented in machines of all sizes. Before a cache system is implemented, a thorough study of the behavior of the memory system under expected operating conditions must be conducted. In this section we will study some of the mechanisms utilized by cache systems, and determine their effectiveness in different conditions. For a relatively complete discussion of a number of the techniques and their relative merits, see [Simt82].

The virtual memory mechanisms discussed in the previous section allow programs to execute using a virtual memory space, a space that appears different to a program than the actual space being utilized. The program need not have a correct understanding of the amount of memory actually available. Programs can run using very large virtual spaces with a relatively small actual main store, or the program can, by its inherent instruction and reference limitations, access only a portion of the actual memory available. In either case, systems that utilize virtual memory tend to have only portions of the program loaded into main store at any one time. These portions are sometimes referred to as the active portions of the programs, and during the execution of a program the active portions will change.

One effect of the use of virtual memory techniques is that the apparent processing speed of the system is higher, because the CPU is more effectively utilized by a number of programs, and the amount of time that the CPU is idle is minimized. Of course, one exception to this speed enhancement will occur when the processing being done is limited not by the processor, but rather by the I/O capabilities of the system. That is, a set of I/O bound jobs will not experience the speedup improvements that would be seen by a mixture of I/O intensive and compute intensive programs. Nevertheless, the system benefits from having only the active portions of the programs reside in the main store at any one time.

Cache memories operate on the same basic principal: keep in the memory (in this case the cache) only those portions of the information needed and active. In this manner, the cache and the virtual memory mechanisms are similar.

However, there are some major differences between the virtual memory and cache memory implementations. The two most obvious differences are the visibility of the mechanism and the ratio of access times.

A virtual memory system has high visibility to a program and to the operating system, since the "virtual machine" as seen by a program is accessed by the virtual memory system, which in turn is managed by the operating system. For example, a user has the capability to access more memory than the system actually has through the use of virtual memory, and the OS must maintain page tables and other information in the system to control the various facets of the system operation. The cache, on the other hand, is usually hidden from the user and the system. The decisions as to the operational modes of the cache are made at design time and built into the system. Thus, a program will not know that a cache is being used, except by the speed of processing.

The ratio of access speeds for the cache, R_{CA}, also differs drastically from R_{VM}. The definition of R_{CA} will be similar to R_{VM}:

$$R_{CA} = \frac{T_{A_{\text{MAIN STORE}}}}{T_{A_{\text{CACHE}}}}$$

Access times for main store and cache memories improve each year, but typical times might be 250 nsec for $T_{A_{\text{MAIN STORE}}}$ and 40 nsec for $T_{A_{\text{CACHE}}}$. Using these times, R_{CA} becomes:

$$R_{CA} = \frac{T_{A_{\text{MAIN STORE}}}}{T_{A_{\text{CACHE}}}}$$

$$= \frac{250 \text{ nsec}}{40 \text{ nsec}}$$

$$= 6.25$$

Instead of a ratio in excess of 110,000 as for R_{VM}, R_{CA} is on the order of 6. This ratio will vary from system to system, but the effect will be the same: there is not enough time to change the task in the processor. Thus, the processing element is halted until the information which was not in cache has been obtained, and then the processing continues.

One of the basic questions is how good the cache memories are, and how to quantify the effect. The term "good" is a relative measure, and indicates how fast the processor is operating with the cache compared to the operating rate without the benefit of the cache. To identify the effects involved with the cache, let us consider a system organized as shown in Figure 7.28. This simple figure indicates the logical organization of the system, but not necessarily the physical organization. The figure of merit that interests us here is the T_{EFF}, which is the effective access time of the memory system, considering the cache and main store memories together as a single system. A very simplistic formula for this time is given by:

$$T_{\text{EFF}} = h \times T_{CA} + (1 - h) \times (T_{CA} + T_{MS})$$

where T_{CA} is the access time of the cache and T_{MS} is the access time of the main store. The other term in the equation, h, is the hit rate, or the fraction of the references found in the cache. Thus, $(1 - h)$ is the miss rate, the fraction of the

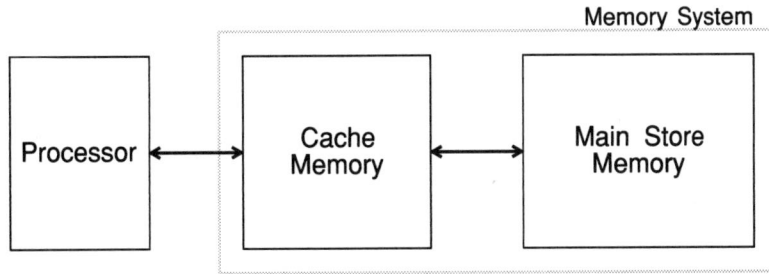

Figure 7.28. System with Cache and Main Store Memories.

references not found in the cache. The first term, $h \times T_{CA}$, indicates that of all the references to memory, the fraction h will incur a penalty of T_{CA}. And the second term, $(1-h) \times (T_{CA}+T_{MS})$, indicates that the remainder of the references, $1 - h$, will incur a penalty of $T_{CA} + T_{MS}$. The T_{CA} term appears here to identify the amount of time that is required to ascertain that the desired reference is not in the cache, and the T_{MS} term identifies the amount of time then required to go to main store to obtain the requested information. With a little algebra, the equation can be further reduced:

$$T_{EFF} = T_{CA} + (1 - h) \times T_{MS}$$

This is a very simplistic formula, since it does not include the effects of many of the real problems that occur in caches. But it is sufficient to give some insight into the effectiveness of a cache memory organization.

The formula for T_{EFF} is a linear equation, and will specify straight lines on a linear plot. Figure 7.29 gives a plot of T_{EFF} as a function of the hit rate, h. Four different lines appear in the figure, for R_{CA} values of 2.5, 5, 10, and 20. The access time is given in terms of T_{MS}, so that, if T_{EFF} exceeds 1.0, then the response time of the memory system with cache would be worse than the response time of the system without cache. The figure identifies that indeed this situation can occur, but the hit rate must be very poor for T_{EFF} to be greater than 1.0.

A graph that gives a more intuitively pleasing observation of the effect of using a cache is given in Figure 7.30. Here we plot the speedup of the system, where the speedup, S, is defined as a ratio of the access times without and with cache memory:

$$S = \frac{T_{MS}}{T_{EFF}}$$

The plot indicates that, as the hit rate approaches 1.0, the speedup improves dramatically. This agrees with expectations concerning the use of caches.

This simple formula is not an accurate model of the exact behavior of a cache memory, since it does not account for many details. We will return later to the calculation of T_{EFF}, but let us now consider some of the implementation methods.

Implementation details vary for cache memories, and the following descriptions can be modified to produce results slightly different from those included here. For example, the addressable units in a cache will vary depending on the application, from small units in caches that are inherently small, to large units, for

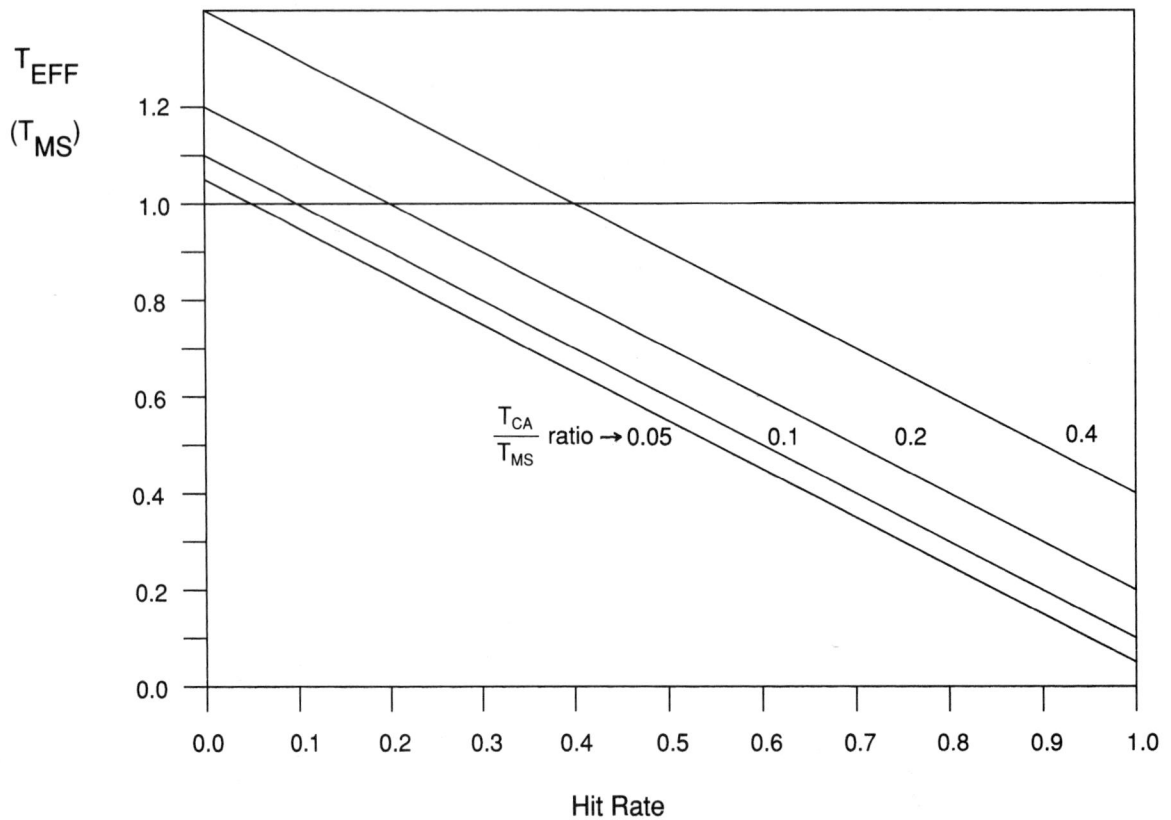

Figure 7.29. Effective Memory Access Time, T_{EFF} as a Function of Hit Rate, h.

caches with an increased memory capacity. But the basic principles of operation will be the same regardless of the implementation.

For our example cache organization we will use a cache size of 32 Kbytes. The system memory may be 16 Mbytes or larger, so the cache can only hold a fraction of the information resident in main store. The cache is organized to access information in some basic unit, which we will call a line. We will let the line size be 32 bytes, so the cache will contain 1,024 lines. The main store will also be organized as lines, so that lines can be exchanged between the cache and main store. This basic organization is depicted in Figure 7.31. Whenever there is a hit, the cache provides to the processor the information that was requested. This will occur at the speeds of the processor itself, and only the specified information (byte, word, double word, etc.) is transferred. However, if there is a cache miss, then the data must be brought from the main store into the cache. The information is transferred from the main store to the cache by moving an entire line. Some cache organizations also have the capability of requesting a transfer involving multiple lines.

To this point we have placed no restriction on the location of information in the cache. If the system permits any line from main store to reside in any line in the cache, then we say that the system is a fully associative organization. Thus, when the processor identifies an address, all of the lines in the cache must be interrogated to ascertain if the desired information is in the cache. This leads to very expensive hardware, since, for the example of Figure 7.31, 1,024 locations

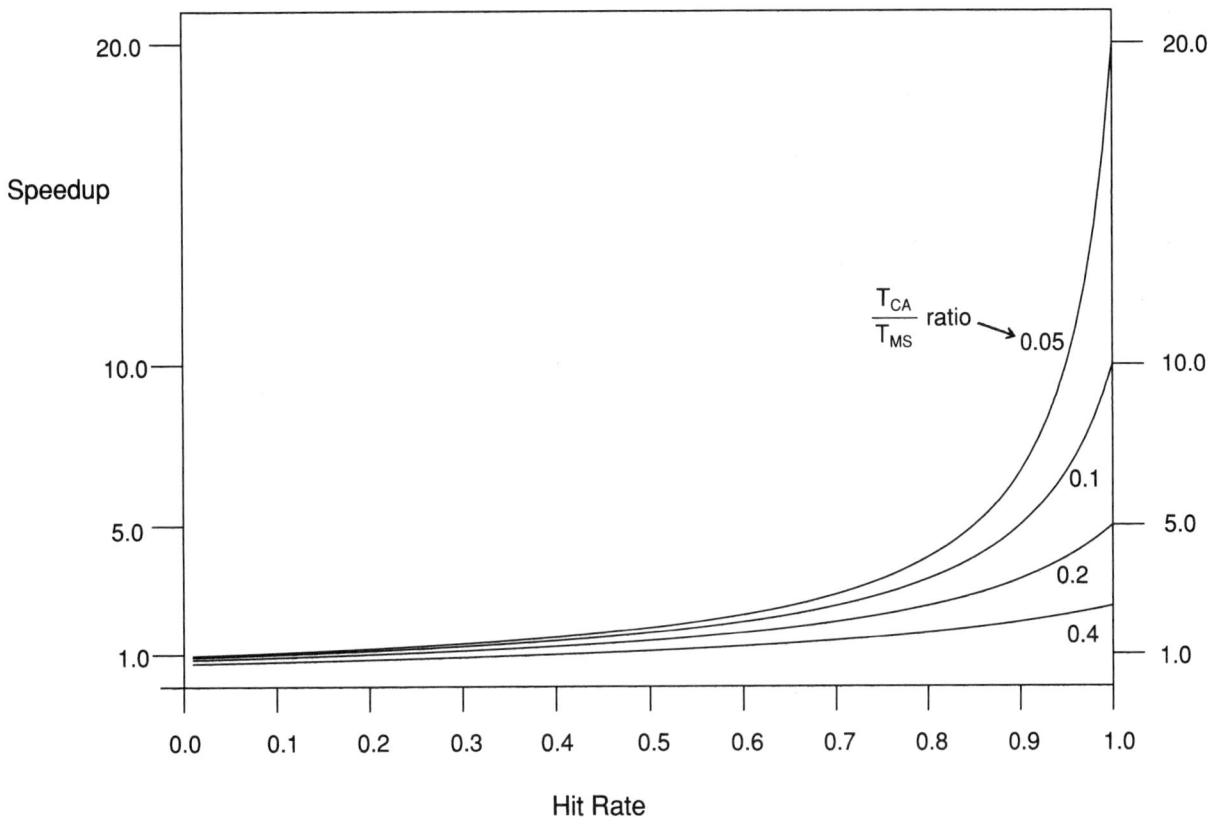

Figure 7.30. Effective Speedup (T_{MS} / T_{EFF}) of a Cache System.

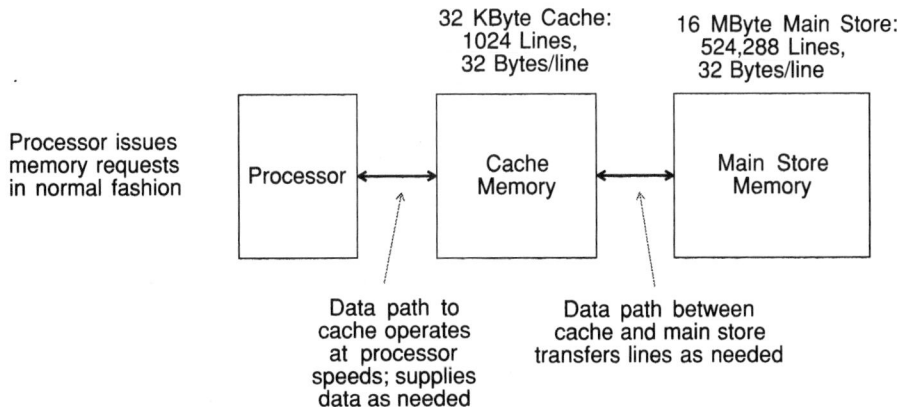

Figure 7.31. Organization of Cache and Main Store Memories.

must be searched. The hardware required to search for the address in question will be greatly reduced if restrictions are place on the allowable locations in the cache of the lines in main store. If a line in main store has exactly one location in the cache where it can be found, we say that the cache has direct mapping. With direct mapping, only one location in the cache needs to be queried to find out if the addressed information is available or not. With direct mapping in the organization of Figure 7.31, each line in the cache can hold information from any of 512 lines in the main store. But each line in main store maps to only one line in the cache.

A compromise between the fully associative and direct mapping mechanisms involves a technique known as "set associativity." If, instead of only one location in the cache, a line in main store could be located in one of two locations, we say that the cache is two way set associative, or set associative with a set size of two. Likewise, if the line can be located in one of four locations, then the organization is four way set associative, or set associative with a set size of four. Other set sizes are possible, such as eight and sixteen. The more elements in a set, then the more hardware is required to implement the cache. With set associativity, a line can be found in a limited number of locations, and the hardware needed for the parallel search of those locations is manageable.

If the cache of Figure 7.31 is organized as a four way set associative cache, then there are 256 sets, each with four lines. The organization of the system is

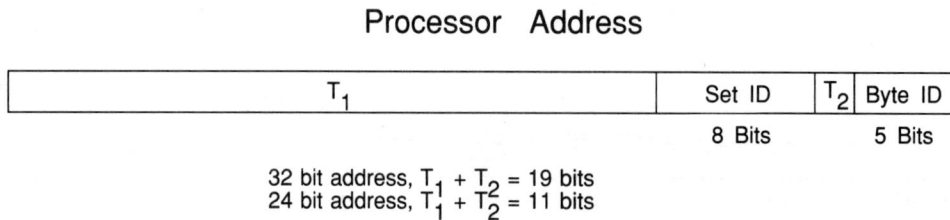

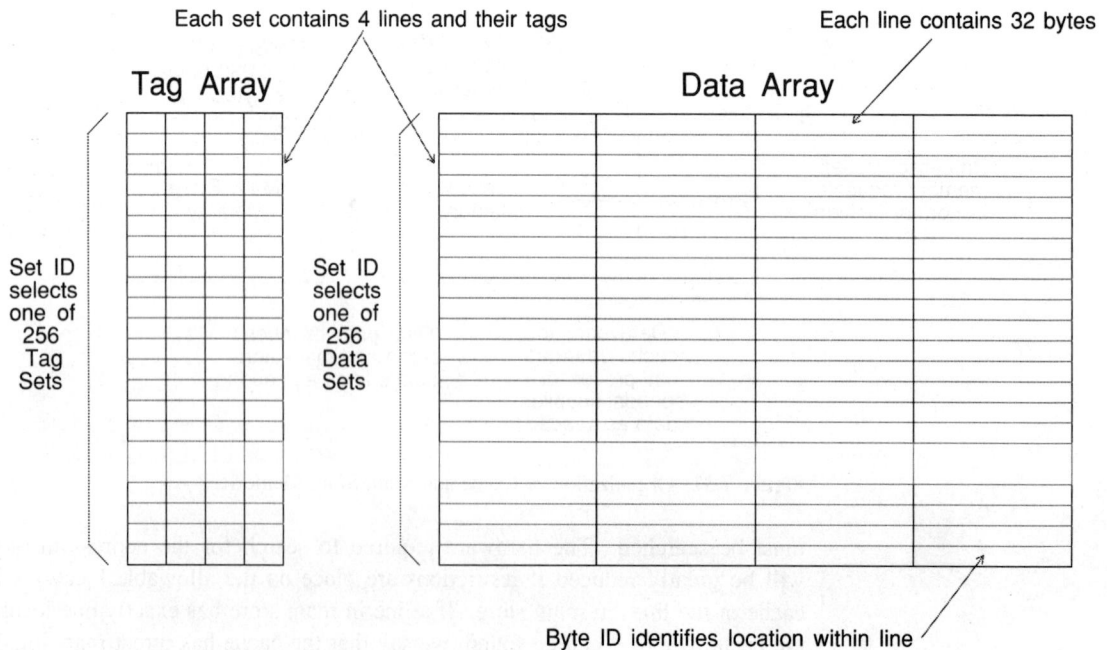

Figure 7.32. Organization of a Set Associative Cache with Four Sets.

shown in Figure 7.32. The address, as supplied by the processor is divided into fields, each of which has a specific function. Since there are 32 bytes in a line, then the 5 least significant bits are required to identify the target location within the line. If the architecture is not byte-addressable, then this requirement changes accordingly. Since most general purpose machines have byte-addressable memories, we will proceed under that assumption. With 256 sets, then 8 bits of the address are needed to specify the appropriate set. The remainder of the bits form part of a collection of information called a tag, and are stored in a memory that mirrors the organization of the data area of the cache. The tag bits include the remaining bits of the address, a method to identify if there is data in the line (since the cache will be empty upon startup), a dirty bit (to indicate if the line has been changed since it was brought into the cache), and other information that is needed by the system. For example, one of the useful things to know is the order of use of the lines in a set. If this information is available, then when one of the lines needs to be removed to make room for a new line, the least recently used line can provide the location for the new information. Thus, each line in the data section has associated with it a tag in the tag section. The line resident in the tag section is uniquely identified by that tag. The process of ascertaining the presence or absence of information in a cache then consists of examining M tags, where there are M elements in each set.

One of the characteristics of the cache mechanism is the order in which the lines of a cache are accessed for a given set of physical addresses. Consider, for example, a large set of addresses that is monotonically and uniformly increasing, each address being 4 bytes greater than its predecessor. In Figure 7.32 the processor address is divided into three different groups: set ID bits, byte ID bits, and two groups of tag bits. The byte ID bits are the 5 least significant address bits. The remaining bits in the address comprise the set ID bits and the tag bits. Eight bits are required to specify the set; these 8 bits form the set ID.

The remaining bits are tag bits, and are further divided into two portions, which we call T_1 and T_2. If there are zero bits in T_2 and all of the tag bits are in T_1, then as the address increases successive lines will be placed in successive sets. However, if there is a single bit in T_2 and the set ID bits are relocated in the address accordingly, then a different addressing pattern is formed. As the address increases, then two lines will be located in each set before moving to the next set in sequence. If T_2 has two bits, then four lines are allocated to a set before moving on. The mechanism which is most beneficial may be determined from the expected workload via a simulated address trace.

Example 7.7: Set associative cache system: Give a data path block diagram for a two way set associative cache memory with a capacity of 32 Kbytes. Identify the width of the data paths and the function of each block. Assuming that the memories used in the cache have an access time of 25 nsec, how quickly can the presence of the line in the cache be detected?

With 32 Kbytes in the cache, organized in a two way set associative manner, there are 512 sets, with the previous assumptions. That is, with a line size of 32 bytes, there are 1,024 lines, and with two lines per set, there are 512 sets. Thus, the cache can be made with 512×8 memories in a very natural way. A data path block diagram of such an organization is shown in Figure 7.33. Using byte wide memories, three devices would be needed for each tag array, and 32 devices would be needed for each data array. Thus, 70 memory devices would be needed for the cache. The address is divided

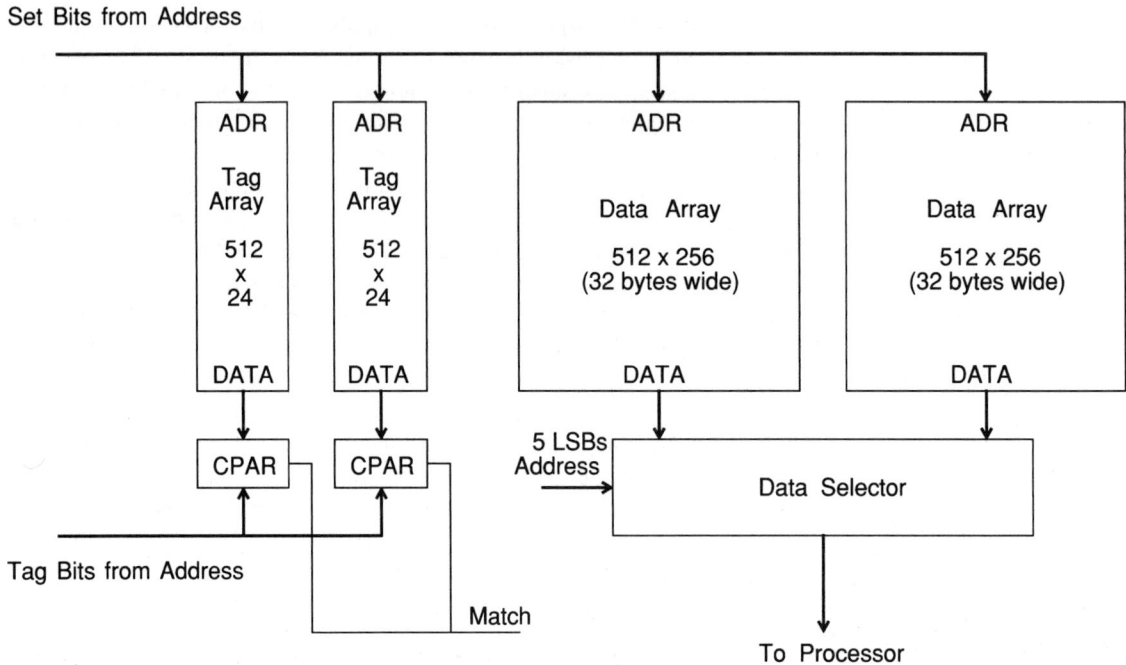

Figure 7.33. Data Path Block Diagram for Cache System of Example 7.7.

into the tag bits, the set bits, and the byte address bits. With a 32-bit address, 18 address lines will be involved in the comparison shown in the figure. Nine address bits are needed to identify the set, and these are fed directly to the memories used in the system. Note that this will probably need some additional drive capability, since 70 individual address lines are being driven by each address bit. At the same time that the tag information is being extracted from the tag arrays, the data information can be obtained from the data arrays. However, the outputs provided by the data arrays contain 32 bytes each. The data selector then has the task of providing the appropriate bytes, based on the five LSBs of the address. Then, if either of the comparators (CPAR) identify a match between the tag bits and the stored lines, the data can be sent to the processor.

The time required to detect the presence of a line will consist of the time to fetch the tag from the tag array (25 nsec) plus the comparison time. Using 'AS866 devices, this can be done in about 17 nsec. Higher speed could be obtained by using individual gates. Thus, the match function would require about 42 nsec.

Cache memories can be very useful to store the information actively used by the CPU. The examination made thus far of the issue has been simplistic in many ways, and we will now endeavor to identify some of the mechanisms that add complexity to the memory system and complicate the analysis. One of the issues to be resolved is the placement/replacement policy. With virtual memory, the system software is responsible for ascertaining the appropriate page to be removed to make way for a new page. However, in a cache system the decision must be made instantaneously, and therefore the decision must be made in hardware. The policy on which the decision is based is made at design time. One policy is to maintain a record of the order of line use, so that, when space is needed for a new line, the least recently used line can be replaced. The amount of hardware required to do this increases with the number of sets, but can be as simple as a flip-flop for an associative scheme with two sets. Another surprisingly effective scheme is a random scheme, where the line to be used is chosen at random from among the available lines.

Another issue that adds complexity to the cache scheme is the data generated by the CPU to write to the memory. That is, in the discussion to this point we have ignored the fact that references to memory consist of both reads (which need information from the system memory) and writes (which generate information to be placed in system memory). A number of schemes have been implemented, but most are variations of two mechanisms: write through and write back.

A write through scheme operates as follows: information written to the memory system is placed directly into main store. If the line also exists in cache, then the cache is updated as well. Thus, the information is written "through" the cache into main memory, which gives rise to the name of the policy. The principal benefit of this mechanism is that the information in main store accurately reflects the state of the system; that is, the cache information is merely a copy of what is in main store. When a replacement is made, only transfers from main store to cache are required; no information is transferred from the cache to the main store.

The write back scheme operates on a different principle. This mechanism calls for writes to change the information in the cache, and not propagate those changes immediately to main store. Then, when the line is replaced in the normal operation of the cache, the line is written back to main store. Hence the reason for the "write back" name associated with the scheme. If the line has not been modified since being loaded into the cache, there is no need to write it back to the main memory, and this will save time.

The effectiveness of the two schemes is dependent upon the work load of the machine. The write through scheme recognizes the fact that many more reads are required than writes in a system. Therefore, when writes occur, the mechanism accepts the larger penalty of a write to main store, which would apparently slow down the response. The reward for this policy is that the system will not need to transfer any lines from the cache to the main store, so when a cache miss does occur, then no time is required for line replacement (to the main store). To minimize the slowing effect of writes to main store each time the system is required to update memory, many systems provide a buffer register for the writes. Thus, the first write will occur at the cache speed (for a system with a single buffer register). The system then continues processing, and a memory controller is responsible for placing the data in main store. If the main store write occurs before any subsequent write, then no time penalty is incurred by the mechanism. Only if a second write occurs while the first is being executed is the system delayed, and then the delay is the time required for the first write to complete. Thus, the write through scheme uses a slightly higher level of complexity to increase the apparent speed of operation.

The effectiveness of the write back scheme is based not on the frequency of write operations, but rather on the locality of reference principle. That is, the write back scheme achieves highest speed when several writes are made to the same line in a short period of time. With the write back scheme, the line is brought into the cache and the multiple writes are executed at cache speeds. Then, when that location in the cache is needed for a new line, then the old one incurs a single main store write penalty for all of the changes that have been made to that line in the cache. Since the memory changes are not immediately communicated to main store, systems with multiple processors that share a common memory will need additional capabilities if this scheme is used. This is sometimes called the "stale data problem," or the "cache coherency problem," and we will examine it in more detail later. The write back mechanism rewards programs that cause writes to memory to occur in clusters, since several writes can be performed at cache speeds before any main store penalty is incurred. When the write occurs, a mechanism to temporarily hold the line being written out will minimize the overall time penalty.

The transfer mechanism with its associated storage buffer is an example of combining the various techniques discussed. For the purposes of discussion, let us use the system shown in Figure 7.34. The overall block diagram indicates that the CPU receives its information from (and provides information to) the cache. Meanwhile, the cache is connected via a bus system to four memory banks. Each bank of memory is essentially an independent unit, with addressing and timing capabilities needed for random access. The coordination of information transfer on the bus is handled by the bus controller. One of the assumptions made in this organization is that line size is 32 bytes, and that each bank holds 8 bytes of each line. Another assumption is that the transfer of information across the 8-byte bus requires 50 nsec, and that the access (read or write) to information in a memory bank requires 200 nsec. So, for a write back memory, the following sequence of events is one mechanism for performing the data transfers required. There is a cache miss, and a line needs to be brought in. Assume that the line currently in the cache in the location in which the new line is to be placed is not dirty — it has not been changed since being retrieved from memory. The accesses for the needed line are invoked in each bank of the memory. When Bank 0 has the required line, which occurs 200 nsec after initiation of the read access, it will transfer the information to the cache. This will be followed by the transfer for Bank 1, which is ready by the end of the transfer of information by Bank 0. The transfers for Banks 2 and 3 follow. Thus, 250 nsec after initiating the request, the first information is available, and 400 nsec after the request starts, the entire line has been accessed and transferred to the cache.

The second case includes the write back of information, as well as the obtaining of information for the cache. This will occur when a "dirty" line is replaced. In this case, one method of implementing the transfers recognizes that the bus is not used for the first 200 nsec of the above cycle. The information is obtained from the cache and sent to the interface modules of the respective memory banks during the first 200 nsec, and the information is then written back to the banks as shown in Figure 7.34(b). As shown in the figure, this policy leads to the desired information being loaded into the cache within 400 nsec, and the write back portion completed within 600 nsec. However, by staggering the requests in time, the effective time can be made 400 nsec. Thus, the write back scheme can benefit from this one level of storage buffer and increase the apparent speed of operation.

Example 7.8: Effective time for cache access: Develop a formula for the effective access time for a cache memory that uses a write back scheme. Assume that the system must bring information into the cache to modify it, rather than to have writes that modify information not in the cache go directly to memory. (This assumption is made to create a simpler formula, not to reflect reality.) Assume that the probability that the access is a read

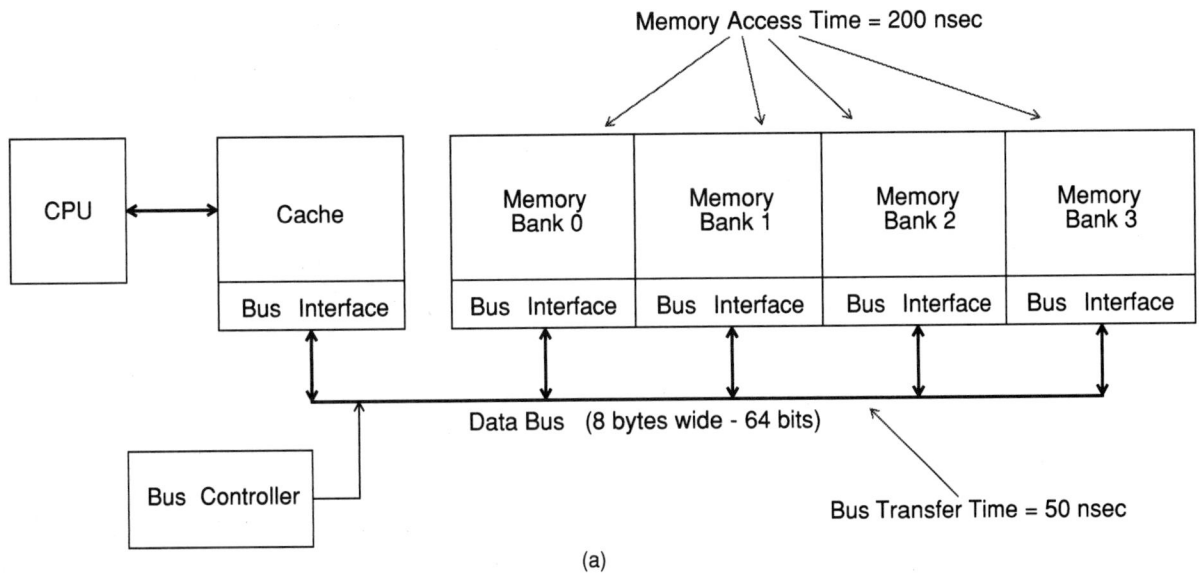

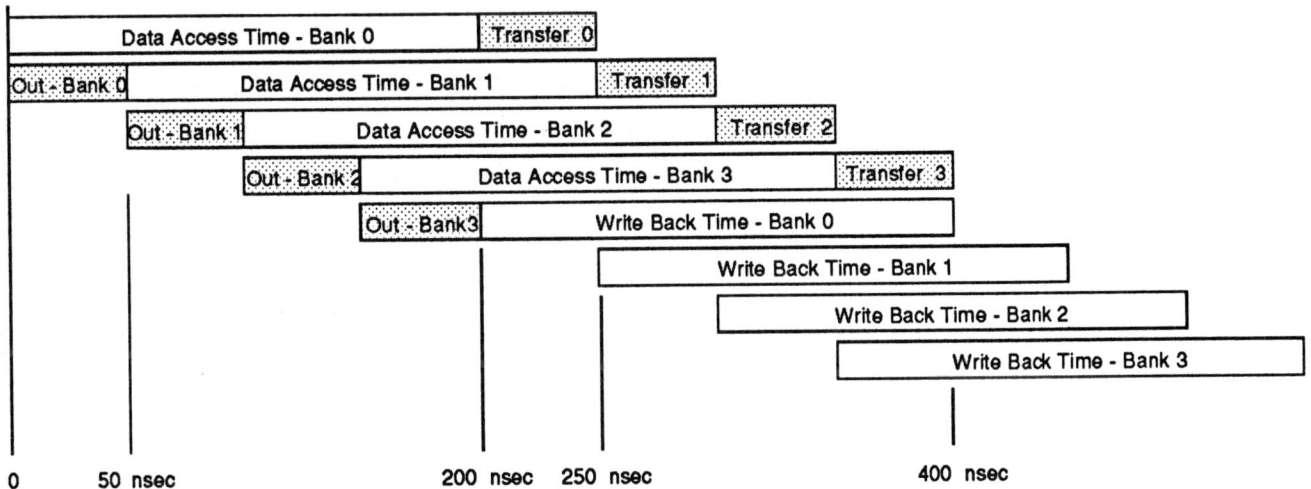

Figure 7.34. Cache Interaction with Banked Memory. (a) Overall Block Diagram. (b) Timing for Write Back Transfer.

is P_{READ}, and that the probability that a cache miss causes a dirty line to be written to main store is P_{DIRTY}. Also assume that reads and writes to main store incur the same penalty, T_{MS}, and that there is no storage buffer in the system. (Again, this assumption is for a simpler formula rather than to reflect reality.)

The assumptions surrounding this problem have been made in such a manner to simplify the resulting formulas, rather than to reflect how a specific cache has been designed. To identify the costs associated with the various accessing mechanisms, we will examine the costs in each of the four obvious cases: read hit, read miss, write hit, and write miss. The total solution will then be a weighted sum of these cases.

- The read and write hit cases are identical: the desired address is in the cache, and the cost of the access is the cache access time: T_{CA}.

- The read miss will incur a penalty of T_{CA} to ascertain that the information is not in the cache, and then a penalty of T_{MS} to bring in the information. However, this is not sufficient, since there may be a need to write back to main store a dirty line. This incurs a penalty of T_{MS} but occurs only with probability P_{DIRTY}.

- The write miss will also incur a penalty of T_{CA} to ascertain the target address is not in the cache. In addition, it will require a time T_{MS} to bring in the desired line. It will also require a time T_{MS} with probability P_{DIRTY} to write out a line being displaced. However, once the line is in the cache, another T_{CA} is required to write to the spot selected.

Thus, the costs can be summarized by the following table:

	Hit	Miss
Read	T_{CA}	$T_{CA} + (1 + P_{DIRTY}) \times T_{MS}$
Write	T_{CA}	$2 \times T_{CA} + (1 + P_{DIRTY}) \times T_{MS}$

The formula for the system is a weighted sum of the above values:

$$T_{EFF} = P_{READ} \times \{ h \times T_{CA} + (1 - h)[T_{CA} + (1 + P_{DIRTY}) \times T_{MS}] \} +$$

$$(1 - P_{READ}) \times$$

$$\{ h \times T_{CA} + (1 - h) \times [2 \times T_{CA} + (1 + P_{DIRTY}) \times T_{MS}] \}$$

$$= T_{CA} \times [1 + (1 - h) \times (1 - P_{READ})] + T_{MS} \times (1 - h) \times (1 + P_{DIRTY})$$

A family of plots of this equation and its inverse are shown in Figure 7.35. The various lines are for different values of the probability of a dirty line (P_{DIR}). The assumption here is that the cache time T_{CA} is one-tenth the main store time T_{MS}. As can be seen from the figure, the probability of a dirty line has a large impact on the performance of the system.

Other equations can be derived to more closely reflect reality. The difference will be in the complexity of the analysis, but the approach will be the same.

A number of other issues need to be dealt with in a real system. For example, how does the hardware handle a request for a word aligned across line boundaries? That is, since the system has been assumed to be byte-addressable, what happens when the request is for 4 bytes, the first of which is on one line and the other three are on another line? A real system must be capable of handling this situation. (Note that one solution is to define the system in such a way that all memory accesses are made on 32-bit boundaries, and obtaining information within must then be done with software rather than hardware. This tradeoff must be made by the system architects at the time of the system definition.) Another real problem concerns the mechanism for physically writing information to the cache. We have not shown in the block diagrams or other examples the data paths nor logic required to write information back to the cache, but this must be done in a

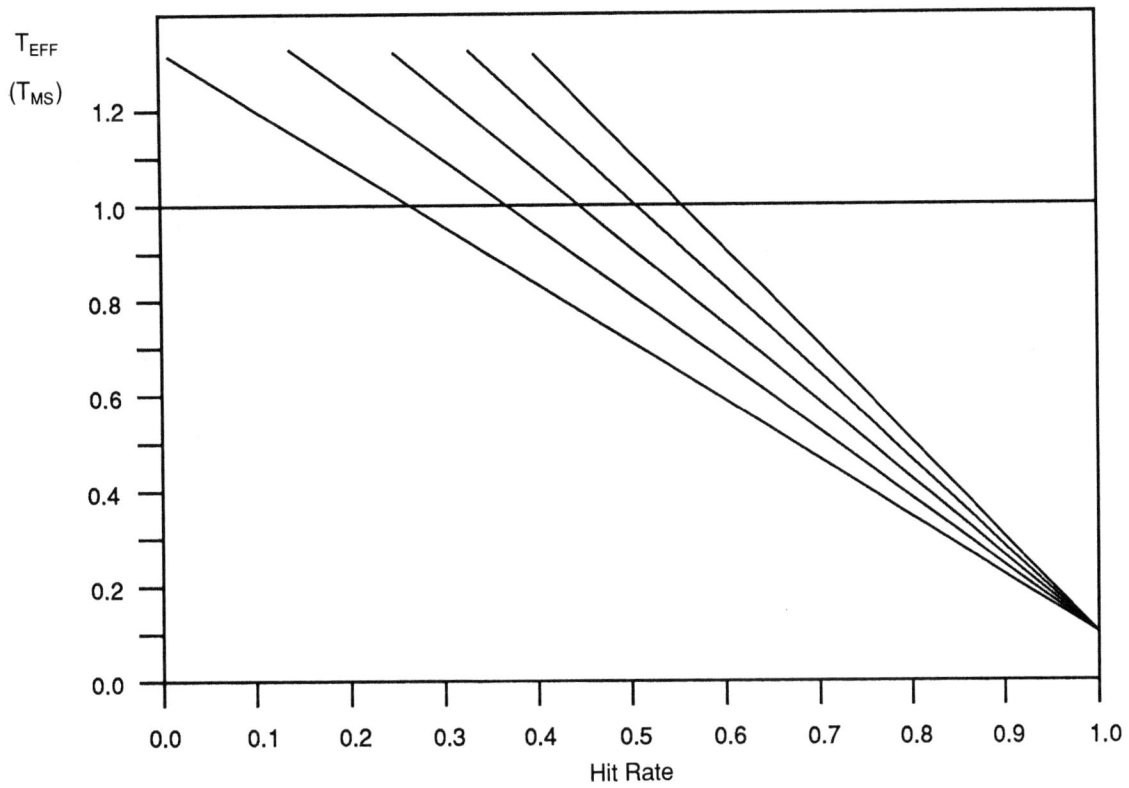

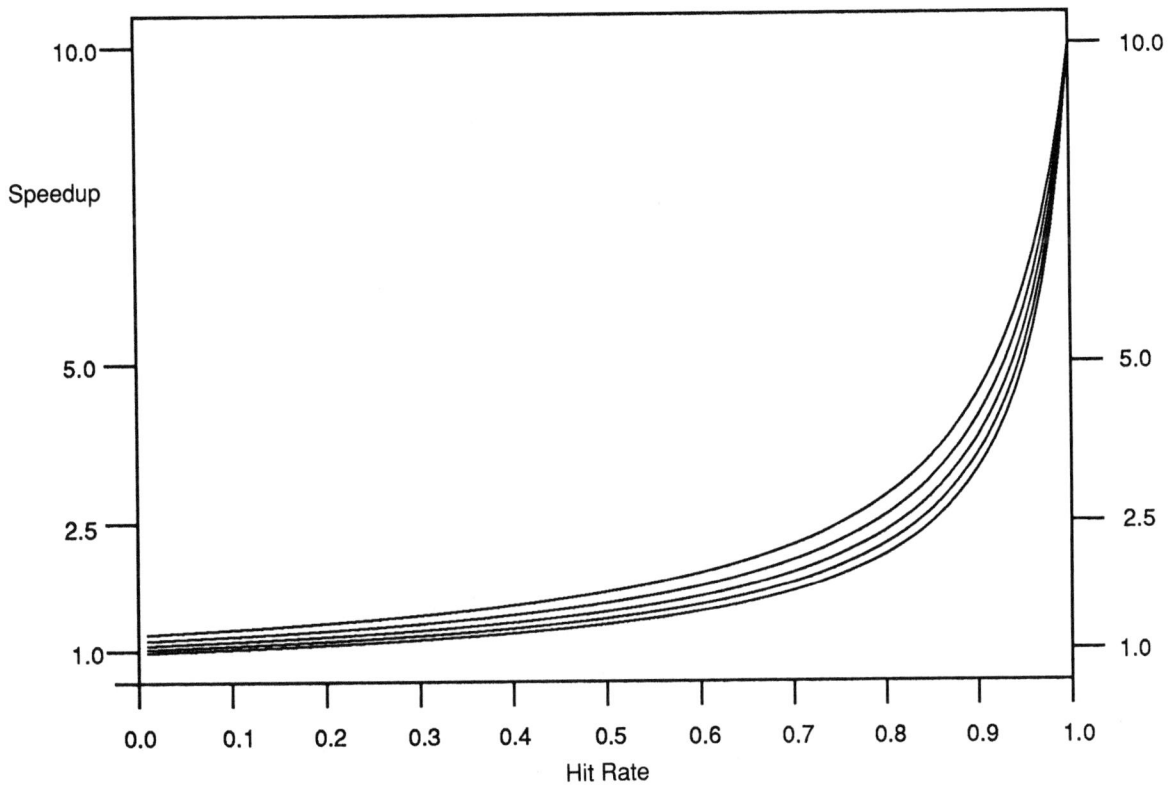

Figure 7.35. Cache Response Characteristics for Cache of Example 7.8. (a) Effective Access Time, T_{EFF} (b) Effective Speedup, $T_{\text{MS}}/T_{\text{EFF}}$.

timely fashion. A third troublesome reality is to coordinate the writes that occur because of the processor with writes occurring because of I/O transfers. Some provisions must be made to keep all of the information current and under control.

One of the side effects is the cache coherency problem, which exists for a system with multiple processors, each of which has its own cache. This situation is depicted in Figure 7.36, which shows a multiprocessor with two processing elements, each of which has its own cache. The cache coherency problem is exemplified by the following sequence of events. Processor A accesses a location in the memory, and the line is then loaded into Cache A. Subsequent accesses to the line will be found in the cache, rather than requiring the main store penalty. Processor B now needs the information in the line, so it accesses main store and gets its own copy of the information into Cache B. Further accesses of Processor B for the information are fielded by Cache B. Processor A now changes the information in the line. Processor B no longer has a valid copy of the line, since the information it has in Cache B has been superceded by the action of Processor A. Thus, the information is not coherent, and the situation has the label of the cache coherence problem.

If the write back scheme is used by the cache, then there is indeed a problem, since not only is the information in Cache B incorrect, but Cache B cannot obtain a valid copy until the information has been updated in main store, which will occur at some indeterminate time in the future. A write through scheme will provide a better basis for action, since the information needed by Cache B will be available in main store. Thus, the action of Processor A in updating the line in Cache A should also mark the line in Cache B invalid, so that when Processor B needs the information, it will be required to go to main store to find it. This is not the only solution to the cache coherency problem, but it does indicate why systems capable of multiprocessing organizations often choose a write through scheme as opposed to the write back scheme.

Example 7.9: A cache coherency solution: The Sequent system is a shared memory multiprocessing organization. What mechanism is used to allow each processor to have its own cache?

The Sequent system is a very interesting combination of the various mechanisms discussed, both for interface methods and for caching policies. A block diagram of a sample Sequent system is shown in Figure 7.37. The CPU module utilized in this system is the 80386, and included with it are the other devices that allow it to create the information needed by the memory

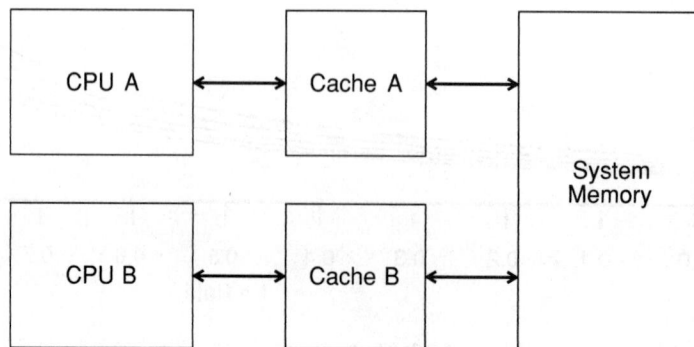

Figure 7.36. Computer System with Two CPUs and Two Caches.

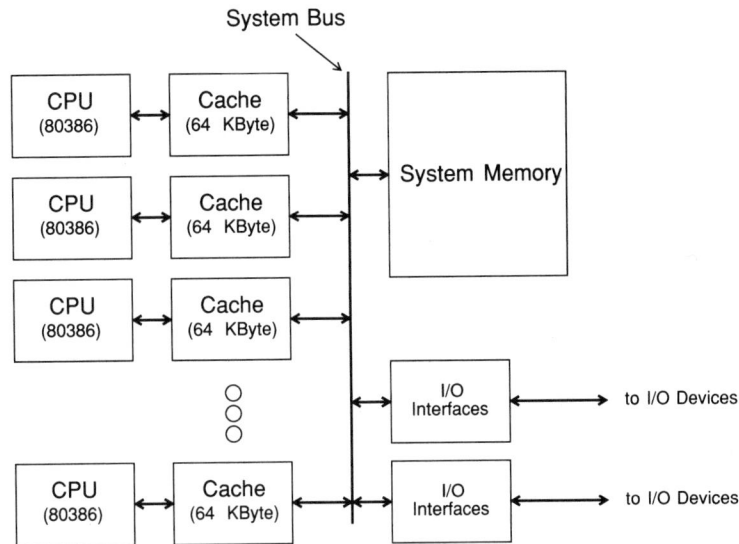

Figure 7.37. Block Diagram of a Sequent Multiprocessing System.

system. That is, there is a virtual-to-real address translation mechanism included with each CPU. Also, high speed floating point units that utilize the IEEE floating point system are available, which will enhance the normal floating point capabilities of the 80386 chip set. The cache system that provides the CPU with the information it needs is a 2 way set associative cache, with a capacity of 64 Kbytes. It is organized with a line size of 16 bytes; this gives 4,096 lines, or 2,048 sets. The mechanism used by the cache to communicate with the main store is a modified write back policy, which violates the intuitive feeling about how cache memory systems for multiple processor/multiple cache systems should work. The reason that the system functions properly can be understood by looking at the mechanisms included with the system bus.

The system bus is a synchronous, time multiplexed bus similar in function to the SBI. However, there are some important differences. The speed of the bus transactions is 100 nsec, and the mechanism for data transfers is address-data-data, as in the SBI. However, the width of the data path is larger in the Sequent than the 4-byte data path of the SBI. During the address portion of the transfer, the address is asserted on the lines. During the data portion of the transfer, 8 bytes of information are placed on the bus. This allows 16 bytes to be transferred in one address-data-data exchange. This is designed to be the amount of information in a line, and so transfers from memory to the caches always occur in increments of one line. With 16 bytes per 300 nsec, this leads to a maximum data rate of over 50 Mbytes/sec.

Solving the cache coherence problem requires the work not only of the system memory, but also of all the cache systems as well. The cache modules are organized such that there is an interface to the CPU for the transfer of information to and from the processor, as well as a watch dog interface, which monitors all of the transactions on the system bus. Since the bus is a synchronous protocol, this can be effectively managed. The interface between the cache and the system bus serves two purposes. The first is to exchange information with the system memory to maintain the cache information as a normal cache system should. The second purpose is to watch for memory transactions that take place with the lines it currently has in the cache. The second function permits the write back policy to be utilized in the system.

The problem explained above in Figure 7.36 involved two processors accessing the same location in memory. That set of events would proceed in a slightly different fashion in the Sequent system:

- Processor A accesses location XYZ in system memory. The system memory responds with the appropriate line. Cache A accepts the line and uses it. However, it keeps track of the fact that it has a private copy of the line.

- Processor B accesses location XYZ in system memory. The system memory responds with the appropriate line. Cache A also has this line; however, Cache A keeps track of the fact that it has not modified the line, so that the copy in system memory and the copy in Cache A are identical. Cache B accepts the line and uses it. However, it keeps track of the fact that it has a *shared* copy of the line. In addition, the watch dog interface on Cache A also notes that the line has been obtained by another cache, and marks it as shared.

- Processor A modifies location XYZ; this takes place in Cache A, and does not propagate to system memory. However, Cache A does send out onto the bus a notice to other caches that the line has been modified. The watch dog interface on Cache B sees this and marks the line as invalid in the cache.

- Processor B accesses location XYZ; the line in Cache B has been marked invalid, and the cache then goes to the system bus to get the information. When Cache A notices that someone needs information from location XYZ, and that it has the updated copy of that information, it signals the system memory not to respond to the request, and the information comes from Cache A instead. Thus, when Cache B requests the information, it does not know from what source the information will come, only that some bus cycles later the information will be provided on the bus.

The use of active interfaces between the cache and the system bus to monitor the data transfers on the bus allows the write back mechanism to function properly. The system will execute the programs as specified by the instruction streams. This organization also allows the creation of the locks needed for system operation. The interlock instructions of the 80386 are executed on a location in memory. The cache first obtains a private copy of the location, and then does not respond itself (nor allows the system memory to respond) until the interlocked transaction is complete.

At this time some comments on cache systems and their utilization are in order. First of all, in our discussion on caches, we assumed that the available address directed the cache to the proper spot to find the information requested. However, the question studiously avoided was, which address should be presented to the cache? Is it a virtual address or a physical address? Machines have been built that utilize virtual addresses for the cache access, but the more common mechanism is to use physical addresses. The problem remains, then to provide the virtual-to-real address translation to direct the request to the proper location. To aid in this process, an often used mechanism is called the translation lookaside buffer (TLB). This table, located in fast registers or fast memory, contains the most recent virtual to real translations, and, with this information, the proper address can be presented to the cache. This unit can be organized in a fashion similar to the cache, or in any manner that will satisfy system requirements for rapid address generation. Basically, this unit provides for the cache memory the same function provided by the 32082 for virtual memory — maintain in a rapidly accessible location the translations needed by the system.

As the relative costs of system resources change, different approaches to the organization of the cache may be appropriate. In this section we have discussed some of the mechanisms used with set associative caches. One of the mechanisms is the replacement of information within a cache. The decision made concerning which member of a set to replace requires hardware to implement — hardware (memory) to remember something about the order in which the members of the set have been accessed, and hardware to use that information to ascertain the proper member to replace. As memory costs continue to drop, one of the approaches that becomes more attractive is to use larger cache sizes and a direct mapping policy. With direct mapping, the hardware needed to maintain replacement information and to determine replacement priorities is nonexistent, since the target location can be found in only one location in a cache. By using this mechanism, the apparent speed can increase, since no multiplexing is needed between members of a set. At the same time, the hit ratio remains high because the cache is sufficiently large to provide the information needed.

Cache systems allow processors to obtain the data that they need in a timely fashion. So long as the information required by a processor is in the cache, then processing continues without unneeded delays for slower memory systems. This mechanism is useful in both "standard" memory systems for uniprocessor systems and for multiprocessing organizations. The added benefit in multiprocessing systems is to localize the information requests and to minimize the requests to system memory.

7.5. Summary

Memory systems in computers are used to maintain the programs and data needed by user and operating system alike. In all system components, information is maintained in devices with two stable states; this enables representation of a "one" and a "zero." Collections of these memory mechanisms allow the system to "remember" information that it needs. The principal requirement for an effective memory mechanism is the ability to store and retrieve the information in an organized fashion.

The speed and retrieval mechanisms used by a memory system lead to differing functions. The slower, serially organized elements are used to maintain large files and other information that can be effectively retrieved in a serial fashion, instead of a random access scheme. The faster storage mechanisms are used to maintain information accessed by the computing system in a time critical fashion. The storage elements that can supply information in the shortest time are used in register and cache systems; elements that are not quite so fast can be effectively used as main memory elements. Organization of the random access elements can be done in a 1-D or 2-D fashion or with similar mechanisms, the requirement being that only one of the various locations is accessed at any one time.

Virtual memory systems allow the user to operate in "virtual space," which is not the same as the actual physical space. The virtual machine is the view of the system as seen by the user, and includes those resources of which the user is aware. The physical machine can be quite different; the physical model is limited by the exact configuration of the system. The virtual machine concept allows users to use more resources than the system actually has, such as larger memory spaces. The same concept allows more memory resources to be shared among many users who are not aware of the entire extent of the system. The virtual memory mechanisms, segmentation and paging, translate requests from the virtual system to the actual physical system. This results in systems with a higher apparent system speed because of the locality observed in programs: during a small portion of the program, only a fraction of the total memory is used by the system.

The locality of programs also allows cache systems to function effectively. The cache allows a small, high speed memory to keep only the most active portions of a program and its data accessible to the CPU. But, since it operates at CPU speeds, the cache mechanism speeds up the overall processing rate of the computer.

7.6. Problems

7.1 Design a 16 element register bank using 1-D techniques. For register elements use the '299 as shown in Figure 7.9.

7.2 Design a 16 element register bank using 2-D techniques. For register elements use the '299 as shown in Figure 7.9.

7.3 The IDT7164 is an 8K × 8 static RAM with 13 address lines and 8 input/output lines, as well as two chip selects (CS1-l, CS2-H), a write enable (WE-L), and an output enable (OE-L). Using this device, design a 64-Kbyte memory using 1-D organizational techniques. How many nonmemory devices are required for this memory system?

7.4 Use the IDT7164 described in Problem 7.3 to create a 128-Kbyte memory system. Use 2-D organizational techniques. How many nonmemory devices are required for the memory system?

7.5 Design the dynamic RAM controller shown in Figure P7.5. The inputs are an 18 line data address, a 9 line refresh address, a refresh request line (REF-H), and a data read line (READ-H) that initiates a read action. The outputs are a 9 line address, which is to go to the dynamic RAM, the row address strobe (RAS-L), the column address strobe (CAS-L), and the ready line (READY-H).

The behavior of the device is as follows: A refresh cycle is accomplished by asserting the refresh address on the RAM address lines (and allowing 50 nsec settling time), then asserting the RAS signal for 150 nsec, and releasing both RAS and the address lines. A read cycle is accomplished by asserting 9 bits of the address (and waiting the 50 nsec required for settling), asserting RAS, waiting another 50 nsec, then changing to the other 9

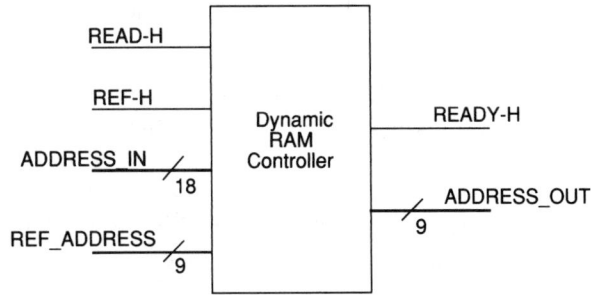

Figure P7.5. Dynamic RAM Controller.

address bits, (and another 50 nsec wait) asserting CAS, waiting 100 nsec, and then asserting the ready line. This condition remains until the READ is released, whereupon the system returns to the quiescent state. Assume a system clock at 20 MHz. To complete the design:

a. Give a data path block diagram. Assume the existance of *N*-bit 2-1 muxes with tri-state outputs and *N*-bit tri-state drivers. (These could be constructed from multiple copies of a '257.)

b. Give a state diagram describing the action of the device. Include signal names and assertion levels.

c. Design a circuit to do the work of part b.

d. Describe what modifications or additional logic would be required to implement the write capability as well as the read capability.

7.6 The block diagram for a general purpose system shown with Problem 4.7 is included here as Figure P7.6. Modify the block diagram to include a segmentation register. That is, provide a way that all addresses to memory can be offset by the value in a segment register. Describe the modifications that

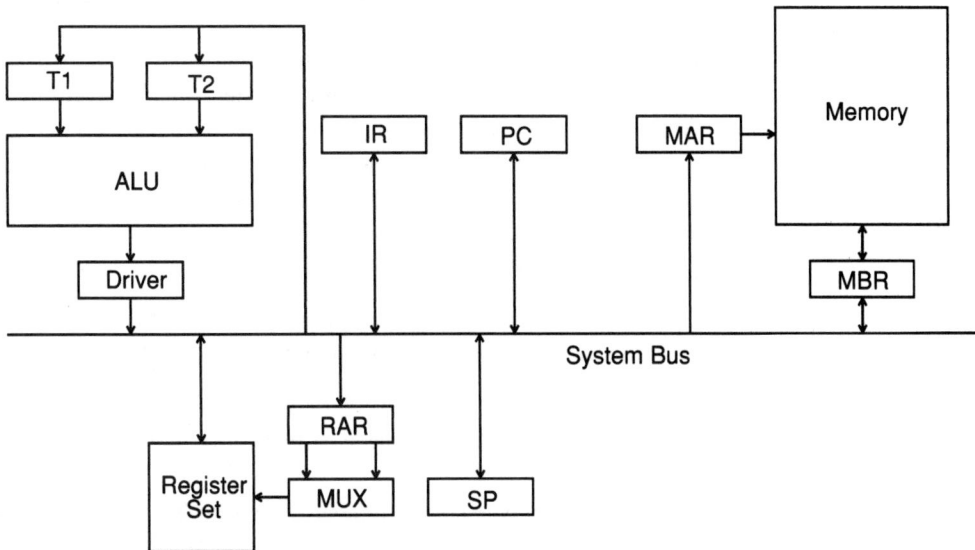

Figure P7.6. Block Diagram for General Purpose Machine.

must be made to an instruction set to control the system with this modification.

7.7 In general, the single segment register of Problem 7.6 does not provide sufficient capabilities to a computer system; a system must be capable of handling several segments. Modify the block diagram of Figure P7.6 to include the capability of several segment addresses. What contributions are made by this enhancement of the arrangement of Problem 7.6?

7.8 Access to a memory system by a number of programs can be enhanced by the use of paging. Modify the block diagram of Figure P7.6 to include a hardware page table, and specify the manner in which the page table is used to generate the effective memory address. Why will this method be faster than the segmentation mechanism of Problem 7.7?

7.9 A computer system is configured with a disk to provide high speed file storage. The disk system has 32 sectors per track, and stores 512 bytes per sector. The rotational speed of the disk is 3,600 RPM. The average seek time is 30 msec. The average instruction execution time is 1.5 μsec. When a page fault occurs, how much time will be required before execution can continue on that program? Identify each of the contributing times, and describe what is happening during that time. How much would the delay be modified if the seek time of the disk were reduced to 24 msec?

7.10 Consider a cache organization with the following characteristics:

Main memory size:	16 Mbytes
Cache memory size:	32 Kbytes
Cache line size:	64 bytes
Cache cycle time:	50 nanoseconds
Main memory cycle:	500 nanoseconds
Probability of cache hit:	.7
Probability of write:	.25
Probability line dirty:	.2
Cache organization:	4 way set associative

a. Give a representation of the address space. That is, what bits in the address are for what? Assume that there are 2 bits between the byte identifying bits and the set identifying bits.

b. Assume that 128×8 memories are used to build the cache. Give a data path block diagram of the cache system. Assume that no parity checking is needed, and that the cache is a write back cache.

c. Find the effective time for a memory access.

7.11 A certain cache memory machine uses a cache that can store 512 blocks of 64 words each. Assume a main memory size of 1,048,576 words.

a. Which bits of the word address should specify the block number?

b. If a set associative scheme is used, which bits should specify the set number?

c. Describe the worst case reference pattern (for maximum cache miss) assuming (i) direct addressing, (ii) set associative with two blocks per set, (iii) set associative with four blocks per set, (iv) fully associative cache allocation. How likely are these worst cases?

7.12 A certain computer has a 16-Mbyte main memory, cycle time of 350 nsec. It also has a 32-Kbyte cache, cycle time of 25 nsec. The cache is set associative, four lines per set, 32 bytes per line.

a. The address space is partially defined below. Complete the specification.

Tag Bits	Set Bits	Tag Bits	Byte in Line
		3	5

b. Assume that an address trace of a program is such that the lines in use are accessed in the following order ... 0 1 2 3 0 1 2 4 0 1 2 3 0 1 2 4 ... If this addressing pattern is continued, what will the effective memory access time be?

7.13 Develop a formula for the effective access time for a cache memory that uses a write through scheme. Assume that writes that are cache misses do not have any effect on the cache at all, except for the time involved in the transaction. Assume also that no buffering is provided for the writes to main store. State all assumptions that you make in the process of problem solution.

7.14 Repeat Problem 7.13 assuming that a buffer is available between the cache and main store. This buffer will allow the operation of the memory system to continue once a write has been initiated. However, if a write is needed and the buffer is in use, the system must wait until the data in the buffer has been transferred to main store.

7.7. References and Readings

[AMD85] Advanced Micro Devices, *Bipolar Microprocessor Logic and Interface Data Book*. Sunnyvale, CA: Advanced Micro Devices, 1985.

[AhDe71] Aho, A. V., P. J. Denning, and J. D. Ullman, "Principles of Optimal Page Replacement," *Journal of the ACM*. Vol. 18, No. 1, January 1971, pp. 80–93.

[Baer84] Baer, J. L., "Computer Architecture," *Computer*. Vol 17, No 10, October 1984, pp. 77–87.

[Baer80] Baer, J. L., *Computer Systems Architecture*. Rockville, MD: Computer Science Press, 1980.

[Bart85] Bartee, T. C., *Digital Computer Fundamentals* 6th edition, New York: McGraw Hill Book Company, 1985.

[BaBr77] Batson, A. A., and R. E. Brundage, "Segment Sizes and Lifetimes in Algol 60 Programs," *Communications of the ACM*. Vol. 20, No. 1, January 1977, pp. 36–44.

[BaJu70] Batson, A., S. Ju, and D. C. Wood, "Measurements of Segment Size," *Communications of the ACM*. Vol. 13, No. 3, March 1970, pp. 155–159.

[BeNe69] Belady, L. A., R. A. Nelson, and G. S. Shedler, "An Anomaly in the Space-Time Characteristics of Certain Programs Running in Paging Machines," *Communications of the ACM*. Vol. 12, No. 6, June 1969, pp. 349–353.

[BeNe71] Bell, C. G. and A. Newell, *Computer Structures: Readings and Examples*. New York: McGraw Hill Book Company, 1971.

[BiSh88] Bic, L., and A. C. Shaw, *The Logical Design of Operating Systems*. Englewood Cliffs, NJ: Prentice Hall, 1988.

[BrHa73] Brinch Hansen, P., *Operating Systems Principles*. Englewood Cliffs, NJ: Prentice Hall, 1973.

[BuGo46] Burks, A. W., H. H. Goldstine, and J. von Neumann, "Preliminary Discussion of the Logical Design of an Electronic Computing Instrument," Institute for Advanced Studies, 1946, reprinted in [Swar76].

[ChOp76] Chu, W. W., and H. Opderbeck, "Program Behavior and the Page-Fault-Frequency Replacement Algorithm," *Computer*. Vol. 9, No. 11, November 1976, pp. 29–38.

[Deit84] Deitel, H. M., *An Introduction to Operating Systems*. Reading, MA: Addison-Wesley Publishing Company, 1984.

[Denn70] Denning, P. J., "Virtual Memory," *ACM Computing Surveys*. Vol. 2, No. 3, September 1970, pp. 153–189.

[Denn80] Denning, P. J., "Working Sets Past and Present," *IEEE Transactions on Software Engineering*. Vol. SE-6, No. 1, January 1980, pp. 64–84.

[Flet80] Fletcher, W. I., *An Engineering Approach to Digital Design*. Englewood Cliffs, NJ: Prentice Hall, 1980.

[FoME85] Fossum, T., J. B. McElroy, and W. English, "An Overview of the VAX 8600 System," *Digital Technical Journal*. Hudson, MA: Digital Equipment Corporation, 1985, pp. 8–23.

[GeTi83] Gelenbe, E., P. Tiberio, and J. Boekhorst, "Page Size in Demand Paging Systems," *Acta Informatica*. Vol. 3, No. 1, 1973, pp. 1–23.

[BuFr78] Gupta, R. K., and M. A. Franklin, "Working Set and Page Fault Frequency Replacement Algorithms: A Performance Comparison," *IEEE Transactions on Computers*. Vol. C-27, No. 8, August 1978, pp. 706–712.

[HaVr78] Hamacher, V. C., Z. G. Vranesic, and S. G. Zaky, *Computer Organization*. New York: McGraw Hill Book Company, 1984.

[Haye88] Hayes, J. P., *Computer Architecture and Organization*, 2nd Edition. New York: McGraw Hill Book Company, 1988.

[Kain89] Kain, R. Y., *Computer Architecture, Software and Hardware*. Englewood Cliffs, NJ: Prentice Hall, 1989.

[KaWi73] Kaplan, K. R., and R. O. Winder, "Cache-Based Computer Systems," *Computer* Vol. 6, No. 3, March 1973, pp. 30–36.

[KnRa75] Knuth, D. E., and G. S. Rao, "Activity in Interleaved Memory," *IEEE Transactions on Computers*. Vol. C-24, No. 9, September 1975, pp. 943–944.

[Kuck78] Kuck, D. J., *The Structure of Computers and Computations*. New York: John Wiley & Sons, 1978.

[Lang82] Langdon, G. G., Jr., *Computer Design*. San Jose, CA: Computeach Press Inc., 1982.

[Lipt68] Liptay, J. S., "Structural Aspects of the System/360 Model 85 — The Cache," *IBM Systems Journal*. Vol. 7, No. 1, 1968., pp. 15–21.

[Mati80] Matick, R. E., "Memory and Storage," in [Ston80], pp. 205–274.

[Mati77] Matick, R. E., *Computer Storage Systems and Technology*. New York: John Wiley & Sons, 1977.

[MaGe70] Mattson, R. L., J. Gecsei, D. L. Slutz, et al., "Evaluation Techniques for Storage Hierarchies," *IBM System Journal*. Vol. 9, No. 2, 1970, pp. 78–117.

[PeSi83] Peterson, J. L., and A. Silberschatz, *Operating System Concepts*. Reading, MA: Addison-Wesley Publishing Company, 1983.

[Pohm84] Pohm, A. V., "High Speed Memory Systems," *Computer*. Vol. 17, No. 10, October 1984, pp. 162–171.

[Rand69] Randell, B., "A Note on Storage Fragmentation and Program Segmentation," *Communications of the ACM*. Vol. 12, No. 7, July 1969, pp. 365–369.

[Schn85] Schneider, G. M., *The Principles of Computer Organization*. New York: John Wiley & Sons, 1985.

[Shiv85] Shiva, S. G., *Computer Design and Architecture*. Boston, MA: Little, Brown, 1985.

[SiBe82] Siewiorek, D. P., C. G. Bell, and A. Newell, *Computer Structures: Principles and Examples*. New York: McGraw Hill Book Company, 1982.

[Simt82] Smith, A. J., "Cache Memories," *ACM Computing Surveys*. Vol. 14, No. 3, September 1982, pp. 473–530.

[Smit85] Smith, A. J., "Cache Evaluation and the Impact of Workload Choice," *Proceedings of the 12th Annual International Symposium on Computer Architecture, Silver Springs, MD: IEEE Computer Society Press,* June 1985, pp. 64–73.

[Smit00] Smith, A. J., "Disk-Cache-Miss Ratio Analysis and Design Considerations," *ACM Transactions on Computer Systems*. Vol. 3, No. 3, August 1985, pp. 161–203.

[SmGo83] Smith, J. E., and J. R. Goodman, "A Study of Instruction Cache Organizations and Replacement Policies," *Proceedings of the 10th Annual Symposium on Computer Architecture*. June 1983, pp. 117–123.

[Ston87] Stone, H. S., *High-Performance Computer Architecture*. Reading, MA: Addison-Wesley Publishing Company, 1987.

[Stre83] Strecker, W. D., "Transient Behavior of Cache Memories," *ACM Transactions on Computer Systems*. Vol. 1, No. 4, November 1983, pp. 281–293.

[Swar76] Swartzlander, E. E., Jr. (Ed.), *Computer Design Development: Principal Papers*. Rochelle Park, NJ: Hayden Book Company, Inc., 1976.

[Tane84] Tanenbaum, A. S., *Structured Computer Organization*. Englewood Cliffs, NJ: Prentice Hall, 1984.

[TI85] Texas Instruments, *The TTL Data Book,* Volume 2. Dallas, TX: Texas Instruments, 1985.

[ThKn86] Thakkar, S. S., and Knowles, A. E., "A High Performance Memory Management Scheme," *Computer*. Vol. 19, No. 5, May 1986, pp. 8–19.

[Wilk87] Wilkinson, B., *Digital System Design*. Englewood Cliffs, NJ: Prentice Hall International, 1987.

8

Pipelined Systems: Low Level Parallelism

Regardless of the application of a computer system, there is always some motivation to enhance the speed of execution of the system. One way to achieve this is to use a technology that operates at a higher speed, and many machines have used this method to produce a system that performs more work in a given amount of time. However, there are practical limits to this method, since there are practical limits to how fast signals will travel. If speed increases are to be achieved without a faster technology, then some degree of concurrency is necessary. If the circuits can't function faster, then to increase the apparent speed of the machine, the basic modules of the machine should perform functions simultaneously. This can be done if the functions to be performed are independent. That is, if the results of one instruction are not needed for the execution of another, then the two functions can be done at the same time. If this technique is successful, then instead of one operation per unit time, N operations per unit time are performed (for N independent units).

A variety of ways have been utilized to increase the amount of concurrent execution in computers. One method is to organize a number of identical functional units in such a way that they can all perform the same operation on different sets of data simultaneously. This is called single instruction stream, multiple data stream processing (SIMD), since many processors are executing simultaneously, but the action is controlled by a single unit. For certain classes of problems, this can be a very beneficial organization. Machines that have used this method of organization include the Illiac IV [BaBr68, Thur76], the Massively Parallel Processor [Batc80, HwBr84], and the Connection Machine [Hill85].

Another method of performing simultaneous tasks is to divide the work to be done into portions that can operate in the same period. For example, von Neumann suggested that the I/O operations could occur simultaneous with processing [BuGo46], which is a common practice in computer systems today. Overlap can also be achieved by dividing instruction execution into its constituent parts: fetch, decode, and execute. That is, while one instruction is being decoded, it may be possible to fetch the next instruction. And at the same time perform the work prescribed by the previous instruction. In this type of mechanism, the results of one step are used by the following step, and the process resembles a pipeline, which is why the method is called pipelining.

We are familiar with the use if pipelines to transport fluids across long distances. The fluid is placed into the pipe at the origin, and after some delay, the fluid becomes available at the destination. The material is kept flowing through the pipe by forcing more material into the beginning or front of the pipe. Because of the length of the pipe, a great deal of material may be sent into the pipe before anything is available at the end. But once the flow has begun, then there is a direct correlation between what enters the pipe and what leaves the pipe.

Other relatively common processes fit this description for pipelining. Manufacturing uses pipelines, called "assembly lines," to produce goods in a timely fashion. When the "pipeline" is flowing in an automobile factory, a new car exits the pipe every few seconds. This is an interesting example since the pipe is not homogeneous. That is, since not all automobiles are exactly alike, as the basic unit (in this case a car) moves through the pipe (the assembly line), features are added at the respective stations in the pipe according to a specification accompanying the unit through the pipe.

Other processes that form pipelines are plentiful. One example is food preparation in restaurants, where individuals perform specific functions on the food as it is processed. Another example is an automatic car wash system, where cars to be cleaned follow one another though a system where the various cleaning steps are applied successively to each unit. Even school systems can be considered a pipeline process, since one class follows another through the educational process, each learning concepts in a predetermined order.

In this chapter we will examine more closely this concept of pipelining, and apply the principles to the design of pipelined computer systems. Two basic kinds of pipes are used in computers: data pipes and control pipes. Both result in higher execution rates, since more answers are available per unit time. And both achieve effective results by overlapping independent functions. First we will identify the limits to the process, and then examine practical implementations of the mechanism. The information in this section is intended to be an introduction to the concept of pipelining, and an examination of some of its characteristics. Additional details can be determined by examining pipelines of real computer systems, and by looking at the implementations of some of the classical machines. Of particular interest are the scoreboard technique for reservation of time slots [Thor64], and the Tomasulo algorithm for utilization of multiple functional units with a pipeline [Toma67]. In addition, some texts present a more complete discussion of many of the aspects of pipelining than presented here [Kogg81, Ston80, HwBr84].

8.1. Pipelined Systems: Overlap of Independent Processes

The use of pipelining in computer systems is used to allow processes that can proceed independently to do so. For an example, consider the process of doing a floating point addition. A block diagram of one method of doing this is shown in Figure 3.25, which is repeated with a few modifications in Figure 8.1. It is possible to perform the addition function as shown in Figure 8.1, but since the

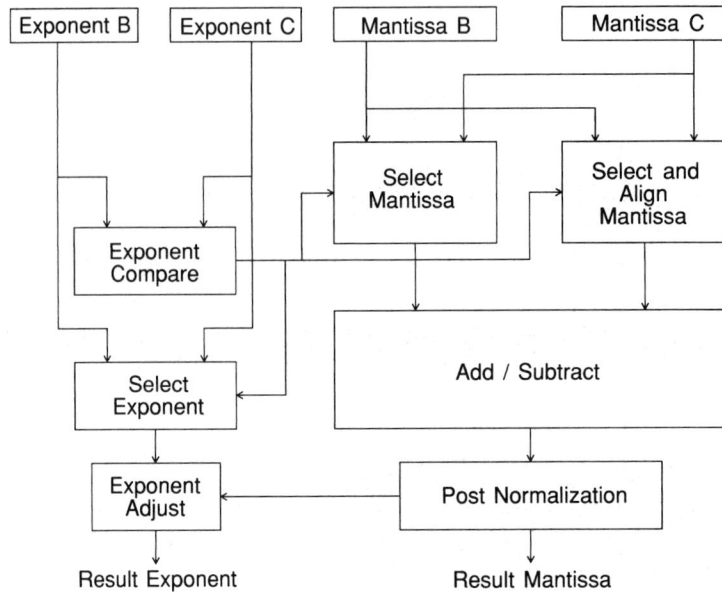

Figure 8.1. Block Diagram of Floating Point Addition.

individual operations are sequential in nature, it is also possible to create a pipeline to perform this function. Such a pipeline is shown in Figure 8.2, which adds to the functional diagram of Figure 8.1 some storage capability. The registers allow different addition operations to utilize different portions of the hardware simultaneously. For the function shown in Figure 8.2, up to three different additions can be in process simultaneously.

The figure indicates that one operation can be utilizing the postnormalization stage, while a second operation is adding the mantissas, and a third operation is being aligned for addition. To achieve this overlap, the data for these operations must be available to be placed in the pipe, and the results must also be extracted in a timely fashion. This places constraints on the data paths for the system, as well as the timing required. For this system, let us assume that the times involved are:

T_{FPA}	Time for floating point addition without pipelining
T_{ALIGN}	Time for the alignment process
T_{ADD}	Time for the addition of the aligned mantissas
T_{PN}	Time for the postnormalization process
T_{REG}	Time required for the registers
T_{MC}	Clock cycle time; time of operation of a stage of the pipe

Obviously, the time for the arithmetic is simply

$$T_{FPA} = T_{ALIGN} + T_{ADD} + T_{PN}$$

If $T_{ALIGN} = T_{ADD} = T_{PN}$, then T_{MC} is simply $T_{FPA} / 3 + T_{REG}$. In general, the clock cycle time is based on the maximum time for a stage,

$$T_{MC} = \max [T_{ALIGN}, T_{ADD}, T_{PN}] + T_{REG}$$

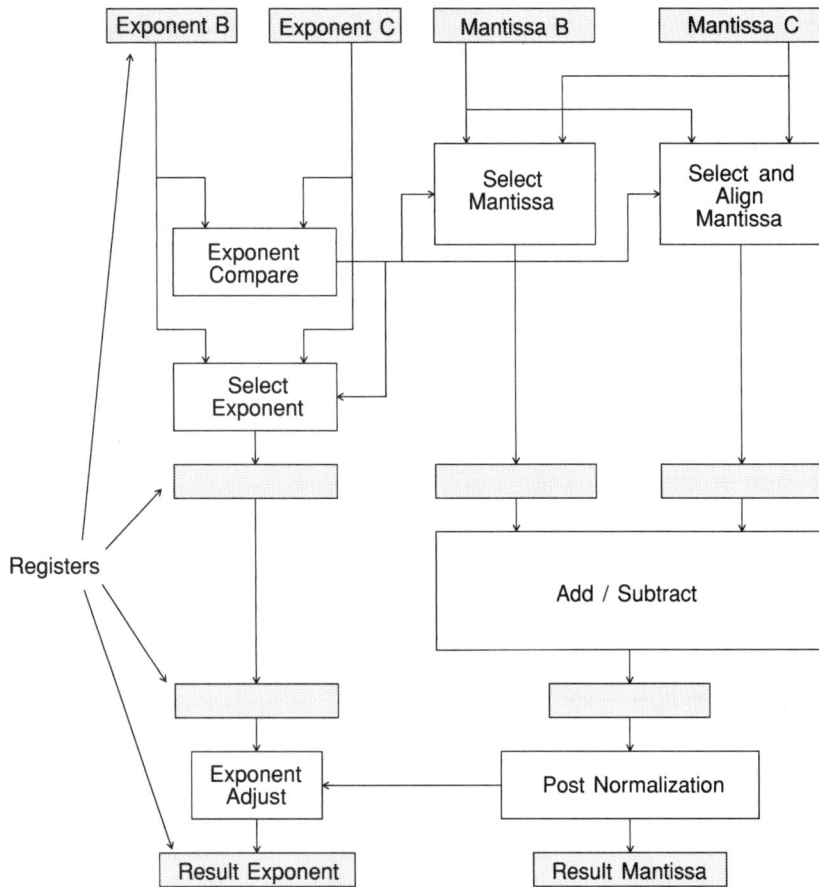

Figure 8.2. Block Diagram of Floating Point Addition with Storage Registers.

But for ease of understanding we will initially assume that the basic operations are of the same length. Thus, we would hope that the floating point addition pipe would produce results three times faster than the nonpipelined operation of the system. The cost of this increase in performance is the addition of the storage elements within the pipe, and the fact that the data movement requirements increase over a nonpipelined implementation. In each clock cycle, two input operands must be supplied and one result must be stored or used in a reasonable fashion.

This simple floating point example identifies some of the properties that are important in analyzing the effectiveness of pipelining. The desired effect is to increase the apparent processing rate, and this is accomplished by overlapping the execution of independent operations. Let us assume that we have a process to pipeline, and that the time for the process without pipelining is T_P. Figure 8.3 presents a block diagram of this process. Data is supplied to the process, some operations are performed on the data, and the output is available to be stored or to form an input to another process. We will also assume that the process is divisible into as many sections as desired. This is not a realistic assumption, but it will identify some interesting characteristics of pipelining. In Figure 8.3, the process has been divided into six sections, and the output from one section is supplied to the following section. The time per section is T_S; we will also make the

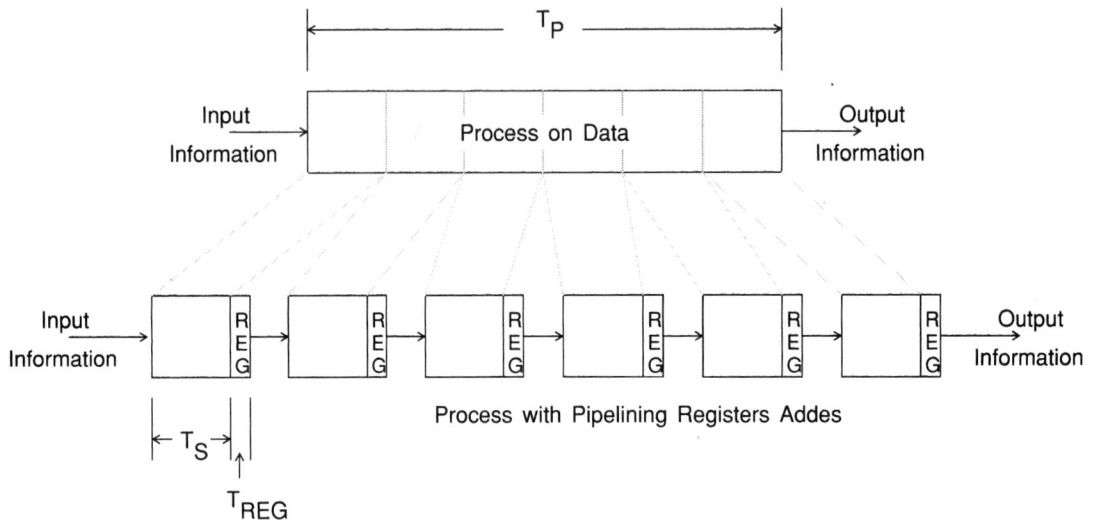

Figure 8.3. Processing with Nonpipelined and Pipelined Mechanisms.

unrealistic assumption that T_S is the same for all sections. The results from the section are saved in a register, and the register time is represented as T_{REG}. The total time for a section, then is $T_S + T_{REG}$. Using this model of processing, let us follow the execution of the process in a nonpipelined and a pipelined system.

To perform M different operations on a nonpipelined implementation would require the application of the processing hardware M different times, as shown in Figure 8.4. Thus, the total processing time for the M instructions would be $M \times T_P$.

On the other hand, the use of pipelining allows different sections of the unit to be used in a single clock cycle. One way to visualize this is to construct a space-time diagram for the hardware; that is, time is shown on the X axis, and the functional units (in this case, sections of the pipelined process) are shown on the Y axis. Then the progress of the M instructions can be followed through the system. Such a diagram is shown in Figure 8.5 for the six section pipe of Figure 8.3. The time for the first instruction will be $N \times (T_S + T_{REG})$, where there are N sections of a pipe. In this case, $N = 6$. If we assume that the cost of the register is not included ($T_{REG} = 0$), and the initial process is equally divisible, so that $T_S = T_P / N$, then the first instruction takes the same amount of time as the first instruction of a nonpipelined implementation, T_P. The benefit comes from the other instructions, since the second instruction will be finished T_S after the first instruction, and so on. So, the total time required for M instructions is just the time required for the first instruction $[N \times (T_S + T_{REG})]$, plus $M - 1$ additional section times $[(M - 1) \times$

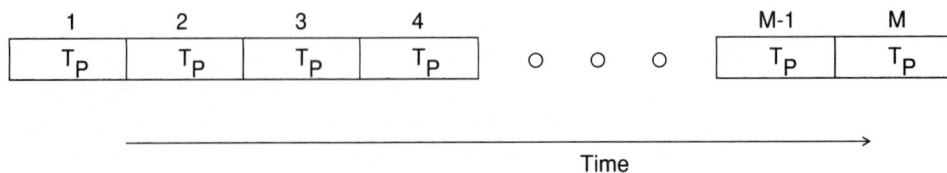

Figure 8.4. Timing Requirements for Nonpipelined Implementations.

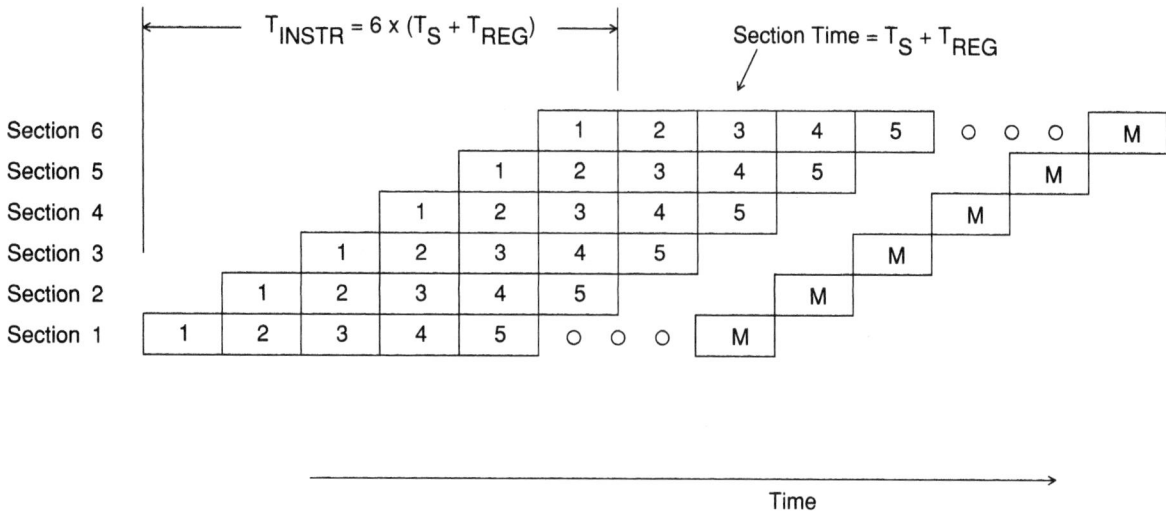

Figure 8.5. Overlapped Execution of Instructions.

$(T_S + T_{REG})$]. So, the total time for M instructions is $(N + M - 1) \times (T_S + T_{REG})$. To see what the speedup is, we then calculate:

$$\text{Speedup} = \frac{\text{Time for } M \text{ instructions without pipelining}}{\text{Time for } M \text{ instructions with pipelining}}$$

From the above times, this becomes:

$$\text{Speedup} = \frac{M \times T_P}{(N + M - 1) \times (T_S + T_{REG})}$$

$$= \frac{T_P}{(1 + \dfrac{N - 1}{M}) \times (T_S + T_{REG})}$$

For large M, the $(N-1)/M$ term becomes negligible, and the speedup is:

$$= \frac{T_P}{T_S + T_{REG}}$$

$$\approx \frac{T_P}{T_S}, \qquad \text{if } T_S \gg T_{REG}$$

$$= N$$

If we assume that T_{REG} is negligible, then the speedup is merely N, the number of sections in the pipe. This agrees with our intuitive feeling of how much faster a pipelined implementation should be; indeed, we expect a six section pipe to produce results six times faster than the nonpipelined implementation. At the same time, we must remember that this observation is valid only if we disregard the time required for the storage function, and we also assume a steady state condition where M is large.

It is instructive to also examine some of the other information evident from the above discussion. First, pipelining implementations do not reduce the time for an instruction. That is, the time from the start to the finish of a single instruction will not decrease with the use of pipelining. If anything, the actual time to accomplish an instruction will be longer than the nonpipelined implementation, since the cycle time will be geared to the longest section time, and the registers will add real delays to the system. Thus, from the initiation of the operation to the completion of the first instruction will take a time dependent on the cycle time and the number of stages in the pipe. This time is sometimes called the "fill time," since it is the time required to fill all of the stages of the pipe. Obviously, for a larger number of stages in the pipe the fill time will be longer. This time may become important in the operation of the pipelined process, as we shall see.

Once the first operation has been completed, the remaining operations will follow at the rate of one result per clock cycle. This will continue as long as operations are available to perform, or until there is a conflict within the pipe for a resource. We will identify possible conflicts and some mechanisms for handling them in a later section. When the pipe is full and producing new results at the rate of one result per clock cycle, the system is operating at its highest efficiency. One of the tasks of the system architect is to create a unit capable of supporting the data movement needed to permit the pipeline to operate at maximum efficiency.

Another observation concerns the effective speedup over a nonpipelined system. The above equations can be plotted to identify the speedup achieved by using the pipeline technique. To give some physical "feel" for the observation, we will make some assumptions about the process we are pipelining. Assume that the nonpipelined system requires 100 nsec to complete. Thus, with no pipelining, the process will have a speedup of 1. Then, as the amount of pipelining increases, the speedup will increase. First, we will assume that the time required by the registers can be ignored, which is not a realistic assumption. That is, we will assume that T_{REG} is zero. With a T_S of 50 nsec, the speedup is 2; with a T_S of 25 nsec, the speedup is 4; and as the time per section, T_S, gets smaller, the effective speedup increases. It is evident from the equations that the effective speedup will asymptotically approach the Y axis. Thus, if the process were infinitely divisible, then the speedup could be infinitely large. A plot of effective speedup versus T_S is shown in Figure 8.6. The circled places on the curve are the effective speedups for $N = 1$ to 12.

The real gains available with pipelining are limited by two different mechanisms. The first is the fact that a real process is neither infinitely nor equally divisible. Thus, the time that needs to be considered is not T_P/N, but rather the maximum section time resulting from dividing the initial process into N sections. The second mechanism is the delay time added into the system by the use of registers or latches. If we assume a register delay of 10 nsec, then the curve of Figure 8.6 must be altered accordingly. This gives rise to the second curve of Figure 8.6, which indicates that the effective speedup is directly impacted by the register delays. An interesting observation can be made by following this second curve until the T_S is zero. At this point the effective speedup is only 10. Thus, even if the processing were free, the time penalty incurred by the use of real registers limits the speedup achievable with pipelining.

One of the assumptions implicit in the above observations is that there is no problem with keeping the pipe full. However, in real pipelines this is a challenging problem, and later in this chapter we will identify some techniques used to

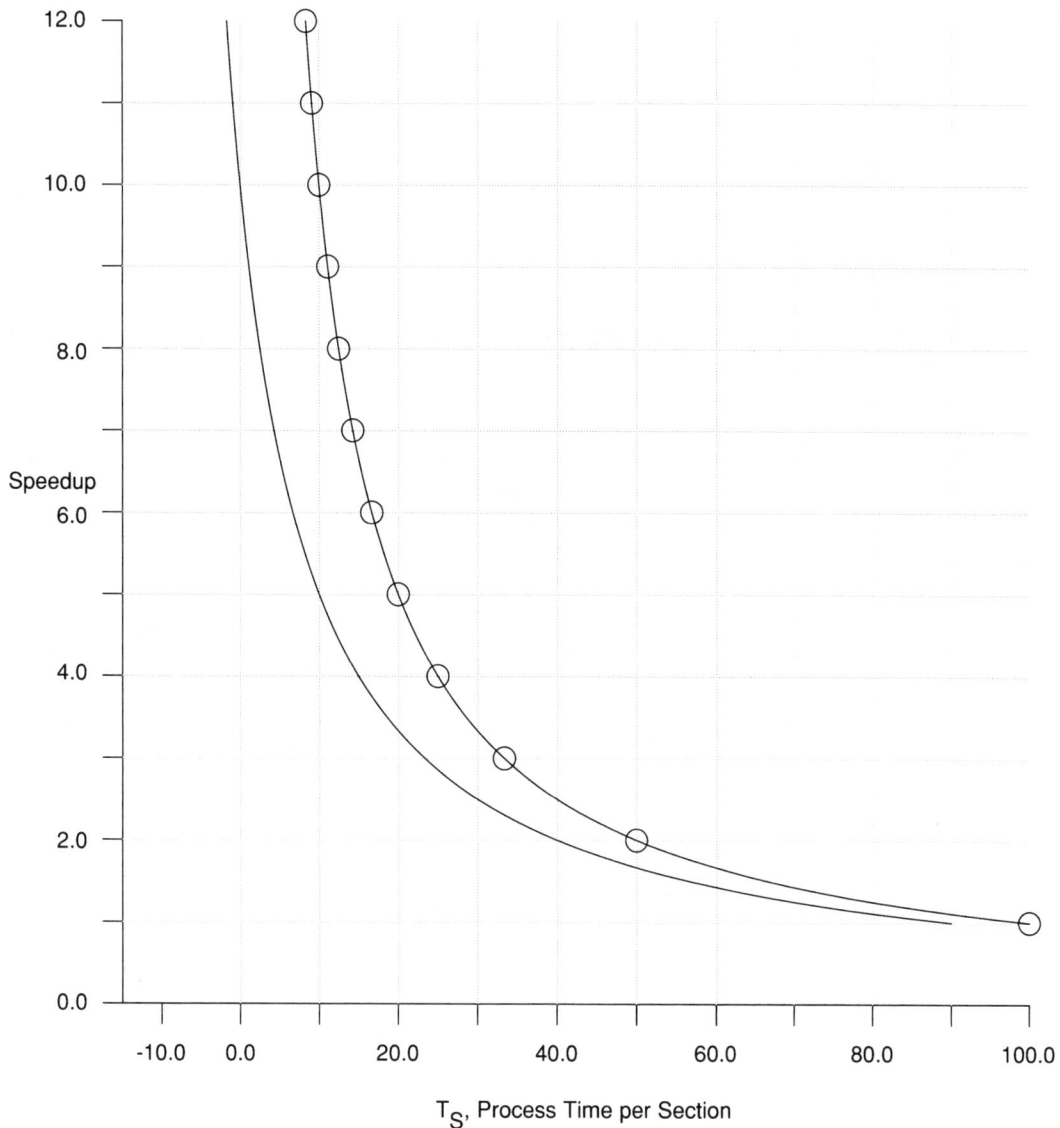

Figure 8.6. Speedup Achievable by Pipelining.

keep the pipe as full as possible. But suppose that the system is not able to keep the pipe full, but for some reason the sections of the pipe are not utilized for a fraction of clock cycles. How is the speedup affected? To answer this question, let us return to the speedup calculation:

$$\text{Speedup} = \frac{\text{Time for } M \text{ instructions without pipelining}}{\text{Time for } M \text{ instructions with pipelining}}$$

Assume that a fraction of the cycles are unused, and let that fraction be represented by f. With this assumption, the amount of time required to execute M functions is not $N + M - 1$, but rather $(N + M - 1) \times (1 + f)$. And the equation developed above changes to become:

$$\text{Speedup} = \frac{M \times T_P}{(N + M - 1) \times (1 + f) \times (T_S + T_R)}$$

$$= \frac{T_P}{\left(1 + \dfrac{N - 1}{M}\right) \times (1 + f) \times (T_S + T_R)}$$

$$= \frac{T_P}{(1 + f) \times (T_S + T_R)}$$

$$= \frac{\text{Best speedup}}{1 + f}$$

Obviously, a pipelined processor is designed in such a way that f is kept as small as possible. However, it is instructive to note the effective degradation in performance that occurs with different values of f. Consider the previous example of a process requiring 100 nsec to complete, and assume that the process is divided into 6 equal sections. Figure 8.7 gives a plot of the effective speedup versus the

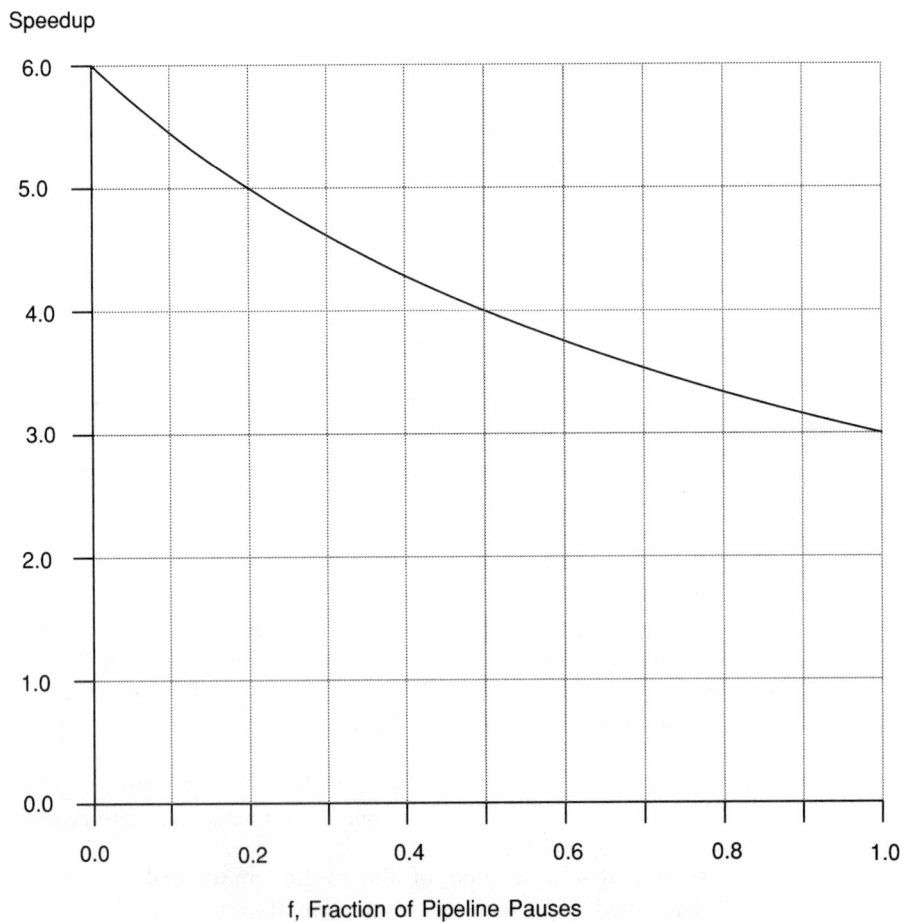

Figure 8.7. Effective Speedup as a Function of f, the Frequency of Pipeline Pauses.

Chap. 8: Pipelined Systems: Low Level Parallelism

frequency of the pauses of the pipe. If the frequency is 1, then the effective speedup is 3. That is, even if there are as many pause cycles as there are work cycles, then the effective speed is still 3 times faster than a nonpipelined implementation. Thus, the pipelining technique is effective for improving the speed of a process, even if the pipe cannot be kept full all of the time.

Pipelining is a technique that can be applied in any situation in which sequentially related events can proceed on independent operations in the same time frame. This will occur in the processing of data in arithmetic units and in the processing of instructions in control units. Let us examine these two mechanisms and identify some of the techniques that can be used.

8.2. Arithmetic Pipes: High Speed Calculations

In Chapter 3 we identified several mechanisms for doing high speed arithmetic. We will now examine some of these mechanisms with the intent of applying pipelining techniques to speed up the arithmetic process. Many metrics are considered during the process of dividing an arithmetic function into pipeline sections, and each designer will arrive at a compromise that meets the system design goals. As stated in the previous section, the objective of utilizing pipelining in arithmetic units is to achieve a speedup by performing operations concurrently for independent data sets. The questions to be asked by a designer in search of higher performance deal with timing issues and overall system issues:

- How can the initial process be subdivided to obtain the best results?
- What clock cycle time satisfies the various components of the process?
- What changes need to be made in the system to provide the overall data movement needed to sustain continuous operation by the pipeline?
- What metric is most meaningful to the overall system design goals?

The divisibility issue is one that can be dealt with in different ways to meet different design criteria. Let us look at floating point multiplication for an example of a data operation which can be pipelined. The basic organization for this system is shown in Figure 8.8. The data movement within the system must

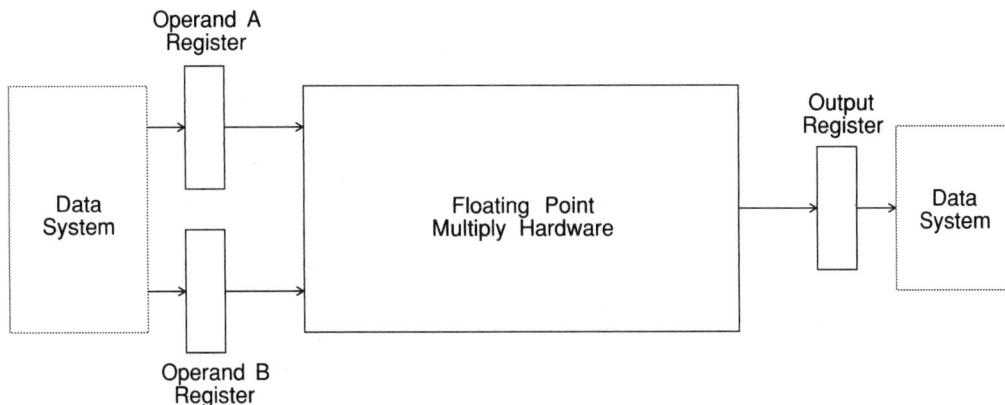

Figure 8.8. Diagram of Floating Point Multiplication Unit in System.

provide the operands for the unit in question, and in this case the multiply unit will perform the operation. The desired improvement is to speed up the operation as much as possible or feasible.

As can be seen from the diagram, one degree of pipelining is already available. That is, the floating point multiply unit can provide the action of multiplication, but the data system is responsible for supplying operands and handling the results. Thus, three operations can be overlapped in time, or pipelined: the fetching of the input operands to provide data to the multiplier, the multiplication function itself, and the storage of the result. Our concern here is with the actual floating point hardware, and the steps taken to pipeline the unit. We will examine the particular questions raised by this example, and also examine some of the other system questions.

As described in Chapter 3, the floating point multiplication can be accomplished in a number of ways. We will assume that the floating point number is in a 32-bit format, with a sign bit, an 8-bit exponent, and a 23-bit fractional mantissa, with hidden bit. Thus, to obtain

$$\text{Output} = A \times B$$

where the output and both inputs are in this format, then

$$\text{MANTISSA}_{\text{OUT}} \times 2^{\text{EXP}_{\text{OUT}}} = \text{MANTISSA}_A \times 2^{\text{EXP}_A} \times \text{MANTISSA}_B \times 2^{\text{EXP}_B}$$

$$= \text{MANTISSA}_A \times \text{MANTISSA}_B \times 2^{(\text{EXP}_A + \text{EXP}_B)}$$

The exponent is the sum of the two operand exponents, and the mantissa is the product of the mantissas of the two input operands. With a base two representation, the product can either be correct or require a 1-bit normalization step. Hardware can be configured in many ways to perform the operations identified above, some more efficient than others. For the purposes of illustration of principles, we will select a mechanism and attempt to pipeline it.

The formation of the floating point product can be broken into different sections depending on the desired results. The initial hardware organization is shown in Figure 8.9. The process is performed in three steps: partial product formulation, partial product addition, postnormalization, and exponent formulation. The initial exponent formulation can be done in parallel with partial product formulation and addition, and then adjusted appropriately when the necessary postnormalization is performed.

The partial products are formed by Am27S558s, which are 8×8-bit multipliers. Thus, for 24-bit mantissas, nine individual multipliers are needed. This forms three rows of partial products, but the significance of the partial products formed in this process overlap one another. These partial products are identified as P1 through P9, with the significance of the bits identified in Figure 8.9. These partial products are then summed in an adder tree made of 74AS881s, 74AS882s, and 74AS182s. The net result is a 48-bit number that may or may not have a "1" in the most significant bit position. Thus, a normalization step is required, and this is formed by a set of multiplexers, 74AS157s. The addition of the exponents is handled by 74AS881s. The element not shown is the sign bit, and the sign bit of the result will merely be the exclusive-OR of the sign bits of the two input operands.

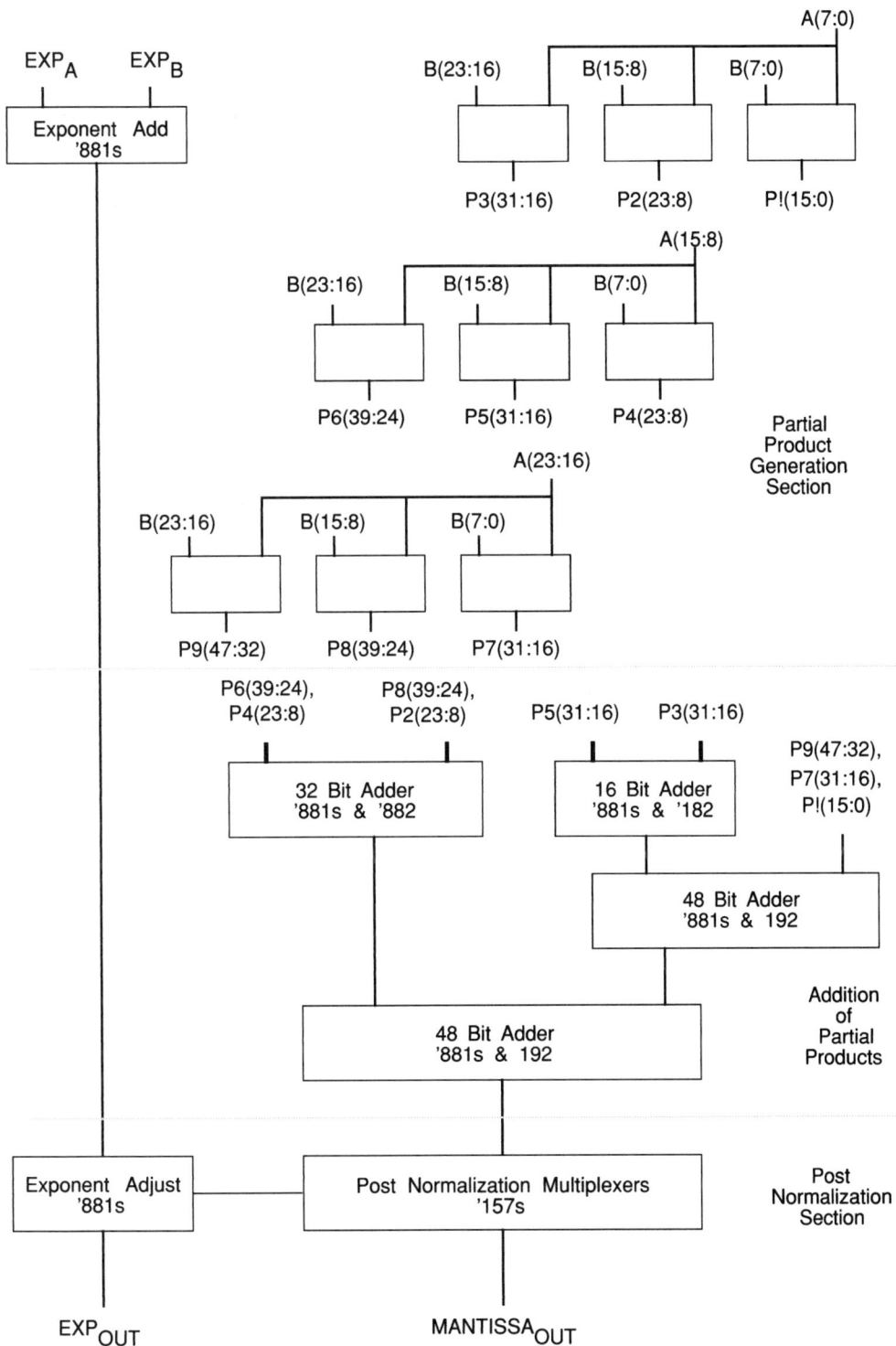

Figure 8.9. Block Diagram Level Representation of Hardware Floating Point Mechanism.

The time required for the hardware shown in Figure 8.9 is the sum of the time required for each of the three sections. The formation of the partial products requires 75 nsec. The addition of the partial products requires another 73 nsec. And the mantissa out will be available 11 nsec later. However, the adjustment of the exponent requires 18 nsec, so the mantissa is actually available about 9 nsec before the exponent. Thus, the whole process can be accomplished in 166 nsec. If this is to fit in a structure as shown in Figure 8.8, then an additional 14 nsec is required for the setup time, hold time, and the propagation delay time through a register, such as the 74AS574. Thus, the entire operation will require 180 nsec.

If we place registers in the process between the major sections, then the result could be represented as shown in Figure 8.10. With the initial process broken into three sections, we would like to see a speedup of three. But the clock cycle time of the system must be adjusted to accommodate the maximum time of the individual sections. Thus, for this example, $T_{\text{CLOCK CYCLE}} = T_P + T_{\text{REG}} = 75 + 14 = 89$ nsec. This results in a speedup of almost exactly two, which could be disappointing. However, in the process of doing this type of a design, locations that need attention if more speedup is required are identified. In this case, we are limited by the formation of the partial products. Slower speed parts can be used in the postnormalization section, and other changes can be made to the partial product addition section. But until a faster method of determining the partial products is obtained, the system will not run faster.

The multiplication example identifies several problems that need to be solved. The description above is for a very simple multiplier, and several things need to be done to the design to make it a real system. For example,

- How is overflow/underflow checked?

- How much hardware is required, and how does it affect the speed of the system?

- With respect to the allowable numbers, is unnormalized operation to be permitted? If so, how is the overall system to be changed?

- Is it necessary to compute the entire partial product array? Of the 48 bits which result from the multiplication, only 24 will actually be a part of the result. Therefore, may it be acceptable to create only the most significant portions of the partial product array under some conditions?

- When the appropriate bits are available, what kind of scheme is used for dealing with the extra bits? Truncation? Rounding? Round-to-zero? And is this to be done before or after post normalization?

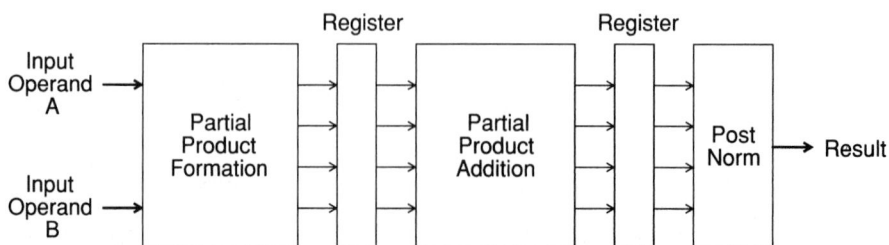

Figure 8.10. Block Diagram Level Representation of Hardware Floating Point Mechanism.

All of these questions must be addressed in a real implementation, and the answers will reflect the priorities of the designers.

Example 8.1: Costs of pipelining: Consider the floating point multiply example discussed above. With the use of pipelining, the speed of the system was doubled. What costs are associated with this speed increase?

Many different costs are associated with various designs, so we will identify only two: board space and power. The chip count is indicative of the amount of logic required by the system, and using board space is a more accurate measure of how "big" the system becomes. It is also indicative of how good the job of subdividing the system has been done. Another view of the system being used for this example is shown in Figure 8.11. The basic parts that could be used in a TTL implementation are identified with each major section. A summary of the parts needed is:

Part Name	Quantity	Unit Area (sq. in.)	Tot. Area (sq. in.)	Unit Power (W)	Total Power (W)
25S558	9	1.47	13.23	1.4	12.6
74AS881	36	.52	18.72	.675	24.3
74AS882	4	.52	2.08	.36	1.44
74AS182	1	.36	.36	.1	.1
74AS157	6	.36	2.16	.1	.6
			36.55		39.04

The total area needed by this system is 36.55 square inches, using DIP packages. A system that used leadless chip carriers would be smaller, but the

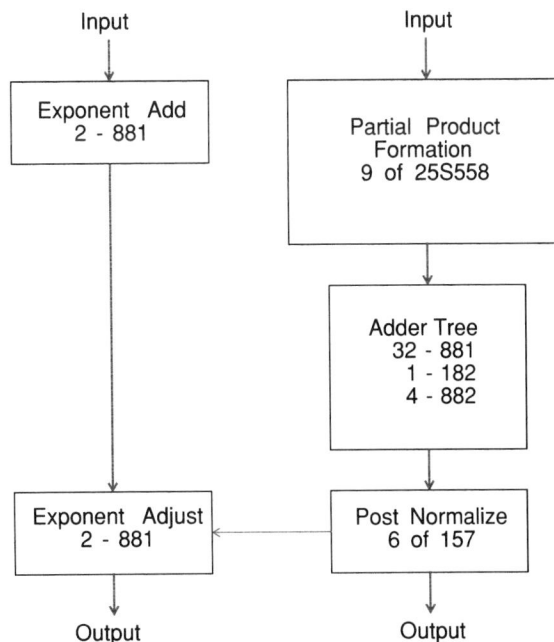

Figure 8.11. IC Requirements for the Hardware Floating Point Unit.

same method of comparison would apply. We will assume that the registers between stages will be comprised of 74AS574s, which are 20 pin chips. Counting all of the lines that need to be saved from partial product formation to the adder tree (and the corresponding exponent), there are 153 bits of information to save. And between the adder tree and postnormalization there are an additional 33 bits. Thus, 25 register chips are needed, which will require an additional 11 square inches of space.

The power required by the devices is similar to the board space. The overall power for the unpipelined version is 39.04 watts. The register chips will require an additional 0.395 watts each, for a total of 9.875 watts. Thus, the speedup by a factor of two has caused an increase of board space of 30%, and an increase of power of 25%. For a resource investment of 25–30% the rate of operation of the floating point multiplier has been doubled.

The above example underscores some of the promises and pitfalls of pipelining. The original process was divided into three separate functions, but the speedup was not three. Because of the real effect of adding registers, and the requirement that the clock cycle time be the maximum of the times for each of the individual functions, the resulting operational rate was twice the original rate. Thus, the actual maximum speedup is a function of all of the factors involved in the design of the system.

One of the basic tenets of pipelining is that to achieve the maximum available speedup ($T_P / \{T_S + T_R\}$) the pipeline must be kept full. To achieve this, the pieces of the "Data System" shown in Figure 8.8 must supply the appropriate operands in a timely fashion, and also handle the results as they become available. For the example system shown above, this means that every 180 nsec, two 4-byte operands must be made available to the floating point unit, and one 4-byte operand must be removed. This leads to a data rate of 12 bytes/180 nsec = 66.6 Mbytes/sec. If this data rate can be sustained, then the floating point unit is capable of achieving an operation rate of 5.55 MFLOPs. The rate of operation for the pipelined system is twice the rate of the unpipelined system, so to maintain the advantage of the speedup available with the pipelined implementation, the data system must be capable of handling information at a rate of 133.3 Mbytes/sec. This places a severe restriction on the types of information systems that can effectively be utilized by systems with data pipelines.

Example 8.2: Data rates for pipelined systems: The CRAY-2 computer system has a clock cycle time of 4.1 nsec. Assuming a single data pipeline system, what is the data rate necessary to keep a pipeline full?

A single pipeline will be full when two input operands and one result are handled in each data cycle. The CRAY-2 system, as well as other scientific systems, has a word width of 64 bits, or 8 bytes. Thus, for a full pipe, $3 \times 8 = 24$ bytes must be handled every 4.1 nsec. This is a data rate of 5854 Mbytes/sec. To achieve these data rates, multibank memories, wide data paths, and short transfer times are required.

As we have seen, the effectiveness of data pipelines is limited by several factors involved in real machines, such as the divisibility of the original process, the addition of registers to the system, and the problems associated with transferring information at the high data rates needed to keep a pipe full. In addition to the problem of physically supplying the information, there is a problem with the availability of the correct information. That is, even with a data system capable of extremely high data rates, there will be a problem when one operation cannot enter the pipe because of data conflicts. Data conflicts will occur when the results of one operation are needed by a following operation. Consider the following pair of operations:

$$A = B \times C$$
$$D = A \times E$$

The value of A is needed before the second operation can proceed. This same behavior is also observed in some array operations:

$$\text{for } (I = 1 ; I < 1000 ; I++)$$

$$X[I] = X[I - 1] + Y[I];$$

In this operation, the calculation for $X[9]$ cannot proceed until the value for $X[8]$ has been obtained, and so on. Both of these operations exemplify the fact that a data calculation cannot proceed because a value is not available. The calculation that follows cannot proceed until the data from the preceding operation has been made available. Thus, the pipeline must halt until the data is ready, at which point it can proceed. This reduces the effective speedup, and hence it is a situation to be avoided as much as possible.

One observation about the interaction between the pipeline and the data processing concerns the length of the pipe. The longer the pipe, the longer it will take to get information from a previous operation. That is, if a process is subdivided into three sections, then the largest number of clock cycles needed to obtain a previous result is two. However, if the same process is divided into six sections, then up to five clock cycles can be needed to obtain the results of a previous calculation. Thus, two different arguments can be made for the optimal number of stages in a pipeline: for a large speedup, divide the initial process into many sections; to minimize the penalty of data conflicts, keep the number of sections small. The designer must then trade off the benefits and costs of processing with a data pipeline.

Another observation concerning the effective use of data pipelines deals with the operands used in the calculations. So long as the operands are independent, there is no possibility of penalties due to data conflicts. Thus, streams of operations constructed in such a fashion as to minimize the data conflicts will result in the highest performance. The guaranteed independence of vector operands is the mechanism used by vector machines to achieve very high data rates. For example, consider the problem of adding two linear arrays of information together. The organization of the data into arrays corresponds to storing the information into vectors, where a vector is an organized set of data. The addition of the two arrays is then accomplished by streaming the information out of the storage locations to the arithmetic unit, and the results back again. Such an arrangement is shown in Figure 8.12. The two input operands actually consist of N pairs of numbers to be added. And the result consists of N numbers, each of which is the sum of the corresponding elements from the original vectors. Since all elements of the vector are available before the operation begins, the processing unit can process information without any conflicts.

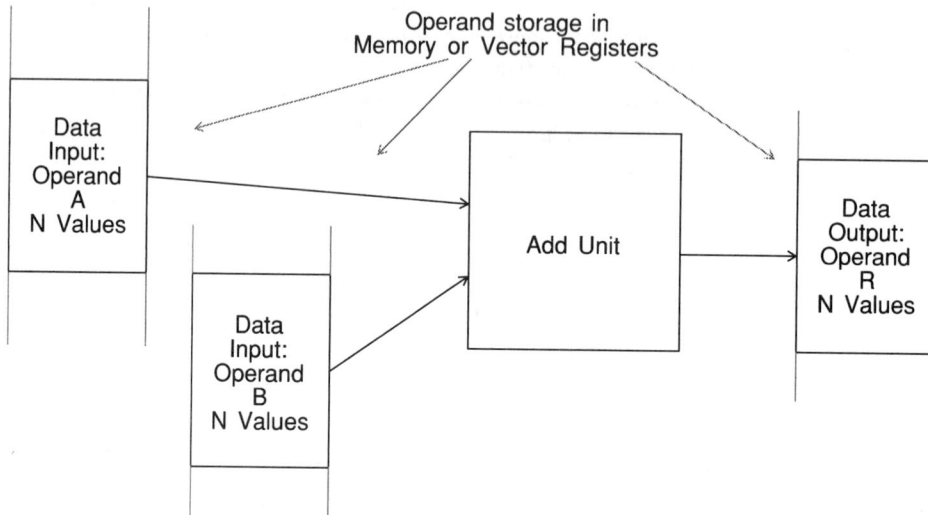

Figure 8.12. Processing Information with Vectors: Vector Addition.

The location of the vectors A, B, and R is dependent on the type of instruction level architecture used by the vector machine. One mechanism is to hold all of the vectors in memory, and stream the operands to the functional units directly from memory, and return the results to memory. This is a memory-to-memory architecture, and was the design mechanism used, for example, in the Cyber 205 vector machine. The instruction must then identify the locations of the vectors in memory and the length of the vectors (how many numbers in each).

A more common mechanism is to use vector registers, a concept similar to the use of general purpose register sets in a "standard" general purpose machine. The operands for vector instructions are then supplied directly from high speed registers, and the results also stored in the registers. The vector instructions for this type of a machine need not identify memory locations, which require long addresses, but rather vector registers, which can be specified with a few bits. However, before the vectors can be combined from the registers the vectors must be moved there from memory. This type of architecture balances the probability that the information in the vectors can be used more than once before memory interaction is needed with the additional instructions required to transfer the data to and from memory.

Regardless of the mechanisms used for storage of the vector operands, one of the reasons that vector machines achieve high operational rates is the guaranteed independence of the operands being sent to the arithmetic units. The operand independence ensures that the pipeline will be kept full, and that there will be no data conflicts. This situation leads to the highest computational rates achievable by a pipelined machine.

Example 8.3: Pipelines in a vector system: The CRAY-1 computer system was one of the first "popular" vector machines, and made extensive use of data pipelines to provide high computation rates. Other members of the CRAY family have added multiprocessing capabilities to the system, and extended some of the features available to the user. What are the data pipelines used in the CRAY-2 computer system? What is the peak floating point operation rate for the system?

The CRAY-2 computer is actually a multiprocessing system, with four processors available for use on programs. A block diagram of one computational section of a CRAY-2 is shown in Figure 8.13. As can be seen from the diagram, this system is not a memory-to-memory architecture. Information is transferred from the memory system to the vector registers (or scalar registers), and all arithmetic is done in the registers. Nine different data pipelines are available for use in the system, and they are:

Data Pipe	Pipe Sections
Address add	
Address multiply	
Scalar integer	
Scalar shift	
Scalar logical	
Vector integer	
Vector logical	
Floating point add	
Floating point multiply	

The complexity of the arithmetic to be done determines the number of sections required in the pipe for that arithmetic unit. The simpler operations listed in the table result in pipelines containing fewer sections than the more complex operations. The vector registers are each capable of storing 64 numbers, and so the vector instructions can operate on sets of data containing up to 64 values (vector length $\leq$ 64). Longer vectors must be divided into sections of 64 elements or less.

When vector operands are being supplied to a pipelined functional unit, a new result is generated at the rate of one value each 4.1 nsec. This is a computational rate of 243.9 Mflops. When circumstances permit, two functional units can be utilized simultaneously, which gives a computational rate of 487.8 Mflops.

As we have seen, the time required for a pipeline section is dependent on several factors. We have partitioned the function performed in a section into two parts: the arithmetic or logical portion, and the storage or register function. In general, a designer will attempt to minimize the time required for both of these portions, so that the system will have a small clock cycle time. This situation is shown in Figure 8.14. Since any combinational function can be formed in two gate delays, if enough gates with a high enough fan in are used, a tradeoff is performed between the number of levels of logic and the total amount of gating required to accomplish the function. This may result in implementations that utilize many gate delays to accomplish their work, but that are beneficial because of a small gate count (or silicon area). The output of the function is directed to the storage element to be sent to the next section of the pipeline.

The ingenuity of the designer in using the available logic has a direct impact on the performance of the system. For example, consider the circuit shown in Figure 8.15(a). The logic portion is a two level gating circuit that implements the sum function, given proper logic levels for the two inputs and the carry. The output from this gating system is directed to a gated latch. When the CLOCK-H line is asserted, the output will be set to agree with the level of the sum network. The total delay through this circuit, if the clock line is asserted, is six gate delays.

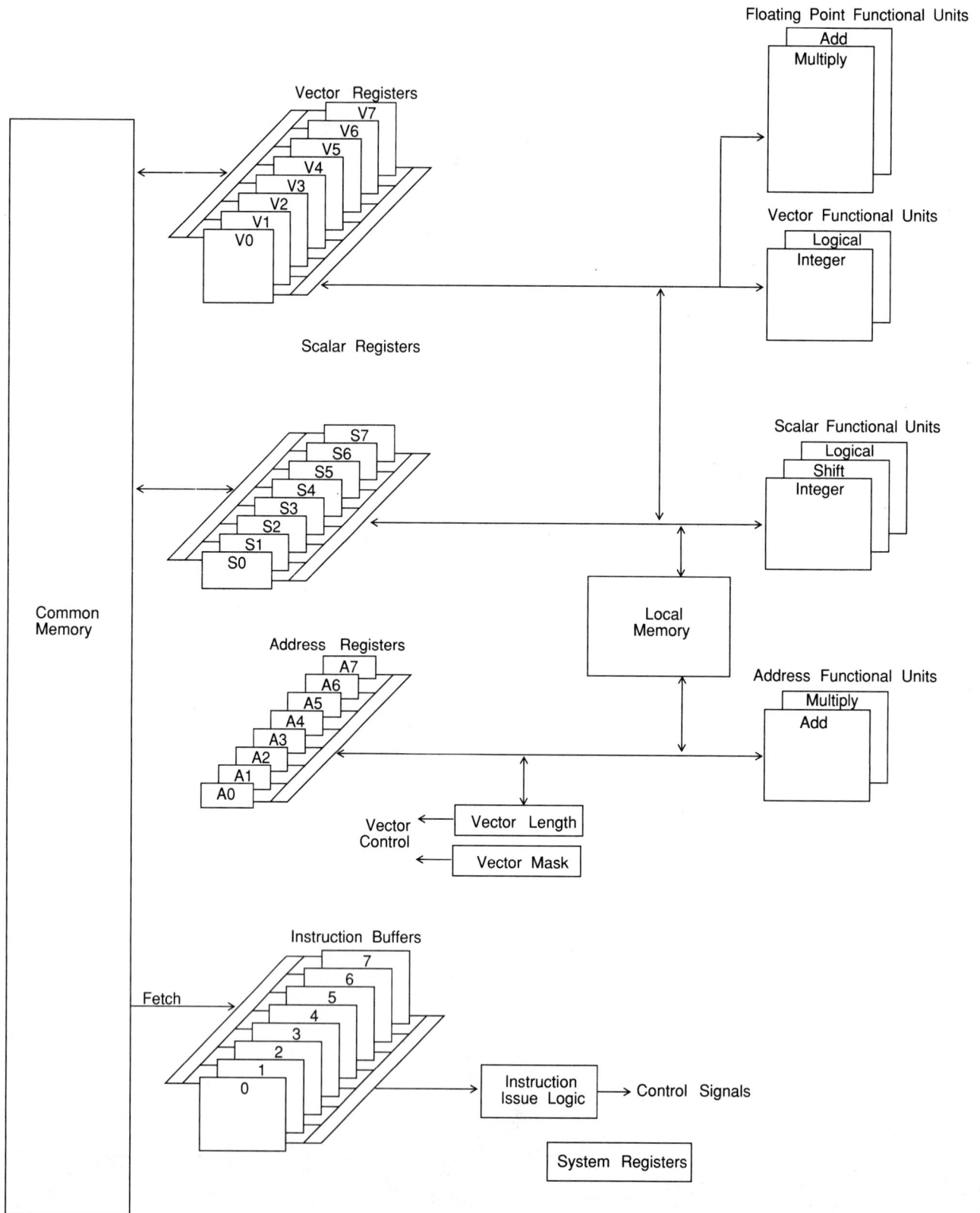

Figure 8.13. Block Diagram of the CRAY-2 Computer System.

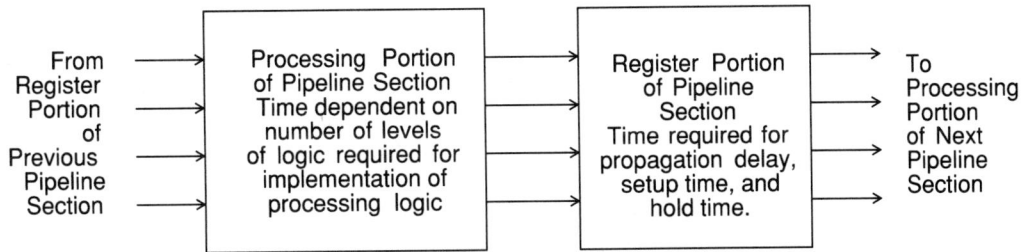

Figure 8.14. Elements of a Pipeline Section.

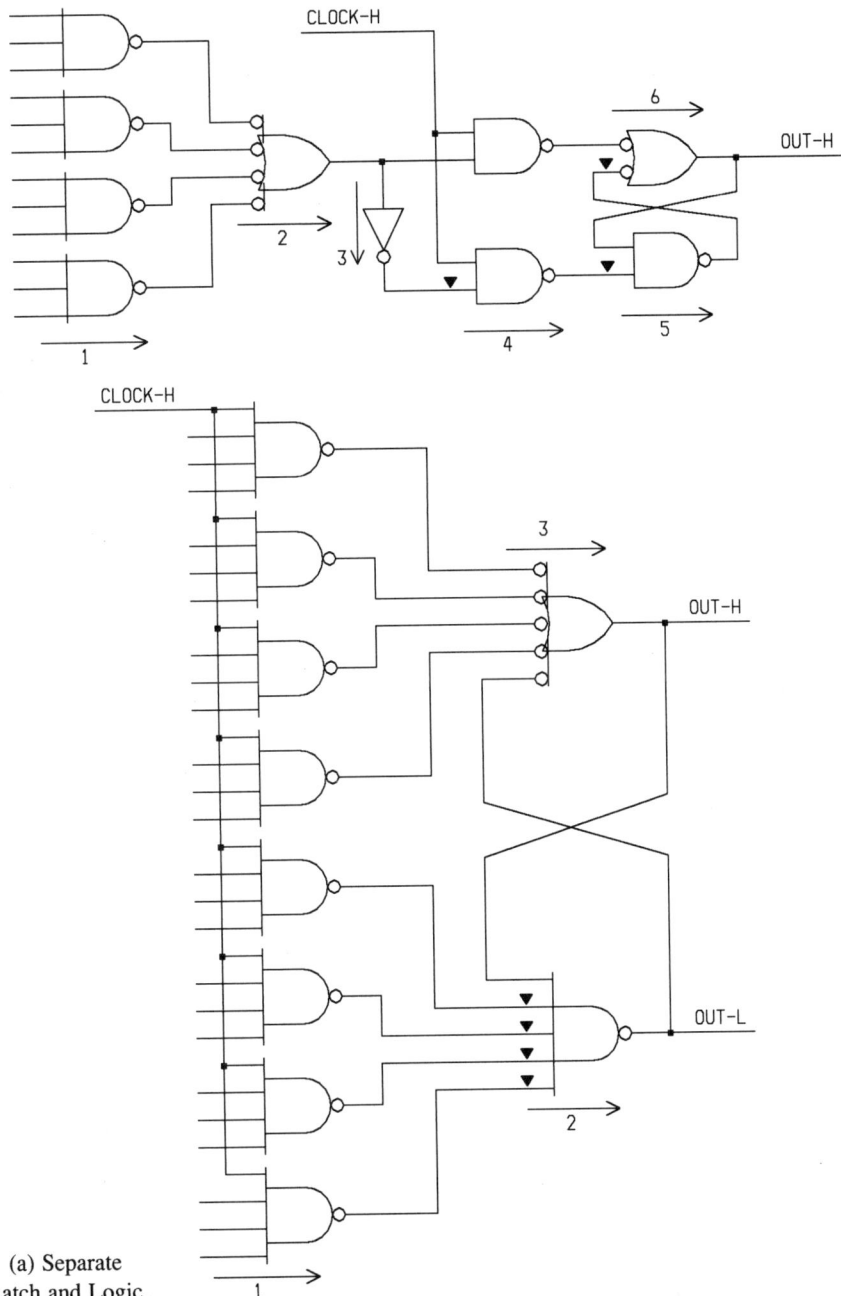

Figure 8.15. Pipeline Segments: (a) Separate
Latch and Logic; (b) Combined Latch and Logic.

However, since this is a gated latch rather than an edge-triggered register, care must be taken to be sure that the value does not propagate too far while the clock is asserted.

The amount of time required for the sum and register functions of Figure 8.15(a) can be reduced by combining the sum logic with the latching logic. The function of Figure 8.15(a) is accomplished by the logic of Figure 8.15(b), with some obvious changes. The ORing function of the logic has been combined with the ORing function of the latching gates, and the ANDing function of the gated latch has been combined with the ANDing gates of the required logic function. The net result is a system that requires only three gate delays to complete, from clock and data stable to outputs stable. Note that both asserted high and asserted low outputs are available in the Figure 8.15(b). This will be useful for functions that follow this stage in the pipe.

Obviously, it would not be reasonable to combine all of the logic of a stage of a pipeline with the latching function, but the mechanism shown above of combining one level of the logic with the latch will reduce the timing impact of adding the latching function to the logic required by the function.

One of the disadvantages of the latches implemented in Figure 8.15 is that the time to output stable from the clock is not always equal. That is, the required time for the data to become stable is a function not only of logic input and the clock, but it is also a function of the level stored in the latch before the assertion of the clock. Consider the four possible combinations of the input data [LAT_IN-H in Figure 8.15(a)] and latch output:

LAT_IN-H	OUT-H	Delay from CLOCK-H
0	0	No change = zero delay
0	1	2 gate delays
1	0	3 gate delays
1	1	No change = zero delay

This difference in time required for the function results in an unwanted skew in the time for a section of logic. With latches designed as shown in Figure 8.15, the problem will always exist.

A number of different solutions to the problem have been suggested, one of which is the Earle Latch, which was used extensively in the IBM 360 pipelined machines. This latch is shown in Figure 8.16(a). One obvious difference is that the latch does not need (nor does it provide) both asserted high and asserted low inputs to function properly. If we repeat the above table to identify the speeds of the Earle Latch, we have:

LAT_IN-H	OUT-H	Delay from CLOCK-H
0	0	No change = zero delay
0	1	2 gate delays
1	0	2 gate delays
1	1	No change = zero delay

Thus the maximum time to data stable is always two gate delays, assuming that the propagation time through a gate is always the same. The only major difficulty with the system shown in Figure 8.16 is that both asserted high and asserted low clocks are required. This requirement is not restrictive since the clock signals will be needed by all of the stages.

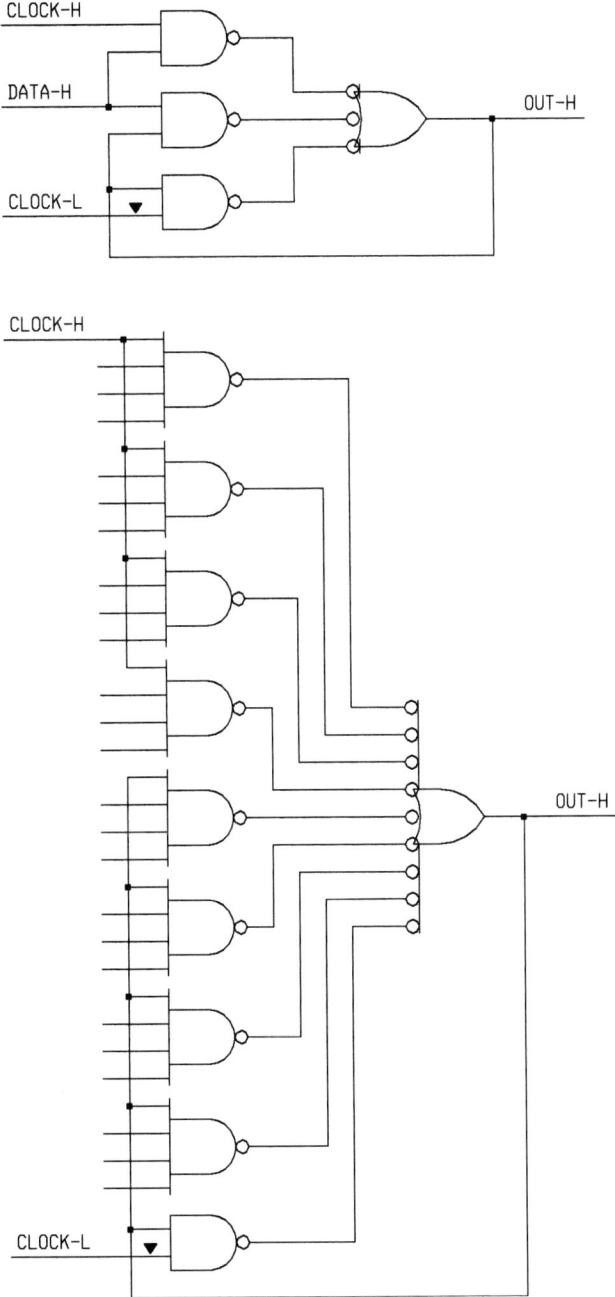

Figure 8.16. Earl Latch Designs: (a) Basic Latch;
(b) Combined Latch and Logic.

The technique applied above of combining the logic of the function with the logic of the latch can also be utilized with the Earle Latch. The sum function of Figure 8.15 is combined with the Earl Latch as shown in Figure 8.16(b). Again, the designer must identify which combination of function and latch logic, with their associated costs (number of gates, or semiconductor area, or ...), matches the design goals of the system.

The use of pipelining techniques to speed up the processing of data manipulations results in enhanced throughput for data operations. The operations that must be performed are identified, and these are partitioned into appropriate sections. Storage elements are inserted between the sections to synchronize the actions of the system and to hold the data needed by the sections that follow. The performance achievable by the use of pipelining is a function of many factors, as we have seen. The divisibility of the original process, the register delays, and the amount of available logic all influence the basic data rate at which the pipe can operate. External influences that affect the operation of the pipe include the independence of the operands needed by the function, and the ability of the system to handle data at a sufficiently high rate to keep the pipeline full. A system that satisfies the internal and external requirements for correctness and data movement can achieve substantial speed improvements over nonpipelined implementations.

Example 8.4: Pipelining in data systems: The concept of pipelining for data operations can be used in many applications where an increase of speed is needed, even if the operations do not lend themselves to division. Consider a hardware system constructed to calculate the fast fourier transform (FFT), as shown in Figure 8.17(a). Can pipelining be used to increase the speed of operation of the system?

In the system depicted in Figure 8.17(a), the data is stored in a memory and extracted as needed to perform the calculations. The arithmetic is performed in a set of special purpose hardware. One method for calculating the butterfly is shown in the data diagram: two values (D_U and D_L) form the inputs, and the outputs (D_U' and D_L') are returned to the memory. The values are complex in nature, and as such consist of two parts, the real and the imaginary. The arithmetic involved consists of a complex multiply, a complex add, and a complex subtract. The weighting factor (W) is derived from a set of constants, and supplied by a memory not shown in the diagram. The complex arithmetic required by each set of butterfly calculations can be accomplished by four multiplications and six additions. With memory transactions, additions, and multiplications all requiring about the same amount of time, the system is fairly well matched at this point. That is, each butterfly will require a minimum of eight cycles, since that much time is required to extract a real and imaginary value for each of D_U and D_L, and place the calculated values back into memory. For six of the eight cycles the adder will be busy, and for four of the eight cycles the multiplier will be busy.

Pipelining can be applied to this system by recognizing that the FFT requires a number of passes through the data set. The number of passes is $\log_2 N$, where N is the total number of data points, and also a factor of 2. The results of one pass form the information needed by the next pass. Thus, the basis for a pipeline exists, since the data is to be passed from one

FFT System

(a)

(b)

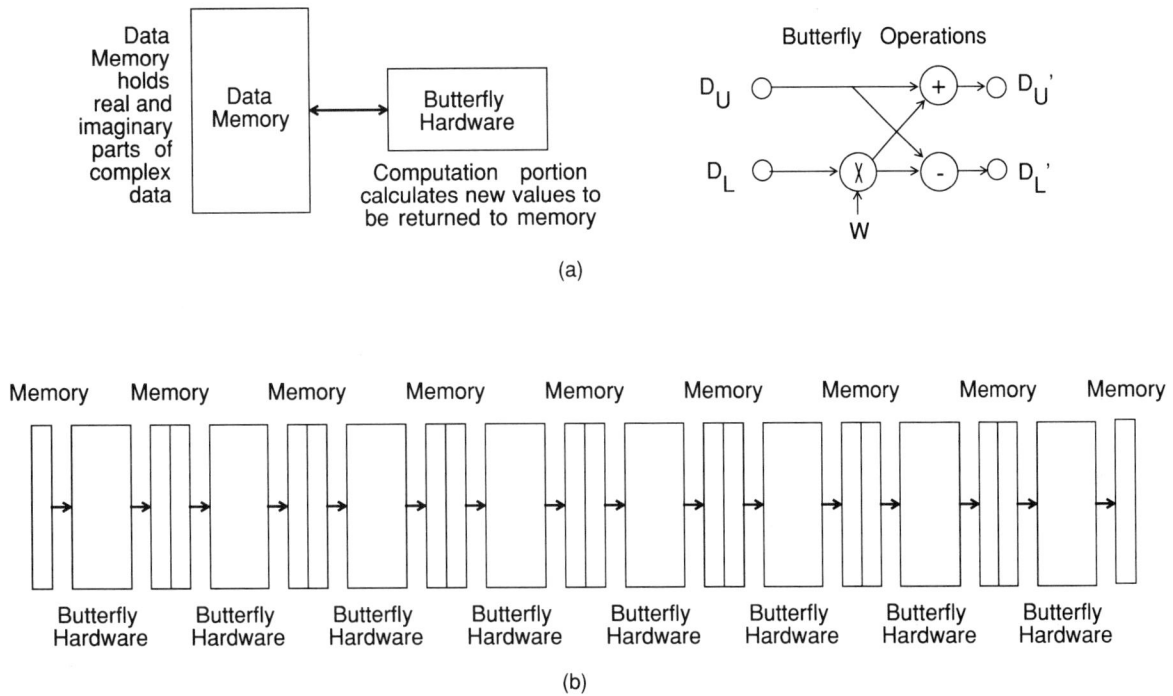

Figure 8.17. Fast Fourier Transform Systems: (a) Nonpipelined Implementation; (b) Pipelined Implementation.

module to another, where each module is responsible for one pass of the butterfly through the data. This arrangement is depicted in Figure 8.17(b) for a system which computes a 256 point transform. Eight stages are needed, and the memory output from one stage feeds the memory input of the next stage. The memories are depicted as duals, since the information will be input by one stage and extracted from the next. Thus, the memories must either "ping-pong" between two sections, or be interleaved in such a way that the desired information is available as needed.

Pipelining as shown in the figure will produce results eight times faster than a nonpipelined implementation, but requires eight times as much hardware. Nevertheless, if the speed is needed to maintain real time operation, then the hardware resources may be justified.

8.3. Control Pipelines: Overlap of Independent Control Operations

In the preceding section we looked at improving the speed of data operations by executing different, independent portions of the calculations at the same time in specifically designed portions of hardware. The principal requirement for correct functionality is that the operations be independent: one stage of the pipe cannot produce correct results until all of the input information is correct. Pipelining is also applicable to other types of processing, so long as the independence requirement is satisfied, and the necessary processing can be appropriately partitioned.

In this section we will examine some of the mechanisms for pipelining control functions, and identify some of the limitations of the achievable performance.

As discussed in Chapter 4, a stored program computer basically operates on a fetch-decode-execute mechanism. An instruction is fetched from memory, decoded, and then the work specified by that instruction is executed. These processes are sequential in nature, and basically independent, so they satisfy the fundamental requirements for pipelining. The responsibility of the designer and system architect is to organize the data paths and registers in such a way that the various functions can be executed concurrently. If this can be accomplished, then the same type of speedup enjoyed by the data pipes of the preceding section can be realized.

One of the simplest pipelines of this nature is demonstrated by the fetch-execute mechanism of microcoded engines, one example of which is shown in Figure 5.31. This is shown in block diagram form in Figure 8.18. The address sequencer has the responsibility of identifying the next microinstruction to execute, and obtaining that instruction from microcode memory. This instruction is loaded into the microinstruction register. During the next clock cycle, the execute section will decode the control bits contained in the microinstruction register and perform the requested work. These two functions form a two stage pipeline, since the fetch section is always obtaining the instruction one clock period before the execute section performs the work. For this reason, the microinstruction register is sometimes referred to as the "pipeline register."

Each of the basic processes of instruction execution can be divided further than the microcode engine example, and many machines utilize this technique internal to the control unit. We will partition the activities of a control unit into the six units shown in Figure 8.19. These units have the following responsibilities:

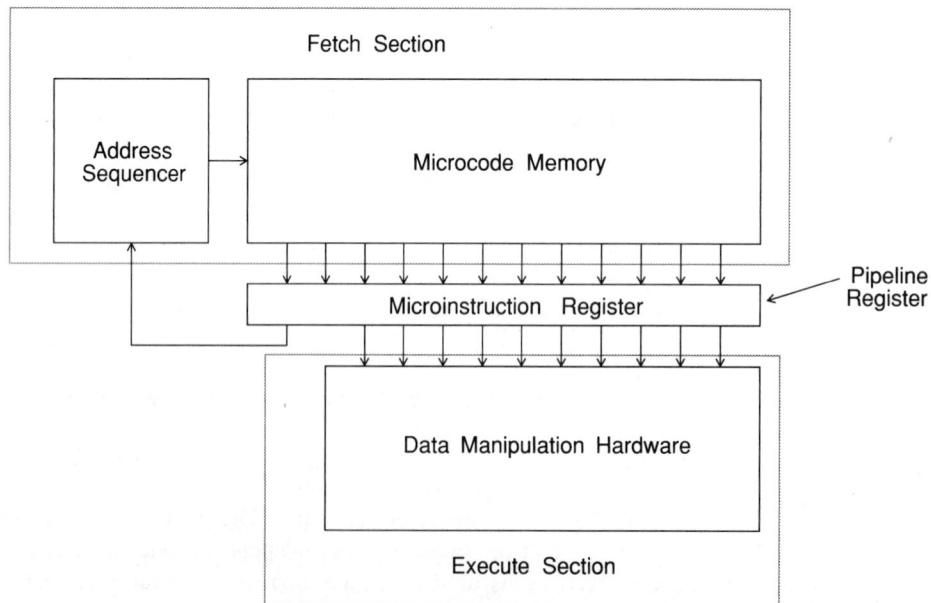

Figure 8.18. Fetch-Execute Mechanism of a Pipelined Engine.

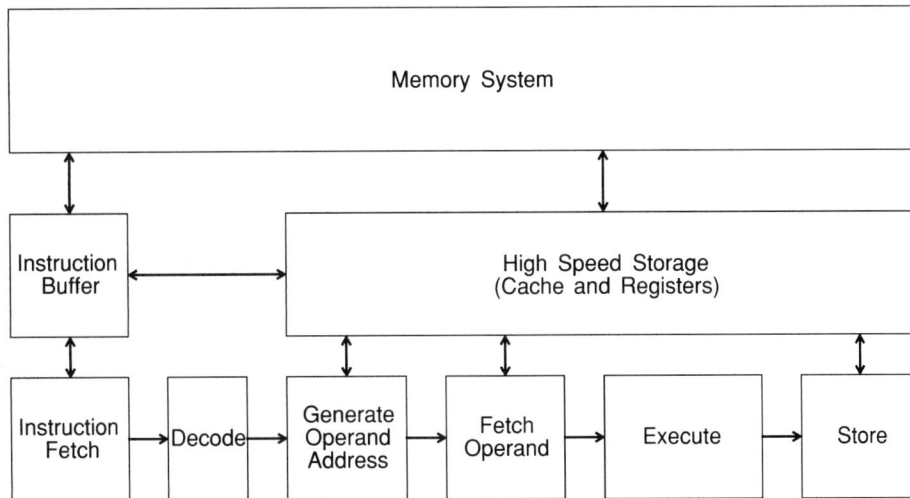

Figure 8.19. Block Diagram of Control Pipeline for Basic Machine.

- *Memory System:* The memory system contains all of the memory utilized by the computer system. This includes the mass storage devices as well as the main store. This portion of the system is responsible for providing the needed instructions and data as rapidly as possible.

- *High Speed Storage:* The high speed storage section contains both the cache memory and the registers utilized by the system. The active data is stored in such a way that it is available as needed by the program. In the discussions that follow, the high speed storage section will be considered perfect. This is not a reasonable assumption in real systems, but will facilitate understanding of the issues related to the pipeline, and remove from consideration the problems resulting from the interaction of the pipeline with an imperfect memory system.

- *Instruction Buffer:* The instruction buffer is a small storage area that contains the instructions currently executing. This storage area is managed by the instruction fetch hardware, and contains the active portion of the currently executing program. Real sizes of instruction buffers vary with manufacturer and purpose from a few bytes to a few kilobytes. The information contained in the instruction buffer may come from directly from the memory system, or it may be provided by the cache memory. As with the high speed storage, we will assume that the instruction buffer is perfect, so that any information needed by the instruction fetch unit is immediately available.

- *Instruction Fetch:* Instructions needed by the program are obtained by the instruction fetch section. This unit identifies the next instruction to execute and presents it to the decode section.

- *Decode:* The decode section obtains an instruction from the instruction fetch unit and identifies the work to be done. It then prepares the information that will be used by succeeding sections to identify operands and actions, and these bits will be forwarded to the sections as required by the instruction flow.

- *Generate Operand Address:* This unit is responsible for identifying addresses of operands. For example, in the two address move instruction:

MOV *R1, R0

data is moved from memory to R0. The generate operand address section would identify the fact that R1 contains an address, and provide that address to the high speed storage section. More complicated addressing mechanisms are possible, and this section of the pipe must be able to provide the requested address. Any address generated by this section of the pipe will be utilized by the next pipe section to obtain the required data.

- *Fetch Operand:* The fetch operand unit identifies the location of the data needed by the instruction, and fetches that information from the high speed storage unit. The data is available to be utilized by the functional units in the data path during the cycle controlled by the execute section.

- *Execute:* The execute unit has the responsibility of doing the work called for by the instruction. The previous sections of the pipe will have prepared the data, and so both data and instruction information will be available. The result of the instruction will be provided to the store unit to be saved as needed.

- *Store:* The store unit takes the information resulting from the execution of the instruction and saves it as necessary in the high speed storage unit. Thus, any necessary modifications to registers or memory locations are performed by the store unit.

With the original process divided into six sections, it would appear that we should be able to get a speed up of six over a nonpipelined implementation. As we have seen with the data pipes, this will not be the case for various reasons: the process will not be equally divisible into six sections; the delays caused by registers adds a real increment of time to the process; and increased speed of data transfers may not be physically possible. However, if we assume that solutions to these problems have been provided, then we can envision the execution of the instructions as shown in Figure 8.20. This is essentially the same as Figure 8.5, but we have added a few more instructions. The reason for this will become evident in the following paragraphs. As with the data pipe, there is an inherent delay caused by the various stages of the pipe, and instructions will require a time (T_I) to complete. If instructions can be inserted into the pipe on each clock, then the effective instruction time will equal the clock cycle time.

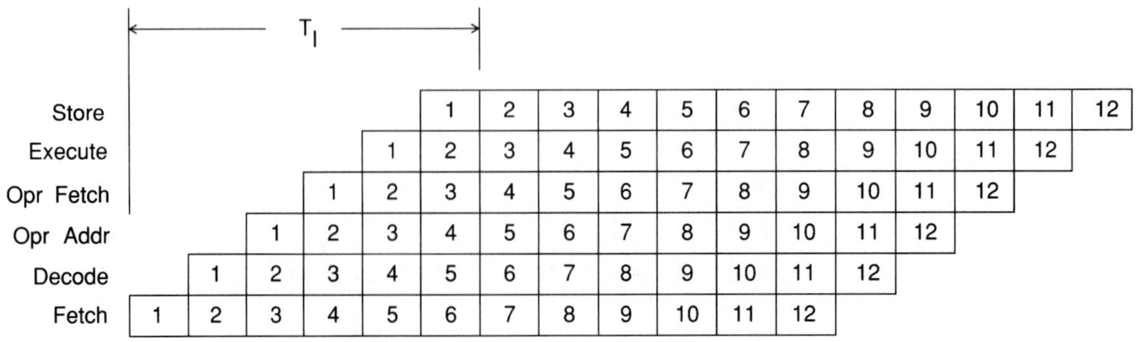

Figure 8.20. Space Time Representation of Instructions in Control Pipe.

Chap. 8: Pipelined Systems: Low Level Parallelism

Aside from the physical problems that we have assumed can be handled in a reasonable way by a complex hardware system, the conflict problem limits the achievable performance. With a data pipe, we used the term "conflict" to describe the case when one operation could not proceed because it needed information from an operation that had not yet completed. Instructions in a pipe interact with one another in much the same way, which prevents the pipe from remaining full at all times. We will describe three different types of conflicts:

- A data conflict
- An address conflict
- A branch conflict

1. As in a data pipe, a *data conflict* results when one instruction cannot proceed because an operand is needed that is the result of a previous instruction, and that instruction has not yet completed. For example, consider the following set of instructions:

1	ADD	R0, R3
2	MOV	R0, R7
3	ADD	R0, R5
4	ADD	R5, R4
5	SUB	R8, R9
6	MOV	R1, R2
7	ADD	R1, R3
8	ADD	R2, R6

The flow of these instructions through the pipeline is shown in Figure 8.21. The first three instructions have no difficulty executing, assuming that all of the information initially needed is available. However, there is a conflict between instruction 3 and instruction 4: the work specified by instruction 4 is to add the contents of R5 to the contents of R4; however, before this can occur, instruction 3 must first modify the contents of R5. Thus, the operand fetch section of the pipe will be unable to fetch the desired value until the store section of the pipe has placed the result of instruction 3 into the register. This results in the two penalty cycles shown in Figure 8.21. The instructions waiting in the pipeline pause until the request can be satisfied, and then proceed. Similarly, instruction 8 collides with instruction 6. When instruction 6 has modified R2, then instruction 8 can obtain the value and proceed. However, as shown in the figure, since there is an independent instruction between 6 and 8, the effective penalty incurred is only one cycle instead of two.

Store					1	2	3			4	5	6	7		8	
Execute				1	2	3			4	5	6	7		8		
Opr Fetch			1	2	3	P1	P2	4	5	6	7	P1	8			
Opr Addr		1	2	3	4	5	5	5	6	7	8					
Decode	1	2	3	4	5	6	6	6	7	8						
Fetch	1	2	3	4	5	6	7	7	7	8						

Figure 8.21. Penalties Associated with Data Conflicts.

The analysis of the effective execution rate is performed in the same manner as the analysis of the pauses which were discussed in the previous section. In fact, the resulting formula will have the same form:

$$\text{Effective speedup} = \frac{\text{Best speedup}}{1 + \sum p_i \times P_i}$$

Here p_i is the probability that there will be a conflict, and P_i is the penalty associated with that conflict. Figure 8.21 identifies a conflict with a penalty of two clock cycles, and a conflict with a penalty of one clock cycle. A plot of the above equation is shown in Figure 8.22. Curves are included for the case where all conflicts incur two penalty cycles and the case in which all conflicts require a single cycle. In practice, the actual penalty incurred because of conflicts in a system of this type would result from a combination of conflicts that incur both penalties, and hence a line representing the effective conflict penalty would be found between the two lines in the figure. Obviously, it is beneficial to reduce the required number of penalty cycles, and we will identify some mechanisms for doing that later in this section.

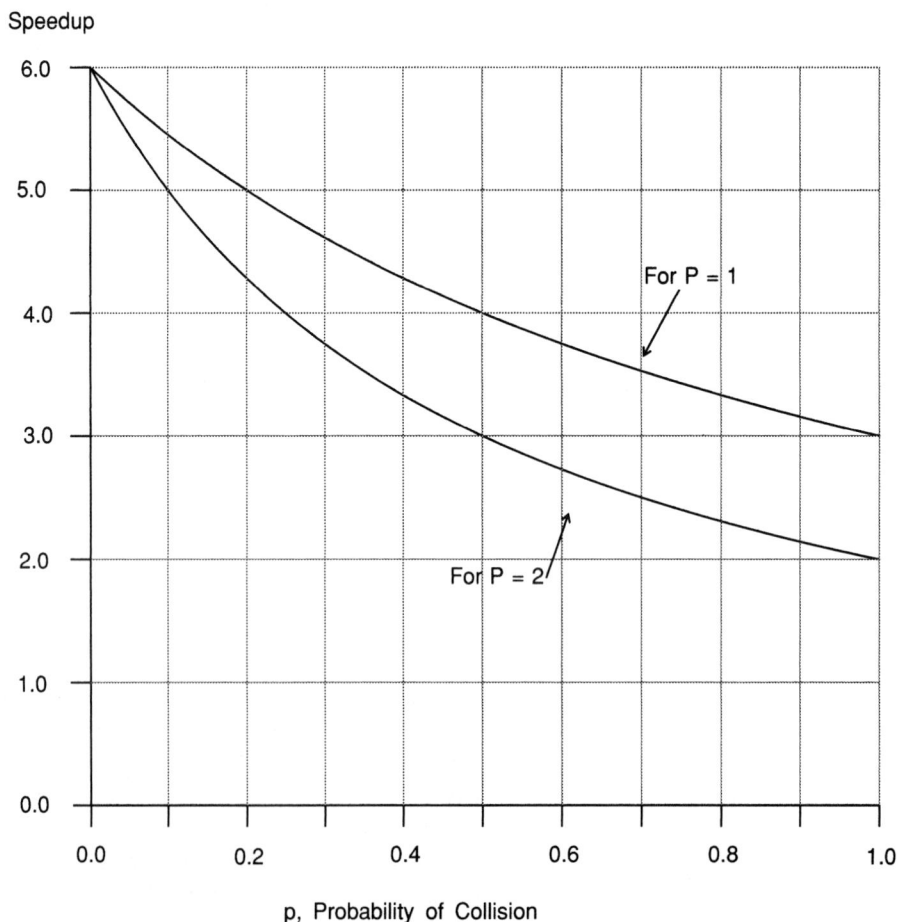

Figure 8.22. Effect of Conflicts on Speedup.

The pipeline must be designed in such a way that the resources needed by each instruction are properly coordinated. Two instructions that use the same resource, such as a register, can either read or write to the resource. This gives rise to four possible orderings:

First Instruction	Second Instruction	Conflict Handling
READ	READ	No conflict; instructions need not coordinate access to resource.
READ	WRITE	First instruction must obtain correct value before second instruction is allowed to modify it.
WRITE	READ	Second instruction must wait until first instruction has appropriately modified resource before obtaining the value.
WRITE	WRITE	Sequence conflict only. The control must assure that the value of the resource is that set by the second instruction.

The control system must examine the resources being utilized and the ordering of the instructions, and assure that the results are compatible with an implementation that does not make use of pipelining. Therefore, the control unit of the pipeline must coordinate the use of the resources identified by the instruction set; independent resources need no special care, while resources utilized by more than one instruction need to be closely monitored. Thus, the control unit becomes more complex as the amount of overlap increases, which results in a pipeline which contains more stages.

2. Like a data conflict, an *address conflict* results because of the unavailability of information. However, rather than a penalty that is the result of unavailability of data, the address conflict occurs because the system cannot generate the address of the data. In the organization of the system as shown in Figure 8.19, the generate operand address block has the responsibility of identifying the location of the data. If the location of the information is specified by values that have not yet been updated, then the system must wait until that information is available. For example, consider the following set of instructions:

```
1   MOV   R1, R9
2   MOV   constant, R8
3   INC   R0
4   MOV   (R7 i R0), R6
5   ADD   R4, R3
6   ADD   (R6), R2
```

The resource utilization diagram corresponding to these instructions is shown in Figure 8.23. Instruction 4 moves a value to R6; the location of that value is identified by indexing R7 by R0. However, instruction 3 increments R0. Therefore, the value contained in R0 cannot be used in the calculation of the address until it has been modified by instruction 3. This causes a penalty that is one greater than the data conflict penalty. The conflict between instruction 3 and instruction 4 causes a penalty of three clock times, while the conflict between instruction 4 and instruction 6 incurs a penalty of two clock times. The analysis of the effect on the overall speedup proceeds exactly as the above analysis of data conflict effects, except that the penalties are larger.

3. *Branch conflicts* occur for the same reasons as other conflicts: the information needed is not available. However, the penalty for branch conflicts is

Figure 8.23 table:

	1	2	3	4	5	6	7	8	9	10	11	12	13	14	15	16
Store						1	2	3				4	5			6
Execute					1	2	3				4	5			6	
Opr Fetch				1	2	3				4	5			6		
Opr Addr			1	2	3	P1	P3	P3	4	5	P1	P2	6			
Decode		1	2	3	4	5	5	5	5	6						
Fetch	1	2	3	4	5	6	6	6	6							

Figure 8.23. Penalties Associated with Address Conflicts.

greater than the other types, since the fetch and decode portions of the pipe occur first. When a conditional branch occurs, the instruction to be executed next is not known until the target of the branch is properly identified. That is, since the condition on which the branch will be made is not available, it is not certain whether or not the branch will be taken. For example, consider the following instructions:

1	label	ADD	R3, R4
2		SUB	R3, R9
3		MOV	R4, (R7 i R1)
4		CMP	R1, R3
5		JNE	label
6		ADD	R0, R1

Instruction 5 determines whether the program flow returns to instruction 1 or moves on to instruction 6. However, the condition on which that decision is based is not available until the comparison of R1 and R3 (instruction 4) is accomplished, and the result of that comparison has been placed in the status register. The resource utilization for this instruction is shown in Figure 8.24 for one implementation and branch path. Other implementations will incur different costs, and different branch paths will result in different resource utilizations. As shown in the figure, the system does not know which instruction follows instruction 5 until instruction 4 completes. This results in a penalty of four clock times.

As we have seen, conflicts in a control pipeline result when information is not available because the action specified by prior instructions has not been completed. Data conflicts occur because an instruction needs data that will not be available until a previous instruction completes. Address conflicts occur when an instruction cannot calculate the address of a data reference because the information needed to identify an address will not be available until a previous instruction

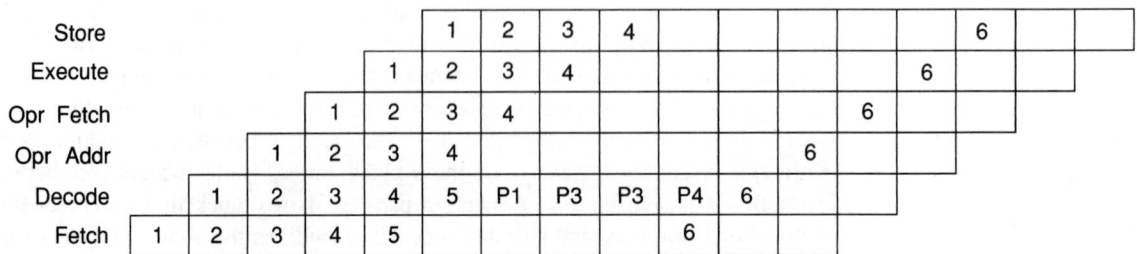

Figure 8.24 table:

	1	2	3	4	5	6	7	8	9	10	11	12	13	14	15
Store						1	2	3	4						6
Execute					1	2	3	4						6	
Opr Fetch				1	2	3	4						6		
Opr Addr			1	2	3	4						6			
Decode		1	2	3	4	5	P1	P3	P3	P4	6				
Fetch	1	2	3	4	5				6						

Figure 8.24. Branch Conflict Penalty for One System Implementation.

completes. And branch conflicts occur when the next instruction to execute will not be known until the results of a previous instruction are available.

A number of techniques have been utilized to minimize the overall effect of conflicts, and we will examine four of the methods. Each of the methods uses a different mechanism to reduce the resource utilization, but the goal is the same: minimize penalty cycles due to conflicts.

The first technique has little to do with hardware and much to do with the way that the program is configured for the machine. We have seen that the effect of the conflicts is minimized when the instructions are independent. Thus, one method to reduce the overall effect of conflicts is to arrange the instructions in an order that will result in the same answers, but that will execute faster. For an example of this technique, consider the simple statements:

$$VX = VCC + (RES1 + RES2) \times I1$$
$$VY = VCC + (RES3 + RES4) \times I2$$

If we assume that these instructions are to be executed by a machine of the type that we have been discussing, then a very simple translation of the above statements into an assembly language might produce code similar to:

1	MOV #<VCC>, R0	Get VCC to R0.
2	MOV #<RES1>, R1	Get RES1 to R1.
3	MOV #<RES2>, R2	Get RES2 to R2.
4	ADD R1, R2	Add RES1 and RES2.
5	MULT #<I1>, R2	Multiply by I1.
6	ADD R0, R2	Add in VCC.
7	MOV R2, @<VX>	Store result in VX.
8	MOV #<RES3>, R3	Get RES3 to R3.
9	MOV #<RES4>, R4	Get RES4 to R4.
10	ADD R3, R4	Add RES3 and RES4.
11	MULT #<I2>, R4	Multiply by I2.
12	ADD R0, R4	Add in VCC.
13	MOV R4, @<VY>	Store result in VY.

This is a very simple set of code, yet it contains a number of data conflicts. If the code is executed as it appears above, then the resource utilization would appear as shown in Figure 8.25(a). The instructions that cause conflicts are instructions 4, 5, 6, 7, 10, 11, 12, and 13. Since all of the conflicts are data conflicts, they each incur a penalty of two clock times. The resulting time to complete the code segment, not including the fill time, is 29 cycles.

If some information is available about the organization of the pipeline, then appropriate choices can be made concerning the methods used by the assembly language implementations of the high level language statements like those shown above. By optimizing the order to help the conflict problem, then the time required to execute the code segment will decrease. In Figure 8.25(b), the same set of instructions is executed, but not in the order specified above. Rather, the order is specified in such a way as to guarantee that the operands are ready when needed by instructions which follow. In this way, the time required to wait for operands is minimized. The results of the calculation will be the same as those shown in Figure 8.25(a), but the number of cycles required has been reduced to 16 cycles. Notice that independent instructions could be inserted into three spaces in the figure. If this were to be accomplished, then the pipeline would be functioning at maximum efficiency.

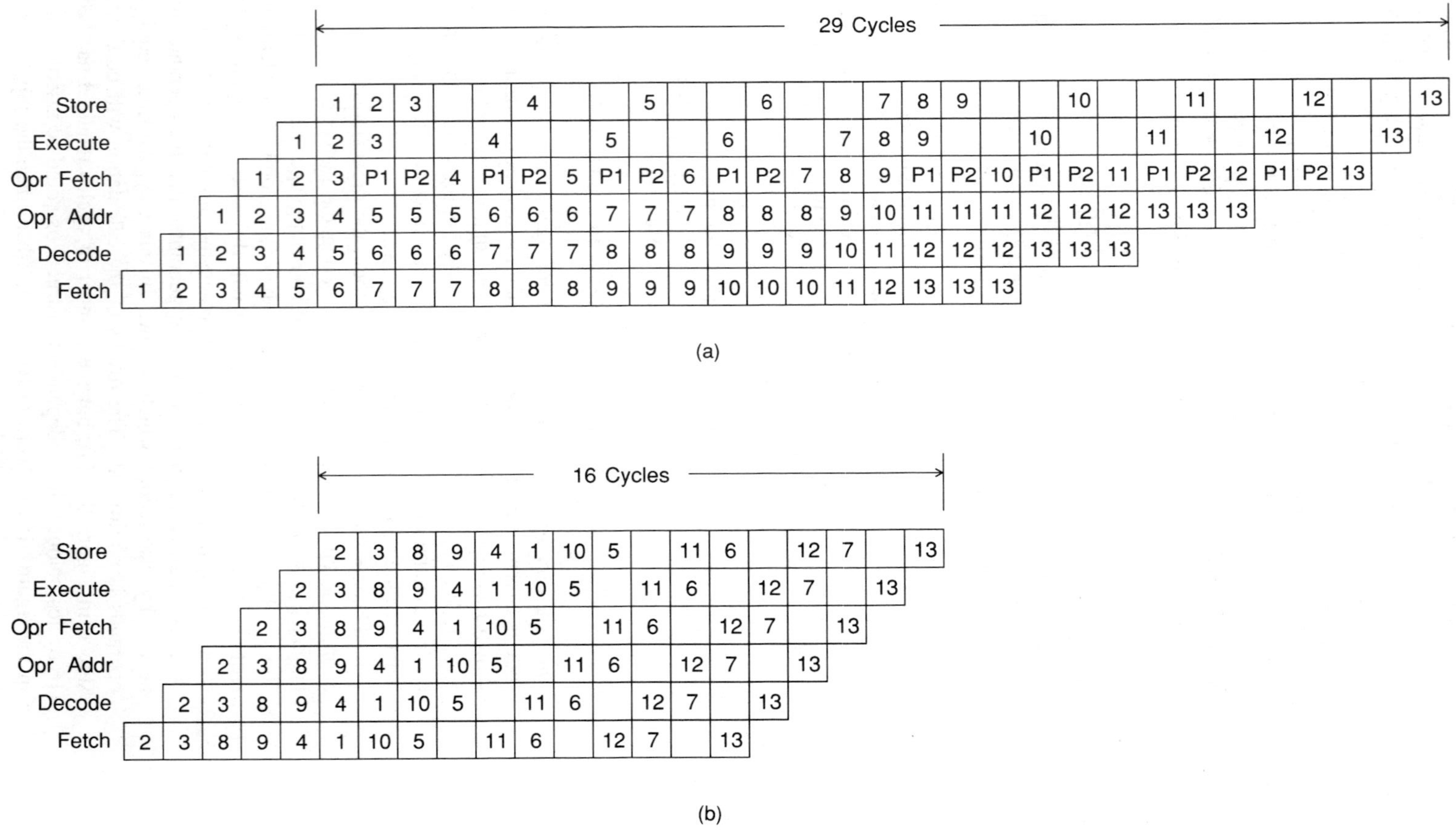

Figure 8.25. Resource Utilization for Code with Data Conflicts: (a) Simple Arrangement of Instructions; (b) Instructions Reordered to Minimize Conflicts.

(a) — 29 Cycles

Store	1	2	3	4	5	6	7	8	9	10	11	12	13	13				
Execute	1	2	3	P1	4	P2	5	P1	6	P2	7	8	9	P1	10	P2	11	P1	12	P2	13
Opr Fetch	1	2	3	P1	4	P2	5	P1	6	P2	7	8	9	P1	10	P2	11	12	13
Opr Addr	1	2	3	4	5	6	7	8	9	10	11	12	13	13
Decode	1	2	3	4	5	6	7	8	9	10	11	12	13
Fetch	1	2	3	4	5	6	7	8					

(b) — 16 Cycles

Store	2	3	8	9	4	1	10	5	11	6	12	7	13
Execute	2	3	8	9	4	1	10	5	11	6	12	7	13
Opr Fetch	2	3	8	9	4	1	10	5	11	6	12	7	13
Opr Addr	2	3	8	9	4	1	10	5	11	6	12	7	13
Decode	2	3	8	9	4	1	10	5	11	6	12	7	13
Fetch	2	3	8	9	4	1	10	5	11	6	12	7	13

434

Example 8.5: Pipeline speedups for real systems: The effective speedup of a pipeline is a function of the probability of conflict and the penalty of that conflict. For the pipeline as shown in Figure 8.25, is the formula a reasonable representation of the actual speedup?

Since we are assuming ideal conditions, we will assume that execution of the instructions in a nonpipelined system will require six cycles per instruction. Thus, the 13 instructions of the code segment will require 78 cycles to complete. If the pipeline is kept full, and there are no conflicts, we would expect a speedup of six. From the code segment and from Figure 8.25(a), we identify that 8 instructions cause conflicts, and that the penalty of each is 2 cycles. Thus,

$$\text{Effective speedup} = \frac{\text{Best speedup}}{1 + p \times P}$$

$$= \frac{6}{1 + (\frac{8}{13}) \times 2}$$

$$= 2.6896$$

The analytical approach says that we should see a speedup on the order of 2.69. Using the steady state number of 29 cycles, the speedup of the system that executes according to the method demonstrated by Figure 8.25(a) is:

$$\text{Effective speedup} = \frac{78}{29}$$

$$= 2.6896$$

which agrees with the calculated speedup. If the instructions are reordered as shown in Figure 8.25(b), then a different calculation is in order. Here three instructions (11, 12, and 13) have penalties associated with them, and the penalties are only one cycle. Thus,

$$\text{Effective speedup} = \frac{\text{Best speedup}}{1 + p \times P}$$

$$= \frac{6}{1 + (\frac{3}{13}) \times 1}$$

$$= 4.875$$

The actual time demonstrated by Figure 8.25(b) is 16 cycles:

$$\text{Effective speedup} = \frac{78}{16}$$

$$= 4.875$$

It is interesting to note that the reordering technique, while not modifying the hardware in any way, resulted in an increase in the effectiveness of the pipeline from an effective speedup of 2.689 to an effective speedup of 4.875. This is an increase of 81%.

The reordering scheme can be utilized by those who program the machine at the assembly language level. But more importantly, the technique can be used by compiler writers to generate code that will execute in a minimum amount of time. For example, one observation concerning the use of system resources in the above example is that better use could be made of the registers as temporary storage. By specifying different registers for each temporary variable, the conflicts could be minimized.

Performance enhancement can be accomplished by reordering since the technique works to organize the operations in an independent fashion, and independence leads to operation without conflicts. Another technique is to recognize that there will be conflicts in the instruction stream, and to attempt to minimize the penalty of a conflicts. One way to reduce the time required by many of the conflicts is to expand the capability of the storage function so that results are not only stored in a cycle, but they are also made available to other stages of the pipe. That is, when the execute unit has completed an operation, the results can be supplied not only to the store unit, but they can also be provided to the other elements of the pipeline as needed. One representation of this path is shown in Figure 8.26, where the execute unit has a private data path that it can use to transfer information to other units in the pipeline.

The addition of the feedback path will reduce the penalty of many of the conflicts by one cycle, since the pipe sections need not wait until the store unit places the information into the memory or a register. The fetch operand section can obtain the data required for instructions following in the pipe. The generate operand address section can receive the information needed to specify operand addresses. And the instruction fetch/decode sections can identify the target address one cycle earlier, since the status information is made available at the same time that the status register is being updated. The overall effect is to greatly reduce the cycles consumed by all types of conflicts.

Example 8.6: Pipeline penalty reduction with internal data path: Assume that a feedback path exists in a pipelined unit as shown in Figure 8.26.

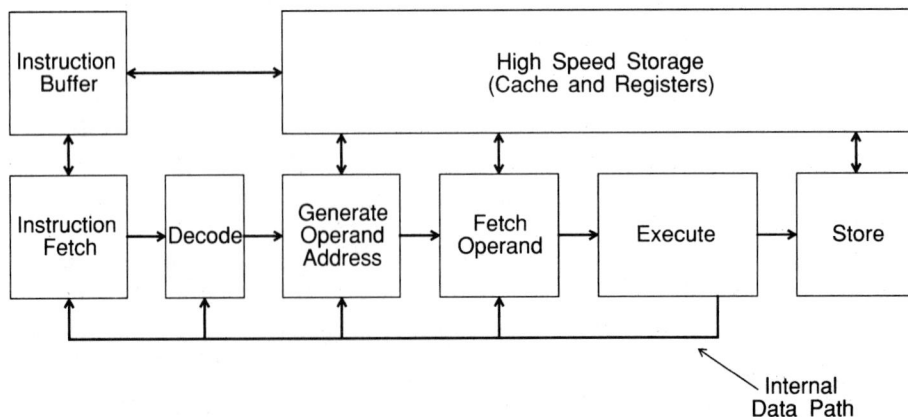

Figure 8.26. Block Diagram of Control Pipeline with Internal Data Feedback Path.

What will the effect be on the execution of the assembly language code used in the previous example?

The addition of the feedback path reduces the data conflicts penalty by one cycle, and this should be evident in the graph of resource utilization for the pipe. The code is repeated here for convenience:

```
1    MOV #<VCC>, R0
2    MOV #<RES1>, R1
3    MOV #<RES2>, R2
4    ADD R1, R2
5    MULT #<I1>, R2
6    ADD R0, R2
7    MOV R2, @<VX>
8    MOV #<RES3>, R3
9    MOV #<RES4>, R4
10   ADD R3, R4
11   MULT #<I2>, R4
12   ADD R0, R4
13   MOV R4, @<VY>
```

The graph of the resource utilization is included as Figure 8.27. As shown in part a, the simple, nonoptimized code now executes in 21 cycles, not

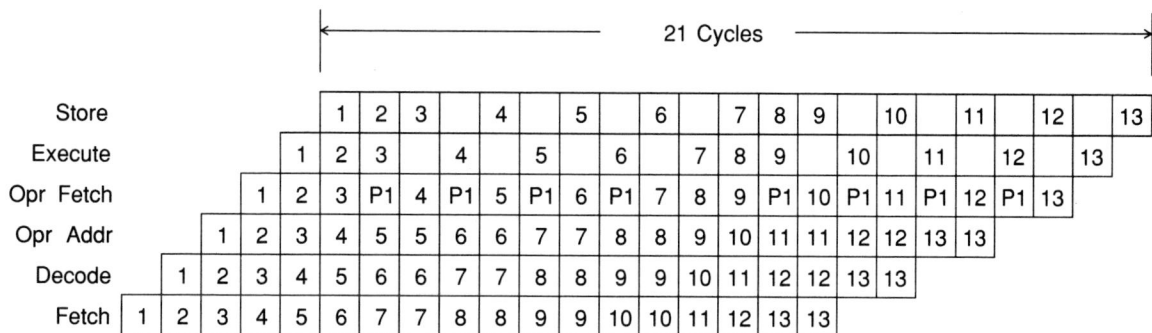

(a)

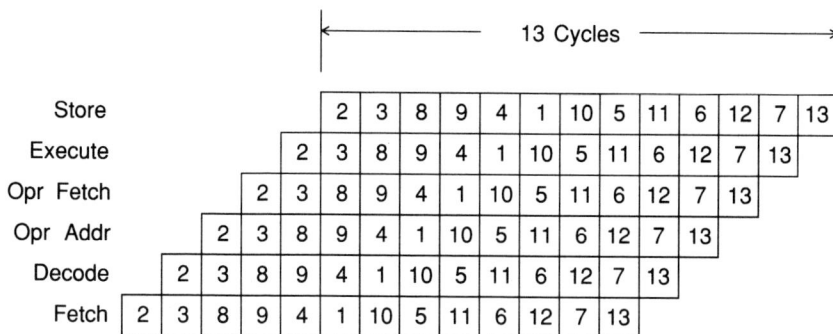

(b)

Figure 8.27. Resource Utilization for Reduced Penalty Data Conflicts: (a) Simple Arrangement of Instructions; (b) Instructions Reordered to Minimize Conflicts.

including the fill time. Instructions 4, 5, 6, 7, 10, 11, 12, and 13 still incur penalties, but now the penalties require only a one cycle delay. The resulting speedup becomes:

$$\text{Effective speedup} = \frac{\text{Best speedup}}{1 + p \times P}$$

$$= \frac{6}{1 + (\frac{8}{13}) \times 1}$$

$$= 3.71$$

The reduction of the penalty from two cycles to one cycle has increased the speedup from 2.689 to 3.71, an increase of 38%. And examination of Figure 8.27(b) indicates that there are no unused cycles, so for the optimized case the speedup is at a maximum. By including the feedback path, the reordering technique in will produce results that are more effective than a system without the ability to bypass the storage function.

Reordering of instructions can be effective because of the use of independent instructions, since independent instructions do not compete for resources. Enhancing the data transfer capabilities of a pipeline to bypass the storage function reduces the penalties associated with all kind of conflicts. As we have seen, the penalties associated with the branch conflict are some of the largest penalties, so various techniques have been devised to try to minimize the overall branch conflict penalty. We will now describe one of these techniques and identify some of the additional problems created by the solution.

The main reason that branch conflicts cause delay is not that the functions cannot be performed, but rather that the machine does not know which of the functions (instructions) are to be done. The correct "next" instruction following a conditional branch will not be identified until the condition on which the branch is based is known. However, one method to minimize the overall effect is to make a guess as to which of the instruction paths will be followed, and start execution along that path. Then, if the guess was correct, the penalty reduces to zero. However, if the guess was not correct, the time penalty will be the same as if no guess had been made.

To visualize this process, consider a set of instructions similar to those already examined. We will construct the set of instructions so that the only delay is a branch conflict, but with some problems that will demonstrate the added capabilities needed by the pipeline. The following instructions could be used to move data from one location to another:

1		MOV #<FROM>, R0	R0 points to source of info.
2		MOV #<TO>, R1	R1 points to where it goes.
3		MOV #<1024>, R2	R2 is counter.
4	label	MOV *R0+, *R1+	Move data, bump pointers.
5		DEC R2	Decrement counter.
6		JNZ label	If not zero, more data to move.
7		MOV R5, R2	When done moving data, do this.

The pipeline system will make a guess as to the appropriate next instruction from 6. In this case, it is obvious that 1,023 times the next instruction is located at "label," so most of the time the correct choice will be instruction 4. If the designers of the system find that the JNZ instruction is indeed found principally at the end of a loop of this nature, then the system can be designed to assume that the branch is taken. Then the resource utilization graph for an iteration of the loop may appear as shown in Figure 8.28. The sequence of instructions indicated by the graph assumes that the next instruction after the jump will be instruction 4. Thus, that instruction is initiated, and the pipeline continues as if it were an unconditional jump. This should cause no problem until the operand fetch portion of the next instruction 4 that is to execute. Instruction 4 causes R0 and R1 to increment, and if the branch is not taken, the values should not change. Therefore, a pipeline system that allows a conditional branch to follow one of the paths must be capable of flushing the pipe of the effects of the instructions if the path turns out to be the incorrect action. Thus, the operand fetch portion of the instruction circled in Figure 8.28 must not cause changes (in R0 or R1) until after the validity of the path has been established.

By allowing the machine to continue execution, branch prediction techniques allow a system to minimize the time required to wait for conflicts to be resolved. This results in an overall speedup, even if the guesses are correct for only a fraction of the instructions. The larger the fraction, the greater the speedup. The cost of this speed enhancement is the additional hardware needed to allow the effects of a branch that should not have been taken to be removed from the pipe.

The final mechanism we will examine is another technique for minimizing the effect of conditional branches. This technique requires a combination of hardware and software to be effective, and hence must be applied in a system solution. That is, the hardware can provide the capability, but unless the software (compiler in conjunction with the operating system) makes use of the technique, no benefit will result.

One of the observations made earlier concerning the conditional branch penalties is that the target of the branch is not known until the condition on which the branch is based has been resolved. One approach to pipeline implementation is to cause the action of the system to stop until the condition has been determined. Since the desired effect of pipelining is to utilize the stages of the pipe as much of the time as possible, another approach is to design the pipeline in such a way that the instruction following a conditional branch is *always* executed. With this technique, an instruction that is always executed in the body of a loop can be placed directly after the conditional branch that determines the end of the loop, and it will produce the correct results.

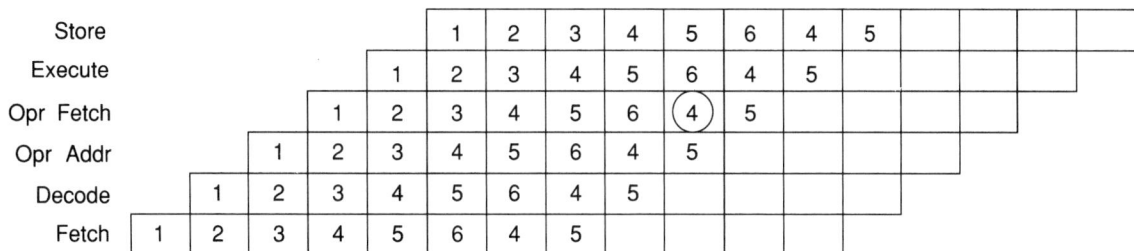

Store						1	2	3	4	5	6	4	5
Execute					1	2	3	4	5	6	4	5	
Opr Fetch				1	2	3	4	5	6	(4)	5		
Opr Addr			1	2	3	4	5	6	4	5			
Decode		1	2	3	4	5	6	4	5				
Fetch	1	2	3	4	5	6	4	5					

Figure 8.28. Resource Utilization for Pipeline with Branch Guess.

This technique results in more effective utilization of the stages of the pipeline, since an independent instruction is executed during the time required to identify the target of a conditional branch. To visualize this process consider the following set of instructions:

1	label	ADD R1, R3	Add two regs together.
2		ADD R2, R4	Add two other regs.
3		INC R0	Bump another reg.
4		CMP R3, R8	Do a comparison and if ...
5		BNE label	Values are equal, branch.

This code segment may result from a loop in a high level language. Note that instructions 1, 2, and 3 are executed each iteration of the loop. The result of applying this technique to the pipeline used as an example throughout this section is shown in Figure 8.29. Part a of the figure indicates that the above loop will execute in 8 cycles, assuming that instruction 5 must wait until the execute portion of instruction 4 determines that the next instruction will be instruction number 1. With this assumption, as soon as instruction 4 completes the execute section, instruction 1 can begin. Reordering the instructions to take advantage of the fact that an instruction following a conditional branch would result in the resource utilization shown in part b of the figure. Instruction 3 has been placed

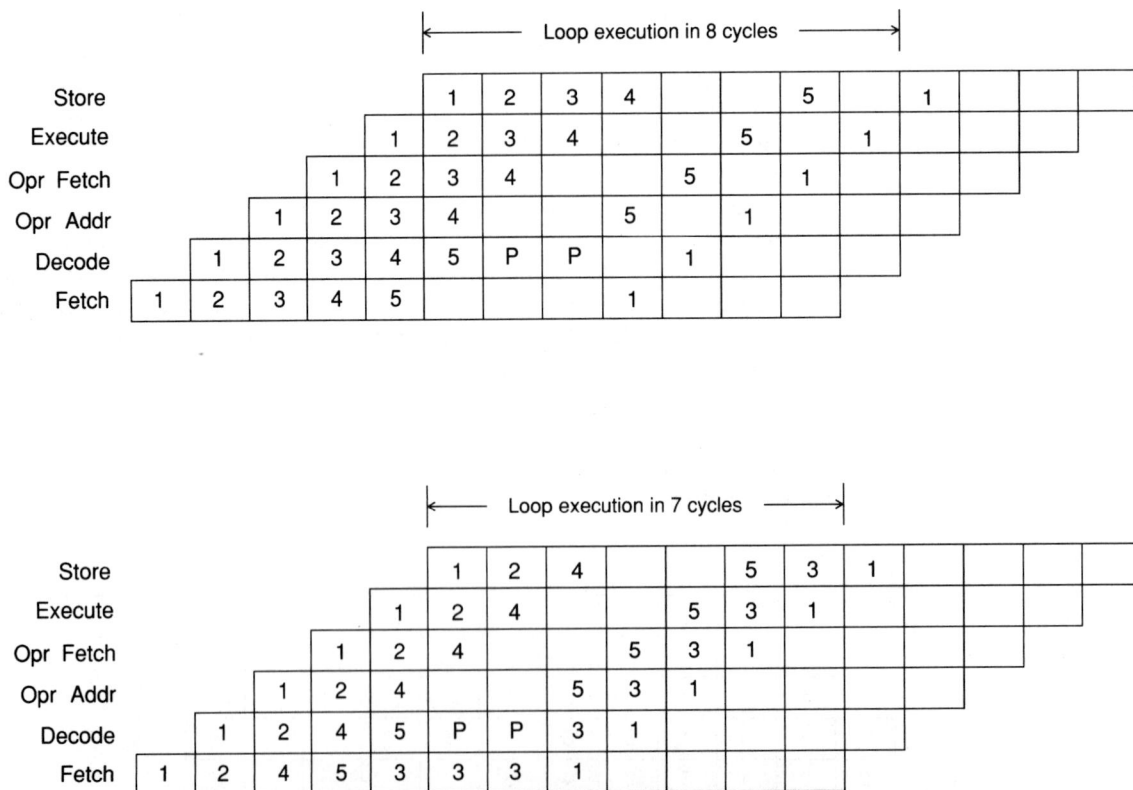

Loop execution in 8 cycles

Store						1	2	3	4		5		1
Execute					1	2	3	4		5		1	
Opr Fetch				1	2	3	4		5		1		
Opr Addr			1	2	3	4		5		1			
Decode		1	2	3	4	5	P	P	1				
Fetch	1	2	3	4	5			1					

Loop execution in 7 cycles

Store						1	2	4			5	3	1
Execute					1	2	4			5	3	1	
Opr Fetch				1	2	4			5	3	1		
Opr Addr			1	2	4			5	3	1			
Decode		1	2	4	5	P	P	3	1				
Fetch	1	2	4	5	3	3	3	1					

Figure 8.29. Resource Utilization With and Without Using Technique That Always Executes Instruction After Branch: (a) Execution of Instructions in "Normal" Fashion; (b) Instruction Execution When Instruction Following Branch Always Executes.

after the branch, and the system is designed so that the instruction will execute regardless of the result of the branch. With this technique applied to this pipeline, the resulting loop execution time is reduced by one cycle.

Studies have shown that this mechanism can be effectively utilized from 60–80% of the time, depending on the job type and the mechanisms involved. If it is determined that the instruction that follows the branch cannot be effective utilized, then a NOP (no operation) instruction is used in that slot. The net result is that when the instruction following the branch is not a NOP, the branch penalty is reduced by one.

Example 8.7: RISC system pipeline: One of the available RISC systems is made by MIPS Corporation. What are the pipeline stages involved with the system? The pipeline of the MIPS system is shown in Figure 8.30. Basically, five sections are identified in the figure. The time for execution is indicated in the figure, and each section utilizes a time of one cycle, except the write back section. The first section is used for instruction fetch, and it has the responsibility of determining the real address of the instruction using the translation lookaside buffer, and then initiating the cache request for this information. This architecture calls for two separate cache systems, one for the instruction stream and one for the data stream. The instruction will not actually be provided until the first part of the decode stage.

The read/decode section obtains the instruction, decodes it, and reads any needed operands from the appropriate CPU registers. (RF stands for register fetch.) The information is then presented to the ALU stage.

The ALU stage performs any required work on operands obtained by the decode section. In the instruction is a LOAD or STORE, the TLB is interrogated to perform the virtual to real address translation to identify a spot in the data cache.

The memory section is responsible for handling LOAD and STORE instructions. The system does not allow operands used in arithmetic or logic instructions to be located in memory, so this section is responsible for moving the information needed for instructions to the appropriate system registers, and also for transferring information from registers back to memory. The addresses needed for this are generated in the half cycle preceding the memory request.

The final section has the task of writing back ALU results or values loaded from the data cache to the register file.

This pipeline is capable of having five instructions executing at any one time, each in its appropriate section of the pipe. Note that TLB access is required for both the instruction address and the data address, and that these requests occur in different halves of a clock cycle. Thus, the TLB accesses will not slow the execution rate of the pipe.

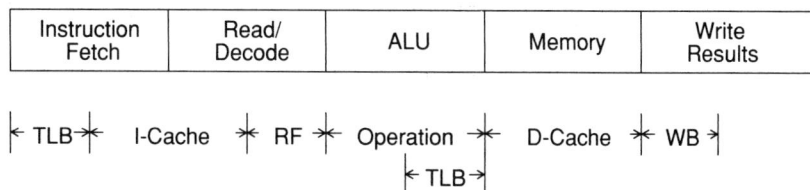

Instruction Fetch	Read/ Decode	ALU	Memory	Write Results

|← TLB →|← I-Cache →|← RF →|← Operation →|← D-Cache →|← WB →|

|← TLB →|

Figure 8.30. Pipeline Stages for MIPS System.

The pipeline utilizes the delayed instruction technique for conditional branches, which we discussed above. However, the delayed availability of operands when performing load operations creates a condition similar to the conditional branch. The system utilizes the same technique with loads and stores as with branches: interlocks are not built into the hardware, but the software must be configured to assure that data not yet available is not requested for an operation. If there is no independent instruction which can be placed in the "delayed slot" after a branch or between fetching information from memory and using it, then a NOP *must* be inserted in the code. This policy makes the hardware easier to build, since conditions for halting the pipe are removed by careful attention to the software before the program runs.

Pipelines for control and instruction functions appear in virtually all high speed processors, and many microprocessors and smaller systems as well. The benefits obtained by execution of independent instructions in different sections of a pipeline justify the complexity of the system. In those systems with a possibility of using multiple system resources, interlocks must be provided to assure that the instructions will produce the proper results. Other systems, especially systems with short pipelines and systems that are RISC in nature, use software systems that create programs so that the results are correct, by presenting sequences of instructions that do not have resource conflicts.

8.4. Summary

The execution rate of computing systems can be increased by dividing the processing that needs to be done into small pieces and executing these pieces for different operations in the same time period. The division process breaks the required processing into sections each of which perform a portion of the overall function; the computational action is accomplished by passing information from one section to the next, and an operation is complete only when it has accomplished the work needed by all of the sections. Both data functions and control or instruction functions can be divided into basic sections and utilize the concept of pipelining.

With this technique, many different operations can be in progress at the same time, and each operation occupying a different stage of the pipeline. The highest rate for execution of operations with pipelining occurs when the pipeline is entirely full. When this is the case, each clock cycle results in another completed function, and extremely high computational rates can occur. To support this high execution rate, the data transfer mechanisms of the computational element that move information to and from memory, and to and from registers within the system, must be able to transfer operands and instructions at a rate sufficiently high to keep the system busy. If the data system is not capable of this high transfer rate, then the full benefits of pipelining will not be realized.

If the data system is capable of supporting the data transfers needed to maintain high data rates within a computer, then performance degradations will occur only when operations within the system are not independent. If the results of one operation are required by the next, then the appropriate pipeline section must wait until the data is available to proceed. The independence must be maintained in pipelines for both computational functions and control or instruction functions. Pipelines can be required to wait for data information (data conflicts), for information needed to generate operand addresses (address conflicts), and for status information needed to identify the target of a conditional branch (branch conflicts). These conditions arise when operations within the pipe are not independent.

Performance improvements will occur in pipeline systems whenever steps are taken to reduce the penalties associated with nonindependent operations. The four techniques presented in this chapter all seek to reduce the time required to resolve conflicts incurred by use of common system resources. The first technique requires no hardware commitments; rather, the software is manipulated in such a way that the instructions are fed into the pipelined instruction unit in such a way that the operations are independent. This results in a higher apparent execution rate. The second technique is to provide an internal data path within the pipeline, so that operands can be obtained by sections of the pipe when the operands become available, rather than waiting for them to be stored. This reduces the time needed to wait for results.

Another technique presented is to allow the pipeline to identify the expected target of a conditional branch and begin execution at that point. This reduces to zero the penalty associated with the branch if the guess is correct, but incurs the cost of being able to flush from the pipe the effects of those instructions followed if the guess is incorrect. The final technique presented is to design the system in such a way that the instruction following a conditional branch is always executed, and rely on the users of the system (compiler writers, assembly language programmers, etc.) to create the programs in such a way that the instruction after the branch is effectively utilized.

8.5. Problems

8.1 Develop a formula for T_{TOT}, the total time required to perform N independent arithmetic operations in an arithmetic pipe. Assume that the arithmetic pipe contains 6 stages, and that each stage executes in 100 nsec.

8.2 Design a pipelined floating point add unit. To accomplish this:

a. Give a block diagram of the floating point add operation.

b. Describe each element in the block diagram, and specify the hardware needed to perform the work of that block.

c. Identify the delays associated with each of the blocks in the block diagram.

d. Insert registers at appropriate locations in the block diagram. (What delays are associated with the registers?)

e. Assuming that collision avoidance is handled by another piece of the system, identify the controls needed in the pipelined unit, and show how the control is handled.

f. What is the data rate needed to keep the pipeline full?

8.3 Assume that a high speed floating point multiply part is available at a reasonable cost. Give a block diagram of a pipeline used to provide a divide operation. If a ROM is available to specify the first coefficient to 15 bits, how many stages are required to provide a result correct to 56 bits (double precision floating point)? If the multiply takes 120 nsec, and the register requires 10 nsec, what is the floating point divide rate? What must the data rate of the memory system be to sustain the highest operation rate?

8.4 Show a block diagram level design for a pipelined vector floating point add system. Include vector registers capable of holding up to 64 elements of a vector. Show on a time plot the action of each of the elements of the system for a period of 10 clock cycles.

8.5 Give a detailed logic diagram for the pipelined system of Problem 8.4. Assume that you have memories which are 64 × 8 to work with, and that these come in 20 pin packages. For this problem:

a. Use the block diagram of Problem 8.4. Remember to include whatever address registers are needed to identify the elements of the vectors.

b. Specify the devices needed to implement the system.

c. Identify the control lines needed to control the flow of data in the system.

d. Create a control system that will assert the control signals in the proper fashion to do the calculation as specified.

e. Provide the logic diagrams of the system.

8.6 Discuss possible alternatives, as well as their advantages and disadvantages, for the organization of a memory system to be used with the pipelined system of Problem 8.4, and the interconnection between the memory and the vector registers.

8.7 Identify the modifications required to add another pipelined functional unit to the system of Problem 8.4. That is, the system as specified is capable of doing a floating point add for vectors of values. What would be required to add a functional unit that would utilize the same vector registers, but that would do a floating point multiply for vectors of numbers?

8.8 A pipelined control unit has six separate stages. The various collisions that can occur in the system can produce penalties of one cycle, two cycles, three cycles, or four cycles. Develop a formula that will give the effective speedup for the system as a function of the probability of each of the four penalties. Plot the formula such that the abscissa is the effective speedup, and the ordinate is the probability of collisions. For the plot, vary only one probability at a time, leaving the other three probabilities zero.

8.9 The instruction portion of a certain computer has been broken into five distinct parts for purposes of pipelining: instruction fetch, instruction decode, operand fetch, instruction execution, and storage of results, where necessary. Assume that all instructions must take all five cycles to execute. Assume also that results are not available until after the end of the fifth section. The code segment that is to run on this fictitious machine is:

```
           LOAD R1 with -512
           LOAD R2 with 4000
           LOAD R3 with 5000
           LOAD R4 with 6000
OVER:      MOVE *R2, R8     * is indirection, destination is R8.
           MOVE *R3, R9
           ADD R8, R9
```

```
          MOVE R9, *R4
          ISZ R2                    ISZ is increment and skip if zero.
          ISZ R3
          ISZ R4
          ISZ R1
          JNZ OVER
```

a. If there were never any problem with collisions, how much faster would the pipelined system run than unpipelined system?

b. How long will it take to execute the above section of code? Assume that the time step is 100 nsec.

8.10 Consider a two address computer designed with a pipelined control section. The sections are instruction fetch, decode, operand 1 fetch, operand 2 fetch, execute, and store. Each section does its work in one cycle. The store section can be bypassed for data needed for either operand fetch section. The status bits are available for testing directly after the execute section. The branch guess is the next instruction in line. How many cycles does it take to compute the following section of code:

```
          MOV    100, R0     100 decimal to counter.
label     MOV    R0, R2      Count to temporary.
          ADD    R3, R2      Add constant to temporary.
          MOV    R2, *R0     Store in memory.
          DEC    R0          Decrement counter.
          BNZ    label       Loop til done.
```

8.11 Consider a computer with an instruction time of 8t units. Assume that conditions are ideal and that this computer can be redesigned to take advantage of pipelining, and that the pipeline consists of four equal segments. For this new machine:

a. How long will it take to start and complete a sequence of 40 instructions?

b. A time penalty is associated with collisions in the pipeline. That is, the pipeline must halt for some period of time when an applicable collision occurs. (Remember that independent instructions do not cause collisions, and that collisions result in modified data/address do not incur a penalty.) How long does it take to completely execute the following code to add two vectors? (I, J, K, L stored in registers.)

```
                 10  → I      I,J,K can be used as addresses.
                 20  → J
                 30  → K
                -20  → L
          label: CLA          Clear the accumulator.
                 ADD M[I]      Add in one value.
                 INC I         Bump the Address.
                 ADD M[J]      Add in another value.
                 INC J         Bump the address.
                 STO M[K]      Store the result.
                 INC K         Bump the address.
                 ISZ L         Check to see if done.
                 JMP label     If not done, go back.
                 HALT          Otherwise, quit.
```

8.12 Consider the instruction unit of a computer; a design team wants to pipeline the system. Currently the process of fetching, decoding, and executing instructions takes 600 nsec. By very clever work, you have been able to divide the unit into six separate actions: fetch, decode, operand 1 fetch, operand 2 fetch, execute, store result. Each of these actions will take 100 nsec, and single operand instructions do nothing during operand 2 fetch. A data collision in a register must wait for the correct value to reach the register. By being extremely clever the design team has eliminated the address collision problem.

a. If this machine executes 60 instructions, all independent so there are no collisions, how much time elapses between initiation of the first instruction and completion of the last?

b. The following set of instructions adds two vectors together and stores the final value in a new vector. The conditional jump instruction here is designed to assume that the jump will be successful. How long will it take to complete this set of instructions?

```
               300 → J  (a register)
               400 → K  (a register)
               20 → L   (a register)
LABEL:         MOVE MEM[L],N  (N is a register)
               ADD MEM[J],N
               DEC J
               STORE N,MEM[K]
               DEC K
               DEC L
               JNZ LABEL
               HALT
```

c. If the machine were to stay in the above loop (LABEL-JNZ) forever, what would the effective instruction time be?

8.6. References and Readings

[AnSp67] Anderson, D. W., F. J. Sparacio and R. M. Tomasulo, "The IBM System/360 Model 91: Machine Philosophy and Instruction-Handling," *IBM Journal of Research and Developments.* Vol. 11, No. 1, January 1967, pp. 8–24.

[Baer84] Baer, J. L., "Computer Architecture," *Computer.* Vol. 17, No. 10, October 1984, pp. 77–87.

[Baer80] Baer, J. L., *Computer Systems Architecture.* Rockville, MD: Computer Science Press, 1980.

[BaBr68] Barnes, G. H., R. M. Brown, M. Kato, et al., "The Illiac IV Computer," *IEEE Transactions on Computers.* Vol. C-17, No. 8, August 1968, pp. 746–757.

[Batc80] Batcher, K. E., "The Design of a Massively Parallel Processor," *IEEE Transactions on Computers.* Vol. C-29, No. 9, September 1980, pp. 836–840.

[BeNe71] Bell, C. G. and A. Newell, *Computer Structures: Readings and Examples.* New York: McGraw-Hill Book Company, 1971.

[BuGo46] Burks, A. W., H. H. Goldstine, and J. von Neumann, "Preliminary Discussion of the Logical Design of an Electronic Computing Instrument," Institute for Advanced Studies, 1946, reprinted in [Swar76].

[Chen80] Chen, T. C., "Overlap and Pipeline Processing," in [Ston80], pp. 427–485.

[Chen71] Chen, T. C., "Parallelism, Pipelining, and Computer Efficiency," *Computer Design.* Vol. 10, No. 1, January 1971, pp. 69–74.

[Davi71] Davidson, E. S., "The Design and Control of Pipelined Function Generators," *Proceedings of the IEEE International Conference on Systems Networks and Computers.* 1971, pp. 19–21.

[DRGl85] DeRosa, J., R. Glackemeyer, and T. Knight, "Design and Implementation of the VAX 8600 Pipeline," *Computer.* Vol. 18, No. 5, May 1985, pp. 38–48.

[FoME85] Fossum, T., J. B. McElroy, and W. English, "An Overview of the VAX 8600 System," *Digital Technical Journal.* Hudson, MA: Digital Equipment Corporation, 1985, pp. 8–23.

[BrHe82] Gross, T. R., and J. L. Hennessy, "Optimizing Delayed Branches," *Proceedings of the 15th Annual Workshop on Microprogramming.* New York, NY: IEEE Computer Society Press, 1982, pp. 114–120.

[Hill85] Hillis, W. D., *The Connection Machine.* Cambridge, MA: MIT Press, 1985.

[HwBr84] Hwang, K., and F. A. Briggs, *Computer Architecture and Parallel Processing.* New York: McGraw-Hill, 1984.

[Kane87] Kane, Gerry, *MIPS R2000 RISC Architecture.* Englewood Cliffs, NJ: Prentice Hall, 1987.

[Kell75] Keller, R. M., "Lookahead Processers," *ACM Computing Surveys.* Vol. 7, No. 4, 1975, pp. 177–195.

[Kogg81] Kogge, P. M., *The Architecture of Pipelined Computers.* New York: McGraw-Hill, 1981.

[KuSm86] Kunkel, S. R., and J. E. Smith, "Optimal Pipelining in Supercomputers," *Proceedings of the 13th International Symposium on Computer Architecture.* Washington, DC: IEEE Computer Society Press, 1986, pp. 404–411.

[RaLi77] Ramamoorthy, C. V., and H. F. Li, "Pipeline Architecture," *ACM Computing Surveys.* Vol. 9, No. 1, March 1977, pp. 61–102.

[Russ78] Russell, R. M., "The CRAY-1 Computer System," *Communications of the ACM.* Vol. 21, No. 1, January 1978, pp. 63–72.

[Ryma82] Rymarczyk, J., "Coding Guidelines for Pipelined Processors," *Proceedings of the ACM Symposium on Architectural Support for Programming Languages and Operating Systems.* New York: ACM, 1982, pp. 12–19.

[SiBe82] Siewiorek, D. P., C. G. Bell, and A. Newell, *Computer Structures: Principles and Examples.* New York: McGraw-Hill Book Company, 1982.

[Site78] Sites, R. L., "An Analysis of the CRAY-1 Computer," *Proceedings of the 5th Symposium on Computer Architecture,* New York: IEEE Computer Society Press 1978, pp. 101–106.

[Ston80] Stone, H. S., (Ed.), *Introduction to Computer Architecture.* Chicago, IL: Science Research Associates, 1980.

[Ston87] Stone, H. S., *High-Performance Computer Architecture.* Reading MA: Addison-Wesley Publishing Company, 1987.

[Swar76] Swartzlander, E. E., Jr. (Ed.), *Computer Design Development: Principal Papers.* Rochelle Park, NJ: Hayden Book Company, Inc., 1976.

[Thor64] Thornton, J. E., "Parallel Operation in the Control Data 6600," *Proceedings of the Fall Joint Computer Conference.* AFIPS, Montvale, NJ:AFIPS Press, Vol. 24, 1964, pp. 33–40.

[Thur76] Thurber, K. J., *Large Scale Computer Architecture, Parallel and Associative Processers.* Rochelle Park, NJ: Hayden Book Company, Inc., 1976.

[Toma67] Tomasulo, R. M., "An Efficient Algorithm for Exploiting Multiple Arithmetic Units," *IBM Journal of Research and Development.* Vol. 11, No. 1, January 1967, pp. 25–33.

[TrCh85] Troiani, M., S. S. Ching, N. N. Quaynor, et al., "The VAX 8600 I Box, A Pipelined Implementation of the VAX Architecture," *Digital Technical Journal.* Hudson, MA: Digital Equipment Corp., 1985, pp. 24–42.

[WeRo84] Wedig, R. G., and A. Rose, "The Reduction of Branch Instruction Execution Overhead Using Structured Control Flow," *Eleventh Annual International Conference on Computer Architecture,* Silver Springs, MD: IEEE Computer Society Press, June 1984, pp. 119–125.

[WeSm84] Weiss, S., and J. E. Smith, "Instruction Issue Logic for Pipelined Supercomputers," *Transactions on Computers.* Vol. C-33, No. 11, November 1984, pp. 1013–1022.

Character Codes

ASCII Code

The following code was adopted as the American Standard Code for Information Interchange.

Table of ASCII Code Combinations
Format: HEX Representation of Bit Pattern, ASCII Coded Character

H	E	H	E	H	E	H	E	H	E	H	E	H	E	H	E
00	NUL	01	SOH	02	STX	03	ETX	04	EOT	05	ENQ	06	ACK	07	BEL
08	BS	09	HT	0A	LF	0B	VT	0C	FF	0D	CR	0E	SO	0F	SI
10	DLE	11	DC1	12	DC2	13	DC3	14	DC4	15	NAK	16	SYN	17	ETB
18	CAN	19	EM	1A	SUB	1B	ESC	1C	FS	1D	GS	1E	RS	1F	US
20	SP	21	!	22	"	23	#	24	$	25	%	26	&	27	'
28	(	29	)	2A	*	2B	+	2C	,	2D	–	2E	.	2F	/
30	0	31	1	32	2	33	3	34	4	35	5	36	6	37	7
38	8	39	9	3A	:	3B	;	3C	<	3D	=	3E	>	3F	?
40	@	41	A	42	B	43	C	44	D	45	E	46	F	47	G
48	H	49	I	4A	J	4B	K	4C	L	4D	M	4E	N	4F	O
50	P	51	Q	52	R	53	S	54	T	55	U	56	V	57	W
58	X	59	Y	5A	Z	5B	[	5C	\	5D	]	5E	^	5F	_
60	`	61	a	62	b	63	c	64	d	65	e	66	f	67	g
68	h	69	i	6A	j	6B	k	6C	l	6D	m	6E	n	6F	o
70	p	71	q	72	r	73	s	74	t	75	u	76	v	77	w
78	x	79	y	7A	z	7B	{	7C			7D	}	7E	~	7F	DEL

EBCDIC Code

The following code is the Extended Binary Coded Decimal Interchange Code.

Table of EBCDIC Code Combinations
Format: HEX Representation of Bit Pattern, EBCDIC Coded Character

H	E	H	E	H	E	H	E	H	E	H	E	H	E	H	E
00	NUL	01	SOH	02	STX	03	ETX	04	SEL	05	HT	06	RNL	07	DEL
08	GE	09	SPS	0A	RPT	0B	VT	0C	FF	0D	CR	0E	SO	0F	SI
10	DLE	11	DC1	12	DC2	13	DC3	14	RES/ENP	15	NL	16	BS	17	POC
18	CAN	19	EM	1A	UBS	1B	CU1	1C	IFS	1D	IGS	1E	IRS	1F	ITB/IUS
20	DS	21	SOS	22	FS	23	WUS	24	BYP/INP	25	LF	26	ETB	27	ESC
28	SA	29	SFE	2A	SM/SW	2B	CSP	2C	MFA	2D	ENQ	2E	ACK	2F	BEL
30		31		32	SYN	33	IR	34	PP	35	TRN	36	NBS	37	EOT
38	SBS	39	IT	3A	RFF	3B	CU3	3C	DC4	3D	NAK	3E		3F	SUB
40	SP	41		42		43		44		45		46		47	
48		49		4A	¢	4B	.	4C	<	4D	(	4E	+	4F	|
50	&	51		52		53		54		55		56		57	
58		59		5A	!	5B	$	5C	*	5D	)	5E	;	5F	¬
60	-	61	/	62		63		64		65		66		67	
68		69		6A		6B	,	6C	%	6D	_	6E	>	6F	?
70		71		72		73		74		75		76		77	
78		79		7A	:	7B	#	7C	@	7D	'	7E	=	7F	"
80		81	a	82	b	83	c	84	d	85	e	86	f	87	g
88	h	89	i	8A		8B		8C		8D		8E		8F	
90		91	j	92	k	93	l	94	m	95	n	96	o	97	p
98	q	99	r	9A		9B		9C		9D		9E		9F	
A0		A1	~	A2	s	A3	t	A4	u	A5	v	A6	w	A7	x
A8	y	A9	z	AA		AB		AC		AD		AE		AF	
B0		B1		B2		B3		B4		B5		B6		B7	
B8		B9		BA		BB		BC		BD		BE		BF	
C0	{	C1	A	C2	B	C3	C	C4	D	C5	E	C6	F	C7	G
C8	H	C9	I	CA	SHY	CB		CC		CD		CE		CF	
D0	}	D1	J	D2	K	D3	L	D4	M	D5	N	D6	O	D7	P
D8	Q	D9	R	DA		DB		DC		DD		DE		DF	
E0	\	E1	NSP	E2	S	E3	T	E4	U	E5	V	E6	W	E7	X
E8	Y	E9	Z	EA		EB		EC		ED		EE		EF	
F0	0	F1	1	F2	2	F3	3	F4	4	F5	5	F6	6	F7	7
F8	8	F9	9	FA		FB		FC		FD		FE		FF	EO

Control Character Representations Used In ASCII and EBCDIC Tables

ACK	Acknowledge		IT	Indent tab
BEL	Bell		IUS	Interchange unit separator
BS	Backspace		ITB	Intermediate transmission block
BYP	Bypass		LF	Line feed
CAN	Cancel		MFA	Modify field attribute
CR	Carriage return		NAK	Negative acknowledge
CSP	Control sequence prefix		NBS	Numeric backspace
CU1	Customer use 1		NL	New line
CU3	Customer use 3		NUL	Null
DC1	Device control 1		POC	Program operator communciation
DC2	Device control 2		PP	Presentation position
DC3	Device control 3		RES	Restore
DC4	Device control 4		RFF	Required form feed
DEL	Delete		RNL	Required new line
DLE	Data link escape		RPT	Repeat
DS	Digit select		SA	Set attribute
EM	End of medium		SBS	Subscript
ENP	Enable presentation		SEL	Select
ENQ	Enquiry		SFE	Start field extended
EO	Eight ones		SI	Shift in
EOT	End of transmission		SM	Set mode
ESC	Escape		SO	Shift out
ETB	End of transmission block		SOH	Start of heading
ETX	End of text		SOS	Start of significance
FF	Form feed		SPS	Superscript
FS	Field seperator		STX	Start of text
GE	Graphic escape		SUB	Substitute
HT	Horizontal tab		SW	Switch
IFS	Interchange file separator		SYN	Synchronous idle
IGS	Interchange group separator		TRN	Transparent
INP	Inhibit presentation		UBS	Unit backspace
IR	Index return		VT	Vertical tab
IRS	Interchange record seperator		WUS	Word underscore

Detailed Logic Diagrams

The logic diagrams contained in this appendix provide additional details for examples and systems used in the various chapters. A fuller understanding of the designs and the methods used can be obtained by examining the details included here. Along with each design is an expanded version of the description contained within the text. This expanded description identifies details important to the design and observations concerning the techniques used. Additional insight can be obtained by carrying the design process beyond the point shown here. Additional information can be used as metrics to compare design techniques. This information includes such things as power dissipation (for different logic families), board space required, and speed of operation (for different logic families).

B.1.   Multiplier with Reverse Order Partial Products

This multiplier is included in Chapter 3, and involves adding the partial products in reverse order; that is, the most significant partial product is the first to be added to the product register. This design is shown in Figures B.1 and B.2. To add the partial products in reverse order, an adder that is as wide as the final product is required. In this design we have used four '283s, which will be fast enough for most systems. If higher speed is required, then an adder system composed of units that use the look-ahead technique could be used. These would include arithmetic devices like the '181 or '381, and carry look-ahead generators like the '182. In this design the product register consists of '273s, which are 8-bit edge-triggered registers capable of being cleared. Since the clearing of the product register is required to begin the multiplication process, other 8-bit registers without the ability of being cleared, such as the '574, cannot be used.

The value of the product register forms one input of the adder system. Note that there is no built-in shift in the connection arrangement of the product register,

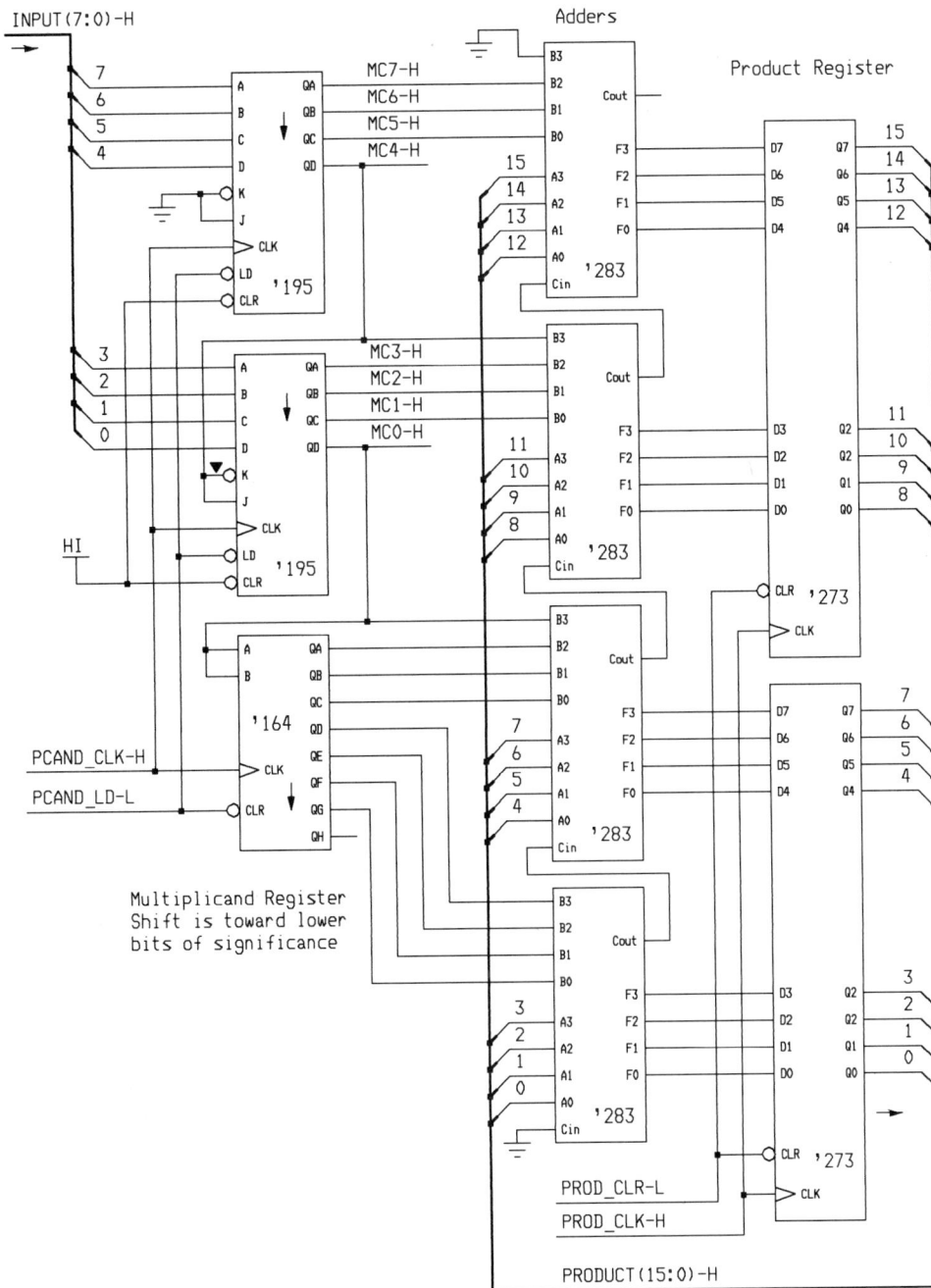

Figure B.1. Logic Diagram of Multiplier System. Multiplicand Register, Adders, and Product Register.

a technique used in some of the examples in Chapter 3. No shifting is required at the product register, since the multiplicand is being shifted to values of lower significance. The multiplicand register consists of an 8-bit loadable shift register section (two '195s) for the most significant bits, and an 8-bit serial to parallel shift register section ('164) for the least significant bits. At the beginning of the process, the multiplicand is loaded into the most significant bits, and the least significant bits are cleared. Both the load and the clear can be accomplished by using a single signal (PCAND_LD-L) in conjunction with the clock (PCAND_CLK-H). The required action is to assert the load line (PCAND_LD-L goes low), and then, while the load line is asserted, cause a low to high transition on the clock line. That sequence of action on the control lines will cause the value available on the input lines (INPUT(7:0)-H) to be loaded into the '195s, and since the '164 has a direct clear, the bits of lesser significance will be set to zero.

The multiplier register is also composed of '195s. This register is loaded in the same way as the multiplicand register, with a low to high transition occurring on the clock line (PLIER_CK-H) while the load line (PLIER_LD-L) is asserted. However, while the multiplicand register is set up to shift toward bits of lesser

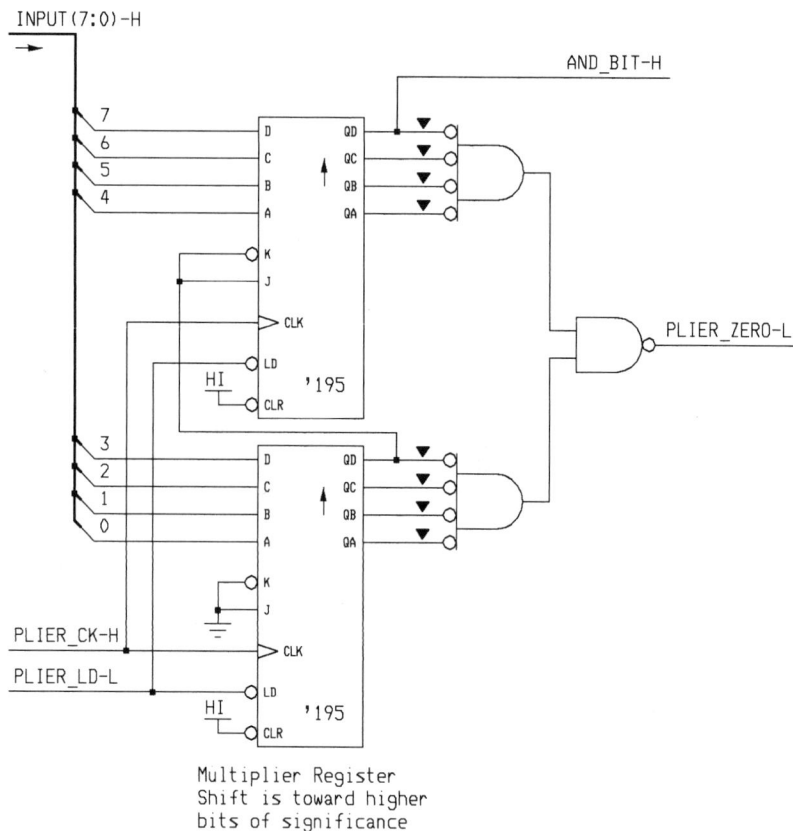

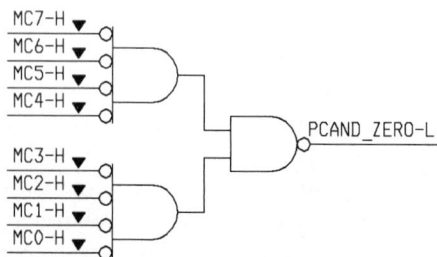

Figure B.2. Logic Diagram of Multiplier System. Multiplier Register, Multiplicand Zero Gates.

significance, the multiplier register is set up to shift towards bits of higher significance. Note that the signal tested by the control section to determine whether the partial product should be added or not (AND_BIT-H) is the most significant bit. As the shift occurs, each bit tested represents a partial product of lesser significance, which is exactly what is required by the algorithm. Note that the ANDing gates (which are actually two four input NOR gates and a two input NAND gate) on the output of the multiplier register look for the condition of all zeros. When that condition exists, all of the appropriate partial products have been added into the final result, and the process can terminate. Note also that a similar AND system is used to test the value of the multiplicand. However, the multiplicand is tested only once, when the multiplication process is being initiated. If at that time the multiplicand is zero, then the product is zero, and the correct answer will be obtained by clearing the product register.

The control section is responsible for the assertion of the various clock lines (PLIER_CK-H, PCAND_CLK-H, and PROD_CLK-H). The best system speed will come when all of these events happen simultaneously. Then all of the action (the shifting of the multiplier register and the multiplicand register, and the loading of the product register) will occur together, and the change of the multiplicand (because of the shift) will occur at the same time as the change of the product (from loading a new product value). The inputs to the product register will then be stable after the clock to output stable time of the registers (take the maximum of the product register and the multiplicand register), plus the add time for the '283s. Once the data is stable at the input to the product register, the system must allow sufficient time for the setup requirements of the product register before a new set of clock lines can occur. For the system shown, using typical times for low power Schottky circuits, the cycle time is 90 nsec.

B.2. Direct Divider System

A direct divide system is shown in Figure 3.23, and the logic diagrams for this system are shown in Figures B.3, B.4, and B.5. The algorithm calls for three registers for storing values during the division process. The divisor register receives its input from the 16-bit input bus, and is shown in Figure B.3. The divisor register consists of two '564s. These registers are used because the output is inverted from the input; this provides the complement portion of the complement and increment process of subtraction. The subtractor actually consists of four '283s, which are 4-bit adders. The increment portion of the complement and increment needed for the divisor is provided by asserting the carry-in of the least significant adder. The value of the R register is provided by the bus labeled R_REG(15:0)-H, and the difference output from the subtractor is provided on the bus labeled DIFF(15:0)-H. This bus provides one of the two possible inputs to the R register.

The R register is shown in Figure B.4. Since the R register must be loadable, readable, and shiftable, this register is composed of two '198s. These shift registers have a parallel load capability, 2-state parallel outputs that can provide the needed value to the subtractor (over bus R_REG(15:0)-H), and are also capable of the shift needed by the algorithm. The R register needs to be loaded either from the data bus or from the output of the subtractor (over the DIFF bus), and so a set of multiplexers is provided ('157s). This allows the control section to determine the appropriate input by controlling the SEL_INPUT-H line. At the

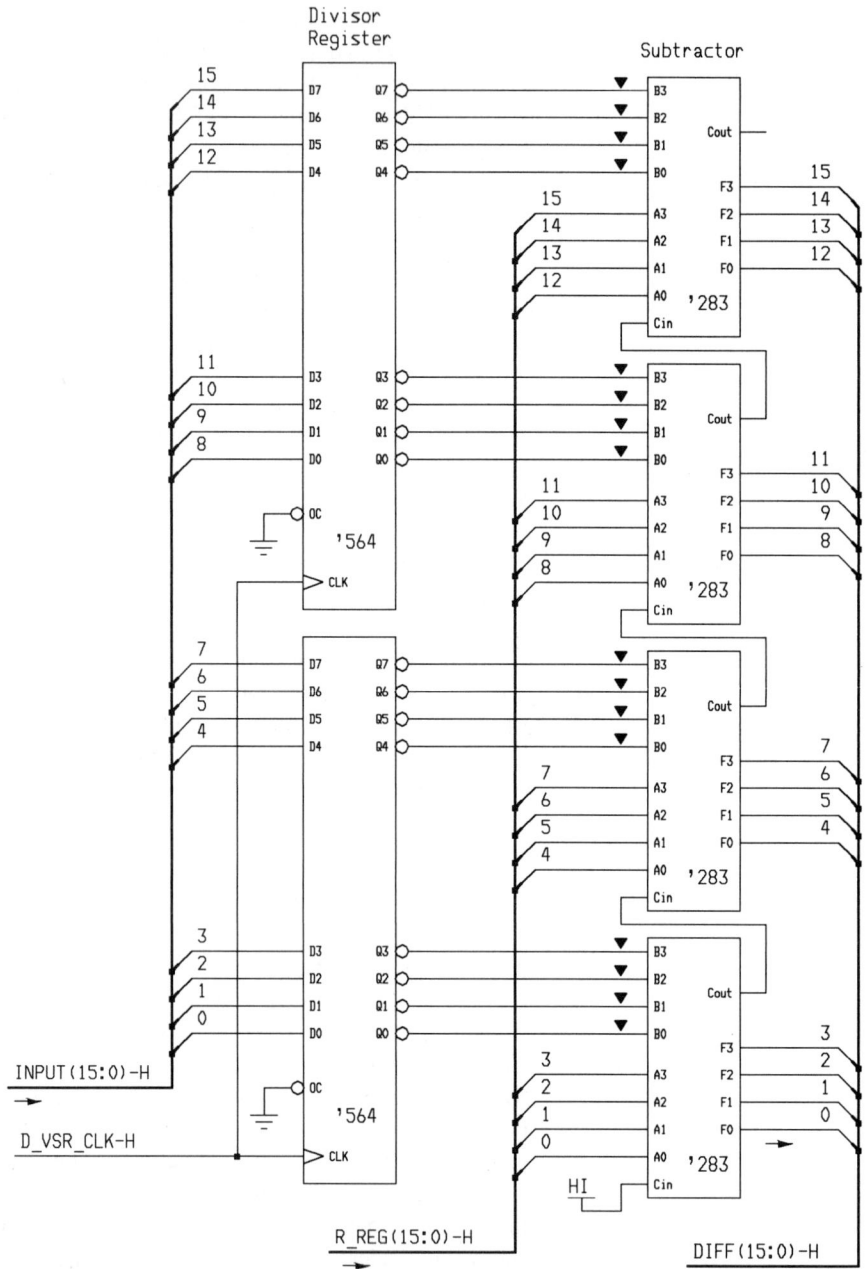

Figure B.3. Logic Diagram of Direct Divide System. Divisor Register and Subtractor.

beginning of the process the dividend (D_D) is loaded into the R register, and after that the appropriate loads are made from the output of the subtractor. The control section also causes either the loading or the shifting of the R register by appropriately asserting the S1 control input (with R_LD-H) and the clock line (R_CLK-H). The shift is always toward higher significance, and the serial input is provided by the Q register (via the Q_REG(15)-H line). The remaining components in Figure B.4 are tri-state drivers, which assert the contents of the R register on the output lines when the R_REG_OUT-L line is asserted.

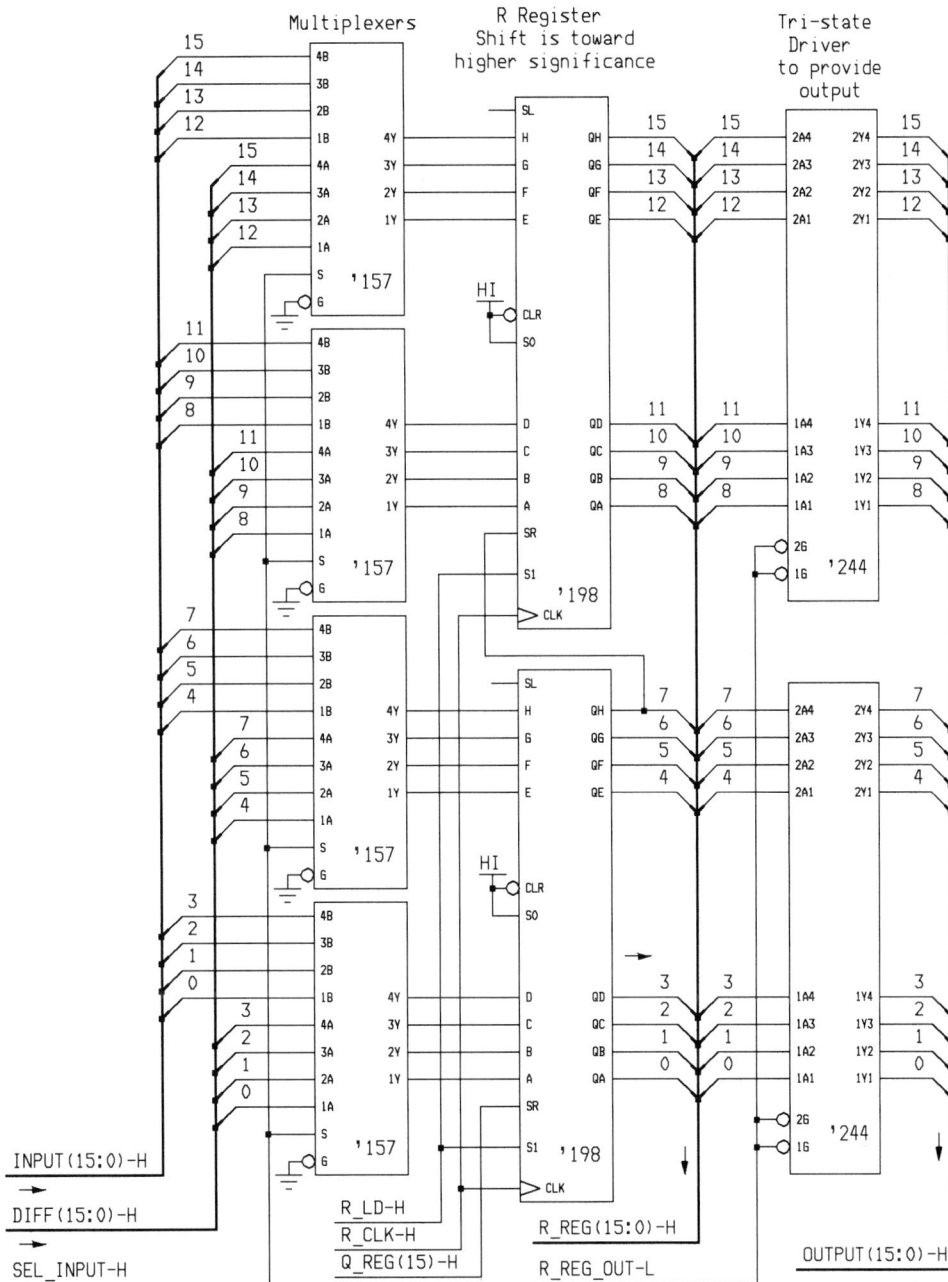

Figure B.4. Logic Diagram of Direct Divide System. R Register with Multiplexers and Output Drivers.

The Q register is shown in Figure B.5. This register also consists of a pair of '198s, to allow loading, reading, and shifting. The input is provided by the input bus (INPUT(15:0)-H), and the contents of the register is asserted on the output lines (OUTPUT(15:0)-H) when the Q_REG_OUT-L line is asserted. The tri-state drivers shown are '244s, but any appropriate driver could be used. The most significant bit (Q_REG(15)-H) is used as an input to the R register, and so the combination of the Q register and R register is a 32-bit shift register. The serial input

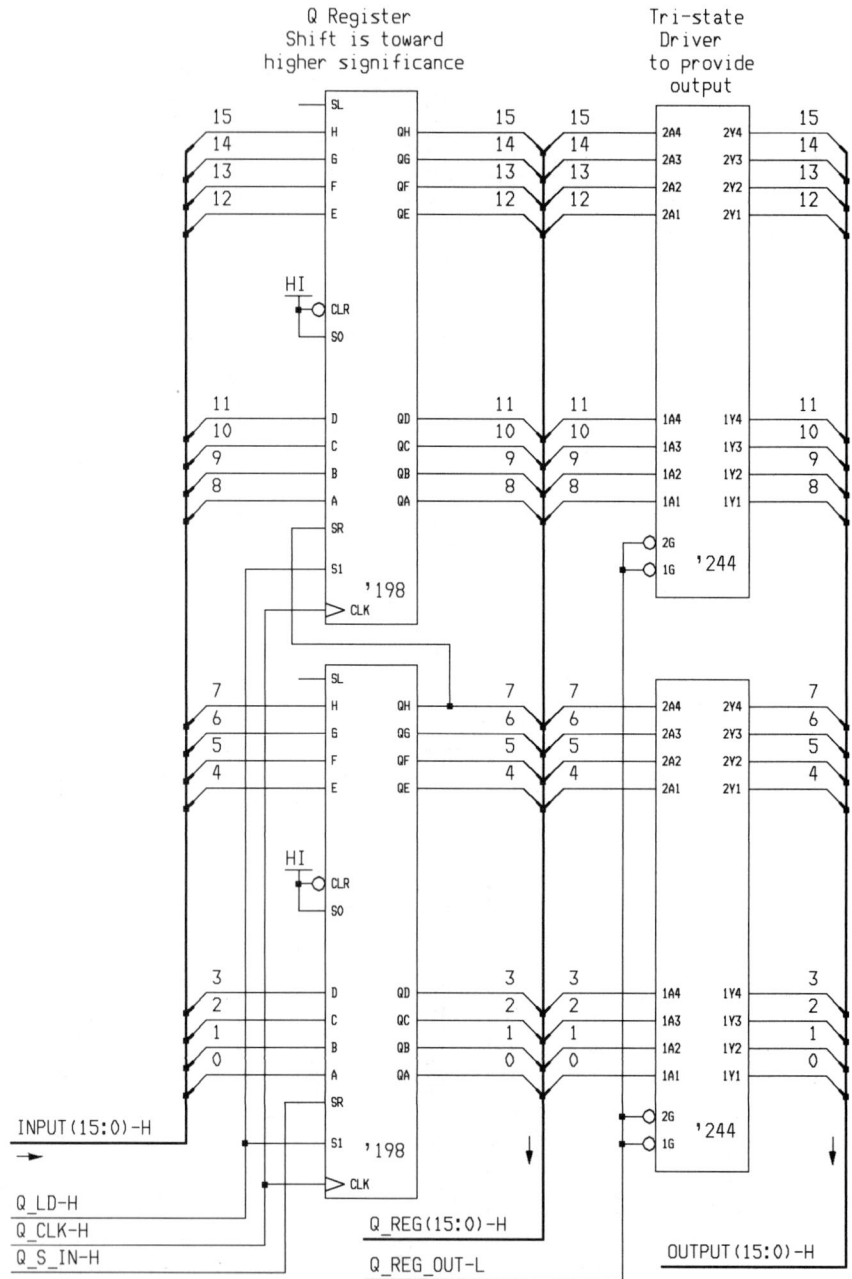

Figure B.5. Logic Diagram of Direct Divide System. Q Register and Output Drivers.

of the Q register (Q_S_IN-H) is provided by the control system, based on the result of the subtraction and the algorithm being used in the division process.

The logic not shown is the control section. The control lines must be appropriately activated to load the values into the divisor register, Q register, and R register to initialize the process. Once the process is started, the control section must appropriately load the R register, and shift both the R register and Q register, as well as provide the correct serial input to the Q register. When the process is completed, the desired outputs (from the R register or the Q register) are asserted on the output bus (OUTPUT(15:0)-H) by the control section.

B.3. Shift Network for Alignment

One of the methods that can be used to align operands by shifting is shown in Figure 3.26. This method uses a set of 2-1 multiplexers to select the appropriate value at each step in the process. Figures B.6 and B.7 show a more detailed version of Figure 3.26, detailing the wiring needed at each set of multiplexers.

The initial set of multiplexers accepts the input (on DATA(23:0)-H) and provides a value to the second set of multiplexers. The value provided is either the original value, or a shifted version of the original value. The selection is made by controlling the A_BY_16-H line. In the diagram the most significant bits of the shifted version are set to zero, but a signed mechanism could be provided by using the most significant bit of the input to determine the appropriate level for the most significant bits of the shifted version. The second set of multiplexers accepts the input from the first, and the output of this set of muxes is either not shifted or shifted by 8. The shifted version will be obtained when the A_BY_8-H control line is asserted; otherwise, the unshifted input is available on the output. This process is repeated in the third set of multiplexers, where a shifted copy of the output of the second stage is available if the A_BY_4-H line is asserted. If the A_BY_4-H line is not asserted, the unshifted copy of the input is available at the output. The number of bit positions shifted here is four.

The final two stages are shown in Figure B.7. These two stages provide a shift of two bits (if the A_BY_2-H line is asserted) and one bit (if the A_BY_1-H line is asserted). The number of stages needed in aligning numbers by this method is determined by the number of bits needed to represent the number of bit positions to shift. In this diagram, the shift has been provided for 24 bits, and $\lceil \log_2 (24) \rceil = 5$. With five control bits, shifts up to 31 bit positions are possible; a system with six multiplexer stages could provide alignment up to 63 bits.

A final observation can be made concerning the alignment requirement and the base of the floating point system involved. With a base two system, alignment must be possible to each bit position, and a system such as shown in Figures B.6 and B.7 is needed. However, with a base 4 system, alignment would only be needed to every other bit position, since 2 bits are required for base 4 digits. Hence, the final stage shown in Figure B.7 would not be needed for a base 4 system. For base 8 systems, the alignment requirement is for base 8 digits, or every 3 bits. For base 16 systems, the alignment requirement is for alignment of base 16 digits, which is every 4 bits. Thus, a base 16 system would not need either of the stages shown in Figure B.7, and for a 24-bit system, only the three stages shown in Figure B.6 would be used. The complexity of the alignment system is directly related to the type of floating point number system being used.

B.4. Horizontal Microcode System

Horizontal microcode receives its name from the fact that the control logic grows "horizontally," and the number of bits in the microinstruction register increases with each control bit needed by the data path. Figure 5.40 shows a diagram of a the logic resulting from a horizontal approach to microcode for the computer system included in Chapter 5. In this section we include the details missing from Figure 5.40. The resulting logic diagrams are shown in Figures B.8 to B.12.

The sequencer section is built around the capabilities of the 2910 sequencer. This device provides address control for up to 12 bits, which will address up to

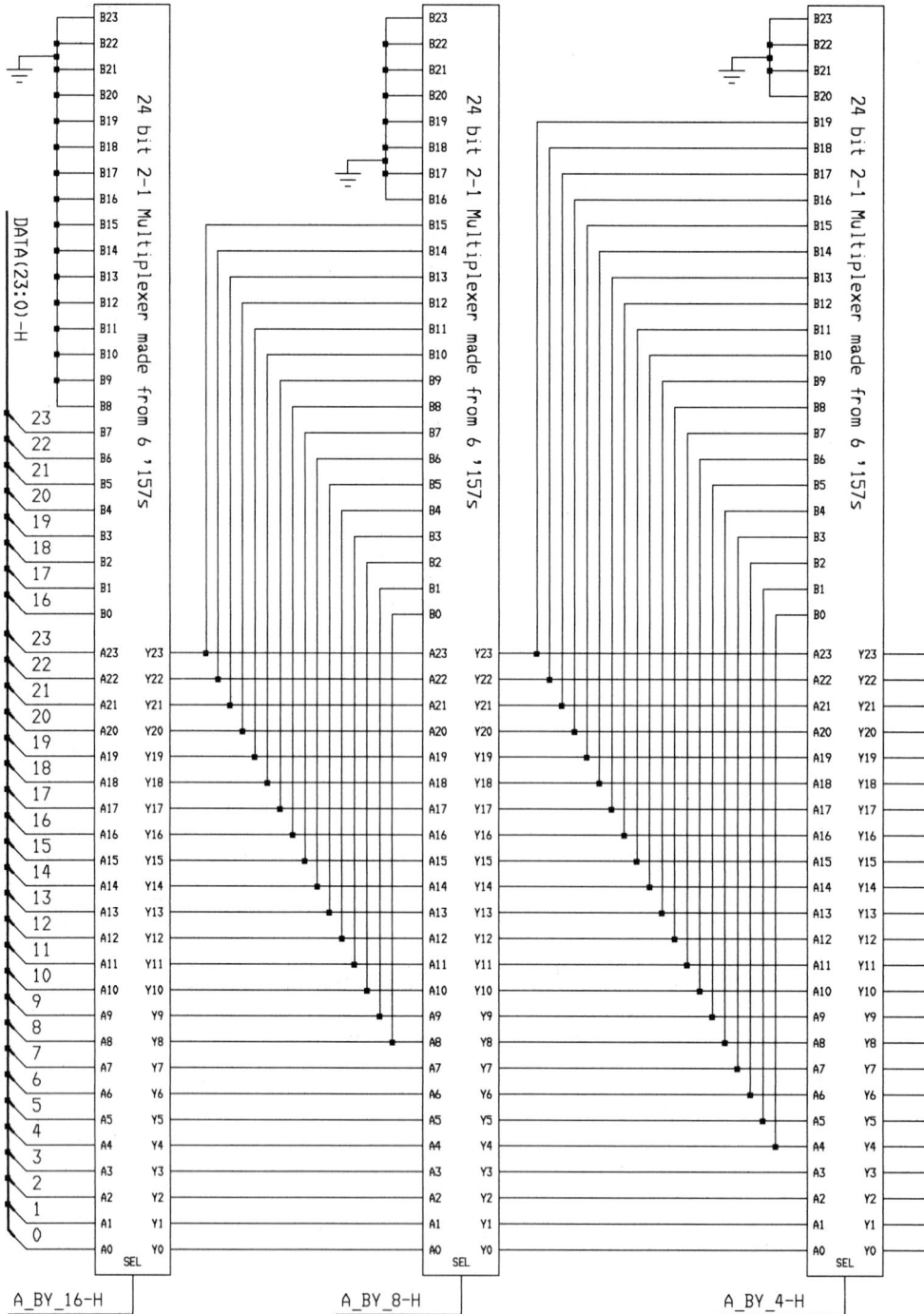

Figure B.6. Logic Diagram of Alignment Network Composed of Multiplexers. Shifts by 16 Bits, 8 Bits, and 4 Bits.

4,096 microcode memory locations. The system shown here uses only ten of those bits, so the microcode address bus (MICODE_ADR(9:0)-H) is shown connected to only ten of the address outputs. If a larger microcode memory is

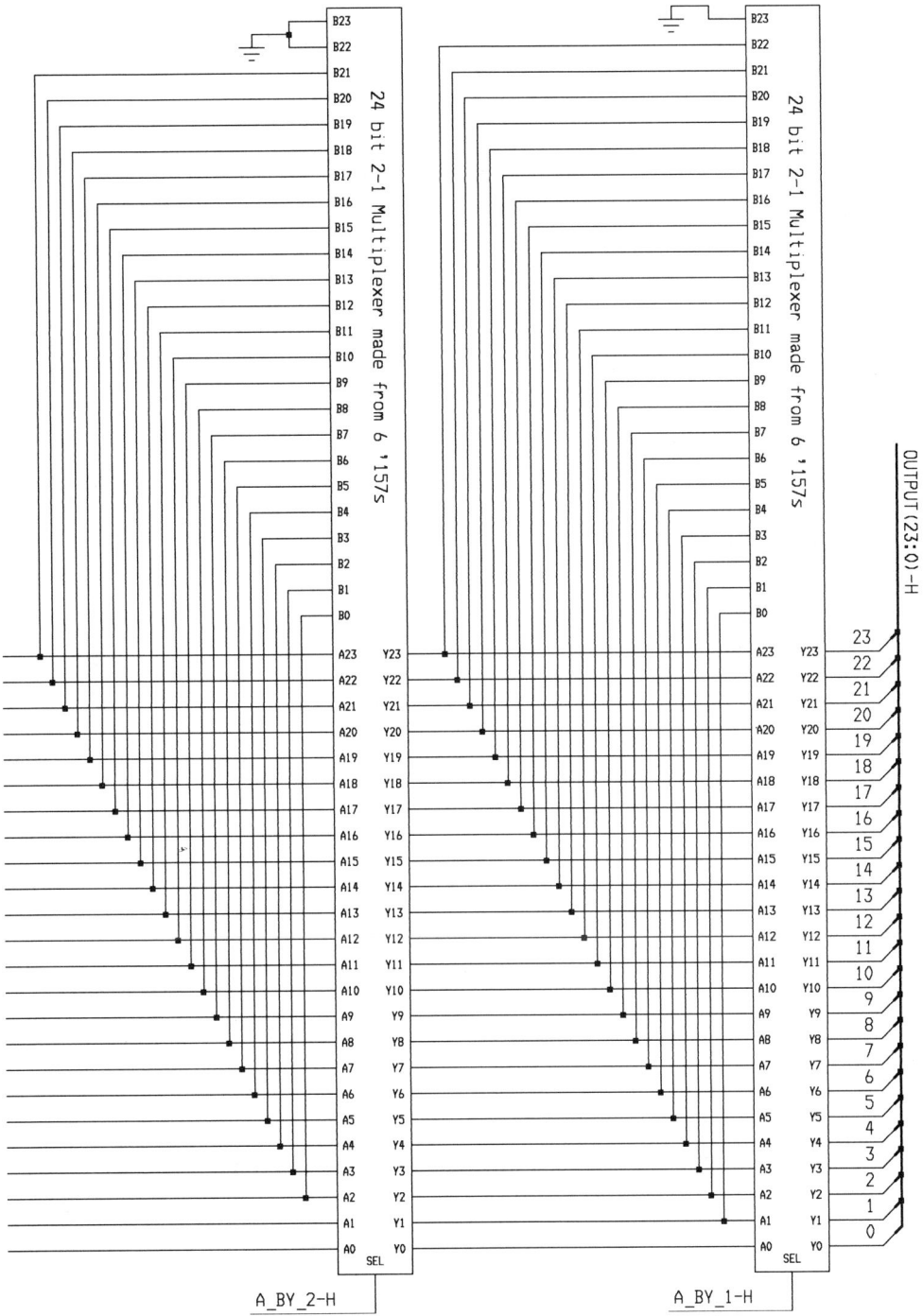

Figure B.7. Logic Diagram of Alignment Network Composed of Multiplexers. Shifts by 2 Bits and 1 Bit.

needed, then more address lines will be required. The 2910 sequencer is capable of normal sequencing (providing the next address in sequence), jumping to an address stored within the 2910 itself, jumping to an address provided on the input

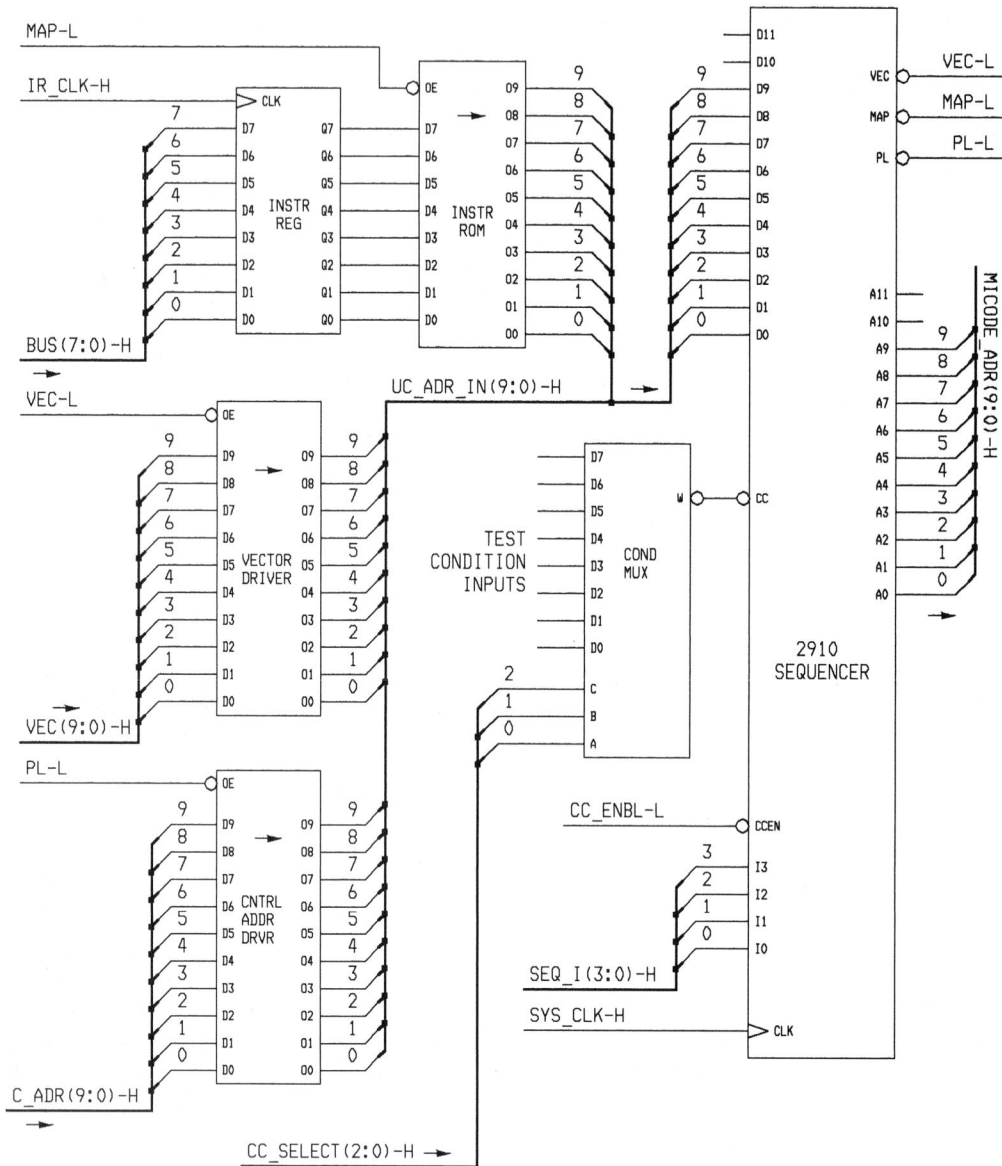

Figure B.8. Logic Diagram for Horizontal Microcode Control. Sequencer Control Logic.

lines for either conditional or unconditional jumps and subroutines, or returning from a subroutine. The path shown in Figure B.8 to provide addresses to the 2910 (UC_ADR_IN(9:0)-H) is capable of providing ten bits of address; for systems with more microcode memory, this path will need to be wider.

The action of the sequencer is controlled by the four instruction lines (SEQ_I(3:0)-H), and the outputs change with the active edge of the clock (SYS_CLK-H). When the instruction lines specify a conditional instruction, such as a conditional jump or a conditional return from subroutine, the conditional action will be enabled if both the condition code enable line (CC_ENBL-L) and the condition code itself (the CC pin on the sequencer) are asserted. The multiplexer connected to the condition code input of the sequencer permits selection of one of

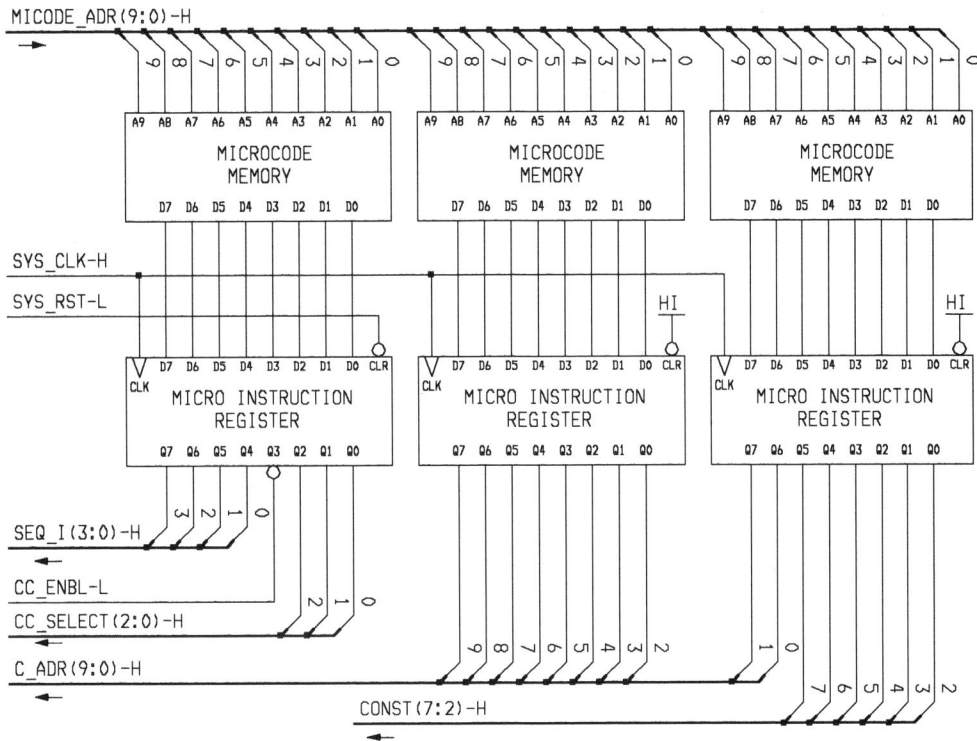

Figure B.9. Logic Diagram for Horizontal Microcode Control. Microcode Memory and Microinstruction Register for Sequencer Control and Constant.

eight different conditions, and the selection is determined by the condition code select lines (CC_SELECT(2:0)-H). More conditions could be handled by a larger multiplexer, which in turn require more select lines.

In addition to the microcode address, three outputs from the sequencer are used in conjunction with the other parts provided in Figure B.8: VEC-L, MAP-L, and PL-L. Only one of these three will be asserted during any clock period, but during every clock period one of them will be asserted. The line asserted is determined by the instruction being executed by the sequencer. These lines can be used as enables that determine the source of the value available at the data inputs of the sequencer. One source of information is the microinstruction register; these ten lines are labeled C_ADR(9:0)-H. The value from the C_ADR lines is available at the data input of the sequencer when the PL-L line is asserted. Another source of information is based on an address provided by the system, called a "vector address." The system identifies a condition that needs attention, and provides the address of a set of microcode (on the VEC(9:0)-H lines) that will handle the situation. When the sequencer is ready to respond to the condition, it asserts the VEC-L line to obtain the address, whereupon the microcode action moves to the new address and continues execution. The tri-state drivers shown both for the path from the microinstruction register (CNTRL ADDR DRVR) and for the vector information (VECTOR DRIVER) are '244s; other tri-state devices with low true enables would function equally well. The other source of address information is enabled when the MAP-L line is asserted. This is shown as an instruction ROM (INSTR ROM), the address of which is provided by an 8-bit register (INSTR REG). This arrangement assumes a mode of operation as follows: an 8-bit instruction is loaded into the instruction register; this is then used as an address into a mapping memory, which provides a microcode address to the sequencer. When the sequencer is ready to do the work needed to perform the instruction, it asserts the MAP-L line and jumps to the address provided by the instruction memory. The instruction ROM is therefore a table look-up mechanism used to provide the microcode address, at which a set of microinstructions can be found to perform the work required by the instruction.

The microcode memory and associated microinstruction register are included in Figures B.9 to B.12. The lines included in Figure B.9 basically control the flow of the microinstructions. The instruction lines to the sequencer (INTSTR(3:0)-H) control the operation of the sequencer. Note that the clear line of the microinstruction register device used to generate the instruction lines has its clear line asserted by the system reset (SYS_RST-L). When all zeros are placed on the instruction lines of the 2910, the result is to force a zero address. Thus, the result of the assertion of system reset is to cause the microcode memory to access location zero, which should be the first instruction required upon initialization. Included in the same register chip as the instruction lines are the condition code enable (CC_ENBL-L) and the condition code select lines (CC_SELECT(2:0)-H). These lines control the behavior of the sequencer when conditional instructions are being executed. The next ten lines are used to provide the address to the sequencer for jumps and subroutines. The remaining lines shown in Figure B.9 are used to allow the control section to place data into the data section. Only 6 of

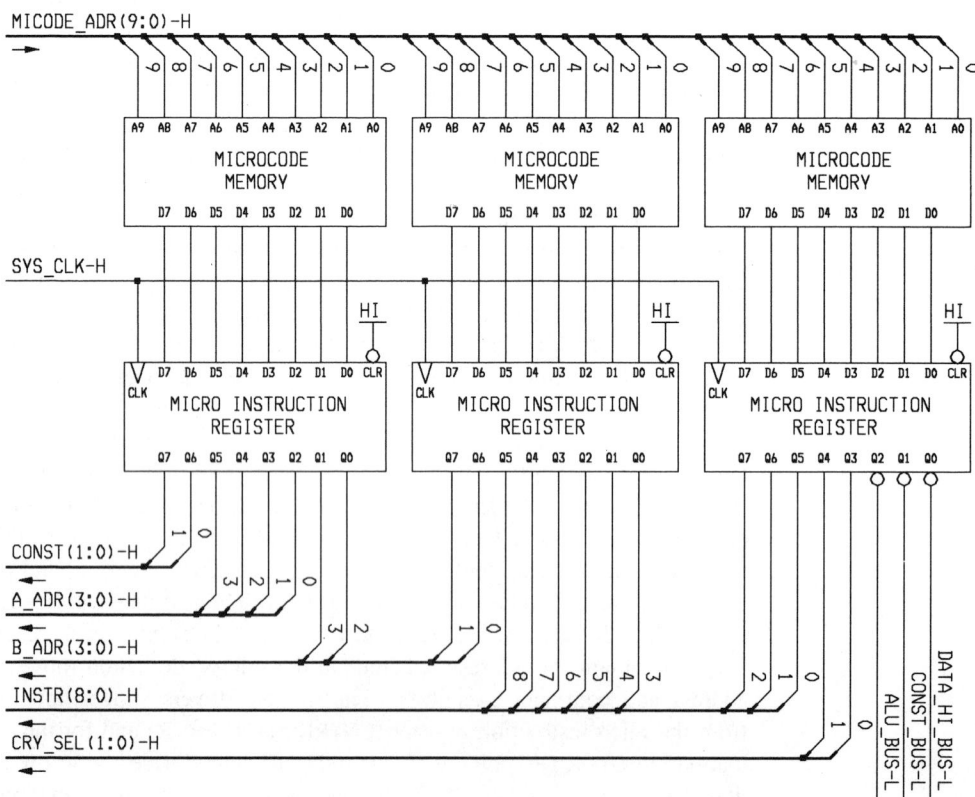

Figure B.10. Logic Diagram for Horizontal Microcode Control. Microcode Memory and Microinstruction Register for ALU Control.

the 8 bits are shown in the figure; the remaining 2 bits are found in Figure B.10. One of the sources of information for the 8-bit system bus is the the information stored in this field, so that constants can be loaded into the registers of the system.

The bits shown in the microcode memory and microinstruction register of Figure B.10 deal mostly with the control of the 2901 processor. Two sets of address lines (A_ADR(3:0)-H and B_ADR(3:0)-H) are used by the sequencer to identify one of sixteen registers internal to the 2901s. Nine instruction lines (INSTR(8:0)-H) are used to control the action of the processor. These instruction lines specify what is to be done with the values extracted from the registers identified (by A_ADR(3:0)-H and B_ADR(3:0)-H), from the internal Q register, or from the data inputs of the 2901. In addition, the instruction lines specify where the results should be stored. The carry select lines (CRY_SEL(1:0)-H) control the carry input to the least significant bit slice processor, as explained in Chapter 5. The remaining lines in Figure B.10 are used to enable values onto the system data bus. Care must be taken to be sure that only one of the enables is asserted in any cycle to prevent damage to the tri-state drivers which are used, as well as to prevent erroneous data as two drivers are enabled simultaneously.

Additional bus enable lines are found in Figure B.11. Also, the lines controlling the action of the devices that receive their information from the bus are included as well. Finally, the control lines used to effect the I/O transfers are included in this figure.

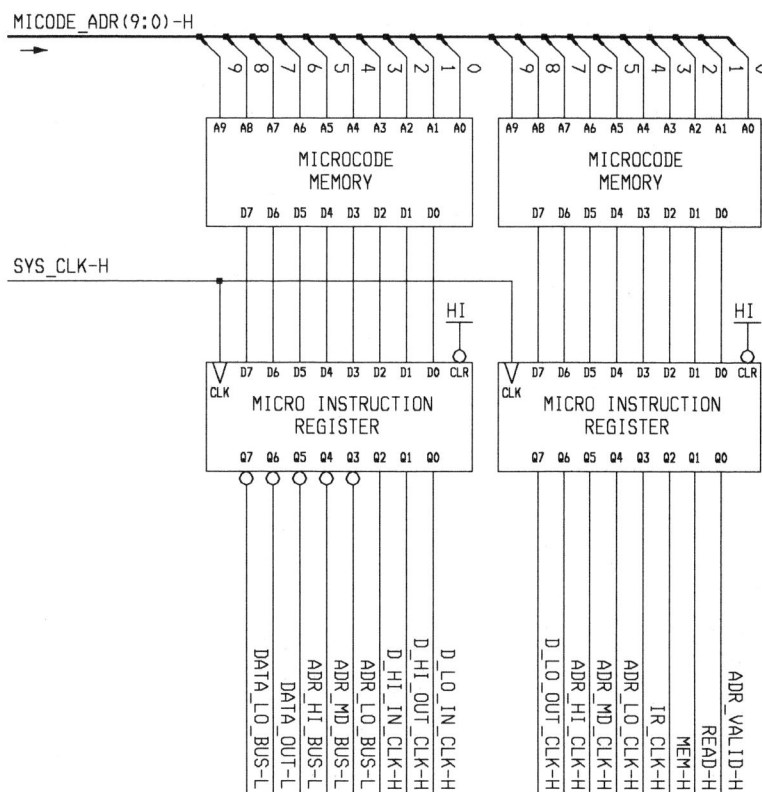

Figure B.11. Logic Diagram for Horizontal Microcode Control. Microcode Memory and Microinstruction Register for Bus Control.

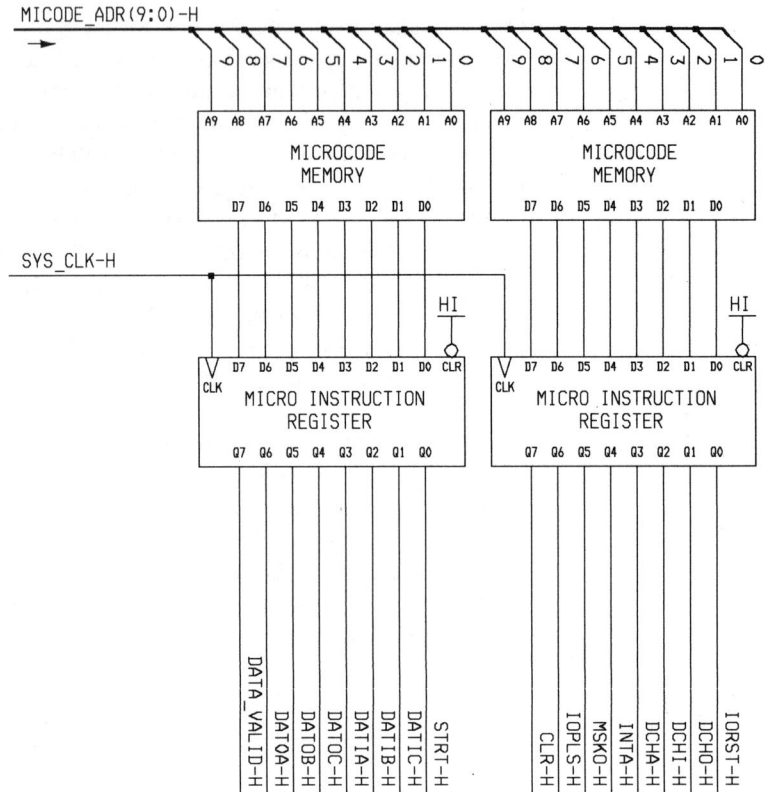

Figure B.12. Logic Diagram for Horizontal Microcode Control. Microcode Memory and Microinstruction Register for I/O Control.

With the horizontal approach, each control line has a dedicated bit in the microinstruction register used to control the action of that device. Therefore, in preparing the microcode used to do work in the system, a designer can identify the levels that should be on each line during a clock cycle and cause that level to be stored in the appropriate location of the microcode memory. As more control lines are required, the microcode memory and the microinstruction register must expand to accommodate them.

B.5. Vertical Microcode System

Vertical microcode receives its name from the fact that the control logic grows "vertically." That is, the number of control lines in the system (the number of bits in the microinstruction register) does not grow with each new control line. Rather, the lines in the microinstruction register are encoded with patterns decoded by logic that is connected to the MIR. This decode logic allows multiple use of the fields and lines making up the microinstruction register, but also slows down the effective speed, since the minor cycle time must now include time for the decode function. With fewer bits in the MIR, fewer memories and instruction register parts are required to build the system. However, more microinstructions may be needed to do the same work of a horizontally organized system. Thus, the growth for added function is "vertical," or more microinstructions, rather than "horizontal," or more control lines.

A vertical implementation of the microcoded system in Chapter 5 is shown in Figure 5.41. Details of this system are shown in the logic diagrams of Figure B.13 to B.15. The sequencer logic shown in Figure B.13 is essentially identical to the sequencer logic of the horizontal system, which is shown in Figure B.8. This is not surprising, since the action of the sequencer control is identical for both systems. The difference between the two systems is apparent when considering the source of information for address information. In Figure B.8, this information is presented on a bus labeled C_ADR(9:0)-H, which has its own field in the microinstruction register. In Figure B.13, the input to the control address driver is derived from a bus labeled CON_LINES(9:0)-H. These lines combine the function

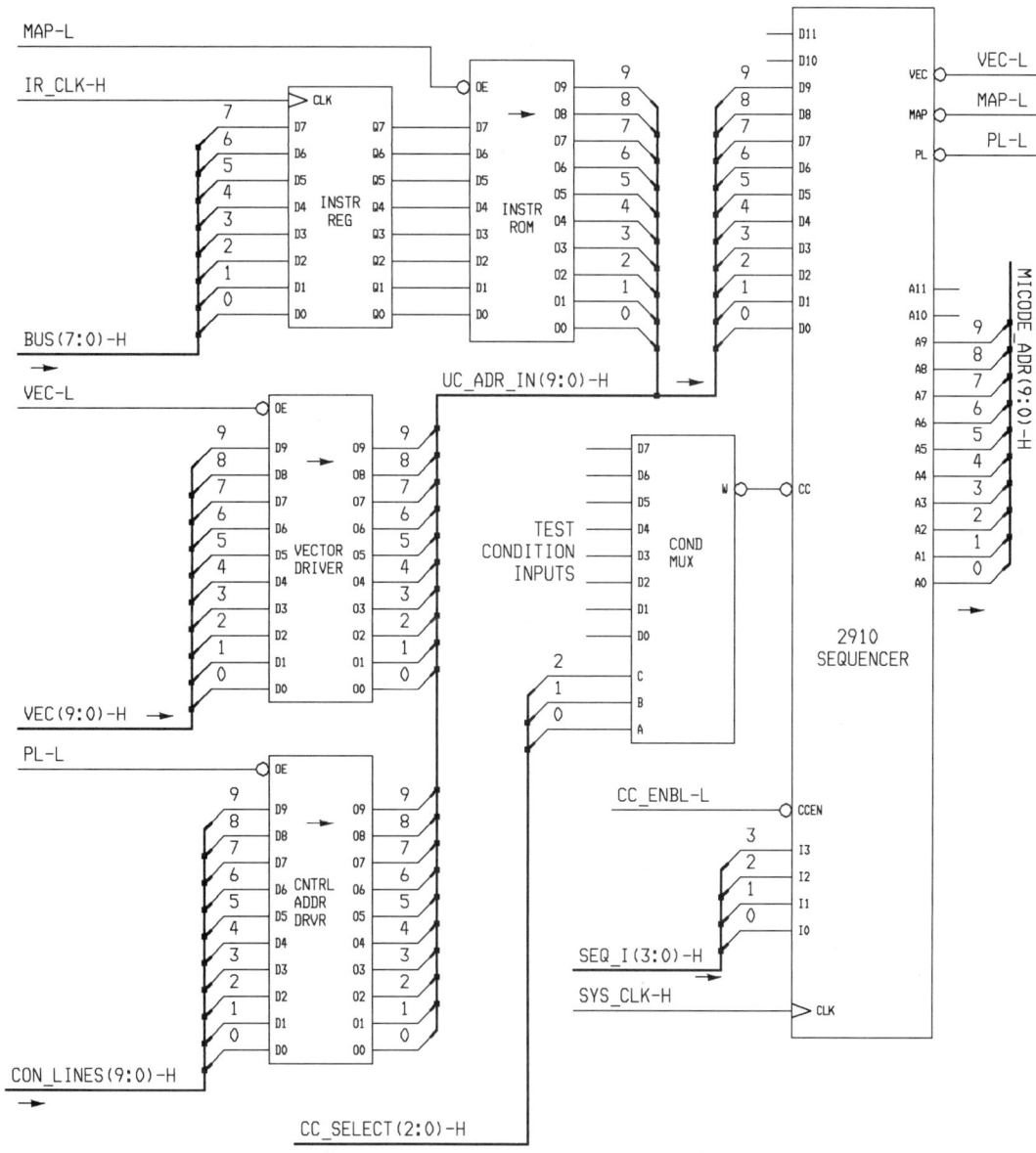

Figure B.13. Logic Diagram for Vertical Microcode Control. Sequencer Control Logic.

of several fields of the horizontal method. As can be seen from Figure B.13, the lines are used to provide an address for jumps or subroutines when needed. In addition, four of the lines (CON_LINES(7:4)-H) are used to provide the A addresses for the 2901s, and another four lines (CON_LINES(3:0)-H) are used to provide the four B address lines for the 2901s. Eight of the lines (CON_LINES(7:0)-H) are used to provide constants to the bus. Finally, two of the lines (CON_LINES(9:8)-H) are used to control the carry selection for the 2901s. The net result is that 27 lines in the horizontal implementation have been replaced by 10 lines in the vertical implementation. However, since the functions have been combined, the lines cannot provide more than one function at a time. For example, an address and a data constant cannot be provided in the same cycle, unless the address and the data happen to be the same. Also, constants cannot be directly moved from the bus to the registers within the 2901. An intermediate register, such as the Q register of the 2901, must be used in the transfer, since the B address lines are also connected to the wires that hold the constant being loaded.

The diminishing of the number of lines needed for implementation of the microcoded system is evident by examining the portion of the microcode memory and microinstruction register shown in Figure B.14. Since the sequencer section

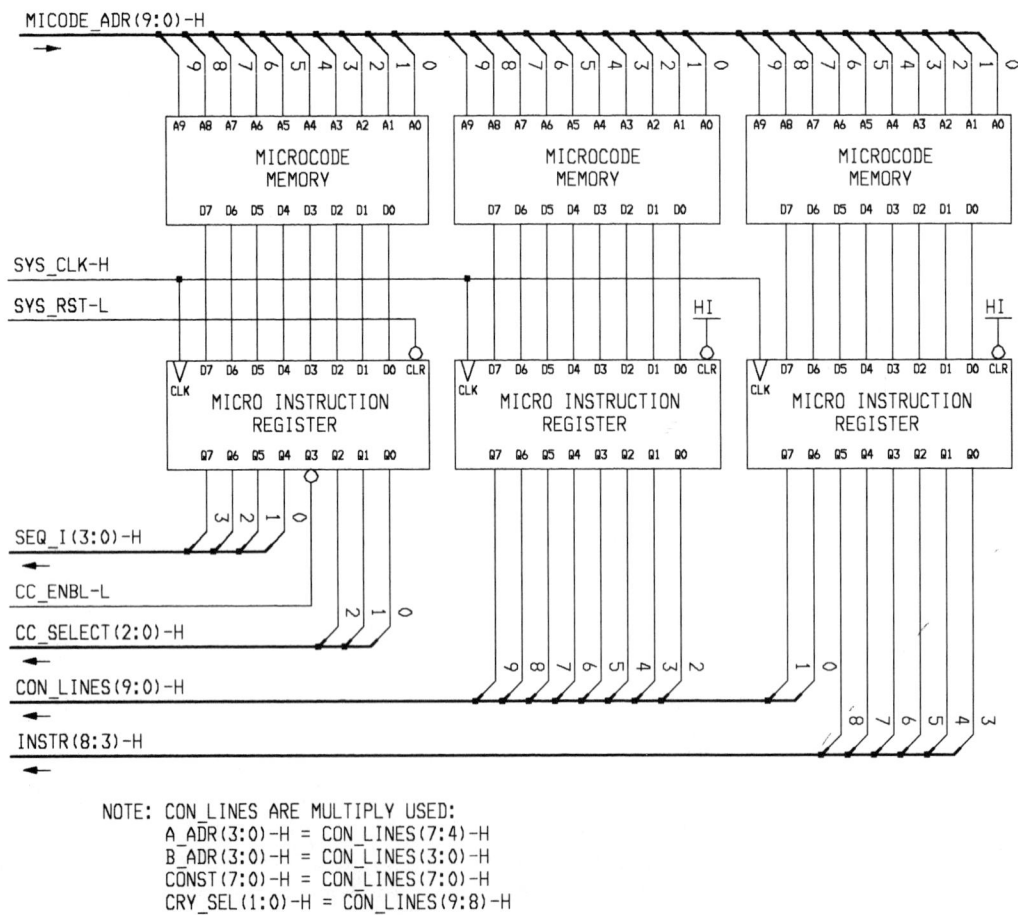

Figure B.14. Logic Diagram for Vertical Microcode Control. Microcode Memory and Microinstruction Register Sequencer and Processor Control.

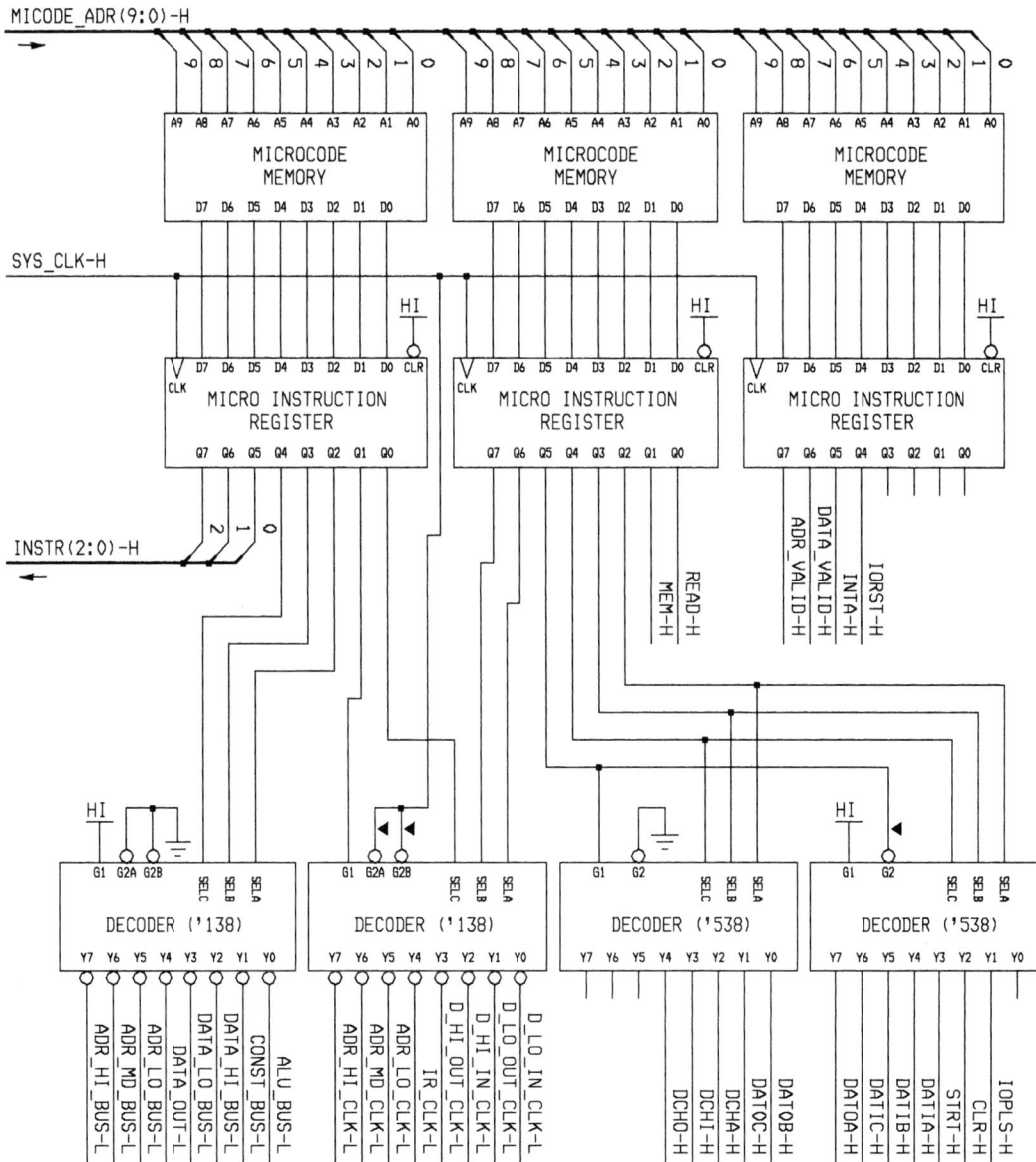

Figure B.15. Logic Diagram for Vertical Microcode Control. Microcode Memory and Microinstruction Register for System Bus and I/O Control.

is identical to the horizontal system, the sequencer instruction lines (SEQ_I(3:0)-H), as well as the condition code enable (CC_ENBL-L) and the condition code select lines (CC_SELECT(2:0)-H), are the same as the horizontal system. This includes the initialization mechanism provided for the system by clearing the first element of the microinstruction register. However, as explained above, the CON_LINES are used to provide several functions, and these are shown in Figure B.14. The next lines are the instruction lines for the processor. Figure B.14 contains six of these lines (INSTR(8:3)-H), and Figure B.15 contains the remaining three (INSTR(2:0)-H).

The remaining elements of the microcode memory and the microinstruction register are included in Figure B.15. Three of the bits are used to select one of eight possible sources of information for the system bus. Since the 3-line-to-8-line decoder is always enabled, information is always enabled onto the bus. An additional 3 bits are used to identify the destination of the information on the bus. However, four lines are used for this function: 3 bits select which of the eight possible destinations is to be the target of the transfer, and 1 bit is used to enable the function. Note also that SYS_CLK-H is connected to the low true enable of the decoder. This has the effect of causing the assertion of the appropriate clock signal only during the last half of a clock cycle. Thus, any glitches that would occur because the of the real nature of the decoder will not be transferred to the outputs, since the outputs are enabled only after the inputs have been allowed to stabilize in the first half of the cycle. Note also that these clock lines will be connected, in general, to clock lines that cause action on the low to high transition of the clock. Therefore, transferring information from one register to another is accomplished by asserting both the enable signal and the clock signal in the same cycle: the enable line causes the data to become stable on the bus, and then at the end of the cycle the low to high transition loads the data into the destination register.

The remaining bits of the microinstruction register shown in Figure B.15 are used to provide the I/O functions. The signals that can be created in a mutually exclusive manner are generated by decoding four bits of the MIR. The decoders used to perform this action are '538s, instead of the '138s, which are used elsewhere. The reason for this is that the '538s can be configured to provide a high assertion level, which is required by the function being performed. Another observation is that no enable is provided for the decoders used to create the mutually exclusive signals. However, if all four of the lines are low, then the asserted line is not connected, and this action effectively leaves the I/O lines in a quiescent state. In addition to the 4 bits required for the mutually exclusive signals, six lines are used to provide the remainder of the functions.

B.6. Tape Recorder Interface System

In Chapter 6 a tape recorder interface is discussed, and the basic diagrams for this interface appear in Figure 6.18. Details of the logic to implement this interface are given in Figures B.16 to B.25. In the paragraphs that follow we will discuss the various aspects of the interface design, and describe some of the details of the interface system.

The UNIBUS interface contains 16 data lines and 18 address lines. However, in Figure B.16 the buffered bus address (BADDR(23:0)-H) is shown with 24 address lines. As the amount of real memory available increases in computer systems the number of address lines required will continue to increase. The 18 address lines of the UNIBUS only allow direct access to 256 Kbytes of memory; the 24 address lines shown in Figure B.16 permit access to 16 Mbytes of memory. Newer systems contain address buses with 32 address lines, which allow access to 4 Gbytes of memory. The type of interface bus used to communicate with the I/O devices will determine the number of address lines that must be included for the address comparisons shown in Figure B.16.

The devices shown in Figure B.16 for address comparison are '520s, which provide a comparison of 8 bits. The P lines are connected to the buffered address bus, while the Q lines are connected to switches that allow the specification of the

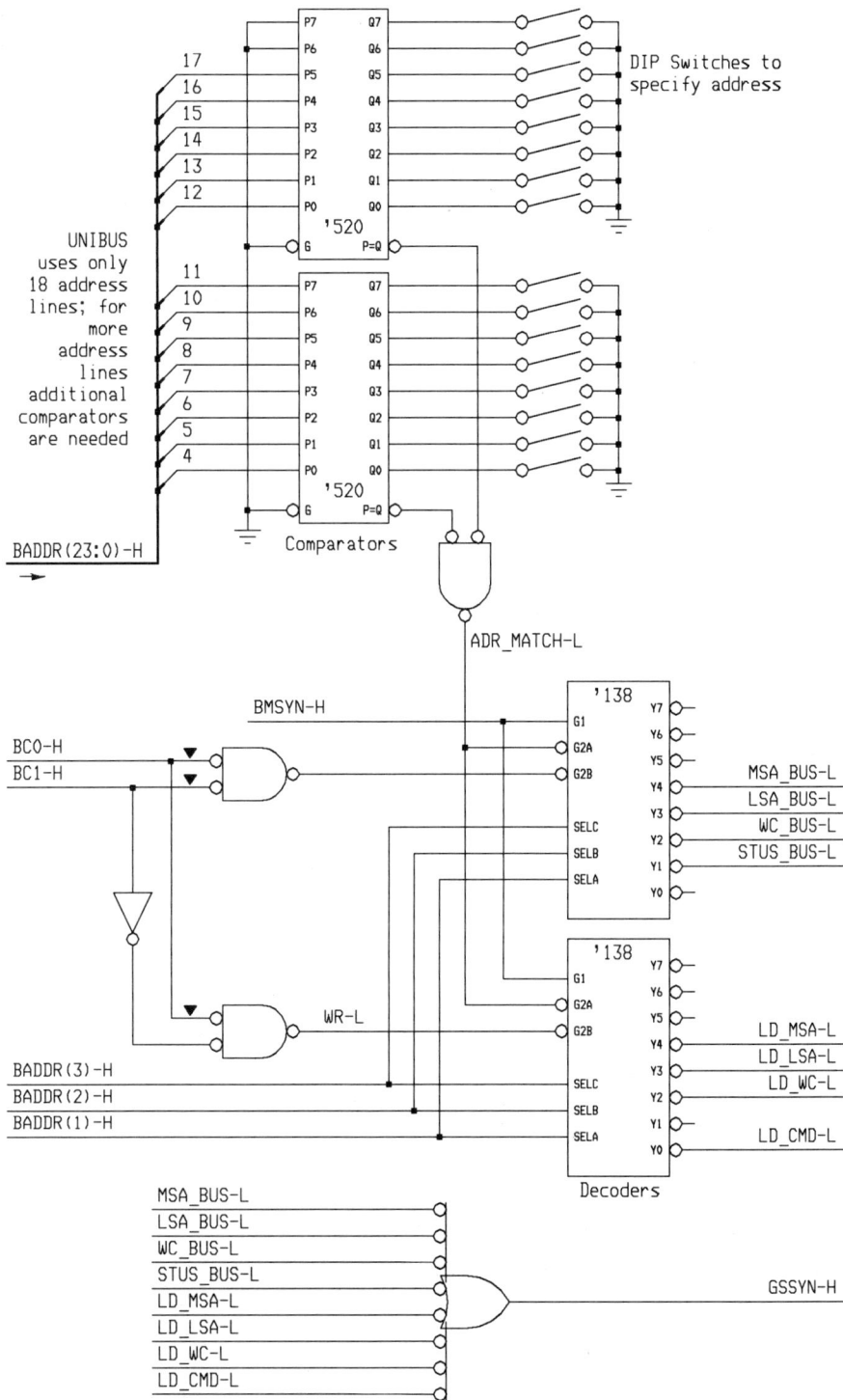

Figure B.16. Logic Diagram Tape Recorder Interface System. Address Decode and Programmed I/O Signal Generation.

address that will be utilized by the interface to be done at installation time, rather than at design time. Also, the Q lines contain internal pullup resistors used to guarantee a high level when the switch is open; this removes the need for resistors connected to the switches themselves, and reduces the number of parts needed. When the address available on the buffered address bus matches the address entered in the switches, the address match line (ADR_MATCH-L) will be asserted, enabling the action of the decoders. Note that the address lines directed to the decoders do not include the least significant address line (BADDR(0)-H); this interface assumes that the interaction is aligned on word boundaries, and that the least significant line would not be required. The type of bus interaction (read or write) to be used is determined by the BC0-H and BC1-H lines, which are buffered versions of the C1 and C0 lines available on the UNIBUS. The bus transfer type is identified by these lines as follows:

Control Lines		Type of Transfer
C1	*C0*	
0	0	DATI (read)
0	1	DATIP (read, to be followed by DATO)
1	0	DATO (write)
1	1	DATOB (write, byte)

The only transactions we are going to recognize with this simple interface are DATI and DATO transactions, and so the two OR gates used in an ANDing function in Figure B.16 are used to appropriately enable the two decoders. Thus, if the address matches, and it is a DATI transaction, then when the request is asserted, the read decoder is enabled. If the address matches and it is a DATO transaction, then the write decoder is enabled when the request is asserted. Thus, when the request line is asserted (buffered master sync, or BMSYN-H), the appropriate action is taken. The action is identified in the following table:

Address	Read Action	Signal Name	Write Action	Signal Name
xxx0	None		Load command register	LD_CMD-L
xxx1	Read status register	STUS_BUS-L	None	
xxx2	Read word count	WC_BUS-L	Load word count	LD_WC-L
xxx3	Read LSB of address	LSA_BUS-L	Write LSB of address	LD_LSA-L
xxx4	Read MSB of address	MSA_BUS-L	Write MSB of address	LD_MSA-L

Note that, when any of the signals listed in the table are asserted, the NAND gate used in an ORing function generates GSSYN-H. This signal causes assertion of the bus line SSYN L, which is the correct handshake response to the bus master.

The command register and the control line drivers for the tape recorder interface are shown in Figure B.17. The command register actually consists of two portions: command register A and command register B. Command register A is loaded from the buffered data bus by a programmed I/O instruction; thus it is not synchronous with the clock of the interface. Command register B is used by the state machine controller, and is loaded by the system clock so that the contents change synchronously with the changes made by the state machine. Command register A accepts the 8 least significant bits of the bus. The action of filling the register also sets a flag (CMD_FLAG-H), which will be tested by the

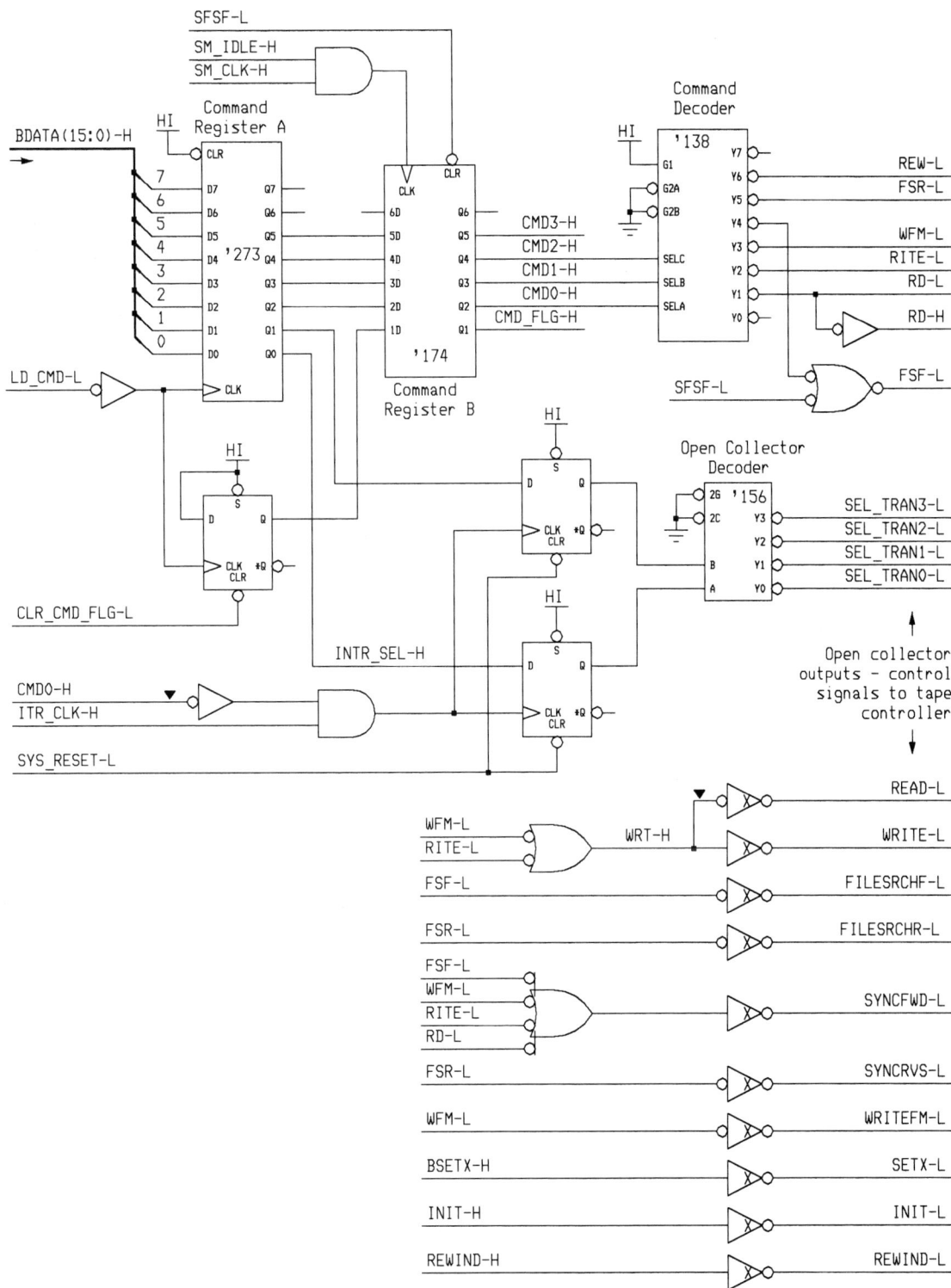

Figure B.17. Logic Diagram Tape Recorder Interface System. Command Register and Tape Control Lines.

state machine directing the interaction with the tape controller. The 4 bits of the command register that identify the desired function, as well as the command flag, are input to a 6-bit register ('174); the register is clocked by the state machine whenever the system is in an idle state. This has two purposes. As mentioned above, one reason is to synchronize the filling of the command register with the clock of the state machine system. Without this mechanism the system would fail when the contents of the command register changed during the sensitive time before the active edge of the state machine clock. The second reason for the second register is to prevent any change in the command register from affecting a function in progress. Associated with the command register in Figure B.17 is the selection of the active transport. This information is taken directly from the two least significant bits of the command register into flip-flops, which are decoded by a '156; the '156 is an open collector device, and hence directly compatible with the tape controller.

The contents of the command register determine the command currently being executed. Thus, 3 bits are directed to a '138, which will identify the command; these are then gated together in an appropriate fashion and sent to the tape controller through open collector drivers. Note that the controller is informed of a synchronous forward command (SYNCFWD) whenever the command register contains a file space forward (FSF) command, a write file mark (WFM) command, a write (RITE) command, or a read (RD) command. The appropriate action will not be initiated until the SETX signal is asserted by the state machine. The open collector devices driving the control lines of the recorder interface are also included in Figure B.17.

The word count register is shown in Figure B.18. Both the word count and the address registers have been implemented with 8-bit up/down counters ('869). These are synchronous load, synchronous count registers, and thus two clocking sources must be provided. When the state machine is idle, SM_IDLE will be asserted, and the clock is derived from the programmed I/O signals. However, when the state machine is not idle, the word count register is decremented by a signal from the state machine itself (WC_DEC-L). Also, when the state machine is idle, the control lines are configured to load the counter; otherwise, the unit is configured to count down. One feature of the system that will not be used in the normal action of transfers is the ability to read the contents of the word count register. This is provided by the tri-state drivers ('541) included with the word count register; when the enable signal is asserted (WC_BUS-L) the information in the word count register is enabled onto the internal data bus (BDATA) and then to the UNIBUS.

The address register is shown in Figure B.19. The UNIBUS address space includes only 18 bits; however, the circuitry shown is for a 24-bit address. This would be useful for machines that use a larger address space. Note that the 24-bit register could easily be extended to include 32 bits. One not so obvious thing in the diagram is the treatment of the least significant bit. When the address (ADR_OUT(23:0)-H) is buffered to the bus, it is shifted by 1 bit, so that the least significant bit is forced to 0. We are assuming that the system will always be aligned to a 16-bit boundary, and this action allows the counters, which increment by one, to be used in the byte-addressable environment. As with the word count register, the clocking for the registers is derived from the state machine for incrementing and from the programmed I/O signals for loading. In addition to the address, which is to be buffered and asserted onto the address bus, the output of the register is also available to the data bus (BDATA(15:0)-H) to be read under

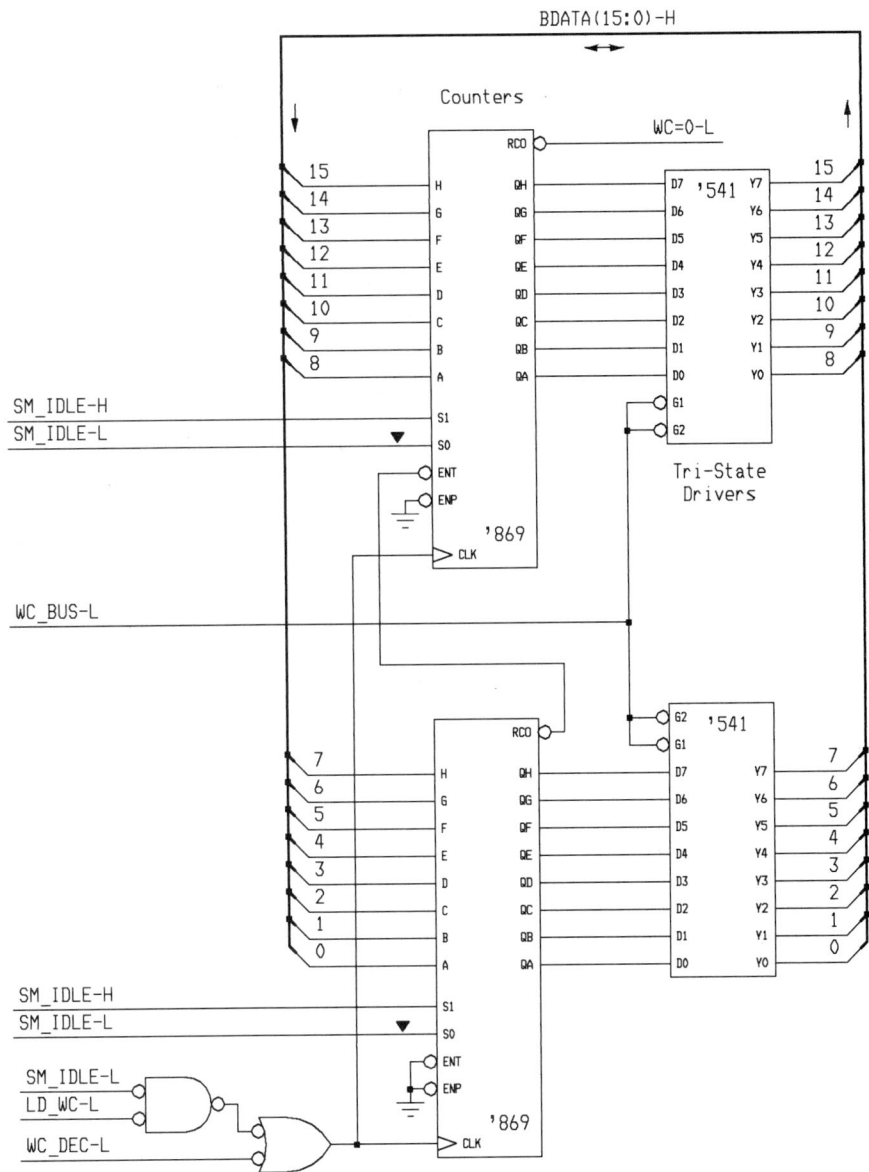

Figure B.18. Logic Diagram Tape Recorder Interface System. Word Count Register.

program control. Since the assumption here is a 16-bit system, loading and reading the register must be done with two transfers. Loading the 16 least significant bits is accomplished by asserting LD_LSA-L, and loading the 8 most significant bits is accomplished by asserting LD_MSA-L. Similarly, reading the least significant 16 bits is accomplished by asserting LSA_BUS-L; reading the most significant 8 bits occurs when MSA_BUS-L is asserted.

The data path is included in Figure B.20. The path to and from the bus is provided by a pair of bidirectional registers ('646). These devices contain two registers, one for each direction. During a write operation, information from the bus is obtained 16 bits at a time, and loaded into the register by a signal derived from the request line (DMA_OUT_CLK-L). The NAND gate generating the signal

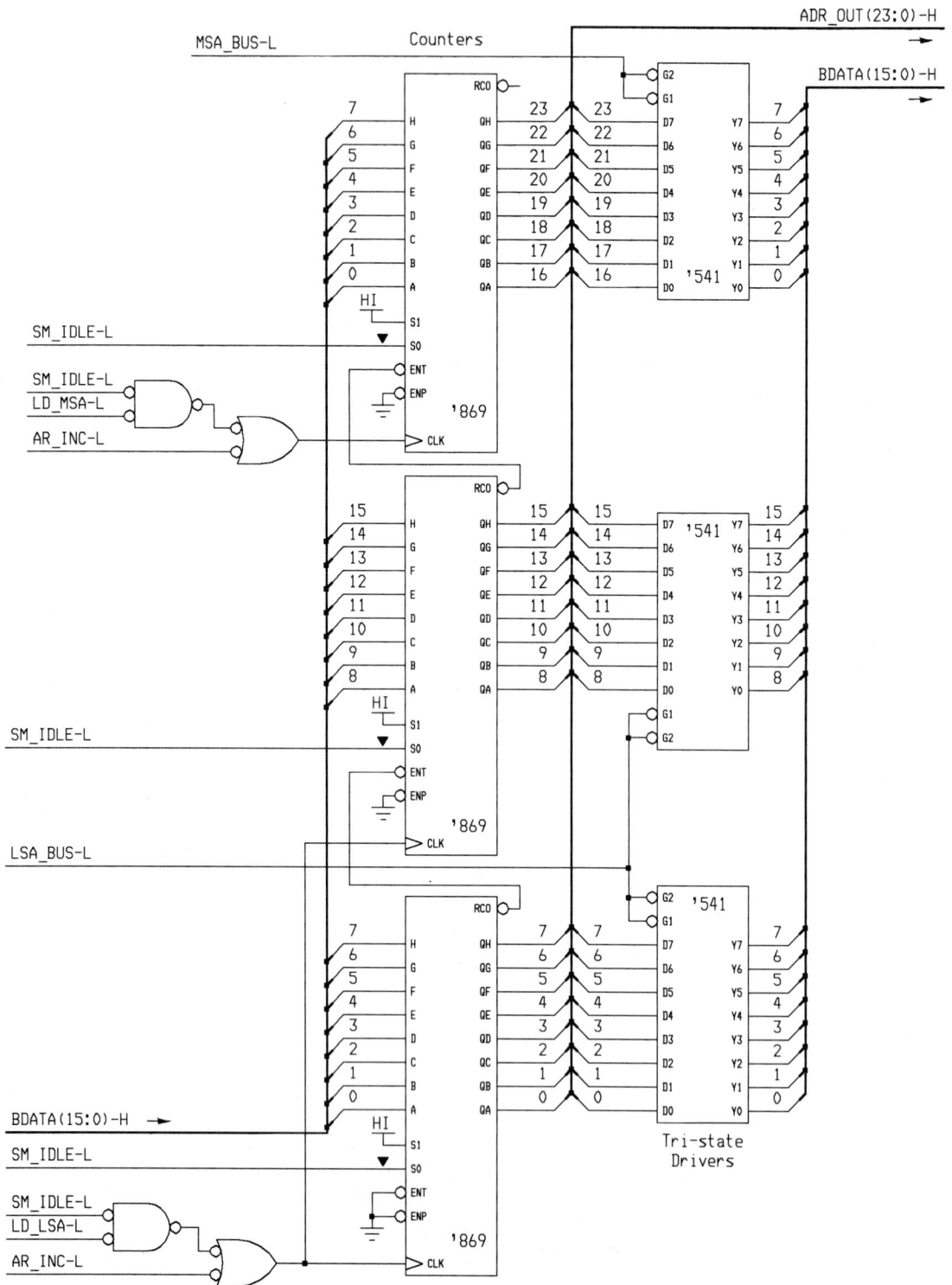

Figure B.19. Logic Diagram Tape Recorder Interface System. Address Register.

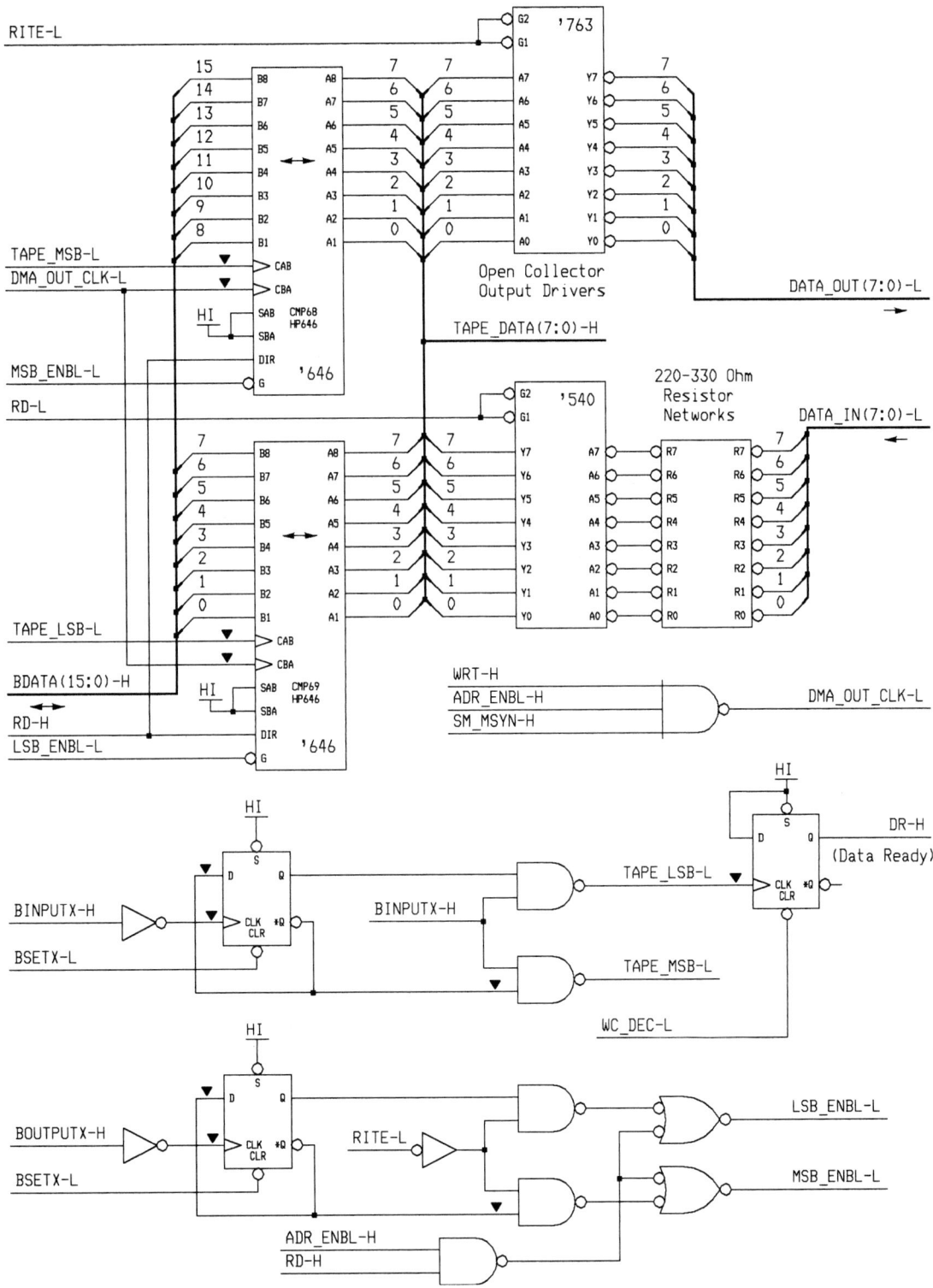

Figure B.20. Logic Diagram Tape Recorder Interface System. Data Exchange Interface Logic.

is asserted when it is a write function, the address has been enabled onto the bus, and the request line has been asserted. When the request line is unasserted, the clock line (DMA_OUT_CLK-L) makes a low to high transition, and the data is latched into the registers. This information is then fed 1 byte at a time to the controller, using the TAPE_DATA lines. The selection of the byte to send to the controller is handled by the enable lines (LSB_ENBL-L, MSB_ENBL-L), which are alternately enabled during a write operation. The logic to accomplish this is located at the bottom of the diagram.

During a read operation, the data path is reversed. The registers contained in the '646 used for the reverse direction are loaded by signals derived from the control lines of the tape controller (TAPE_MSB-L, TAPE_LSB-L). The timing for these signals is derived from the control lines from the tape controller. The resulting values are enabled onto the data bus whenever the address enable (ADR_ENBL-H) line is asserted by the DMA control circuitry, and it is a read function. This places the data onto the UNIBUS at the same time that the address is asserted, which will allow the appropriate slave device to accept the data. As noted earlier, the data lines to the controller are asserted with open collector drivers (note the '763, which not only provides the open collector capability, but also the inversion needed), and the lines from the controller are received with resister networks. The state machine controller is responsible for asserting the appropriate information onto the TAPE_DATA(7:0)-H lines, either from the DMA output registers ('646) or from the data input lines (through the '540).

The status register is included in Figure B.21. The 10 least significant bits of this information, as well as the most significant bit, can be derived directly from the information provided form the tape controller. These lines from the tape controller are fed into resister networks and the inverting buffer. The other bits are obtained from information present in the interface itself. The interrupt enable bit is a value contained in a flip-flop that is reset with the system reset, and otherwise derived from the least significant bit of the command register (INTR_SEL-H) at the appropriate time. This time is determined by the instruction in the command register, which will identify either the transport select function (1000xx) or the interrupt selection function (10010x). The error bit identifies the condition that the number of words read from the tape does not agree with the expected number of words. It is reset at the beginning of each motion command, and set only if an error is detected. Finally, the state machine idle bit can be interrogated to identify if the state machine itself is busy. Note that the signals are maintained in a register with a tri-state output capability ('374). The mechanism shown for the clock and enable line will cause the current value of all of the status bits to be loaded into the register when a request is made to read the status bits (by STUS_BUS-L). This prevents any change in the individual status bits to propagate to the bus during a read operation.

In addition to the status register bits, Figure B.21 also contains the buffers needed for some of the control signals coming from the tape controller. INPUTX is a clock signal that identifies when the controller is accepting a byte, and the next byte can be supplied. Likewise, OUTPUTX is a clock signal that identifies when data is available for the interface. DSTP is a signal that identifies when the command has been completed, and the transport will begin to stop. And FLCL is a signal asserted when the selected transport is slowing down, and the interface can proceed to the idle state. These signals are buffered and supplied to flip-flops that act as edge detectors. The outputs of the edge detectors are used by the state machine to determine the logical sequence of control signals.

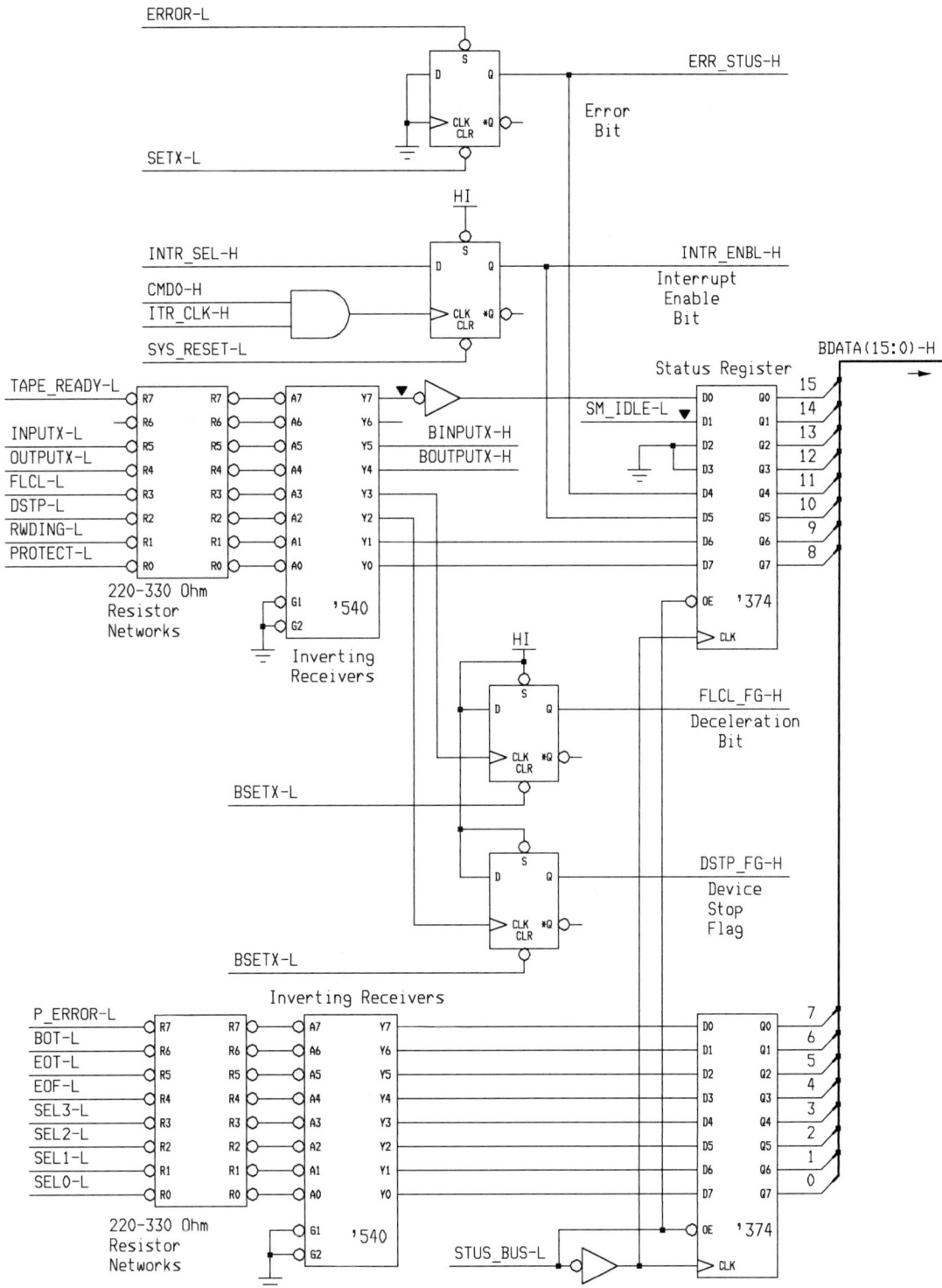

Figure B.21. Logic Diagram Tape Recorder Interface System. Status Register Logic.

Some of the logic for controlling the interface is shown in Figure B.22, which contains one of the two state machines used in this implementation. The state machine controller shown in Figure B.22 is for the action of the interface itself; the other state machine is shown in Figure B.23 (page 483) and controls the DMA interaction. The controller specification calls for command pulses that are a minimum of 200 nsec. For that reason, the state machine controlling the action of the interface is clocked at 5 MHz, which provides a 200 nsec state time. The state diagrams describing the behavior of the system are included as Figures B.26 and B.27, and in some paragraphs that follow we will describe in detail the action they specify. The interface control state machine is constructed from two registered PROMs, each of which contains 2,048 words of 8 bits. This requires 11 bits of address. Five of the 11 bits are provided by the present state of the system; the remaining 6 bits are derived from the inputs to the system. Fourteen different inputs provide information needed by the state machine, and the appropriate six are selected by using two multiplexers. The outputs of the registered PROMs provide the needed control and state information. The two devices together have sixteen outputs; five of these are used for present state information, and eleven are used for control signals. These signals control the function of the device as follows:

Signal	Function
BSETX-H	The tape controller initiates a prescribed action, except for rewind.
INIT-H	This signal is used by the tape controller to initialize internal conditions and reset flags.
REWIND-H	This signal must be held for 2 μsec; it causes the selected transport to rewind to load point.
DO_DMA-H	When the action of the interface necessitates a direct memory data transfer or an interrupt cycle, this signal will be asserted.
DR_CLR-L	Clears the data ready flag.
ERROR-L	Sets the record length error bit for the status register.
SFSF-L	This is a special file space forward signal. When the action of the interface needs a special file space forward action, this signal will be asserted.
WC_DEC-L	Decrement the contents of word count register.
AR_INC-L	Increment the contents of the address register.
CLR_CMD_FLG-L	Assertion of this signal will cause the command flag to be cleared, as well as the contents of the command register.
ITR_CLK-H	This signal is used to clock either the transport select flip-flops or the interrupt enable flip-flop, depending on the value in the command register.

The action supplied by some of the lines is modified by the state of the system; note that ITR_CLK-H is used for both the interrupt enable function (in Figure B.16) and the transport select function (in Figure B.21). It is possible to add another PROM, with its eight outputs, to remove this condition. Such a device could contain bits for SM_IDLE-H, separate bits for interrupt and transport select functions, separate bits for clearing the command flag and the command register, and so on. The designer is faced with the choice of mechanism: additional parts

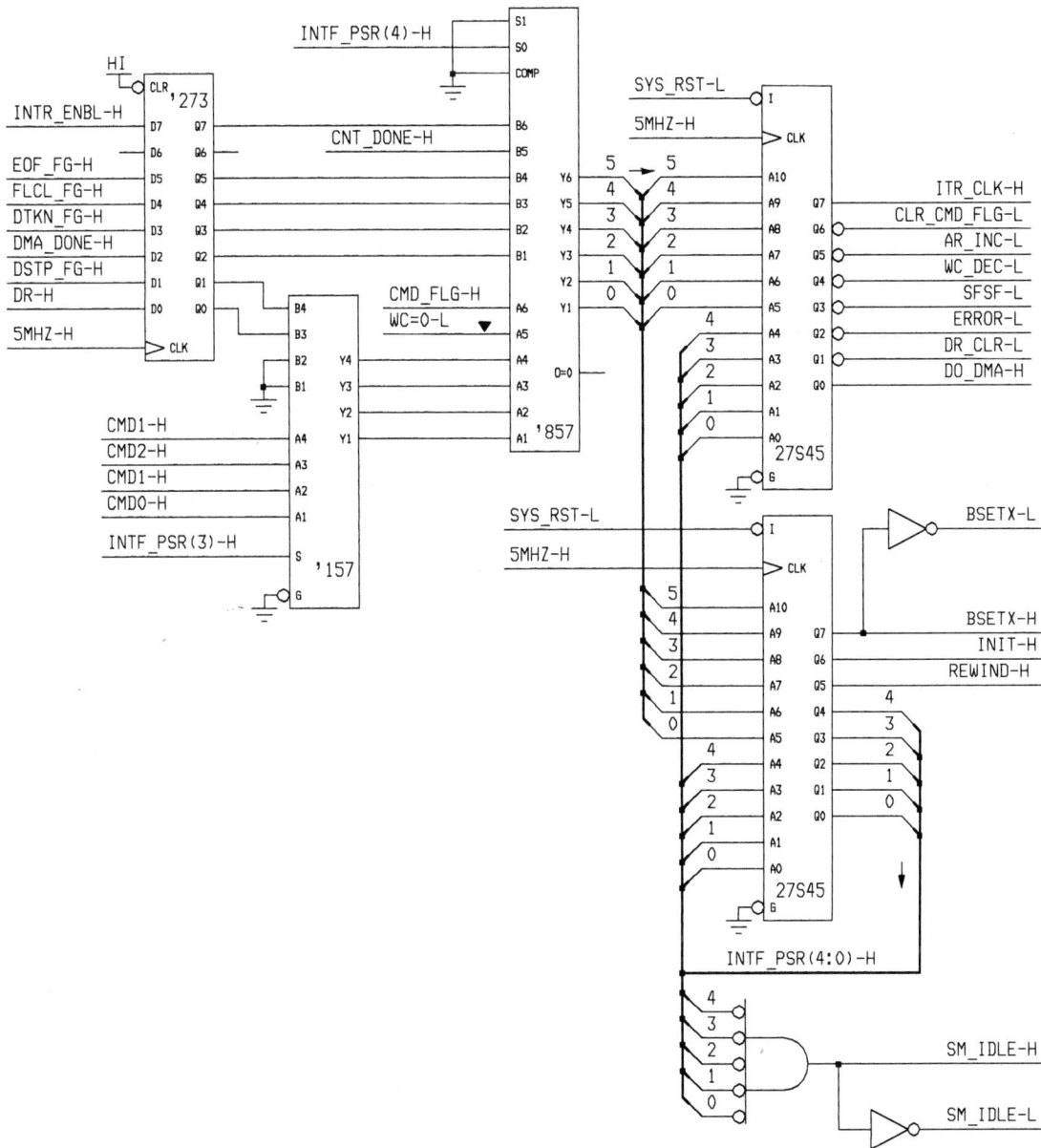

Figure B.22. Logic Diagram Tape Recorder Interface System. Control System State Machine Logic.

will allow more specialized control over the system; fewer parts result in a smaller system that may provide all necessary functions.

The state machine used for DMA and interrupt requests is shown in Figure B.23. This consists of two parts: a synchronizing register ('174) and a registered PAL (16R8). These parts need to be capable of fairly high speed, since the cycle time for the unit is 50 nsec. The function of the DMA controller is to control the interaction with the bus for direct access to memory. The appropriate action is described by the state diagram in Figure B.27, which is detailed below. The control outputs of the state machine are:

Signal	Function
DMA_PSR(2:0)-H	These lines identify the present state of the controller. They allow up to eight different states in the system definition. The lines are fed back internally to be used as inputs in the system.
SM_MSYN-H	The request line for the bus interaction; this is generated by the interface system and buffered to the bus.
SM_ADR_ENBL-H	Address enable; this line is asserted when the address is to be enabled to the UNIBUS; for interrupt cycles, the address is not needed.
SM_SACK-H	Selection acknowledge. In the process of obtaining control of the bus, this signal is used to signal the arbitration unit that it is ready to command the bus. Buffered to the bus.
SM_BBSY-H	Bus busy. When this interface has control of the bus, this signal is asserted to prevent other bus interface devices from asserting bus control lines. The signal is also inverted and used to clear the DMA request.
DMA_REQ_CLR-L	DMA request clear. When the request for the DMA or interrupt action has been recognized, this signal is asserted to clear the request.

Also included with the control circuitry are some flags that handle communication between the two state machines, and a timer used to create a rewind signal that is longer than 2 µsec.

The circuitry contained in Figure B.24 forms part of the interface buffers needed to connect to the bus. The address and data buses are buffered coming into the interface, as well as going from the interface. Also, the interrupt vector address can be specified. Other bus protocols will contain different mechanisms for supplying the interrupt information.

The devices used to buffer the control signals are shown in Figure B.25 (page 485). Each of these signals (MSYN, SSYN, etc.) are isolated from the bus, and asserted onto the bus with special gates that add a minimal electrical load onto the bus.

The diagrams contained in Figures B.16 to B.25 specify about 90 integrated circuits; the total area required by these chips is about 35 square inches on a very densely packed board. Thus, the interface could easily be placed on a board which fits into a UNIBUS, since there is over 60 square inches of active space on a standard board.

The action of the interface is described by the state diagrams included as Figures B.26 (page 486), and B.27 (page 487). As mentioned above, the minimum time for the tape controller is 200 nsec, whereas the UNIBUS will be most effectively used if the state times are much less than 200 nsec. Thus, the state time for the interface controller itself is 200 nsec, while the DMA controller operates with a 50 nsec clock. It would be possible to combine the two state machines, but that would result in a much larger system. Hence, the decision was made to use two different state machines.

Figure B.26 deals with the behavior of the interface itself. The states the unit goes through to perform the work of directing the tape controller are identified, and the signals that need to be asserted are identified in each state. To understand the action of the system, we will now identify each state and the purpose of it. The ordering of the following states is in a logical sequence, rather than a numerical sequence. State numbers can be selected in many ways; the

App. B: Detailed Logic Diagrams

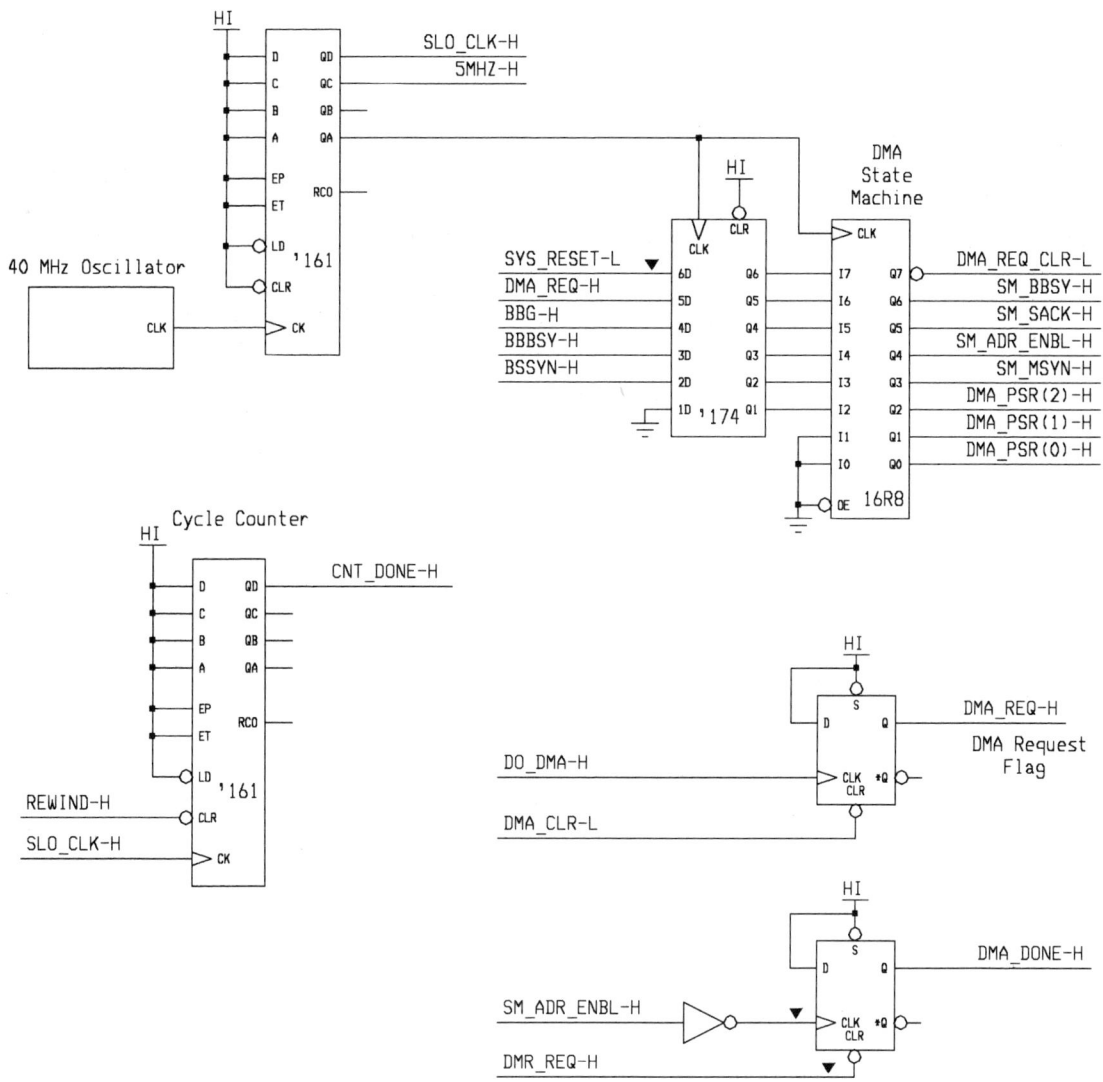

Figure B.23. Logic Diagram Tape Recorder Interface System. Bus Interface State Machine Logic.

primary selection criteria for the given system was to be able to use the most significant present state lines to select the proper value in the multiplexers for the determination of next state.

- *State 0:* This is the initialization state; upon power up or system reset the unit will be forced to this state. The result is to send an INIT signal to the tape controller to reset the internal electronics, and then to go to the idle state. The 27S45 devices used to implement the system have a programmable initialization value; hence this state can easily be achieved with a reset signal.

- *State 1:* This is the idle state, where the system will spend most of the time. No signal is asserted in this state. The system will leave the state only if a command is detected. The possible next states are 3, for setting the interrupt enable condition, and 4, which is used for tape motion commands.

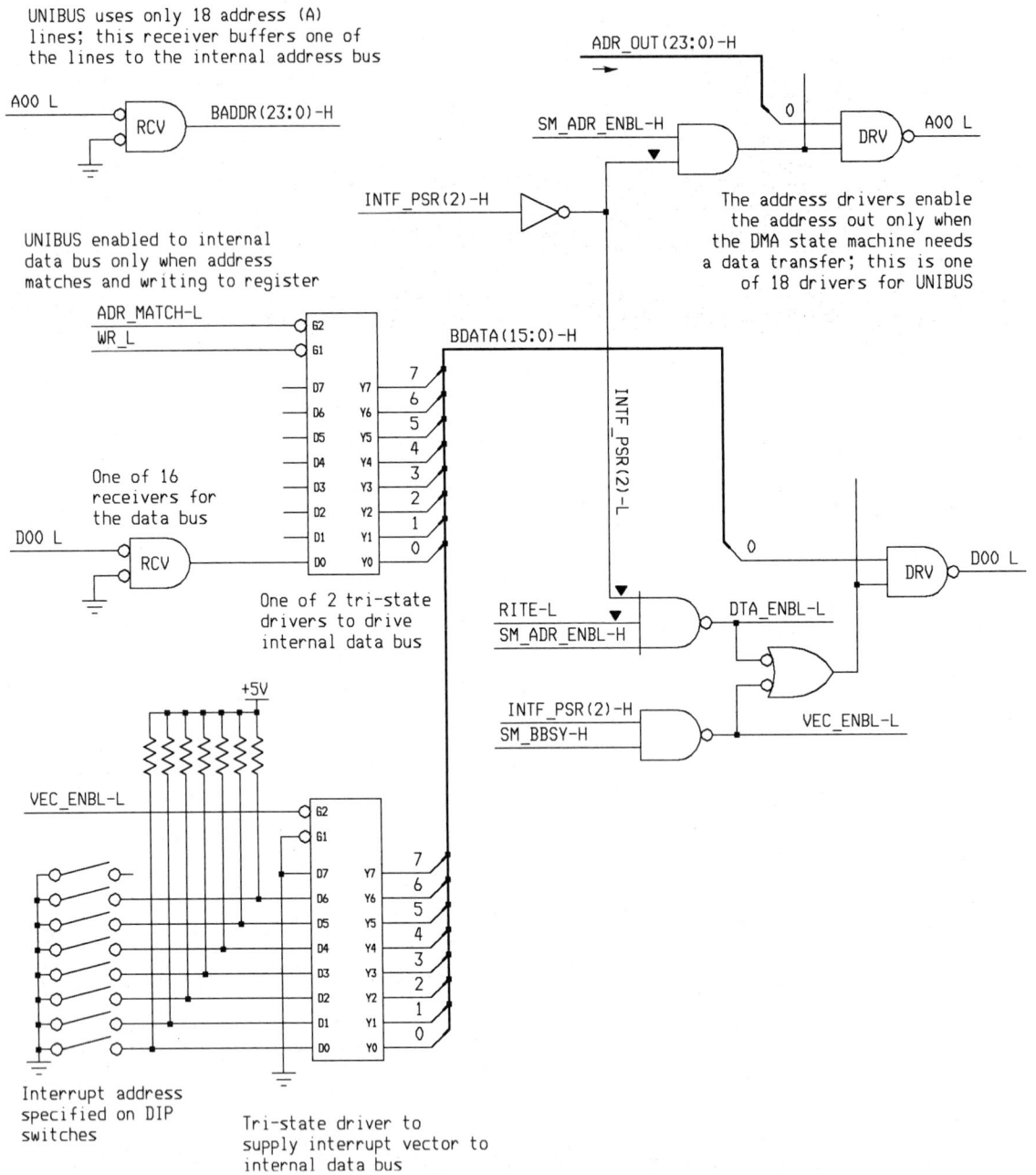

Figure B.24. Logic Diagram Tape Recorder Interface System. Bus Interface Buffers and Drivers.

- *State 3:* This state is used to do the work for nontape motion commands. A clock signal (ITR_CLK) is asserted, and this is gated either to the transport select flip-flops, or to the interrupt enable flip-flop, depending on the state of CMD0. Also, the command register is cleared. The next state is the always the idle state.

- *State 4:* This state is used for tape motion commands. Asserting the initialization signal for the tape controller clears the necessary flags and prepares the

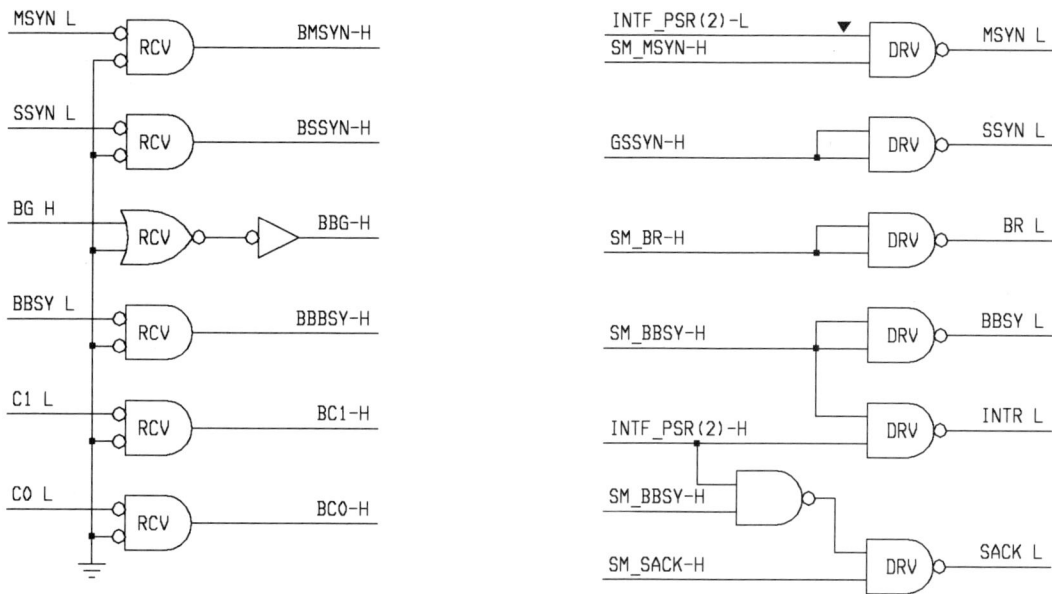

Figure B.25. Logic Diagram Tape Recorder Interface System. Buffers and Drivers Bus Control Lines..

tape controller for the work to follow. The possible next states are State 20 for rewind, State 7 for file space commands, State 8 for a read command, State 9 for a write command, and State 6 for a write file mark command. Also, if the word count is already equal to zero, then the system returns to the idle state, unless the request is for a rewind.

- *State 20:* The tape controller specification calls for a pulse of at least 2 µsec for the rewind command. The REWIND signal is asserted in this state, and this signal also allows a counter to increment. When the counter has incremented to 8, 3.6 µsec have passed, the count done signal is asserted, and the system moves to State 23 to await the completion of the task.

- *State 6:* If the command is a write file mark command, then all that is required of the system is to assert the SETX signal and wait for the completion of the task. The wait is done by State 23, which is the only next state.

- *State 7:* This state is entered if the system is to do a file search command. The gating associated with the command register asserts the appropriate direction signals, and the action starts when SETX is asserted in this state. At the same time, the word count is decremented to allow checking the number of file marks skipped. The next state is State 21.

- *State 21:* The system waits in this state for the assertion of the end of file signal, which indicates that the file mark has been reached. At that point the action moves to State 5.

- *State 5:* The INIT signal is generated in this state to reset the EOF flag of the tape controller. Then a decision is made as to the proper next state. If the word count is not equal to zero, then we haven't found the proper file mark, and the action moves back to State 7 to find another file mark. However, if the word count is zero, then the proper next state is determined by the contents of the command register. If it is a file search forward command, then we are done

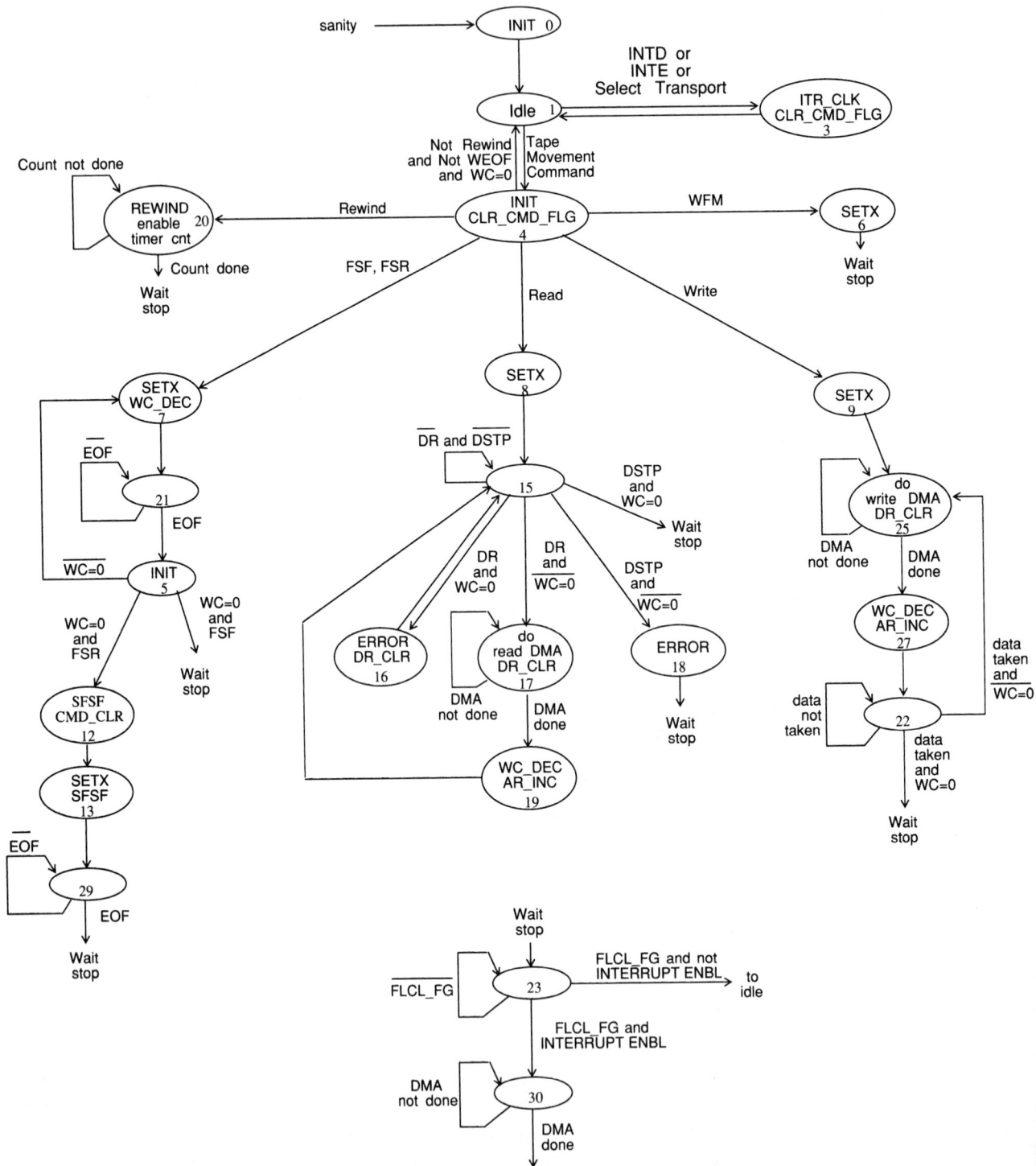

Figure B.26. State Diagram for Tape Controller Interface.

and the action moves to State 23 to wait for the tape motion to cease. If, however, the command is a file search reverse, then the action moves to State 12 to move forward one file mark.

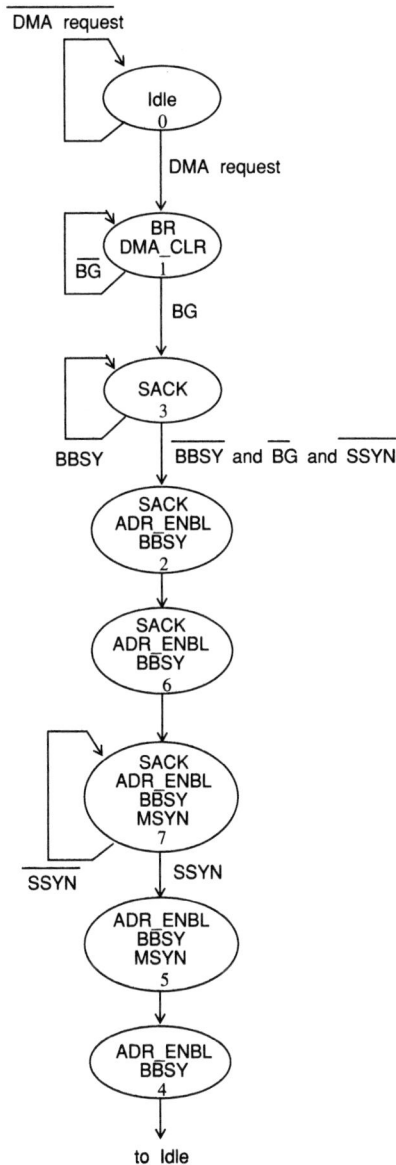

Figure B.27. State Diagram for DMA
Bus Interaction.

- *State 12:* This state is used to set up a file space forward action. The SFSF (special file space forward) signal is asserted, which creates the proper signal levels at the tape controller. The next state is State 13.

- *State 13:* This state completes the command action initiated in State 12. The SETX signal sends the request to the tape controller, and the SFSF signal is asserted to satisfy the timing requirements of the tape controller. The next state is State 29.

- *State 29:* The system waits in this state for the arrival of the next EOF signal from the controller, indicating that the job has been accomplished. The system then moves to State 23 to await the termination of motion.

- *State 8:* The gates associated with the command register have prepared the tape controller with the correct control signals, and when SETX is asserted in this state tape system begins its appointed action. The next state is State 15.

- *State 15:* The system waits in this state for signals indicating that further action is necessary; the two signals are the DR flag, which indicates that data is ready, and the DSTP flag, which indicates that the tape transport has completed its task and will begin to stop the tape. If the DR flag occurs and the word count is zero, then a record length error has occurred, and the system moves to State 16. If the DR flag occurs and the word count is not zero, then new data is available, and the system moves to State 17 to perform the necessary data transfer. If the DSTP flag occurs, then the read action is over. If the word count is zero, the expected number of words was read from the tape, and the system moves to State 23 to await the transport stop. However, if DSTP occurs and the word count is not equal to zero, then there has been a record length error, and the system moves to State 18 to set the appropriate flip flop.

- *State 16:* This state is entered when more data is read than expected. The error condition flag is set, and the DR flag is cleared. Action then moves back to State 15.

- *State 17:* This is the state for a successful read. The DMA flag is set for the DMA state machine, and the DR flag is cleared. When the DMA is complete, action moves on to State 19.

- *State 19:* This state is used to adjust the address and word count registers before moving to State 15 to wait for the next event needing action.

- *State 18:* If fewer words were read than expected, the word count will not be equal to zero, and this state is visited. The effect is to set the error flag, and then proceed to State 23 to wait for the transport system to stop.

- *State 9:* When a write command is detected, the system will move to this state. The SETX signal is asserted to initiate tape movement. And the system moves to State 25 to get the data. Asserting the SETX signal before obtaining the data assumes that the DMA action will be completed before the tape can move far enough to need the data.

- *State 25:* This is a wait state. The DMA request signal is asserted, and when the signal is received that the action has been completed, the system moves on to State 27.

- *State 27:* The word count register and the address register values are adjusted, and the action moves to State 22.

- *State 22:* The system waits in this state for the tape controller to accept the 2 bytes of data obtained by the DMA action. When the data has been taken, then the system moves on. If the word count is not equal to zero, then not all of the information has been written to the tape, and the action moves back to State 25. If the word count is equal to zero, then all of the necessary information has been moved, and the action moves to State 23 to wait for the transport to slow.

- *State 23:* This state is used to wait for the transport to signal that it is slowing the tape action. When that condition exists, the controller will assert the FLCL signal. This signals the state machine to move on to the next state. The next state will depend on the contents of the interrupt enable flip-flop. If the interrupt is not enabled, then the system returns to idle. However, if the interrupt is enabled, then the system moves to State 30, which will request the interrupt interaction.

- *State 30:* The system enters this state when an interrupt interaction is needed at the completion of a motion command. The interrupt itself is controlled by the DMA state machine, so the action of this state is to assert the DMA request line. When the interrupt cycle is complete, the DMA_DONE flag will be set, and the system returns to the idle state.

The interaction between the two state machines is handled with a simple flag arrangement, and, when a DMA interaction is needed, the DMA_REQ flag is set. The DMA state machine is then enabled to direct the interaction with the UNIBUS. This interaction is shown in Figure B.27, and is described as follows:

- *State 0:* This is the idle state, and the system will remain here until the DMA request flag is detected. Then it will move to State 1.

- *State 1:* When a DMA or interrupt cycle is needed, this state is entered. The result is to assert the bus request flag and clear the DMA request flag. The system will remain in this state until the assertion of the bus grant line, at which point the action moves to State 3.

- *State 3:* The response to the detection of bus grant is to assert the selection acknowledge (SACK) line. The bus has now been acquired, and the interface will move to State 2 to use the bus when the bus busy signal is unasserted (the current transaction is done), the bus grant signal is released (arbitration is completed), and the slave sync signal is released (previous slave has completed transaction).

- *State 2:* In this state the address is enabled onto the address bus (ADR_ENBL), and the bus busy signal is asserted (BBSY). The effect is to initiate a transaction as a master. The next state is State 6.

- *State 6:* The BBSY and ADR_ENBL signals are continued in this state. The net effect of the two states (2 and 6) is to assert these signals for 100 nsec before the request line is asserted in the next state. This meets the timing requirement for the UNIBUS. The next state is always State 7.

- *State 7:* This state calls for the continuation of the previous signals (BBSY, ADR_ENBL, SACK), and also for the assertion of the request line (MSYN). The request line signals the slave devices that an interaction is needed, and, when the appropriate slave is ready, it will respond with the acknowledge signal (SSYN). When that happens, the system will move to State 5.

- *State 5:* When the slave has responded (detection of SSYN), the action enters this state. The effect is to delay the release of MSYN to meet the bus timing requirements, and then to move on to State 4. The SACK signal is also released by entering this state, so other masters are informed of the imminent release of the bus. For the write to tape operation, which reads data from memory, data is clocked into the interface registers on the trailing edge of the MSYN signal, which has been created to provide time for data deskewing.

- *State 4:* This state is used to delay the release of the address and bus busy signals after the release of the request signal. From this state the system returns to the idle state.

If the action is an interrupt sequence rather than a data transfer, then the same action is needed, but not all of the same signals are used. Thus, the gating of Figure B.25 is used to allow both interrupt and DMA transfers to be controlled by the DMA sequencer. For example, the request signal (MSYN) is not used for the interrupt sequence, and hence the bus driver for that signal is disabled during that operation.

The interface presented here is a relatively straightforward implementation that utilizes the concepts of bus interaction and sequential circuits. The system can be made much more complex in its interaction by including additional instructions and expanding the state diagram. For example, the controller has the capability to read and write when the tape motion is in reverse. This ability can be harnessed by including appropriate instructions in the interface definition, and then including appropriate action definitions in the state machine. Other action, such as block searchs and unloading the tape, are also possible with more a more complex system.

B.7. Dynamic Memory System

The dynamic memory system shown in Figure 7.13 is composed of SIPs: single in line packages. Each SIP contains nine individual memory chips, and each memory chip contains a 256-Kbit memory. Thus, each SIP contains a quarter of a megabyte of memory. The ninth bit can be used to add parity to the byte of memory; this capability is not shown in the logic diagrams of this memory system. Each SIP in the system is represented by the following symbol:

The symbol represents a module with nine address lines, nine date lines, a column address strobe (CAS) line, a row address strobe (RAS) line, and a write enable (WE) line. These signal lines, plus power and ground, fit into a module three inches long that contains 30 pins. The CAS lines for each memory module in the SIP are connected together; hence the CAS pin for the whole module has an effective load of nine devices. Similarly, the RAS and WE lines are connected together for all of the memory modules of the SIP. This same technique also applies to all of the address lines of the SIP. Therefore, the devices used to drive these lines must be capable of handling a sufficiently large current fast enough to get the job done.

The logic diagrams for the memory are shown in Figures B.28 to B.32. The memory modules themselves are shown in Figure B.28 and B.29. The memory is designed to interface to a 32-bit data bus, and as such it is organized to present data (or accept data) 4 bytes at a time. Each byte has its own write enable line (WE(0)-L to WE(3)-L); this permits writing to individual bytes within the addressed word by asserting only the appropriate write enable lines. Each byte also has its own tri-state transceiver to connect it with the data bus, and these transceivers are separately enabled. The memory organization is also organized in a megabyte fashion. That is, four 256-Kbyte modules together constitute a megabyte, and are addresses as such. Thus, each set of four modules has its own RAS and CAS lines. The address presented is decoded to determine which of the RAS and CAS lines must be activated to identify the appropriate location. Because of the loads of all of the individual memory modules, the address lines are connected into four

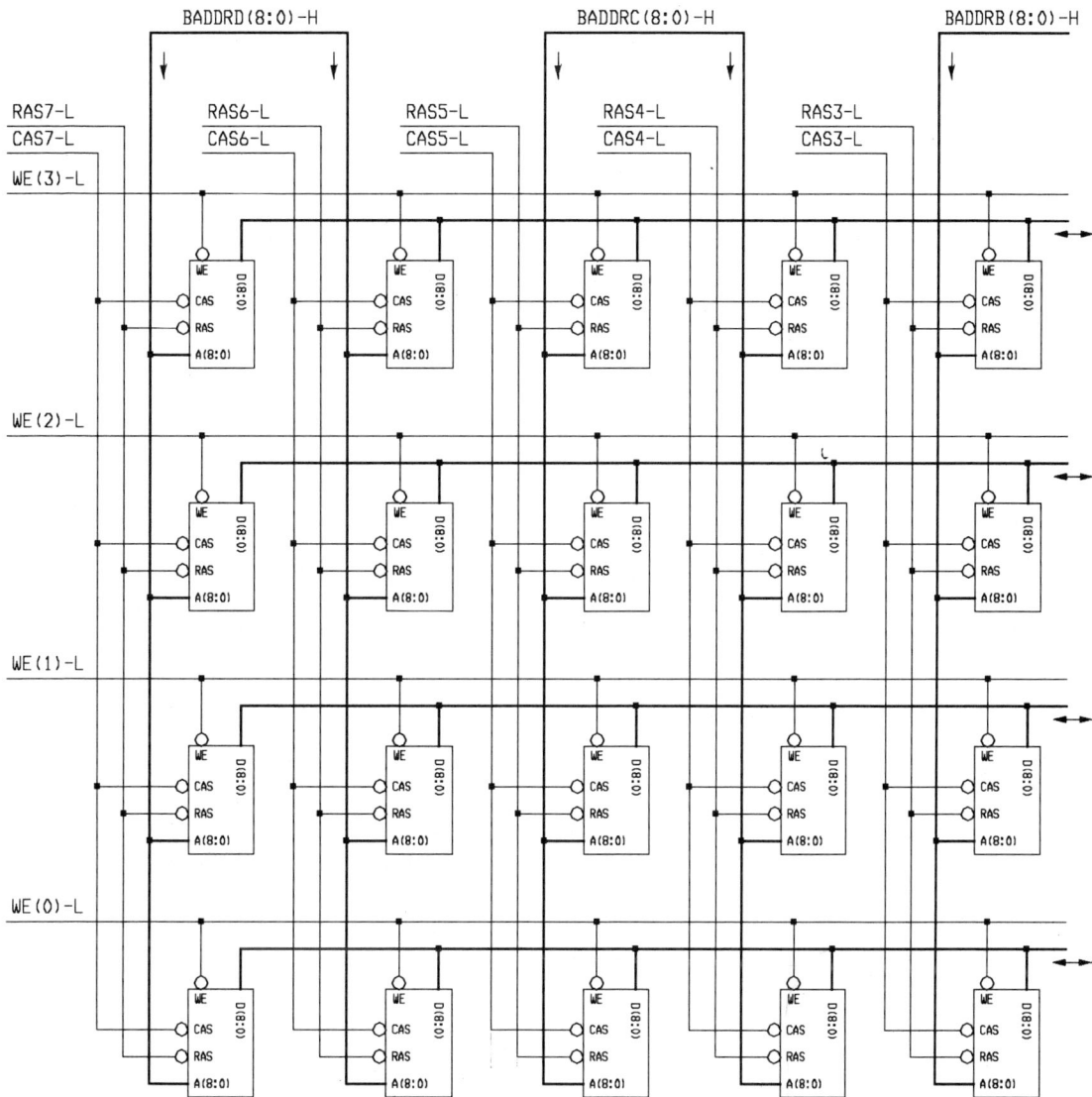

Figure B.28. Logic Diagram for Dynamic Memory System. Dynamic Memory Modules.

address groups (named buffered address lines A through D, or BADDRA(8:0)-H through BADDRD(8:0)-H), and individual driver circuits are used for each group. Nine lines are required to alternately present the half of the 18 lines needed to address 262,144 locations.

The individual drivers for the row and address strobes are shown in Figure B.30. The '804 gates were chosen because they are capable of handling the current required by four SIPs, which together contain 36 memory devices. The time at which the row address strobe should be asserted is identified by the assertion of DO_RAS-H, which is created by the system controller. Similarly, the time for the column address strobe is determined by DO_CAS-H, which is also created by the system controller. The selection of the RAS and CAS lines to be asserted is determined from the address lines by the decoder ('538). The '538 was chosen for this function for two reasons. The first is that the decoder can be configured to

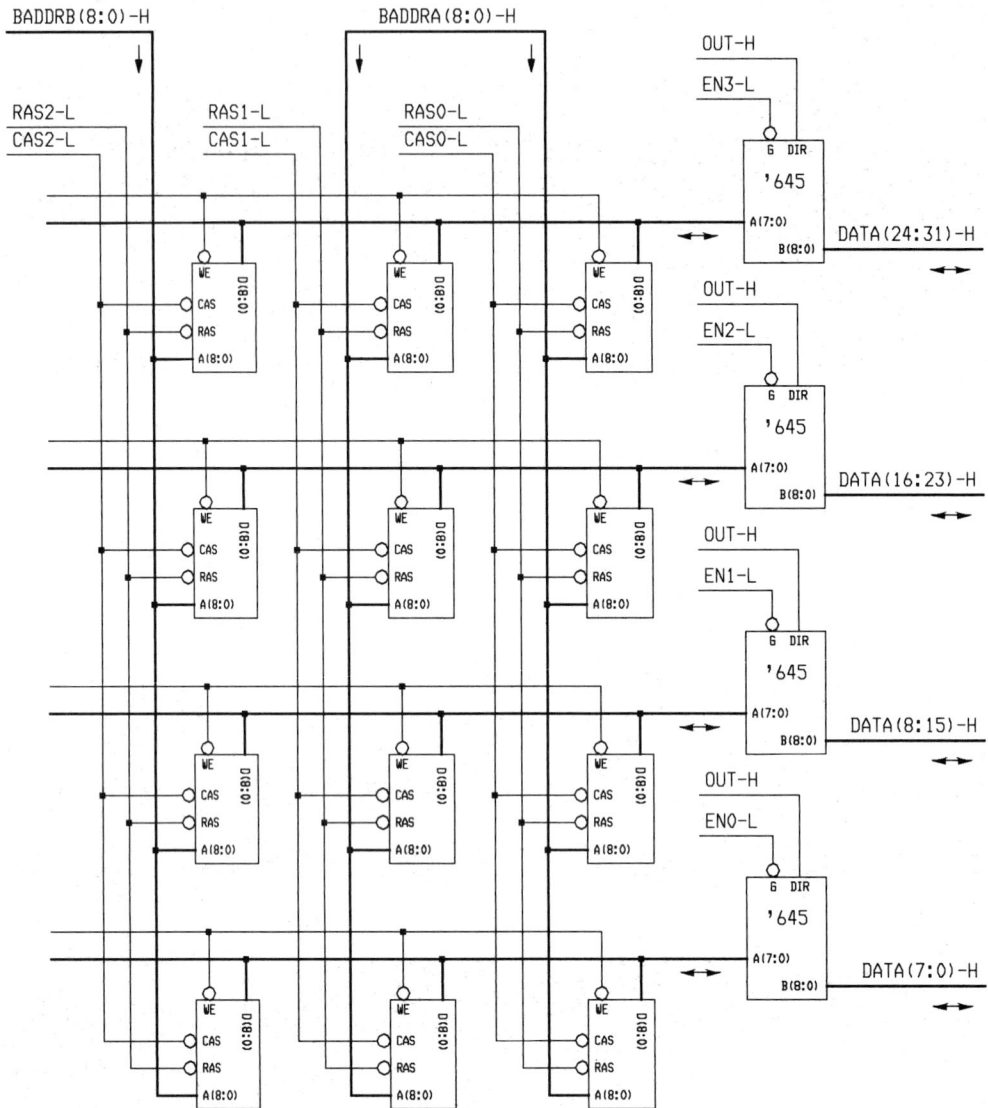

Figure B.29. Logic Diagram for Dynamic Memory System. Dynamic Memory Modules and Bus Interface.

provide an output that is asserted high, as opposed to decoders like the '138, which provide only asserted low outputs. The second reason is that the output lines of the decoder, if the control lines are appropriately configured, can all be asserted simultaneously. This is useful for refresh, when all of the memory modules can be refreshed simultaneously.

Figure B.31 contains the address drivers and the refresh row counter. In the figure, the address latches are connected to the data lines; this will be the configuration for a bus that time-shares the 32 bus lines between the address and the data. When the ADDRESS-H line is asserted, the value on the bus (which is assumed to be the address) is loaded into the address latch devices. The '843s will each accept 9 bits, which is what is needed for the individual row and address components for the memory modules. The '373 accepts the most significant lines,

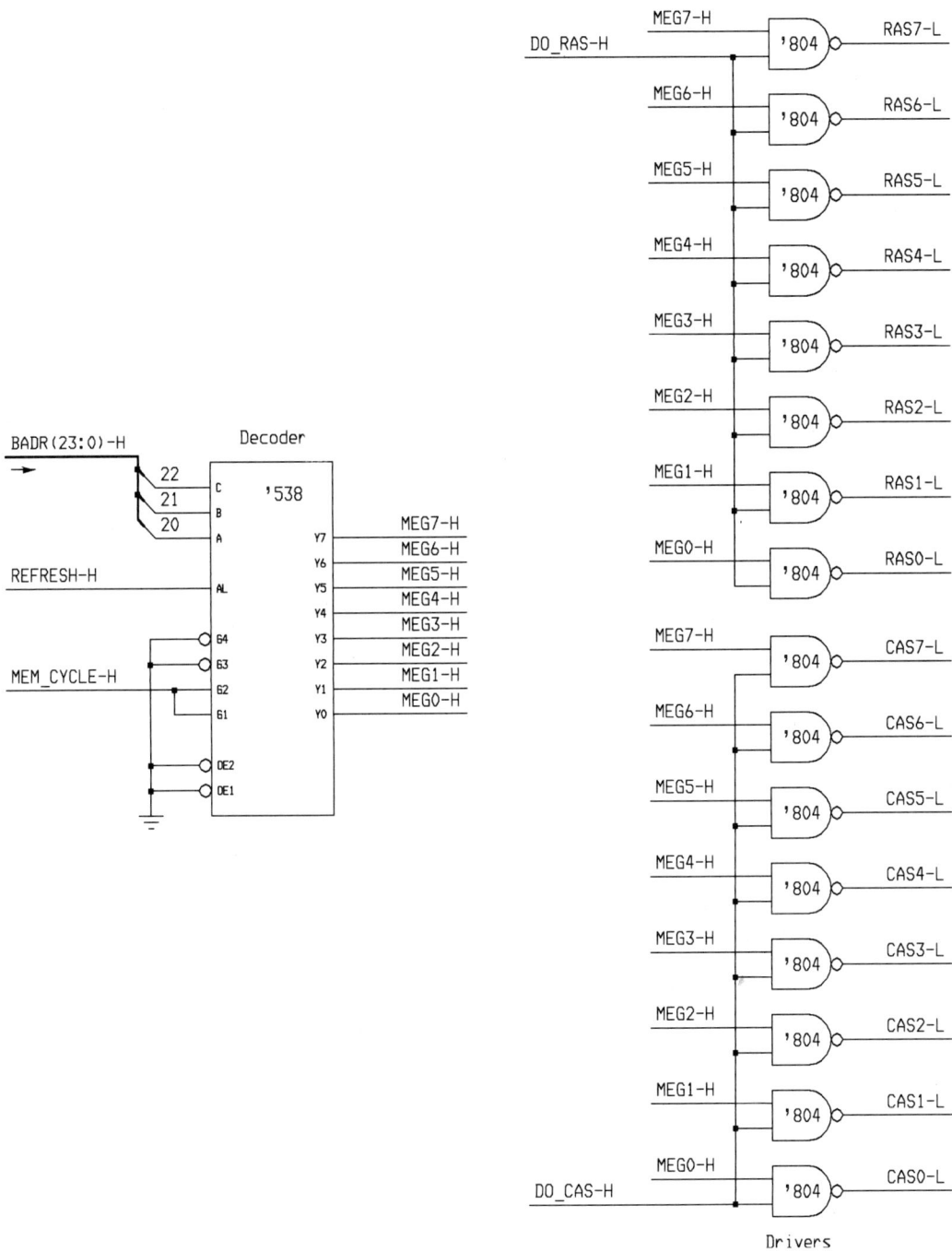

Figure B.30. Logic Diagram for Dynamic Memory System. RAS and CAS Logic and Drivers.

which are then sent to the decoder in Figure B.30 to determine the proper mega-byte to assert. The row and column information is asserted onto RC_BUS(8:0)-H by ROW-L and COLUMN-L, respectively. Four individual buffer systems then send this information to the individual memory modules via BADDRA(8:0)-H through BADDRD(8:0)-H. The buffer systems are made with 84244 devices, which

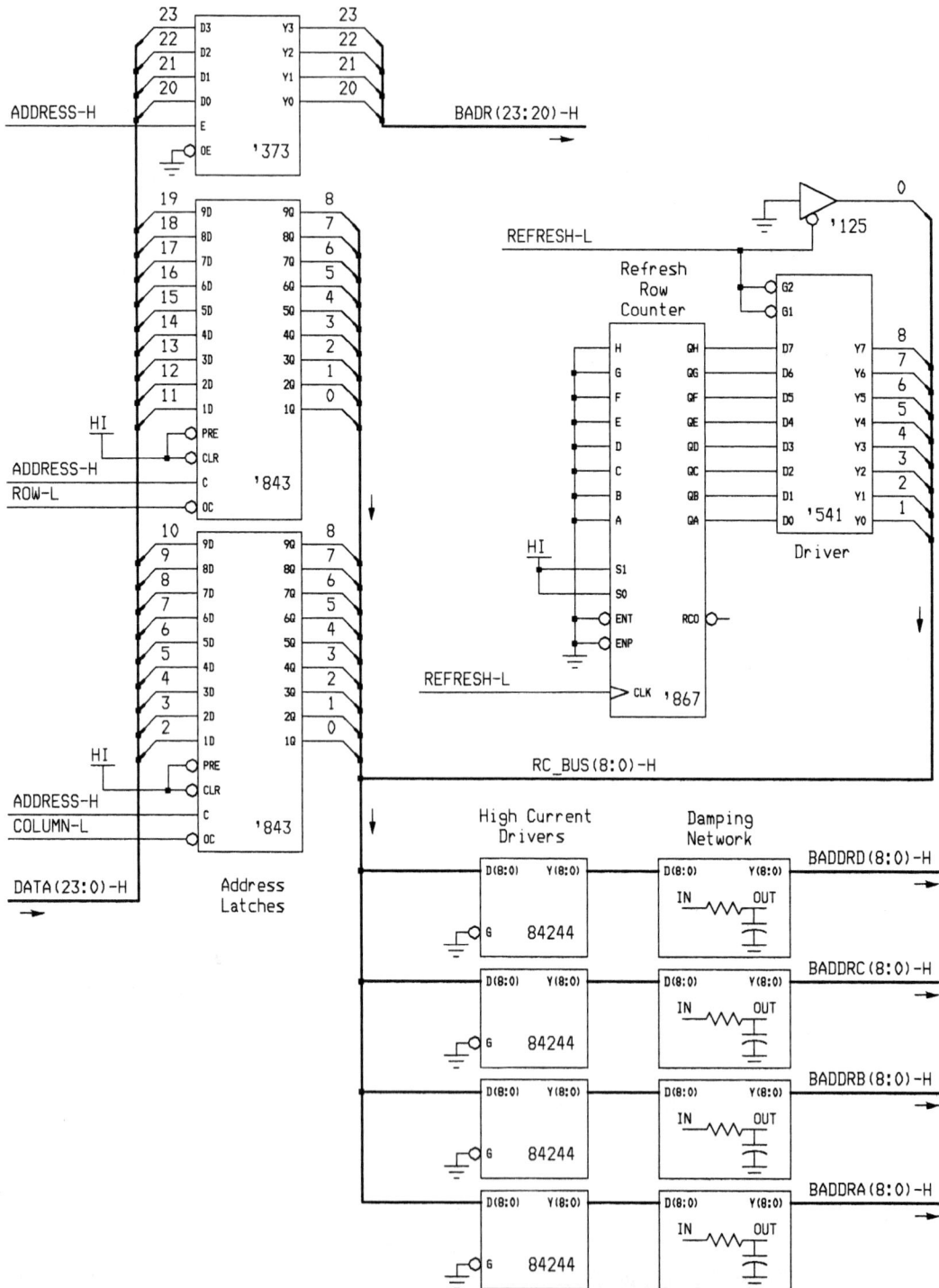

Figure B.31. Logic Diagram for Dynamic Memory System. Address Drivers and Refresh Counter.

are specifically designed to be used in high current requirements such as this. Also, the output of each 84244 is sent through a resistor-capacitor combination as shown, which provides a damping network to reduce the noise on the address

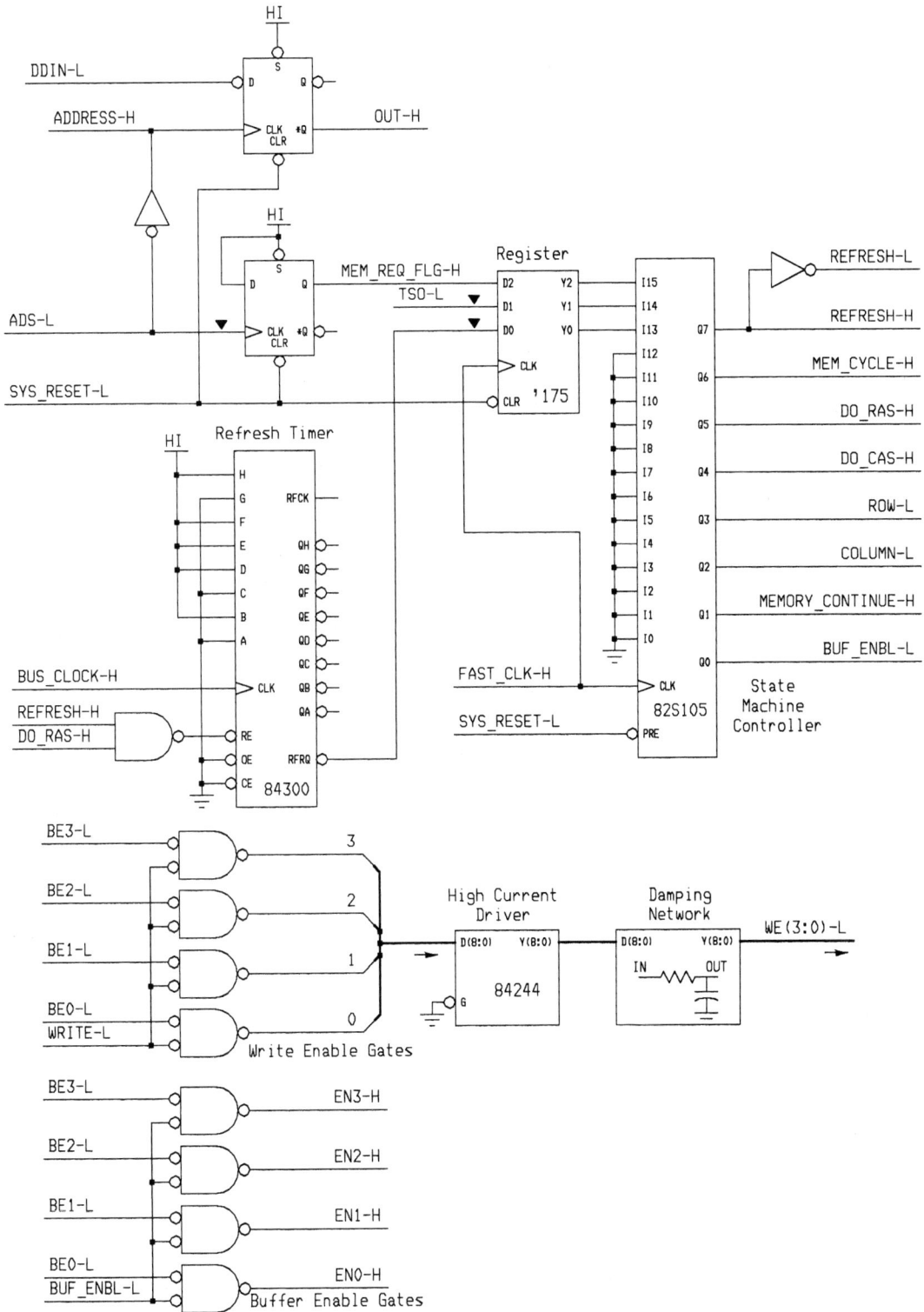

Figure B.32. Logic Diagram for Dynamic Memory System. Write Enable Drivers and System Controller.

lines. The remaining portion of the logic in Figure B.31 is the refresh row counter. This counter is configured to count up by one each time the clock line is asserted (REFRESH-L). Thus, each time a refresh occurs, the row counter increments to point to the next row that needs to be refreshed. The memory modules used in this design are capable of refreshing two rows simultaneously, so the least significant address line of RC_BUS(8:0)-H is not involved in the count, and is driven low each time the refresh occurs.

The controller for the memory system is shown in Figure B.32. Dynamic RAM controllers are commercially available, so the system shown in the figure could be considered a "homemade" version of a RAM controller. The address is available when the ADS-L signal is asserted. Assertion of ADS-L sets a flag used by the controller (MEM_REQ_FLG-H), as well as identifying the direction of the transfer (with OUT-H). The controller itself is a state machine controller made with an 82S105 programmable device. This contains the logic and the register needed to control the memory system. The only requirement is to synchronize the inputs with the state machine, which is done by the '175 register. The controller asserts the signals needed (DO_RAS-H, DO_CAS-H, etc.) in the order needed to perform the work. Even though they work on the same principle, different dynamic RAMs have different timing requirements, and the system controller must be configured to meet the timing requirements of the modules being used. One of the characteristics of a dynamic RAM is the time permitted between refresh cycles. The 84300 shown in the figure is a refresh timer, and the input lines are configured to create a flag whenever a refresh cycle is needed to maintain the contents of the memory system. When the refresh request is satisfied, the flag is reset. The refresh takes priority over normal memory requests, so a system using a dynamic RAM memory must be capable of waiting for the results, since the memory request could occur when a refresh is in progress. Also included in the figure are the gates used to buffer the write enable lines. Since each write enable is connected to eight SIP modules, the drivers must be capable of handling the load of 72 individual devices. Finally, the transceivers that provide buffering for the individual bytes of the memory are separately enabled, and the gates that enable the transceivers are shown at the bottom of the drawing.

ICs Used in the Text

IC	Description
'00	Two input NAND gate
'02	Two input NOR gate
'04	Inverter
'05	Inverter — open collector output
'07	Inverter — open collector output, high voltage
'08	Two input AND gate
'10	Three input NAND gate
'20	Four input NAND gate
'30	Eight input NAND gate
'32	Two input OR gate
'74	Edge triggered D flip-flop
'86	Two input exclusive-OR gate
'125	Tri-state driver with low true enable
'133	Thirteen input NAND gate

'138	3-line-to-8-line decoder
	    Inputs: 3 enables: 2 asserted low and 1 asserted high;
	      3 data inputs, asserted high
	    Outputs: 8, asserted low

'139	2-line-to-4-line decoder
	    Inputs: 2 data inputs, asserted high
	    Outputs: 4, asserted low

'148	8-line-to-3-line priority encoder
	    Inputs: 8 data lines, 1 enable line, all asserted low
	    Outputs: 3 data outputs, 2 enable outputs, asserted low

IC	Description
'151	1-of-8 data selector/multiplexer: Inputs: 8 data, 3 select, asserted high; 1 enable, asserted low Outputs: high and low asserted data
'156	2-line-to-4-line decoder with open collector outputs Inputs: 2 data, asserted high; 2 enables, asserted low Outputs: 4, asserted low, open collector
'157	Quad 2-line-to-1-line data selector/multiplexer Inputs: 8 data lines, 1 select line, asserted high; 1 enable line, asserted low Outputs: 4 data lines, asserted high
'161	Synchronous 4-bit binary counter with direct clear Inputs: 4 data, 2 enables, one clock, asserted high; clear, load, asserted low Outputs: 4 data, 1 ripple carry out, asserted high
'164	8-Bit parallel out serial shift register Inputs: 2 data, 1 clock, asserted high; clear, asserted low Outputs: 8 data, asserted high
'165	8-Bit parallel in serial shift register Inputs: 8 data lines, serial in, clock, clock inhibit, asserted high load line, asserted low Outputs: 1 data line asserted both high and low
'174	6-Bit D-type register Inputs: 6 data, clock, asserted high; clear, asserted low Outputs: 6 data, asserted high
'175	4-Bit D-type register Inputs: 4 data, clock, asserted high; clear, asserted low Outputs: 4 data, asserted both high and low

'181	4-bit arithmetic logic unit/function generator
	Inputs: 8 data (2 4-bit data words), carry in, mode,
	  4 select lines, asserted high
	Outputs: 4 data (1 4-bit word), carry out, A=B out,
	  asserted high, generate and propagate, asserted low

'182	Look-ahead carry generator Inputs: Generate and Propagate from 4 units, asserted low Outputs: 3 carry out lines, asserted high, generate and propagate, asserted low

'191	4-bit binary synchronous up/down counter
	Inputs: 4 data, clock, asserted high; load, count up,
	  count enable, asserted low
	Outputs: 4 data, min/max, asserted high; ripple carry
	  out, asserted low

'192	4-bit BCD up/down counter with dual clock
	Inputs: 4 data lines, two clocks, clear, asserted high;
	  load, asserted low
	Outputs: 4 data lines, asserted high; two clocks,
	  asserted low

'195	4-bit parallel access shift register
	Inputs: 4 data, J (for serial in), clock,
	  asserted high; load, clear, K bar,
	  (for serial in) asserted low
	Outputs: 4 data asserted high; one data asserted low

IC	Description
'198	8-bit bidirectional shift register Inputs: 8 data lines, left serial in, right serial in, two select lines, clock, asserted high; clear line, asserted low Outputs: 8 data lines, asserted high
'244	8-bit noninverting tri-state driver Inputs: 8 data, asserted high; two enable, asserted low Outputs: 8 data, asserted high
'245	8-bit noninverting tri-state bus transceiver Inputs: direction, asserted high; enable, asserted low I/O: two sets of 8 lines (bi-directional), asserted high
'260	5 Input NOR gate
'273	8-bit D-type flip-flop Inputs: 8 data lines, clock line, asserted high; clear line, asserted low Outputs: 8 data lines, asserted high
'283	4-bit binary adder Inputs: 8 data lines (2 4-bit words), carry in, asserted high Outputs: 4 data lines, carry out, asserted high
'286	9-bit parity generator/checker Inputs: 9 data lines, asserted high; transmit, asserted low Outputs: parity error, asserted low I/O: parity (generated or tested)
'299	8-bit bidirectional shift register with tri-state I/O Inputs: 2 select lines, right serial in, left serial in, clock, asserted high; clear, 2 enables, asserted low Outputs: two data outs (for serial shift), asserted high I/O: 8 data lines
'373	8-bit latch with tri-state outputs Inputs: 8 data lines, enable line, asserted high; output enable, asserted low Outputs: 8 data lines, tri-state
'374	8-bit register with tri-state outputs Inputs: 8 data lines, clock line, asserted high; output enable, asserted low Outputs: 8 data lines, tri-state
'520	8-bit identity comparator (2 8-bit words) Inputs: 16 data lines (2 8-bit words),asserted high; enable line, asserted low Outputs: equal, asserted low
'538	3-line-to-8-line decoder/demultiplexer with tri-state outputs Inputs: 3 data lines, output level select, 2 enable lines, asserted high; 2 enable lines, 2 output enables, asserted low Outputs: 8 data lines, asserted high or low
'540	8-bit tri-state driver with inverted outputs Inputs: 8 data lines, asserted high; 2 enables, asserted low Outputs: 8 data lines, asserted low
'541	8-bit tri-state driver Inputs: 8 data lines, asserted high; 2 enables, asserted low Outputs: 8 data lines, asserted high

IC	Description
'550	8-bit registered transceiver Inputs: 2 clocks, 2 flag clear lines, asserted high; 2 clock enables, 2 output enables, asserted low Outputs: two flags, asserted high I/O: 16 data lines (2 8-bit bidirectional groups)
'564	8-bit D registers with inverted tri-state outputs Inputs: 8 data lines, clock, asserted high; output enable, asserted low Outputs: 8 data lines, asserted low
'574	8-bit register with tri-state outputs Inputs: 8 data lines, clock line, asserted high; output enable, asserted low Outputs: 8 data lines, tri-state
'612	Memory mapper Inputs: 4 address lines, 4 register select lines, asserted high; chip select, map enable, map mode, write, asserted low Outputs: 12 data lines, asserted high I/O: 12 data lines, bidirectional
'620	8-bit noninverting tri-state bus transceiver Inputs: enable, asserted high; enable, asserted low I/O: two sets of 8 lines (bi-directional), asserted high
'645	8-bit noninverting tri-state bus transceiver Inputs: direction, asserted high; enable, asserted low I/O: two sets of 8 lines (bi-directional), asserted high
'646	8-bit bus transceiver and registers with tri-state outputs Inputs: 2 clocks, 2 source lines, direction, asserted high; enable, asserted low I/O: 16 lines (2 8-bit words, bidirectional)
'763	8-bit buffer with open collector outputs Inputs: 8 data lines, asserted high; 2 enables, asserted low Outputs: 8 data lines, asserted low (open collector)
'804	Two input NAND with high current capability
'843	9-bit register with tri-state output Inputs: 9 data lines, clock, asserted high; output enable, preset, clear, asserted low Outputs: 9 data lines (tri-state outputs)

'857	6-bit 2-line-to-1-line multiplexer
	Inputs: 12 data (2 6-bit words), 2 select, output polarity
	  select, asserted high
	Outputs: 6 data (tri-state, polarity determined by input),
	  input equal to zero, asserted high

'867	8-bit synchronous up/down counter Inputs: 8 data lines, clock, 2 select lines, asserted high; 2 enables, asserted low Outputs: 8 data lines, asserted high; ripple carry out, asserted low
'869	8-bit synchronous up/down counter Inputs: 8 data lines, clock, 2 select lines, asserted high; 2 enables, asserted low Outputs: 8 data lines, asserted high; ripple carry out, asserted low
'881	4-bit ALU, similar to '181

IC	Description
'882	32-bit look-ahead carry generator Inputs: generate, propagate from 8 stages, asserted low; carry in, asserted high Outputs: 4 carry outs, asserted high
82S105	Field programmable sequencer
84244	8-Bit Non-Inverting Tri-State Driver, Trapazoidal Drive Inputs: 8 data, asserted high; two enable, asserted low Outputs: 8 data, asserted high

84300	Programmable refresh timer
	Inputs: 8 data lines, clock, asserted high; refresh,
	   chip enable, chip enable, asserted low
	Outputs: 8 data lines, refresh request asserted low;
	   refresh clock, asserted high

AM2901	4-bit microprocessor slice
	Inputs: 4 A address lines, 4 B address lines,
	   9 instruction lines, 4 data lines, carry in, clock,
	   asserted high; output enable asserted low
	Outputs: 4 data lines, overflow, equal, sign, carry out, asserted high;
	   propagate, generate, asserted low
	I/O: 4 shift lines

AM2910	Microprogram controller
	Inputs: 12 data lines, 4 instruction lines, carry in, clock,
	   asserted high; output enable, condition code, condition
	   code enable, register load, asserted low
	Outputs: 12 data lines, asserted high; map enable, PL enable,
	   VEC enable, full, asserted low

IDT7423	16×16 Multiplier/accumulator
L16R8	Programmable logic array
27S45	Registered PROM

Index